Professional JavaScript™ for Web Developers

Professional JavaScript™ for Web Developers

Nicholas C. Zakas

WILEY
Wiley Publishing, Inc.

Professional JavaScript™ for Web Developers

Published by Wiley Publishing, Inc., Indianapolis, Indiana

Published simultaneously in Canada

Library of Congress Cataloging-in-Publication Data is available from the publisher.

ISBN-13: 978-0-7645-7908-0

ISBN-10: 0-7645-7908-8

Printed in the United States of America

10 9 8 7 6 5 4 3 2 1

About the Author

Nicholas C. Zakas is a user interface designer for Web applications, specializing in client-side technologies such as JavaScript, HTML, and CSS. Nicholas currently works as Senior Software Engineer, Design Engineering, at MatrixOne, Inc. located in Westford, Massachusetts, USA.

Nicholas has a B.S. in Computer Science from Merrimack College, where he learned traditional programming in C and C++. During college, he began investigating the World Wide Web and HTML in his spare time, eventually teaching himself enough to be hired as Webmaster of a small software company named Radnet, Inc. in Wakefield, Massachusetts, USA. It was there that Nicholas began learning JavaScript and working on Web applications.

Nicholas can be reached through his Web site, `http://www.nczonline.net/`.

Credits

Vice President and Executive Group Publisher:
Richard Swadley

Vice President and Publisher:
Joseph B. Wikert

Acquisitions Editor:
Jim Minatel

Editorial Manager:
Mary Beth Wakefield

Development Editor:
Sharon Nash

Senior Production Editor:
Angela Smith

Technical Editor:
Jean-Luc David, Wiley-Dreamtech India Pvt Ltd

Text Design & Composition:
Wiley Composition Services

Acknowledgments

It takes more than just one person to write a book of this nature, despite the single name on the front cover. Without the help of numerous individuals, this book would not have been possible.

First are foremost, thanks to everyone at Wiley Publishing, especially Jim Minatel and Sharon Nash, for providing all the guidance and support that a new author needs.

Thanks to all those who offered their ideas on what a good JavaScript book should include: Keith Ciociola, Ken Fearnley, John Rajan, and Douglas Swatski.

A special thanks to everyone who reviewed the subject matter ahead of time: Erik Arvidsson, Bradley Baumann, Guilherme Blanco, Douglas Crockford, Jean-Luc David, Emil A. Eklund, Brett Fielder, Jeremy McPeak, and Micha Schopman. All your input was excellent and made for a much better book.

Thanks to Drs. Ed and Frances Bernard for keeping me in tip-top health during the writing of this book and the past few years.

Last, but certainly not least, thanks to my family, mom, dad, and Greg, and my extremely understanding girlfriend, Emily. Your love and support helped take me from the proposal to the final published copy.

Contents

Introduction

Although once supported by Netscape Enterprise Server and Active Server Pages (ASP) on the server, JavaScript is primarily a client-side scripting language for use in Web browsers. Its main focus today is to help developers interact with Web pages and the Web browser window itself.

JavaScript is very loosely based on Java, an object-oriented programming language popularized for use on the Web by way of embedded applets. Although JavaScript has a similar syntax and programming methodology, it is not a "light" version of Java. Instead, JavaScript is its own language, finding its home in Web browsers around the world and enabling enhanced user interaction on Web sites and Web applications alike.

In this book, JavaScript is covered from its very beginning in the earliest Netscape browsers to the present-day incarnations flush with support for XML and Web Services. You learn how to extend the language to suit specific needs and how to create seamless client-server communication without intermediaries such as Java or hidden frames. In short, you learn how to apply JavaScript solutions to business problems faced by Web developers everywhere.

What Does This Book Cover?

Professional JavaScript for Web Developers provides a developer-level introduction along with the more advanced and useful features of JavaScript.

Starting at the beginning, the book explores how JavaScript originated and evolved into what it is today. A detailed discussion of the components that make up a JavaScript implementation follows, with specific focus on standards such as ECMAScript and the Document Object Model (DOM). The differences in JavaScript implementations used in different popular Web browsers are also discussed.

Building on that base, the book moves on to cover basic concepts of JavaScript including its version of object-oriented programming, inheritance, and its use in various markup languages such as HTML. An in-depth examination of events and event handling is followed by an exploration of browser detection techniques and a guide to using regular expressions in JavaScript. The book then takes all this knowledge and applies it to creating dynamic user interfaces.

The last part of the book is focused on issues related to the deployment of JavaScript solutions in Web applications. These topics include error handling, debugging, security, optimization/obfuscation, XML, and Web Services.

Who Is This Book For?

This book is aimed at three groups of readers:

- Experienced developers familiar with object-oriented programming who are looking to learn JavaScript as it relates to traditional OO languages such as Java and C++.
- Web application developers attempting to enhance the usability of their Web sites and Web applications.
- Novice JavaScript developers aiming to better understand the language.

In addition, familiarity with the following related technologies is a strong indicator that this book is for you:

- XML
- XSLT
- Java
- Web Services
- HTML
- CSS

This book is not aimed at beginners lacking a basic computer science background or those looking to add some simple user interactions to Web sites. These readers should instead refer to Wrox's *Beginning JavaScript*, Second Edition (Wiley Publishing, Inc., ISBN 0-7645-5587-1).

What You Need to Use This Book

To run the samples in the book, you need the following:

- Windows 2000, Windows Server 2003, Windows XP, or Mac OS X
- Internet Explorer 5.5 or higher (Windows), Mozilla 1.0 or higher (all platforms), Opera 7.5 or higher (all platforms), or Safari 1.2 or higher (Mac OS X).

The complete source code for the samples is available for download from the Web site at `http://www.wrox.com/`.

How Is This Book Structured?

1. **What Is JavaScript?**
   This chapter explains the origins of JavaScript: where it came from, how it evolved, and what it is today. Concepts introduced include the relationship between JavaScript and ECMAScript, the Document Object Model (DOM), and the Browser Object Model (BOM). A discussion of the relevant standards from the European Computer Manufacturer's Association (ECMA) and the World Wide Web Consortium (W3C) is also included.

2. **ECMAScript Basics**
   This chapter examines the core technology upon which JavaScript is built, ECMAScript. This chapter describes the basic syntax and concepts necessary to write JavaScript code, from declaring variables and functions to using and understanding primitive and reference values.

3. **Object Basics**
   This chapter focuses on the foundations of object-oriented programming (OOP) in JavaScript. Topics covered include defining custom objects using a variety of different methods, creating object instances, and understanding the similarities and differences to OOP in JavaScript and Java.

4. **Inheritance**
   This chapter continues the exploration of OOP in JavaScript, describing how inheritance works. The various methods of achieving inheritance are discussed, and these methods are compared and contrasted with inheritance in Java.

5. **JavaScript in the Browser**
   This chapter explains how to include JavaScript in Web pages made with a variety of languages, including Hyper Text Markup Language (HTML), Scalable Vector Graphics (SVG), and XML User Interface Language (XUL). This chapter also introduces the Browser Object Model (BOM) and its various objects and interfaces.

6. **DOM Basics**
   This chapter introduces the DOM as implemented in JavaScript. It includes an introduction to DOM concepts of specific value to Web developers. These concepts are applied later in examples using HTML, SVG, and XUL.

7. **Regular Expressions**
   This chapter focuses on the JavaScript implementation of regular expressions, which are a powerful tool for data validation and string manipulation. The origins of regular expressions are explored, as well as its syntax and usage across a variety of programming languages. The chapter ends with an explanation of the similarities and differences in JavaScript's implementation.

8. **Browser and Operating System Detection**
   This chapter explains the importance of writing JavaScript to run on a variety of Web browsers. The two methods of browser detection, object/feature detection and user-agent string detection, are discussed; the advantages and disadvantages of each approach are listed.

9. **All about Events**
   This chapter discusses one of the most important concepts in JavaScript: events. Events are the main way to tie JavaScript to a Web-user interface regardless of the markup language being used. This chapter describes the various methods of handling events and the concept of event flow (including bubbling and capturing).

10. **Advanced DOM Techniques**
    This chapter introduces some of the more advanced features of the DOM, including ranges and style-sheet manipulation. I give examples of when and how to use these technologies, and I also discuss how to achieve cross-browser support given the differences in implementations.

11. **Forms and Data Integrity**
    This chapter discusses the importance of data validation when using forms. As I introduce techniques for handling validation, I apply concepts introduced earlier, such as regular expressions, events, and DOM manipulation.

12. **Sorting Tables**
    This chapter applies a number of language features described earlier to accomplish dynamic sorting of tables on the client. It includes an in-depth discussion of sorting in JavaScript as well as using events, DOM manipulation, and comparison operators to develop a generic table-sorting protocol that can be used in a number of different Web browsers.

13. **Drag and Drop**
    This chapter explains the concept of drag and drop as it applies to JavaScript and Web browsers. The concept of system drag and drop versus simulated drag and drop is discussed, ending with the creation of a standard drag-and-drop interface that can be used across browsers.

14. **Error Handling**
    This chapter introduces the concept of error handling in JavaScript by discussing the use of the `try...catch` statement and the `onerror` event handler. Other topics explored are the creation of custom errors using the `throw` statement and the use of JavaScript debuggers.

15. **XML in JavaScript**
    This chapter presents the features of JavaScript used to read and manipulate eXtensible Markup Language (XML) data. I explain the differences in support and objects in various Web browsers, and I offer suggestions for easier cross-browser coding. This chapter also covers the use of eXtensible Stylesheet Language Transformations (XSLT) to transform XML data on the client.

16. **Client-Server Communication**
    This chapter explores the various JavaScript methods of communicating back to the server. These methods include the use of cookies and JavaScript-based HTTP requests. This chapter also explains how to achieve both GET and POST HTTP requests without the use of hidden frames.

17. **Web Services**
    This chapter looks at how to consume Web Services using JavaScript. The different methods used in Internet Explorer and Mozilla are discussed, along with a basic solution to the problem of adding Web Service support to browsers that don't have built-in support.

18. **Interacting with Plugins**
    This chapter explains the various methods of communication between JavaScript and browser plugins such as Java applets, SVG documents, and ActiveX controls. Other topics include how to program plugins for use with JavaScript.

19. **Deployment Issues**
    This chapter focuses on what happens after the completion of JavaScript coding. Specifically, it describes what should happen before you deploy a JavaScript solution on either a Web site or in a Web application. Topics covered include security issues, internationalization, optimization, intellectual property protection, and Section 508 compliance.

20. **The Evolution of JavaScript**
    This chapter looks into the future of JavaScript to see where the language is headed. ECMAScript 4 and XML for ECMAScript are discussed.

Conventions

To help you get the most from the text and keep track of what's happening, I've used a number of conventions throughout the book.

> **Boxes like this one hold important, not-to-be forgotten information that is directly relevant to the surrounding text.**

Tips, hints, tricks, and asides to the current discussion are offset and placed in italics like this.

As for styles in the text:

- We *highlight* important words when we introduce them
- We show keyboard strokes like this: Ctrl+A
- We show file names, URLs, and code within the text like so: `persistence.properties`
- We present code in two different ways:

```
In code examples we highlight new and important code with a gray background.
```

```
The gray highlighting is not used for code that's less important in the present
context or has been shown before.
```

Source Code

As you work through the examples in this book, you may choose either to type in all the code manually or to use the source code files that accompany the book. All the source code used in this book is available for download at `http://www.wrox.com`. Once at the site, simply locate the book's title (either by using the Search box or by using one of the title lists) and click the Download Code link on the book's detail page to obtain all the source code for the book.

Because many books have similar titles, you may find it easiest to search by ISBN; for this book the ISBN is 0-7645-7908-8.

After you download the code, just decompress it with your favorite compression tool. Alternately, you can go to the main Wrox code download page at `http://www.wrox.com/dynamic/books/download.aspx` to see the code available for this book and all other Wrox books.

Errata

We make every effort to ensure that there are no errors in the text or in the code. However, no one is perfect, and mistakes do occur. If you find an error in one of our books, like a spelling mistake or faulty piece of code, we would be very grateful for your feedback. By sending in errata you may save another reader hours of frustration and, at the same time, you will be helping us provide even higher quality information.

To find the errata page for this book, go to http://www.wrox.com and locate the title using the Search box or one of the title lists. Then, on the book details page, click the Book Errata link. On this page you can view all errata that has been submitted for this book and posted by Wrox editors. A complete book list including links to each book's errata is also available at www.wrox.com/misc-pages/booklist.shtml.

If you don't spot "your" error on the Book Errata page, go to www.wrox.com/contact/techsupport.shtml and complete the form there to send us the error you have found. We'll check the information and, if appropriate, post a message to the book's errata page and fix the problem in subsequent editions of the book.

p2p.wrox.com

For author and peer discussion, join the P2P forums at p2p.wrox.com. The forums are a Web-based system for you to post messages relating to Wrox books and related technologies and to interact with other readers and technology users. The forums offer a subscription feature to e-mail you topics of interest of your choosing when new posts are made to the forums. Wrox authors, editors, other industry experts, and your fellow readers are present on these forums.

At http://p2p.wrox.com you will find a number of different forums that will help you, not only as you read this book, but also as you develop your own applications. To join the forums, just follow these steps:

1. Go to p2p.wrox.com and click the Register link.
2. Read the terms of use and click Agree.
3. Complete the required information to join as well as any optional information you wish to provide and click Submit.
4. You will receive an e-mail with information describing how to verify your account and complete the joining process.

You can read messages in the forums without joining P2P, but in order to post your own messages, you must join.

After you join, you can post new messages and respond to messages other users post. You can read messages at any time on the Web. If you would like to have new messages from a particular forum e-mailed to you, click the Subscribe to This Forum icon by the forum name in the forum listing.

For more information about how to use the Wrox P2P, be sure to read the P2P FAQs for answers to questions about how the forum software works as well as to see many common questions specific to P2P and Wrox books. To read the FAQs, click the FAQ link on any P2P page.

1

What Is JavaScript?

When JavaScript first appeared in 1995, its main purpose was to handle some of the input validation that had previously been left to server-side languages such as Perl. Prior to that time, a round trip to the server was needed to determine if a required field had been left blank or an entered value was invalid. Netscape Navigator sought to change that with the introduction of JavaScript. The capability to handle some basic validation on the client was an exciting new feature at a time when use of telephone modems (operating at 28.8 kbps) was widespread. Such slow speeds turned every trip to the server into an exercise in patience.

Since that time, JavaScript has grown into an important feature of every major Web browser on the market. No longer bound to simple data validation, JavaScript now interacts with nearly all aspects of the browser window and its contents. Even Microsoft, with its own client-side scripting language called VBScript, ended up including its own JavaScript implementation in Internet Explorer from its very earliest version.

In this chapter, you will learn how and why JavaScript came about, from its humble beginnings to its modern-day, feature-packed implementations. To be able to use JavaScript to its full potential, it is important to understand its nature, history, and limitations. Specifically, this chapter examines:

- ❑ The origins of JavaScript and client-side scripting
- ❑ The different parts of the JavaScript language
- ❑ The standards related to JavaScript
- ❑ JavaScript support in popular Web browsers

A Short History

Around 1992, a company called Nombas began developing an embedded scripting language called C-minus-minus (Cmm for short). The idea behind Cmm was simple: a scripting language powerful enough to replace macros, but still similar enough to C (and C++) that developers could learn it quickly. This scripting language was packaged in a shareware product called CEnvi, which first exposed the power of such languages to developers. Nombas eventually changed the name Cmm to ScriptEase because the latter sounded "too negative" and the letter C "frightened people" (`http://www.nombas.com/us/scripting/history.htm`). ScriptEase is now the driving force behind Nombas products. When the popularity of Netscape Navigator started peaking, Nombas developed a version of CEnvi that could be embedded into Web pages. These early experiments were called *Espresso Pages*, and they represented the first client-side scripting language used on the World Wide Web. Little did Nombas know that its ideas would become an important foundation for the Internet.

As Web surfing gained popularity, a gradual demand for client-side scripting languages developed. At the time, most Internet users were connecting over a 28.8 kbps modem even though Web pages were growing in size and complexity. Adding to users' pain was the large number of round-trips to the server required for simple form validation. Imagine filling out a form, clicking the Submit button, waiting 30 seconds for processing, and then being met with a message telling you that you forgot to complete a required field. Netscape, at that time on the cutting edge of technological innovation, began seriously considering the development of a client-side scripting language to handle simple processing.

Brendan Eich, who worked for Netscape at the time, began developing a scripting language called LiveScript for the upcoming release of Netscape Navigator 2.0 in 1995, with the intention of using it both in the browser and on the server (where it was to be called LiveWire). Netscape entered into a development alliance with Sun Microsystems to complete the implementation of LiveScript in time for release. Just before Netscape Navigator 2.0 was officially released, Netscape changed the name to JavaScript in order to capitalize on Java as a new Internet buzzword. Netscape's gamble paid off and JavaScript became a must-have from that point on.

Because JavaScript 1.0 was such a hit, Netscape released version 1.1 in Netscape Navigator 3.0. Right around that time, Microsoft decided to throw its hat into the ring and released Internet Explorer 3.0 with a JavaScript-clone called JScript (so-called in order to avoid any possible licensing issues with Netscape). This major step for Microsoft into the realm of Web browsers is now a date that lives in infamy for Netscape, but it also represented a major step in the development of JavaScript as a language.

After Microsoft threw its hat into the ring, three different JavaScript versions were floating around: JavaScript in Netscape Navigator, JScript in Internet Explorer, and CEnvi in ScriptEase. Unlike C and many other programming languages, JavaScript had no standards governing its syntax or features, and the three different versions only highlighted this problem. With industry fears mounting, it was decided that the language must be standardized.

In 1997, JavaScript 1.1 was submitted to the European Computer Manufacturers Association (ECMA) as a proposal. Technical Committee #39 (TC39) was assigned to "standardize the syntax and semantics of a general purpose, cross-platform, vendor-neutral scripting language" (`http://www.ecma-international.org/memento/TC39.htm`). Made up of programmers from Netscape, Sun, Microsoft, Borland, and other companies with interest in the future of scripting, TC39 met for months to hammer out ECMA-262, a standard defining a new scripting language named ECMAScript.

The following year, the International Organization for Standardization and International Electrotechnical Commission (ISO/IEC) also adopted ECMAScript as a standard (ISO/IEC-16262). Since that time, Web browsers have tried, with varying degrees of success and failure, to use ECMAScript as a basis for their JavaScript implementations.

JavaScript Implementations

Although ECMAScript is an important standard, it is not the only part of JavaScript, and certainly not the only part that has been standardized. Indeed, a complete JavaScript implementation is made up of three distinct parts (see Figure 1-1):

- The Core (ECMAScript)
- The Document Object Model (DOM)
- The Browser Object Model (BOM)

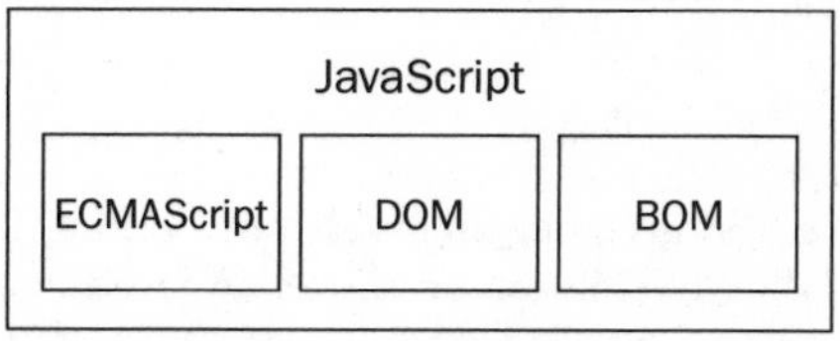

Figure 1-1

ECMAScript

ECMAScript doesn't have ties to any browser in particular and, actually, has no methods for user input or output to speak of. (It is not unlike languages such as C, which rely on external libraries to accomplish such tasks.) So what is ECMAScript? ECMA-262 (p. 2) describes it like this:

> *"ECMAScript can provide core scripting capabilities for a variety of host environments, and therefore the core scripting language is specified...apart from any particular host environment."*

A Web browser is considered a host environment for ECMAScript, but it is not the only host environment. Indeed, numerous other environments (such as Nombas's ScriptEase and Macromedia's ActionScript, used in both Flash and Director MX) can host ECMAScript implementations. So what does ECMAScript specify outside of a browser? To put it simply, ECMAScript describes the following:

- Syntax
- Types
- Statements
- Keywords
- Reserved Words
- Operators
- Objects

ECMAScript is simply a description, defining all the properties, methods, and objects of a scripting language. Other languages implement ECMAScript, as JavaScript does (see Figure 1-2), as the baseline for functionality.

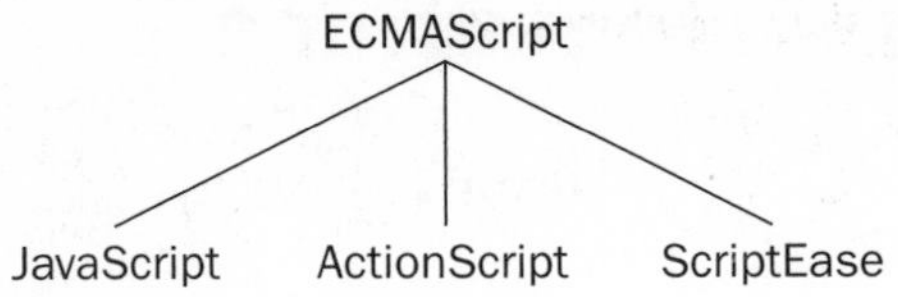

Figure 1-2

Each browser has its own implementation of the ECMAScript interface, which is then extended to contain the DOM and BOM (discussed in the following sections). There are other languages that also implement and extend ECMAScript such as Windows Scripting Host (WSH), ActionScript in Macromedia Flash and Director, and Nombas ScriptEase.

ECMAScript editions

ECMAScript is separated into editions rather than versions because it is defined in a standard called ECMA-262. Like any standard, ECMA-262 can be edited and updated. When a major update occurs, a new edition of the standard is published. The most recent edition of ECMA-262 is edition 3, released in December of 1999. The first edition of ECMA-262 was essentially the same as Netscape's JavaScript 1.1 with all browser-specific code removed, but with a few changes. First, ECMA-262 required support for the Unicode Standard (to support multiple languages). Second, it required that objects be platform-independent (Netscape's JavaScript 1.1 actually had different implementations of objects, such as the Date object, depending on the platform). This was a major reason why JavaScript 1.1 and 1.2 did not conform to the first edition of ECMA-262.

The second edition of ECMA-262 was largely editorial in nature. The standard was updated in order to get into strict agreement with ISO/IEC-16262 and didn't feature any additions, changes, or omissions. ECMAScript implementations typically don't use the second edition as a measure of conformance.

The third edition of ECMA-262 was the first real update to the standard. It provides updates to string handling, the definition of errors, and numeric outputs. It also adds support for regular expressions, new control statements, try...catch exception handling, and small changes to better prepare the standard for internationalization. To many, this marked the arrival of ECMAScript as a true programming language.

What does ECMAScript conformance mean?

In ECMA-262, the definition of ECMAScript conformance is laid out. A scripting language must subscribe to four basic tenets:

- A conforming implementation must support all "types, values, objects, properties, functions, and program syntax and semantics" (ECMA-262, p. 1) as they are described in ECMA-262.
- A conforming implementation must support the Unicode Character Standard.
- A conforming implementation may add "additional types, values, objects, properties, and functions" that are not specified in ECMA-262. ECMA-262 describes these additions as primarily new objects or new properties of objects not given in the specification.
- A conforming implementation may support "program and regular expression syntax" that are not defined in ECMA-262 (meaning that the built-in regular expression support is allowed to be altered and extended).

All implementations of ECMAScript must be in agreement with these criteria.

ECMAScript support in Web browsers

Netscape Navigator 3.0 shipped with JavaScript 1.1 in 1996. That same JavaScript 1.1 specification was then submitted to the ECMA as a proposal for a new standard. With JavaScript's explosive popularity, Netscape was very happy to start developing version 1.2. One problem: ECMA hadn't yet accepted Netscape's proposal.

A little after Netscape Navigator 3.0 was released, Microsoft introduced Internet Explorer 3.0. This version of IE shipped with JScript 1.0 (Microsoft's name for its JavaScript implementation), which was supposed to be equivalent to JavaScript 1.1. However, because of undocumented and improperly replicated features, JScript 1.0 fell far short of JavaScript 1.1.

Netscape Navigator 4.0 was shipped in 1997 with JavaScript 1.2 before the first edition of ECMA-262 was finalized; ECMA-262 was accepted and standardized later that year. As a result, JavaScript 1.2 is not compliant to the first edition of ECMAScript, even though ECMAScript was supposed to be based on JavaScript 1.1.

The next update to JScript occurred in Internet Explorer 4.0 with version JScript 3.0 (version 2.0 was released in Microsoft's Internet Information Server version 3.0 but was never included in a browser). Microsoft put out a press release touting JScript 3.0 as the first truly ECMA-compliant scripting language in the world. At that time, ECMA-262 hadn't yet been finalized, so JScript 3.0 suffered the same fate as JavaScript 1.2: It did not comply with the final ECMAScript standard.

Netscape opted to update its JavaScript implementation in Netscape Navigator 4.06. JavaScript 1.3 brought Netscape into full compliance with ECMAScript Edition 1. Netscape added support for the Unicode standard and made all objects platform-independent while keeping the features that were introduced in JavaScript 1.2.

When Netscape released its source code to the public as the Mozilla project, it was anticipated that JavaScript 1.4 would be shipped with Netscape Navigator 5.0. However, a radical decision to completely redesign the Netscape code from the bottom up threw a monkey wrench into the works. JavaScript 1.4 was only released as a server-side language for the Netscape Enterprise Server and never made it into a Web browser.

Today, all popular Web browsers comply with the third edition of ECMA-262. The following table lists ECMAScript support in the most popular Web browsers:

Browser	ECMAScript Compliance
Netscape Navigator 2.0	–
Netscape Navigator 3.0	–
Netscape Navigator 4.0–4.05	–
Netscape Navigator 4.06–4.79	Edition 1
Netscape 6.0+ (Mozilla 0.6.0+)	Edition 3
Internet Explorer 3.0	–
Internet Explorer 4.0	–

Table continued on following page

Browser	ECMAScript Compliance
Internet Explorer 5.0	Edition 1
Internet Explorer 5.5+	Edition 3
Opera 6.0–7.1	Edition 2
Opera 7.2+	Edition 3
Safari 1.0+/Konqueror ~2.0+	Edition 3

The Document Object Model (DOM)

The *Document Object Model* (DOM) is an application programming interface (API) for HTML as well as XML. The DOM maps out an entire page as a document composed of a hierarchy of nodes. Each part of an HTML or XML page is a derivative of a node. Consider the following HTML page:

```
<html>
    <head>
        <title>Sample Page</title>
    </head>
    <body>
        <p>Hello World!</p>
    </body>
</html>
```

This code can be diagrammed into a hierarchy of nodes using the DOM (see Figure 1-3).

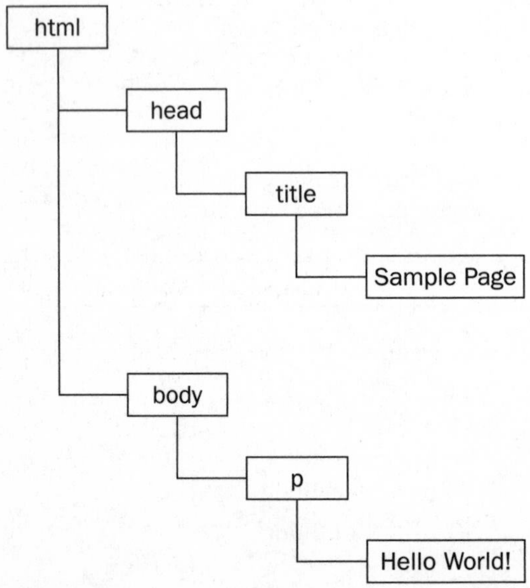

Figure 1-3

By creating a tree to represent a document, the DOM allows developers an unprecedented level of control over its content and structure. Nodes can easily be removed, added, and replaced by using the DOM API.

Why the DOM is necessary

With Internet Explorer 4.0 and Netscape Navigator 4.0 each supporting different forms of Dynamic HTML (DHTML), developers for the first time could alter the appearance and content of a Web page without reloading it. This represented a tremendous step forward in Web technology, but also a huge problem. Netscape and Microsoft each went its own way in developing DHTML, thus ending the period when Web developers could write a single HTML page that could be accessed by any Web browser.

It was decided that something had to be done to preserve the cross-platform nature of the Web. The fear was that, if someone didn't rein in Netscape and Microsoft, the Web would develop into two distinct factions that were exclusive to targeted browsers. It was then that the World Wide Web Consortium (W3C), the body charged with creating standards for Web communication, began working on the DOM.

DOM levels

DOM Level 1 became a W3C recommendation in October of 1998. It consisted of two modules: the DOM Core, which provided a way to map the structure of an XML-based document to allow for easy access to and manipulation of any part of a document, and the DOM HTML, which extended the DOM Core by adding HTML-specific objects and methods.

Note that the DOM is not JavaScript-specific, and indeed has been implemented in numerous other languages. For Web browsers, however, the DOM has been implemented using ECMAScript and now makes up a large part of the JavaScript language.

Whereas DOM Level 1's only goal was to map out the structure of a document, DOM Level 2's aims were much broader. This extension to the original DOM added support for mouse and user interface events (long supported by DHTML), ranges, traversals (methods to iterate over a DOM document), and support for Cascading Style Sheets (CSS) through object interfaces. The original DOM Core introduced in Level 1 was also extended to include support for XML namespaces.

DOM Level 2 introduced several new modules of the DOM to deal with new types of interfaces:

- DOM Views — describes interfaces to keep track of the various views of a document (that is, the document before CSS styling and the document after CSS styling)
- DOM Events — describes interfaces for events
- DOM Style — describes interfaces to deal with CSS-based styles
- DOM Traversal and Range — describes interfaces to traverse and manipulate a document tree

DOM Level 3 further extends the DOM with the introduction of methods to load and save documents in a uniform way (contained in a new module called DOM Load and Save) as well as methods to validate a document (DOM Validation). In Level 3, the DOM Core is extended to support all of XML 1.0, including XML Infoset, XPath, and XML Base.

When reading about the DOM, you may come across references to DOM Level 0. Note that there is no standard called DOM Level 0; it is simply a reference point in the history of the DOM (DOM Level 0 is considered to be the original DHTML supported in Internet Explorer 4.0 and Netscape Navigator 4.0).

Other DOMs

Aside from the DOM Core and DOM HTML interfaces, several other languages have had their own DOM standards published. The languages are XML-based and each DOM adds methods and interfaces unique to that language:

- Scalable Vector Graphics (SVG) 1.0
- Mathematical Markup Language (MathML) 1.0
- Synchronized Multimedia Integration Language (SMIL)

Additionally, other languages have developed their own DOM implementations, such as Mozilla's XML User Interface Language (XUL). However, only the languages in the preceding list are standard recommendations from W3C.

DOM support in Web browsers

The DOM was already a standard for some time before Web browsers started implementing it. Internet Explorer took first stab in version 5.0, but it actually didn't have any realistic DOM support until version 5.5, when it implemented most of DOM Level 1. Internet Explorer hasn't introduced new DOM functionality since that time.

For Netscape, no DOM support existed until Netscape 6 (Mozilla 0.6.0) was introduced. To date, Mozilla has the best support for the DOM, implementing all of Level 1, nearly all of Level 2, and some parts of Level 3. (The goal of the Mozilla development team was to build a 100% standards-compliant browser, and their work paid off.)

Latecomers such as Opera, which didn't add DOM support until version 7.0, and Safari, which has implemented most of DOM Level 1, are mostly on par with Internet Explorer 5.5; and in some cases, they exceed it. However, all the browsers are still a distant second to Mozilla as far as DOM support goes. The following table shows DOM support for popular browsers:

Browser	DOM Compliance
Netscape Navigator 1.0–4.x	–
Netscape 6.0+ (Mozilla 0.6.0+)	Level 1, Level 2, Level 3 (partial)
Internet Explorer 2.0–4.x	–
Internet Explorer 5.0	Level 1 (minimal)
Internet Explorer 5.5+	Level 1 (almost all)
Opera 1.0–6.0	–
Opera 7.0+	Level 1 (almost all), Level 2 (partial)
Safari 1.0+/Konqueror ~2.0+	Level 1

The Browser Object Model (BOM)

The Internet Explorer 3.0 and Netscape Navigator 3.0 browsers feature a *Browser Object Model* (BOM) that allows access and manipulation of the browser window. Using the BOM, developers can move the window, change text in the status bar, and perform other actions that do not directly relate to the page content. What makes the BOM truly unique, and often problematic, is that it is the only part of a JavaScript implementation that has no related standard.

Primarily, the BOM deals with the browser window and frames, but generally any browser-specific extension to JavaScript is considered to be a part of the BOM. Such things include:

- The capability to pop up new browser windows.
- The capability to move, resize, and close browser windows.
- The navigator object, which provides detailed information about the Web browser.
- The location object, which gives detailed information about the page loaded in the browser.
- The screen object, which gives detailed information about the user's screen resolution.
- Support for cookies.
- Internet Explorer extends the BOM to include the ActiveXObject class, which can be used to instantiate ActiveX objects through JavaScript.

Because no standards exist for the BOM, each browser has its own implementation. There are some *de facto* standards, such as having a window object and a navigator object, but each browser defines its own properties and methods for these and other objects. Chapter 5, "JavaScript in the Browser," goes into more detail about the implementation differences.

Summary

This chapter introduced JavaScript as a client-side scripting language for Web browsers. You learned about the various parts that make up a complete JavaScript implementation:

- ECMAScript, the core of JavaScript, describes the language syntax and basic objects.
- The Document Object Model (DOM) describes methods and interfaces for working with the content of a Web page.
- The Browser Object Model (BOM) describes methods and interfaces for interacting with the browser.

Additionally, you explored the history of JavaScript to gain an understanding of how various parts of the language developed and how browsers historically have dealt with the implementation of standards.

2

ECMAScript Basics

Some simple JavaScript functionality is easy to accomplish in the browser. Numerous articles on the Internet show you how to accomplish what many term "stupid Web tricks" using JavaScript. These tricks include how to pop up notices to the user, swap images, and create simple games. Although these are all interesting pieces of functionality to add to Web sites, copying and pasting code doesn't provide an understanding of why or how something works. This chapter aims to provide you with a deeper knowledge base about how JavaScript works by examining its core, ECMAScript.

As described in the previous chapter, ECMAScript provides JavaScript with syntax, operators, and basic objects necessary to complete common programming tasks.

Syntax

Developers familiar with languages such as Java, C, and Perl will find ECMAScript syntax easy to pick up because it borrows syntax from each. Java and ECMAScript have several key syntax features in common, as well as some that are completely different.

The basic concepts of ECMAScript are the following:

- **Everything is case-sensitive.** Just as with Java, variables, function names, operators, and everything else is case-sensitive, meaning that a variable named `test` is different from one named `Test`.
- **Variables are loosely typed.** Unlike Java and C, variables in ECMAScript are not given a specific type. Instead, each variable is defined using the `var` operator and can be initialized with any value. This enables you to change the type of data a variable contains at any point in time (although you should avoid doing so whenever possible). Some examples:

```
var color = "red";
var num = 25;
var visible = true;
```

- **End-of-line semicolons are optional.** Java, C, and Perl require that every line end with a semicolon (`;`) to be syntactically correct; ECMAScript allows the developer to decide whether or not to end a line with a semicolon. If the semicolon is not provided, ECMAScript considers the end of the line as the end of the statement (similar to Visual Basic and VBScript), provided that this doesn't break the semantics of the code. Proper coding practice is to always include the semicolons because some browsers won't run properly without them, but according to the letter of the ECMAScript standard, both of the following lines are proper syntax:

```
var test1 = "red"
var test2 = "blue";
```

- **Comments are the same as in Java, C, and Perl.** ECMAScript borrowed its comments from these languages. There are two types of comments: single-line and multiline. The single-line comments begin with two forward-slashes (`//`), whereas multiline comments begin with a forward-slash and asterisk (`/*`) and end with an asterisk followed by a forward-slash (`*/`).

```
//this is a single-line comment

/* this is a multi-
   line comment */
```

- **Braces indicate code blocks.** Another concept borrowed from Java is the code block. Code blocks are used to indicate a series of statements that should be executed in sequence and are indicated by enclosing the statements between an opening brace (`{`) and a closing brace (`}`). For example:

```
if (test1 == "red") {
    test1 = "blue";
    alert(test1);
}
```

If you are interested in the specifics of ECMAScript's grammar, The ECMAScript Language Specification (ECMA-262) is available for download from ECMA's Web site, at **`www.ecma-international.org`**.

Variables

As I mentioned, variables in ECMAScript are defined by using the `var` operator (short for *variable*), followed by the variable name, such as:

```
var test = "hi";
```

In this example, the variable `test` is declared and given an initialization value of `"hi"` (a string). Because ECMAScript is loosely typed, the interpreter automatically creates a string value for `test` without any explicit type declaration. You can also define two or more variables using the same `var` statement:

```
var test = "hi", test2 = "hola";
```

The previous code defines the variable `test` to have a value of `"hi"` and the variable `test2` to have a value of `"hola"`. Variables using the same `var` statement don't have to be of the same type, however, as shown in the following:

```
var test = "hi", age = 25;
```

This example defines `test` (yet again) in addition to another variable named `age` that is set to the value of `25`. Even though `test` and `age` are two different data types, this is perfectly legal in ECMAScript.

Unlike Java, variables in ECMAScript do not require initialization (they are actually initialized behind the scenes, which I discuss later). Therefore, this line of code is valid:

```
var test;
```

Also unlike Java, variables can hold different types of values at different times; this is the advantage of loosely typed variables. A variable can be initialized with a string value, for instance, and later on be set to a number value, like this:

```
var test = "hi";
alert(test);     //outputs "hi"
//do something else here
test = 55;
alert(test);     //outputs "55"
```

This code outputs both the string and the number values without incident (or error). As mentioned previously, it is best coding practice for a variable to always contain a value of the same type throughout its use.

In terms of variables names, a name must follow two simple rules:

- The first character must be a letter, an underscore (_), or a dollar sign ($).
- All remaining characters may be underscores, dollar signs, or any alphanumeric characters.

All the following variable names are legal:

```
var test;
var $test;
var $1;
var _$te$t2;
```

Of course, just because variable names are syntactically correct doesn't mean you should use them. Variables should adhere to one of the well-known naming conventions:

- Camel Notation — the first letter is lowercase and each appended word begins with an uppercase letter. For example:

```
var myTestValue = 0, mySecondTestValue = "hi";
```

- Pascal Notation — the first letter is uppercase and each appended word begins with an uppercase letter. For example:

```
var MyTestValue = 0, MySecondTestValue = "hi";
```

- Hungarian Type Notation — prepends a lowercase letter (or sequence of lowercase letters) to the beginning of a Pascal Notation variable name to indicate the type of the variable. For example, `i` means integer and `s` means string in the following line:

```
var iMyTestValue = 0, sMySecondTestValue = "hi";
```

The following table list prefixes for defining ECMAScript variables with Hungarian Type Notation. These prefixes are used throughout the book to make sample code easier to read:

Type	Prefix	Example
Array	`a`	`aValues`
Boolean	`b`	`bFound`
Float (Number)	`f`	`fValue`
Function	`fn`	`fnMethod`
Integer (Number)	`i`	`iValue`
Object	`o`	`oType`
Regular Expression	`re`	`rePattern`
String	`s`	`sValue`
Variant (can be any type)	`v`	`vValue`

Another interesting aspect of ECMAScript (and a major difference from most programming languages) is that variables don't have to be declared before being used. For example:

```
var sTest = "hello ";
sTest2 = sTest + "world";
alert(sTest2);     //outputs "hello world"
```

In the previous code, `sTest` is declared with a string value of `"hello"`. The next line uses a variable named `sTest2` to create a concatenation of `sTest` and the string `"world"`. The variable `sTest2` hasn't been defined using the `var` operator; it has just been inserted as if it has already been declared.

When the ECMAScript interpreter sees an identifier that hasn't been declared, it creates a global variable with the given name of the identifier and initializes it with the value specified. This is a handy feature of the language, but it can also be dangerous if you don't keep track of variables closely. Best practice is always to declare all variables as you would with other programming languages (for more information on why you should always declare variables, see Chapter 19, "Deployment Issues").

Keywords

ECMA-262 describes a set of *keywords* that ECMAScript supports. These keywords indicate beginnings and/or endings of ECMAScript statements. By rule, keywords are reserved and cannot be used as variable or function names. Here is the complete list of ECMAScript keywords:

```
break        else         new        var
case         finally      return     void
catch        for          switch     while
continue     function     this       with
default      if           throw
delete       in           try
do           instanceof   typeof
```

If you use a keyword as a variable or function name, you will probably be greeted with an error message like this: "Identifier expected."

Reserved Words

ECMAScript also defines a number of *reserved words*. The reserved words are, in a sense, words that are reserved for future use as keywords. Because of this, reserved words cannot be used as variable or function names. The complete list of reserved words in ECMA-262 Edition 3 is as follows:

```
abstract     enum         int          short
boolean      export       interface    static
byte         extends      long         super
char         final        native       synchronized
class        float        package      throws
const        goto         private      transient
debugger     implements   protected    volatile
double       import       public
```

If you use a reserved word as a variable or function name, more than likely you *will not* receive an error...until a future browser implements one of them. Then the word will be considered a keyword, and you will get a keyword error.

Primitive and Reference Values

In ECMAScript, a variable can hold one of two types of values: primitive values and reference values.

- *Primitive values* are simple pieces of data that are stored on the *stack*, which is to say that their value is stored directly in the location that the variable accesses.
- *Reference values*, on the other hand, are objects that are stored in the *heap*, meaning that the value stored in the variable location is a *pointer* to a location in memory where the object is stored.

When a value is assigned to a variable, the ECMAScript interpreter must decide if it is a primitive or reference value. To do this, the interpreter tries to determine if the value is one of the ECMAScript *primitive types*: Undefined, Null, Boolean, Number, or String. Because each one of these primitive types takes up a fixed amount of space, it can be stored in the small memory area known as the stack. Doing so allows for quick look up of variable values.

In many languages, strings are considered a reference type and not a primitive type because a string can vary in length. ECMAScript breaks from this tradition.

If the value is a reference, then space is allocated on the heap. Because a reference value's size can vary, it cannot be placed on the stack because it would reduce the speed of variable lookup. Instead, the value placed in the variable's stack space is an address of a location in the heap where the object is stored. This address does have a fixed size; so storing it in the stack has no negative effect on variable performance (Figure 2-1).

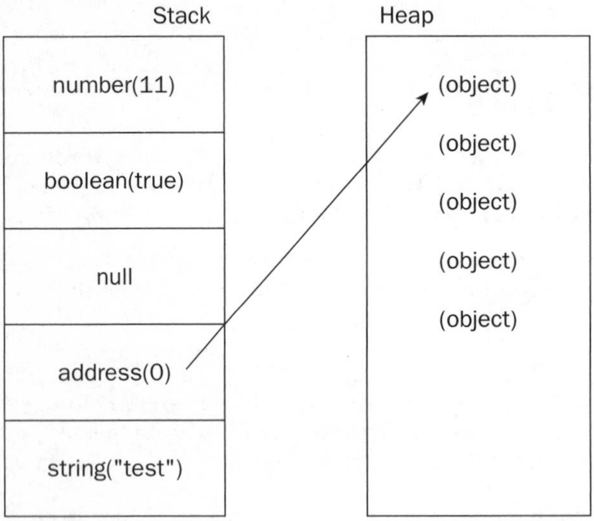

Figure 2-1

Primitive Types

As mentioned previously, ECMAScript has five *primitive types*: Undefined, Null, Boolean, Number, and String. ECMA-262 defines the term *type* as a set of values, and each of the primitive types defines a range of values it can contain as well as literal representations of that type. To determine if a value is in the range of values for a particular type, ECMAScript provides the `typeof` operator. This operator can be used to determine if a value represents a primitive type and, if so, which primitive type it represents.

The typeof operator

The `typeof` operator takes one parameter: the variable or value to check. For example:

```
var sTemp = "test string";
alert(typeof sTemp);     //outputs "string"
alert(typeof 95);    //outputs "number"
```

Calling `typeof` on a variable or value returns one of the following values:

- `"undefined"` if the variable is of the Undefined type.
- `"boolean"` if the variable is of the Boolean type.
- `"number"` if the variable is of the Number type.
- `"string"` if the variable is of the String type.
- `"object"` if the variable is of a reference type or of the Null type.

> **You may wonder why the `typeof` operator returns "object" for a value that is `null`. This was actually an error in the original JavaScript implementation that was then copied in ECMAScript. Today, it is rationalized that `null` is considered a placeholder for an object, even though, technically, it is a primitive value.**

The Undefined type

As previously mentioned, the Undefined type has only one value, `undefined`. When a variable is declared and not initialized, it is given the value of `undefined` by default.

```
var oTemp;
```

The previous line of code declares a variable named `oTemp`, which has no initialization value. This variable is given a value of `undefined`, which is the literal representation of the Undefined type. You can test that the variable is equal to the literal yourself by running this code snippet:

```
var oTemp;
alert(oTemp == undefined);
```

This code displays an alert with the word `"true"`, indicating that these two values are indeed equal. You can also use the `typeof` operator to show that the variable has a value of `undefined`.

```
var oTemp;
alert(typeof oTemp);     //outputs "undefined"
```

Note that a variable having the value of `undefined` is different from a value being undefined. However, the `typeof` operator doesn't actually distinguish between the two. Consider the following:

```
var oTemp;

//make sure this variable isn't defined
//var oTemp2;

//try outputting
```

```
alert(typeof oTemp);      //outputs "undefined"
alert(typeof oTemp2);     //outputs "undefined"
```

The previous code outputs `"undefined"` for both variables, even though only one of them (`oTemp2`) is undefined. If you try to use `oTemp2` with any operator other than `typeof`, it causes an error because operators can only be applied to defined variables. For example, this causes an error:

```
//make sure this variable isn't defined
//var oTemp2;

//try outputting
alert(oTemp2 == undefined);    //causes error
```

The value `undefined` is also returned when a function doesn't explicitly return a value, as in the following:

```
function testFunc() {
   //leave the function blank
}
alert(testFunc() == undefined);    //outputs "true"
```

The Null type

Another type with just one value, the Null type, has only the special value `null`, which is also its literal. The value `undefined` is actually a derivative of the value `null`, so ECMAScript defines them as equal to each other.

```
alert(null == undefined);    //outputs "true"
```

Even though the values are both true, they are considered to have different meanings. Whereas `undefined` is the value assigned when a variable is declared and not initialized, `null` is the value used to represent an object that doesn't exist (which I touched upon briefly in the discussion of the `typeof` operator). If a function or method is supposed to return an object, it usually returns `null` when the object isn't found.

The Boolean type

The Boolean type is one of the most frequently used in the language. It has two values, `true` and `false` (which are also the two Boolean literals). Even though `false` isn't equal to `0`, `0` is converted to `false` when necessary, making it safe to use either in a Boolean statement.

```
var bFound = true;
var bLost = false;
```

The Number type

The most unique type defined in ECMA-262 is the Number type. The Number type can represent both 32-bit integer and 64-bit floating-point values. A Number type literal is considered any number entered directly (not accessed from another variable). For example, the following line of code declares a variable to hold an integer value, which is defined by the literal `55`:

```
var iNum = 55;
```

Integers can also be represented as either octal (base 8) or hexadecimal (base 16) literals. For an octal literal, the first digit must be a zero (0), and the following digits can be any octal digit (0 through 7), as in this line of code:

```
var iNum = 070;     //070 is equal to 56 in decimal
```

To create a hexadecimal literal, the first digit must be a zero (0) followed by the letter `x`, followed by any number of hexadecimal digits (0-9 and A-F). The digits may be in uppercase or lowercase. For example:

```
var iNum = 0x1f;     //0x1f is equal to 31 in decimal
var iNum2 = 0xAB;    //0xAB is equal to 171 in decimal
```

Even though integers can be represented as octal and hexadecimal literals, all mathematical operations return decimal results.

To define a floating-point value, you must include a decimal point and one digit after the decimal point (for instance, use 1.0 not 1.). This is considered a floating-point number literal. Example:

```
var fNum = 5.0;
```

The interesting thing about this form of floating-point literal is that it is actually stored as a string until it's needed for calculation.

For very large or very small numbers, floating-point values can be represented using *e-notation*. In e-notation, a number is represented by digits (including decimal digits), followed by an `e` (or an `E`), followed by the number of times to multiply it by 10. Confused? Here's an example:

```
var fNum = 3.125e7;
```

This notation represents the number 31250000. You can get this value by converting the e-notation to a calculation: 3.125×10^7, which is exactly equal to $3.125 \times 10 \times 10 \times 10 \times 10 \times 10 \times 10 \times 10$.

E-notation can also be used to represent very small numbers, such as 0.00000000000000003, which can be written as 3e-17 (here, 10 is raised to the –17 power, meaning that you will actually be dividing by 10 17 times). ECMAScript, by default, converts any floating-point number with six or more leading zeros into e-notation.

Floating-point values are stored in a 64-bit IEEE 754 format, meaning that decimal values can have up to 17 decimal places. After that, the values are truncated, resulting in small mathematical errors.

A few special values are also defined as part of the Number type. The first two are `Number.MAX_VALUE` and `Number.MIN_VALUE`, which define the outer bounds of the Number value set. All ECMAScript numbers must fall between these two values, without exception. A calculation can, however, result in a number that does not fall in between these two numbers.

When a calculation results in a number greater than `Number.MAX_VALUE`, it is assigned a value of `Number.POSITIVE_INFINITY`, meaning that it has no numeric value anymore. Likewise a calculation that results in a number less than `Number.MIN_VALUE` is assigned a value of `Number.NEGATIVE_INFINITY`, which also has no numeric value. If a calculation returns an infinite value, the result cannot be used in any further calculations.

> *There is actually a special value for infinity named (you guessed it)* ***`Infinity`***. ***`Number.POSITIVE_INFINITY`*** *has a value of* ***`Infinity`***, *whereas* ***`Number.NEGATIVE_INFINITY`*** *has a value of* ***`-Infinity`***.

Because an infinite number can be positive or negative, a method can be used to determine if a number is finite (instead of testing for each infinite number separately). The `isFinite()` method can be called on any number to ensure that the number isn't infinite. For example:

```
var iResult = iNum* some_really_large_number;
if (isFinite(iResult)) {
    alert("Number is finite.");
} else {
    alert("Number is infinite.");
}
```

The final special number value is `NaN`, which stands for *Not a Number*. `NaN` is an odd special value. In general, this occurs when conversion from another type (String, Boolean, and so on) fails. For example, trying to convert the word *blue* into a number value will fail because there is no numeric equivalent. Just like the infinity values, `NaN` cannot be used in mathematical calculations. Another oddity of `NaN` is that it is not equal to itself, meaning that the following will return `false`:

```
alert(NaN == NaN);    //outputs "false"
```

For this reason, it is not recommended to use the `NaN` value itself. Instead, the function `isNaN()` will do the job quite nicely:

```
alert(isNaN("blue"));    //outputs "true"
alert(isNaN("123"));     //outputs "false"
```

The String type

The String type is unique in that it is the only primitive type that doesn't have a definite size. A string can be used to store zero or more Unicode characters, represented by 16-bit integers (Unicode is an international character set that is discussed later in this book).

Each character in a string is given a position, starting with the first character in position 0, the second character in position 1, and so on. This means that the position of the final character in a string is always the length of the string minus 1 (see Figure 2-2).

The string "hello!" has a length of 6.

	h	e	l	l	o	!
Position	0	1	2	3	4	5

Figure 2-2

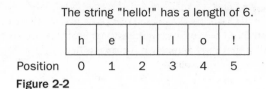

String literals are specified by using either double quotes (") or single quotes ('). This differs from Java, where double quotes are used to specify strings and single quotes are used to specify characters. However, because ECMAScript has no character type, it is permissible to use either notation. For example, the following two lines are valid:

```
var sColor1 = "blue";
var sColor2 = 'blue';
```

The string type also encompasses several character literals, which should be very familiar to Java, C, and Perl developers. The following table lists the ECMAScript character literals:

Literal	Meaning
\n	Newline
\t	Tab
\b	Backspace
\r	Carriage return
\f	Formfeed
\\	Backslash
\'	Single quote
\"	Double quote
\0*nnn*	A character represented by octal code *nnn* (where *n* is an octal digit 0-7)
\x*nn*	A character represented by hexadecimal code *nn* (where *n* is a hexadecimal digit 0-F)
\unnnn	A Unicode character represented by hexadecimal code nnnn (where n is a hexadecimal digit 0-F)

Conversions

One of the most important features of any programming language is the capability to convert between types, and ECMAScript provides developers with a number of easy conversion routines. Most types contain methods that provide for simple conversion, and several global methods are available for more complex conversion. In either case, type conversion is a short, one-step process in ECMAScript.

Converting to a string

The interesting thing about ECMAScript primitive values for Booleans, numbers, and strings is that they are pseudo-objects, meaning that they actually have properties and methods. For example, to get the length of a string, you can do the following:

```
var sColor = "blue";
alert(sColor.length);     //outputs "4"
```

Even though the value `"blue"` is a primitive string, it still has a `length` property holding the size of the string. To that end, the three main primitive values, Booleans, numbers, and strings, all have a `toString()` method to convert their value to a string.

*You may be asking, "Isn't it ridiculously redundant to have a **`toString()`** method for a string?" Yes, it is. But ECMAScript defines all objects, whether they are pseudo-objects representing primitive values or full-fledged objects, to have a **`toString()`** method. Because the string type falls in the category of pseudo-object, it also must have a **`toString()`** method.*

The Boolean `toString()` method simply outputs the string `"true"` or `"false"`, depending on the value of the variable:

```
var bFound = false;
alert(bFound.toString());     //outputs "false"
```

The Number `toString()` method is unique in that it has two modes: default and radix mode. In default mode, the `toString()` method simply outputs the numeric value in an appropriate string (whether that is integer, floating point, or e-notation), like this:

```
var iNum1 = 10;
var fNum2 = 10.0;
alert(iNum1.toString());     //outputs "10"
alert(fNum2.toString());     //outputs "10"
```

*In default mode, the Number's **`toString()`** method always returns the decimal representation of the number, regardless of how you originally specified it. Therefore, numbers specified by octal or hexadecimal literals are output as decimal.*

When you use the Number's `toString()` method in radix mode, it is possible to output the number using a different base, such as 2 for binary, 8 for octal, or 16 for hexadecimal. The *radix* is just a fancy name for the base to convert to, and it is specified as an argument to the `toString()` method:

```
var iNum = 10;
alert(iNum1.toString(2));     //outputs "1010"
alert(iNum1.toString(8));     //outputs "12"
alert(iNum1.toString(16));   //outputs "A"
```

In the previous example, the number 10 is output in three different ways: binary, octal, and hexadecimal. This functionality can be very useful for dealing with numbers in HTML, which use hexadecimal representations for each color.

*Calling **toString(10)** on a number is the same as calling **toString()**; they both return the decimal equivalent of the number.*

Converting to a number

ECMAScript provides two methods for converting non-number primitives into numbers: `parseInt()` and `parseFloat()`. As you may have guessed, the former converts a value into an integer whereas the latter converts a value into a floating-point number. These methods only work properly when called on strings; all other types return `NaN`.

Both `parseInt()` and `parseFloat()` look at a string carefully before deciding what its numeric value should be. The `parseInt()` method starts with the character in position 0 and determines if this is a valid number; if it isn't, the method returns `NaN` and doesn't continue. If, however, the number is valid, the method goes on to the character in position 1 and does the same test. This process continues until a character isn't a valid number, at which point `parseInt()` takes the string (up to that point) and converts it into a number. For example, if you want to convert the string `"1234blue"` to an integer, `parseInt()` would return a value of `1234` because it stops processing one it reaches the character `b`. Any number literal contained in a string is also converted correctly, so the string `"0xA"` is properly converted into the number 10. However, the string `"22.5"` will be converted to `22`, because the decimal point is an invalid character for an integer. Some examples:

```
var iNum1 = parseInt("1234blue");  //returns 1234
var iNum2 = parseInt("0xA");       //returns 10
var iNum3 = parseInt("22.5");      //returns 22
var iNum4 = parseInt("blue");      //returns NaN
```

The `parseInt()` method also has a radix mode, allowing you to convert strings in binary, octal, hexadecimal, or any other base into an integer. The radix is specified as a second argument to `parseInt()`, so a call to parse a hexadecimal value looks like this:

```
var iNum1 = parseInt("AF", 16);    //returns 175
```

Of course, this can also be done for binary, octal, and even decimal (which is the default mode):

```
var iNum1 = parseInt("10", 2);    //returns 2
var iNum2 = parseInt("10", 8);    //returns 8
var iNum2 = parseInt("10", 10);   //returns 10
```

If decimal numbers contain a leading zero, it's always best to specify the radix as 10 so that you won't accidentally end up with an octal value. For example:

```
var iNum1 = parseInt("010");        //returns 8
var iNum2 = parseInt("010", 8);     //returns 8
var iNum3 = parseInt("010", 10);    //returns 10
```

In this code, both lines are parsing the string `"010"` into a number. The first line thinks that the string is an octal value and parses it the same way as the second line (which specifies the radix as 8). The last line specifies a radix of 10, so `iNum3` ends up equal to 10.

The `parseFloat()` method works in a similar way to `parseInt()`, looking at each character starting in position 0. It also continues until the first invalid character and then converts the string it has seen up to that point. For this method, however, the decimal point is a valid character the first time it appears. If two decimal points are present, the second is considered invalid and the `parseFloat()` method converts the string up until that position. This means that the string `"22.34.5"` will be parsed into `22.34`.

Another difference when using `parseFloat()` is that the string must represent a floating-point number in decimal form, not octal or hexadecimal. This method ignores leading zeros, so the octal number `0908` will be parsed into `908`, and the hexadecimal number `0xA` will return `NaN` because `x` isn't a valid character for a floating-point number. There is also no radix mode for `parseFloat()`.

Some examples of using `parseFloat()`:

```
var fNum1 = parseFloat("1234blue");   //returns 1234.0
var fNum2 = parseFloat("0xA");        //returns NaN
var fNum3 = parseFloat("22.5");       //returns 22.5
var fNum4 = parseFloat("22.34.5");    //returns 22.34
var fNum5 = parseFloat("0908");       //returns 908
var fNum6 = parseFloat("blue");       //returns NaN
```

Type Casting

It's also possible to convert values using a process called *type casting*. Type casting allows you to access a specific value as if it were of a different type. Three type casts are available in ECMAScript:

- `Boolean(value)` – casts the given value as a Boolean
- `Number(value)` – casts the given value as a number (either integer or floating-point)
- `String(value)` – casts the given value a string

Casting a value using one of these three functions creates a new value that is a direct conversion of the original. This can lead to some unexpected results.

The `Boolean()` type cast returns `true` when the value is a string with at least one character, a number other than 0, or an object (discussed in the next section); it returns `false` when the value is an empty string, the number 0, `undefined`, or `null`. The following code snippet can be used to test type casting as a Boolean:

```
var b1 = Boolean("");                //false - empty string
var b2 = Boolean("hi");              //true - non-empty string
var b3 = Boolean(100);               //true - non-zero number
var b4 = Boolean(null);              //false - null
var b5 = Boolean(0);                 //false - zero
var b6 = Boolean(new Object());      //true - object
```

The `Number()` type cast works in a manner similar to `parseInt()` and `parseFloat()`, except that it converts the entire value, not just part of it. Remember that `parseInt()` and `parseFloat()` only convert up to the first invalid character (in strings), so `"4.5.6"` becomes `"4.5"`. Using the `Number()` type cast, `"4.5.6"` becomes `NaN` because the entire string value cannot be converted into a number. If a string value can be converted entirely, `Number()` decides whether to use `parseInt()` or `parseFloat()`. The following table illustrates what happens when `Number()` is used on various values:

Usage	Result
`Number(false)`	0
`Number(true)`	1
`Number(undefined)`	NaN
`Number(null)`	0
`Number("5.5")`	5.5
`Number("56")`	56
`Number("5.6.7")`	NaN
`Number(new Object())`	NaN
`Number(100)`	100

The last type cast, `String()`, is the simplest because it can accurately convert any value to a string value. To execute the type cast, it simply calls the `toString()` method of the value that was passed in, which converts 1 to "1", true to "true", false to "false", and so on. The only difference between type casting as a string and using `toString()` is that the type cast can produce a string for a `null` or `undefined` value without error:

```
var s1 = String(null);     //"null"
var oNull = null;
var s2 = oNull.toString(); //won't work, causes an error
```

Type casting is very helpful when dealing with the loosely typed nature of ECMAScript, although you should ensure that only proper values are used.

Reference Types

Reference types are commonly referred to as *classes*, which is to say that when you have a reference value, you are dealing with an object. The vast number of predefined ECMAScript reference types are discussed throughout the book. For now, the discussion focuses around the reference types that are closely related to the primitive types just discussed.

ECMAScript doesn't actually have classes in the traditional sense. In fact, the word "class" doesn't appear in ECMA-262 except to explain that there are no classes. ECMAScript defines "object definitions" that are logically equivalent to classes in other programming languages. This book chooses to use the term "class" because it is more familiar to most developers.

Objects are created by using the `new` operator and providing the name of the class to instantiate. For example, this line creates an instance of the Object class:

```
var o = new Object();
```

This syntax is similar to Java, although ECMAScript requires parentheses to be used only if there are one or more parameters. If there are no parameters, such as in the previous line of code, then the parentheses can be safely omitted:

```
var o = new Object;
```

Chapter 3, "Object Basics," contains a more in-depth look at objects and their behaviors. This section focuses on those reference types that have primitive equivalents.

> **Although the parentheses aren't required, it's always best to include them in order to avoid confusion.**

The Object class

The `Object` class itself isn't very useful, but you should understand it before moving on to the other classes. Why is that? Because the `Object` class in ECMAScript is similar to `java.lang.Object` in Java: It is the base class from which all ECMAScript classes inherit. All the properties and methods of the Object class are also present in the other classes, and so to understand the `Object` class is to understand all the others better.

The `Object` class has the following properties:

- `constructor` — A reference value (pointer) to the function that created the object. For the `Object` class, this points to the native `Object()` function.
- `prototype` — A reference value to the object prototype for this object. Prototypes are discussed further in Chapter 3. For the all classes, this returns an instance of `Object` by default.

The `Object` class also has several methods:

- `hasOwnProperty(`*`property`*`)` — Determines if a given property exists for the object. The property must be specified as a string (for example, `o.hasOwnProperty("name")`).
- `isPrototypeOf(`*`object`*`)` — Determines if the object is a prototype of another object.
- `propertyIsEnumerable(`*`property`*`)` — Determines if a given property can be enumerated by using the `for...in` statement (discussed later in this chapter).
- `toString()` — Returns a primitive string representation of the object. For the `Object` class, this value is undefined in ECMA-262 and, as such, differs in each implementation.
- `valueOf()` — Returns the most appropriate primitive value of this object. For many classes, this returns the same value as `toString()`.

Each of the properties and methods listed previously are designed to be overridden by other classes.

The Boolean class

The `Boolean` class is the reference type for the Boolean primitive type. To create a `Boolean` object, you need only pass in a Boolean value as a parameter:

```
var oBooleanaobject = new Boolean(true);
```

`Boolean` objects override the `valueOf()` method of the `Object` class to return a primitive value of either `true` or `false`; the `toString()` method is also overridden to return a string of "`true`" or "`false`" when called. Unfortunately, not only are Boolean objects of little use in ECMAScript, they can actually be rather confusing.

The problem typically occurs when trying to use `Boolean` objects in Boolean expressions. For example:

```
var oFalseObject = new Boolean(false);
var bResult = oFalseObject && true;      //outputs true
```

In this code, a `Boolean` object is created with a value of `false`. That same object is then ANDed with the primitive value `true`. In Boolean math, `false` AND `true` is equal to `false`. However, in this line of code it is the `oFalseObject` being evaluated, not its value (`false`). As discussed earlier, all objects are automatically converted to `true` in Boolean expressions, so `oFalseObject` actually is given a value of `true` in the expression. Then, `true` ANDed with `true` is equal to `true`.

> **Although you should understand that the `Boolean` object is available, it's best to use Boolean primitives only to avoid the problems mentioned in this section.**

The Number class

As you might have assumed, the `Number` class is the reference type for the Number primitive type. To create a `Number` object, do the following:

```
var oNumberObject = new Number(55);
```

You may recognize the `Number` class from earlier in this chapter, where the special number values are discussed (such as `Number.MAX_VALUE`). All the special values are static properties of the `Number` class.

To get the Number primitive value for a number object, simply use the `valueOf()` method:

```
var iNumber = oNumberObject.valueOf();
```

Of course, the `Number` class also has a `toString()` method, which was discussed at length in the section on conversions. Aside from the standard methods inherited from the `Object` class, the `Number` class has several methods specifically for working with number values.

The `toFixed()` method returns a string representation of a number with a specified number of decimal points. For example:

```
var oNumberObject = new Number(99);
alert(oNumberObject.toFixed(2));    //outputs "99.00"
```

Here, the `toFixed()` method is given an argument of `2`, which indicates how many decimal places should be displayed. As a result, the method returns the string `"99.00"`, filling out the empty decimal places with 0s. This method can be very useful for applications dealing with currency. The `toFixed()` method can represent numbers with 0 to 20 decimal places; other values may cause errors.

Another method related to formatting numbers is the `toExponential()` method, which returns a string with the number formatted in e-notation. Just as with `toFixed()`, `toExponential()` accepts one argument, which is the number of decimal places to output. For example:

```
var oNumberObject = new Number(99);
alert(oNumberObject.toExponential(1));    //outputs "9.9e+1"
```

This code outputs `"9.9e+1"` as the result, which you may remember from the earlier explanation, represents 9.9×10^1. The question is, what if you don't know the proper format to use for a number: fixed or exponential? That's where the `toPrecision()` method comes in.

The `toPrecision()` method returns either the fixed or exponential representation of a number, depending on which makes the most sense. This method takes one argument, which is the total number of digits to use to represent the number (not including exponents). Example:

```
var oNumberObject = new Number(99);
alert(oNumberObject.toPrecision(1));    //outputs "1e+2"
```

In this example, the task is to represent the number `99` with a single digit, which results in `"1e+2"`, otherwise known as 100. Yes, `toPrecision()` rounded the number to get as close as possible to the actual value. Because you can't represent 99 with any fewer than 2 digits, this rounding had to occur. If, however, you want to represent 99 using two digits, well, that's easy:

```
var oNumberObject = new Number(99);
alert(oNumberObject.toPrecision(2));    //outputs "99"
```

Of course the output is `"99"`, because that is the exact representation of the number. But what if you specify more than the number of digits needed?

```
var oNumberObject = new Number(99);
alert(oNumberObject.toPrecision(3));    //outputs "99.0"
```

In this case, `toPrecision(3)` is exactly equivalent to `toFixed(1)`, outputting `"99.0"` as the result.

The **`toFixed()`**, **`toExponential()`**, *and* **`toPrecision()`** *methods round up or down to accurately represent a number with the correct number of decimal places.*

> **Similar to the `Boolean` object, the `Number` object is important, but it should be used sparingly in order to avoid potential problems. Whenever possible, you should use numeric primitives instead.**

The String class

The `String` class is the object representation of a String primitive and is created in the following manner:

```
var oStringObject = new String("hello world");
```

Both `valueOf()` and `toString()` return the String primitive value for a `String` object:

```
alert(oStringObject.valueOf() == oStringObject.toString());    //outputs "true"
```

If you run this code, the output is `"true"`, indicating that the values are indeed equal.

*The **`String`** class is one of the more complicated reference types in ECMAScript. As such, this section focuses only on the basic functionality of the **`String`** class. More advanced functionality is split into suitable topics throughout the book.*

The `String` class has one property, `length`, which gives the number of characters in the string:

```
var oStringObject = new String("hello world");
alert(oStringObject.length);    //outputs "11"
```

This example outputs `"11"`, the number of characters in `"hello world"`. Note that even if the string contains a double-byte character (as opposed to an ASCII character, which uses just one byte), each character is still counted as one.

The `String` class also has a large number of methods. The first two, `charAt()` and `charCodeAt()`, have to do with accessing the individual characters in the string. As described in the section on String primitives, the first character is in position 0, the second is in position 1, and so on. Both these methods accept one argument, the position of the character to act on. The `charAt()` method returns a string containing the character in that position:

```
var oStringObject = new String("hello world");
alert(oStringObject.charAt(1));    //outputs "e"
```

The character in position 1 of `"hello world"` is `"e"`, so calling `charAt(1)` returns `"e"`. If instead of the actual character you want the character code, then calling `charCodeAt()` is the appropriate choice:

```
var oStringObject = new String("hello world");
alert(oStringObject.charCodeAt(1));    //outputs "101"
```

This example outputs `"101"`, which is the character code for the lowercase `e` character.

Next up is the `concat()` method, which is used to concatenate one or more strings to the primitive value of the `String` object. This method actually returns a String primitive value as a result and leaves the original `String` object intact:

```
var oStringObject = new String("hello ");
var sResult = oStringObject.concat("world");
alert(sResult);     //outputs "hello world"
alert(oStringObject);    //outputs "hello "
```

The result of calling the `concat()` method in the previous code is `"hello world"`, whereas the contents of the `String` object remains `"hello "`. For this reason, it is much more common to use the add operator (+) to concatenate strings because it more logically indicates the actual behavior:

```
var oStringObject = new String("hello ");
var sResult = oStringObject + "world";
alert(sResult);     //outputs "hello world"
alert(oStringObject);    //outputs "hello "
```

So far, you have seen methods of concatenating strings and accessing individual characters in strings, but what if you are unsure if a character exists in a particular string? That's where the `indexOf()` and `lastIndexOf()` methods are useful.

Both the `indexOf()` and `lastIndexOf()` methods return the position of a given substring within another string (or –1 if the substring isn't found). The difference between the two is that the `indexOf()` method begins looking for the substring at the beginning of the string (character 0) whereas the `lastIndexOf()` method begins looking for the substring at the end of the string. For example:

```
var oStringObject = new String("hello world");
alert(oStringObject.indexOf("o"));     //outputs "4"
alert(oStringObject.lastIndexOf("o"));    //outputs "7"
```

Here, the first occurrence of the string `"o"` occurs at position 4, which is the `"o"` in `"hello"`. The last occurrence of the string `"o"` is in the word `"world"`, at position 7. If there is only one occurrence of `"o"` in the string, then `indexOf()` and `lastIndexOf()` return the same position.

The next method is `localeCompare()`, which helps sort string values. This method takes one argument, the string to compare to, and it returns one of three values:

- If the `String` object should come alphabetically before the string argument, a negative number is returned (most often this is –1, but it is up to each implementation as to the actual value).
- If the `String` object is equal to the string argument, 0 is returned.
- If the `String` object should come alphabetically after the string argument, a positive number is returned (most often this is 1, but once again, this is implementation-specific).

Example:

```
var oStringObject = new String("yellow");
alert(oStringObject.localeCompare("brick"));      //outputs "1"
alert(oStringObject.localeCompare("yellow"));     //outputs "0"
alert(oStringObject.localeCompare ("zoo"));      //outputs "-1"
```

In this code, the string "yellow" is compared to three different values, "brick", "yellow", and "zoo". Because "brick" comes alphabetically before "yellow", localCompare() returns 1; "yellow" is equal to "yellow", so localCompare() returns 0 for that line; "zoo" comes after "yellow", so localCompare() returns –1. Once again, because the values are implementation-specific, it is best to use localCompare() in this way:

```
var oStringObject1 = new String("yellow");
var oStringObject2 = new String("brick");
var iResult = sTestString.localeCompare("brick");
if(iResult < 0) {
    alert(oStringObject1 + " comes before " + oStringObject2);
} else if (iResult > 0) {
    alert(oStringObject1 + " comes after " + oStringObject2);
} else {
    alert("The two strings are equal");
}
```

By using this sort of construct, you can be sure that the code works correctly in all implementations.

The unique part of localeCompare() is that an implementation's locale (country and language) indicates exactly how this method operates. In the United States, where English is the standard language for ECMAScript implementations, localCompare() is case-sensitive, determining that uppercase letters come alphabetically after lowercase letters. However, this may not be the case in other locales.

ECMAScript provides two methods for creating string values from a substring: slice() and substring(). Both methods return a substring of the string they act on, and both accept either one or two arguments. The first argument is the position where capture of the substring begins; the second argument, if used, is the position **before** which capture is stopped (which is to say that the character at this position is not included in the returned value). If the second argument is omitted, it is assumed that the ending position is the length of the string. Just as with the concat() method, slice() and substring() do not alter the value of the String object itself: They simply return a primitive String value as the result, leaving the String object unchanged.

```
var oStringObject = new String("hello world");
alert(oStringObject.slice(3));          //outputs "lo world"
alert(oStringObject.substring(3));      //outputs "lo world"
alert(oStringObject.slice(3, 7));       //outputs "lo w"
alert(oStringObject.substring(3,7));    //outputs "lo w"
```

In this example, slice() and substring() are used in the same manner and, ironically enough, return the same values. When given just one argument, 3, both methods return "lo world", as the second "l" in "hello" is in position 3. When given two arguments, 3 and 7, both methods return "lo w" (the "o" in "world" is in position 7, so it is not included). Why have two methods that do the exact same thing? Truthfully, the methods aren't identical, but they differ only in how they deal with arguments that are negative numbers.

For the slice() method, a negative argument is treated as the length of the string plus the negative argument; the substring() method treats a negative argument as 0 (which means that it is ignored). For example:

```
var oStringObject= new String("hello world");
alert(oStringObject.slice(-3));         //outputs "rld"
```

```
alert(oStringObject.substring(-3));     //outputs "hello world"
alert(oStringObject.slice(3, -4));      //outputs "lo w"
alert(oStringObject.substring(3,-4));   //outputs "hel"
```

Here, you see the main difference between `slice()` and `substring()`. When you call each with one argument, `-3`, `slice()` returns `"rld"` while `substring()` returns `"hello world"`. This occurs because `slice(-3)` translates into `slice(7)` for the string `"hello world"` whereas `substring(-3)` translates into `substring(0)`. Likewise, the difference is apparent when using the parameters `3` and `-4`. For the `slice()` method, this translates into `slice(3,7)`, the same as the previous example, which returns `"lo w"` as the result. However the `substring()` method interprets this as `substring(3,0)`, which is essentially `substring(0, 3)` because `substring()` always considers the smaller number as the start and the larger number as the end. As a result, `substring(3,-4)` returns `"hel"`. The bottom line here is to be clear about how you are using these two methods.

The last set of methods to be discussed involves case conversion. Four methods perform case conversion: `toLowerCase()`, `toLocaleLowerCase()`, `toUpperCase()`, and `toLocaleUpperCase()`. The uses for these methods are pretty obvious from their names — two convert the string into all lowercase and two convert the string into all uppercase. The `toLowerCase()` and `toUpperCase()` methods are the originals, modeled after the same methods in `java.lang.String`; the `toLocaleLowerCase()` and `toLocaleUpperCase()` methods are intended to be implemented based on a particular locale (in the same way `localeCompare()` is intended to be used). In many locales, the locale-specific methods are identical to the generic ones; however, a few languages apply special rules to Unicode case conversion (such as Turkish), and this necessitates using the locale-specific methods for proper conversion.

```
var oStringObject= new String("Hello World");
alert(oStringObject.toLocaleUpperCase());   //outputs "HELLO WORLD"
alert(oStringObject.toUpperCase());         //outputs "HELLO WORLD"
alert(oStringObject.toLocaleLowerCase());   //outputs "hello world"
alert(oStringObject.toLowerCase());         //outputs "hello world"
```

This code outputs `"HELLO WORLD"` for both `toLocaleUpperCase()` and `toUpperCase()`, just as `"hello world"` is output for both `toLocaleLowerCase()` and `toLowerCase()`. Generally speaking, if you do not know the language in which the code will be running, it is safer to use the locale-specific methods.

*Remember, all the methods and properties for the **`String`** class also apply to String primitive values because they are pseudo-objects.*

The instanceof operator

One of the problems with using reference types to store values has been the use of the `typeof` operator, which returns `"object"` no matter what type of object is being referenced. To provide a solution, ECMAScript introduced another Java operator: `instanceof`.

The `instanceof` operator works in a similar way to the `typeof` operator: It identifies the type of object you are working with. Unlike `typeof`, `instanceof` requires the developer to explicitly ask if an object is of a particular type. For example:

```
var oStringObject = new String("hello world");
alert(oStringObject instanceof String);     //outputs "true"
```

Here, the code asks, "Is variable s an instance of the class String?" Yes it is, so the result is "true". Although not as versatile as typeof, instanceof does offer enough help for the cases when typeof returns "object".

Operators

ECMA-262 describes a set of *operators* that can be used to manipulate variables. The operators range from mathematical operators (such as addition and subtraction) and bitwise operators to relational operators and equality operators. Any time a native action is performed on a value, it is considered an operator.

Unary operators

Unary operators take only one parameter: the object or value to operate on. They are the simplest operators in ECMAScript.

delete

The delete operator erases a reference to an object property or method that was previously defined. Example:

```
var o = new Object;
o.name = "Nicholas";
alert(o.name);      //outputs "Nicholas"
delete o.name;
alert(o.name);     //outputs "undefined"
```

In this example, the name property is deleted, which means that it is forcibly de-referenced and set to undefined (which you will remember is the same value a variable has when it is created and not initialized).

The delete operator *cannot* be used to delete properties and methods that are not defined by the developer. For instance, the following line causes an error:

```
delete o.toString;
```

Even though toString is a valid name of a method, this code line causes an error because the toString() method is native to ECMAScript and not developer-defined.

void

The void operator returns undefined for any value. This is typically used to avoid outputting a value that shouldn't be output, such as when calling a JavaScript function from an HTML <a> element. To do this properly, the function cannot return a valid value; otherwise the browser erases the page and displays only the result of the function. For example:

```
<a href="javascript:window.open('about:blank')">Click Me</a>
```

If you place this line of code into an HTML page, and click the link, you see `"[Object]"` printed on the screen (Figure 2-3). This occurs because `window.open()` returns a reference to the newly opened window (this and other methods of the window are discussed further in Chapter 5, "JavaScript in the Browser"). That object is then converted to a string for display.

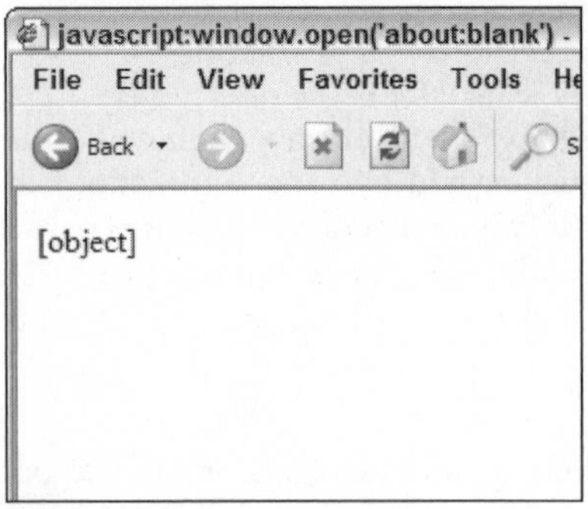

Figure 2-3

To avoid this, use the `window.open()` call with the void operator:

```
<a href="javascript:void(window.open('about:blank'))">Click Me</a>
```

This makes the `window.open()` call return `undefined`, which is not a valid value and is not displayed in the browser window. Remember, functions that have no return value actually return `undefined`.

Prefix increment/decrement

Two operators taken directly from C (and Java) are prefix increment and prefix decrement. Prefix increment, which adds one to a number value, is indicated by placing two plus signs (++) in front of a variable:

```
var iNum = 10;
++iNum
```

The second line increments `iNum` to `11`. This is effectively equal to:

```
var iNum = 10;
iNum = iNum + 1;
```

Likewise, the prefix decrement subtracts one from a value. The prefix decrement is indicated by two minus signs (– –) placed before the variable:

```
var iNum = 10;
--iNum;
```

In this example, the second line decreases the value of `iNum` to `9`.

When you use prefix operators, note that the increment/decrement takes place *before* the expression is evaluated. Consider the following example:

```
var iNum = 10;
--iNum;
alert(iNum);              //outputs "9"
alert(--iNum);            //outputs "8"
alert(iNum);              //outputs "8"
```

The second line decrements num, and the third line displays the result ("9"). The fourth line displays num once again, but this time the prefix decrement is applied in the same statement, which results in the number "8" being displayed. To prove that all decrements are complete, the fifth line once again outputs "8".

The prefix increment and decrement are equal in terms of order of precedence when evaluating a mathematical expression and, therefore, are evaluated left to right. For instance:

```
var iNum1 = 2;
var iNum2 = 20;
var iNum3 = --iNum1 + ++iNum2;    //equals 22
var iNum4 = iNum1 + iNum2;        //equals 22
```

In the previous code, iNum3 is equal to 22 because the expression evaluates to 1 + 21. The variable iNum4 is also equal to 22 and also adds 1 + 21.

Postfix increment/decrement

Two operators, also taken directly from C (and Java), are the postfix increment and postfix decrement. They also add one to a number value, as indicated by the two plus signs (++) placed *after* a variable:

```
var iNum = 10;
iNum++
```

As you might expect, postfix decrement subtracts one from a value and is indicated by two minus signs (– –) placed after the variable:

```
var iNum = 10;
iNum--;
```

The second line of code decreases the value of iNum to 9.

Unlike the prefix operators, postfix operators increment or decrement *after* the containing expression is evaluated. Consider the following example:

```
var iNum = 10;
iNum--;
alert(iNum);              //outputs "9"
alert(iNum--);            //outputs "9"
alert(iNum);              //outputs "8"
```

Just as in the prefix example, the second line decrements iNum, and the third line displays the result (9). The fourth line displays num once again, but this time the postfix decrement is applied in the same statement. However, because the decrement doesn't happen until after the expression is evaluated, this alert also displays the number 9. When the fifth line is executed, the alert displays 8, because the postfix decrement was executed after line 4 but before line 5.

The postfix increment and decrement are also equal in terms of order of precedence when evaluating a mathematical expression, and they are both evaluated left to right. For instance:

```
var iNum1 = 2;
var iNum2 = 20;
var iNum3 = iNum1-- + iNum2++;     //equals 22
var iNum4 = iNum1 + iNum2;         //equals 22
```

In the previous code, `iNum3` is equal to `22` because the expression evaluates to 2 + 20. The variable `iNum4` is also equal to `22`, although it evaluates 1 + 21 because the increment and decrement aren't completed until after the value of `iNum3` has been assigned.

Unary plus and minus

The unary plus and minus are familiar symbols to most people and operate the same way in ECMAScript as they do in high school math. The unary plus essentially has no effect on a number:

```
var iNum= 25;
iNum = +iNum;
alert(iNum);      //outputs "25"
```

In this code, the unary plus is applied to the number `25`, which returns the exact same value. Although unary plus has no effect on numbers, it has an interesting effect on strings: It converts them to numbers.

```
var sNum = "25";
alert(typeof sNum);      //outputs "string"
var iNum = +sNum;
alert(typeof iNum);      //outputs "number"
```

This code converts a string representation of `25` into the actual number. When the unary plus operates on strings, it evaluates strings the same way as `parseInt()` with one major difference: Unless the string begins with `"0x"` (indicating a hexadecimal number), the string is converted as if it were decimal. So `"010"` is always 10 when converted using unary plus, however, `"0xB"` is converted to 11.

The unary minus, on the other hand, negates the value of a number (for example, converting `25` into `-25`):

```
var iNum= 25;
iNum = -iNum;
alert(iNum);      //outputs "-25"
```

Similar to unary plus, unary minus converts a string into a number with one slight difference: Unary minus also negates the value. For example:

```
var sNum = "25";
alert(typeof sNum);      //outputs "string"
var iNum = -sNum;
alert(iNum);             //outputs "-25"
alert(typeof iNum);      //outputs "number"
```

The unary minus converted the string "25" into the number -25 in the previous code (unary minus also acts the same way as unary plus regarding hexadecimal and decimal values, but it also negates the value).

Bitwise operators

The following set of operators work on numbers at their very base level, with the 32 bits that represent them. Before examining these operators, I begin with a more detailed look into integers in ECMAScript.

Integers revisited

ECMAScript integers come in two specific flavors: signed (allowing both positive and negative values) and unsigned (allowing only positive numbers). In ECMAScript, all integer literals are signed by default. But what exactly does this mean?

Signed integers use the first 31 bits to represent the numeric value of the integer, whereas the 32nd bit represents the sign of the number, 0 for positive or 1 for negative. The number values can range from –2147483648 to 2147483647.

You can store signed integers in binary form in two different ways, one for positive numbers and one for negative numbers. Positive numbers are stored in true binary format, with each of the first 31 bits representing a power of 2, starting with the first bit (called bit 0), which represents 2^0; the second bit (bit 1) represents 2^1, and so on. If any bits are unused, they are filled with 0s and essentially ignored. For example, the number 18 is represented as shown in Figure 2-4.

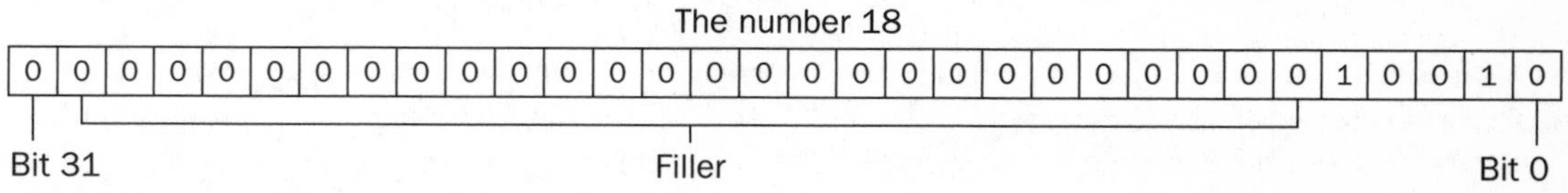

Figure 2-4

The binary version of 18 uses only the first five bits, which are the significant bits for this number. When converting a number into a binary string (as discussed earlier), you see only the significant bits:

```
var iNum = 18;
alert(iNum.toString(2));     //outputs "10010"
```

This code outputs only "10010" instead of the whole 32-bit representation. The other bits really aren't important because using just these five bits makes possible to determine the decimal value (Figure 2-5).

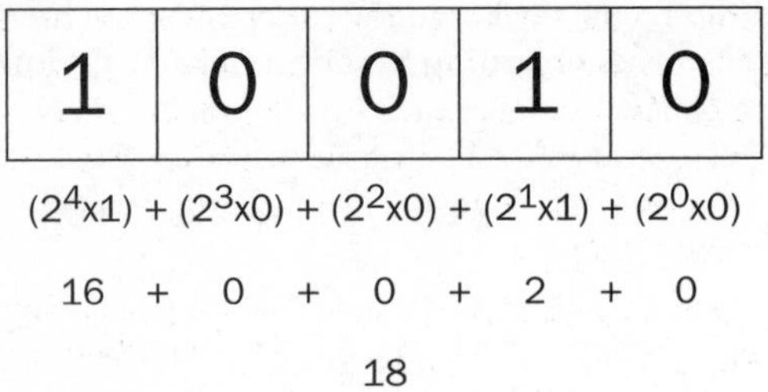

Figure 2-5

Negative numbers are also stored in binary code, but in a format called *two's complement*. The two's complement of a number is calculated in three steps:

1. Determine the binary representation of the non-negative version (for example, to find –18, first determine the binary representation of 18).
2. Find the one's complement of the number, which essentially means that every 0 must be replaced with 1 and vice versa.
3. Add 1 to the one's complement.

To determine the binary representation for –18, you must first take the binary representation of 18, which is:

```
0000 0000 0000 0000 0000 0000 0001 0010
```

Next, take the one's complement, which is the inverse:

```
1111 1111 1111 1111 1111 1111 1110 1101
```

Finally, add 1 to the one's complement:

```
1111 1111 1111 1111 1111 1111 1110 1101
                                       1
---------------------------------------
1111 1111 1111 1111 1111 1111 1110 1110
```

So, the binary equivalent of –18 is 1111 1111 1111 1111 1111 1111 1110 1110. Keep in mind that the developer has no access to bit 31 when dealing with signed integers.

The interesting thing about negative integers is that conversion to a binary string does not show the two's complement form. Instead, ECMAScript outputs the standard binary code for the number's absolute value preceded by a minus sign. For example:

```
var iNum = -18;
alert(iNum.toString(2));     //outputs "-10010"
```

This code outputs only `"-10010"` instead of the two's complement in order to protect bit 31 from being accessed. To put it simply, ECMAScript aims to deal with integers in such a simple way that developers need not spend any time worrying about their usage.

Unsigned integers, on the other hand, treat the final bit just like the other bits. In this mode, the 32nd bit doesn't represent the sign of the number but rather the value 2^{31}. Because of this extra bit, unsigned integers range in value from 0 to 4294967295. For numbers less than or equal to 2147483647, unsigned integers look the same as positive signed integers; numbers greater than 2147483647 require the use of bit 31 (which is always 0 in a signed positive integer). Unsigned integers only return the significant bits when they are converted into a binary string.

Remember, all integer literals are stored as signed integers by default. Unsigned integers can only be created by using one of the ECMAScript bitwise operators.

Bitwise NOT

The bitwise NOT is represented by a tilde (~) and is one of just a few ECMAScript operators related to binary mathematics. The bitwise NOT is a three-step process:

1. The operand is converted to a 32-bit number.
2. The binary form is converted into its one's complement.
3. The one's complement is converted back to a floating-point number.

Example:

```
var iNum1 = 25;          //25 is equal to 00000000000000000000000000011001
var iNum2 = ~iNum1;      //convert to 11111111111111111111111111100110
alert(iNum2);            //outputs "-26"
```

The bitwise NOT essentially negates a number and then subtracts 1 from it, so 25 becomes –26. Really, the same effect can be achieved by doing this:

```
var iNum1 = 25;
var iNum2 = -iNum1 - 1;
alert(iNum2);     //outputs "-26"
```

Bitwise AND

The bitwise AND operator is indicated by the ampersand (&) and works directly on the binary form of numbers. Essentially, bitwise AND lines up the bits in each number and then, using the following rules, performs an AND operation between the two bits in the same position:

Bit from First Number	Bit from Second Number	Result
1	1	1
1	0	0
0	1	0
0	0	0

For example, if you wanted to AND the numbers 25 and 3 together, the code looks like this:

```
var iResult = 25 & 3;
alert(iResult);    //outputs "1"
```

The result of a bitwise AND between 25 and 3 is 1. Why is that? Take a look:

```
 25 = 0000 0000 0000 0000 0000 0000 0001 1001
  3 = 0000 0000 0000 0000 0000 0000 0000 0011
---------------------------------------------
AND = 0000 0000 0000 0000 0000 0000 0000 0001
```

As you can see, only one bit (bit 0) contains a 1 in both 25 and 3. Because of this, every other bit of the resulting number is set to 0, making the result equal to 1.

Bitwise OR

The bitwise OR operator is indicated by the pipe (|) and also works directly on the binary form of numbers. Essentially, bitwise OR follows these rules when evaluating bits:

Bit from First Number	Bit from Second Number	Result
1	1	1
1	0	1
0	1	1
0	0	0

Using the same example as for bitwise AND, if you want to OR the numbers 25 and 3 together, the code looks like this:

```
var iResult = 25 | 3;
alert(iResult);    //outputs "27"
```

The result of a bitwise OR between 25 and 3 is 27:

```
 25 = 0000 0000 0000 0000 0000 0000 0001 1001
  3 = 0000 0000 0000 0000 0000 0000 0000 0011
---------------------------------------------
 OR = 0000 0000 0000 0000 0000 0000 0001 1011
```

As you can see, four bits contain 1 in either number, so these are passed through to the result. The binary code 11011 is equal to 27.

Bitwise XOR

The bitwise XOR operator is indicated by a caret (^) and, of course, works directly on the binary form of numbers. Bitwise XOR is different from bitwise OR in that it returns 1 only when exactly one bit has a value of 1. Here is the truth table:

Bit from First Number	Bit from Second Number	Result
1	1	0
1	0	1
0	1	1
0	0	0

To XOR the numbers 25 and 3 together, use the following code:

```
var iResult = 25 ^ 3;
alert(iResult);    //outputs "26"
```

The result of a bitwise XOR between 25 and 3 is 26:

```
 25 = 0000 0000 0000 0000 0000 0000 0001 1001
  2 = 0000 0000 0000 0000 0000 0000 0000 0011
---------------------------------------------
XOR = 0000 0000 0000 0000 0000 0000 0001 1010
```

As you can see, four bits contain 1 in either number, so these are passed through to the result. The binary code 11010 is equal to 26.

Left shift

The left shift is represented by two *less-than* signs (<<). It shifts all bits in a number to the left by the number of positions given. For example, if you take the number 2 (which is equal to 10 in binary) and shifted it 5 bits to the left, you end up with 64 (which is equal to 1000000 in binary):

```
var iOld = 2;              //equal to binary 10
var iNew = iOld << 5;       //equal to binary 1000000 which is decimal 64
```

Note that when the bits are shifted, five empty bits remain to the right of the number. The left shift fills these bits with the value in the 32nd bit (the sign bit) to make the result a complete 32-bit number (Figure 2-6).

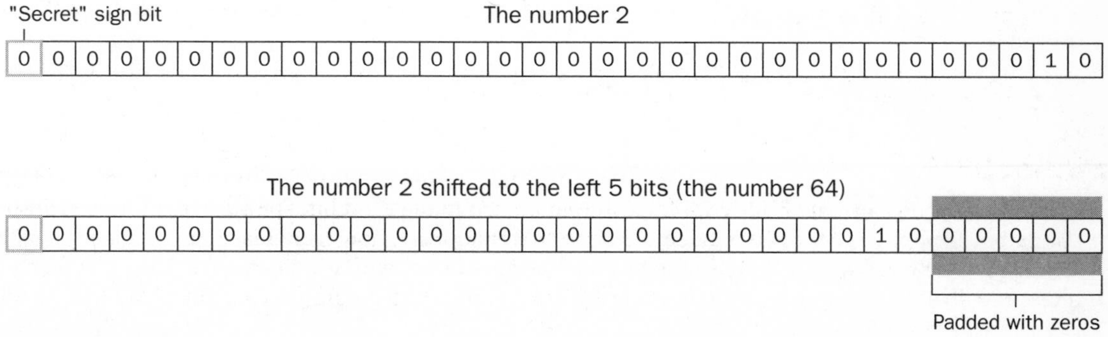

Figure 2-6

Note that left shift preserves the sign of the number it's operating on. For instance, if –2 is shifted to the left by 5 spaces, it becomes –64, not positive 64. "But isn't the sign stored in the 32nd bit?" you ask. Yes it is, but that is behind the scenes of ECMAScript. The developer can never have access to that 32nd bit directly. Even printing out a negative number as a binary string shows the negative sign (for instance, –2 is displayed as –10 instead of 10000000000000000000000000000010).

Signed right shift

The signed right shift is represented by two *greater-than* signs (>>) and shifts all bits in a 32-bit number to the right while preserving the sign (positive or negative); signed right shift is the exact opposite of left shift. For example, if 64 is shifted to the right five bits, it becomes 2:

```
var iOld = 64;            //equal to binary 1000000
var iNew = iOld >> 5;     //equal to binary 10 with is decimal 2
```

Once again, when bits are shifted, the shift creates empty bits. This time, the empty bits occur at the left of the number, but after the sign bit (see Figure 2-7). Once again, ECMAScript fills these empty bits with the value in the sign bit to create a complete number.

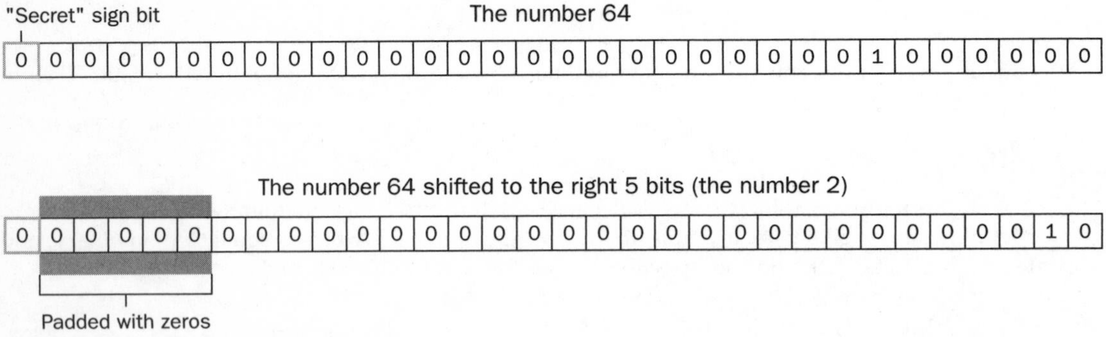

Figure 2-7

Unsigned right shift

The unsigned right shift is represented by three greater-than signs (>>>) and shifts all bits in an unsigned 32-bit number to the right. For numbers that are positive, the effect is the same as a signed right shift. Using the same example as for the signed right shift example, if 64 is shifted to the right five bits, it becomes 2:

```
var iOld = 64;            //equal to binary 1000000
var iNew = iOld >>> 5;    //equal to binary 10 with is decimal 2
```

For numbers that are negative, however, something quite different happens. You see, the unsigned right shift operator fills all empty bits with the value contained in the 32nd bit. For positive numbers, this bit is 0; so the empty bits are filled with zero. For negative numbers, however, this bit is 1, meaning that all empty bits are filled with 1. Because the result of unsigned right shift is an unsigned 32-bit number, you end up with a very large number. For example, if you shift –64 to the right by five bits, you end up with 2147483616. How does this happen?

First, look at the true 32-bit representation of –64. To do so, you need to create an unsigned version of the number, which can be attained by using unsigned right shift with a bit count of 0:

```
var iUnsigned64 = 64 >>> 0;
```

Then, to get the actual bit representation, use the `toString()` method of the Number type with a radix of 2:

```
alert(iUnsigned64.toString(2));
```

This yields a value of 11111111111111111111111111000000, which is the two's complement representation of –64 for a signed integer, but it is equal to 4294967232 as an unsigned integer. For this reason, use caution with the unsigned right shift operator.

Boolean operators

Almost as important as equality operators, Boolean operators are what make a programming language function. Without the capability to test relationships between two values, statements such as `if...else` and loops wouldn't be useful. There are three Boolean operators: NOT, AND, and OR.

Logical NOT

The logical NOT operator in ECMAScript is the same as in C and Java, indicated by an exclamation point (`!`). Unlike logical OR and logical AND operators, the logical NOT always returns a Boolean value. The logical NOT operator behaves in the following way:

- If the operand is an object, `false` is returned.
- If the operand is the number 0, `true` is returned.
- If the operand is any number other than 0, `false` is returned.
- If the operand is `null`, `true` is returned.
- If the operand is `NaN`, `true` is returned.
- If the operand is `undefined`, an error occurs.

This operator is typically used in control loops (discussed later):

```
var bFound = false;
var i = 0;

while (!bFound) {
    if (aValues[i] == vSearchValue) {
        bFound = true;
    } else {
        i++;
    }
}
```

In this example, a Boolean variable (`found`) keeps track of the success of a search. When the item in question is located, `found` is set to `true`, which causes `!found` to equal `false`, meaning that execution will escape the `while` loop.

The logical NOT operator is also useful in determining the Boolean equivalent of an ECMAScript variable. In order to do this, you use two logical NOT operators in a row. The first NOT returns a Boolean value no matter what operand it is given. The second NOT negates that Boolean value and so gives the true Boolean value of a variable.

```
var bFalse = false;
var sBlue = "blue";
var iZero = 0;
var iThreeFourFive = 345;
var oObject = new Object;
document.write("The Boolean value of bFalse is " + (!!bFalse));
document.write("<br />The Boolean value of sBlue is " + (!!sBlue));
document.write("<br />The Boolean value of iZero is " + (!!iZero));
document.write("<br />The Boolean value of iThreeFourFive is " +
(!!iThreeFourFive));
document.write("<br />The Boolean value of oObject is " + (!!oObject));
```

Running this example yields the following output:

```
The Boolean value of bFalse is false
The Boolean value of sBlue is true
The Boolean value of iZero is false
The Boolean value of iThreeFourFive is true
The Boolean value of oObject is true
```

Logical AND

The logical AND operator in ECMAScript is indicated by the double ampersand (`&&`):

```
var bTrue = true;
var bFalse = false;
var bResult = bTrue && bFalse;
```

Logical AND behaves as described in the following truth table:

Operand 1	Operand 2	Result
true	true	true
true	false	false
false	true	false
false	false	false

Logical AND can be used with any type of operands, not just Boolean values. When either operand is not a primitive Boolean, logical AND does not always return a Boolean value:

- If one operand is an object and one is a Boolean, the object is returned.
- If both operands are objects, the second operand is returned.
- If either operand is `null`, `null` is returned.
- If either operand is `NaN`, `NaN` is returned.
- If either operand is `undefined`, an error occurs.

Just as in Java, logical AND is a short-circuited operation, meaning that if the first operand determines the result, the second operand is never evaluated. In the case of logical AND, if the first operand is false, no matter what the value of the second operand, the result can't be equal to true. Consider the following example:

```
var bTrue = true;
var bResult = (bTrue && bUnknown);     //error occurs here
alert(bResult);            //this line never executes
```

This code causes an error when the logical AND is evaluated because the variable `bUnknown` is undefined. The value of variable `bTrue` is `true`, so the logical AND operator continued on to evaluate variable `bUnknown`. When it did, an error occurred because `bUnknown` is undefined and, therefore, cannot be used in a logical AND operation. If this example is changed so that `a` is set to `false`, the error won't occur:

```
var bFalse = false;
var bResult = (bFalse && bUnknown);
alert(bResult);     //outputs "false"
```

In this code, the script writes out the string `"false"`, the value returned by the logical AND operator. Even though the variable `bUnknown` is undefined, it never gets evaluated because the first operand is `false`. You must always keep in mind short-circuiting when using logical AND.

Logical OR

The logical OR operator in ECMAScript is the same as in Java, using the double pipe (||):

```
var bTrue = true;
var bFalse = false;
var bResult = bTrue || bFalse;
```

Logical OR behaves as described in the following truth table:

Operand 1	Operand 2	Result
true	true	true
true	false	true
false	true	true
false	false	false

Just like logical AND, if either operand is not a Boolean, logical OR will not always return a Boolean value:

- If one operand is an object and one is a Boolean, the object is returned.
- If both operands are objects, the first operand is returned.
- If both operands are `null`, `null` is returned.
- If either operand is `NaN`, `NaN` is returned.
- If either operand is undefined, an error occurs.

Also like the logical AND operator, the logical OR operator is short-circuited. In this case, if the first operand evaluates to `true`, the second operand is not evaluated. For example:

```
var bTrue = true;
var bResult = (bTrue || bUnknown);
alert(bResult);              //outputs "true"
```

As with the previous example, the variable `c` is undefined. However, because the variable `bTrue` is set to `true`, variable `bUnknown` is never evaluated and thus the output is `"true"`. If the value of `bTrue` is changed to `false`, an error occurs:

```
var bFalse = false;
var bResult = (bTrue || bUnknown);    //error occurs here
alert(bResult);              //this line never executes
```

Multiplicative operators

This next section deals with the three multiplicative operators: multiple, divide, and modulus. These operators work in a manner similar to their counterparts in languages such as Java, C, and Perl, but they also include some automatic type conversions you need to be aware of.

Multiply

The multiply operator is represented by an asterisk (*) and is used, as one might suspect, to multiply two numbers. The syntax is the same as in C:

```
var iResult = 34 * 56;
```

However, the multiply operator also has some unique behaviors when dealing with special values:

- If the operands are numbers, regular arithmetic multiply is performed, meaning that two positives or two negatives equal a positive, whereas operands with different signs yield a negative. If the result is too high or too low, the result is either `Infinity` or `–Infinity`.
- If either operand is `NaN`, the result is `NaN`.
- If `Infinity` is multiplied by 0, the result is `NaN`.
- If `Infinity` is multiplied by any number other than 0, the result is either `Infinity` or `–Infinity`, depending on the sign of the second operand.
- If `Infinity` is multiplied by `Infinity`, the result is `Infinity`.

Divide

The divide operator is represented by a slash (`/`) and divides the first operand by the second operand:

```
var iResult = 66 / 11;
```

The divide operator, like the multiply operator, has special behaviors for special values:

- If the operands are numbers, regular arithmetic division is performed, meaning that two positives or two negatives equal a positive, whereas operands with different signs yield a negative. If the result is too high or too low, the result is either `Infinity` or – `Infinity`.
- If either operand is `NaN`, the result is `NaN`.
- If `Infinity` is divided by `Infinity`, the result is `NaN`.
- If `Infinity` is divided by any number, the result is `Infinity`.
- Division of a non-infinite number by 0 always equals `NaN`.
- If `Infinity` is divided by any number other than 0, the result is either `Infinity` or – `Infinity`, depending on the sign of the second operand.

Modulus

The modulus (remainder) operator is represented by a percent sign (`%`) and is used in the following way:

```
var iResult = 26 % 5;    //equal to 1
```

Just like the other multiplicative operators, the modulus operator behaves differently for special values:

- If the operands are numbers, regular arithmetic division is performed, and the remainder of that division is returned.
- If the dividend is `Infinity` or the divisor is 0, the result is `NaN`.
- If `Infinity` is divided by `Infinity`, the result is `NaN`.
- If the divisor is an infinite number, the result is the dividend.
- If the dividend is 0, the result is 0.

Additive operators

The additive operators, add and subtract, are typically the simplest mathematical operators in programming languages. In ECMAScript, however, a number of special behaviors are associated with each operator.

Add

The add operator (+) is used just as one would expect:

```
var iResult = 1 + 2;
```

Just like the multiplicative operators, additive operators also behave in special ways when dealing with special values. If the two operands are numbers, they perform an arithmetic add and return the result according to these rules:

- If either number is `NaN`, the result is `NaN`.
- If `Infinity` is added to `Infinity`, the result is `Infinity`.
- If `–Infinity` is added to `–Infinity`, the result is `–Infinity`.
- If `Infinity` is added to `–Infinity`, the result is `NaN`.
- If +0 is added to +0, the result is +0.
- If –0 is added to +0, the result is +0.
- If –0 is added to –0, the result is –0.

If, however, one of the operands is a string, then the following rules are applied:

- If both operands are strings, the second string is concatenated to the first.
- If only one operand is a string, the other operand is converted to a string and the result is the concatenation of the two strings.

For example:

```
var result1 = 5 + 5;      //two numbers
alert(result);     //outputs "10"
var result2 = 5 + "5";     //a number and a string
alert(result);     //outputs "55"
```

This code illustrates the difference between the two modes for the add operator. Normally, `5 + 5` equals `10` (a primitive number value), as illustrated by the first two lines of code. However, if one of the operands is changed to a string, `"5"`, the result becomes `"55"` (which is a primitive string value) because the first operand gets translated to `"5"` as well.

> **To avoid one of the most common mistakes made in JavaScript, always double check the data types when using the add operator.**

Subtract

The subtract operator (–) is another that is used quite frequently:

```
var iResult = 2 - 1;
```

Just like the add operator, the subtract operator has special rules to deal with the variety of type conversions present in ECMAScript:

- If the two operands are numbers, perform arithmetic subtract and return the result.
- If either number is `NaN`, the result is `NaN`.

- If `Infinity` is subtracted from `Infinity`, the result is `NaN`.
- If `-Infinity` is subtracted from `-Infinity`, the result is `NaN`.
- If `-Infinity` is subtracted from `Infinity`, the result is `Infinity`.
- If `Infinity` is subtracted from `-Infinity`, the result is `-Infinity`.
- If +0 is subtracted from +0, the result is +0.
- If –0 is subtracted from +0, the result is –0.
- If –0 is subtracted from –0, the result is +0.
- If either of the two operands is not a number, the result is `NaN`.

Relational operators

The less-than (<), greater-than (>), less-than-or-equal (<=), and greater-than-or-equal (>=) relational operators perform comparisons between numbers in the same way that you learned in math class. Each of these operators returns a Boolean value:

```
var bResult1 = 5 > 3;     //true
var bResult2 = 5 < 3;     //false
```

When a relational operator is used on two strings, however, a different behavior occurs. Many expect that less-than means "alphabetically before" and greater-than means "alphabetically after," but this is not the case. For strings, each of the first string's character codes is numerically compared against the character codes in a corresponding location in the second string. After this comparison is complete, a Boolean value is returned. The problem here is that the character codes of uppercase letters are all lower than the character codes of lowercase letters, meaning that you can run into situations like this:

```
var bResult = "Brick" < "alphabet";
alert(bResult);     //outputs "true"
```

In this example, the string `"Brick"` is considered to be less than the string `"alphabet"` because the letter `B` has a character code of 66 and letter `a` has a character code of 97. To force a true alphabetic result, you must convert both operands into a common case (upper or lower) and then compare:

```
var bResult = "Brick".toLowerCase() < "alphabet".toLowerCase();
alert(bResult);     //outputs "false"
```

Converting both operands to lowercase ensures that `"alphabet"` is correct identified as alphabetically before `"Brick"`.

Another sticky situation occurs when comparing numbers that are strings, for example:

```
var bResult = "23" < "3";
alert(bResult);     //outputs "true"
```

This code will output `"true"` when comparing the string `"23"` to `"3"`. Because both operands are strings, they are compared by their character codes (the character code for `"2"` is 50; the character code for `"3"` is 51). If, however, one of the operands is changed to a number, the result makes more sense:

```
var bResult = "23" < 3;
alert(bResult);     //outputs "false"
```

Here, the string `"23"` is converted into the number `23` and then compared to `3`, giving the expected result. Whenever a number is compared to a string, ECMAScript says that the string should be converted into a number and then numerically compared with the other number. This works well for cases like the previous example, but what if the string can't be converted into a number? Consider this example:

```
var bResult = "a" < 3;
alert(bResult);
```

What would you expect this to output? The letter `"a"` can't be meaningfully converted into a number. After all, if you were to use `parseInt()` on it, `NaN` would be returned. As a rule, any relational operation that contains `NaN` returns `false`, so this code also outputs `false`:

```
var bResult = "a" >= 3;
alert(bResult);
```

Typically, if two values return `false` for a less-than operation, they must return `true` for a greater-than-or-equal operation, but this is not the case when one number is `NaN`.

Equality operators

Determining whether two variables are equivalent is one of the most important operations in programming. This is fairly straightforward when dealing with primitive values, but the task gets a little complicated when you take objects into account. To deal with this problem, ECMAScript provides two sets of operators: equal and not equal to deal with primitive values, and identically equal and not identically equal to deal with objects.

Equal and not equal

The equal operator in ECMAScript is the double equal sign (==), and it returns `true` if—and only if—both operands are equal. The not equal operator is the exclamation point followed by an equal sign (!=), and it returns `true` if—and only if—two operands are not equal. Both operators do conversions in order to determine if two operands are equal.

When performing conversions, follow these basic rules:

- If an operand is a Boolean value, convert it into a numeric value before checking for equality. A value of `false` converts to 0; whereas a value of `true` converts to 1.
- If one operand is a string and the other is a number, attempt to convert the string into a number before checking for equality.
- If one operand is an object and the other is a string, attempt to convert the object to a string (using the `toString()` method) before checking for equality.
- If one operand is an object and the other is a number, attempt to convert the object to a number before checking for equality.

The operators also follow these rules when making comparisons:

- Values of `null` and `undefined` are equal.
- Values of `null` and `undefined` cannot be converted into any other values for equality checking.
- If either operand is `NaN`, the equal operator returns `false` and the not equal operator returns `true`. Important note: Even if both operands are `NaN`, the equal operator returns `false` because, by rule, `NaN` is not equal to `NaN`.
- If both operands are objects, then the reference values are compared. If both operands point to the same object, then the equal operator returns `true`. Otherwise, the two are not equal.

The following table lists some special cases and their results:

Expression	Value
null == undefined	true
"NaN" == NaN	false
5 == NaN	false
NaN == NaN	false
NaN != NaN	true
false == 0	true
true == 1	true
true == 2	false
undefined == 0	false
null == 0	false
"5" == 5	true

Identically equal and not identically equal

The brothers of the equal and not equal operators are the identically equal and not identically equal operators. These two operators do the same thing as equal and not equal, except that they do not convert operands before testing for equality. The identically equal operator is represented by three equal signs (===) and only returns `true` if the operands are equal without conversion. For example:

```
var sNum = "55";
var iNum = 55;
alert(sNum == iNum);     //outputs "true"
alert(sNum === iNum);    //outputs "false"
```

In this code, the first alert uses the equal operator to compare the string `"55"` and the number `55` and outputs `"true"`. As mentioned previously, this happens because the string `"55"` is converted to the number `55` and then compared with the other number `55`. The second alert uses the identically equal operator to compare the string and the number without conversion, and of course, a string isn't equal to a number, so this outputs `"false"`.

The not identically equal operator is represented by an exclamation point followed by two equal signs (`!==`) and returns `true` only if the operands are not equal without conversion. For example:

```
var sNum = "55";
var iNum = 55;
alert(sNum != iNum);     //outputs "false"
alert(sNum !== iNum);    //outputs "true"
```

Here, the first alert uses the not equal operator, which converts the string `"55"` to the number `55`, making it equal to the second operand, also the number `55`. Therefore, this evaluates to `false` because the two are considered equal. The second alert uses the not identically equal operator. It helps to think of this operation as saying, "is `sNum` different from `iNum`?" The answer to this is yes (`true`), because `sNum` is a string and `iNum` is a number, so they are very different.

Conditional operator

The conditional operator is one of the most versatile in ECMAScript, and it takes on the same form as in Java:

```
variable = boolean_expression ? true_value : false_value;
```

This basically allows a conditional assignment to a variable depending on the evaluation of the *`boolean_expression`*. If it's true, then *`true_value`* is assigned to the variable; if it's false, then *`false_value`* is assigned to the variable. For instance:

```
var iMax = (iNum1 > iNum2) ? iNum1 : iNum2;
```

In this example, `iMax` is to be assigned the number with the highest value. The expression states that if `iNum1` is greater than `iNum2`, `iNum1` is assigned to `iMax`. If, however, the expression is false (meaning that `iNum2` is less than or equal to `iNum1`), `iNum2` is assigned to `iMax`.

Assignment operators

Simple assignment is done with the equals sign (=) and simply assigns the value on the right to the variable on the left. For example:

```
var iNum = 10;
```

Compound assignment is done with one of the multiplicative, additive, or bitwise shift operators followed by an equals sign (=). These assignments are designed as shorthand for such common situations as:

```
var iNum = 10;
iNum = iNum + 10;
```

The second line of code can be replaced with a compound assignment:

```
var iNum = 10;
iNum += 10;
```

Compound assignment operators exist for each of the major mathematical operations and a few others as well:

- Multiply/Assign (*=)
- Divide/Assign (/=)
- Modulus/Assign (%=)
- Add/Assign (+=)
- Subtract/Assign (-=)
- Left Shift/Assign (<<=)
- Signed Right Shift/Assign (>>=)
- Unsigned Right Shift/Assign (>>>=)

Comma operator

The comma operator allows execution of more than one operation in a single statement. Example:

```
var iNum1=1, iNum2=2, iNum3=3;
```

Most often, the comma operator is used in the declaration of variables.

Statements

ECMA-262 describes several *statements* for ECMAScript. Essentially, statements define most of the syntax of ECMAScript and, typically, use one or more keywords to accomplish a given task. Statements can be simple, such as telling a function to exit, or complicated, such as specifying a number of commands to be executed repeatedly. This section introduces all the standard ECMAScript statements.

The if statement

One of the most frequently used statements in ECMAScript (and indeed, in many languages), is the `if` statement. The `if` statement has the following syntax:

```
if (condition) statement1 else statement2
```

The condition can be any expression; it doesn't even have to evaluate to an actual Boolean value. ECMAScript converts it to a Boolean for you. If the condition evaluates to `true`, statement1 is executed; if the condition evaluates to `false`, statement2 is executed. Each of the statements can be either a single line or a code block (a group of code lines enclosed within braces). For example:

```
if (i > 25)
    alert("Greater than 25.");     //one-line statement
else {
    alert("Less than or equal to 25.");  //block statement
}
```

It's considered best coding practice to always use block statements, even if only one line of code is to be executed. Doing so can avoid confusion about what should be executed for each condition.

You can also chain `if` statements together like so:

```
if (condition1) statement1 else if (condition2) statement2 else statement3
```

Example:

```
if (i > 25) {
    alert("Greater than 25.")
} else if (i < 0) {
    alert("Less than 0.");
} else {
    alert("Between 0 and 25, inclusive.");

}
```

Iterative statements

Iterative statements, also called loop statements, specify certain commands to be executed repeatedly until some condition is met. The loops are often used to iterate the values of an array (hence the name) or to work though repetitious mathematical tasks. ECMAScript provides four types of iterative statements to aid in the process.

do-while

The `do-while` statement is a post-test loop, meaning that the evaluation of the escape condition is only done after the code inside the loop has been executed. This means that the body of the loop is always executed at least once before the expression is evaluated. Syntax:

```
do {
    statement
} while (expression);
```

For example:

```
var i = 0;
do {
   i += 2;
} while (i < 10);
```

while

The `while` statement is a pretest loop. This means the evaluation of the escape condition is done before the code inside the loop has been executed. Because of this, it is possible that the body of the loop is never executed. Syntax:

```
while(expression) statement
```

For example:

```
var i = 0;
while (i < 10) {
   i += 2;
}
```

for

The `for` statement is also a pretest loop with the added capabilities of variable initialization before entering the loop and defining postloop code to be entered. Syntax:

```
for (initialization; expression; post-loop-expression) statement
```

For example:

```
for (var i=0; i < iCount; i++){
    alert(i);
}
```

This code defines a variable `i` that begins with the value `0`. The `for` loop is entered only if the conditional expression (`i < iCount`) evaluates to `true`, making it possible that the body of the code might not be executed. If the body is executed, the postloop expression is also executed, iterating the variable `i`.

for-in

The `for-in` statement is a strict iterative statement. It is used to enumerate the properties of an object. Syntax:

```
for (property in expression) statement
```

For example:

```
for (sProp in window) {
     alert(sProp);
}
```

Here, the `for-in` statement is used to display all the properties of the BOM `window` object. The method `propertyIsEnumerable()`, discussed earlier, is included in ECMAScript specifically to indicate whether or not a property can be accessed using the `for-in` statement.

Labeled statements

It is possible to label statements for later use with the following syntax:

```
label: statement
```

For example:

```
start: var iCount = 10;
```

In this example, the label `start` can later be referenced by using the `break` or `continue` statements.

The break and continue statements

The `break` and `continue` statements provide stricter control over the execution of code in a loop. The `break` statement exits the loop immediately, preventing any further repetition of the code while the `continue` statement exits the current repetition. It does, however, allow further repetition based on the control expression. For example:

```
var iNum = 0;

for (var i=1; i < 10; i++) {
    if (i % 5 == 0) {
        break;
    }
    iNum++;
}

alert(iNum);    //outputs "4"
```

In the previous code, the `for` loop is to iterate the variable `i` from 1 to 10. In the body of loop, an `if` statement checks to see if the value of `i` is evenly divisible by 5 (using the modulus operator). If so, the `break` statement is executed and the alert displays `"4"`, indicating the number of times the loop has been executed before exiting. If this example is updated to use `continue` instead of `break`, a different outcome occurs:

```
var iNum = 0;

for (var i=1; i < 10; i++) {
    if (i % 5 == 0) {
        continue;
    }
    iNum++;
}

alert(iNum);    //outputs "8"
```

Here, the alert displays `"8"`, the number of times the loop has been executed. The total number of times that the loop can possibly be executed is 9, but when `i` reaches a value of `5`, the `continue` statement is executed, causing the loop to skip the expression `iNum++` and return to the top.

Both the `break` and `continue` statements can be used in conjunction with labeled statements to return to a particular location in the code. This is typically used when there are loops inside of loops, as in the following example:

```
var iNum = 0;

outermost:
for (var i=0; i < 10; i++) {
     for (var j=0; j < 10; j++) {
        if (i == 5 && j == 5) {
            break outermost;
        }
        iNum++;
    }
}

alert(iNum);     //outputs "55"
```

In this example one label, `outermost`, indicates the first `for` statement. Each loop normally executes 10 times a piece, meaning that the `iNum++` statement is normally executed 100 times and, consequently, `iNum` should be equal to 100 when the execution is complete. The `break` statement here is given one argument, the label to break to. Doing this allows the break statement not just to break out of the inner `for` statement (using the variable `j`) but also out of the outer `for` statement (using the variable `i`). Because of this, `iNum` ends up with a value of `55` because execution is halted when both `i` and `j` are equal to `5`. The `continue` statement can also be used in the same way:

```
var iNum = 0;

outermost:
for (var i=0; i < 10; i++) {
     for (var j=0; j < 10; j++) {
        if (i == 5 && j == 5) {
            continue outermost;
        }
        iNum++;
    }
}

alert(iNum);     //outputs "95"
```

In this case, the `continue` statement forces execution to continue—not in the inner loop, but in the outer loop. Because this occurs when `j` is equal to 5, that means the inner loop misses five iterations, leaving `iNum` equal to 95.

As you can tell, using labeled statements in conjunction with **`break`** *and* **`continue`** *can be powerful, but this practice can also make debugging code a problem, if it is overused. Make sure to always use descriptive labels and try not to nest more than a handful of loops.*

The with statement

The `with` statement is used to set the scope of the code within a particular object. Its syntax is the following:

```
with (expression) statement;
```

For example:

```
var sMessage = "hello world";
with(sMessage) {
    alert(toUpperCase());      //outputs "HELLO WORLD"
}
```

In this code, the `with` statement is used with a string, so when the `toUpperCase()` method is called, the interpreter checks to see if this is a local function. If not, it checks the `sMessage` pseudo-object to see if `toUpperCase()` is a method for it, which it is. The alert then outputs `"HELLO WORLD"` because the interpreter finds the implementation of `toUpperCase()` on the `"hello world"` string.

> **The `with` statement is a very slow segment of code, especially while the values of properties are being set. Most of the time, it's best to avoid using it if possible.**

The switch statement

The cousin of the `if` statement, the `switch` statement, allows a developer to provide a series of *cases* for an expression. The syntax for the switch statement is:

```
switch (expression)  {
  case value: statement
    break;
  case value: statement
    break;
  case value: statement
    break;
  ...
  case value: statement
    break;
  default: statement
}
```

Each case says "if *expression* is equal to *value*, execute *statement*". The `break` keyword causes code execution to jump out of the `switch` statement. Without the `break` keyword, code execution falls through the original case into the following one.

The `default` keyword indicates what is to be done if the expression does not evaluate to one of the cases (in effect, it is an `else` statement).

Essentially, the `switch` statement prevents a developer from having to write something like this:

```
if (i == 25)
  alert("25");
else if (i == 35)
  alert("35");
else if (i == 45)
  alert("45");
else
  alert("Other");
```

The equivalent `switch` statement is:

```
switch (i) {
    case 25: alert("25");
        break;
    case 35: alert("35");
        break;
    case 45: alert("45");
        break;
    default: alert("Other");
}
```

Two big differences exist between the `switch` statement in ECMAScript and Java. In ECMAScript, the `switch` statement can be used on strings, and it can indicate case by nonconstant values:

```
var BLUE = "blue", RED = "red", GREEN = "green";

switch (sColor) {
    case BLUE: alert("Blue");
        break;
    case RED: alert("Red");
        break;
    case GREEN: alert("Green");
        break;
    default: alert("Other");
}
```

Here, the `switch` statement is used on the string `sColor`, whereas the `cases` are indicated by using the variables `BLUE`, `RED`, and `GREEN`, which is completely valid in ECMAScript.

Functions

Functions are the heart of ECMAScript: a collection of statements that can be run anywhere at anytime. Functions are declared with the keyword function, followed by a set of arguments, and finally by the code to execute enclosed in braces. The basic syntax is:

```
function functionName(arg0, arg1,...,argN) {
    statements
}
```

For example:

```
function sayHi(sName, sMessage) {
    alert("Hello " + name + "," + sMessage);
}
```

This function can then be called by using the function name, followed by the function arguments enclosed in parentheses (and separated by commas, if there are multiple arguments). The code to call the `sayHi()` function looks like this:

```
sayHi("Nicholas", "how are you today?");
```

This code results in the alert displayed in Figure 2-8.

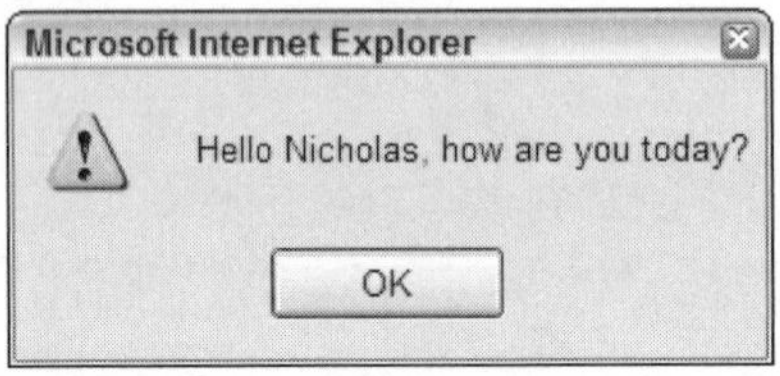

Figure 2-8

The `sayHi()` function doesn't specify a return value, but it requires no special declaration (such as `void` is used in Java) to do so. Likewise, a function doesn't need to explicitly declare a return value type if the function does indeed return a value. The function need only use the `return` operator followed by the value to return:

```
function sum(iNum1, iNum2) {
    return iNum1 + iNum2;
}
```

The value of the `sum` function is returned and assigned to a variable like this:

```
var iResult = sum(1,1);
alert(iResult);    //outputs "2"
```

Another important concept is that, just as in Java, the function stops executing code after a `return` statement is executed. Therefore, any code that comes after a `return` statement is not executed. For example, the alert in the following function is never displayed:

```
function sum(iNum1, iNum2) {
    return iNum1 + iNum2;
    alert(iNum1 + iNum2);    //never reached
}
```

It is possible to have more than one `return` statement in a function, as in this function:

```
function diff(iNum1, iNum2) {
    if (iNum1 > iNum2) {
```

```
            return iNum1 - iNum2;
        } else {
            return iNum2 - iNum1;
        }
    }
```

The previous function is designed to return the difference between two numbers. To do so, it must always subtract the smaller number from the larger, which results in an `if` statement to determine which `return` statement to execute.

If a function doesn't return a value, it can use the return operator without any parameters to exit a function at any time. Example:

```
function sayHi(sMessage) {
    if (sMessage == "bye"){
        return;
    }

    alert(sMessage);
}
```

In this code, the alert will never be displayed if the message is equal to the string `"bye"`.

> **When a function doesn't explicitly return a value or uses the return statement without a value, the function actually returns `undefined` as its value.**

No overloading

ECMAScript functions cannot be overloaded. This may come as a surprise, considering ECMAScript closely resembles other higher-level programming languages that support overloading. You can define two functions with the same name in the same scope without an error; however, the last function becomes the one that is used. Consider the following example:

```
function doAdd(iNum) {
    alert(iNum + 100);
}

function doAdd(iNum) {
    alert(iNum + 10);
}

doAdd(10);
```

What do you think will be displayed from this code snippet? The alert will show `"20"`, because the second `doAdd()` definition overwrites the first. Although this can be annoying to a developer, you have a way to work around this limitation by using the `arguments` object.

The arguments object

Within a function's code, a special object called `arguments` gives the developer access to the function's arguments without specifically naming them. For example, in the `sayHi()` function, the first argument is given the name `message`. The same value can also be accessed by referencing `arguments[0]`, which asks for the value of the first argument (the first argument is in position 0, the second is in position 1, and so on.). Therefore, the function can be rewritten without naming the argument explicitly:

```
function sayHi() {
    if (arguments[0] == "bye") {
        return;
    }

    alert(arguments[0]);
}
```

The `arguments` object can also be used to check the number of arguments passed into the function by referencing the `arguments.length` property. The following example outputs the number of arguments each time the function is called:

```
function howManyArgs() {
    alert(arguments.length);
}

howManyArgs("string", 45);     //outputs "2"
howManyArgs();                 //outputs "0"
howManyArgs(12);               //outputs "1"
```

This snippet shows alerts displaying `"2"`, `"0"`, and `"1"` (in that order). In this way, the `arguments` object puts the responsibility on the developer to check the arguments that are passed into a function.

Unlike other programming languages, ECMAScript functions don't validate the number of arguments passed against the number of arguments defined by the function; any developer-defined function accepts any number of arguments (up to 255, according to Netscape's documentation) without causing an error. Any missing arguments are passed in as **`undefined`***; any excess arguments are ignored.*

By using the arguments object to determine the number of arguments passed into the function, it is possible to simulate the overloading of functions:

```
function doAdd() {
    if(arguments.length == 1) {
        alert(arguments[0] + 10);
    } else if (arguments.length == 2) {
        alert(arguments[0] + arguments[1]);
    }
}

doAdd(10);        //outputs "20"
doAdd(30, 20);    //outputs "50"
```

The function doAdd() adds 10 to a number only if there is one argument; if there are two arguments, they are simply added together and returned. So doAdd(10) outputs "20" whereas doAdd(30,20) outputs "50". It's not quite as good as overloading, but it is a sufficient workaround for this ECMAScript limitation.

The Function class

Perhaps the most interesting aspect of ECMAScript is that functions are actually full-fledged objects. A Function class represents each and every function a developer defines. The syntax for creating a function using the Function class directly is as follows:

```
var function_name = new Function(argument1, argument2,..,argumentN, function_body);
```

In this form, each of the function arguments is one parameter, with the final parameter being the function body (the code to execute). Each of these parameters must be a string. Remember this function?

```
function sayHi(sName, sMessage) {
    alert("Hello " + sName + "," + sMessage);
}
```

It can also be defined like this:

```
var sayHi = new Function("sName", "sMessage", "alert(\"Hello \" + sName + \", \" +
sMessage + \");");
```

Admittedly, this form is a little bit harder to write because of the nature of strings, but understand that functions are just reference types and they always behave as if using the Function class explicitly created for them. Remember this example?

```
function doAdd(iNum) {
    alert(iNum + 100);
}

function doAdd(iNum) {
    alert(iNum + 10);
}

doAdd(10);    //outputs "20"
```

As you remember, the second function overrides the first, making doAdd(10) output "20" instead of "110". This concept becomes a whole lot clearer if this block is rewritten as follows:

```
doAdd = new Function("iNum", "alert(iNum + 100)");
doAdd = new Function("iNum", "alert(iNum + 10)");
doAdd(10);
```

Looking at this code, it is clear that the value of doAdd has changed to point to a different object. Yes, function names are just reference values pointing to a function object and behave just as other pointers do. It is even possible to have two variables point to the same function:

```
var doAdd = new Function("iNum", "alert(iNum + 10) ");
var alsoDoAdd = doAdd;
doAdd(10);        //outputs "20"
alsoDoAdd(10);    //outputs "20"
```

Here, the variable `doAdd` is defined as a function, and then `alsoDoAdd` is declared to point to the same function. Both can then be used to execute the function's code and output the same result, `"20"`. So if a function name is just a variable pointing to a function, is it possible to pass a function as an argument to another function? Yes!

```
function callAnotherFunc(fnFunction, vArgument) {
    fnFunction(vArgument);
}

var doAdd = new Function("iNum", "alert(iNum + 10)");

callAnotherFunc(doAdd, 10);    //outputs "20"
```

In this example, `callAnotherFunction()` accepts two arguments: a function to call and an argument to pass to the function. This code passes the `doAdd()` function into `callAnotherFunction()` with an argument of `10`, outputting `"20"`.

> **Even though it's possible to create a function using the `Function` constructor, it's best to avoid it because it's slower than defining the function in the traditional manner. However, all functions are considered instances of `Function`.**

Because functions are reference types, they can also have properties and methods. The one property defined in ECMAScript is `length`, which indicates the number of arguments that a function expects. Example:

```
function doAdd(iNum) {
    alert(iNum + 10);
}

function sayHi() {
    alert("Hi");
}

alert(doAdd.length);    //outputs "1"
alert(sayHi.length);    //outputs "0"
```

The function `doAdd()` defines one argument to pass in, so its `length` is `1`; `sayHi()` defines no arguments, so its length is `0`. Remember, ECMAScript functions can accept any number of arguments (up to 255) regardless of how many are defined. The `length` property just gives a convenient way to check how many arguments are expected by default.

Function objects also have the standard `valueOf()` and `toString()` methods shared by all objects. Both of these methods return the source code for the function and are particularly useful in debugging. For example:

```
function doAdd(iNum) {
    alert(iNum + 10);
}

alert(doAdd.toString());
```

This code outputs the exact text of the `doAdd()` function (see Figure 2-9).

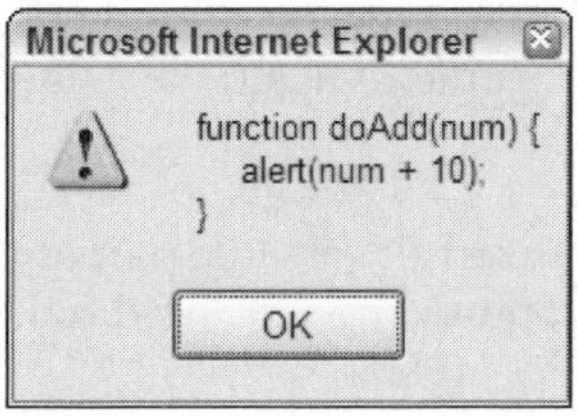

Figure 2-9

> **There are a couple of other methods of the `Function` class that are more relevant to the discussion of objects and so are described in the next chapter.**

Closures

One of the most misunderstood aspects of ECMAScript is its support for *closures.* Closures are functions whose lexical representation includes variables that aren't evaluated, meaning that functions are capable of using variables defined outside of the function itself. Using global variables in ECMAScript is a simple example of a closure. Consider the following example:

```
var sMessage = "Hello World!";

function sayHelloWorld() {
    alert(sMessage);
}

sayHelloWorld();
```

In this code, the variable `sMessage` isn't evaluated for the function `sayHelloWorld()` while the scripts is being loaded into memory. The function *captures* `sMessage` for later use, which is to say that the interpreter knows to check the value of `sMessage` when the function is called. When `sayHelloWorld()` is called (on the last line), the value of `sMessage` is assigned and the message `"Hello World!"` is displayed.

Closures can get more complicated, as when you are defining a function inside of another function, as shown here:

```
var iBaseNum = 10;

function addNumbers(iNum1, iNum2) {
    function doAddition() {
```

```
            return iNum1 + iNum2 + iBaseNum;
        }
        return doAddition();
    }
```

Here, the function `addNumbers()` contains a function (the closure) named `doAddition()`. The internal function is a closure because it captures the arguments of the outer function, `iNum1` and `iNum2`, as well as the global variable `iBaseNum`. The last step of `addNumbers()` calls the inner function, which adds the two arguments and the global variable and returns the value. The important concept to grasp here is that `doAddition()` doesn't accept any arguments at all; the values it uses are captured from the execution environment.

As you can see, closures are a very powerful, versatile part of ECMAScript that can be used to perform complex calculations. Just as when you use any advanced functionality, exercise caution when using closures because they can get extremely complex.

Summary

This chapter looked at the basics of ECMAScript:

- General syntax
- Defining variables using the `var` keyword
- Primitive and reference values
- The basic primitive types (Undefined, Null, Boolean, Number, and String)
- The basic reference types (Object, Boolean, Number, and String)
- Operators and statements
- Functions

Understanding ECMAScript is an important part of JavaScript programming, which is why this chapter is perhaps the most important in this book. A good grasp of the core is vital to comprehending the rest of the topics in the book.

The next chapter focuses on more of the object-oriented aspects of ECMAScript, including how to create your own classes and how to establish inheritance.

3

Object Basics

ECMAScript objects are one of the unique (and useful) features of JavaScript. Chapter 2, "ECMAScript Basics," introduced the concept that everything is an object, including functions. This chapter focuses on how to manipulate and use those objects, as well as how to create your own objects to add functionality specific to your needs.

Object-Oriented Terminology

ECMA-262 defines an *object* as an "unordered collection of properties each of which contains a primitive value, object, or function." Strictly speaking, this means that an object is an array of values in no particular order. Although this is ECMAScript's interpretation, an *object* is more generically defined to be a code-based representation of a noun (person, place, or thing).

Each object is defined by a *class*, which can be thought of as a recipe for an object. The class defines both the *interface* of an object (the properties and methods that can be accessed by developers) as well as the inner workings of the object (the code that makes the properties and methods work). The compiler or interpreter uses the class to build objects according to its specifications.

When a program uses a class to create an object, the resulting object is said to be an *instance* of the class. The only limit to the number of instances that can be created from a single class is the physical memory limitations of the machine on which the code is running. Each instance behaves the same way, but each can handle separate sets of data. The process of creating an object instance from a class is called *instantiation*.

As I discussed briefly in Chapter 1, ECMAScript has no formal classes. Instead, ECMA-262 describes *object definitions* as the recipes for an object. This is a logical compromise for ECMAScript, because object definitions actually are objects in and of themselves (which I explain shortly). Even though classes don't actually exist, this book refers to object definitions as classes because the term is more familiar to most developers and, functionally, the two are equivalent.

The object definition is contained within a single function called a *constructor*. The constructor isn't a special kind of function; it's just a regular function that is used to create an object. Later in this chapter, you learn how to create your own constructors.

Requirements of object-oriented languages

Before a language can be called object-oriented, it must provide four basic capabilities to developers:

1. *Encapsulation* — the capability to store related information, whether data or methods, together in an object
2. *Aggregation* — the capability to store one object inside of another object
3. *Inheritance* — the capability of a class to rely upon another class (or number of classes) for some of its properties and methods
4. *Polymorphism* — the capability to write one function or method that works in a variety of different ways

ECMAScript supports all four of these requirements and so is considered to be object-oriented.

Composition of an object

In ECMAScript, objects are composed of *attributes*, which are either primitive or reference values. If an attribute contains a function, it is considered to be a *method* of the object; otherwise, the attribute is considered a *property*.

Working with Objects

The previous chapter touched briefly on how to work with objects, but now it's time to go into more detail. Objects are created and destroyed throughout the execution of JavaScript code, and understanding the implications of this paradigm is vital to your understanding of the language as a whole.

Declaration and instantiation

Objects are created by using the `new` keyword followed by the name of the class you wish to instantiate:

```
var oObject = new Object();
var oStringObject = new String();
```

The first line creates a new instance of `Object` and stores it in the variable `oObject`; the second line creates a new instance of `String` and stores it in the variable `oStringObject`. The parentheses aren't required when the constructor doesn't require arguments, so these two lines could be rewritten as follows:

```
var oObject = new Object;
var oStringObject = new String;
```

Object references

In Chapter 1, the concept of reference types was introduced. In ECMAScript, it is not possible to access the physical representation of the object; it is only possible to access *references* to the object. Every time you create an object, a reference to the object is stored in the variable, not the actual object itself.

Dereferencing objects

ECMAScript has a *garbage collection* routine, meaning that you don't have to specifically destroy objects in order to free up the memory. When there are no remaining references to an object, the object is said to be *dereferenced*. When the garbage collector is run, all dereferenced objects are destroyed. The garbage collector runs whenever a function has completed its code, freeing up all local variables, and at other not-so-predictable times.

It is possible to forcibly dereference objects by setting all its references equal to `null`. For example:

```
var oObject = new Object;
//do something with the object here
oObject = null;
```

When the variable `oObject` is set to `null`, there are no longer any references to the object created in the first line. This means that the next time the garbage collector is run, this object will be destroyed.

It's always a good idea to dereference an object as soon as you're done using it in order to free up memory. Doing so can also prevent programming errors by ensuring that you aren't using an object that should no longer be accessible. Additionally, older browsers (such as IE/Mac) don't have conscientious garbage collectors, so objects may not be properly destroyed when a page is unloaded. Dereferencing an object and all its properties is the best way to ensure proper memory usage.

> **Be careful to dereference all references to an object. If you have two or more references to the same object, all of them must be set to `null` in order to for you properly dereference the object.**

Early versus late binding

The concept of *binding* describes the method whereby an object's interface is bound to an object instance.

Early binding means that properties and methods are defined for an object (via its class) before it is instantiated so the compiler/interpreter can properly assemble the machine code ahead of time. In languages such as Java and Visual Basic, early binding allows for the use of IntelliSense (the capability that gives the developer a list of available properties and methods for a particular object) in development environments. ECMAScript isn't strongly typed, so it does not support early binding.

Late binding, on the other hand, means that the compiler/interpreter doesn't know what type of object is being held in a particular variable until runtime. With late binding, no check is made to determine the particular type of object, only whether the object supports the property or method. ECMAScript uses late binding for all variables, which allows a large amount of object manipulation to occur without penalty.

Types of Objects

In ECMAScript, all objects are not created equal. Generally speaking, three specific types of objects can be used and/or created.

Native objects

ECMA-262 defines *native objects* as "any object supplied by an ECMAScript implementation independent of the host environment." Simply put, native objects are the classes (reference types) defined by ECMA-262. They include all the following:

```
Object        Function    Array        String
Boolean       Number      Date         RegExp
Error         EvalError   RangeError   ReferenceError
SyntaxError   TypeError   URIError
```

Some of these native objects you are already familiar with from the previous chapter (`Object`, `Function`, `String`, `Boolean`, and `Number`), and some will be discussed later in the book. For now, the two native objects of importance are `Array` and `Date`.

The Array class

In ECMAScript, unlike in Java, there is an actual `Array` class. You create an `Array` object like this:

```
var aValues = new Array();
```

If you know ahead of time how many items you need in the array, you can pass in the array size as a parameter:

```
var aValues = new Array(20);
```

Using either of these two methods, you must populate the array by using bracket notation, similar to how it is done in Java:

```
var aColors = new Array();
aColors[0] = "red";
aColors[1] = "green";
aColors[2] = "blue";
```

Here, an array is created and given three items, `"red"`, `"green"`, and `"blue"`. The array dynamically grows in size with each additional item

Also, if you know the values that the array should contain, you can specify those as arguments, creating an `Array` object with a length equal to the number of arguments. For example, the following line of code creates an array of three strings:

```
var aColors = new Array("red", "green", "blue");
```

As in strings, the first item in an array is in position 0, the second is in position 1, and so on. To access a particular item, use square brackets enclosing the position of the item to retrieve. For instance, to output the string `"green"` from the array defined previously, you do this:

```
alert(aColors[1]);     //outputs "green"
```

The full size of the array can be determined by using the `length` property. Like the same property in strings, the length property is always one more than the position of the last item, meaning that an array with three items has items in positions 0 through 2.

```
var aColors = new Array("red", "green", "blue");
alert(aColors.length);     //outputs "3"
```

As mentioned previously, the size of an array can grow and shrink as necessary. So, if you wanted to add another item to the array defined previously, you can just place the value in the next open position:

```
var aColors = new Array("red", "green", "blue");
alert(aColors.length);     //outputs "3"
aColors[3] = "purple";
alert(aColors.length);     //outputs "4"
```

In this code, the next open position is 3, so the value `"purple"` is assigned to it. This addition changes the length of the array from 3 to 4. But what would happen if you placed a value in position 25 of this array? ECMAScript fills in all positions from 3 to 24 with the value `null`; then it places the appropriate value in position 25, increasing the size of the array to 26:

```
var aColors = new Array("red", "green", "blue");
alert(aColors.length);     //outputs "3"
aColors[25] = "purple";
aColors(arr.length);     //outputs "26"
```

Arrays can contain a maximum of 4294967295 items, which should be plenty for almost all programming needs. If you try to add more than that number, an exception occurs.

You can also define an `Array` object by using the literal representation, which is indicated by using square brackets ([and]) and separating the values with commas. For instance, the previous example can be rewritten in the following form:

```
var aColors = ["red", "green", "blue"];
alert(aColors.length);     //outputs "3"
aColors[25] = "purple";
alert(aColors.length);     //outputs "26"
```

Note that, in this case, the `Array` class is never mentioned explicitly. The square brackets imply that the enclosed values are to be made into an `Array` object. Arrays declared in this way are exactly equal to arrays declared in the more traditional manner.

The `Array` object overrides the `toString()` and `valueOf()` methods to return a special string. This string is made by calling the `toString()` method on each item in the array and then combining them using commas. For example, an array with the items `"red"`, `"green"`, and `"blue"` return the string `"red,green,blue"` when either of the methods is called.

```
var aColors = ["red", "green", "blue"];
alert(aColors.toString());     //outputs "red,green,blue"
alert(aColors.valueOf());      //outputs "red,green,blue"
```

Similarly, the `toLocaleString()` method returns a string made up of the items in the array. The one difference here is that each of the items' `toLocaleString()` methods is called to get the value. In many cases, this returns the same value as `toString()`, with the strings joined by commas.

```
var aColors = ["red", "green", "blue"];
alert(aColors.toLocaleString());      //outputs "red,green,blue"
```

Because developers may also want to create such values out of arrays, ECMAScript provides a method called `join()`, whose sole purpose it is to create concatenated string values. The `join()` method accepts one argument, which is the string to use between the items. Consider the following example:

```
var aColors = ["red", "green", "blue"];
alert(aColors.join(","));     //outputs "red,green,blue"
alert(aColors.join("-spring-"));     //outputs "red-spring-green-spring-blue"
alert(aColors.join("]["));     //outputs "red][green][blue"
```

Here, the `join()` method is used to create three different string representations of the array. The first, using the comma, is essentially equal to calling the `toString()` or `valueOf()` method; the second and third use different strings to create odd (and probably not that useful) separators between the array items. The point to understand is that any string can be used as a separator.

You may be wondering at this point, if the `Array` has a way to convert itself into a string, does the `String` have a way to convert itself into an array? The answer is yes. The `String` class has a method called `split()` that does exactly that. The `split()` method takes only one parameter. That parameter, as you probably guessed, is the string that should be considered the separator between items. So, if you have a string separated by commas, you can do the following to convert it into an `Array`:

```
var sColors = "red,green,blue";
var aColors = sColors.split(",");
```

If you specify an empty string as the separator, the `split()` method returns an array in which each item is equal to one character in the string, for example:

```
var sColors = "green";
var aColors = sColors.split("");
alert(aColors.toString());     //outputs "g,r,e,e,n"
```

Here, the string `"green"` is transformed into an array of the strings `"g"`, `"r"`, `"e"`, `"e"`, and `"n"`. This functionality can be useful if you need to parse strings character-by-character.

The `Array` object has a couple of methods that have equivalents in the `String` class, namely the `concat()` and `slice()` methods. The `concat()` method works almost exactly the same as it does with strings: The arguments are appended to the end of the array, and a new `Array` object (one containing both the items in the original array and the new items) is returned as the function value. For example:

```
var aColors = ["red", "green", "blue"];
var aColors2 = arr.concat("yellow", "purple");
alert(aColors2.toString());     //outputs "red,green,blue,yellow,purple"
alert(aColors.toString());        //outputs "red,green,blue"
```

In this example, the strings `"yellow"` and `"purple"` are added to the array using the `concat()` method. The `aColors2` array contains five values whereas the original array, `aColors`, still contains only three. This can be proved by calling the `toString()` method on each array.

The `slice()` method is also very similar to `String` class equivalent in that it returns a new array containing the specified items. Just like the `String`'s method, the `Array`'s `slice()` method can accept one or two arguments: the starting and stopping positions of the items to extract. If only one argument is present, the method returns all items between that position and the end of the array; if there are two arguments, the method returns all items between the first position and second position, not including the item in the second position. For example:

```
var aColors = ["red", "green", "blue", "yellow", "purple"];
var aColors2 = arr.slice(1);
var aColors3 = arr.slice(1, 4);
alert(aColors2.toString());        //outputs "green,blue,yellow,purple"
alert(aColors3.toString());        //outputs "green,blue,yellow"
```

Here, `aColors2` contains all the items in `arr` from position 1 on. Because the string `"green"` is in position 1, this is the first item in the new array. For `aColors3`, the `slice()` method is called with two arguments, 1 and 4. The string `"green"` is in position 1 and the string `"purple"` is in position 4, so `aColors3` contains `"green"`, `"blue"`, and `"yellow"` because `slice()` only includes the item immediately before the last position.

One of the interesting things about the ECMAScript `Array` class is that it provides methods to make an array behave like other types of data structures. An `Array` object, for example, can act just like a stack, which is one of a group of data structures that restrict the insertion and removal of items. A stack is referred to as a *last-in-first-out* (LIFO) structure, meaning that the most recently added item is the first one removed. The insertion and removal of items in a stack occur at only one point: the top of the stack.

It helps to think of a stack in literal terms, such as a stack of plates. If you want to add a plate to the stack of plates, you place the plate on top of the stack. When an item is added to a stack data structure, it is said to be *pushed* onto the stack; it is added at the top (Figure 3-1).

When it comes time to remove a plate for dinner, what do you do? You remove the top plate from the stack of plates and put it on the table. Again, the stack data structure works the same way, removing only the topmost item. When an item is removed from a stack, it is said to be *popped* from the stack (Figure 3-2).

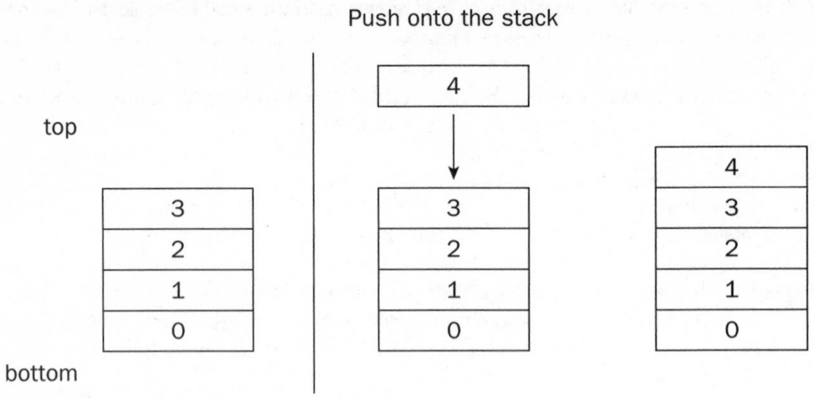

Figure 3-1

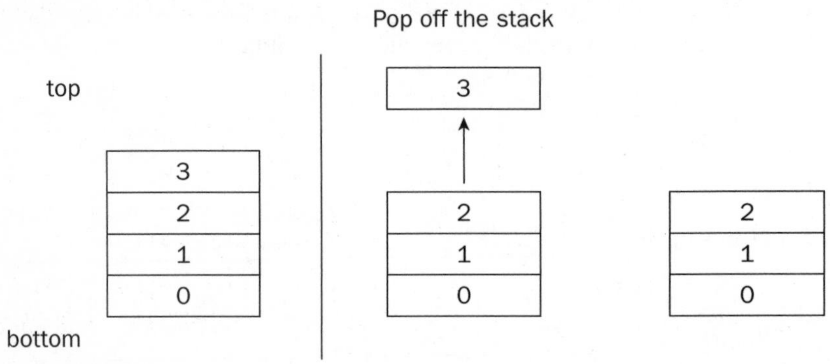

Figure 3-2

To facilitate such functionality, the `Array` object provides two methods, `push()` and `pop()`. As you might expect, the `push()` method adds one or more items to the end of the `Array` whereas the `pop()` method removes the very last item (`length - 1`) from the array and returns it as the function value. Consider the following example:

```
var stack = new Array;
stack.push("red");
stack.push("green");
stack.push("yellow");
alert(stack.toString());      //outputs "red,green,yellow"
var vItem = stack.pop();
alert(vItem);                  //outputs "yellow"
alert(stack.toString());      //outputs "red,green"
```

In the previous code, an empty `Array` object is created and then populated by using the `push()` method numerous times (note that even though this example shows only one argument for the `push()` method, you can, in fact, pass as many arguments as you wish). After the array is filled, the string value is output (`"red,green,yellow"`) to assure that all items have been added. Then, the `pop()` method is called, which returns only the last item, "yellow", and stores it in the variable vItem. The array is then left with only the strings "red" and "green".

The push() method is actually the same as manually adding the array items as shown in previous examples. This example could be rewritten as the following:

```
var stack = new Array;
stack[0] = "red";
stack[1] = "green";
stack[2] = "yellow";
alert(stack.toString());       //outputs "red,green,yellow"
var vItem = stack.pop();
alert(vItem);                   //outputs "yellow"
alert(stack.toString());       //outputs "red,green"
```

The Array also provides methods to manipulate the very first item. The shift() method removes the first item in the array and returns it as the function value. On the other end of the spectrum, the unshift() method places an item into the first position of the array, shifting all other items down one position in the process. Example:

```
var aColors = ["red", "green", "yellow"];
var vItem = aColors.shift();
alert(aColors.toString());        //outputs "green,yellow"
alert(vItem);                   //outputs "red"
aColors.unshift("black");
alert(aColors.toString());        //outputs "black,green,yellow"
```

In this example, the string "red" is removed (shift()ed) from the array, leaving only "green" and "yellow". By using the unshift() method, the string "black" is placed at the front of the array, effectively replacing "red" as the new value in the first position.

By using shift() and push(), it is possible to make an Array object behave like a queue. A queue is a member of the group of data structures that restricts the insertion and removal of elements. A queue is referred to as a *last-in-last-out* (LILO) structure, meaning that the most recently added element is the last one removed. The insertion of elements always occurs only at the back of the queue whereas the removal of elements occurs only at the front of the queue.

When you think of a queue, think of a line at the movies. When new people arrive to get tickets, they go to the back of the line (Figure 3-3). This is traditionally called *put* or *enqueue*.

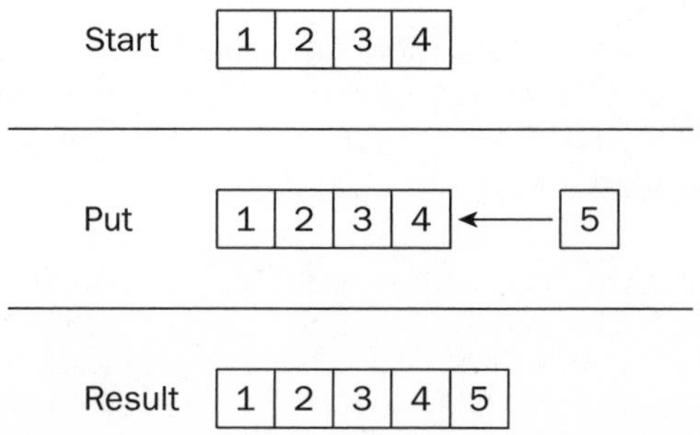

Figure 3-3

They wait their turns, eventually moving to the front of the line where they buy their tickets. After the purchase is complete, the people leave the front of the line and go into the movies (Figure 3-4). This is traditionally called *get* or *dequeue*.

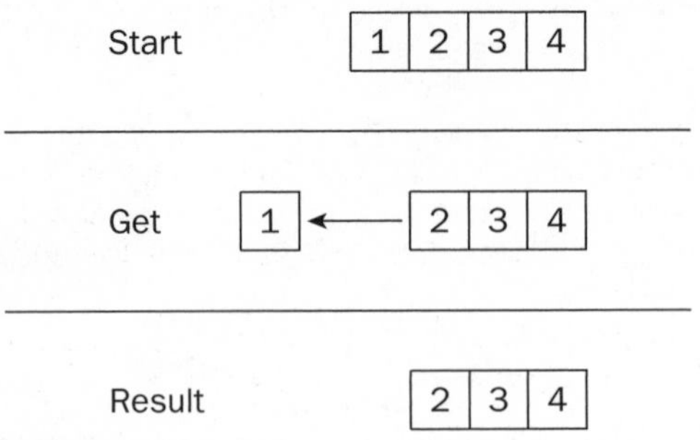

Figure 3-4

Although the names of the methods aren't the same, the functionality is the same. You add items to the queue using the `push()` method (adding items to the back of the array) and remove items from the queue by using the `shift()` method:

```
var queue = ["red", "green", "yellow"];
queue.push("black");
alert(queue.toString());              //outputs "red,green,yellow,black"
var sNextColor = queue.shift();
alert(sNextColor);                     //outputs "red"
alert(queue.toString());              //outputs "green,yellow,black"
```

In this example, the string `"black"` is added to the back of the queue by using the `push()` method. In order to get the next color, the `shift()` method is used to retrieve `"red"`, leaving the queue with only `"green"`, `"yellow"`, and `"black"`.

Two methods relate to the ordering of items in arrays, the `reverse()` and `sort()` methods. The `reverse()` method, as one might expect, simply reverses the order of the items in an array. So if you want to reverse the order of `"red"`, `"green"`, `"blue"`, you do this:

```
var aColors = ["red", "green", "blue"];
aColors.reverse();
alert(aColors.toString());     //outputs "blue,green,red"
```

The `sort()` method, on the other hand, arranges the item in the array by sorting them into ascending order based on their values. To do this sort, transform all values into strings by calling their `toString()` method. The items are compared by character code (as I described in the section on using the less-than operator on strings). For example:

```
var aColors = ["red", "green", "blue", "yellow"];
aColors.sort();
alert(aColors.toString());     //outputs "blue,green,red,yellow"
```

This code sorts the strings `"red"`, `"green"`, `"blue"`, and `"yellow"` into alphabetical order by using their character codes. Because all values are strings, this sort order is logical. If, however, the values are numbers, the result becomes bizarre:

```
var aColors = [3, 32, 2, 5]
aColors.sort();
alert(aColors.toString());    //outputs "2,3,32,5"
```

When trying to sort the numbers 3, 32, 2, and 5, the `sort()` method reorders the items into 2, 3, 32, and 5. As mentioned before, this occurs because the numbers are converted to strings and then compared by character code. This problem can be overcome. I discussed this further in Chapter 12, "Sorting Tables."

The most complicated method by far is `splice()`. The purpose of this method is quite simple really: to insert items into the middle of an array. The variety of ways that `splice()` uses to insert these items, however, takes some getting used to:

- *Deletion* — You can delete any number of items from the array by specifying just two parameters, the starting position of the first item to delete and the number of items to delete. For example: `arr.splice(0, 2)` deletes the first two items in the array `arr`.
- *Replacement without delete* — You can insert items into a specific position by specifying three parameters: the starting position, 0 (the number of items to delete), and the item to insert. You can optionally specify fourth, fifth, or any number of other parameters to insert. For example, `arr.splice(2, 0, "red", "green")` inserts the strings `"red"` and `"green"` into the array `arr` at position 2.
- *Replacement with delete* — You can insert items into a specific position while simultaneously deleting items by specifying three parameters: the starting position, the number of items to delete, and the item to insert. Here, you can also specify extra parameters to insert. The number of items to insert doesn't have to match the number of items to delete. For example, `arr.splice(2, 1, "red", "green")` deletes one item at position `2` and then inserts the strings `"red"` and `"green"` into the array `arr` at position `2`.

As you can tell, the `Array` class is an extremely versatile and helpful object. Chapter 12 explores using arrays in a more practical manner, but for now, this information is all you need to know.

The Date class

The `Date` class in ECMAScript is based on earlier versions of `java.util.Date` from Java. ECMAScript, as well as Java, stores the date as the number of milliseconds since 12 AM on January 1, 1970 UTC. UTC stands for Universal Time Code (also known as Greenwich Mean Time), which is the standard time upon which all time zones are based. Storing the number of milliseconds ensures that both Java and ECMAScript were immune from the dreaded "Y2K" problems that plagued older mainframe computers in the late 1990s. Dates can accurately be represented 285,616 years before or after January 1, 1970, meaning that you won't have any problems with date storage unless you live to be over 200,000 years old.

To create a new `Date` object, you simply do the following:

```
var d = new Date();
```

This line creates a new Date object with the current date and time. You can also set the date and time value when creating a new Date object in one of two ways. The first is to just specify the number of milliseconds since 12 AM on January 1, 1970:

```
var d = new Date(0);
```

Two class methods (which would be static methods in Java) called parse() and UTC() can also be used in conjunction with this method of creating Date objects. The parse() method accepts a string as an argument and tries to convert that string into a date value (meaning the millisecond representation). ECMA-262 doesn't define the date formats that the parse() method accepts, so this is purely implementation-specific and often locale-specific. For instance, in the United States, most implementations support the following date formats:

- mm/dd/yyyy (such as 6/13/2004)
- mmmm dd, yyyy (such as January 12, 2004)

For instance, if you wanted to create a Date object for May 25, 2004, you could use the parse() method to get the millisecond representation and then pass that value into the Date constructor:

```
var d = new Date(Date.parse("May 25, 2004"));
```

If the string passed in to parse() can't be turned into a date, the function returns NaN.

The UTC() method also returns the millisecond representation of a date, but with different arguments: year, month, day of the month, hours, minutes, seconds, and milliseconds. When using this method, you must always specify the year and month, but the other information is optional. Be very careful when setting the month because the values go from 0 to 11, where 0 is equal to January and 11 is equal to December, so to set a date equal to February 5, 2004, you do this:

```
var d = new Date(Date.UTC(2003, 1, 5));
```

Here, the 1 represents February, the second month. This is obviously a very important difference to keep track of when accepting user input to create a date. The other information is as you would expect, with the possible exception that the hours are given in military time (0 through 23) instead of AM/PM. So, to set a date equal to February 5, 2004 at 1:05 PM, you use this code:

```
var d = new Date(Date.UTC(2003, 1, 5, 13, 5));
```

The second method of creating a date is to specify the same arguments that UTC() accepts directly:

```
var d = new Date(2003, 1, 5);
```

The arguments are specified in the same order, and they don't all need to be present (except for the year and month).

The Date class is one of the few that overrides toString() and valueOf() differently. The valueOf() method always return the millisecond representation of the date whereas the toString() method returns a string in an implementation-specific, human-readable format. For this reason, it is impossible to depend on the toString() method for any consistent behavior. As an example, in the United States,

Internet Explorer displays February 2, 2003 as "Sat Feb 2 00:00:00 EST 2003" while Mozilla displays it as "Tue Feb 2 2003 00:00:00 GMT-0400 (Eastern Daylight Time)".

Several other methods are also designed to create alternate string representations of a particular date:

- `toDateString()` — displays only the date part of a `Date` (only the month, day, and year) in an implementation-dependent format
- `toTimeString()` — displays only the time part of a `Date` (hours, minutes, seconds, and time zone) in an implementation-dependent format
- `toLocaleString()` — displays the date and time of a `Date` in a locale-specific format
- `toLocaleDateString()` — displays the date part of a `Date` value in a locale-specific format
- `toLocaleTimeString()` — displays the time part of a `Date` in a locale-specific format
- `toUTCString()` — displays the UTC date of a Date in an implementation-specific format

Each of these methods outputs different values in different implementations and locales, and for this reason, care must be exercised when using them.

In case you haven't figured it out yet, the `Date` class relies heavily on the UTC date and time. In order to indicate a particular time zone's relationship to UTC, the `Date` class provides a method called `getTimezoneOffset()`. This method returns the number of minutes that the current time zone is ahead or behind UTC. For instance, `getTimezoneOffset()` returns 300 for U.S. Eastern Daylight Saving Time, which is 5 hours (or 300 minutes) behind UTC.

It is possible to determine if a particular time zone makes use of daylight saving time by using the `getTimezoneOffset()`. To do this, create a date of January 1 of any year, and then create a date of July 1 in the same year. Then, compare the time zone offset. If the minutes aren't equal, the time zone uses daylight saving time; if they are equal, the time zone doesn't use daylight saving time.

```
var d1 = new Date(2004, 0, 1);
var d2 = new Date(2004, 6, 1);
var bSupportsDaylightSavingTime = d1.getTimezoneOffset() != d2.getTimezoneOffset();
```

The remaining methods of the `Date` class (listed in the following table) are simply used to set and get particular parts of a date value.

Method	Description
`getTime()`	Returns the milliseconds representation of the date.
`setTime(`*`milliseconds`*`)`	Sets the milliseconds representation of the date.
`getFullYear()`	Returns the year of the date, represented by four digits (such as 2004 instead of just 04).
`getUTCFullYear()`	Returns the year of the UTC date, represented by four digits.

Table continued on following page

Method	Description
`setFullYear(year)`	Sets the year of the date, which must be given as a four-digit year.
`setUTCFullYear(year)`	Sets the year of the UTC date, which must be given as a four-digit year.
`getMonth()`	Returns the month of the date, represented by the numbers 0 (for January) through 11 (for December).
`getUTCMonth()`	Returns the month of the UTC date, represented by the numbers 0 (for January) through 11 (for December).
`setMonth(month)`	Sets the month of the date, which is any number 0 or greater. Numbers greater than 11 begin to add years.
`setUTCMonth(month)`	Sets the month of the UTC date, which is any number 0 or greater. Numbers greater than 11 begin to add years.
`getDate()`	Returns the date, which is the day of the month, of the date value.
`getUTCDate()`	Returns the date, which is the day of the month, of the UTC date value.
`setDate(date)`	Sets the day of the month of the date.
`setUTCDate(date)`	Sets the day of the month of the UTC date.
`getDay()`	Returns the day of the week of the date.
`getUTCDay()`	Returns the day of the week of the UTC date.
`setDay(day)`	Sets the day of the week of the date.
`setUTCDay(day)`	Sets the day of the week of the UTC date.
`getHours()`	Returns the hours of the date time.
`getUTCHours()`	Returns the hours of the UTC date time.
`setHours(hours)`	Sets the hours of the date time.
`setUTCHours(hours)`	Sets the hours of the UTC date time.
`getMinutes()`	Returns the minutes of the date time.
`getUTCMinutes()`	Returns the minutes of the UTC date time.
`setMinutes(minutes)`	Sets the minutes of the date time.
`setUTCMinutes(minutes)`	Sets the minutes of the UTC date time.
`getSeconds()`	Returns the seconds of the date time.
`getUTCSeconds()`	Returns the seconds of the UTC date time.
`setSeconds(seconds)`	Sets the seconds of the date time.

Method	Description
`setUTCSeconds(seconds)`	Sets the seconds of the UTC date time.
`getMilliseconds()`	Returns the milliseconds of the date time. Note that this does not refer to the milliseconds since January 1, 1970, but rather the number of milliseconds in the current time, such as 4:55:34.20, where 20 is the number of milliseconds of the time.
`getUTCMilliseconds ()`	Returns the milliseconds of the UTC date time.
`setMilliseconds (milliseconds)`	Sets the milliseconds of the date time.
`setUTCMilliseconds (millseconds)`	Sets the milliseconds of the UTC date time.

Built-in objects

ECMA-262 defines a *built-in object* as "any object supplied by an ECMAScript implementation, independent of the host environment, which is present at the start of the execution of an ECMAScript program." This means the developer does not need to explicitly instantiate a built-in object; it is already instantiated. Only two built-in objects are defined by ECMA-262: `Global` and `Math` (which are also both native objects because by definition, every built-in object is a native object).

The Global object

The `Global` object is the most unique in ECMAScript because, for all intents and purposes, it doesn't exist. If you try typing the following line, you get an error:

```
var pointer = Global;
```

The error would say that `Global` is not an object, but didn't I just say that it is an object? Yes. The main concept to understand is this: In ECMAScript no standalone functions exist; all functions must be methods of some object to actually exist. So functions covered earlier in this book such as `isNaN()`, `isFinite()`, `parseInt()`, and `parseFloat()` only look like they are standalone functions. In reality, they are all methods of the `Global` object. But these are not the only methods for the `Global` object.

The `encodeURI()` and `encodeURIComponent()` methods are used to encode URIs (Uniform Resource Identifiers) to be passed to the browser. To be valid, a URI cannot contain certain characters, such as spaces. These methods help to encode the URIs so that a browser can still accept and understand them, replacing all invalid characters with a special UTF-8 encoding.

The `encodeURI()` method is designed to work on an entire URI (for instance, `http://www.wrox.com/illegal value.htm`), whereas `encodeURIComponent()` is designed to work solely on a segment of a URI (such as `illegal value.htm` from the previous URI). The main difference between the two methods is that `encodeURI()` does not encode special characters that are part of a URI such as the colon, forward slash, question mark, and pound sign; `encodeURIComponent()` encodes every non-standard character it finds. For example:

```
var sUri = "http://www.wrox.com/illegal value.htm#start";
alert(encodeURI(sUri));
alert(encodeURIComponent(sUri));
```

This code outputs two values:

```
http://www.wrox.com/illegal%20value.htm#start
http%3A%2F%2Fwww.wrox.com%2Fillegal%20value.htm%23start
```

As you can see, the first URI was left intact except for the space, which was replaced with `%20`. The second URI replaced all non-alphanumeric characters with their encoded equivalents, which essentially makes this URI useless. This is why `encodeURI()` can be used on full URIs, whereas `encodeURIComponent()` can only be used on strings that are appended to the end of an existing URI.

Naturally, there are also two methods to decode URIs that have already been encoded, called `decodeURI()` and `decodeURIComponent()`. As you might expect, these methods do the exact opposite of their counterparts. The `decodeURI()` method only decodes characters that have been replaced by using `encodeURI()`. For instance `%20` is replaced with a space, but `%23` is not replaced because it represents a pound sign (#), which `encodeURI()` does not replace. Likewise, `decodeURIComponent()` decodes all characters encoded by `encodeURIComponent()`, essentially meaning it decodes all special values. Example:

```
var sUri = "http%3A%2F%2Fwww.wrox.com%2Fillegal%20value.htm%23start";
alert(decodeURI(sUri));
alert(decodeURIComponent(sUri));
```

This code outputs two values:

```
http%3A%2F%2Fwww.wrox.com%2Fillegal value.htm%23start
http://www.wrox.com/illegal value.htm#start
```

In this example, the `uri` variable contains a string that is encoded using `encodeURIComponent()`. The resulting values show what happens when you apply the two decoding methods. The first value is the output of `decodeURI()`, which replaced only `%20` with a space; the second value is the output of `decodeURIComponent()`, which replaces all the special characters.

> **These URI methods, `encodeURI()`, `encodeURIComponent()`, `decodeURI()`, and `decodeURIComponent()`, replace the BOM methods `escape()` and `unescape()`. The URI methods are always preferable because they encode all Unicode characters, whereas the BOM methods encode only ASCII characters correctly. Avoid using `escape()` and `unescape()`.**

The final method is perhaps the most powerful in the entire ECMAScript language, the `eval()` method. This method works like an entire ECMAScript interpreter and accepts one argument, a string of ECMAScript (or JavaScript) to execute. For example:

```
eval("alert('hi')");
```

This line is functionally equivalent to the following:

```
alert("hi");
```

When the interpreter finds an `eval()` call, it interprets the argument into actual ECMAScript statements and then inserts it into place. This means that variables can be referenced inside of an `eval()` call that is defined outside of its argument:

```
var msg = "hello world";
eval("alert(msg)");
```

Here, the variable `msg` is defined outside of the context of the `eval()` call, yet the alert is still displayed with the text `"hello world"` because the second line is replaced with a real line of code. Likewise, you can define a function or variables inside of an `eval()` call that can be referenced by the code outside of itself:

```
eval("function sayHi() { alert('hi'); }");
sayHi();
```

Here, the `sayHi()` function is defined inside of an `eval()` call. Because that call is replaced with the actual function, it is possible to call `sayHi()` on the following line.

> **This capability is very powerful, but also very dangerous. Use extreme caution with `eval()`, especially when passing user-entered data into it. A mischievous user could insert values that could compromise your site or application security (this is called *code injection*).**

The `Global` object doesn't just have methods, it also has properties. Remember those special values `undefined`, `NaN`, and `Infinity`? They are all properties of the `Global` object. Additionally, all native object constructors are also properties of the `Global` object. The following table describes all the properties in more detail.

Property	Description
`undefined`	The literal for the Undefined type.
`NaN`	The special Number value for *Not a Number*.
`Infinity`	The special Number value for an infinite value.
`Object`	Constructor for `Object`.
`Array`	Constructor for `Array`.
`Function`	Constructor for `Function`.
`Boolean`	Constructor for `Boolean`.
`String`	Constructor for `String`.
`Number`	Constructor for `Number`.
`Date`	Constructor for `Date`.
`RegExp`	Constructor for `RegExp`.

Table continued on following page

Property	Description
`Error`	Constructor for `Error`.
`EvalError`	Constructor for `EvalError`.
`RangeError`	Constructor for `RangeError`.
`ReferenceError`	Constructor for `ReferenceError`.
`SyntaxError`	Constructor for `SyntaxError`.
`TypeError`	Constructor for `TypeError`.
`URIError`	Constructor for `URIError`.

The Math object

The `Math` object is the built-in object that you wish you had during those high school math classes: It knows all the formulas for the most complicated mathematical problems, and it can figure them out for you if you give it the numbers to work with.

The `Math` object has several properties, consisting mostly of special values in the world of mathematics. The following table describes these properties:

Property	Description
`E`	The value of e, the base of the natural logarithms.
`LN10`	The natural logarithm of 10.
`LN2`	The natural logarithm of 2.
`LOG2E`	The base 2 logarithm of `E`.
`LOG10E`	The base 1 logarithm of `E`.
`PI`	The value of π.
`SQRT1_2`	The square root of ½.
`SQRT2`	The square root of 2.

Although the meanings and uses of these values is outside the scope of this book, if you know what they are, they are available when you need them.

The `Math` object also contains many methods aimed at performing both simple and complex mathematical calculations.

The methods `min()` and `max()` are used to determine which number is the lowest or highest in a group of numbers. Each of these methods accepts any number of parameters:

```
var iMax = Math.max(3, 54, 32, 16);
alert(iMax);     //outputs "54"
```

```
var iMin = Math.min(3, 54, 32, 16);
alert(iMin);     //outputs "3"
```

Out of the number 3, 54, 32, and 16, `max()` returns the number 54 whereas `min()` returns the number 3. These methods are useful to avoid extra loops and `if` statements to determine the maximum value out of a group of numbers.

Another method is `abs()`, which returns the absolute value of a number. The absolute value is the positive version of a negative number (positive numbers are their own absolute values).

```
var iNegOne = Math.abs(-1);
alert(iNegOne);     //outputs "1"
var iPosOne = Math.abs(1);
alert(iPosOne);     //outputs "1"
```

In this example, `abs(-1)` returns `1` and so does `abs(1)`.

The next group of methods has to do with rounding decimal values into integers. Three methods, `ceil()`, `floor()`, and `round()`, handle rounding in different ways.

- The `ceil()` method represents the *ceiling* function, which always rounds numbers up to the nearest value.
- The `floor()` method represents the *floor* function, which always rounds numbers down to the nearest value.
- The `round()` method represents a standard round function, which rounds up if the number is more than halfway to the next value (0.5 of the way there) and rounds down if not. This is the way you were taught to round in elementary school.

To illustrate how each of these methods works, consider using the value 25.5:

```
alert(Math.ceil(25.5));      //outputs "26"
alert(Math.round(25.5));     //outputs "26"
alert(Math.floor(25.5));     //outputs "25"
```

For `ceil()` and `round()`, passing in 25.5 returns 26, whereas `floor()` returns 25. Be careful not to use these methods interchangeably because you could end up with some unexpected results.

Another group of methods relates to the use of exponents. These methods include the following: `exp()`, which raises `Math.E` to a given power; `log()`, which returns the natural logarithm of a particular number; `pow()`, which raises a given number to a given power; and `sqrt()`, which returns the square root of a given number.

Essentially, `exp()` and `log()` reverse each other, whereas `exp()` raises `Math.E` to a specific power and `log()` determines what exponent of `Math.E` is needed to equal the given value. For example:

```
var iNum = Math.log(Math.exp(10));
alert(iNum);
```

Here, `Math.E` is first raised to the power of 10 by using `exp()`, and then `log()` returns 10 as the exponent necessary to equal that number. If you are confused, you're not alone. This type of stuff stumps high school and college math students worldwide. Chances are if you don't know what the natural logarithm is, you'll probably never need to code it.

The `pow()` method is used to raise a number to a given power, such as raising 2 to the power of 10 (represented in math as 2^{10}):

```
var iNum = Math.pow(2, 10);
```

The first argument of `pow()` is the base number, in this case, 2. The second argument is the power to raise it to, which is 10 in this example.

> **It is not recommended to use `Math.E` as a base for the `pow()` method. Always use `exp()` for this because it does special calculations to determine the value more accurately.**

The last method in this group is `sqrt()`, which returns the square root of a given number. It takes only one argument, which is the number whose square root you want to find. So to find the square root of 4, you need only this line of code:

```
var iNum = Math.sqrt(4);
alert(iNum);    //outputs "2"
```

Of course, the square root of 4 is 2, which is output in this code.

You may ask, "What does the square root have to do with exponents?" The square root of a number is actually that number raised to the one-half power; for example, $2^{1/2}$ is the square root of 2.

There is also a complete set of geometric methods included in the `Math` object. These are displayed in the following table.

Method	Description
`acos(x)`	Returns the arc cosine of *x*.
`asin(x)`	Returns the arc sine of *x*.
`atan(x)`	Returns the arc tangent of *x*.
`atan2(y, x)`	Returns the arc cosine of *y/x*.
`cos(x)`	Returns the cosine of *x*.
`sin(x)`	Returns the sine of *x*.
`tan(x)`	Returns the tangent of *x*.

Even though these methods are defined by ECMA-262, the results are implementation-dependent because you can calculate each value in many different ways. Consequently, the precision of the results may also vary from one implementation to another.

The last method of the `Math` object is `random()`. This method returns a random number between the 0 and 1, not including 0 and 1. This is a favorite tool of Web sites that are trying to display random quotes or random facts upon entry. You can use `random()` to select numbers within a certain range by using the following formula:

```
number = Math.floor(Math.random() * total_number_of_choices + first_possible_value)
```

The `floor()` method is used here because `random()` always returns a decimal value, meaning that multiplying it by a number and adding another still yields a decimal value. Most of the time, you want to select a random integer. Because of that, the `floor()` method is needed. So, if you wanted to select a number between 1 and 10, the code looks like this:

```
var iNum = Math.floor(Math.random() * 10 + 1);
```

You see 10 possible values (1 through 10) with the first possible value being 1. If you want to select a number between 2 and 10, then the code looks like this:

```
var iNum = Math.floor(Math.random() * 9 + 2);
```

There are only nine numbers when counting from 2 to 10, so the total number of choices is 9 with the first possible value being 2. Many times, it's just easier to use a function that handles the calculation of the total number of choices and the first possible value:

```
function selectFrom(iFirstValue, iLastValue) {
    var iChoices = iLastValue - iFirstValue + 1;
    return Math.floor(Math.random() * iChoices + iFirstValue);
}

//select from between 2 and 10
var iNum = selectFrom(2, 10);
```

Using the function, it's easy to select a random item from an `Array`:

```
var aColors = ["red", "green", "blue", "yellow", "black", "purple", "brown"];
var sColor = aColors[selectFrom(0, aColors.length-1)];
```

Here, the second parameter to `selectFrom()` is the length of the array minus 1, which (as you remember) is the last position in an array.

Host objects

Any object that is not native is considered to be a *host object*, which is defined as an object provided by the host environment of an ECMAScript implementation. All BOM and DOM objects are considered to be host objects and are discussed later in the book.

Scope

Programmers in any language understand the concept of *scope*, meaning the area in which certain variables are accessible.

Public, protected, and private

In traditional object-oriented programming, a lot of focus is placed on the public and private scopes. An object's properties in the *public* scope can be accessed from outside the object, meaning that after a developer creates an instance of the object, that property can be used. Properties in the *private* scope, however, can only be accessed from within the object itself, meaning that these properties don't exist to the outside world. This also means that subclasses of the class defining the private properties and methods can't access them either.

More recently, another scope has become popular: *protected*. Although different languages have different rules for the protected scope, it generally is used to define properties and methods that act private except that they are accessible by subclasses.

The discussion of these scopes in reference to ECMAScript is almost a moot point because only one scope of these three exists: the public scope. All properties and methods of all objects in ECMAScript are public. You must take great care, therefore, when defining your own classes and objects. Keep in mind that all properties and methods are public by default.

This problem has been tackled by many developers online trying to come up with effective property scoping schemes. Due to the lack of a private scope, a convention was developed to indicate which properties and methods should be considered private. This convention involves adding two underscores before and after the actual property name. For example:

```
obj.__color__ = "red";
```

In this code, the `color` property is intended to be private. Remember, adding these underscores doesn't change the fact that the property is public; it just indicates to other developers that it should be considered private.

Some developers also prefer to use a single underscore to indicate private members, such as ***`obj._color`***.

Static is not static

The *static* scope defines properties and methods accessible all the time from one location. In Java, classes can have static properties and methods that are accessible without instantiating an object of that class, such as `java.net.URLEncoder`, whose function `encode()` is a static method.

Strictly speaking, ECMAScript doesn't have a static scope. It can, however, provide properties and methods on constructors. Remember, constructors are just functions. Functions are objects, and objects can have properties and methods. For instance:

```
function sayHi() {
    alert("hi");
}
```

```
sayHi.alternate = function() {
    alert("hola");
};

sayHi();                //outputs "hi"
sayHi.alternate();      //outputs "hola"
```

Here, the method `alternate()` is actually a method on the function `sayHi`. It is possible to call the `sayHi()` as a regular function to output `"hi"` as well as calling `sayHi.alternate()` to output `"hola"`. Even so, `alternate()` is considered to be a method of the function `sayHi()` in the public scope, not a static method.

The this keyword

One of the most important concepts to grasp in ECMAScript is the use of the `this` keyword, which is used in object methods. The `this` keyword always points to the object that is calling a particular method, for example:

```
var oCar = new Object;
oCar.color = "red";
oCar.showColor = function () {
    alert(this.color);     //outputs "red"
};
```

Here, the `this` keyword is used in the `showColor()` method of an object. In this context, `this` is equal to `car`, making this code functionality equivalent to the following:

```
var oCar = new Object;
oCar.color = "red";
oCar.showColor = function () {
    alert(oCar.color);     //outputs "red"
};
```

So why use `this`? Because you can never be sure of the variable name a developer will use when instantiating an object. By using `this`, it is possible to reuse the same function in any number of different places. Consider the following example:

```
function showColor() {
    alert(this.color);
}

var oCar1 = new Object;
oCar1.color = "red";
oCar1.showColor = showColor;

var oCar2 = new Object;
oCar2.color = "blue";
oCar2.showColor = showColor;

oCar1.showColor();     //outputs "red"
oCar2.showColor();     //outputs "blue"
```

In this code, the function `showColor()` is defined first (using `this`). Then, two objects (`oCar1` and `oCar2`) are created, one with a `color` property set to `"red"`, and the other with a `color` property set to `"blue"`. Both objects are assigned a property called `showColor` that points to the original function named `showColor()` (note that no naming problem exists because one is a global function and the other is a property of an object). When calling `showColor()` on each object, the `oCar1` outputs `"red"` whereas `oCar2` outputs `"blue"`. This happens because the this keyword in the function is equal to `car1` when `oCar1.showColor()` is called and equal to `oCar2` when `oCar2.showColor()` is called.

Note that the `this` keyword *must* be used when referring to properties of an object. For instance, `showColor()` wouldn't work if it were written like this:

```
function showColor() {
    alert(color);
}
```

Whenever a variable is referenced without an object or `this` before it, ECMAScript thinks that it is a local or global variable. This function then looks for a local or global variable named `color`, which it won't find. The result? The function displays `"null"` in the alert.

Defining Classes and Objects

The capability to use predefined objects is only one part of an object-oriented language. The true power comes because you can create your own classes and objects for specific uses. As with many things in ECMAScript, you can accomplish this in a variety of ways.

Factory paradigm

Because properties of an object can be defined dynamically after its creation, a lot of developers wrote code similar to the following when JavaScript was first introduced:

```
var oCar = new Object;
oCar.color = "red";
oCar.doors = 4;
oCar.mpg = 23;
oCar.showColor = function () {
    alert(this.color);
};
```

In this code, an object is created named `car`. The object is then given several properties: Its color is red, it has four doors, and it gets 23 miles per gallon. The last property is actually a pointer to a function, which means the property is a method. After this code is executed, you can use an object called `car`. The problem is that you may need to create more than one instance of a car.

To solve the problem, developers created *factory functions*, which create and return an object of a specific type. For example, a function called `createCar()` could be used to encapsulate the creation of the `car` object described previously:

```
function createCar() {
    var oTempCar = new Object;
    oTempCar.color = "red";
    oTempCar.doors = 4;
    oTempCar.mpg = 23;
    oTempCar.showColor = function () {
        alert(this.color)
    };

    return oTempCar;
}

var oCar1 = createCar();
var oCar2 = createCar();
```

Here, all the previous lines of code are contained within the `createCar()` function, including one extra line, which returns the car (`oTempCar`) as the function value. When this function is called, it creates a new `Object` and assigns all the properties necessary to replicate the car object described earlier. Using this method, it is easy to create two (or more) versions of a car object (`oCar1` and `oCar2`) that have the exact same properties. Of course, the `createCar()` function can also be modified to allow the passing in of default values for the various properties instead of just assigning default values:

```
function createCar(sColor, iDoors, iMpg) {
    var oTempCar = new Object;
    oTempCar.color = sColor;
    oTempCar.doors = iDoors;
    oTempCar.mpg = iMpg;
    oTempCar.showColor = function () {
        alert(this.color)
    };

    return oTempCar;
}

var oCar1 = createCar("red", 4, 23);
var oCar1 = createCar("blue", 3, 25);
oCar1.showColor();    //outputs "red"
oCar2.showColor();    //outputs "blue"
```

By adding arguments to the `createCar()` function, it is possible to assign values to the color, doors, and mpg properties of the car object being created. This leaves two objects with the same properties but different values for those properties.

As ECMAScript became more formalized, however, this method of creating objects fell out of favor and is typically frowned upon today. Part of the reason for this was semantic (it doesn't look as appropriate as using the `new` operator with a constructor), and part was functional. The functional problem has to do with the creation of object methods using this paradigm. In the previous example, every time the `createCar()` function is called, a new function is created called `showColor()`, meaning that every object has its own version of `showColor()` when, in reality, each object should share the same function.

Some got around this problem by defining the object methods outside of the factory functions and then pointing to them:

```
function showColor() {
    alert(this.color);
}

function createCar(sColor, iDoors, iMpg) {
    var oTempCar = new Object;
    oTempCar.color = sColor;
    oTempCar.doors = iDoors;
    oTempCar.mpg = iMpg;
    oTempCar.showColor = showColor;
    return oTempCar;
}

var oCar1 = createCar("red", 4, 23);
var oCar2 = createCar("blue", 3, 25);
oCar1.showColor();     //outputs "red"
oCar2.showColor();     //outputs "blue"
```

In this rewritten code, the `showColor()` function is defined before the `createCar()` function. Inside `createCar()`, the object is assigned a pointer to the already existing `showColor()` function. Functionally, this solves the problem of creating duplicate function objects; but semantically, the function doesn't look like it is a method of an object.

All these problems led to the creation of developer-defined constructors.

Constructor paradigm

Creating a constructor is just as easy as defining a factory function, if not easier. The first step is selection of a class name, which becomes the name of the constructor. Traditionally, this name begins with a capital letter to differentiate it from variable names, which typically begin with lowercase letters. Other than this difference, a constructor looks a lot like a factory function. Consider the following example:

```
function Car(sColor, iDoors, iMpg) {
    this.color = sColor;
    this.doors = iDoors;
    this.mpg = iMpg;
    this.showColor = function () {
        alert(this.color)
    };
}

var oCar1 = new Car("red", 4, 23);
var oCar2 = new Car("blue", 3, 25);
```

The first difference you may notice is that no object is created inside the constructor; instead, the `this` keyword is used. When a constructor is called with the `new` operator, an object is created before the first line of the constructor is executed; that object is accessible (at that point) only by using `this`. It is then possible to assign properties directly to `this` that are returned as the function value by default (no need to explicitly use the `return` operator).

Creating the object is now much more like general object creation in ECMAScript by using the `new` operator with the class name `Car`. You may be wondering if this paradigm has the same problems as the previous one with managing functions. The answer is yes.

Just like factory functions, constructors duplicate functions, effectively creating a separate copy of a function for each object. Also similar to factory functions, constructors can be rewritten with external functions, but again, semantically they don't make sense. This is where the prototype paradigm becomes advantageous.

Prototype paradigm

This paradigm makes use of an object's `prototype` property, which is considered to be the prototype upon which new objects of that type are created. Here, an empty constructor is used only to set up the name of the class. Then, all properties and methods are assigned directly to the `prototype` property. Rewriting the previous example, the code looks like this:

```
function Car() {
}

Car.prototype.color = "red";
Car.prototype.doors = 4;
Car.prototype.mpg = 23;
Car.prototype.showColor = function () {
    alert(this.color);
};

var oCar1 = new Car();
var oCar2 = new Car();
```

In this code, the constructor (`Car`) is defined first and contains no code. The next few lines of code define the object's properties by adding them to the `prototype` property of `Car`. When `new Car()` is called, all the properties of prototype are immediately assigned to the object that was created, meaning that all instances of `Car` contain pointers to the same `showColor()` function. Semantically, everything looks like it belongs to an object, so the two problems of the previous paradigms have been solved. As an added bonus, this method allows the use of the `instanceof` operator to check what kind of object a given variable points to. So the following line outputs `true`:

```
alert(oCar1 instanceof Car);    //outputs "true"
```

It seems like this is a great solution. Unfortunately, not everything is better here.

First, you may notice that the constructor has no arguments. When using the prototype paradigm, it is impossible to set the initial values of properties by passing arguments to the constructor, so both `car1` and `car2` have `color` equal to `"red"`, `doors` equal to `4`, and `mpg` equal to `23`. This means any changes to the default values must be done after the object is created, which is annoying—but not the end of the world. The real problem arises when one of the properties points to an object other than a function. Functions can be shared without any consequences, but objects are rarely meant to be shared across all instances. Consider the following example:

```
function Car() {
}
```

```
Car.prototype.color = "red";
Car.prototype.doors = 4;
Car.prototype.mpg = 23;
Car.prototype.drivers = new Array("Mike", "Sue");
Car.prototype.showColor = function () {
    alert(this.color);
};

var oCar1 = new Car();
var oCar2 = new Car();

oCar1.drivers.push("Matt");

alert(oCar1.drivers);     //outputs "Mike,Sue,Matt"
alert(oCar2.drivers);     //outputs "Mike,Sue,Matt"
```

Here, a property called `drivers` is a pointer to an `Array` containing two names, `Mike` and `Sue`. Because `drivers` is a reference value, both instances of `Car` point to the same array. This means that when `"Matt"` is added to `car1.drivers`, it is also reflected in `car2.drivers`. Outputting either one of these pointers results in the string `"Mike,Sue,Matt"` being displayed.

With so many problems in creating objects, you must be wondering if there is any way to create objects in a rational way. The answer is to combine the best of both constructor and prototype paradigms.

Hybrid constructor/prototype paradigm

By using both the constructor and prototype paradigms, you can create an object just as you would when using other programming languages. The concept is very simple: Use the constructor paradigm to define all nonfunction properties of the object and use the prototype paradigm to define the function properties (methods) of the object. The result is that functions are only created once, but each object can have its own instance of object properties. If you once again rewrite this example, the code becomes the following:

```
function Car(sColor, iDoors, iMpg) {
    this.color = sColor;
    this.doors = iDoors;
    this.mpg = iMpg;
    this.drivers = new Array("Mike", "Sue");
}

Car.prototype.showColor = function () {
    alert(this.color);
};

var oCar1 = new Car("red", 4, 23);
var oCar2 = new Car("blue", 3, 25);

oCar1.drivers.push("Matt");

alert(oCar1.drivers);     //outputs "Mike,Sue,Matt"
alert(oCar2.drivers);     //outputs "Mike,Sue"
```

Now that's more like it. All the nonfunction properties are defined in the constructor, meaning that once again it is possible to assign default values by passing arguments into the constructor. Only one instance of the `showColor()` function is being created, so there is no wasted memory. Additionally, when `oCar1` adds `"Matt"` to the `drivers` array, it has no effect on `oCar2`'s array, so when it output these arrays, `oCar1.drivers` displays `"Mike,Sue,Matt"` whereas `oCar2.drivers` displays `"Mike,Sue"`. Because the prototype paradigm is used, it is still possible to use the `instanceof` operator to determine the type of object.

In case you haven't figured it out, this paradigm is the dominant form used in ECMAScript because it combines the positive attributes of the other paradigms without any of the harsh side effects. However, some developers feel this is still not enough.

Dynamic prototype method

For developers coming from other languages, using the hybrid constructor/prototype paradigm is a little jarring. After all, most object-oriented languages provide some sort of visual encapsulation of properties and methods when defining classes. Consider the following Java class:

```
class Car {
    public String color = "red";
    public int doors = 4;
    public int mpg = 23;

    public Car(String color, int doors, int mpg) {
        this.color = color;
        this.doors = doors;
        this.mpg = mpg;
    }

    public void showColor() {
        System.out.println(color);
    }
}
```

Java provides a nice wrap of all properties and methods of the `Car` class, so the code really looks more like what it does: It defines information for one object. Critics of the hybrid constructor/prototype paradigm say that it isn't logical to look for some properties inside of the constructor and others outside of it. So, the dynamic prototype method was devised to provide a more friendly coding style.

The basic idea behind dynamic prototyping is the same as the hybrid constructor/prototype paradigm: Nonfunction properties are defined in the constructor, whereas function properties are defined on the prototype property. The one difference is where the assignment of the methods takes place. Take a look at the `Car` class rewritten using dynamic prototyping:

```
function Car(sColor, iDoors, iMpg) {
    this.color = sColor;
    this.doors = iDoors;
    this.mpg = iMpg;
    this.drivers = new Array("Mike", "Sue");

    if (typeof Car._initialized == "undefined") {
```

```
            Car.prototype.showColor = function () {
                alert(this.color);
            };

            Car._initialized = true;
        }
    }
```

The constructor is identical until the line that checks if `typeof Car._initialized` is equal to `"undefined"`. This line is the most important part of the dynamic prototype method. If this value is undefined, the constructor continues on to define the methods of the object using the prototype paradigm and then sets `Car._initialized` to `true`. If the value is defined (when it's true, its `typeof` is Boolean), then the methods aren't created again. Simply put, this method uses a flag (`_initialized`) to determine if the prototype has been assigned any methods yet. The methods are only created and assigned once, and to the delight of traditional OOP developers, the code looks more like class definitions in other languages.

Hybrid factory paradigm

This paradigm is typically used as a workaround when the previous paradigms don't work. Here, the aim is to create a dummy constructor that simply returns a new instance of another type of object. The code looks very similar to the class paradigm's factory function:

```
function Car() {
    var oTempCar = new Object;
    oTempCar.color = "red";
    oTempCar.doors = 4;
    oTempCar.mpg = 23;
    oTempCar.showColor = function () {
        alert(this.color)
    };

    return oTempCar;
}
```

Unlike the classic paradigm, this paradigm uses the `new` keyword to make it seem like an actual constructor is being called:

```
var car = new Car();
```

Because the `new` operator is called within the `Car()` constructor, the second `new` operator (called outside of the constructor) is essentially ignored. The object created inside the constructor is passed back into the variable `car`.

This paradigm has the same problems as the classic paradigm regarding memory management of object methods. It is highly recommended that you avoid using this method unless absolutely necessary (see Chapter 15, "XML in JavaScript," for an example of such a case).

Which one to use?

As mentioned previously, the hybrid constructor/prototype paradigm is the one most widely used at present. That being said, dynamic prototyping is catching on in popularity and is functionally equivalent. Using either of these two methods is perfectly fine. Don't ever get caught using the classic, constructor or prototype paradigms alone, however, because you may introduce problems into code.

A practical example

Part of the appeal of objects is the way they can be used to solve problems. One of the common problems in ECMAScript is the performance of string concatenation. Similar to other languages, ECMAScript strings are *immutable*, meaning that their value cannot be changed. Consider the following code:

```
var str = "hello ";
str += "world";
```

This code actually executes the following steps behind the scenes:

1. Create a string to store `"hello "`.
2. Create a string to store `"world"`.
3. Create a string to store the result of concatenation.
4. Copy the current contents of `str` into the result.
5. Copy the `"world"` into the result.
6. Update `str` to point to the result.

Steps 2–6 occur every time a string concatenation is completed, making this a very expensive operation. If this process is repeated hundreds or even thousands of times, performance suffers. The solution is to use an `Array` object to store the strings and then use the `join()` method (with an empty string as an argument) to create the final string. Imagine writing this code instead:

```
var arr = new Array;
arr[0] = "hello ";
arr[1] = "world";
var str = arr.join("");
```

Using this method, it doesn't matter how many strings are introduced into the array because the only concatenation occurs when the `join()` method is called. At that point, the following steps are executed:

1. Create a string to store the result.
2. Copy each string into the appropriate spot in the result.

Although this solution is good, it could be better. The problem is that the code doesn't accurately reflect its intent. To make it more understandable, this functionality can be wrapped in a `StringBuffer` class:

```
function StringBuffer() {
    this.__strings__ = new Array;
}
```

```
StringBuffer.prototype.append = function (str) {
    this.__strings__.push(str);
};

StringBuffer.prototype.toString = function () {
    return this.__strings__.join("");
};
```

The first thing to note about this code is the `strings` property, which is intended to be private. It has only two methods: `append()` and `toString()`. The `append()` method takes an argument and appends it to the strings array and the `toString()` method returns the actual concatenated string by using the array's `join()` method. To concatenate a group of strings using a `StringBuffer` object, use the following code:

```
var buffer = new StringBuffer();
buffer.append("hello ");
buffer.append("world");
var result = buffer.toString();
```

You can test the performance of the `StringBuffer` object versus traditional string concatenation with the following code:

```
var d1 = new Date();
var str = "";
for (var i=0; i < 10000; i++) {
    str += "text";
}
var d2 = new Date();

document.write("Concatenation with plus: " + (d2.getTime() - d1.getTime()) + "
milliseconds");

var oBuffer = new StringBuffer();
d1 = new Date();
for (var i=0; i < 10000; i++) {
    oBuffer.append("text");
}
var sResult = buffer.toString();
d2 = new Date();

document.write("<br />Concatenation with StringBuffer: " + (d2.getTime() -
d1.getTime()) + " milliseconds");
```

The code runs two tests on string concatenation, the first by using the additive operator and the second by using the `StringBuffer`. Each operation concatenates 10,000 strings. The dates `d1` and `d2` are used to determine how much time it takes to complete the operation. Remember, when you create a new `Date` object without any arguments, it is assigned current date and time. To figure out how much time elapsed during the concatenation, the millisecond representation of the dates (returned by the `getTime()` method) are subtracted. This is a common method of measuring JavaScript performance. The results of this test should show a savings of 100–200% over using the additive operator.

Modifying Objects

Creating your own objects is just part of the fun in ECMAScript. How would you like to modify the behavior of existing objects? This is completely possible in ECMAScript, so dream up whatever methods you'd like for a `String`, `Array`, `Number`, or any other object, because the possibilities are endless.

Remember the `prototype` object from an earlier section in this chapter? You already know that each constructor has a `prototype` property that can be used to define methods. What you don't already know is that each of the native objects in ECMAScript also has a `prototype` property that can be used in the exactly same way.

Creating a new method

You can define a new method for any existing class by using its `prototype` property, just as you would with your own classes. For instance, remember the `toString()` method of `Number` that outputs a hexadecimal string if you pass in 16 as an argument? Wouldn't it be nicer to have a `toHexString()` method to handle the process? It's simple to create it:

```
Number.prototype.toHexString = function () {
    return this.toString(16);
};
```

In this context, the `this` keyword points to the instance of `Number` and so has full access to all the `Number` methods. With this code, it is possible to do this:

```
var iNum = 15;
alert(iNum.toHexString());    //outputs "F"
```

Because the number 15 is equal to hexadecimal F, the alert displays `"F"`. And remember the discussion about using an `Array` as a queue? The only thing missing was properly named methods. You can add `enqueue()` and `dequeue()` to `Array` and just have them call the existing `push()` and `shift()` methods respectively:

```
Array.prototype.enqueue = function(vItem) {
    this.push(vItem);
};

Array.prototype.dequeue = function() {
    return this.shift();
};
```

You can also, of course, add methods that don't rely on existing methods at all. For example, say that you want to determine the position of a particular item in an array. You have no native method to do such a thing. You can easily create a method that does this:

```
Array.prototype.indexOf = function (vItem) {

    for (var i=0; i < this.length; i++) {
        if (vItem == this[i]) {
            return i;
```

```
        }
    }

    return -1;
}
```

This method, named `indexOf()` to keep it consistent with the `String` method of the same name, searches each item in the array until it finds the equivalent of the item passed in. If the item is found, the method returns the position; if not, the method returns `-1`. With this defined, the following code is possible:

```
var aColors = new Array("red", "green", "yellow");
alert(aColors.indexOf("green"));    //outputs "1"
```

Lastly, if you want to add a new method to every native object in ECMAScript, you must define it on the `Object`'s prototype property. As discussed in the last chapter, all native objects inherit from `Object`, and so any changes to `Object` are reflected in all native objects. For example, if you want to add a method that outputs the current value of the object in an alert, you do the following:

```
Object.prototype.showValue = function () {
    alert(this.valueOf());
};

var str = "hello";
var iNum = 25;
str.showValue();    //outputs "hello"
iNum.showValue();    //outputs "25"
```

Here, both the `String` and `Number` objects inherit the `showValue()` method from `Object`, displaying `"hello"` and `"25"` when called on their respective objects.

Redefining an existing method

Just as it is possible to define new methods for existing classes, it is also possible to redefine existing methods. As discussed in the previous chapter, function names are simply pointers to functions, and as such, can be easily changed to point to other functions. What happens if you change a native method, such as `toString()`?

```
Function.prototype.toString = function () {
    return "Function code hidden";
};
```

The previous code is perfectly legal and works as expected:

```
function sayHi() {
    alert("hi");
}

alert(sayHi.toString());    //outputs "Function code hidden"
```

You may recall from Chapter 2 that the `Function`'s `toString()` method normally outputs the source code of the function. By overriding that method, you can supply a different string to return (in this case, `"Function code hidden"`). But what happened to the original function that `toString()` was pointing to? Well, it has gone on to the garbage collector because it was fully dereferenced. You have no way to get that original function back, which is why it is always safer to store a pointer to the original method that you are overriding, just in case you need it later. You may even want to call that original method under certain circumstances in your new method:

```
Function.prototype.originalToString = Function.prototype.toString;

Function.prototype.toString = function () {
    if (this.originalToString().length > 100) {
        return "Function too long to display.";
    } else {
        return this.originalToString();
    }
};
```

In this code, the first line saves a reference to the current `toString()` method in a property called `originalToString`. Then, the `toString()` method is overridden with a custom method. This new method checks to see if the length of the function source code is longer greater than 100. If so, the method returns a small error message stating that the function code is too long; otherwise, it returns the source code by calling `originalToString()`.

Very late binding

Technically speaking, there is no such thing as very late binding. The term is used in this book to describe a phenomenon in ECMAScript where it is possible to define a method for a type of object after the object has already been instantiated. For example:

```
var o = new Object;

Object.prototype.sayHi = function () {
    alert("hi");
};

o.sayHi();
```

In most programming languages, you must define object methods well in advance of object instantiation. Here, the `sayHi()` method is added to the `Object` class after an instance has been created. Not only is that unheard of in traditional languages, but the instance of `Object` is then automatically assigned the method and it can be used immediately (on the following line).

> **It is not recommended that you use very late binding because it can be difficult to keep track of and document. However, you should understand that it is possible.**

Summary

ECMAScript provides JavaScript implementations with complete object-oriented language capabilities. In this chapter, you have learned about the three different types of objects defined in ECMA-262: native objects, built-in objects, and host objects.

You explored the `Array` and `Date` objects, learning about their methods, properties, and various quirks. You also learned about the two built-in objects, `Global` and `Math`, as well as gained understanding about how the `Global` object is different from others.

This chapter also introduced the capability to define your own objects from the ground up. Several different methods of accomplishing this were explored and their pros and cons discussed.

Finally, you learned how to modify existing objects to include new methods as well as to override existing methods.

The next chapter finishes up the introduction to the JavaScript Core, ECMAScript, with a discussion of inheritance.

4

Inheritance

A truly object-oriented language must support inheritance, the capability of a class to reuse (*inherit*) methods and properties from another class. In the previous chapter, you learned how to define properties and methods of a class, but what if you want two classes to use the same methods? This is where inheritance comes in.

Inheritance in Action

The easiest way to describe inheritance is through a classic example, geometric shapes. There are really two types of shapes: ellipses (which are rounded) and polygons (which have a certain number of sides). Circles are a type of ellipse with one focus; triangles, rectangles, and pentagons are types of polygons with a different number of sides. A square is a type of rectangle with all sides equal. This describes a perfect inheritance relationship.

In this example, Shape is the *base class* (the class to be inherited from) of Ellipse and Polygon. An Ellipse has one property called *foci,* indicating the number of foci the Ellipse has. Circle inherits from Ellipse, so Circle is a *subclass* of Ellipse and Ellipse is a *superclass* of Circle. Likewise, Triangle, Rectangle, and Pentagon are subclasses of Polygon and Polygon is a superclass to each of these shapes. Finally, Square inherits from Rectangle.

The inheritance relationship is best explained through diagrams, which is where the Universal Modeling Language (UML) comes in. One of UML's many purposes is to visually represent complex object relationships such as inheritance. Figure 4-1 is a UML diagram explaining the relationship of Shape to its subclasses:

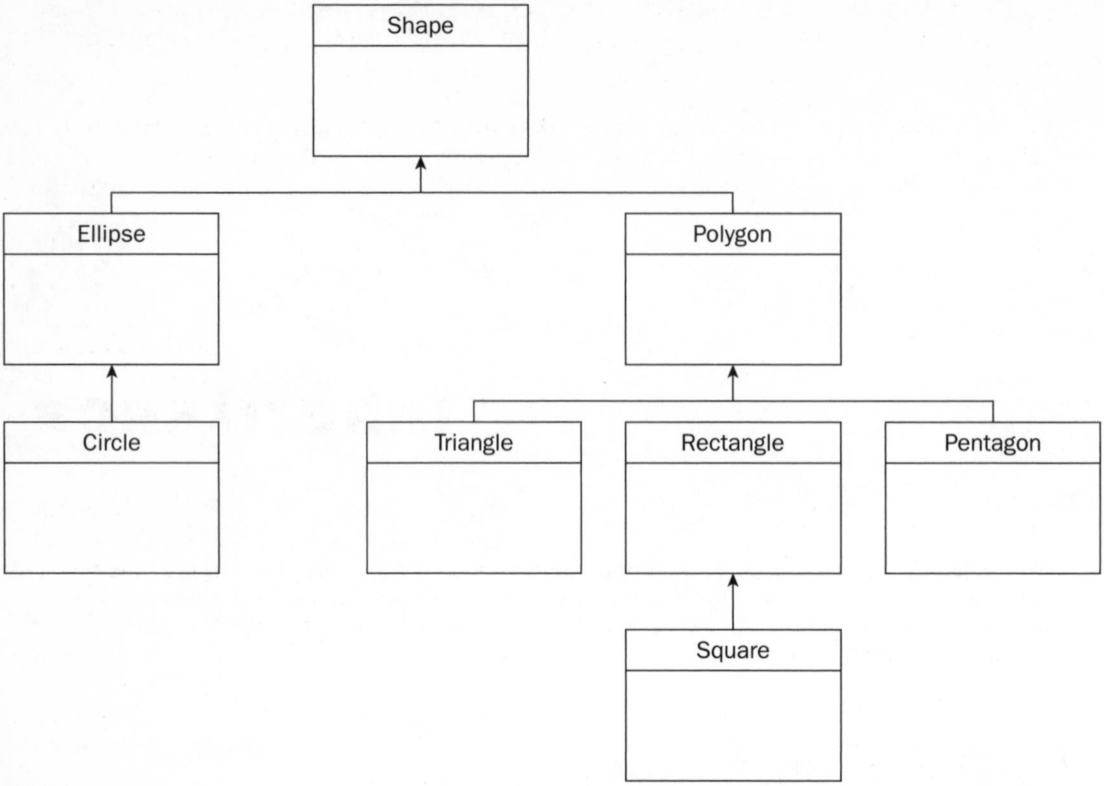

Figure 4-1

In UML, each box represents a class, indicated by the class name. Lines coming from the top of Triangle, Rectangle, and Pentagon converge and point at Shape, indicating that each of these classes inherits from Shape. Likewise, the arrow pointing from Square to Rectangle indicates the inheritance relationship there.

If you are interested in learning more about UML, refer to Instant UML (Wrox Press, ISBN 1861000871).

Implementing Inheritance

In order to implement inheritance in ECMAScript, you start out with a base class from which to inherit. All developer-defined classes are candidate base classes. As a security precaution, native or host objects cannot be base classes; this prevents giving the public access to compiled browser-level code that could potentially be used in a malicious way.

After the base class has been selected, you can proceed to create its subclasses. It's completely up to you whether or not the base class should be used at all. Sometimes, you may want to create a base class that isn't intended to be used directly. Instead, it only provides common functionality to subclasses. In this case, the base class is considered *abstract*.

Although ECMAScript doesn't strictly define abstract classes as some other languages do, it sometimes creates certain base classes that aren't supposed to be used. Usually these are simply documented as abstract.

The subclasses you create inherit all properties and methods from the superclass, including the constructor and method implementations. Remember, all the properties and methods are public, so subclasses may access these directly. Subclasses may add new properties and methods not present in the superclass or override properties and methods of the superclass with new implementations.

Methods of inheritance

As usual with ECMAScript, you have more than one way to implement inheritance. This is because inheritance in JavaScript isn't explicit; it's emulated. This means that the interpreter doesn't handle all the inheritance details. It is up to you, as the developer, to handle inheritance in a way that is most appropriate for your situation.

Object masquerading

Object masquerading was never intended when the original ECMAScript was conceived. Instead, it evolved as developers began to understand exactly how functions worked and, specifically, how to use the `this` keyword in the context of functions.

The reasoning goes like this: A constructor assigns all properties and methods (with the Constructor Paradigm of class declaration) using the `this` keyword. Because a constructor is just a function, you can make the constructor of `ClassA` into a method of `ClassB` and call it. `ClassB` then receives the properties and methods defined in `ClassA`'s constructor. For example, `ClassA` and `ClassB` are defined in this way:

```
function ClassA(sColor) {
    this.color = sColor;
    this.sayColor = function () {
        alert(this.color);
    };
}

function ClassB(sColor) {
}
```

As you remember, the `this` keyword references the currently created object in a constructor; in a method, however, `this` points to the owning object. The theory is that treating `ClassA` as a regular function instead of as a constructor establishes a type of inheritance. This can be done in the constructor `ClassB` like so:

```
function ClassB(sColor) {
    this.newMethod = ClassA;
    this.newMethod(sColor);
    delete this.newMethod;
}
```

In this code, the method named `newMethod` is assigned to `ClassA` (remember, the name of a function is just a pointer to it). Then, the method is called, passing the `color` argument from the `ClassB` constructor. The final line of code deletes the reference to `ClassA` so that it cannot be called later on.

All new properties and methods must be added after the line that deletes the new method. Otherwise, you run the risk of overwriting the new properties and methods with those of the superclass:

```
function ClassB(sColor, sName) {
    this.newMethod = ClassA;
    this.newMethod(sColor);
    delete this.newMethod;

    this.name = sName;
    this.sayName = function () {
        alert(this.name);
    };
}
```

To prove that this works, you can run the following example:

```
var objA = new ClassA("red");
var objB = new ClassB("blue", "Nicholas");
objA.sayColor();     //outputs "red"
objB.sayColor();     //outputs "blue"
objB.sayName();      //outputs "Nicholas"
```

As an interesting side note, object masquerading supports *multiple inheritance*, meaning that a class can inherit from multiple superclasses. Multiple inheritance is represented in UML by showing the previous superclasses of the subclass as shown in Figure 4-2.

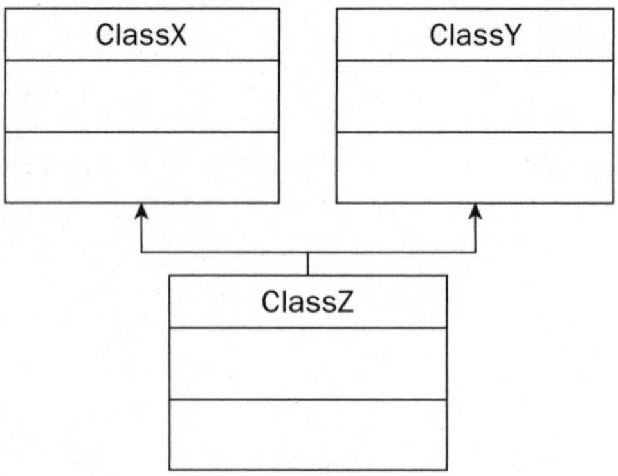

Figure 4-2

For example, if two classes, ClassX and Class Y, exist, and ClassZ wishes to inherit from both, then the following code can be used:

```
function ClassZ() {
    this.newMethod = ClassX;
    this.newMethod();
    delete this.newMethod;

    this.newMethod = ClassY;
```

```
        this.newMethod();
        delete this.newMethod;
    }
```

The one downside to this is that if `ClassX` and `ClassY` have a property or method with the same name, `ClassY`'s takes priority because it is inherited from last. Besides that minor issue, multiple inheritance with object masquerading is a breeze.

Because this method of inheritance caught on, the third edition of ECMAScript includes two new methods of the `Function` object: `call()` and `apply()`.

The call() method

The `call()` method is the method most similar to the classic object-masquerading method. Its first argument is the object to be used for `this`. All other arguments are passed directly to the function itself. For example:

```
function sayColor(sPrefix, sSuffix) {
    alert(sPrefix + this.color + sSuffix);
};

var obj = new Object();
obj.color = "red";

//outputs "The color is red, a very nice color indeed. "
sayColor.call(obj, "The color is ", ", a very nice color indeed. ");
```

In this example, the function `sayColor()` is defined outside of an object, and it references the `this` keyword even though it is not attached to any object. The object `obj` is given a `color` property equal to `"red"`. When `call()` is, well, called, the first argument is `obj`, which indicates that the `this` keyword in `sayColor()` should be assigned the value of `obj`. The second and third arguments are strings. They are matched up with the `prefix` and `suffix` arguments of `sayColor()`, resulting in the message `"The color is red, a very nice color indeed."` being displayed.

To use this with the object masquerading method of inheritance, just replace the three lines that assign, call, and delete the new method:

```
function ClassB(sColor, sName) {
    //this.newMethod = ClassA;
    //this.newMethod(sColor);
    //delete this.newMethod;
    ClassA.call(this, sColor);

    this.name = sName;
    this.sayName = function () {
        alert(this.name);
    };
}
```

Here, you want the `this` keyword in `ClassA` to be equal to the newly created `ClassB` object, so this is passed in as the first argument. The second argument is the `color` argument, the only one for either class.

The apply() method

The `apply()` method takes two arguments: the object to be used for `this` and an array of arguments to be passed to the function. For example:

```
function sayColor(sPrefix, sSuffix) {
    alert(sPrefix + this.color + sSuffix);
};

var obj = new Object();
obj.color = "red";

//outputs "The color is red, a very nice color indeed. "
sayColor.apply(obj, new Array("The color is ",", a very nice color indeed."));
```

This is the same example as before, but now the `apply()` method is being called. When `apply()` is called, the first argument is still `obj`, which indicates that the `this` keyword in `sayColor()` should be assigned the value of `obj`. The second argument is an array consisting of two strings, which are matched up with the `prefix` and `suffix` arguments of `sayColor()`. This also results in the message `"The color is red, a very nice color indeed."` being displayed.

This method is also used in place of the three lines to assign, call, and delete the new method:

```
function ClassB(sColor, sName) {
    //this.newMethod = ClassA;
    //this.newMethod(sColor);
    //delete this.newMethod;
    ClassA.apply(this, new Array(sColor));

    this.name = sName;
    this.sayName = function () {
        alert(this.name);
    };
}
```

Once again, you pass `this` in as the first argument. The second argument is an array with just one value: `color`. You can, alternatively, pass in the entire `arguments` object of `ClassB` as the second argument of the `apply()` method:

```
function ClassB(sColor, sName) {
    //this.newMethod = ClassA;
    //this.newMethod(sColor);
    //delete this.newMethod;
    ClassA.apply(this, arguments);

    this.name = sName;
    this.sayName = function () {
        alert(this.name);
    };
}
```

Of course, passing in the object of the arguments only works if the order of the arguments in the superclass constructor is exactly the same as the order of the arguments in the subclass. When this is not the case, you must create a separate array to place the arguments into the correct order. You could also use the `call()` method.

Prototype chaining

The form of inheritance actually intended for use in ECMAScript is prototype chaining. The last chapter introduced the prototype paradigm for defining classes. Prototype chaining builds off this paradigm to accomplish inheritance in an interesting way.

In the last chapter, you learned that the `prototype` object is the template upon which an object is based when instantiated. To summarize: Any properties or methods on the `prototype` object will be passed on all instances of that class. Prototype chaining uses this functionality to accomplish inheritance.

If the classes from the previous example are redefined using the prototype paradigm, they become the following:

```
function ClassA() {
}

ClassA.prototype.color = "red";
ClassA.prototype.sayColor = function () {
    alert(this.color);
};

function ClassB() {
}

ClassB.prototype = new ClassA();
```

The magic in prototype chaining occurs in the highlighted previous line. Here, you are setting the `prototype` property of `ClassB` to be an instance of `ClassA`. This makes perfect sense because you want all the properties and methods of `ClassA`, but you don't want to have to assign each of them separately to `ClassB`'s prototype property. What better way to do this than just to make the `prototype` into an instance of `ClassA`?

> **Note that no parameters are passed into the `ClassA` constructor call. This is standard in prototype chaining. Be sure that your constructor functions properly without any arguments.**

Similar to object masquerading, all new properties and methods of the subclass must come after the assignment of the `prototype` property because all methods assigned before will be deleted. Why? Because the `prototype` property is being completely replaced with a new object; the original object to which you would have added the methods is destroyed. So to add the name property and the `sayName()` method to `ClassB`, the code looks like this:

```
function ClassB() {
}

ClassB.prototype = new ClassA();
```

```
ClassB.prototype.name = "";
ClassB.prototype.sayName = function () {
    alert(this.name);
};
```

You can test this code by running the following example:

```
var objA = new ClassA();
var objB = new ClassB();
objA.color = "red";
objB.color = "blue";
objB.name = "Nicholas";
objA.sayColor();     //outputs "red"
objB.sayColor();     //outputs "blue"
objB.sayName();      //outputs "Nicholas"
```

As a bonus, the `instanceof` operator works in a rather unique way in prototype chaining. For all instances of `ClassB`, `instanceof` returns `true` for both `ClassA` and `ClassB`. For example:

```
var objB = new ClassB();
alert(objB instanceof ClassA);    //outputs "true";
alert(objB instanceof ClassB);    //outputs "true"
```

In the loosely typed world of ECMAScript, this can be an incredibly useful tool, one that is not available when you use object masquerading.

The downside to prototype chaining is that it has no support for multiple inheritance. Remember, prototype chaining involves overwriting the prototype property of the class with another type of object.

Hybrid method

You may have noticed that this method of inheritance uses the constructor paradigm to define classes without any use of prototyping. The main problem with object masquerading is that you must use the constructor paradigm, which (as you learned in the last chapter) is not optimal. But if you go with prototype chaining, you lose the capability to have constructors with arguments. What's a developer to do? The answer is simple: Use both.

In the previous chapter, you learned that the best way to create classes is to use the constructor paradigm to define the properties and to use the prototype paradigm to define the methods. The same goes for inheritance; you use object masquerading to inherit properties from the constructor and prototype chaining to inherit methods from the `prototype` object. Take a look at the previous example rewritten using both methods of inheritance:

```
function ClassA(sColor) {
    this.color = sColor;
}

ClassA.prototype.sayColor = function () {
    alert(this.color);
};

function ClassB(sColor, sName) {
```

```
        ClassA.call(this, sColor);
        this.name = sName;
    }

    ClassB.prototype = new ClassA();

    ClassB.prototype.sayName = function () {
        alert(this.name);
    };
```

In this example, inheritance is accomplished with the two highlighted lines. First, in the `ClassB` constructor, object masquerading is used to inherit the `color` property from `ClassA`. In the second highlighted line, prototype chaining is used to inherit the methods of `ClassA`. Because this hybrid method uses prototype chaining, the `instanceof` operator still works correctly.

The following example tests this code:

```
var objA = new ClassA("red");
var objB = new ClassB("blue", "Nicholas");
objA.sayColor();    //outputs "red"
objB.sayColor();    //outputs "blue"
objB.sayName();     //outputs "Nicholas"
```

A more practical example

In real Web sites and applications, chances are you won't be creating classes named `ClassA` and `ClassB`. It's far more likely that you will create classes that represent specific things, such as shapes. If you consider the shapes example from the beginning of the chapter, the `Polygon`, `Triangle`, and `Rectangle` classes form a nice set of data to explore.

Creating the base class

Think of the `Polygon` class first. What sort of properties and methods are necessary? First, it's important to know the number of sides the polygon has, so an integer property named `sides` should be included. What else might be necessary for a polygon? You may want to determine the area of polygon, so add a method named `getArea()` to calculate it. Figure 4-3 shows the UML representation of this class.

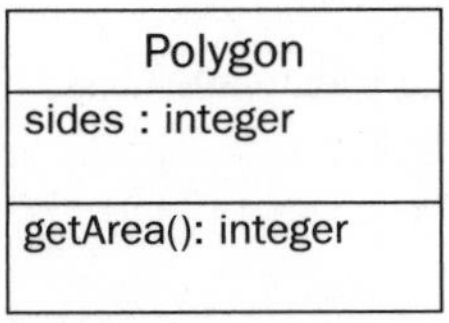

Figure 4-3

In UML, properties are represented by the property name and type in the section immediately under the class name. Methods are located under the properties, indicating the method name and the type of the return value.

In ECMAScript, the class can be written like this:

```
function Polygon(iSides) {
    this.sides  = iSides;
}

Polygon.prototype.getArea = function () {
    return 0;
};
```

Note that the `Polygon` class isn't specific enough to be used by itself; `getArea()` returns `0` because it is just a placeholder for the subclasses to override.

Creating the subclasses

Now consider the `Triangle` class. A triangle has three sides, so this class has to override the `Polygon` class's `sides` property and set it to `3`. The `getArea()` method also has to be overridden to use the area formula for a triangle, which is ½ × base × height. But how does the method get the values for base and height? They must be entered specifically, and so you must create a `base` property and a `height` property. The UML representation for `Triangle` is displayed in Figure 4-4.

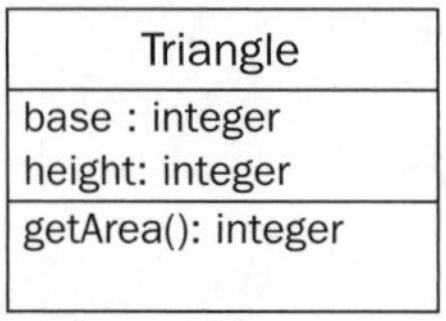

Figure 4-4

This diagram shows only the new properties and overridden methods of `Triangle`. If `Triangle` doesn't override `getArea()`, the method is not listed in the diagram. It would be considered as retained from `Polygon`. The complete UML diagram showing the relationship between `Polygon` and `Triangle` (Figure 4-5) makes it a little bit clearer.

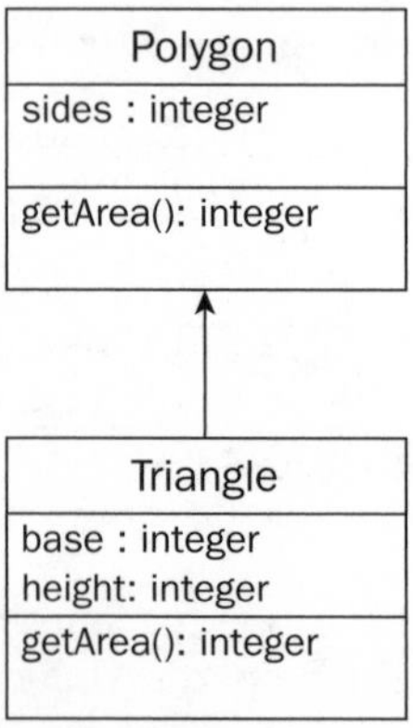

Figure 4-5

In UML, you never duplicate properties or methods that are inherited unless a method is being overridden (or overloaded, which is not possible in ECMAScript).

The code for the `Triangle` class is:

```
function Triangle(iBase, iHeight) {
    Polygon.call(this, 3);
    this.base = iBase;
    this.height = iHeight;
}

Triangle.prototype = new Polygon();
Triangle.prototype.getArea = function () {
    return 0.5 * this.base * this.height;
};
```

Note that the `Triangle` constructor accepts two arguments, `base` and `height`, even though the `Polygon` constructor accepts just one, `sides`. This is because you already know the number of sides in a triangle, and you don't want to allow the developer to change that. So, when you use object masquerading, the number `3` is passed to the `Polygon` constructor as the number of sides for this object. Then, the values for `base` and `height` are assigned the appropriate properties.

After using prototype chaining to inherit the methods, `Triangle` then overrides the `getArea()` method to provide the custom calculation required for the calculation of triangle areas.

The last class is `Rectangle`, which also inherits from `Polygon`. Rectangles have four sides and the area is calculated by multiplying the length by the width, which are two properties needed for the class. `Rectangle` fits into the earlier UML diagram next to `Triangle` because both have `Polygon` as a superclass (see Figure 4-6).

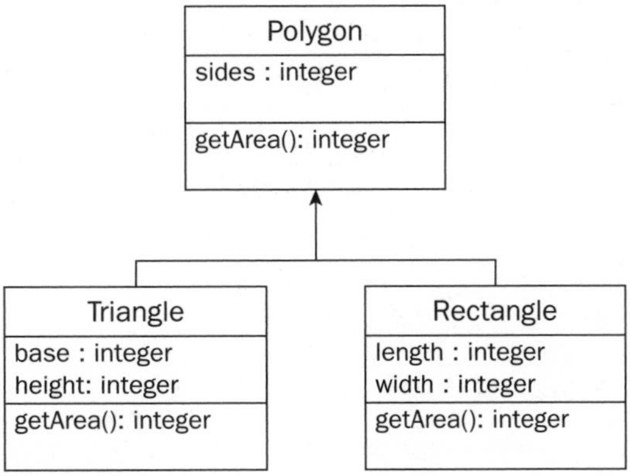

Figure 4-6

The ECMAScript code for `Rectangle` is as follows:

```
function Rectangle(iLength, iWidth) {
    Polygon.call(this, 4);
    this.length = iLength;
    this.width = iWidth;
```

```
}

Rectangle.prototype = new Polygon();
Rectangle.prototype.getArea = function () {
    return this.length * this.width;
};
```

Notice that the `Rectangle` constructor also doesn't accept `sides` as an argument, and once again a constant value (`4`) is passed directly to the `Polygon` constructor. Also similar to `Triangle`, `Rectangle` introduces two new properties as arguments to the constructor and then overrides the `getArea()` method.

Testing the code

You can test the code created for this example by running the following code:

```
var triangle = new Triangle(12, 4);
var rectangle = new Rectangle(22, 10);

alert(triangle.sides);          //outputs "3"
alert(triangle.getArea());      //outputs "24"

alert(rectangle.sides);         //outputs "4"
alert(rectangle.getArea());     //outputs "220"
```

This code creates a triangle, with a base of `12` and a height of `4`, and a rectangle, with a length of `22` and a width of `10`. Then, both the number of sides and the area of each shape are output to prove that the `sides` property is being properly filled and the `getArea()` method is returning the correct value. The area of the triangle should be `24` and the area of the rectangle should be `220`.

What about dynamic prototyping?

The previous example uses the hybrid constructor/prototype paradigm of object definition to show inheritance, but does it work with dynamic prototyping? The answer is no.

The reason that inheritance doesn't work with dynamic prototyping is because of the unique nature of the `prototype` object. Take a look at the following code (which is incorrect, but important to study nonetheless):

```
function Polygon(iSides) {
    this.sides  = iSides;

    if (typeof Polygon._initialized == "undefined") {

        Polygon.prototype.getArea = function () {
            return 0;
        };

        Polygon._initialized = true;
    }
}

function Triangle(iBase, iHeight) {
```

```
        Polygon.call(this, 3);
        this.base = iBase;
        this.height = iHeight;

        if (typeof Triangle._initialized == "undefined") {

            Triangle.prototype = new Polygon();
            Triangle.prototype.getArea = function () {
                return 0.5 * this.base * this.height;
            };

            Triangle._initialized = true;
        }
    }
```

The previous code illustrates both `Polygon` and `Triangle` defined using dynamic prototyping. The mistake is in the highlighted line, where `Triangle.prototype` is set. Logically, this is the correct location; but functionally, it doesn't work. Technically, by the time that code is run, the object is already instantiated and tied to the original `prototype` object. Although changes to that prototype object are reflected properly with very late binding, replacing the `prototype` object has no effect on that object. Only future object instances reflect the change, making the first instance incorrect.

To correctly use dynamic prototyping with inheritance, you must assign the new `prototype` object outside of the constructor, like this:

```
function Triangle(iBase, iHeight) {
    Polygon.call(this, 3);
    this.base = iBase;
    this.height = iHeight;

    if (typeof Triangle._initialized == "undefined") {

        Triangle.prototype.getArea = function () {
            return 0.5 * this.base * this.height;
        };

        Triangle._initialized = true;
    }
}

Triangle.prototype = new Polygon();
```

This code works because the `prototype` object is assigned before any objects are instantiated. Unfortunately, this means the code isn't completely encapsulated in the constructor, which is the main purpose of dynamic prototyping.

Alternative Inheritance Paradigms

Due to the limitations of ECMAScript inheritance (for instance, lack of a private scope and the inability to easily access superclass methods), developers around the world have constantly pushed their code to the limit in an effort to create other ways of implementing inheritance. This section examines some of the alternatives to the standard ECMAScript inheritance paradigms.

zInherit

Prototype chaining essentially copies all methods from an object to a class's `prototype` object. But what if there were a different way to accomplish this? There is. Using the zInherit library (available at `http://www.nczonline.net/downloads`), it's possible to accomplish method inheritance without using prototype chaining. This small library supports all modern browsers (Mozilla, IE, Opera, Safari) as well as some older browsers (Netscape 4.x, IE/Mac).

In order to use the zInherit library, you must include zinherit.js using the **`<script/>`** *tag. Chapter 5, "JavaScript in the Browser," discusses including external JavaScript files in detail.*

The zInherit library adds two methods to the `Object` class: `inheritFrom()` and `instanceOf()`. As you may have guessed, the `inheritFrom()` method does the heavy lifting, copying the methods from a given class. The following line uses prototype chaining to inherit methods from `ClassA` to `ClassB`:

```
ClassB.prototype = new ClassA();
```

This line can be replaced with the following:

```
ClassB.prototype.inheritFrom(ClassA);
```

The `inheritFrom()` method accepts one argument, which is the class from which to copy the methods. Note that, as opposed to prototype chaining, this paradigm doesn't actually create a new instance of the class to inherit from, making it a little safer and freeing the developer from worrying about the constructor arguments.

> **The `inheritFrom()` method call must be used exactly where the prototype assignment normally occurs in order to ensure proper inheritance.**

The `instanceOf()` method is a replacement for the `instanceof` operator. Because this paradigm doesn't use prototype chaining at all, this line of code won't work:

```
ClassB instanceof ClassA
```

The `instanceOf()` method makes up for this loss, working with `inheritFrom()` to keep track of all superclasses:

```
ClassB.instanceOf(ClassA);
```

Polygons revisited

The entire polygon example can be rewritten using the zInherit library by replacing just two lines (highlighted):

```
function Polygon(iSides) {
    this.sides  = iSides;
}

Polygon.prototype.getArea = function () {
    return 0;
};

function Triangle(iBase, iHeight) {
    Polygon.call(this, 3);
    this.base = iBase;
    this.height = iHeight;
}

Triangle.prototype.inheritFrom(Polygon);

Triangle.prototype.getArea = function () {
    return 0.5 * this.base * this.height;
};

function Rectangle(iLength, iWidth) {
    Polygon.call(this, 4);
    this.length = iLength;
    this.width = iWidth;
}

Rectangle.prototype.inheritFrom(Polygon);

Rectangle.prototype.getArea = function () {
    return this.length * this.width;
};
```

To test this code, you can use the same example as before and add in a couple extra lines to test out the `instanceOf()` method:

```
var triangle = new Triangle(12, 4);
var rectangle = new Rectangle(22, 10);

alert(triangle.sides);
alert(triangle.getArea());

alert(rectangle.sides);
alert(rectangle.getArea());

alert(triangle.instanceOf(Triangle));    //outputs "true"
alert(triangle.instanceOf(Polygon));     //outputs "true"

alert(rectangle.instanceOf(Rectangle));  //outputs "true"
alert(rectangle.instanceOf(Polygon));    //outputs "true"
```

The last four lines test `instanceOf()` and should all return `true`.

Dynamic prototyping support

As mentioned earlier, prototype chaining can't be used in the true spirit of dynamic prototyping, which is to keep all code for a class inside of its constructor. The zInherit library fixes this problem by allowing the `inheritFrom()` method to be called from inside the constructor.

Take a look at the polygon dynamic prototyping example used earlier, now with the addition of the zInherit library:

```
function Polygon(iSides) {
    this.sides  = iSides;

    if (typeof Polygon._initialized == "undefined") {

        Polygon.prototype.getArea = function () {
            return 0;
        };

        Polygon._initialized = true;
    }
}

function Triangle(iBase, iHeight) {
    Polygon.call(this, 3);
    this.base = iBase;
    this.height = iHeight;

    if (typeof Triangle._initialized == "undefined") {

        Triangle.prototype.inheritFrom(Polygon);
        Triangle.prototype.getArea = function () {
            return 0.5 * this.base * this.height;
        };

        Triangle._initialized = true;
    }
}

function Rectangle(iLength, iWidth) {
    Polygon.call(this, 4);
    this.length = iLength;
    this.width = iWidth;

    if (typeof Rectangle._initialized == "undefined") {

        Rectangle.prototype.inheritFrom(Polygon);
        Rectangle.prototype.getArea = function () {
            return this.length * this.width;
        };

        Rectangle._initialized = true;
    }
}
```

The two highlighted lines in the previous code implement inheritance from the `Polygon` class for both the `Triangle` and the `Rectangle` classes. The reason this works is that the `prototype` object isn't being overwritten when using the `inheritFrom()` method; methods are just being added to it. Using this method, it's possible to get around the prototype chaining restriction and implement dynamic prototyping the way it is intended.

Multiple Inheritance support

One of the most useful features of the zInherit library is its capability to support multiple inheritance, which is not available using prototype chaining. Again, the key fact that makes this possible is that `inheritFrom()` doesn't replace the `prototype` object.

The `inheritFrom()` method must be used in combination with object masquerading in order to inherit properties and methods. Consider the following example:

```
function ClassX() {
    this.messageX = "This is the X message. ";

    if (typeof ClassX._initialized == "undefined") {

        ClassX.prototype.sayMessageX = function () {
            alert(this.messageX);
        };

        ClassX._initialized = true;
    }
}

function ClassY() {
    this.messageY = "This is the Y message. ";

    if (typeof ClassY._initialized == "undefined") {

        ClassY.prototype.sayMessageY = function () {
            alert(this.messageY);
        };

        ClassY._initialized = true;
    }
}
```

Both `ClassX` and `ClassY` are small classes, each with one property and one method. Suppose you now have `ClassZ` that needs to inherit from both. The class can be defined like this:

```
function ClassZ() {
    ClassX.apply(this);
    ClassY.apply(this);
    this.messageZ = "This is the Z message. ";

    if (typeof ClassZ._initialized == "undefined") {

        ClassZ.prototype.inheritFrom(ClassX);
        ClassZ.prototype.inheritFrom(ClassY);
```

```
        ClassZ.prototype.sayMessageZ = function () {
            alert(this.messageZ);
        };

        ClassZ._initialized = true;
    }
}
```

Note that two lines inherit the properties (using the `apply()` method), and two lines inherit the methods (using the `inheritFrom()`) method. As discussed earlier, the order in which the inheritance happens is important, and it is generally better to always inherit methods in the same order as the properties (meaning that if properties are inherited from `ClassX` and then `ClassY`, the methods should be inherited in that same order).

The following code tests the multiple inheritance example:

```
var objZ = new ClassZ();
objZ.sayMessageX();     //outputs "This is X message. "
objZ.sayMessageY();     //outputs "This is Y message."
objZ.sayMessageZ();     //outputs "This is Z message."
```

The previous code calls three methods:

1. `sayMessageX()`, which is inherited from `ClassX`, accesses the `messageX` property, also inherited from `ClassX`.
2. `sayMessageY()`, which is inherited from `ClassY`, accesses the `messageY` property, also inherited from `ClassY`.
3. `sayMessageZ()`, which is defined in `ClassZ`, accesses the `messageZ` property, also defined in `ClassZ`.

These three methods should output the appropriate message from the appropriate property, indicating that the multiple inheritance has succeeded.

xbObjects

Netscape's DevEdge site (`http://devedge.netscape.com`) contains a lot of useful information and scripting tools for Web developers. One such tool is xbObjects (available for download from `http://archive.bclary.com/xbProjects-docs/xbObject/`), written by Bob Clary of Netscape Communications in 2001, when Netscape 6 (Mozilla 0.6) was first released. It supports all versions of Mozilla since that time as well other modern browsers (IE, Opera, Safari).

Purpose

The purpose of xbObjects is to provide a stronger object-oriented paradigm to JavaScript, allowing not only for inheritance but also for overloading of methods and the capability to call superclass methods. To do this, xbObjects requires a number of steps be followed.

First, you must *register* the class, and in doing so, define which class to inherit from. This is done using the following call:

```
_classes.registerClass("Subclass_Name", "Superclass_Name");
```

Here, the subclass and superclass names are passed in as strings, not as pointers to their constructors. This call must come before the constructor for the given subclass.

> *You can also call* **`registerClass()`** *with only the first argument if the new class doesn't inherit from another class.*

The second step is to call the `defineClass()` method inside of the constructor, passing in the name of the class as well as a pointer to what Clary calls a *prototype function*, which is used to initialize all properties and methods for the object (more on that later). For example:

```
_classes.registerClass("ClassA");

function ClassA(color) {
    _classes.defineClass("ClassA", prototypeFunction);

    function prototypeFunction() {
        //...
    }
}
```

As you can see, the prototype function (aptly named `prototypeFunction()`) is located inside of the constructor. Its main purpose is to assign all methods to the class when appropriate (it works like dynamic prototyping in this way).

The next step (that's three so far) is to create an `init()` method for the class. This method is responsible for setting up all properties for the class and must accept the same arguments as the constructor itself. By convention, the `init()` method is always called after the `defineClass()` method is called. For example:

```
_classes.registerClass("ClassA");

function ClassA(sColor) {
    _classes.defineClass("ClassA", prototypeFunction);

    this.init(sColor);

    function prototypeFunction() {

        ClassA.prototype.init = function (sColor) {
            this.parentMethod("init");
            this.color = sColor;
        };

    }
}
```

You may have noticed a method named `parentMethod()` being called in the `init()` method. This is the way that xbObjects allows a class to call a superclass method. The `parentMethod()` accepts any number of arguments, but the first argument is always the name of the parent class method to call (this argument must be a string, not a function pointer); all other arguments are passed to the superclass method.

In this case, the superclass `init()` method is being called first, which is required for xbObjects to work. Even though `ClassA` didn't register a superclass, a default superclass for all classes is created using xbObjects, which is where this superclass `init()` method comes from.

The fourth and final step is to add the other class methods inside of the prototype function:

```
_classes.registerClass("ClassA");

function ClassA(sColor) {
    _classes.defineClass("ClassA", prototypeFunction);

    this.init(sColor);

    function prototypeFunction() {

        ClassA.prototype.init = function (sColor) {
            this.parentMethod("init");
            this.color = sColor;
        };

        ClassA.prototype.sayColor = function () {
            alert(this.color);
        };

    }
}
```

Then, you can create an instance of `ClassA` in the normal way:

```
var objA = new ClassA("red");
objA.sayColor();    //outputs "red"
```

Polygons reloaded

At this point, surely you're wondering if you will have a chance to see the polygon example redone using xbObjects, so here it goes.

First, rewrite the `Polygon` class, which is very simple:

```
_classes.registerClass("Polygon");

function Polygon(sides) {

    _classes.defineClass("Polygon", prototypeFunction);

    this.init(sides);

    function prototypeFunction() {

        Polygon.prototype.init = function(iSides) {
            this.parentMethod("init");
            this.sides = iSides;
        };
```

```
        Polygon.prototype.getArea = function () {
            return 0;
        };

    }
}
```

Next, rewrite the `Triangle` class, which is the first taste of real inheritance in this example:

```
_classes.registerClass("Triangle", "Polygon");

function Triangle(iBase, iHeight) {

    _classes.defineClass("Triangle", prototypeFunction);

    this.init(iBase,iHeight);

    function prototypeFunction() {
        Triangle.prototype.init = function(iBase, iHeight) {
            this.parentMethod("init", 3);
            this.base = iBase;
            this.height = iHeight;
        };

        Triangle.prototype.getArea = function () {
            return 0.5 * this.base * this.height;
        };
    }

}
```

Note the `registerClass()` call just before the constructor, where the inheritance relationship is set up. Also, the first line of the `init()` method calls the superclass (`Polygon`) `init()` with an argument of `3`, which sets the `sides` property to `3`. Other than that, the `init()` method is very similar: a simple constructor, assigning the `base` and `height`.

The `Rectangle` class ends up looking very similar to `Triangle`:

```
_classes.registerClass("Rectangle", "Polygon");

function Rectangle(iLength, iWidth) {

    _classes.defineClass("Rectangle", prototypeFunction);

    this.init(iLength, iWidth);

    function prototypeFunction() {
        Rectangle.prototype.init = function(iLength, iWidth) {
            this.parentMethod("init", 4);
            this.length = iLength;
            this.width = iWidth;
        }
```

```
        Rectangle.prototype.getArea = function () {
            return this.length * this.width;
        };

    }
}
```

The main difference between this and the `Triangle` class (aside from the different `registerClass()` and `defineClass()` calls) is calling the superclass `init()` method with an argument of `4`. Other than that, the additional `length` and `width` properties are added and the `getArea()` method is overridden.

Summary

This chapter introduced the concept of object inheritance in ECMAScript (and, therefore, in JavaScript) using object masquerading and prototype chaining. You learned that using these methods together is the optimal way to establish inheritance between classes.

Finally, a couple of alternate methods of establishing inheritance were introduced: zInherit and xbObjects. These JavaScript libraries, available free on the Internet, introduce new and different capabilities for object inheritance.

This wraps up the discussion of ECMAScript, the core of JavaScript. The following chapters build upon this base and introduce you to more Web-specific aspects of the language.

5

JavaScript in the Browser

In the preceding chapters, you learned about JavaScript's core, ECMAScript, and how the basics of the language work. Beginning with this chapter, the focus switches to using JavaScript inside its natural habitat: the Web browser.

Web browsers have come a long way since JavaScript was first introduced in Netscape Navigator 2.0. Browsers today are capable of handling a variety of file formats, not just conventional HTML. Ironically enough, JavaScript is used in most of these file formats as a way to dynamically change content on the client. This chapter explores how JavaScript fits into HTML and other languages, as well as introduces you to some basic concepts of the Browser Object Model (BOM).

JavaScript in HTML

Of course, it was HTML that first made use of embedded JavaScript, so the natural first discussion point is how JavaScript is used in HTML. The evolution of HTML to include JavaScript began with the introduction of tags to be used in conjunction with JavaScript, as well as the addition of new attributes for several common parts of HTML.

The <script/> tag

JavaScript is included in HTML pages by using the `<script/>` tag. Typically located within the `<head/>` tag of a page, the `<script/>` tag was originally defined to have one or two attributes: `language` that indicates the scripting language being used and, optionally, `src` that indicates an external JavaScript file to include in the page. The `language` attribute is traditionally set to `JavaScript`, but it can also be used to indicate the exact version of JavaScript, such as `JavaScript1.3` (if the `language` attribute is omitted, the browser defaults to the most current version of JavaScript available).

Although originally created for JavaScript, the **`<script/>`** *tag can be used to specify any number of different client-side scripting languages with the* **`language`** *attribute indicating the type of code being used. For example,* **`language`** *can be set to* **`VBScript`** *to use Internet Explorer's VBScript (Windows only).*

JavaScript code can be written free form within a `<script/>` tag, but only if the `src` attribute isn't specified; when `src` is specified, the code inside a `<script/>` tag may not work (depending on the browser). Example:

```
<html>
    <head>
        <title>Title of Page</title>
        <script language="JavaScript">
            var i = 0;
        </script>
        <script language="JavaScript" src="../scripts/external.js"></script>
    </head>
    <body>
        <!-- body goes here -->
    </body>
</html>
```

This example shows both inline JavaScript code and a link to an external JavaScript file. When using the `src` attribute, an external JavaScript file is referenced in the same way as images and style sheets.

By convention, external JavaScript files should have a .js extension, although it is not required by most browsers (this leaves open the possibility of dynamically generating JavaScript code using JSP, PHP, or another server-side scripting language).

External file format

External JavaScript files have a very simple format. Essentially, they are just plain text files containing JavaScript code. No `<script/>` tags are needed inside of external files, because the `<script/>` tag referencing the file is present in the HTML page. This makes external JavaScript files look very similar to source code files for other programming languages.

For example, consider the following inline code:

```
<html>
    <head>
        <title>Title of Page</title>
        <script language="JavaScript">
            function sayHi() {
                alert("Hi");
            }
        </script>
    </head>
    <body>
        <!-- body goes here -->
    </body>
</html>
```

To externalize the `sayHi()` function into a file named `external.js`, you copy the function text itself (Figure 5-1).

external.js

```
function sayHi() {
  alert("Hi");
}
```

Figure 5-1

Then the HTML code can be updated to include the external file:

```
<html>
    <head>
        <title>Title of Page</title>
        <script language="JavaScript" src="external.js"></script>
    </head>
    <body>
        <!-- body goes here -->
    </body>
</html>
```

> **No rules exist about what you can include in a single JavaScript source file, meaning that you are free to include any number of class definitions, functions, and so on, in a single file.**

Inline code versus external files

When should you write code inline versus writing the code in an external file? Although no hard and fast rules exist about when to use either method, the general consensus is that large amounts of JavaScript should never be included inline for a number of reasons:

- *Security* — Anyone can see exactly what the code is doing just by viewing the source of the page. If a malicious developer examines the code, he might find security holes that could compromise the site or application. Additionally, copyright and other intellectual property notices can be included in external files without interrupting the flow of the page.

- *Code Maintenance*—If JavaScript code is sprinkled throughout various pages, code maintenance becomes a nightmare. It is much easier to have a directory for all JavaScript files so that when a JavaScript error occurs, there is no question about where the code is located.
- *Caching*—Browsers cache all externally linked JavaScript files according to specific settings, meaning that if two pages are using the same file, it is only downloaded once. This ultimately means faster loading times. Including the same code in multiple pages is not only wasteful, but also increases the page size and thus increases the download time.

Tag placement

Generally speaking, it is common to place all code and function definitions in the `<head/>` tag of an HTML page so that the code is fully loaded and ready for use once the body is rendered. The only code that should appear within the `<body/>` tag is code that calls the functions defined previously.

When the `<script/>` tag is placed inside of the `<body/>` tag, the script is executed as soon as that part of the page is downloaded to the browser. This makes it possible to execute JavaScript code before the entire page is loaded. For example:

```
<html>
    <head>
        <title>Title of Page</title>
        <script language="JavaScript">
            function sayHi() {
                alert("Hi");
            }
        </script>
    </head>
    <body>
        <script language="JavaScript">
              sayHi();
        </script>
        <p>This is the first text the user will see.</p>
    </body>
</html>
```

In this code, the `sayHi()` method is called before any text is displayed on the page, meaning that the alert pops up before the text "This is the first text the user will see." is ever rendered. This method of calling JavaScript inside the `<body/>` of a page is not recommended and should be avoided whenever possible. Instead, it is recommended to use JavaScript only as an *event handler* in the body of a page, such as:

```
<html>
    <head>
        <title>Title of Page</title>
        <script language="JavaScript">
            function sayHi() {
                alert("Hi");
            }
        </script>
    </head>
    <body>
```

```
        <input type="button" value="Call Function" onclick="sayHi()" />
    </body>
</html>
```

Here, the <input/> tag is used to create a button that calls sayHi() when clicked. The onclick attribute specifies an *event handler*, which is the code that responds to a given event. Events and event handlers are discussed further in Chapter 9, "All about Events."

Note that JavaScript begins running as soon as the page begins loading, so it is possible to call function that doesn't exist yet. In the previous example, you can cause an error by placing the original <script/> tag after the function call:

```
<html>
    <head>
        <title>Title of Page</title>
    </head>
    <body>
        <script language="JavaScript">
             sayHi();
        </script>
        <p>This is the first text the user will see.</p>
        <script language="JavaScript">
            function sayHi() {
                alert("Hi");
            }
        </script>
    </body>
</html>
```

This example causes an error because sayHi() is called before it is defined. Because JavaScript is loading top-down, the function sayHi() does not exist until the second <script/> tag is encountered. Be aware of this problem and, as mentioned previously, use events and event handlers to call your JavaScript functions.

To hide or not to hide

When JavaScript was first introduced, only one browser supported it, so concern arose over how the nonsupporting browsers would deal with the <script/> tag and the code contained within. To that end, a format was devised to hide code from older browsers (which is a phrase that can still be found in the source code of a great many Web sites on the Internet today). The following method uses HTML comments around inline code so that other browsers won't render the code to the screen:

```
<script language="JavaScript"><!-- hide from older browsers
     function sayHi() {
        alert("Hi");
     }
//-->
</script>
```

The first line begins an HTML comment immediately after the opening <script> tag. This works because the browser still considers the rest of that line as part of HTML, with JavaScript code beginning on the following line. Next, you see the function definition as usual. The second-to-last line is the most interesting because it starts with a JavaScript single-line comment (the two forward slashes) and then continues with the close of the HTML comment (-->). This line is still considered part of the JavaScript code, so the single-line comment notation is necessary to avoid a syntax error. However, older browsers only acknowledge the close of the HTML comment and, therefore, ignore all the JavaScript code. A browser that supports JavaScript, however, just ignores this line and continues on to the closing `</script>` tag.

Although this method of code-hiding was very prevalent in the early days of the Web, it is not as necessary today. Presently, most of the popular Web browsers support JavaScript, and those that don't often are smart enough to ignore the code on their own. It is completely up to you whether you choose to use this method, but keep in mind that using external JavaScript files inside of inline code is a much easier method of hiding code from older browsers.

The <noscript/> tag

Another concern over browsers without JavaScript is how to provide alternate content. Hiding the code was part of the solution, but developers wanted a way to specify content that should appear only if JavaScript wasn't available. The solution came in the form of the `<noscript/>` tag, that can contain any HTML code (aside from `<script/>`). This HTML code is ignored by browsers that support JavaScript and have it enabled; any browser that doesn't support JavaScript or has it disabled renders the content of `<noscript/>`. For example:

```
<html>
    <head>
        <title>Title of Page</title>
        <script language="JavaScript">
            function sayHi() {
                alert("Hi");
            }
        </script>
    </head>
    <body>
        <script language="JavaScript">
             sayHi();
        </script>
        <noscript>
            <p>Your browser doesn't support JavaScript. If it did support
JavaScript, you would see this message: Hi!</p>
        </noscript>
        <p>This is the first text the user will see if JavaScript is enabled. If
JavaScript is disabled this is the second text the user will see.</p>
    </body>
</html>
```

In this example, the `<noscript/>` tag is included with a message telling the user that the browser doesn't support JavaScript. Chapter 8, "Browser and Operating System Detection," explains a practical way of using `<noscript/>`.

Changes in XHTML

Recently, with the advent of the XHTML standard (eXtensible HTML), the `<script/>` tag has undergone a change. Instead of the `language` attribute, the tag is now expected to have a `type` attribute to indicate the mime type of the inline code or external file being included; the mime type for JavaScript is `"text/javascript"`. For example:

```
<html>
    <head>
        <title>Title of Page</title>
        <script type="text/javascript">
            var i = 0;
        </script>
        <script type="text/javascript" src="../scripts/external.js"></script>
    </head>
    <body>
        <!-- body goes here -->
    </body>
</html>
```

Even though many browsers don't fully support XHTML, most developers are now using the `type` attribute in place of the `language` attribute in anticipation of better XHTML support. Omitting the `language` attribute doesn't cause any problems because, as noted earlier, all browsers default to JavaScript for the `<script/>` tag.

The second change in XHTML is the use of CDATA sections. CDATA sections are used in XML (and, therefore, in XHTML) to indicate text that should not be parsed as tags, allowing the use of special characters such as the less-than (<), greater-than (>), ampersand (&), and double quotes (") without using their character entities. Consider the following code:

```
<script type="text/javascript">
    function compare(a, b) {
        if (a < b) {
            alert("A is less than B");
        } else if (a > b) {
            alert("A is greater than B");
        } else {
            alert("A is equal to B");
        }
    }
</script>
```

This is a fairly simple function, which just compares two numbers, `a` and `b`, and then displays a message indicating their relationship. In XHTML, however, this code is invalid because it uses three special characters, less-than, greater-than, and double-quote. To fix this, you must replace these characters with their XML entities, `<`, `>`, and `"`, respectively:

```
<script type="text/javascript">
    function compare(a, b) {
        if (a &lt; b) {
            alert(&quot;A is less than B&quot;);
        } else if (a &gt; b) {
```

```
            alert(&quot;A is greater than B&quot;);
        } else {
            alert(&quot;A is equal to B&quot;);
        }
    }
</script>
```

This code raises two problems. First, developers aren't used to writing code using XML entities. It makes the code harder to read. Second, this is actually considered a syntax error in JavaScript because the interpreter has no idea what the XML entities mean. Using a CDATA section, it is possible to write JavaScript code in its normal, readable syntax. The official way to include a CDATA section is as follows:

```
<script type="text/javascript"><![CDATA[
    function compare(a, b) {
        if (a < b) {
            alert("A is less than B");
        } else if (a > b) {
            alert("A is greater than B");
        } else {
            alert("A is equal to B");
        }
    }
]]></script>
```

Although this it the official way, remember that XHTML isn't fully supported by most browsers, which raises a major problem: This is a JavaScript syntax error because most browsers don't recognize CDATA sections yet!

The solution currently being used is a takeoff on the old "hide from older browsers" code. By using single-line JavaScript comments, you can embed the CDATA section without affecting the syntax of the code:

```
<script type="text/javascript">
//<![CDATA[
    function compare(a, b) {
        if (a < b) {
            alert("A is less than B");
        } else if (a > b) {
            alert("A is greater than B");
        } else {
            alert("A is equal to B");
        }
    }
//]]>
</script>
```

This code now works in browsers that don't support XHTML as well as those that do.

Like the use of the `type` attribute, the use of CDATA sections in this way is becoming more prevalent as developers prepare for better support of XHTML in browsers. Ultimately, however, it's best to include JavaScript using external files in order to avoid the CDATA problem altogether.

JavaScript in SVG

Scalable Vector Graphics (SVG) is an up-and-coming XML-based language used to draw vector graphics on the Web. Vector graphics are different from raster (or bitmap) graphics in that they define angles, lines, and their relationship to each other instead of simply specifying one color per pixel of an image. The result is an image that looks the same no matter what size the rendering. Vector graphic programs such as Adobe Illustrator have begun to include SVG export functions as the language gains popularity.

Although no browsers natively support SVG at present (although Mozilla 2.0 will), a number of companies, notably Adobe and Corel, are making SVG plugins that enable most browsers to display SVG graphics.

Basic SVG

Introducing SVG as a language is out of the scope of this book; however, it is helpful to understand a little about the language for the JavaScript discussion.

Here is a simple SVG example:

```
<?xml version="1.0"?>
<!DOCTYPE svg PUBLIC "-//W3C//DTD SVG 1.0//EN"
"http://www.w3.org/TR/2001/REC-SVG-20010904/DTD/svg10.dtd">
<svg xmlns="http://www.w3.org/2000/svg" xmlns:xlink="http://www.w3.org/1999/xlink"
width="100%" height="100%">
    <desc>
         An image of a square and a circle.
    </desc>
    <defs>
        <rect id="rect1" width="200" height="200" fill="red" x="10" y="10"
stroke="black"/>
        <circle id="circle1" r="100" fill="white" stroke="black" cx="200"
cy="200"/>
    </defs>
    <g>
        <use xlink:href="#rect1" />
        <use xlink:href="#circle1" />
    </g>
</svg>
```

This example places a circle at the lower-right corner of a square (see Figure 5-2).

Note that SVG files begin with the XML prolog `<?xml version="1.0"?>`, which indicates that this language is XML-based. Following that is the SVG DTD, which is optional but typically included.

The outermost tag is `<svg/>`, which defines the file as an SVG image. The `width` and `height` attributes can be set to anything, including percentages and pixels, but are set to 100% here for simplicity. Notice that two XML namespaces are specified, one for SVG and one for XLink. XLink defines the behavior of links such as `href` and will most likely be supported in future versions of XHTML. For now, SVG leads the way in supporting basic XLink.

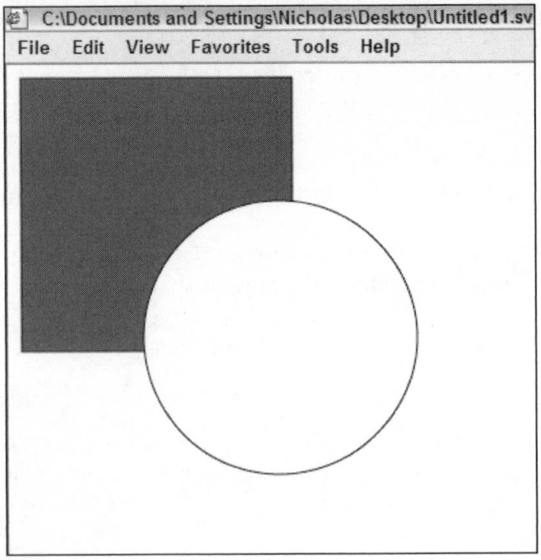

Figure 5-2

The next tag is `<desc/>`, which contains a description of the image. You can think of `<desc/>` as being similar to the `<title/>` tag in HTML because it provides a description of what is in the image but does not render it on the page. Immediately following is the `<defs/>` tag, which is where you can define resources and shapes that are to be used later in the image. In this case, a rectangle and a circle are defined. These shapes won't be displayed unless specifically used in the actual image.

After `<defs/>` is the `<g/>` tag, which is short for *group*. This `<g/>` is special because it is the outermost one and, therefore, encapsulates the visible image. `<g/>` tags can be used multiple times to form groups of shapes within the outermost `<g/>` (think of it as a `<div/>` in HTML).

In this example, two `<use/>` tags point to a shape in the `<defs/>` section. The `<use/>` tag points its `xlink:href` attribute to the ID of a shape (preceded by the pound sign, #) and, therefore, brings the shape into the visible image. Shapes defined in `<defs/>` can be used multiple times in the image if you include multiple `<use/>` tags. This capability makes SVG a shining example of code reuse among XML-based languages.

Of course, one of the most exciting parts of SVG is its excellent support for JavaScript that can be used to manipulate all parts of an SVG image.

The <script/> tag in SVG

SVG adopted a similar version of the `<script/>` tag for including JavaScript in its pages. This `<script/>` tag, however, is different from its HTML sibling:

- **The `type` attribute is required.** This can be set to `text/javascript` or `text/ecmascript`, though the former is technically the correct one.
- **The `language` attribute is illegal.** Including this attribute causes SVG code to be invalid.

- **CDATA sections are required for inline code.** Because SVG is a true XML-based language, it properly supports CDATA sections and, therefore, requires them when inline code uses special XML characters.
- **Uses `xlink:href` instead of `src`.** In SVG, no `src` attribute is used on a `<script/>` tag. Instead, SVG uses the `xlink:href` attribute to indicate an external file to reference.

For example:

```
<?xml version="1.0"?>
<!DOCTYPE svg PUBLIC "-//W3C//DTD SVG 1.0//EN"
"http://www.w3.org/TR/2001/REC-SVG-20010904/DTD/svg10.dtd">
<svg xmlns="http://www.w3.org/2000/svg" xmlns:xlink="http://www.w3.org/1999/xlink"
width="100%" height="100%">
    <desc>
         An image of a square and a circle.
    </desc>
    <script type="text/javascript"><![CDATA[
            var i = 0;
    ]]></script>
    <script type="text/javascript" xlink:href="../scripts/external.js"></script>
    <defs>
        <rect id="rect1" width="200" height="200" fill="red" x="10" y="10"
stroke="black"/>
        <circle id="circle1" r="100" fill="white" stroke="black" cx="200"
cy="200"/>
    </defs>
    <g>
        <use xlink:href="#rect1" />
        <use xlink:href="#circle1" />
    </g>
</svg>
```

In this code, the two `<script/>` tags are correct for SVG. The first, containing inline code, is surrounded by a CDATA section so no problems arise if you use special characters; the second uses the `xlink:href` attribute to reference an external file.

Tag placement in SVG

Because no `<head/>` area exists in SVG, `<script/>` tags can be placed nearly anywhere. Typically, however, they are placed:

- Immediately after the `<desc/>` tag
- Inside of the `<defs/>` tag
- Just before the outermost `<g/>` tag

The `<script/>` tag cannot be placed inside of shapes, such as `<rect/>` or `<circle/>`, nor can they be placed inside of filters, gradients, or other appearance-defining tags.

The Browser Object Model

You can't really talk about JavaScript in the browser without talking about the Browser Object Model (BOM), which provides objects that interact with the browser window independent of the content.

The BOM is made up of a series of objects that are related to one another. Figure 5-3 shows the basic BOM hierarchy.

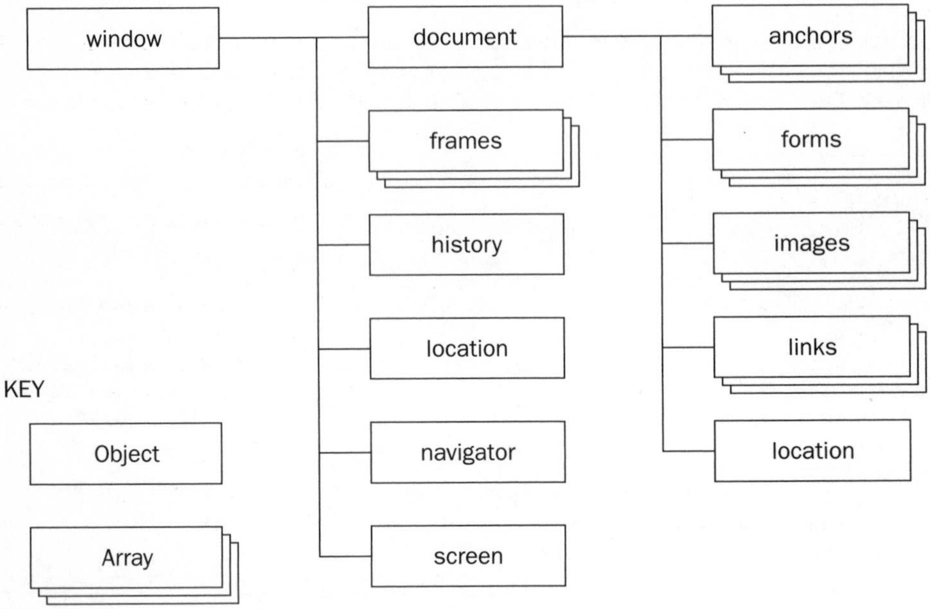

Figure 5-3

As you can see, the `window` object is the center of the BOM universe, with all objects and collections somehow connecting back to it. I begin the discussion of the BOM with this object.

The window object

The `window` object represents an entire browser window, but not necessarily the content that the window contains. Rather, `window` can be used to move, resize, and otherwise affect the browser that it represents.

If a page uses framesets, each frame is represented by its own `window` object and stored in the `frames` collection. Within the `frames` collection, the window objects are indexed both by number (starting at 0, going first left-to-right, then row-by-row) and by the name of the frame. Consider the following example:

```
<html>
    <head>
        <title>Frameset Example</title>
```

```
    </head>
    <frameset rows="100,*">
        <frame src="frame.htm" name="topFrame" />
        <frameset cols="50%,50%">
            <frame src="anotherframe.htm" name="leftFrame" />
            <frame src="yetanotherframe.htm" name="rightFrame" />
        </frameset>
    </frameset>
</html>
```

This code creates a frameset with one frame across the top and two frames underneath. Here, the top frame can be referenced by `window.frames[0]` or `window.frames["topFrame"]`, however, you would probably use the `top` object instead of `window` to refer to these frames (making it `top.frames[0]`, for instance).

The `top` object always points to the very top (outermost) frame, which is the browser window itself. This assures that you are pointing to the correct frame. If you then write code within a frame, the `window` object referenced in it is a pointer to just that frame.

Because the window object is the center of the BOM universe, it enjoys a special privilege: You don't need to explicitly reference it. Whenever a function, object, or collection is referenced, the interpreter always looks to the `window` object, so `window.frames[0]` can be rewritten as just `frames[0]`. To understand the various ways to reference the frames in the previous example, refer to Figure 5-4.

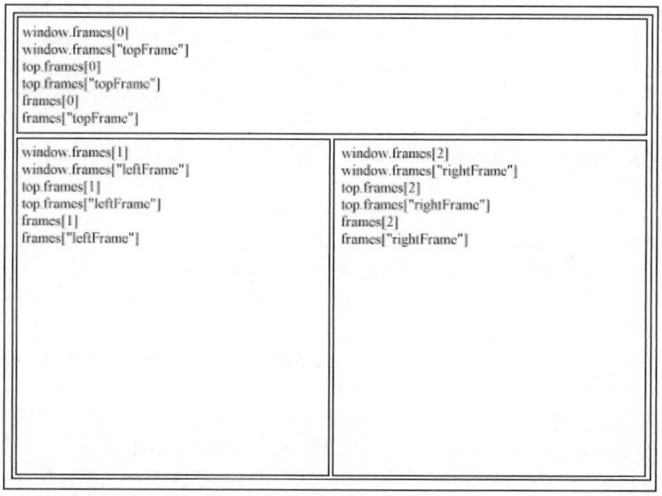

Figure 5-4

It is also possible to access a frame directly using its name, such as **`window.leftFrame`**. *However, using the* **`frames`** *collection is generally more acceptable because it more accurately represents the code's intent.*

Another instance of the window object is called `parent`. The `parent` object is used with framesets that load files that are also framesets. Suppose the file named `frameset1.htm` contains this code:

```
<html>
    <head>
        <title>Frameset Example</title>
    </head>
    <frameset rows="100,* ">
        <frame src="frame.htm" name="topFrame" />
        <frameset cols="50%,50%">
            <frame src="anotherframe.htm" name="leftFrame" />
            <frame src="anotherframeset.htm" name="rightFrame" />
        </frameset>
    </frameset>
</html>
```

Now what if there is also a file named `anotherframeset.htm` containing this code?

```
<html>
    <head>
        <title>Frameset Example</title>
    </head>
    <frameset cols="100,* ">
        <frame src="red.htm" name="redFrame" />
        <frame src="blue.htm" name="blueFrame" />
    </frameset>
</html>
```

When the first file, `frameset1.htm`, is loaded into the browser, it loads `anotherframeset.htm` into `rightFrame`. If code is written in `redFrame` (or `blueFrame`), the `parent` object points to `rightFrame` in `frameset1.htm`. If, however, code is written in `topFrame`, the `parent` object actually points to `top` because the browser window itself is considered the parent of any top-level frameset.

Figure 5-5 proves this fact by accessing the `window` object's `name` property, which stores the name of the frame (but will always be blank for `top`).

One more global window pointer, called `self`, is always equal to `window` (yes, a bit redundant, but it's included as a better fit with `parent`. It clarifies that you are not talking about the frame's parent but the frame itself.)

If there are no frames in the page, **`window`** *and* **`self`** *are equal to* **`top`** *and the* **`frames`** *collection has a length of 0.*

It is also possible to chain references to `window` objects together, such as `parent.parent.frames ["topFrame"]`, although this is generally frowned upon because any change in the frame structure results in code errors.

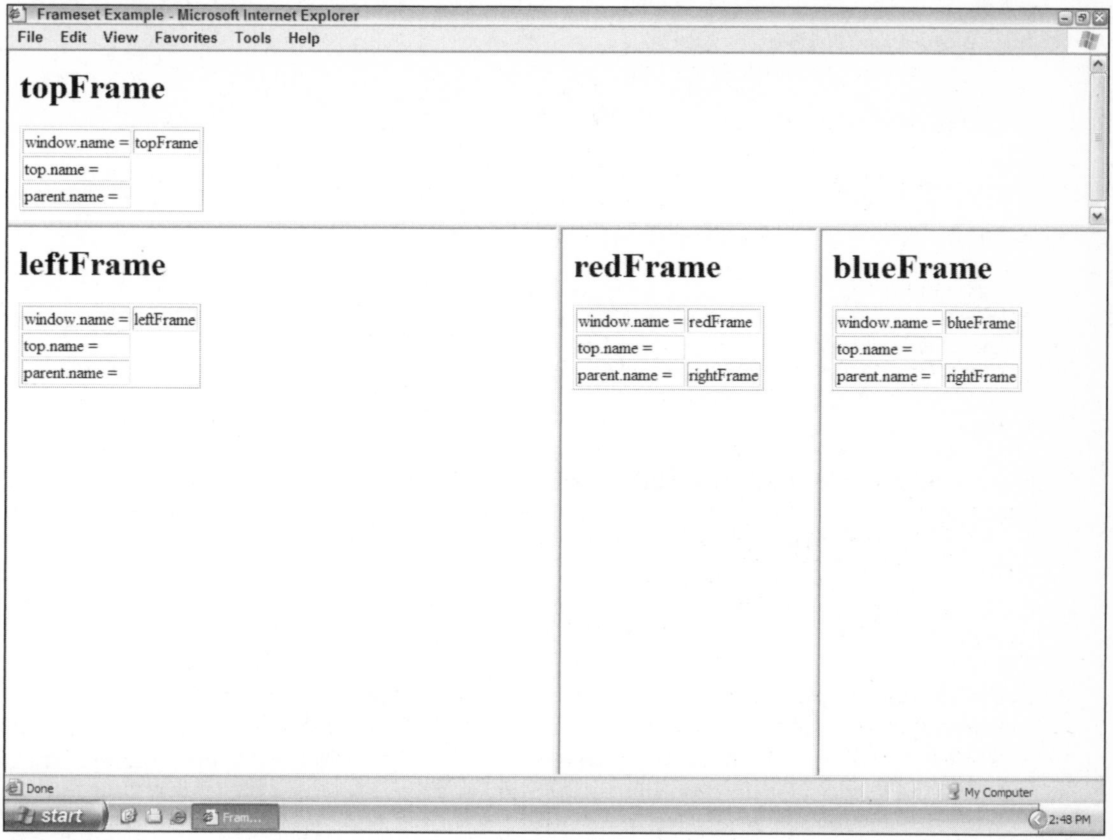

Figure 5-5

Manipulating windows

As mentioned previously, the `window` object is useful to manipulate browser windows (and frames), which means as a developer, you are able to move and resize browser windows. Four methods are available to accomplish this:

- `moveBy(`*`dx`*`, `*`dy`*`)` — moves the browser window `dx` pixels horizontally and `dy` pixels vertically relative to its current position. Negative numbers can be used for `dx` to move the window to the left and for `dy` to move the window up.
- `moveTo(`*`x`*`, `*`y`*`)` — moves the browser window so that its upper-left corner is located at position (x,y) on the user's screen. Negative numbers can be used, but these move part of the window off of the visible screen.
- `resizeBy(`*`dw`*`, `*`dh`*`)` — resizes the browser window's width by `dw` pixels and its height by `dh` pixels relative to the window's current size. Negative numbers can be used for `dw` to shrink the window's width and for `dh` to shrink the window's height.

- `resizeTo(w, h)` — resizes the browser window's width to `w` and its height to `h`. Negative numbers cannot be used.

For example:

```
//move the window right by 10 pixels and down by 20 pixels
window.moveBy(10, 20);

//resize the window to have a width of 150 and a height of 300
window.resizeTo(150, 300);

//resize the window to be 150 pixels wider, but leave the height alone
window.resizeBy(150, 0);

//move back to the upper-left corner of the screen (0,0)
window.moveTo(0, 0);
```

Suppose you went through all this trouble to change the size and position of a window, but you didn't keep track of the changes. Now you need to figure out where on the screen the window is located and what its dimensions are. This is where a lack of standards causes problems.

- Internet Explorer provides `window.screenLeft` and `window.screenTop` to determine the position of the window, but doesn't provide any way of determining the size of the actual window. The size of the viewport (that area where the HTML page is displayed), can be retrieved by using `document.body.offsetWidth` and `document.body.offsetHeight`, although this isn't a standard either.
- Mozilla provides `window.screenX` and `window.screenY` to determine the position of the window. It also provides `window.innerWidth` and `window.innerHeight` to determine the size of the viewport, as well as `window.outerWidth` and `window.outerHeight` to determine the size of the browser window itself.
- Opera and Safari provide the same facilities as Mozilla.

So the question becomes one of understanding the browsers your users have.

> **Even though moving and resizing browser windows is a cool trick, it should be used sparingly. Moving and resizing windows has a jarring effect on users and for this reason is usually avoided in professional Web sites and Web applications.**

Navigating and opening new windows

Using JavaScript, it is possible to navigate to URLs and open new browser windows using the `window.open()` method. This method accepts four arguments: the URL of the page to load in the new window, the name of the new window (for targeting purposes), a string of features, and a Boolean value indicating whether the loaded page should take the place of the currently loaded page. Typically, only the first three arguments are used because the last one has an effect only when calling `window.open()` doesn't open a new window.

If `window.open()` is called with the name of an existing frame as the second argument, the URL is then loaded into the frame with that name. For example, to load a page into the frame named `"topFrame"`, the following code does the trick:

```
window.open("http://www.wrox.com/", "topFrame");
```

This line of code behaves as if a user clicked a link with the `href` set to `http://www.wrox.com/` and the `target` set to `"topFrame"`. The special frame names `_self`, `_parent`, `_top`, and `_blank` are also valid.

If the name specified isn't a valid frame name, then `window.open()` opens a new window with features based on the third argument (feature string) of the method. If the third argument is missing, a new browser window is opened as if you had clicked a link with `target` set to `_blank`. This means that the new browser window is displayed with the exact same settings as the default browser window (toolbars, location, and statusbar are all visible).

When the third argument is used, it is assumed that a new window should be opened. The feature string, which is a comma-separated list of settings, defines certain aspects of the newly created window. The following table displays the various settings:

Setting	Values	Description
`left`	Number	Indicates the left coordinate of the new window. This cannot be a negative number.*
`top`	Number	Indicates the top coordinate of the new window. This cannot be a negative number.*
`height`	Number	Sets the height of the new window. This cannot be a number less than 100.*
`width`	Number	Sets the width of the new window. This cannot be a number less than 100.*
`resizable`	yes,no	Determines if the new window can be resized by dragging on its border. The default is no.
`scrollable`	yes,no	Determines if the new window allows scrolling if the content cannot be fit in the viewport. The default is no.
`toolbar`	yes,no	Determines if the new window has its toolbar showing. The default is no.
`status`	yes,no	Determines if the new window has its status bar showing. The default is no.
`location`	yes,no	Determines if the new window has its location (Web address) area showing. The default is no.

*These security features of the browser are discussed in greater detail in Chapter 19, "Deployment Issues."

As mentioned previously, the feature string is comma-delimited and, therefore, must contain no space before or after a comma or equal sign. For example, the following string is invalid:

```
window.open("http://www.wrox.com/", "wroxwindow",
            "height=150, width= 300, top=10, left= 10, resizable =yes");
```

This string won't work because of the spaces after the commas and other spaces around a couple of equal signs. Just remove the spaces and it works fine:

```
window.open("http://www.wrox.com/", "wroxwindow",
            "height=150,width=300,top=10,left=10,resizable=yes");
```

The `window.open()` method returns a `window` object as its function value that is also the `window` object for the newly created window (or for the frame, if the name given is the name of an existing frame). Using this object, it's possible to manipulate the new window:

```
var oNewWin = window.open("http://www.wrox.com/", "wroxwindow",
                          "height=150,width=300,top=10,left=10,resizable=yes");

oNewWin.moveTo(100, 100);
oNewWin.resizeTo(200, 200);
```

Also using this object, it is possible to close the new window using the `close()` method:

```
oNewWin.close();
```

If there is code in the new window, it can close itself by using:

```
window.close();
```

This only works in the new window. If you try to call `window.close()` in the main browser window, you get a message saying that a script is trying to close the window and asking if you actually want it to close. The general rule to remember is this: Scripts can close any windows that they open, but no others.

A new window also has a reference to the window that opened it stored in the `opener` property. The `opener` property exists only on the topmost `window` object of the new window, making it safer to use `top.opener` to access it. Example:

```
var oNewWin = window.open("http://www.wrox.com/", "wroxwindow",
                          "height=150,width=300,top=10,left=10,resizable=yes");

alert(oNewWin.opener == window);   //outputs "true"
```

In this example, a new window is opened and then its `opener` property is tested against the `window` object to prove that `opener` does indeed point to `window` (this alert displays `"true"`).

Opening new windows can be helpful to users in some instances, but generally speaking it's better to keep pop-up windows to a minimum. A large industry has popped up (no pun intended) selling pop-up ads on Web sites, which most users find incredibly annoying. To this end, many users have installed pop-up blockers that automatically block all pop-up windows unless the user specifically allows them. Remember, pop-up blockers don't know the difference between a legitimate pop-up window and an advertisement, so it's always best to warn a user when a window is going to be popped up.

System dialogs

Aside from popping up new browser windows, several other methods *pop up* information to the user utilizing methods of the `window` object: `alert()`, `confirm()`, and `input()`.

You are already familiar with the syntax of a call to `alert()` because it has been used in a large number of examples up to this point. This method accepts one argument, which is the text to display to the user. When `alert()` is called, the browser creates a system message box that displays the given text with an OK button. For example, the following line of code causes the message box in Figure 5-6 to be displayed:

```
alert("Hello world! ");
```

Figure 5-6

Alert dialogs are typically used when users must be made aware of something that they have no control over, such as errors. Often alert dialogs are displayed when the user has entered invalid data into a form.

The second type of dialog is displayed by calling `confirm()`. A confirm dialog looks similar to an alert dialog in that it displays a message to the user. The main difference between the two is the presence of a Cancel button along with the OK button in the confirm dialog, which allows the user to indicate if a given action should be taken. For example, the following line of code displays the confirm dialog shown in Figure 5-7:

```
confirm("Are you sure? ");
```

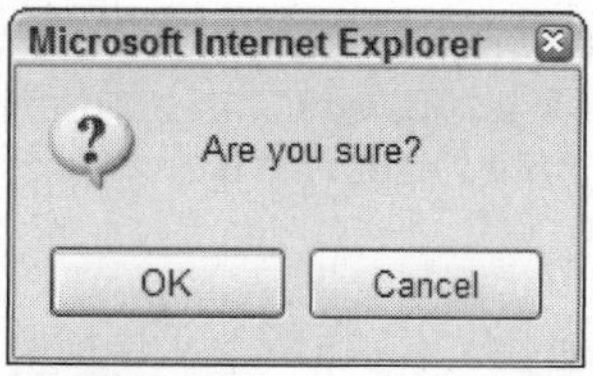

Figure 5-7

To determine if the user clicked OK or Cancel, the `confirm()` method returns a Boolean value: `true` if OK was clicked, `false` if Cancel was clicked. Typical usage of a confirm dialog usually looks like this:

```
if (confirm("Are you sure? ")) {
    alert("I'm so glad you're sure! ");
} else {
     alert("I'm sorry to hear you're not sure. ");
}
```

In this example, the confirm dialog is displayed to the user in the first line, which is a condition of the `if` statement. If the user clicks OK, an alert is displayed saying, "I'm so glad you're sure!" If, however, the Cancel button is clicked, an alert is displayed saying, "I'm sorry to hear you're not sure." This type of construct is often used when the user tries to delete something, such as an e-mail in his or her inbox.

The final dialog is displayed by calling `prompt()`, and as you might expect, this dialog prompts for input from the user. Along with OK and Cancel buttons, this dialog also has a text box where the user is asked to enter some data. The `prompt()` method accepts two arguments: the text to display to the user and the default value for the text box (which can be an empty string if you so desire). The following line results in the window displayed in Figure 5-8 being shown:

```
prompt("What's your name? ", "Michael");
```

Figure 5-8

The value in the text box is returned as the function value if the OK button is clicked; if the Cancel button is clicked, `null` is returned. The `prompt()` method is often used like this:

```
var sResult = prompt("What is your name? ", "");
if (sResult != null) {
  alert("Welcome, " + sResult);
}
```

I have a few final points to cover regarding these three dialogs. First, all the dialog windows are system windows, meaning that they may appear different on different operating systems (and sometimes, on different browsers). This also means that you have no control over the display of the window in terms of fonts, colors, and so on.

Second, the dialogs are all *modal*, meaning that the user cannot do anything else in the browser until the dialog is dismissed by clicking the OK button or Cancel buttons. This is a common method of controlling user behavior to ensure that important information is delivered in a secure way.

The status bar

The status bar is the area in the bottom border that displays information to the user (see Figure 5-9).

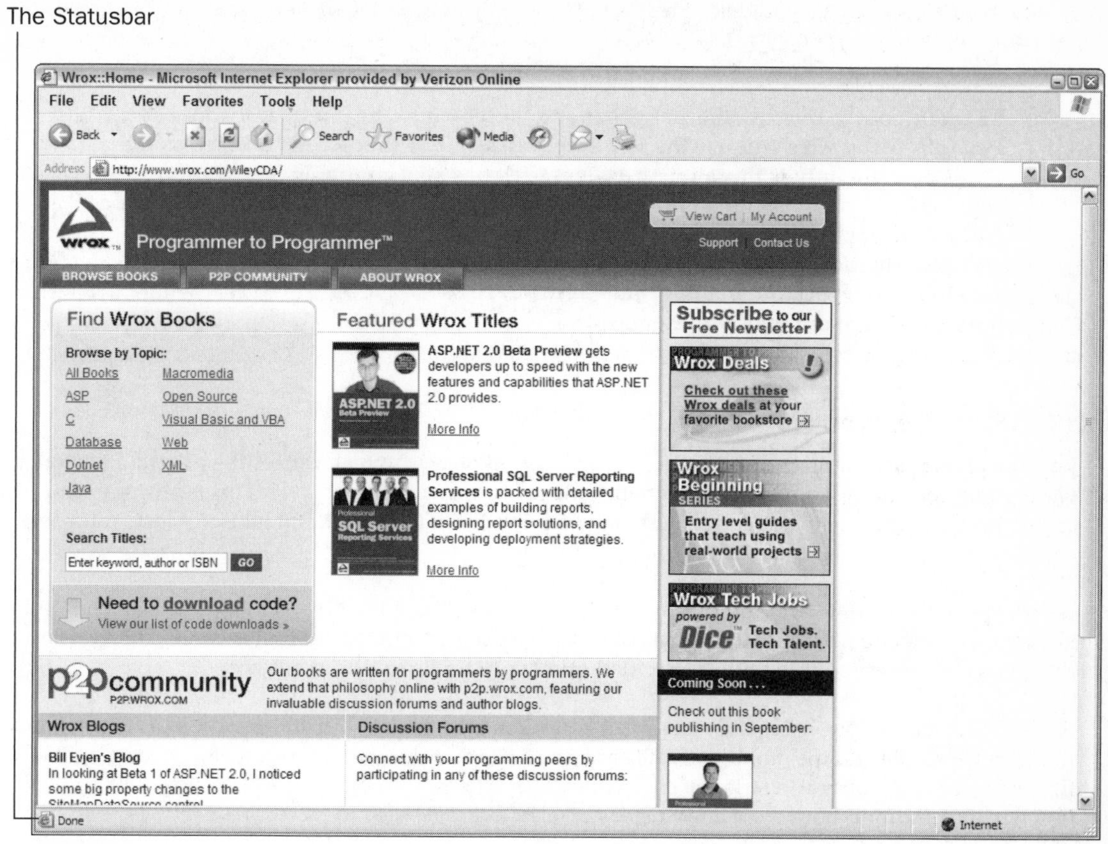

Figure 5-9

Normally, the status bar tells the user when the page is loading and when it has finished loading; however, it is possible to set its value using two properties of the window object: `status` and `defaultStatus`. As you may have guessed, `status` changes the status bar text for a moment while `defaultStatus` changes it as long as the user is on the page. For example, you may use a default status bar message when the page first loads:

```
window.defaultStatus = "You are surfing www.wrox.com. ";
```

You may also want to display information about a certain link when the user moves the mouse over it:

```
<a href="books.htm" onmouseover="window.status='Information on Wrox books.'
">Books</a>
```

This is especially useful when using a JavaScript URL because browsers, by default, display the value of the `href` attribute in the status bar when the user mouses over. Setting `window.status` can keep the details of the link implementation from users:

```
<a href="javascript:goSomewhere(1,2,3,4)" onmouseover="window.status='Information
on Wrox books.' ">Books</a>
```

Be careful not to overuse the status bar and thereby making it a distraction. For example, many sites still use the *scrolling message code* that scrolls text across the status bar. Not only is this a fairly useless trick, it's also annoying, very unprofessional, and adds a very amateurish feeling that a Web site or Web application can do without. Because this book is all about professional JavaScript, the scrolling text code will not be covered. However, if you are interested in playing around with scrolling text, check out `http://javascript.internet.com/scrolls/`, where you can find a large number of these scripts.

Intervals and timeouts

Java developers are familiar with the `wait()` method of objects, which causes the program to stop and wait a specified amount of time before continuing on to the next line of code. This is a very useful piece of functionality and, unfortunately, one that JavaScript doesn't support. But all is not lost. You have a couple of ways around this issue.

JavaScript supports timeouts and intervals, which effectively tell the browser when certain code should be executed: Timeouts execute the given code after a specified number of milliseconds; intervals execute the given code repeatedly, waiting a specified number of milliseconds in between.

Setting a timeout is done using the `window`'s `setTimeout()` method. This method accepts two arguments: the code to execute and the number of milliseconds (1/1000 of a second) to wait before executing it. The first argument can either be a string of code (as would be used with the `eval()` function) or a pointer to a function. For example, both these lines display an alert after one second:

```
setTimeout("alert('Hello world!') ", 1000);
setTimeout(function() { alert("Hello world!"); }, 1000);
```

Of course, you can also reference a previously defined function:

```
function sayHelloWorld() {
    alert("Hello world!");
}

setTimout(sayHelloWorld, 1000);
```

When you call `setTimeout()`, it creates a numeric timeout ID, which is similar to a process ID in an operating system. The timeout ID is essentially an identifier for the delayed process should you decide, after calling `setTimeout()`, that the code shouldn't be executed. To cancel a pending timeout, use the `clearTimeout()` method and pass in the timeout ID:

```
var iTimeoutId = setTimeout("alert('Hello world!')", 1000);

//nevermind
clearTimeout(iTimeoutId);
```

You may be thinking to yourself, "Why would I define a timeout and then cancel it before it executes?" Consider the tooltips available in most applications today. When you move your mouse over a button, it takes a little bit of time before that friendly yellow box appears to tell you what the button does. If you move your mouse over the button for just a short time and then move it to another button, the tooltip isn't displayed. This is precisely why you would cancel a timeout before the code executes: Because you want to wait a specified amount of time before the code is executed. If the user does something that would result in a different outcome, you need the flexibility to cancel that timeout.

Intervals work in much the same way except that they repeat the given code indefinitely at specific time intervals. To set up an interval, use the `setInterval()` method with the same type of arguments as you use with `setTimeout()` — the code to execute and the number of milliseconds to wait between each execution. For example:

```
setInterval("alert('Hello world!') ", 1000);
setInterval(function() { alert("Hello world!"); }, 1000);

function sayHelloWorld() {
    alert("Hello world!");
}

setInterval(sayHelloWorld, 1000);
```

Also similar to timeouts, the `setInterval()` method creates an interval ID to identify the code to be executed. It can be used with the `clearInterval()` method to prevent any further executions. Obviously, this is much more important when using intervals because, if left unchecked, they continue to execute until the page is unloaded. Here is a common example of interval usage:

```
var iNum = 0;
var iMax = 100;
var iIntervalId = null;

function incNum() {
    iNum++;

    if (iNum == iMax) {
        clearInterval(iIntervalId);
    }
}

iIntervalId = setInterval(incNum, 500);
```

In this code, the number `iNum` is incremented every 500 milliseconds until it reaches the maximum (`iMax`), at which point the interval is cleared. You can use timeouts for this, eliminating the need to keep track of a timeout ID, by doing the following:

```
var iNum = 0;
var iMax = 100;

function incNum() {
    iNum++;

    if (iNum != iMax) {
        setTimeout(incNum, 500);
    }
}

setTimeout(incNum, 500);
```

Here, the code uses linked timeouts, meaning that the code being executed by `setTimeout()` also calls `setTimeout()`. If `iNum` is still not equal to `iMax` after it is incremented, another `setTimeout()` call is made. You don't have to keep track of the timeout ID or clear it because after the code is executed, the timeout ID is destroyed.

So which method should you use? It's really depends on the use case. To wait a certain amount of time before executing a certain set of code, use timeouts. If, however, you need some code to be executed repeatedly, then use intervals.

History

It is possible to access the history of a browser window. The history is the list of places the user has been. For security reasons, all you can do is navigate through the history; there is no way to get the URLs of the pages contained in the browser history.

To navigate through history, you don't need a time machine; you use the `window` object's `history` property and its associated methods.

The `go()` method takes only one parameter: the number of pages to go back or forward. If the number is negative, you are going backwards through the browser history. If the number is positive you are going forward (think of it as the difference between the Back and Forward buttons).

So, to go back one page, the following code can be used:

```
window.history.go(-1);
```

Of course, the reference to the `window` object isn't necessary, so this will do:

```
history.go(-1);
```

Most often, this is used to create a custom "Back" button embedded in a Web page, such as:

```
<a href="javascript:history.go(-1)">Back to the previous page</a>
```

To go forward one page, just use a positive one:

```
history.go(1);
```

Alternatively, you can use the `back()` and `forward()` methods to accomplish the same thing:

```
//go back one
history.back();

//go forward one
history.forward();
```

These may be a little more meaningful because they accurately reflect the behavior of the browser Back and Forward buttons.

Although it's not possible to see the URLs in the browser history, you can see how many pages are in it by using the `length` property:

```
alert("There are currently " + history.length + " pages in history.");
```

This capability is helpful if you want to go back or forward by more than one page and want to know if that is possible.

The document object

The `document` object is actually a property of the `window` object, but as you learned earlier, any property or method of the window object may be accessed directly, so this line of code will return `"true"`:

```
alert(window.document == document);
```

It is also unique in that it is the only object that belongs to both the BOM and the DOM (the `document` as it relates to the DOM is discussed in the next chapter). From the BOM perspective, the `document` object is made up of a series of collections that access various parts of the document as well as give information about the page itself. Once again, because the BOM has no standards guiding implementations, each browser tends to have slightly different implementations for `document`; this section focuses on the most common functionality.

The following table lists some of the common properties for the BOM `document` object:

Property	Description
`alinkColor`	The color for active links as defined by `<body alink="color">`*
`bgColor`	The color for the page background as defined by `<body bgcolor="color">`*
`fgColor`	The color for text as defined by `<body text="color">`*
`lastModified`	The date the page was last modified as a string
`linkColor`	The color for links as defined by `<body link="color">`*
`referrer`	The URL one position back in the browser history
`title`	The text displayed in the `<title/>` tag
`URL`	The URL of the currently loaded page
`vlinkColor`	The color for visited links as defined by `<body vlink="color">`*

*These properties are deprecated because they refer to old HTML attributes of the `<body/>` tag. Style sheet scripting should be used instead.

The `lastModified` property retrieves a string representing the date that the page was last modified, which is of marginal use unless you want to display the last modified date on a home page (which can also be done using server-side technology). Likewise, the `referrer` property isn't very useful unless you want to track where users are coming from (perhaps to see if someone visited your site via Google or another search engine). But again, this can also be handled server-side.

The `title` property is read/write, so you can change the title of your page at any time regardless of what the HTML contains. This is particularly useful when a site uses a frameset and only one frame is changing while the overall frameset remains unchanged. Using this property, you can change the title (which is displayed in the overall browser title bar) to reflect the new page loaded into the frame:

```
top.document.title = "New page title";
```

The `URL` property is also read/write, so you can use it to retrieve the URL of the current page, or you can set it to a new URL, which causes the window to navigate there. For example:

```
document.URL = "http://www.wrox.com/";
```

As mentioned previously, the `document` object also has a number of collections providing access to various parts of the loaded page. These collections are outlined in the following table:

Collection	Description
`anchors`	Collection of all anchors in the page (represented by `<a name="anchorname"></a>`)
`applets`	Collection of all applets in the page
`embeds`	Collection of all embedded objects in the page (represented by the `<embed/>` tag)
`forms`	Collection of all forms in the page
`images`	Collection of all images in the page
`links`	Collection of all links in the page (represented by `<a href="somewhere.htm"></a>`)

Similar to the `window.frames` collection, each of the `document` collections is indexed both by number and by name, meaning that you can access an image by `document.images[0]` or `document.images["image_name"]`. Consider the following HTML page:

```
<html>
    <head>
        <title>Document Example</title>
    </head>
    <body>
        <p>Welcome to my <a href="home.htm">home</a> away from home.</p>
        <img src="home.jpg" align="right" name="imgHome" />
        <form method="post" action="submit.cgi" name="frmSubscribe">
            <input type="text" name="txtEmail" />
            <input type="submit" value="Subscribe" />
        </form>
    </body>
</html>
```

Here are the ways to access various parts of this document:

- To access the link, refer to `document.links[0]`.
- To access the image, refer to `document.images[0]` or `document.images["imgHome"]`.
- To access the form, refer to `document.forms[0]` or `document.forms["frmSubscribe"]`.

Additionally, all the attributes of links, images, and so on all become properties of the objects. For example, `document.images[0].src` is the code to get the `src` attribute of the first image.

Finally, several methods exist on the BOM `document` object. One of the most often used is the `write()` method or its sibling `writeln()`. Each of these methods accepts one argument, which is a string to write to the document. The only difference is, as you might expect, `writeln()` adds a new line (`\n`) character at the end of the string.

Both methods insert the string content in the location where it is called. The browser then treats the document as if the string were part of the normal HTML in the page. Consider the following short page:

```
<html>
    <head>
        <title>Document Write Example</title>
    </head>
    <body>
        <h1><script type="text/javascript">document.write("this is a
test")</script></h1>
     </body>
</html>
```

The page is displayed in the browser as if it were the following:

```
<html>
    <head>
        <title>Document Write Example</title>
    </head>
    <body>
        <h1>this is a test</h1>
     </body>
</html>
```

You can use this functionality to dynamically include external JavaScript files as well. For example:

```
<html>
    <head>
        <title>Document Example</title>
        <script type="text/javascript">
            document.write("<script type=\"text/javascript\" src=\"external.js\">"
                           + "</scr" + "ipt>");
        </script>
    </head>
    <body>

    </body>
</html>
```

This code writes a `<script/>` tag to the page, which causes the browser to load the external JavaScript file as it would normally. Note that the string `"</script>"` is split into two parts (`"</scr"` and `"ipt>"`). This is necessary because anytime the browser sees `</script>`, it assumes that the code block is complete (even if it occurs inside of a JavaScript string). Suppose the previous example were written without breaking up the `"</script>"` string:

```
<html>
    <head>
        <title>Document Example</title>
        <script type="text/javascript">
            document.write("<script type=\"text/javascript\" src=\"external.js\">"
                           + "</script>");  //this will cause a problem
        </script>
    </head>
    <body>

    </body>
</html>
```

The browser views this page as:

```
<html>
    <head>
        <title>Document Example</title>
        <script type="text/javascript">
            document.write("<script type=\"text/javascript\" src=\"external.js\">"
        </script>
        </script>
    </head>
    <body>

    </body>
</html>
```

As you can see, forgetting to split up the `"</script>"` string causes major confusion. First, there is a syntax error inside of the `<script/>` tag because the `document.write()` call is missing its closing parenthesis. Second, there are two `</script>` tags. This is why you must always break up the `"</script>"` string when writing `<script/>` tags to the page using `document.write()`.

> **Remember that both `write()` and `writeln()` must be called before the page has been fully loaded in order to insert the content properly. If either method is called after the page is loaded, it erases the page and displays the content specified.**

Related closely to `write()` and `writeln()` are the `open()` and `close()` methods. The `open()` method is used to open an already loaded document for writing; the `close()` method is used to close a document opened with `open()`, essentially telling it to render everything that was written to it. This combination of methods is typically used to write to either a frame or a newly opened window, such as the following:

```
var oNewWin = window.open("about:blank", "newwindow",
                          "height=150,width=300,top=10,left=10,resizable=yes");

oNewWin.document.open();
oNewWin.document.write("<html><head><title>New Window</title></head>");
oNewWin.document.write("<body>This is a new window!</body></html>");
oNewWin.document.close();
```

This example opens a blank page (using the native `"about:blank"` URL) and then writes a new page to it. To do this appropriately, the `open()` method is called before the using `write()`. After the writing is complete, `close()` is called to complete the rendering. This technique is useful when you want to display a page without going back to the server.

The location object

One of the most useful objects in the BOM is `location`, which is a property of both `window` and `document` (this is where a lack of standards leads to some real confusion). The `location` object represents the URL loaded in a window and, as an added bonus, it also parses the URL into various segments:

- `hash` — If the URL contains a pound sign (#), this returns the content after it (for example, `http://www.somewhere.com/index#section1` has a hash equal to `"#section1"`).
- `host` — The name of the server (for example, www.wrox.com)
- `hostname` — Most often equal to `host`, this sometimes eliminates the *www.* from the front.
- `href` — The full URL of the currently loaded page
- `pathname` — Everything after the host in the URL. For example, the `pathname` for `http://www.somewhere.com/pictures/index.htm` is `"/pictures/index.htm"`.
- `port` — The port of the request if specified in the URL. By default, most URLs don't include the port as part of the URL so this property is typically blank. If a URL is used such as `http://www.somewhere.com:8080/index.htm`, the `port` is equal to 8080.
- `protocol` — The protocol used in the URL. This is everything before the two forward slashes (`//`) in the URL. For example, the `protocol` for `http://www.wrox.com` is `http:` and the `protocol` for `ftp://www.wrox.com` is `ftp:`.
- `search` — Otherwise known as the query string, this is everything after a question mark (`?`) in a URL performing a GET request. For example, the `search` for `http://www.somewhere.com/search.htm?term=javascript` is `?term=javascript`.

The `location.href` property is used most often to either get or set the URL of the window (in this regard, it is similar to `document.URL`). You can navigate to a new page just by changing its value:

```
location.href = "http://www.wrox.com/";
```

When navigating this way, the new location is added to the history stack after the previous page, meaning that the Back button goes to the page that made this call.

The method `assign()` accomplishes the same thing:

```
location.assign("http://www.wrox.com");
```

Either way is fine, but most developers use `location.href` because it more accurately represents the intent of the code.

If you don't want the page containing the script to be accessible in the browser history, you can use the `replace()` method. This method does the same thing as `assign()`, but it takes the extra step of removing the page containing the script from history, making it inaccessible using the browser Back and Forward buttons. Try it for yourself:

```
<html>
    <head>
        <title>You won't be able to get back here</title>
    </head>
    <body>
        <p>Enjoy this page for a second, because you won't be coming back here.</p>
        <script type="text/javascript">
            setTimeout(function () {
                location.replace("http://www.wrox.com/");
            }, 1000);
        </script>
    </body>
</html>
```

Load this page in your browser, wait for it to navigate to the new page, and then try hitting the Back button.

The location object also has a method called `reload()` that reloads the current page. The two modes for `reload()` reload from the browser cache or reload from the server. Which of these two modes is used depends on the value of one argument: `false` to load from cache; `true` to load from the server (if the argument is omitted, it is considered `false`).

So, to reload from the server, you use this code:

```
location.reload(true);
```

To reload from the cache, you can use either of these lines:

```
location.reload(false);
location.reload();
```

> **Any code located after a `reload()` call may or may not be executed, depending on factors such as network latency and system resources. For this reason, it is best to have `reload()` as the last line of code.**

The final method of the `location` object is `toString()`, which simply returns the value of `location.href`. Therefore, the following two lines of code are equal:

```
alert(location);
alert(location.href);
```

> **Throughout this section, the `location` object has been used in the examples. Remember, the `location` object is a property of both `window` and `document`, so `window.location` and `document.location` are equal to each other and can be used interchangeably.**

The navigator object

The `navigator` object is one of the earliest implemented BOM objects, introduced in Netscape Navigator 2.0 and Internet Explorer 3.0. It contains a significant amount of information about the Web browser. It is also a property of the `window` object, and as such, can be referenced either as `window.navigator` or just `navigator`.

Although Microsoft originally objected to the term *navigator* as being specific to Netscape's browser, the `navigator` object has become a sort of de facto standard for providing information about a Web browser. (Microsoft does have its own object called `clientInformation` in addition to the `navigator` object, but both provide the exact same data.)

Once again, the lack of standards rears its ugly head with the `navigator` object because each browser decides what properties and methods to support. The following table lists the most popular properties and methods and also which of the four most popular browsers — Internet Explorer, Mozilla, Opera, and Safari — support them.

Property/Method	Description	IE	Moz	Op	Saf
`appCodeName`	String representing code name of the browser (typically `"Mozilla"`)	X	X	X	X
`appName`	String representing official browser name	X	X	X	X
`appMinorVersion`	String representing extra version information	X	–	–	–
`appVersion`	String representing the browser version	X	X	X	X
`browserLanguage`*	String representing the language of the browser or operating system	X	–	X	–
`cookieEnabled`	Boolean indicating if cookies are enabled	X	X	X	–
`cpuClass`	String representing the CPU class (`"x86"`, `"68K"`, `"Alpha"`, `"PPC"`, or `"Other"`)	X	–	–	–
`javaEnabled()`	Boolean indicating if Java is enabled	X	X	X	X
`language`	String representing language of the browser	–	X	X	X
`mimeTypes`	Array of mimetypes registered with the browser	–	X	X	X

Table continued on following page

Property/Method	Description	IE	Moz	Op	Saf
`onLine`	Boolean indicating if the browser is attached to the Internet	X	–	–	–
`oscpu`	String representing the operating system or the CPU	–	X	–	–
`platform`	String representing the computer platform that the browser is running on	X	X	X	X
`plugins`	Array of plugins installed in the browser	X	X	X	X
`preference()`	Function used to set browser preferences	–	X	X	–
`product`	String representing the name of the product (typically `"Gecko"`)	–	X	–	X
`productSub`	String representing extra information about the product (typically the Gecko version)	–	X	–	X
`opsProfile`		–	–	–	–
`securityPolicy`		–	X	–	–
`systemLanguage`*	String representing the operating system's language	X	–	–	–
`taintEnabled()`	Boolean indicating if data tainting is enabled	X	X	X	X
`userAgent`	String representing the user-agent header string	X	X	X	X
`userLanguage`*	String representing the operating system's language	X	–	–	–
`userProfile`	Object allowing access to the browser user profile	X	–	–	–
`vendor`	String representing the name of the branded browser (typically `"Netscape6"` or `"Netscape"`)	–	X	–	X
`vendorSub`	String representing extra information for the branded browser (typically the version of Netscape)	–	X	–	X

* Most of the time, `browserLanguage`, `systemLanguage`, and `userLanguage` are the same.

The `navigator` object is extremely helpful in determining what browser is being used to view a page. A quick search of the Internet reveals any number of methodologies for browser detection, all of which make extensive use of `navigator`. Browser and operating-system detection using the `navigator` object is discussed in greater detail in Chapter 9.

The screen object

Although most information about the user's system is hidden for security reasons, it is possible to get a certain amount of information about the user's monitor using the `screen` object (which, you may have already guessed, is a property of `window` as well).

The screen object typically contains the following properties (although, as usual, many browsers add their own properties):

- availHeight — the height of the screen (in pixels) available for use by windows. This takes into account the space needed by operating system elements such as the Windows taskbar.
- availWidth — the width of the screen (in pixels) available for use by windows
- colorDepth — the number of bits used to represent colors. For most systems, this is 32.
- height — the height of the screen in pixels
- width — the width of the screen in pixels

The availHeight and availWidth properties are useful when determining the new size for a window. For example, to fill up the user's screen, you could use this code:

```
window.moveTo(0, 0);
window.resizeTo(screen.availWidth, screen.availHeight);
```

Besides that, most of this data is used in conjunction with site traffic tools to determine the graphical capabilities of users.

Summary

This chapter introduced using JavaScript inside of Web browsers. It covered how to include JavaScript code in both HTML and SVG pages, explaining the differences between the two. It also discussed how XHTML has changed how JavaScript is included in HTML pages and the best way to prepare for the future in this regard.

Later in the chapter, you learned about the Browser Object Model and the various objects it supplies. You learned that the window object is the center of the JavaScript universe, and all the other BOM objects are actually just properties of window.

The chapter explained how to manipulate browser windows and frames, moving and resizing them using JavaScript. Using the location object, you learned how to access and alter a window's location and, using the history object, how to go back and forward to pages the user has already visited.

Finally, you learned how to retrieve information about a user's Web browser and screen by using the navigator and screen objects.

6

DOM Basics

The Document Object Model (DOM) is perhaps the single greatest innovation on the Web since HTML was first used to connect related documents together over the Internet. The DOM gives developers unprecedented access to HTML, enabling them to manipulate and view HTML as an XML document. The DOM represents the evolution of Dynamic HTML, pioneered by Microsoft and Netscape, into a true cross-platform, language-independent solution.

What Is the DOM?

Before I discuss exactly what the DOM is, you should know what led to its creation. Although the DOM was heavily influenced by the rise of Dynamic HTML in browsers, the W3C took a step backward and first applied it to XML.

Introduction to XML

The eXtensible Markup Language (XML) was derived from an earlier language called Standard Generalized Markup Language (SGML). SGML's main purpose was to define the syntax of markup languages to represent data using tags.

Tags consist of text enclosed between a less-than symbol (<) and a greater-than symbol (>), as in `<tag>`. *Start tags* begin a particular area, such as `<start>`; *end tags* define the end of an area. They look the same as start tags but have a forward slash (/) immediately following the less-than symbol, as in `</end>`. SGML also defines attributes for tags, which are values assigned inside of the less-than and greater-than symbols, such as the `src` attribute in `<img src="picture.jpg">`. If this looks familiar, it should; the most famous implementation of an SGML-based language is the original HTML.

SGML was used to define the Document Type Definition (DTD) for HTML, and it is still used to write DTDs for XML. The problem with SGML is its allowances for odd syntax, which makes creating parsers for HTML a difficult problem:

- Some start tags specifically disallow end tags, such as the HTML `<img>`. Including an end tag causes an error.
- Some start tags have optional or implied end tags, such as the HTML `<p>`, which assumes a closing tag when it meets another `<p>` or several other tags.
- Some start tags require end tags, such as the HTML `<script>`.
- Tags can be embedded in any order. For instance, `<b>This is a <i> sample </b> string</i>` is okay even though the end tags don't occur in reverse order of the start tags.
- Some attributes require values, such as `src` in `<img src="picture.jpg" >`.
- Some attributes don't require values, such as `nowrap` in `<td nowrap>`.
- Attribute can be defined with or without quotation marks surrounding them, so `<img src="picture.jpg">` and `<img src=picture.jpg>` are both allowed.

All these issues make creating SGML language parsers a truly arduous task. The difficultly of knowing when to apply the rules caused a stagnation in the definition of SGML languages. This is where XML begins to fit in.

XML does away with all the optional syntax of SGML that caused so many developers heartache early on. In XML, the following rules apply:

- Every start tag must have end tag.
- An optional shorthand syntax represents both the start and end tags in one. This syntax uses a forward slash (`/`) immediately before the greater-than symbol, such as `<tag />`. An XML parser interprets this as being equal to `<tag></tag>`.
- Tags must be embedded in an appropriate order, so end tags must mirror start tags, such as `<b>this is a <i>sample</i> string</b>`. It helps to think of start and end tags as similar to open and close parentheses in math: You cannot close the outermost parenthesis without first closing all the inner ones.
- All attributes require values.
- All attributes must use quotes around the values.

These rules make an XML parser much simpler to develop and also remove the guesswork of when and where to apply odd syntax rules. Where SGML failed to gain mainstream acceptance, XML has made tremendous inroads because of its simplicity. XML has spawned several languages in just the first six years of its existence, including MathML, SVG, RDF, RSS, SOAP, XSLT, XSL-FO, and the reformulation of HTML into XHTML.

For a technical comparison of SGML and XML, please see the W3C's note located at ***`http://www.w3.org/TR/NOTE-sgml-xml.html`***.

Today XML is one of the fastest-growing technologies in the world. Its main purpose is to represent data in a structured way using plain text. In some ways, XML files are not unlike databases, which also represent a structured view of data. Here is an example XML file:

```
<?xml version="1.0"?>
<books>
    <!-- begin the list of books -->
    <book isbn="0764543555">
        <title>Professional JavaScript for Web Developers</title>
        <author>Nicholas C. Zakas</author>
        <desc><![CDATA[
Professional JavaScript for Web Developers brings you up to speed on the latest
innovations in the world of JavaScript. This book provides you with the details of
JavaScript implementations in Web browsers and introduces the new capabilities
relating to recently-developed technologies such as XML and Web Services.
        ]]></desc>
    </book>
    <?page render multiple authors ?>
    <book isbn="0764570773">
        <title>Beginning XML, 3rd Edition</title>
        <author>David Hunter</author>
        <author>Andrew Watt</author>
        <author>Jeff Rafter</author>
        <author>Jon Duckett</author>
        <author>Danny Ayers</author>
        <author>Nicholas Chase</author>
        <author>Joe Fawcett</author>
        <author>Tom Gaven</author>
        <author>Bill Patterson</author>
        <desc><![CDATA[
Beginning XML, 3rd Edition, like the first two editions, begins with a broad
overview of the technology and then focuses on specific facets of the various
specifications for the reader. This book teaches you all you need to know about XML:
what it is, how it works, what technologies surround it, and how it can best be used
in a variety of situations, from simple data transfer to using XML in your Web
pages. It builds on the strengths of the first and second editions, and provides new
material to reflect the changes in the XML landscape - notably RSS and SVG.
        ]]></desc>
    </book>
    <book isbn="0764543555">
        <title>Professional XML Development with Apache Tools</title>
        <author>Theodore W. Leung</author>
        <desc><![CDATA[
If you're a Java programmer working with XML, you probably already use some of the
tools developed by the Apache Software Foundation. This book is a code-intensive
guide to the Apache XML tools that are most relevant for Java developers, including
Xerces, Xalan, FOP, Cocoon, Axis, and Xindice.
        ]]></desc>
    </book>""""""""
</books>
```

Every XML document begins with the *XML prolog*, which is the first line in the previous code, `<?xml version="1.0"?>`. This line alone tells parsers and browsers that this file should be parsed based on the XML rules discussed earlier. The second line, `<books>`, is the *document element*, which is the outermost start tag in the file (an *element* is considered the contents of a start tag and end tag). All other tags must be contained within this one in order to constitute a valid XML file. The second line of the XML file need not always contain the document element; it can come later if comments or other (???)

The third line in this sample file is a comment, which you may recognize as the same style comment used in HTML. This is one of the syntax elements XML inherited from SGML.

A little bit farther down the page you find a `<desc>` tag with some special syntax inside it. The `<![CDATA[ ]]>` code is used to indicate text that should not be parsed, allowing special characters such as less-than and greater-than to be included without fear of breaking the XML syntax. The text must appear between `<![CDATA[` and `]]>` to be properly shielded from parsing. This is called a *Character Data Section* or *CData Section* for short.

The following line is just before the second book definition:

```
<?page render multiple authors ?>
```

Even though this looks like the XML prolog, it is actually considered a different type of syntax called a *processing instruction*. The purpose of processing instructions (or PIs for short) is to provide extra information to programs that are processing the page, such as XML parsers. PIs are generally free form. Their only requirement is that a letter must follow the first question mark. After that point, a PI can contain any sequence of characters aside from the less-than or greater-than symbols.

The most common PI is used to specify a style sheet for an XML file:

```
<?xml-stylesheet type="text/css"" href="MyStyles.css" ?>
```

This PI is typically placed immediately after the XML prolog and is used by Web browsers to display the XML data using particular styles.

If you're interested in learning more about XML and its many uses, consider picking up Beginning XML, 3rd Edition (Wiley Publishing, Inc., ISBN 0-7645-7077-3).

An API for XML

After XML was defined as a language, the need arose for a way to both represent and manipulate XML code using common programming languages such as Java.

First came the Simple API for XML (SAX) project for Java. SAX provides an event-based API to parse XML. Essentially, SAX parsers start out at the beginning of the file and parse their way through the code in one straight pass, firing events every time it encounters a start tag, end tag, attribute, text, or other XML syntax. It is up to the developer, then, to determine what to do when each of these events occurs.

SAX parsers are lightweight and fast because they just parse the text and continue on their way. Their main downside is the inability to stop, go backward, or access a specific part of the XML structure without starting from the beginning of the file.

The Document Object Model (DOM) is a tree-based API for XML. Its main focus isn't just to parse XML code, but rather to represent that code using a series of interlinked objects that can be modified and accessed directly without reparsing the code.

Using the DOM, code is parsed once to create a tree model; sometimes a SAX parser is used to accomplish this. After that initial parse, the XML is fully represented in a DOM model, and the original code is no longer needed. Although the DOM is slower than SAX and requires more overhead because it creates so many objects, it is the method favored by Web browsers and JavaScript for its ease of use.

Note that the DOM is a language-independent API, meaning that it is not tied to Java, JavaScript, or any other language for implementation. For the purposes of this book, however, I place most focus on the JavaScript implementation.

Hierarchy of nodes

So what exactly is a tree-based API? When talking about DOM trees (which are called *documents*), you are really talking about a hierarchy of *nodes*. The DOM defines the `Node` interface as well as a large number of node types to represent the multiple aspects of XML code:

- `Document` — The very top-level node to which all other nodes are attached
- `DocumentType` — The object representation of a DTD reference using the syntax `<!DOCTYPE >`, such as `<!DOCTYPE HTML PUBLIC "-//W3C//DTD HTML 4.0 Transitional//EN">`. It cannot contain child nodes.
- `DocumentFragment` — Can be used like a `Document` to hold other nodes
- `Element` — Represents the contents of a start tag and end tag, such as `<tag></tag>` or `<tag/>`. This node type is the only one that can contain attributes as well as child nodes.
- `Attr` — Represents an attribute name-value pair. This node type cannot have child nodes.
- `Text` — Represents plain text in an XML document contained within start and end tags or inside of a CData Section. This node type cannot have child nodes.
- `CDataSection` — The object representation of `<![CDATA[ ]]>`. This node type can have only text nodes as child nodes.
- `Entity` — Represents an entity definition in a DTD, such as `<!ENTITY foo "foo">`. This node type cannot have child nodes.
- `EntityReference` — Represents an entity reference, such as `"`. This node type cannot have child nodes.
- `ProcessingInstruction` — Represents a PI. This node type cannot have child nodes.
- `Comment` — Represents an XML comment. This node type cannot have child nodes.
- `Notation` — Represents notation defined in a DTD. This is rarely used and so won't be included in this discussion.

A document is made up of a hierarchy of any number of these nodes. Consider the following XML code:

```
<?xml version="1.0"?>
<employees>
    <!-- only employee -->
    <employee>
        <name>Michael Smith</name>
        <position>Software Engineer</position>
        <comments><![CDATA[
          His birthday is on 8/14/68.
        ]]></comments>
    </employee>""
</employees>
```

This code can be represented in a DOM document as displayed in Figure 6-1.

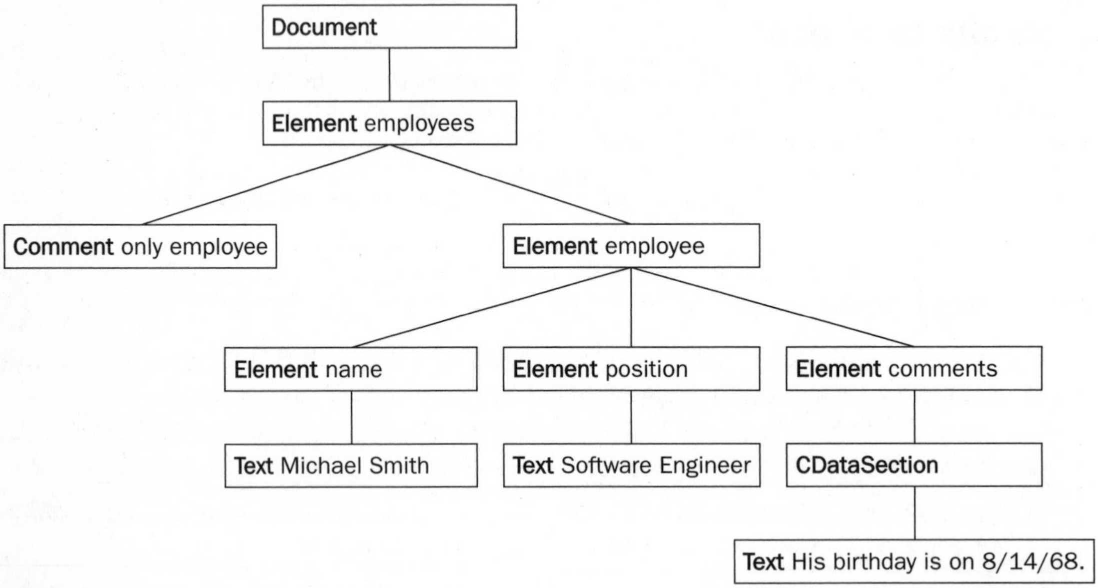

Figure 6-1

In Figure 6-1, each rectangle represents a node in the DOM document tree, with the bold text indicating the node type and the nonbold text indicating the content of that node.

Both the comment and `<employee/>` nodes are considered to be *child nodes* of `<employees/>` because they fall immediately underneath it in the tree. Likewise, `<employees/>` is considered the parent node of the comment and `<employee/>` nodes.

Similarly, `<name/>`, `<position/>`, and `<comments/>` are all considered child nodes of `<employee/>` and are also considered *siblings* of each other because they exist at the same level of the DOM tree and have the same parent node.

The `<employees/>` node is considered the ancestor of all nodes in this section of the tree, including its children (the comment and `<employee/>`) as well as their children (`<name/>`, `<position/>`, and so on, all the way down to the text node `"His birthday is on 8/14/68"`). The document node is considered the ancestor of all nodes in the document.

The `Node` interface defines 12 constants that map to the different node types (and are used by the `nodeType` property discussed later):

- `Node.ELEMENT_NODE` (1)
- `Node.ATTRIBUTE_NODE` (2)
- `Node.TEXT_NODE` (3)
- `Node.CDATA_SECTION_NODE` (4)
- `Node.ENTITY_REFERENCE_NODE` (5)
- `Node.ENTITY_NODE` (6)
- `Node.PROCESSING_INSTRUCTION_NODE` (7)
- `Node.COMMENT_NODE` (8)
- `Node.DOCUMENT_NODE` (9)
- `Node.DOCUMENT_TYPE_NODE` (10)
- `Node.DOCUMENT_FRAGMENT_NODE` (11)
- `Node.NOTATION_NODE` (12)

The `Node` interface also defines a set of properties and methods that all node types contain. These properties and methods are listed out in the following table:

Property/Method	Type/Return Type	Description
`nodeName`	`String`	The name of the node; this is defined depending on the type of node.
`nodeValue`	`String`	The value of the node; this is defined depending on the type of node.
`nodeType`	`Number`	One of the node type constant values
`ownerDocument`	`Document`	Pointer to the document that this node belongs to
`firstChild`	`Node`	Pointer to the first node in the `childNodes` list
`lastChild`	`Node`	Pointer to the last node in the `childNodes` list
`childNodes`	`NodeList`	A list of all child nodes
`previousSibling`	`Node`	Pointer to the previous sibling; `null` if this is the first sibling

Table continued on following page

Property/Method	Type/Return Type	Description
`nextSibling`	`Node`	Pointer to the next sibling; `null` if this is the last sibling
`hasChildNodes()`	`Boolean`	Returns true when `childNodes` contains one or more nodes
`attributes`	`NamedNodeMap`	Contains `Attr` objects representing an element's attributes; only used for `Element` nodes
`appendChild(`*`node`*`)`	`Node`	Adds *`node`* to the end of `childNodes`
`removeChild(`*`node`*`)`	`Node`	Removes *`node`* from `childNodes`
`replaceChild (`*`newnode, oldnode`*`)`	`Node`	Replaces *`oldnode`* in `childNodes` with *`newnode`*
`insertBefore (`*`newnode, refnode`*`)`	`Node`	Inserts *`newnode`* before *`refnode`* in `childNodes`

In addition to nodes, the DOM also defines some helper objects, which are used to work with nodes but are not necessarily part of a DOM document:

- `NodeList` — an array of nodes indexed numerically; used to represent child nodes of an element
- `NamedNodeMap` — an array of nodes indexed both numerically and name; used to represent element attributes

These helper objects provide additional access and traversal methods for dealing with DOM document. Usage specifics are discussed later.

Language-Specific DOMs

Any XML-based language, such as XHTML and SVG, can make use of the core DOM just introduced because they are technically XML. However, many languages go on to define their own DOMs that extend the XML core to provide language-specific features.

Along with developing the XML DOM, the W3C concurrently developed a DOM more specific to XHTML (and HTML). This DOM defines an `HTMLDocument` and `HTMLElement` as the basis for the implementation. Each HTML element is represented by its own `HTMLElement` type, such as `HTMLDivElement` representing `<div>`, with the exception of a small subset of elements that don't require special properties or methods other than those provided by `HTMLElement`. Throughout the rest of the book, you are introduced to various HTML DOM features as well as to the core XML DOM features.

> **Regular HTML is not valid XML; however, most modern Web browsers are forgiving and still parse an HTML document into a proper DOM document (even without the XML prolog). However, it's always best to use XHTML code when programming Web pages to eliminate bad coding habits.**

*The W3C has also published language-specific DOMs defined for SVG (**http://www.w3.org/TR/SVG**), SMIL Animation (**http://www.w3.org/TR/smil-animation**), and MathML (**http://www.w3.org/TR/MathML2**).*

DOM Support

As I said previously, not all browsers are at the same level of DOM support. Generally speaking, Mozilla has the best DOM standards support, supporting almost all DOM Level 2 and parts of DOM Level 3. Behind Mozilla, Opera and Safari have made significant inroads toward closing the support gap, supporting almost all DOM Level 1 and most of DOM Level 2. Lagging behind the field is Internet Explorer, whose incomplete implementation of DOM Level 1 leaves much to be desired.

Using the DOM

Even though the `document` object is considered part of the BOM, it is also is a representation of the HTML DOM's `HTMLDocument` object, which, in turn, is also an XML DOM `Document` object. Most DOM manipulation in JavaScript makes use of the `document` object, so that's a logical place to begin the discussion.

Accessing relative nodes

Consider the following HTML page for the next few sections:

```
<html>
    <head>
        <title>DOM Example</title>
    </head>
    <body>
        <p>Hello World!</p>
        <p>Isn't this exciting?</p>
        <p>You're learning to use the DOM!</p>
    </body>
</html>
```

To access the `<html/>` element (which you should realize is the `document` element of this file), you can use the `documentElement` property of `document`:

```
var oHtml = document.documentElement;
```

> **Because of an incorrect DOM implementation, Internet Explorer 5.5 returns the `<body/>` element for `document.documentElement`. Internet Explorer 6.0 fixes this problem.**

The variable `oHtml` now contains an `HTMLElement` object representing `<html/>`. If you want to get the `<head/>` and `<body/>` elements using `oHtml`, this works:

```
var oHead = oHtml.firstChild;
var oBody = oHtml.lastChild;
```

You can also use the `childNodes` property to accomplish the same thing. Just pretend that it's a regular JavaScript `Array` and use square-bracket notation:

```
var oHead = oHtml.childNodes[0];
var oBody = oHtml.childNodes[1];
```

You can also get the number of child nodes by using the `childNodes.length` property:

```
alert(oHtml.childNodes.length);     //outputs "2"
```

Note that the square-bracket notation is a convenient implementation of the `NodeList` in JavaScript. The formal method of retrieving child nodes from the childNodes list is the `item()` method:

```
var oHead = oHtml.childNodes.item(0);
var oBody = oHtml.childNodes.item(1);
```

The HTML DOM also defines `document.body` as a pointer to the `<body />` element:

```
var oBody = document.body;
```

With the three variables `oHtml`, `oHead`, and `oBody`, you can play around to determine their relationship to one another:

```
alert(oHead.parentNode == oHtml);          //outputs "true"
alert(oBody.parentNode == oHtml);          //outputs "true"
alert(oBody.previousSibling == oHead);     //outputs "true"
alert(oHead.nextSibling == oBody);         //outputs "true"
alert(oHead.ownerDocument == document);    //outputs "true"
```

This little snippet of code tests to make sure that the `parentNode` property of both `oBody` and `oHead` point to `oHtml`, as well as uses the `previousSibling` and `nextSibling` properties to establish their relationship to one another. The last line assures that the `ownerDocument` property of `oHead` actually does point back to the document.

> **There is some discrepancy among browsers regarding what is and isn't a `Text` node. Some browsers, such as Mozilla, consider any white space between elements a `Text` node; whereas others, such as Internet Explorer, ignore the white space altogether. Because it's hard to determine which white space to consider as a `Text` node using the Mozilla method, this book uses the Internet Explorer method.**

Checking the node type

You can check the type of node by using the `nodeType` property:

```
alert(document.nodeType);      //outputs "9"
alert(document.documentElement.nodeType);    //outputs "1"
```

In this example, `document.nodeType` returns `9`, which is equal to `Node.DOCUMENT_NODE`, and `document.documentElement.nodeType` returns `1`, which is equal to `Node.ELEMENT_NODE`.

You can also match up these values with the `Node` constants:

```
alert(document.nodeType == Node.DOCUMENT_NODE);      //outputs "true"
alert(document.documentElement.nodeType == Node.ELEMENT_NODE);    //outputs "true"
```

This code works in Mozilla 1.0+, Opera 7.0+, and Safari 1.0+. Unfortunately, Internet Explorer doesn't support these constant values, so this code causes an error. You can remedy the situation by defining your own constants that match the node type constants, such as the following:

```
if (typeof Node == "undefined") {
    var Node = {
        ELEMENT_NODE: 1,
        ATTRIBUTE_NODE: 2,
        TEXT_NODE: 3,
        CDATA_SECTION_NODE: 4,
        ENTITY_REFERENCE_NODE: 5,
        ENTITY_NODE: 6,
        PROCESSING_INSTRUCTION_NODE: 7,
        COMMENT_NODE: 8,
        DOCUMENT_NODE: 9,
        DOCUMENT_TYPE_NODE: 10,
        DOCUMENT_FRAGMENT_NODE: 11,
        NOTATION_NODE: 12
    }
}
```

The other option is to use the integer literals (although this may get confusing because not many people have memorized the node type values).

Dealing with attributes

As mentioned previously, only `Element` nodes have attributes even though the `Node` interface has an `attributes` method that is inherited by all node types. The attributes property for an `Element` node is a `NamedNodeMap`, which provides several methods for accessing and manipulating its contents:

- `getNamedItem(`*`name`*`)` — returns the node whose `nodeName` property is equal to *`name`*
- `removeNamedItem(`*`name`*`)` — removes the node whose `nodeName` property is equal to *`name`* from the list
- `setNamedItem(`*`node`*`)` — adds the *`node`* into the list, indexing it by its `nodeName` property
- `item(`*`pos`*`)` — just like `NodeList`, returns the node in the numerical position `pos`

> **Keep in mind that each of these methods returns an `Attr` node, not the value of the attribute.**

The `NamedNodeMap` object also has a `length` property to indicate the number of nodes it contains.

When used to represent attributes, each node in the `NamedNodeMap` is an `Attr` node, whose `nodeName` property is set to the attribute name. The `nodeValue` property is set to the attribute value. For example, suppose you had this element:

```
<p style="color: red" id="p1">Hello world!</p>
```

Also, suppose that the variable `oP` that contains a reference to this element. You can access the value of the `id` attribute like this:

```
var sId = oP.attributes.getNamedItem("id").nodeValue;
```

Of course, you could access this `id` attribute numerically, which is a little less intuitive:

```
var sId = oP.attributes.item(1).nodeValue;
```

You can change the `id` attribute by setting a new value to the `nodeValue` property:

```
oP.attributes.getNamedItem("id").nodeValue = "newId";
```

`Attr` nodes also have a `value` property that is exactly equal (and kept in sync with) the `nodeValue` property, as well as a `name` property that is kept in sync with `nodeName`. You use any of these properties to modify or change the attributes.

Because this method is a little bit cumbersome, the DOM also defines three element methods to aid in the assignment of attributes:

- `getAttribute(`*`name`*`)` — same as `attributes.getNamedItem(`*`name`*`).value`
- `setAttribute(`*`name`*`, `*`newvalue`*`)` — same as `attributes.getNamedItem(`*`name`*`).value =` *`newvalue`*
- `removeAttribute(`*`name`*`)` — same as `attributes.removeNamedItem(`*`name`*`)`

These methods are helpful in that they deal directly with the attribute values, completely hiding the `Attr` nodes. So, to retrieve the `id` attribute of the `<p />` used earlier, you can just do this:

```
var sId = oP.getAttribute("id");
```

And to change the ID, you can do this:

```
oP.setAttribute("id", "newId");
```

As you can see, these methods are much less verbose than using the `NamedNodeMap` methods.

Accessing specific nodes

You already know how to access parent and child nodes, but what if you want access to a node (or group of nodes) that are located deep in the document? Certainly, you don't want to count child nodes until you get down to what you're looking for. To help you in this use case, the DOM provides several methods to enable easy access to specific nodes.

getElementsByTagName()

The Core (XML) DOM defines the method `getElementsByTagName()` to return a `NodeList` of all `Element` objects whose `tagName` property is equal to a specific value. In an `Element` object, the `tagName` property is always equal to the name immediately following the less-than symbol — for example, the `tagName` of `<img />` is `"img"`. The following line of code returns a list of all `<img />` elements in a document:

```
var oImgs = document.getElementsByTagName("img");
```

After storing all of the images in `oImgs`, you can access them individually in the same way that you access child nodes, by using either square-bracket notation or the `item()` method (`getElementsByTagName()` returns a `NodeList`, just like `childNodes`):

```
alert(oImgs[0].tagName);    //outputs "IMG"
```

This line of code outputs the `tagName` of the first image, which is output as `"IMG"`. For some reason, most browsers still record the tag name as all uppercase even though XHTML conventions dictate that tag names must be all lowercase.

But suppose you want to get only the images within the first paragraph of a page. This can be accomplished by calling `getElementsByTagName()` on the first paragraph element, like this:

```
var oPs = document.getElementsByTagname("p");
var oImgsInP = oPs[0].getElementsByTagName("img");
```

You can use this one method to get down to any element in the `document` or to get all elements in the `document` by using an asterisk:

```
var oAllElements = document.getElementsByTagName("*");
```

This line of code returns all the elements contained in `document` regardless of their tag names.

> **Internet Explorer 6.0 doesn't return all elements when the argument is an asterisk. You must use `document.all` instead.**

getElementsByName()

The HTML DOM defines `getElementsByName()` to retrieve all elements that have their `name` attribute set to a specific value. Consider the following HTML:

```
<html>
    <head>
        <title>DOM Example</title>
    </head>
    <body>
        <form method="post" action="dosomething.cgi">
            <fieldset>
                <legend>What color do you like?</legend>
                <input type="radio" name="radColor" value="red" /> Red<br />
                <input type="radio" name="radColor" value="green" /> Green<br />
                <input type="radio" name="radColor" value="blue" /> Blue<br />
            </fieldset>
            <input type="submit" value="Submit" />
        </form>
    </body>
</html>
```

This page asks the user which color he/she likes. The radio buttons all have the same `name`, because you only want to return one value for this field, which is the `value` attribute of the selected radio button. To get references to all the radio button elements, you can use the following code:

```
var oRadios = document.getElementsByName("radColor");
```

You can then manipulate the radio buttons the same way as you can any other element:

```
alert(oRadios[0].getAttribute("value"));  //outputs "red"
```

> **Internet Explorer 6.0 and Opera 7.5 have a couple of bugs when using this method. First, they also return elements that have an `id` equal to the given name. Second, they only check `<input/>` and `<img/>` elements.**

getElementById()

The second method defined by the HTML DOM is `getElementById()`, which returns an element with its `id` attribute set to a specific value. In HTML, the `id` attribute is unique — meaning that no two elements can share the same `id`. This is undoubtedly the fastest method of retrieving a single specific element from the document tree.

Suppose you have the following HTML page:

```
<html>
    <head>
        <title>DOM Example</title>
    </head>
    <body>
        <p>Hello World!</p>
        <div id="div1">This is my first layer</div>
    </body>
</html>
```

To access the `<div />` element with the ID `"div1"`, you can use the `getElementsByTagName()` like this:

```
var oDivs = document.getElementsByTagName("div");
var oDiv1 = null;
for (var i=0; i < oDivs.length; i++){
    if (oDivs[i].getAttribute("id") == "div1") {
        oDiv1 = oDivs[i];
        break;
    }
}
```

Or, you could use `getElementById()` like this:

```
var oDiv1 = document.getElementById("div1");
```

As you can see, this is a much more streamlined way to get a reference to a specific element.

> **Internet Explorer 6.0 also returns an element if the given ID matches the `name` attribute of an element. This is a bug, and one that you should be very careful of.**

Creating and manipulating nodes

So far, you've learned how to access various nodes inside of a document, but that's just the beginning of what can be done using the DOM. You can also add, remove, replace, and otherwise manipulate nodes within a DOM document. This functionality is what makes the DOM truly dynamic.

Creating new nodes

The DOM `Document` has a number of methods designed to create various types of nodes, even though the browser `document` object doesn't necessarily support each of these methods in all browsers. The following table lists the methods included in DOM Level 1 and which browsers support each one.

Method	Description	IE	MOZ	OP	SAF
`createAttribute(name)`	Creates an attribute node with the given *`name`*	X	X	X	–
`createCDATASection(text)`	Creates a CDATA Section with a text child node containing *`tex`*	–	X	–	–
`createComment(text)`	Creates a comment node containing *`text`*	X	X	X	X
`createDocumentFragment()`	Creates a document fragment node	X	X	X	X
`createElement(tagname)`	Creates an element with a tag name of *`tagname`*	X	X	X	X

Table continued on following page

Method	Description	IE	MOZ	OP	SAF
`createEntityReference(name)`	Creates an entity reference node with the given *name*	–	X	–	–
`createProcessingInstruction(target, data)`	Creates a PI node with the given *target* and *data*	–	X	–	–
`createTextNode(text)`	Creates a text node containing *text*	X	X	X	X

IE = Internet Explorer 6 for Windows, MOZ = Mozilla 1.5 for all platforms, OP = Opera 7.5 for all platforms, SAF = Safari 1.2 for MacOS.

The most commonly used methods are `createDocumentFragment()`, `createElement()`, and `createTextNode()`; the other methods are either not useful (`createComment()`) or not supported by enough browsers to be useful at this point in time.

createElement(), createTextNode(), appendChild()

Suppose you have the following HTML page:

```
<html>
    <head>
        <title>createElement() Example</title>
    </head>
    <body>

    </body>
</html>
```

To this page, you want to add the following code using the DOM:

```
<p>Hello World!</p>
```

The `createElement()` and `createTextNode()` methods can be used to accomplish this. Here's how.

The first thing to do is create the `<p/>` element:

```
var oP = document.createElement("p");
```

Second, create the text node:

```
var oText = document.createTextNode("Hello World!");
```

Next you need to add the text node to the element. To do this, you can use the `appendChild()` method, which was briefly mentioned earlier in the chapter. The `appendChild()` method exists on every node type and is used to add a given node to the end of another's `childNodes` list. In this case, the text node should be added to the `<p />` element:

```
oP.appendChild(oText);
```

You're not done quite yet. You have created the element and text node and attached them to each other, but the element still doesn't have a spot in the document. To actually be visible, the element must be attached either to the `document.body` element or one of its children. Once again, you can use the `appendChild()` method for this:

```
document.body.appendChild(oP);
```

To put all this into a sample you can run, just create a function containing each of these steps and call it when the page is loaded by using the `onload` event handler (events will be covered in more detail in the Chapter 9, "All About Events"):

```
<html>
    <head>
        <title>createElement() Example</title>
        <script type="text/javascript">
            function createMessage() {
                var oP = document.createElement("p");
                var oText = document.createTextNode("Hello World! ");
                oP.appendChild(oText);
                document.body.appendChild(oP);
            }
        </script>
    </head>
    <body onload="createMessage()">

    </body>
</html>
```

When you run this code, the message `"Hello World!"` is displayed as if it were part of the HTML document all along.

> **At this point, it's prudent to point out that all DOM manipulation must occur *after* the page has fully loaded. It isn't possible to insert code while a page is loading to work with the DOM because the DOM tree isn't fully constructed until the page has been completely downloaded to the client machine. For this reason, all code must be executed using the `onload` event handler.**

removeChild(), replaceChild(), and insertBefore()

Naturally, if you can add a node you can also remove a node, which is where the `removeChild()` method comes in. This method accepts one argument, the node to remove, and then returns that node as the function value. So if, for instance, you start out with a page already containing the `"Hello World!"` message and you wanted to remove it, you can use the method like this:

```
<html>
    <head>
        <title>removeChild() Example</title>
        <script type="text/javascript">
            function removeMessage() {
                var oP = document.body.getElementsByTagName("p")[0];
```

```
                document.body.removeChild(oP);
            }
        </script>
    </head>
    <body onload="removeMessage()">
        <p>Hello World!</p>
    </body>
</html>
```

When this page is loaded, it displays a blank screen because the message is removed even before you have a chance to see it. Although this works, it's always better to use a node's `parentNode` property to make sure you are accessing its real parent:

```
<html>
    <head>
        <title>removeChild() Example</title>
        <script type="text/javascript">
            function removeMessage() {
                var oP = document.body.getElementsByTagName("p")[0];
                oP.parentNode.removeChild(oP);
            }
        </script>
    </head>
    <body onload="replaceMessage()">
        <p>Hello World!</p>
    </body>
</html>
```

But what if you want to replace this message with a new one? In that case, you can use the `replaceChild()` method.

The `replaceChild()` method takes two arguments: the node to add and the node to replace. In this case, you create a new element with a new message and replace the `<p />` element with the `"Hello World!"` message.

```
<html>
    <head>
        <title>replaceChild() Example</title>
        <script type="text/javascript">
            function replaceMessage() {
                var oNewP = document.createElement("p");
                var oText = document.createTextNode("Hello Universe! ");
                oNewP.appendChild(oText);
                var oOldP = document.body.getElementsByTagName("p")[0];
                oOldP.parentNode.replaceChild(oNewP, oOldP);
            }
        </script>
    </head>
    <body onload="replaceMessage()">
        <p>Hello World!</p>
    </body>
</html>
```

This sample page replaces the message "Hello World!" with "Hello Universe!" Note that this code still uses the parentNode property to ensure the correct parent is being manipulated.

Of course, you may want both messages to appear. If you want the new message to come after the old message, use the appendChild() method:

```
<html>
    <head>
        <title>appendChild() Example</title>
        <script type="text/javascript">
            function appendMessage() {
                var oNewP = document.createElement("p");
                var oText = document.createTextNode("Hello Universe! ");
                oNewP.appendChild(oText);
                document.body.appendChild(oNewP);
            }
        </script>
    </head>
    <body onload="appendMessage()">
        <p>Hello World!</p>
    </body>
</html>
```

If, however, you want the new message to come before the old, use the insertBefore() method. This method accepts two arguments: the new node to add and the node that it should be inserted before. In this example, the second argument is the <p /> element containing "Hello World!":

```
<html>
    <head>
        <title>insertBefore() Example</title>
        <script type="text/javascript">
            function insertMessage() {
                var oNewP = document.createElement("p");
                var oText = document.createTextNode("Hello Universe! ");
                oNewP.appendChild(oText);
                var oOldP = document.getElementsByTagName("p")[0];
                document.body.insertBefore(oNewP, oOldP);
            }
        </script>
    </head>
    <body onload="insertMessage()">
        <p>Hello World!</p>
    </body>
</html>
```

createDocumentFragment()

As soon as you add nodes to document.body (or one of its ancestors), the page is updated to reflect the changes. This is fine for a small number of changes, as in the previous examples. However, when a large amount of data has to be added to the document, it can be a very slow process if it adds changes one-by-one. To correct this situation, you can create a document fragment to which you attach all new nodes, and then add the contents of the document fragment to the document.

Suppose you want to create ten new paragraphs. Using the methods you learned previously, you write this code:

```
var arrText = ["first", "second", "third", "fourth", "fifth", "sixth", "seventh",
"eighth", "ninth", "tenth"];

for (var i=0; i < arrText.length; i++) {
    var oP = document.createElement("p");
    var oText = document.createTextNode(arrText[i]);
    oP.appendChild(oText);
    document.body.appendChild(oP);}
```

This code works just fine, the problem is that it's making ten calls to `document.body.appendChild()`, which causes a refresh of the page each time. This is where the document fragment is useful:

```
var arrText = ["first", "second", "third", "fourth", "fifth", "sixth", "seventh",
"eighth", "ninth", "tenth"];

var oFragment = document.createDocumentFragment();

for (var i=0; i < arrText.length; i++) {
    var oP = document.createElement("p");
    var oText = document.createTextNode(arrText[i]);
    oP.appendChild(oText);
    oFragment.appendChild(oP);
}

document.body.appendChild(oFragment);
```

In this code, each new `<p />` element is added to the document fragment. Then, the fragment is passed in as the argument to `appendChild()`. The call to `appendChild()` doesn't actually append the document fragment node itself to the `<body />` element; instead, it just appends the fragment's child nodes. You can see the obvious performance gains: One call to `document.body.appendChild()` instead of 10 means only one screen refresh.

DOM HTML Features

The properties and methods of the Core DOM are generic, designed to work with every XML document in every situation. The properties and methods of the HTML DOM are specific to HTML and make certain DOM manipulations easier. These include the capability to access attributes as properties in addition to element-specific properties and methods that can make common tasks, such as building tables, much more straightforward.

Attributes as properties

For the most part, all attributes are included in HTML DOM elements as properties. For example, suppose you had the following image element:

<img src="mypicture.jpg" border="0" />

To get and set the `src` and `border` attributes using the Core DOM, you use the `getAttribute()` and `setAttribute()` methods:

```
alert(oImg.getAttribute("src"));
alert(oImg.getAttribute("border"));
oImg.setAttribute("src", "mypicture2.jpg");
   oImg.setAttribute("border", "1");
```

However, using the HTML DOM, you can get and set these values using properties with the same name:

```
alert(oImg.src);
alert(oImg.border);
oImg.src = "mypicture2.jpg";
oImg.border = "1";
```

The only instance where the attribute name isn't the same as the property name is in the `class` attribute, which specifies a CSS class to apply to an element, such as in the following:

```
<div class="header"></div>
```

Because `class` is a reserved word in ECMAScript, it cannot be used as a variable, property, or function name in JavaScript. Therefore, the property is `className`:

```
alert(oDiv.className);
oDiv.className = "footer";
```

Using properties to modify attributes instead of `getAttribute()` and `setAttribute()` affords no real advantages aside from decreasing the code's size and making it a little bit easier to read.

> **Internet Explorer has a major problem with `setAttribute()`: When you use it, changes aren't always reflected correctly. If you are planning on supporting Internet Explorer, it is best to use the attribute properties as often as possible.**

Table methods

Suppose you want to create the following HTML table using the DOM:

```
<table border="1" width="100%">    <tbody>
        <tr>
            <td>Cell 1,1</td>
            <td>Cell 2,1</td>
        </tr>
        <tr>
            <td>Cell 1,2</td>
            <td>Cell 2,2</td>
        </tr>
    </tbody>
</table>
```

If you want to accomplish this with the Core DOM methods, your code would look something like this:

```
//create the table
var oTable = document.createElement("table");
oTable.setAttribute("border", "1");
oTable.setAttribute("width", "100%");

//create the tbody
var oTBody = document.createElement("tbody");
oTable.appendChild(oTBody);

//create the first row
var oTR1 = document.createElement("tr");
oTBody.appendChild(oTR1);
var oTD11 = document.createElement("td");
oTD11.appendChild(document.createTextNode("Cell 1,1"));
oTR1.appendChild(oTD11);
var oTD21 = document.createElement("td");
oTD21.appendChild(document.createTextNode("Cell 2,1"));
oTR1.appendChild(oTD21);

//create the second row
var oTR2 = document.createElement("tr");
oTBody.appendChild(oTR2);
var oTD12 = document.createElement("td");
oTD12.appendChild(document.createTextNode("Cell 1,2"));
oTR2.appendChild(oTD12);
var oTD22 = document.createElement("td");
oTD22.appendChild(document.createTextNode("Cell 2,2"));
oTR2.appendChild(oTD22);
//add the table to the document body
document.body.appendChild(oTable);
```

This code is quite verbose and a little hard to follow. To facilitate building tables, the HTML DOM adds several properties and methods to the `<table/>`, `<tbody/>`, and `<tr/>` elements.

The `<table/>` element adds the following:

- `caption` — pointer to the `<caption/>` element (if it exists)
- `tBodies` — collection of `<tbody/>` elements
- `tFoot` — pointer to the `<tfoot/>` element (if it exists)
- `tHead` — pointer to the `<thead/>` element (if it exists)
- `rows` — collection of all rows in the table
- `createTHead()` — creates a `<thead/>` element and places it into the table
- `createTFoot()` — creates a `<tfoot/>` element and places it into the table
- `createCaption()` — creates a `<caption/>` element and places it into the table
- `deleteTHead()` — deletes the `<thead/>` element
- `deleteTFoot()` — deletes the `<tfoot/>` element

- `deleteCaption()` — deletes the `<caption/>` element
- `deleteRow(position)` — deletes the row in the given position
- `insertRow(position)` — inserts a row in the given position in the `rows` collection

The `<tbody/>` element adds the following:

- `rows` — collection of rows in the `<tbody/>` element
- `deleteRow(position)` — deletes the row in the given position
- `insertRow(position)` — inserts a row in the given position in the `rows` collection

The `<tr/>` element adds the following:

- `cells` — collection of cells in the `<tr/>` element
- `deleteCell(position)` — deletes the cell in the given position
- `insertCell(position)` — inserts a cell in the given position in the `cells` collection

What does all of this mean? Essentially, it means that creating a table can be a lot less complicated if you use these convenient properties and methods:

```
//create the table
var oTable = document.createElement("table");
oTable.setAttribute("border", "1");
oTable.setAttribute("width", "100%");

//create the tbody
var oTBody = document.createElement("tbody");
oTable.appendChild(oTBody);
//create the first row
oTBody.insertRow(0);
oTBody.rows[0].insertCell(0);
oTBody.rows[0].cells[0].appendChild(document.createTextNode("Cell 1,1"));
oTBody.rows[0].insertCell(1);
oTBody.rows[0].cells[1].appendChild(document.createTextNode("Cell 2,1"));

//create the second row
oTBody.insertRow(1);
oTBody.rows[1].insertCell(0);
oTBody.rows[1].cells[0].appendChild(document.createTextNode("Cell 1,2"));
oTBody.rows[1].insertCell(1);
oTBody.rows[1].cells[1].appendChild(document.createTextNode("Cell 2,2"));
//add the table to the document body
document.body.appendChild(oTable);
```

In this code, the creation of the `<table/>` and `<tbody/>` elements remain the same. What has changed is the section creating the two rows, which now makes use of the HTML DOM Table properties and methods. To create the first row, the `insertRow()` method is called on the `<tbody/>` element with an argument of 0, which indicates the position in which the row should be placed. After that point, the row can be referenced by `oTBody.rows[0]` because it is automatically created and added into the `<tbody/>` element in position 0.

Creating a cell is done in a similar way — calling `insertCell()` on the `<tr/>` element and passing in the position in which the cell should be placed. The cell can then be referenced by `oTBody.rows[0].cells[0]` because the cell has been created and inserted into the row in position 0.

Using these properties and methods to create a table makes the code much more logical and readable, although technically both sets of code are correct.

DOM Traversal

Up until this point, the features discussed have all been part of DOM Level 1. This section introduces some of the features of DOM Level 2, specifically objects in the DOM Level 2 Traversal and Range specification relating to traversing a DOM document. These features are only available in Mozilla and Konqueror/Safari.

NodeIterator

The first object of interest is the `NodeIterator`, which enables you to do a depth-first search of a DOM tree, which can be useful if you are looking for specific types of information (or elements) in a page. To understand what the `NodeIterator` does, consider the following HTML page:

```
<html>
    <head>
        <title>Example</title>
    </head>
    <body>
        <p>Hello <b>World!</b></p>
    </body>
</html>
```

This page evaluates to the DOM tree represented in Figure 6-2.

When using a `NodeIterator`, it's possible to start from the `document` element, `<html/>`, and traverse the entire DOM tree in a systematic way known as a depth-first search. In this method of searching, the traversal goes as deep as it possibly can from parent to child, to that child's child, and so on, until it can't go any further. Then, the traversal goes back up one level and goes to the next child. For instance, in the DOM tree shown previously, the traversal first visits `<html/>`, then `<head/>`, then `<title/>`, then the text node `"Example"`, before going back up to `<body/>`. Figure 6-3 displays the complete path for the traversal.

The best way to think of a depth-first search is to draw a line that starts from the left of the first node and follows the outline of the tree. Whenever the line passes a node on its left, the node appears next in the search (this line is indicated by the thick line in Figure 6-3).

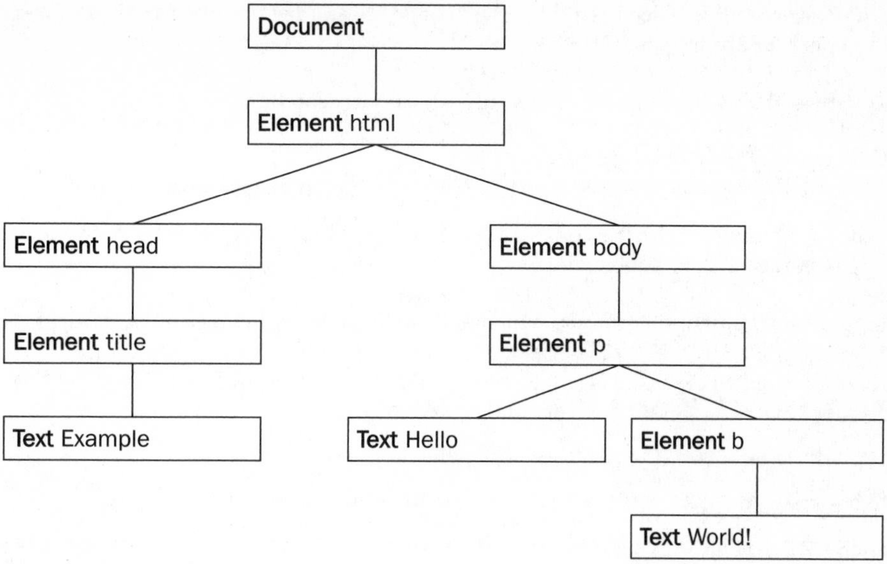

Figure 6-2

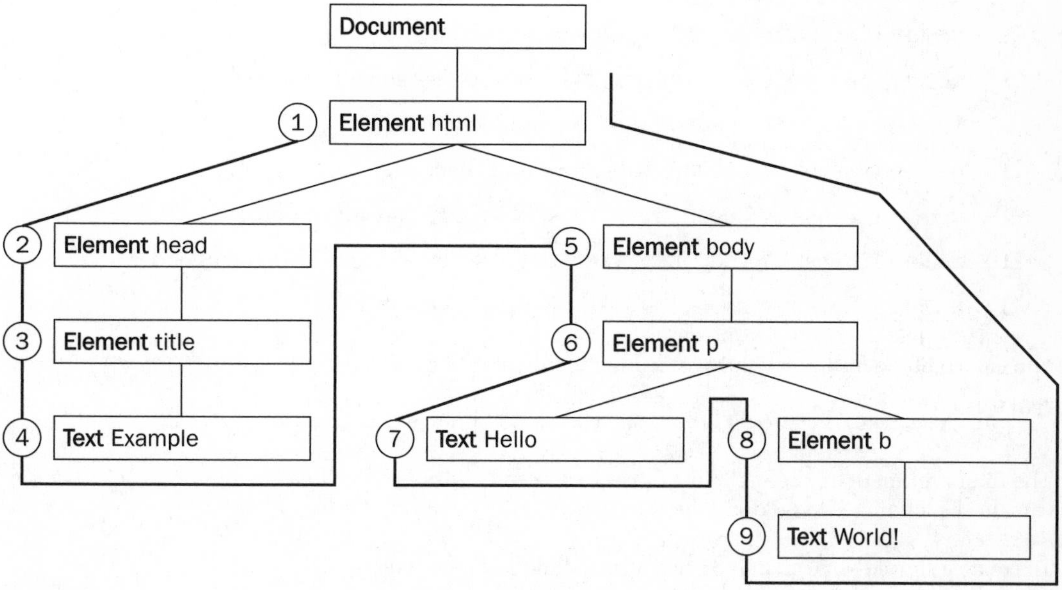

Figure 6-3

To create a NodeIterator object, use the createNodeIterator() method of the document object. This method accepts four arguments:

1. root — the node in the tree that you wish to start searching from
2. whatToShow — a numerical code indicating which nodes should be visited
3. filter — a NodeFilter object to determine which nodes to ignore
4. entityReferenceExpansion — a Boolean value indicating whether entity references should be expanded

The whatToShow argument determines which nodes to visit by applying one or more of the following constants:

- NodeFilter.SHOW_ALL — show all node types
- NodeFilter.SHOW_ELEMENT — show element nodes
- NodeFilter.SHOW_ATTRIBUTE — show attribute nodes
- NodeFilter.SHOW_TEXT — show text nodes
- NodeFilter.SHOW_CDATA_SECTION — show CData section nodes
- NodeFilter.SHOW_ENTITY_REFERENCE — show entity reference nodes
- NodeFilter.SHOW_ENTITY — show entity nodes
- NodeFilter.SHOW_PROCESSING_INSTRUCTION — show PI nodes
- NodeFilter.SHOW_COMMENT — show comment nodes
- NodeFilter.SHOW_DOCUMENT — show document nodes
- NodeFilter.SHOW_DOCUMENT_TYPE — show document type nodes
- NodeFilter.SHOW_DOCUMENT_FRAGMENT — show document fragment nodes
- NodeFilter.SHOW_NOTATION — show notation nodes

You can combine multiple values by using the bitwise OR operator:

```
var iWhatToShow = NodeFilter.SHOW_ELEMENT | NodeFilter.SHOW_TEXT;
```

The filter argument of createNodeIterator() can be used to specify a custom NodeFilter object, but can also be left null if you don't want to use it.

To create a simple NodeIterator that visits all node types, use the following:

```
var iterator = document.createNodeIterator(document, NodeFilter.SHOW_ALL, null,
false);
```

To move forward and backward in the search, use the nextNode() and previousNode() methods:

```
var node1 = iterator.nextNode();
var node2 = iterator.nextNode();
```

```
var node3 = iterator.previousNode();
alert(node1 == node3); ///outputs "true"
```

For example, suppose you wanted to list all elements contained within a specific `<div/>` inside of a specified area on an HTML page. The following code accomplishes this:

```
<html>
    <head>
        <title>NodeIterator Example</title>
        <script type="text/javascript">

           var iterator = null;

           function makeList() {
               var oDiv = document.getElementById("div1");
               iterator = document.createNodeIterator(oDiv,
NodeFilter.SHOW_ELEMENT, null, false);

               var oOutput = document.getElementById("text1");
               var oNode = iterator.nextNode();
               while (oNode) {
                   oOutput.value += oNode.tagName + "\n";
                   oNode = iterator.nextNode();
               }

           }

        </script>
    </head>
    <body>
        <div id="div1">
            <p>Hello <b>World!</b></p>
            <ul>
                <li>List item 1</li>
                <li>List item 2</li>
                <li>List item 3</li>
            </ul>
        </div>
        <textarea rows="10" cols="40" id="text1"></textarea><br />
        <input type="button" value="Make List" onclick="makeList()" />    </body>
</html>
```

When the button is clicked, the `<textarea/>` is filled with the tag names of the elements contained in `div1`:

```
P
B
UL
LI
LI
LI
```

But suppose you don't want to include `<p/>` elements in the results. This can't be accomplished just by using the `whatToShow` argument. In this case, you need a custom `NodeFilter` object.

A `NodeFilter` object has only one method: `acceptNode()`, which returns `NodeFilter.FILTER_ACCEPT` if the given node should be visited or `NodeFilter.FILTER_REJECT` if the given node should not be visited. However, you cannot create an object using the class `NodeFilter` because it is an abstract class. In Java or other languages, you must define a new subclass of `NodeFilter`, but because this is JavaScript you can't do that.

Instead, you just create an object with an `acceptNode()` method and pass that to the `createNodeIterator()` method, like this:

```
var oFilter = new Object;
oFilter.acceptNode = function (oNode) {
    //filter logic goes here
};
```

To disallow `<p/>` element nodes, you just check the `tagName` property and return `NodeFilter.FILTER_REJECT` if it's equal to `"P"`:

```
var oFilter = new Object;
oFilter.acceptNode = function (oNode) {
    return (oNode.tagName == "P") ? NodeFilter.FILTER_REJECT :
NodeFilter.FILTER_ACCEPT;
};
```

If you include this in the previous example, the code becomes the following:

```
<html>
    <head>
        <title>NodeIterator Example</title>
        <script type="text/javascript">

            var iterator = null;

            function makeList() {
                var oDiv = document.getElementById("div1");
                var oFilter = new Object;
                oFilter.acceptNode = function (oNode) {
                    return (oNode.tagName == "P") ?
                            NodeFilter.FILTER_REJECT : NodeFilter.FILTER_ACCEPT;
                };

                iterator = document.createNodeIterator(oDiv,
NodeFilter.SHOW_ELEMENT, oFilter, false);

                var oOutput = document.getElementById("text1");
                var oNode = iterator.nextNode();
                while (oNode) {
                    oOutput.value += oNode.tagName + "\n";
                    oNode = iterator.nextNode();
                }

            }
```

```
        </script>
    </head>
    <body>
        <div id="div1">
            <p>Hello <b>World!</b></p>
            <ul>
                <li>List item 1</li>
                <li>List item 2</li>
                <li>List item 3</li>
            </ul>
        </div>
        <textarea rows="10" cols="40" id="text1"></textarea><br />
        <input type="button" value="Make List" onclick="makeList()" />    </body>
</html>
```

This time when the button is clicked, the `<textarea/>` is filled with the following:

```
UL
LI
LI
LI
```

Note that both `"P"` and `"B"` have disappeared from the list. This is because filtering out the `<p/>` element eliminates it and all its ancestors from the iteration search. Because `<b/>` is a child of `<p/>`, it is also skipped.

The `NodeIterator` object presents an orderly way of traversing an entire DOM tree (or just part of it) from top to bottom. However, you may want to traverse a particular area of the tree and then look at a node's sibling or child. In that case, you use a `TreeWalker`.

TreeWalker

The `TreeWalker` is like the big brother of `NodeIterator`: It has all the same functionality (with `nextNode()` and `previousNode()`) but with added traversal methods:

- `parentNode()` — travels to the current node's parent
- `firstChild()` — travels to the first child of the current node
- `lastChild()` — travels to the last child of the current node
- `nextSibling()` — travels to the next sibling of the current node
- `previousSibling()` — travels to the previous sibling of the current node

To start, you can actually use a `TreeWalker` just like a `NodeIterator` by replacing the call to `createNodeIterator()` with a call to `createTreeWalker()`, which accepts the same arguments:

```
<html>
    <head>
        <title>TreeWalker Example</title>
        <script type="text/javascript">
```

```
            var walker = null;

            function makeList() {
                var oDiv = document.getElementById("div1");
                var oFilter = new Object;
                oFilter.acceptNode = function (oNode) {
                    return (oNode.tagName == "P") ?
                            NodeFilter.FILTER_REJECT : NodeFilter.FILTER_ACCEPT;
                };

                walker = document.createTreeWalker(oDiv, NodeFilter.SHOW_ELEMENT,
oFilter, false);

                var oOutput = document.getElementById("text1");
                var oNode = walker.nextNode();
                while (oNode) {
                    oOutput.value += oNode.tagName + "\n";
                    oNode = walker.nextNode();
                }

            }

        </script>
    </head>
    <body>
        <div id="div1">
            <p>Hello <b>World!</b></p>
            <ul>
                <li>List item 1</li>
                <li>List item 2</li>
                <li>List item 3</li>
            </ul>
        </div>
        <textarea rows="10" cols="40" id="text1"></textarea><br />
        <input type="button" value="Make List" onclick="makeList()" />    </body>
</html>
```

Naturally, the true power of a `TreeWalker` is lost on a simple example such as this; it is much more useful in cases when you don't want to go straight through the entire DOM tree. For example, suppose you only want to visit the `<li/>` elements in the HTML page shown previously. You could write a filter that only accepts elements with the tagName `"LI"`, or you could use a `TreeWalker` to do a purposive traversal:

```
<html>
    <head>
        <title>TreeWalker Example</title>
        <script type="text/javascript">

            var walker = null;

            function makeList() {
                var oDiv = document.getElementById("div1");

                walker = document.createTreeWalker(oDiv, NodeFilter.SHOW_ELEMENT,
null, false);
```

```
                var oOutput = document.getElementById("text1");
                walker.firstChild();   //go to <p>
                walker.nextSibling();  //go to <ul>
                var oNode = walker.firstChild();  //go to first <li>
                while (oNode) {
                    oOutput.value += oNode.tagName + "\n";
                    oNode = walker.nextSibling();
                }

            }

        </script>
    </head>
    <body>
        <div id="div1">
            <p>Hello <b>World!</b></p>
            <ul>
                <li>List item 1</li>
                <li>List item 2</li>
                <li>List item 3</li>
            </ul>
        </div>
        <textarea rows="10" cols="40" id="text1"></textarea><br />
        <input type="button" value="Make List" onclick="makeList()" />
    </body>
</html>
```

In this example, the `TreeWalker` is created and immediately `firstChild()` is called, which points the walker at the `<p/>` element (because `<p/>` is the first child of `div1`). When `nextSibling()` is called on the next line, the walker goes to `<ul/>`, which is the next sibling of `<p/>`. Then, `firstChild()` is called to return the first `<li/>` element under `<ul/>`. After it is inside the loop, the `nextSibling()` method is used to iterate through the rest of the `<li/>` elements.

When you click the button, the output is the following:

```
LI
LI
LI
```

The bottom line is that the `TreeWalker` is much more useful when you have an idea about the structure of the DOM tree you will be traversing, whereas a `NodeIterator` is much more practical when you don't know the structure.

Detecting DOM Conformance

As you can tell, there's a lot to the DOM. For this reason, you have a method to determine which parts of the DOM are supported by any given implementation. The object is named, ironically enough, `implementation`.

The `implementation` object is a property of a DOM Document, and is, therefore, part of the browser `document` object. The sole method of `implementation` is `hasFeature()`, which accepts two parameters: the feature to check and the version of that feature. For instance, if you want to check for support of XML DOM Level 1, the call would be:

```
var bXmlLevel1 = document.implementation.hasFeature("XML", "1.0");
```

The following table lists all the DOM features and the corresponding versions to check for:

Feature	Supported Versions	Description
Core	1.0, 2.0, 3.0	Basic DOM spelling out the use of a hierarchical tree to represent documents
XML	1.0, 2.0, 3.0	XML extension of the Core that adds support for CDATA sections, processing instructions, and entities
HTML	1.0, 2.0	HTML extension of XML that adds support for HTML-specific elements and entities
Views	2.0	Accomplishes formatting of a document based on certain styles
StyleSheets	2.0	Relating style sheets to documents
CSS	2.0	Support for Cascading Style Sheets Level 1
CSS2	2.0	Support for Cascading Style Sheets Level 2
Events	2.0	Generic DOM events
UIEvents	2.0	User interface events
MouseEvents	2.0	Events caused by the mouse (click, mouseover, and so on)
MutationEvents	2.0	Events fired when the DOM tree is changed
HTMLEvents	2.0	HTML 4.01 events
Range	2.0	Objects and methods for manipulating a range in a DOM tree
Traversal	2.0	Methods for traversing a DOM tree
LS	3.0	Loading and saving between files and DOM trees synchronously
LS-Async	3.0	Loading and saving between files and DOM trees asynchronously
Validation	3.0	Methods to modify a DOM tree and still make it valid

Although it is a nice convenience, the drawback of using `implementation.hasFeature()` is that the `implementor` gets to decide if the implementation is indeed conformant with the various parts of the DOM specification. It's very easy to make this method return `true` for any and all values, but that doesn't necessarily mean that the implementation conforms to all the specifications it claims to. At present time, the most accurate browser is Mozilla, which more or less actually does conform to the DOM specs that return `true` for this method.

DOM Level 3

DOM Level 3 was introduced as a W3C Recommendation in April of 2004. To date, no browser has fully implemented it, although Mozilla has implemented parts. It is unknown at what rate Web browsers will begin adding their missing DOM features because Internet Explorer hasn't had an update in nearly four years (meaning no changes to its level of DOM support). Mozilla has pledged to remain as compliant as possible moving forward and continues to be the leader in DOM support. However, Opera rewrote its core browser components to better support the DOM standards and has a newfound zest for keeping up-to-date with the latest technology. Even Apple's Safari browser, which is based on Konqueror, is moving forward with plans to implement as much DOM functionality as possible.

No further development is planned on the DOM after Level 3 rounded out all the missing functionality. Therefore, browsers now have a finite finish line to reach in order to achieve DOM compliance. One can only hope that they all reach it someday.

Summary

This chapter introduced the basic interfaces of the Document Object Model (DOM). You learned how the DOM organizes an XML-based document into a hierarchical tree made up of any number of nodes. You also learned about the different node type that can be present in a document as well as how to manipulate, add, and remove nodes from a DOM tree.

Additionally, this chapter covered HTML DOM-specific features, such as the migrating of attributes into object properties and table-specific methods that make building HTML easier than using the traditional DOM methods.

Finally, you learned about the DOM Traversal specification's `NodeIterator` and `TreeWalker` objects that can be used to traverse DOM trees in a logical way.

The only major parts of the DOM not covered in this chapter were events and event handling, which are covered in Chapter 9, "All about Events."

7

Regular Expressions

Once upon a time, testing for patterns contained within strings was an arduous process. It often involved using string functions such as `charAt()` and `indexOf()`. Languages such as Perl implemented a solution called regular expressions based on a Unix administration tools such as gred and ed.

Regular expressions are strings with a special syntax indicating the occurrence of specific characters or substrings within another string. These patterns range from very simple to very complicated and can be used to do anything from removing white space to validating credit card numbers.

JavaScript has natively supported regular expressions for longer than some high-powered languages, such as Java, which only introduced native regular expression support in JDK 1.4. Entire books are written on the subject of regular expressions because they can be very complicated; this chapter looks specifically at how JavaScript implements regular expressions

Regular Expression Support

JavaScript supports regular expressions through the ECMAScript `RegExp` class. The constructor for a `RegExp` object takes one or two arguments. The first (or only) argument is the string describing the pattern to match; if there is a second argument, it is a string specifying additional processing instructions.

The most basic regular expression is a regular string. For instance, to match the word `"cat"`, you can define the regular expression like this:

```
var reCat = new RegExp("cat");
```

This regular expression matches only the first occurrence of the word "cat" in a string, and it is case-sensitive. To make the regular expression match all occurrences of "cat", you can add the second argument to the constructor:

```
var reCat = new RegExp("cat", "g");
```

In this line, the second argument "g" is short for *global,* meaning that the entire string is searching for occurrences of "cat" instead of stopping after the first occurrence. If you want to make the pattern case-insensitive, you can add the character "i" to the second argument ("i" is short for *insensitive*, as in *case-insensitive*):

```
var reCat = new RegExp("cat", "gi");
```

Some regular expression literals use Perl-style syntax:

```
var reCat = /cat/gi;
```

Regular expression literals begin with a forward slash, followed by the string pattern, followed by another forward slash. If you want to specify additional processing instructions, such as "g" and "i", these come after the second forward slash (as in the previous example).

Using a RegExp object

After creating a RegExp object, you apply it to a string. You can use several methods of both RegExp and String.

The first thing you do with a regular expression is determine if a string matches the specified pattern. For this simple case, the RegExp object has a method called test(), which simply returns true if the given string (the only argument) matches the pattern and false if not:

```
var sToMatch = "cat";
var reCat = /cat/;
alert(reCat.test(sToMatch));    //outputs "true"
```

In this example, the alert outputs "true" because the pattern matches the string. Even if the pattern only occurs once in the string, it is considered a match, and test() returns true. But what if you want access to the occurrences of the pattern? For this use case, you can use the exec() method.

The RegExp exec() method, which takes a string as an argument, returns an Array containing all matches. Consider the following example:

```
var sToMatch = "a bat, a Cat, a fAt baT, a faT cat";
var reAt = /at/;
var arrMatches = reAt.exec(sToMatch);
```

Here, arrMatches contains only one item: the first instance of "at" (which is in the word "bat"). If you want to return all instances of "at", add the g option:

```
var sToMatch = "a bat, a Cat, a fAt baT, a faT cat";
var reAt = /at/g;
var arrMatches = reAt.exec(sToMatch);
```

In this code, arrMatches contains three items: the "at" from "bat", "Cat", and "cat". To return all instances of at, regardless of the case, just add the i option:

```
var sToMatch = "a bat, a Cat, a fAt baT, a faT cat";
var reAt = /at/gi;
var arrMatches = reAt.exec(sToMatch);
```

Now arrMatches contains all of the instances of "at", regardless of position or case. Note that the instances of "at" with uppercase letters will be stored in arrMatches the same way that they appear in sToMatch. Here are the contents of the arrMatches array after this code executes:

Index	Value	From
0	"at"	"bat"
1	"at"	"Cat"
2	"At"	"fAt"
3	"aT"	"baT"
4	"aT"	"faT"
5	"at"	"cat"

The String object has a method called match(), which intentionally mirrors the functionality of the RegExp object's exec() method. The main difference is that the method is called on the String object and the RegExp object is passed in as an argument:

```
var sToMatch = "a bat, a Cat, a fAt baT, a faT cat";
var reAt = /at/gi;
var arrMatches = sToMatch.match(reAt);
```

This code yields the same result as the previous example, with arrMatches containing all the same items.

A String method calls search() that acts the same way as indexOf(), but uses a RegExp object instead of a substring. The search() method returns the index of the first occurrence in the string:

```
var sToMatch = "a bat, a Cat, a fAt baT, a faT cat";
var reAt = /at/gi;
alert(sToMatch.search(reAt));    //outputs "3"
```

In this example, the alert will display "3", because the first occurrence of "at" is at position 3 in the string. Specifying the regular expression as global (with the g) has no effect when using search().

Extended string methods

Two String methods, discussed earlier in the book, also accept regular expressions as parameters. The first is the replace() method, which replaces all occurrences of a substring (the first argument) with a different string (the second argument). For example:

```
var sToChange = "The sky is red. ";
alert(sToChange.replace("red", "blue"));     //outputs "The sky is blue."
```

Here, the substring `"red"` is replaced with the string `"blue"`, making the output `"The sky is blue."` It is possible to pass in a regular expression as the first argument as well:

```
var sToChange = "The sky is red.";
var reRed = /red/;
alert(sToChange.replace(reRed, "blue"));     //outputs "The sky is blue. "
```

This code has the same result as the previous example, producing the output `"The sky is blue."`

You can also specify a function as the second argument of `replace()`. This function accepts one argument, the matching text, and returns the text that should replace it. For example:

```
var sToChange = "The sky is red.";
var reRed = /red/;
var sResultText = sToChange.replace(reRed, function(sMatch) {
     return "blue";
});

alert(sResultText);     //outputs "The sky is blue."
```

In this example, the value of `sMatch` in the function is always `"red"` (because that is the only pattern being matched). The first occurrence of `"red"` is replaced by `"blue"` because it is the value returned by the function. Using functions to deal with text replacement in conjunction with regular expressions is very powerful, enabling you to use all the facilities of JavaScript to determine what the replacement text should be.

> **Note that in the previous three examples, you are replacing only the first occurrence of `"red"` in the given string. In order to replace all occurrences, you must specify the expression as `/red/g`.**

The second method is `split()`, which splits a string into a number of substrings and returns them in an array, like this:

```
var sColor = "red,blue,yellow,green";
var arrColors = sColor.split(",");     //split at each comma
```

The previous code creates an array, `arrColors`, that contains four items, `"red"`, `"blue"`, `"yellow"`, and `"green"`. The same thing can be accomplished using a regular expression instead of the comma:

```
var sColor = "red,blue,yellow,green";
var reComma = /\,/;
var arrColors = sColor.split(reComma);     //split at each comma
```

Note the regular expression `reComma` requires a backslash before the comma character. The comma has special meaning in regular expression syntax, which you don't intend as its meaning in this case.

> **In both of these methods, you may not see the advantage of using regular expressions in place of simple strings. Keep in mind that the examples in this section of the chapter are very simple and are used just for introducing concepts; more complex patterns are discussed later and will truly show the power of using regular expressions in place of simple strings.**

Simple Patterns

The patterns used in this chapter so far have all been simple, constructed of string literals. However, a regular expression has many more parts than just matching specific characters. Metacharacters, character classes, and quantifiers are all important parts of regular expression syntax and can be used to achieve some powerful results.

Metacharacters

In the previous section you discovered that a comma has to be escaped (preceded with a backslash) to be matched correctly. That's because the comma is a *metacharacter*, which is a character that is part of regular expression syntax. Here are all the regular expression metacharacters:

```
( [ { \ ^ $ | ) ? * + .
```

Any time you want to use one of these characters inside of a regular expression, they must be escaped. So, to match a question mark, the regular expression looks like this:

```
var reQMark = /\?/;
```

Or like this:

```
var reQMark = new RegExp("\\?");
```

Did you notice the two backslashes in the second line? This is an important concept to grasp: When a regular expression is represented in this (non-literal) form, every backslash must be replaced with two backslashes because the JavaScript string parser tries to interpret `\?` the same way it tries to interpret `\n`. To ensure that this doesn't happen, place two backslashes (called *double escaping*) in front of the metacharacter in question. This little *gotcha* is why many developers prefer to use the literal syntax.

Using special characters

You can represent characters by using their literals or by specifying a character code using either their ASCII code or Unicode code. To represent a character using ASCII, you must specify a two-digit hexadecimal code preceded by `\x`. For example, the character *b* has an ASCII code of 98, which is equal to hex 62; therefore, to represent the letter *b* you could use `\x62`:

```
var sColor = "blue";
var reB = /\x62/;
alert(reB.test(sColor));    //outputs "true"
```

This code matches the letter *b* in `"blue"`.

Alternatively, you can specify the character code using octal instead of hex by including the octal characters after a backslash. For example, *b* is equal to octal 142, so this will work:

```
var sColor = "blue";
var reB = /\142/;
alert(reB.test(sColor));    //outputs "true"
```

To represent a character using Unicode, you must specify a four-digit hexadecimal representation of the character code. So *b* becomes `\u0062`:

```
var sColor = "blue";
var reB = /\u0062/;
alert(reB.test(sColor));    //outputs "true"
```

Note that to use this method of representing characters with the `RegExp` constructor, you still need to include a second backslash:

```
var sColor = "blue";
var reB = new RegExp("\\u0062")/;
alert(reB.test(sColor));    //outputs "true"
```

Additionally, there are a number of predefined special characters, which are listed in the following table:

Character	Description
`\t`	The tab character
`\n`	The new line character
`\r`	The carriage return character
`\f`	The form feed character
`\a`	The alert character
`\e`	The escape character
`\cX`	The control character corresponding to *X*
`\b`	Backspace character
`\v`	Vertical tab character
`\0`	Null character

All of these characters must also be double-escaped in order to use them with the `RegExp` constructor.

Suppose you want to remove all new line characters from a string (a common task when dealing with user-input text). You can do so like this:

```
var sNewString = sStringWithNewLines.replace(/\n/g, "");
```

Character classes

Character classes are groups of characters to test for. By enclosing characters inside of square brackets, you are effectively telling the regular expression to match the first character, the second character, the third character, or so on. For example, to match the characters a, b, and c, the character class is `[abc]`. This is called a *simple class*, because it specifies the exact characters to look for.

Simple classes

Suppose you want to match `"bat"`, `"cat"`, and `"fat"`. It is very easy to use a simple character class for this purpose:

```
var sToMatch = "a bat, a Cat, a fAt baT, a faT cat";
var reBatCatRat = /[bcf]at/gi;
var arrMatches = sToMatch.match(reBatCatRat);
```

The `arrMatches` array is now be filled with these values: `"bat"`, `"Cat"`, `"fAt"`, `"baT"`, `"faT"`, and `"cat"`. You can also include special characters inside simple classes (and any other type of character class as well). Suppose you replace the *b* character with its Unicode equivalent:

```
var sToMatch = "a bat, a Cat, a fAt baT, a faT cat";
var reBatCatRat = /[\u0062cf]at/gi;
var arrMatches = sToMatch.match(reBatCatRat);
```

This code behaves the same as it did in the previous example.

Negation classes

At times you may want to match all characters except for a select few. In this case, you can use a *negation class*, which specifies characters to exclude. For example, to match all characters except *a* and *b*, the character class is `[^ab]`. The caret (^) tells the regular expression that the character must not match the characters to follow.

Going back to the previous example, what if you only wanted to get words containing *at* but not beginning with *b* or *c*?

```
var sToMatch = "a bat, a Cat, a fAt baT, a faT cat";
var reBatCatRat = /[^bc]at/gi;
var arrMatches = sToMatch.match(reBatCatRat);
```

In this case, `arrMatches` contains `"fAt"` and `"faT"`, because these strings match the pattern of a sequence ending with *at* but not beginning with *b* or *c*.

Range classes

Up until this point, the character classes required you to type all the characters to include or exclude. Suppose that you want to match any alphabet character, but you really don't want to type every letter in the alphabet. Instead, you can use a *range class* to specify a range between *a* and *z*: `[a-z]`. The key here is the dash (-), which should be read as *through* instead of *minus* (so the class is read as *a through z* not *a minus z*).

> **Note that `[a-z]` matches only lowercase letters unless the regular expression is set to case insensitive by using the *i* option. To match only uppercase letters, you must use `[A-Z]`.**

Range classes work whenever the characters you want to test are in order by character code. Consider the following example:

```
var sToMatch = "num1, num2, num3, num4, num5, num6, num7, num8, num9";
var reOneToFour = /num[1-4]/gi;
var arrMatches = sToMatch.match(reOneToFour);
```

After execution, `arrMatches` contains four items: `"num1"`, `"num2"`, `"num3"`, and `"num4"` because they all match `num` and are followed by a character in the range `1 through 4`.

> **You can also negate range classes so as to exclude all characters within a given range. For example, to exclude characters 1 through 4, the class is `[^1-4]`.**

Combination classes

A *combination class* is a character class that is made up of several other character classes. For instance, suppose you want to match all letters `a` through `m`, numbers `1` through `4`, and the new line character. The class looks like this:

```
[a-m1-4\n]
```

Note that there are no spaces between the different internal classes.

> **JavaScript/ECMAScript doesn't support union and intersection classes as do other regular expression implementations. This means you can't make patterns such as `[a-m[p-z]]` or `[a-m[^b-e]]`.**

Predefined classes

Because some patterns are used over and over again, a set of predefined character classes is used to make it easy for you to specify some complex classes. The following table lists all the predefined classes:

Code	Equal To	Matches
`.`	`[^\n\r]`	Any character except new line and carriage return
`\d`	`[0-9]`	A digit
`\D`	`[^0-9]`	A non-digit
`\s`	`[ \t\n\x0B\f\r]`	A white-space character

Code	Equal To	Matches
`\S`	`[^\t\n\x0B\f\r]`	A non-white–space character
`\w`	`[a-zA-Z_0-9]`	A word character (all letters, all numbers, and an underscore)
`\W`	`[^a-zA-Z_0-9]`	A non-word character

Using predefined classes can make pattern matching significantly easier. Suppose you want to match three numbers, without using `\d`. Your code looks like this:

```
var sToMatch = "567 9838 abc";
var reThreeNums = /[0-9][0-9][0-9]/;
alert(reThreeNums.test(sToMatch)); //outputs "true"
```

Using `\d`, the regular expression becomes much cleaner:

```
var sToMatch = "567 9838 abc";
var reThreeNums = /\d\d\d/;
alert(reThreeNums.test(sToMatch)); //outputs "true"
```

Quantifiers

Quantifiers enable you to specify how many times a particular pattern should occur. You can specify both hard values (for example, this character should appear three times) and soft values (for example, this character should appear at least once but can repeat any number of times) when setting how many times a pattern should occur.

Simple quantifiers

The following table lists the various ways to quantify a particular pattern.

Code	Description
`?`	Either zero or one occurrence
`*`	Zero or more occurrences
`+`	One or more occurrences
`{`*n*`}`	Exactly *n* occurrences
`{`*n*`,`*m*`}`	At least *n* but no more than *m* occurrences
`{`*n*`,}`	At least *n* occurrences

For example, suppose you want to match words *bread*, *read*, or *red*. Using the question mark quantifier, you can create just one regular expression to match all three:

```
var reBreadReadOrRed = /b?rea?d/;
```

You can read this regular expression as "zero or one occurrence of *b*, followed by *r*, followed by *e*, followed by zero or one occurrence of *a*, followed by *d*." The preceding regular expression is the same as this one:

```
var reBreadReadOrRed = /b{0,1}rea{0,1}d/;
```

In this regular expression, the question mark has been replaced with curly braces. Inside the curly braces are the numbers 0, which is the minimum number of occurrences, and 1, which is the maximum. This expression reads the same way as the previous one; it's just represented differently. Both expressions are considered correct.

To illustrate the other quantifiers, suppose you had to create a regular expression to match the strings "bd", "bad", "baad", and "baaad". The following table illustrates some possible solutions and which words each match.

Regular Expression	Matches
`ba?d`	"bd", "bad"
`ba*d`	"bd", "bad", "baad", "baaad"
`ba+d`	"bad", "baad", "baad"
`ba{0,1}d`	"bd", "bad"
`ba{0,}d`	"bd", "bad", "baad", "baaad"
`ba{1,}d`	"bad", "baad", "baad"

As you can see, only two of the six expressions adequately solve the problem: `ba*d` and `ba{0,}d`. Notice that these two are exactly equal because the asterisk means *0 or more* just as *{0,}* does. Likewise, the first and fourth expressions are equal, and the third and sixth expressions are equal.

Quantifiers can also be used with character classes, so if you wanted to match the strings "bead", "baed", "beed", "baad", "bad", and "bed", the following regular expression would do so:

```
var reBeadBaedBeedBaadBedBad = /b[ae]{1,2}d/;
```

This expression says that the character class `[ae]` can appear a minimum of one time and a maximum of two times.

Greedy, reluctant, and possessive quantifiers

The three kinds of regular expression quantifiers are *greedy*, *reluctant*, and *possessive*.

A *greedy quantifier* starts by looking at the entire string for a match. If no match is found, it eliminates the last character in the string and tries again. If a match is still not found, the last character is again discarded and the process repeats until a match is found or the string is left with no characters. All the quantifiers discussed to this point have been greedy.

A *reluctant quantifier* starts by looking at the first character in the string for a match. If that character alone isn't enough, it reads in the next character, forming a string of two characters. If still no match is found, a reluctant quantifier continues to add characters from the string until either a match is found or the entire string is checked without a match. Reluctant quantifiers work in reverse of greedy quantifiers.

A *Possessive quantifier* only tries to match against the entire string. If the entire string doesn't produce a match, no further attempt is made. Possessive quantifiers are, in a manner of speaking, a one-shot deal.

What makes a quantifier greedy, reluctant, or possessive? It's really all in the use of the asterisk, question mark, and plus symbols. For example, the question mark alone (`?`) is greedy, but a question mark followed by another question mark (`??`) is reluctant. To make the question mark possessive, append a plus sign (`?+`). The following table shows all the greedy, reluctant, and possessive versions of the quantifiers you've already learned.

Greedy	Reluctant	Possessive	Description
`?`	`??`	`?+`	Zero or one occurrences
`*`	`*?`	`*+`	Zero or more occurrences
`+`	`+?`	`++`	One or more occurrences
`{n}`	`{n}?`	`{n}+`	Exactly *n* occurrences
`{n,m}`	`{n,m}?`	`{n,m}+`	At least *n* but no more than *m* occurrences
`{n,}`	`{n,}?`	`{n,}+`	At least *n* occurrences

To illustrate the differences among the three kinds of quantifiers, consider the following example:

```
var sToMatch ="abbbaabbbaaabbb1234";
var re1 = /.*bbb/g;      //greedy
var re2 = /.*?bbb/g;     //reluctant
var re3 = /.*+bbb/g;     //possessive
```

You want to match any number of letters followed by `bbb`. Ultimately, you'd like to get back as matches `"abbb"`, `"aabbb"`, and `"aaabbb"`. However, only one of the three regular expressions returns this result, can you guess which one?

If you guessed `re2`, congratulations! You now understand the difference between greedy, reluctant, and possessive quantifiers. The first regular expression, `re1`, is greedy and so it starts by looking at the whole string. Behind the scenes, this is what happens:

```
re1.test("abbbaabbbaaabbb1234");    //false - no match
re1.test("abbbaabbbaaabbb123");     //false - no match
re1.test("abbbaabbbaaabbb12");      //false - no match
re1.test("abbbaabbbaaabbb1");       //false - no match
re1.test("abbbaabbbaaabbb");        //true - match!
```

So the only result that `re1` returns is `"abbbaabbbaaabbb"`. Remember, the dot represents any character, and *b* is included, therefore `"abbbaabbbaaa"` matches the `.*` part of the expression and `"bbb"` matches the `bbb` part.

For the second regular expression, `re2`, the following takes place behind the scenes:

```
re2.test("a");                    //false - no match
re2.test("ab");                   //false - no match
re2.test("abb");                  //false - no match
re2.test("abbb");                 //true - match!
//store this result and start with next letter

re2.test("a");                    //false - no match
re2.test("aa");                   //false - no match
re2.test("aab");                  //false - no match
re2.test("aabb");                 //true - match!
re2.test("aabbb");                //true - match!
//store this result and start with next letter

re2.test("a");                    //false - no match
re2.test("aa");                   //false - no match
re2.test("aaa");                  //false - no match
re2.test("aaab");                 //true - match!
re2.test("aaabb");                //false - no match
re2.test("aaabbb");               //true - match!
//store this result and start with next letter

re2.test("1");                    //false - no match
re2.test("12");                   //false - no match
re2.test("123");                  //false - no match
re2.test("1234");                 //false - no match
//done
```

Since `re2` contains a reluctant quantifier, it returns `"abbb"`, `"aabbb"`, and `"aaabbb"`, just as you'd expect.

The final regular expression, `re3`, actually has no result because it's possessive. Here's what it does behind the scenes:

```
re3.test("abbbaabbbaaabbb1234");    //false - no match
```

Because possessive quantifiers only do one test, if that test fails, you get no result. In this case, the `"1234"` at the end of the string causes the expression not to match. If the string were simply `"abbbaabbbaaabbb"`, then `re3` would have returned the same result as `re1`.

> **Browser support for possessive quantifiers leaves much to be desired. Internet Explorer and Opera don't support possessive quantifiers and throw an error when you try to use one. Mozilla won't throw an error, but it treats possessive quantifiers as greedy.**

Complex Patterns

Regular expressions can represent simple patterns, as discussed in the previous sections, or they can represent complex patterns. Complex patterns are made up of more than just character classes and quantifiers: They are made up of groups, backreferences, lookaheads, and other powerful regular expression functions. This section introduces these concepts and more, so you can use you regular expressions to make complex string manipulations easier.

Grouping

So far in this chapter, you've learned how to deal with regular expressions on a character-by-character basis. As you might expect, certain character sequences, instead of containing just individual characters, repeat themselves. To handle character sequences, regular expressions support grouping.

Grouping is used by enclosing a set of characters, character classes, and/or quantifiers inside of a set of parentheses. For instance, suppose you wanted to match the string `"dogdog"`. Using the knowledge gained up to this point, you might predict the expression would probably look like this:

```
var reDogDog = /dogdog/g;
```

Although this is fine, it's a bit wasteful. What if you don't know how many occurrences of *dog* will be in the string? You can rewrite this expression using grouping such as the following:

```
var reDogDog = /(dog){2}/g;
```

The parentheses in this expression say that the sequence `"dog"` will occur twice in a row. But you're not limited to using curly braces with groups; you can use any and all quantifiers:

```
var re1 = /(dog)?/;     //match zero or one occurrences of "dog"
var re2 = /(dog)*/;     //match zero or more occurrences of "dog"
var re3 = /(dog)+/;     //match one or more occurrences of "dog"
```

You can even make some pretty complicated groups using a mixture of character literals, character classes, and quantifiers:

```
var re = /([bd]ad?)*/;  //match zero or more occurrences of "ba", "da", "bad", or 
"dad"
```

And don't be afraid to put groups inside of groups:

```
var re = /(mom( and dad)?)/;    //match "mom" or "mom and dad"
```

This expression says that the string `"mom"` is required, but the entire string `" and dad"` can be there zero or one times. Groups can also be used to make up for language features that JavaScript lacks.

For most programming languages with strings, a method to trim leading and trailing white space is a standard offering. JavaScript, however, has been without such a method since its introduction. Fortunately, regular expressions (with the help of groups) make it easy to create a `trim()` method for strings.

Expressions to match leading and trailing white space are very simple thanks to the `\s` character class that matches all the white space characters:

```
var reExtraSpace = /^\s+(.*?)\s+$/;
```

This regular expression looks for one or more occurrences of white space at the beginning of the string, followed by any number of additional characters (which are captured in a group), followed by one or more occurrences of white space at the end of the string. By using this in conjunction with the `String` object's `replace()` method and backreferences, you can define your own `trim()` method:

```
String.prototype.trim = function () {
    var reExtraSpace = /^\s+(.*?)\s+$/;
    return this.replace(reExtraSpace, "$1");
};
```

With this method, you can create trimmed versions of strings very easily:

```
var sTest = "   this is a test   ";
alert("[" + sTest + "]");    //outputs " [   this is a test   ] "
alert("[" + sTest.trim() + "]");    //outputs " [this is a test]"
```

Backreferences

So what do you do with groups after the expression has been evaluated? Each group is stored in a special location for later use. These special values, stored from your groups, are called *backreferences.*

Backreferences are created and numbered by the order in which opening parenthesis characters are encountered going from left to right. For example, the expression `(A?(B? (c?)))` creates three backreferences numbered 1 through 3:

1. `(A? (B? (c?)))`
2. `(B? (c?))`
3. `(c?)`

The backreferences can then be used in a couple of different ways.

First, the values of the backreferences can be obtained from the `RegExp` constructor itself by using the `test()`, `match()`, or `search()` methods. For example:

```
var sToMatch = "#123456789";
var reNumbers = /#(\d+)/;
reNumbers.test(sToMatch);
alert(RegExp.$1);             //outputs "123456789"
```

This example tries to match the pound sign followed by one or more digits. The digits are grouped so they will be stored. After the `test()` method is called, all backreferences have been stored on the `RegExp` constructor starting with `RegExp.$1`, which stores the first backreference (it continues with `RegExp.$2` if there is a second, `RegExp.$3` if there is a third, and so on). Because the group matches `"123456789"`, that is what is stored in `RegExp.$1`.

You can also include backreferences in the expression that defines the groups. You do this by using the special escape sequences `\1`, `\2`, and so on. For example:

```
var sToMatch = "dogdog";
var reDogDog = /(dog)\1/;
alert(reDogDog.test(sToMatch));     //outputs "true"
```

The regular expression `reDogDog` creates a group for the word *dog*, which is then referenced by the special escape sequence `\1`, effectively making the regular expression equal to `/dogdog/`.

Third, backreferences can be used with the `String`'s `replace()` method by using the special character sequences `$1`, `$2`, and so on. The best example to illustrate this functionality is to reverse the order of two items in a string. Suppose you want to change the string `"1234 5678"` to `"5678 1234"`. The following code accomplishes this:

```
var sToChange = "1234 5678";
var reMatch = /(\d{4}) (\d{4})/;
var sNew = sToChange.replace(reMatch, "$2 $1");
alert(sNew);     //outputs "5678 1234"
```

In this example, the regular expression has two groups each with four digits. In the second argument of the `replace()` method, `$2` is equal to `"5678"` and `$1` is equal to `"1234"`, corresponding to the order in which they appear in the expression.

Alternation

Sometimes it gets very difficult to create a pattern that correctly matches all the possibilities you have in mind. What if you need to match `"red"` and `"black"` with the same expression? These words have no characters in common, so you could write two different regular expressions and test a string against both, like this:

```
var sToMatch1 = "red";
var sToMatch2 = "black";
var reRed = /red/;
var reBlack = /black/;
alert(reRed.test(sToMatch1) || reBlack.test(sToMatch1));     //outputs "true"
alert(reRed.test(sToMatch2) || reBlack.test(sToMatch2));     //outputs "true"
```

This gets the job done, but it is a little too verbose. The other option is to use the regular expression alternation operator.

The alternation operator is the same as the ECMAScript bitwise OR, a pipe (|), and it is placed between two independent patterns, as in this example:

```
var sToMatch1 = "red";
var sToMatch2 = "black";
var reRedOrBlack = /(red|black)/;
alert(reRedOrBlack.test(sToMatch1));     //outputs "true"
alert(reRedOrBlack.test(sToMatch2));     //outputs "true"
```

In this, `reRedOrBlack` matches either `"red"` or `"black"`, and testing against each string yields `"true"`. Because the alternation is contained in a group, whichever alternative is matched is stored in `RegExp.$1` for later use (as well as being available as `\1` in the expression). In the first test, `RegExp.$1` is equal to `"red"`; in the second, it is equal to `"blue"`.

You can specify as many options as you'd like just by adding more alternatives and more alternation operators:

```
var sToMatch1 = "red";
var sToMatch2 = "black";
var sToMatch3 = "green";
var reRedOrBlack = /(red|black|green)/;
alert(reRedOrBlack.test(sToMatch1));     //outputs "true"
alert(reRedOrBlack.test(sToMatch2));     //outputs "true"
alert(reRedOrBlack.test(sToMatch3));     //outputs "true"
```

A more practical use of an OR pattern is to remove inappropriate words from user input, which can be very important in online forums. By using an OR pattern with the inappropriate words and the `replace()` method, you can easily strip out any offensive material before it is posted:

```
var reBadWords = /badword|anotherbadword/gi;
var sUserInput = "This is a string using badword1 and badword2.";
var sFinalText = sUserInput.replace(reBadWords, "****");
alert(sFinalText);  //output "This is a string using **** and ****"
```

This example specifies `"badword1"` and `"badword2"` to be inappropriate. The expression `reBadWords` uses the OR operator to specify both words (note that both the global and case-insensitive flags are set). When the `replace()` method is used, each of the inappropriate words is replaced with four asterisks (the proverbial four-letter word representation).

You can also replace inappropriate words using an asterisk to replace each letter, meaning that the replacement text contains the same number of characters as the word in question. This can be done using a function as the second argument to the `replace()` method:

```
var reBadWords = /badword|anotherbadword/gi;
var sUserInput = "This is a string using badword1 and badword2.";
var sFinalText = sUserInput.replace(reBadWords, function(sMatch) {
    return sMatch.replace(/./g, "*");
});
alert(sFinalText);  //output "This is a string using ******* and **************"
```

In this code, the function passed in as the second argument to `replace()` actually uses another regular expression. When the function is executed, `sMatch` contains one of the inappropriate words. The fastest way to replace each character with an asterisk is to use the `replace()` method on `sMatch`, specifying a pattern that matches any character (the period) and replacing it with an asterisk (note that the global flag has been set as well). Techniques such as this can ensure that inappropriate remarks cannot get posted to your online forum or bulletin board.

Non-capturing groups

Groups that create backreferences are called *capturing groups*. There are also *non-capturing groups*, which don't create backreferences. In very long regular expressions, storing backreferences slows down the matching process. By using non-capturing groups, you can have the same flexibility to match sequences of characters without incurring the overhead of storing the results.

If you want to create a non-capturing group, just add a question mark followed by a colon immediately after the opening parenthesis:

```
var sToMatch = "#123456789";
var reNumbers = /#(?:\d+)/;
reNumbers.test(sToMatch);
alert(RegExp.$1);             //outputs ""
```

The last line of this example outputs an empty string because the group is specified as non-capturing. Because of this, no backreferences can be used with the `replace()` method, accessed via the `RegExp.$x` variables, or used in the regular expression itself. Look what happens when the following code is run:

```
var sToMatch = "#123456789";
var reNumbers = /#(?:\d+)/;
alert(sToMatch.replace(reNumbers, "abcd$1"));  //outputs "abcd$1"
```

This code outputs `"abcd$1"` instead of `"abcd123456789"` because the `"$1"` code isn't recognized as a backreference; instead, it is interpreted literally.

One very popular use of regular expressions is to strip HTML tags out of text. This is typically used on discussion boards and forums to prevent visitors from including malicious or careless HTML in their postings. To strip HTML tags using regular expressions is trivial; you just need one simple expression:

```
var reTag = /<(?:.|\s)*?>/g;
```

This expression matches a less-than symbol (<) followed by any text (specified in a non-capturing group), followed by a greater-than symbol (>), which effectively matches all HTML tags. The non-capturing group is used in this case because it doesn't matter what appears between the less-than and greater-than symbols (it all must be removed). You can use the `replace()` method with this pattern to create your own `stripHTML()` method for a String:

```
String.prototype.stripHTML = function () {
    var reTag = /<(?:.|\s)*?>/g;
    return this.replace(reTag, "");
};
```

To use this method is equally simple:

```
var sTest = "<b>This would be bold</b>";
alert(sTest.stripHTML());    //outputs "This would be bold"
```

Lookaheads

Sometimes you may want to capture a particular group of characters only if they appear before another set of characters. Using lookaheads makes this process easy.

A *lookahead* is just what it sounds like: It tells the regular expression evaluator to look ahead any number of characters without losing its spot. There are both positive and negative lookaheads. Positive lookaheads check whether a certain set of characters comes next. Negative lookaheads determine if a certain set of characters does not come next.

A positive lookahead is created by enclosing a pattern between `(?=` and `)`. Note that this is not a group, even though it uses parentheses. In fact, groups don't recognize that lookaheads (either positive or negative) exist. Consider the following:

```
var sToMatch1 = "bedroom";
var sToMatch2 = "bedding";
var reBed = /(bed(?=room))/;
alert(reBed.test(sToMatch1));     //outputs "true"
alert(RegExp.$1);                 //outputs "bed"
alert(reBed.test(sToMatch2));     //outputs "false"
```

In this example, `reBed` matches `"bed"` only if it is followed by `"room"`. Therefore, it matches `sToMatch1` but not `sToMatch2`. After testing the expression against `sToMatch1`, this code outputs the contents of `RegExp.$1`, which is `"bed"`, not `"bedroom"`. The `"room"` part of the pattern is contained inside of a lookahead and so isn't returned as part of the group.

At the other end of the spectrum is a negative lookahead, created by enclosing a pattern between `(?!` and `)`. The previous example can be changed to use a negative lookahead to match `"bedding"` instead of `"bedroom"`:

```
var sToMatch1 = "bedroom";
var sToMatch2 = "bedding";
var reBed = /(bed(?!room))/;
alert(reBed.test(sToMatch1));     //outputs "false"
alert(reBed.test(sToMatch2));     //outputs "true"
alert(RegExp.$1);                 //outputs "bed"
```

Here, the expression is changed to match `"bed"` only if `"room"` doesn't follow it, so the pattern matches `"bedding"` but not `"bedroom"`. After testing against `sToMatch2`, `RegExp.$1` contains `"bed"` once again, not `"bedding"`.

> **Although JavaScript supports regular-expression lookaheads, it does not support lookbehinds, which match patterns such as `"match b only if it isn't preceded by a"`.**

Boundaries

Boundaries are used in regular expressions to indicate the location of a pattern. The following table lists the available boundaries:

Boundary	Description
`^`	Beginning of the line
`$`	End of the line
`\b`	Word boundary
`\B`	Non-word boundary

Suppose that you want to find a word, but only if it appears at the end of the line. You can use the dollar sign (`$`) to indicate this:

```
var sToMatch = "Important word is the last one.";
var reLastWord = /(\w+)\.$/;
reLastWord.test(sToMatch);
alert(RegExp.$1);          //outputs "one"
```

The regular expression in this example looks for the last word with one or more word characters preceding a period that appears before the end of the line. When this expression is run against `sToMatch`, it returns `"one"`. You can easily change this expression to get the first word in the line by using the caret (`^`) character:

```
var sToMatch = "Important word is the last one.";
var reFirstWord = /^(\w+)/;
reFirstWord.test(sToMatch);
alert(RegExp.$1);          //outputs "Important"
```

In this example, the regular expression looks for the beginning of the line followed by one or more word characters. If a non-word character is encountered, the match stops, returning `"Important"`. This example can be easily updated to use a word boundary instead:

```
var sToMatch = "Important word is the last one.";
var reFirstWord = /^(.+?)\b/;
reFirstWord.test(sToMatch);
alert(RegExp.$1);          //outputs "Important"
```

Here, the regular expression uses a reluctant quantifier to specify any character can appear one or more times before a word boundary (if a greedy quantifier is used, the expression matches the entire string).

Using the word boundary is a great way to extract words from a string.

```
var sToMatch = "First second third fourth fifth sixth"
var reWords = /\b(\S+?)\b/g;
var arrWords = sToMatch.match(reWords);
```

The regular expression `reWords` uses both the word boundary (`\b`) and the non-white space class (`\S`) to extract the words in a sentence. After execution, the `arrWords` array contains `"First"`, `"second"`, `"third"`, `"fourth"`, `"fifth"`, and `"sixth"`. Note that the beginning of the line and the end of the line, normally represented by `^` and `$`, respectively, both count as word boundaries so `"First"` and `"sixth"` are included in the result. This is not the only way to get all the words in a sentence, however.

It is, in fact, easier to use the word character class (`\w`):

```
var sToMatch = "First second third fourth fifth sixth"
var reWords = /(\w+)/g;
var arrWords = sToMatch.match(reWords);
```

This is just the latest example of how the same functionality can be achieved by different means.

Multiline mode

In the last section, you learned about the beginning and end of the line boundaries. If a string has only one line, this is very straightforward. But what if there are multiple lines contained in a string? You could use the `split()` method to separate the string into an array of lines, but then you'd have to match the regular expression against each line.

To illustrate the problem, consider the following example:

```
var sToMatch = "First second\nthird fourth\nfifth sixth"
var reLastWordOnLine = /(\w+)$/g;
var arrWords = sToMatch.match(reLastWordOnLine);
```

The regular expression in this code wants to match a word at the end of a line. The only match contained in `arrWords` is `"sixth"`, because it is at the end of the string. However, there are two line breaks in `sToMatch`, so really both `"second"` and `"fourth"` should also be returned. This is where *multiline mode* comes in.

To specify multiline mode, you need only add an *m* to the options of the regular expression. Doing so causes the `$` boundary to match the new line character (`\n`) as well as the actual end of the string. If you add this option, the previous example returns `"second"`, `"fourth"`, and `"sixth"`:

```
var sToMatch = "First second\nthird fourth\nfifth sixth"
var reLastWordOnLine = /(\w+)$/gm;
var arrWords = sToMatch.match(reLastWordOnLine);
```

Multiline mode also changes the behavior of the ^ boundary so that it matches immediately after a new line character. For example, to retrieve the strings `"First"`, `"third"`, and `"fifth"` from the string in the example, you can do this:

```
var sToMatch = "First second\nthird fourth\nfifth sixth"
var reFirstWordOnLine = /^(\w+)/gm;
var arrWords = sToMatch.match(reFirstWordOnLine);
```

Without specifying multiline mode, the expression would return only `"First"`.

Understanding the RegExp Object

A regular expression in JavaScript is an object just like everything else. You already know that regular expressions are represented by the `RegExp` object, and you also know that it has methods, which have already been discussed in this chapter. But the RegExp object also has properties, both on the constructor and on instances of RegExp. Both sets of properties change as patterns are created and tested.

Instance properties

An instance of RegExp has a number of properties that can be of use to developers:

- global — A Boolean value indicating whether or not the *g* option has been set
- ignoreCase — A Boolean value indicating whether or not the *i* option has been set
- lastIndex — An integer representing the character position where the next match will be attempted (only filled after using exec() or test(), otherwise is 0)
- multiline — A Boolean value indicating whether the *m* option has been set
- source —The string source of the regular expression. For example, the expression /[ba]*/ returns "[ba]*" as its source.

You don't typically use the global, ignoreCase, multiline, and source properties because you often already have the data they provide:

```
var reTest = /[ba]*/i;
alert(reTest.global);         //outputs "false"
alert(reTest.ignoreCase);     //outputs "true"
alert(reTest.multiline);      //outputs "false"
alert(reTest.source);         //outputs "[ba]*"
```

The really useful property is lastIndex, which tells you how far the regular expression has traveled along a string before stopping:

```
var sToMatch = "bbq is short for barbecue";
var reB = /b/g;
reB.exec(sToMatch);
alert(reB.lastIndex);     //outputs "1"
reB.exec(sToMatch);
alert(reB.lastIndex);     //outputs "2"
reB.exec(sToMatch);
alert(reB.lastIndex);     //outputs "18"
reB.exec(sToMatch);
alert(reB.lastIndex);     //outputs "21"
```

In this example, the regular expression reB is looking for the character b. When it is first executed against sToMatch, it finds the b in the first position, position 0; therefore, the lastIndex property is set to 1, which is where the matching picks up when exec() is called again. When it's called again, the expression finds the b in position 1, which sets lastIndex to 2. When called a third time, it finds the b in position 17, setting lastIndex to 18, and so on.

If you want the matching to start at the beginning again, you can always set lastIndex to 0:

```
var sToMatch = "bbq is short for barbecue";
var reB = /b/g;
```

```
reB.exec(sToMatch);
alert(reB.lastIndex);     //outputs "1"
reB.lastIndex = 0;
reB.exec(sToMatch);
alert(reB.lastIndex);     //outputs "1"
```

With the change in this code, both calls to `exec()` find the `b` in position 0, so both times, the alert displays `"1"` as the value of `lastIndex`.

Static properties

The static `RegExp` properties apply to all regular expressions in scope. These properties are also unique because they each have two names: a verbose name and a short name beginning with a dollar sign. The properties are listed in the following table.

Verbose Name	Short Name	Description
`input`	`$_`	The last string matched against (the string passed in to `exec()` or `test()`)
`lastMatch`	`$&`	The last matched characters
`lastParen`	`$+`	The last matched group
`leftContext`	`` $` ``	The substring before the last match
`multiline`	`$*`	A Boolean value specifying whether all expressions should use multiline mode
`rightContext`	`$'`	The substring after the last match

These properties can be used to tell you specific information about the match just completed using `exec()` or `test()`. Example:

```
var sToMatch = "this has been a short, short summer";
var reShort = /(s)hort/g;
reS.test(sToMatch);
alert(RegExp.input);         //outputs "this has been a short, short summer"
alert(RegExp.leftContext);   //outputs "this has been a "
alert(RegExp.rightContext);  //outputs ", short summer"
alert(RegExp.lastMatch);     //outputs "short"
alert(RegExp.lastParen);     //outputs "s"
```

This example illustrates how the various properties are used:

- The `input` property is always equal to the string being tested.
- `RegExp.leftContext` contains everything before the first instance of `"short"` and `RegExp.rightContext` contains everything after the first instance of `"short"`.
- The `lastMatch` property contains the last string that matches the entire regular expression, which is `"short"`.
- The `lastParen` property contains the last matched group, which in this case is `"s"`.

You can also use the short names for these properties, although you must use the bracket notation for most of them because some names use illegal ECMAScript syntax:

```
var sToMatch = "this has been a short, short summer";
var reShort = /(s)hort/g;
reShort.test(sToMatch);
alert(RegExp.$_);          //outputs "this has been a short, short summer"
alert(RegExp["$`"]);       //outputs "this has been a "
alert(RegExp["$'"]);       //outputs ", short summer"
alert(RegExp["$&"]);       //outputs "short"
alert(RegExp["$+"]);       //outputs "s"
```

Keep in mind that every time `exec()` or `test()` is called, all these properties (except `multiline`) are reset. Example:

```
var sToMatch1 = "this has been a short, short summer";
var sToMatch2 = "this has been a long, long summer";
var reShort = /(s)hort/g;
var reLong = /(l)ong/g;

reShort.test(sToMatch1);
alert(RegExp.$_);          //outputs "this has been a short, short summer"
alert(RegExp["$`"]);       //outputs "this has been a "
alert(RegExp["$'"]);       //outputs ", short summer"
alert(RegExp["$&"]);       //outputs "short"
alert(RegExp["$+"]);       //outputs "s"

reLong.test(sToMatch1);
alert(RegExp.$_);          //outputs "this has been a long, long summer"
alert(RegExp["$`"]);       //outputs "this has been a "
alert(RegExp["$'"]);       //outputs ", long summer"
alert(RegExp["$&"]);       //outputs "long"
alert(RegExp["$+"]);       //outputs "l"
```

Here, a second regular expression, `reLong`, is used after `reShort`. All the `RegExp` properties are set to new values.

The `multiline` property is a different type of property because it doesn't depend on the last executed match. Instead, it sets the `m` option for every regular expression in scope:

```
var sToMatch = "First second\nthird fourth\nfifth sixth"
var reLastWordOnLine = /(\w+)$/g;
RegExp.multiline = true;
var arrWords = sToMatch.match(reLastWordOnLine);
```

When this code completes execution, `arrWords` contains `"second"`, `"fourth"`, and `"sixth"`, just as if the `m` option is used in the regular expression.

> **Internet Explorer and Opera don't support `RegExp.multiline`, so it's best to use the `m` setting on individual expressions instead of trying to set this flag globally.**

Common Patterns

On the Web, regular expressions are most often used to validate user input before sending data back to the server. This is, after all, why JavaScript was initially created.

The patterns most commonly tested for on the Web are the following:

- Dates
- Credit Cards
- URLs
- E-mail Addresses

Each of these data types represents a different problem to solve. Some involve numbers only, others involve non-alphanumeric characters, and still others include characters that can be ignored. By studying these four patterns, you can sharpen your regular expression skills.

Validating dates

For many Web developers, dates are a major headache. Despite the advent of nifty layer-based, pop-up calendar systems, users really just want to be able to type in a date. Most developers cringe at the idea of letting a user manually enter a date. Many different date patterns are used around the world, not to mention the internationalized month and day names! Many sites use three form fields for date entry, usually comprised of two combo boxes (one with month names, the other with day numbers) and a text field for the year (although sometimes this, too, is a combo box). Although this approach is okay, it still leaves users wanting to type in a date, which is much faster than tabbing through three fields and clicking up or down to select an item in a combo box.

Think back to Chapter 3, "Object Basics," and the discussion about `Date.parse()`, which can parse several string patterns into millisecond representations of dates. As a quick review, these are the supported patterns:

- m/d/yyyy (such as 6/13/2004)
- mmmm d, yyyy (such as January 12, 2004)

But what if you want to allow users to enter a date in the form dd/mm/yyyy (such as 25/06/2004), which is popular in Europe? This is where regular expressions can help.

To start discerning a pattern, consider the various ways a date in the format can be represented. For instance, a month is always two digits, numbers 01 through 12; the day also must always have two digits that must be numbers 01 through 31. So, the month and day must be two-digit numbers whereas the year must have four digits. Start with a simple pattern, like this:

```
var reDate = /\d{1,2}\/\d{1,2}\/\d{4}/;
```

This pattern matches the basic format of dd/mm/yyyy, but it doesn't take into account the range of valid numbers for days or months. The result of this could be a false positive when matched against a date such as 55/44/2004. To solve this problem, consider a pattern for recording just the day: The first digit can be any number 0–3 and the second digit (which is required) can be any number 0–9. Therefore, a logical pattern for the day would be as follows:

```
var reDay = /[0-3]?[0-9]/;
```

However, this expression also matches 32 through 39, which are never valid days. By using alternation and character classes, you can come up with an all-encompassing day pattern:

```
var reDay = /0[1-9]|[12][0-9]|3[01]/;
```

This regular expression correctly matches all day values where 0 can be before any number 1 through 9, but not another 0, or the number can begin with 1 or 2 and can be followed by any number 0 through 9. Finally, the number can begin with a 3 and be followed by only a 0 or a 1. Now, you move on to formatting the month.

The month pattern is very much like the day pattern except without as many options:

```
var reMonth = /0[1-9]|1[0-2]/;
```

The pattern presented here matches all numbers 01 through 12, without exception. The last step is to create a pattern for the year.

Two modes of thinking exist about allowing users to enter the year. The first is to let them enter whatever year they want (so long as it's numerical) and let them deal with any problems associated with setting a due date in the distant future. The second is to limit the valid years to those from 1900 through 2099, with the logic being that by the time 2099 comes around, chances are any system using this code will have been put out to pasture a long time ago.

For the purpose of building a complete example, consider the second mode of thought. This can be accomplished with the following regular expression:

```
var reYear = /19|20\d{2}/;
```

All years between 1900 and 2099 will match this pattern, which starts by declaring a year must start with either 19 or 20 followed by two more digits.

Combining the patterns for the day, month, and year into one, you get:

```
var reDate = /(?:0[1-9]|[12][0-9]|3[01])\/(?:0[1-9]|1[0-2])\/(?:19|20\d{2})/;
```

Notice that the complete pattern puts each part of the date into a non-capturing group. This is necessary to ensure that the alternations don't run into one another. You can, of course, use capturing groups if you have the need.

Finally, it's much easier to use a function to check if a date is valid, so you can wrap the regular expression and the test in a function called `isValidDate()`:

```
function isValidDate(sText) {
    var reDate = /(?:0[1-9]|[12][0-9]|3[01])\/(?:0[1-9]|1[0-2])\/(?:19|20\d{2})/;
    return reDate.test(sText);
}
```

The `isValidDate()` function is then called like this:

```
alert(isValidDate("5/5/2004"));      //outputs "true"
alert(isValidDate("10/12/2009"));     //outputs "true"
alert(isValidDate("6/13/2000"));     //outputs "false"
```

Validating credit cards

If you own or operate an e-commerce site, chances are you need to deal with credit card validation. Not every incorrect credit card number is a fraudulent buyer; sometimes people just mistype or hit Enter too early. To prevent a trip back to the server, you can create some basic patterns to determine if a given credit card number is valid.

To start, consider a MasterCard credit card number, which must contain 16 digits. Of those 16 digits, the first two digits must be a number between 51 and 55. A simple pattern is the following:

```
var reMasterCard = /^5[1-5]\d{14}$/;
```

Note the use of the caret and dollar sign to indicate the start and end of input to ensure that input matches the entire string, not just part of it. This pattern is okay, but MasterCard numbers can be entered either with spaces or dashes between every four digits, such as 5555-5555-5555-5555, which should also be taken into account.

```
var reMasterCard = /^5[1-5]\d{2}[\s\-]?\d{4}[\s\-]?\d{4}[\s\-]?\d{4}$/;
```

Actual credit card number validation requires using the Luhn algorithm. The Luhn algorithm is a method to validate unique identifiers and is commonly used to validate credit card numbers. To run a number through the algorithm, however, you must extract the numbers from the user input, which means adding capturing groups:

```
var reMasterCard = /^(5[1-5]\d{2})[\s\-]?(\d{4})[\s\-]?(\d{4})[\s\-]?(\d{4})$/;
```

Now you can begin to build a function to validate a MasterCard number. The first step is to test a given string against the pattern. If the string matches, then add the four digit groups back into a string (for example, "5432-1234-5678-9012" should be converted to "5432123456789012"):

```
function isValidMasterCard(sText) {
    var reMasterCard = /^(5[1-5]\d{2})[\s\-]?(\d{4})[\s\-]?(\d{4})[\s\-]?(\d{4})$/;

    if (reMasterCard.test(sText)) {

        var sCardNum = RegExp.$1 + RegExp.$2 + RegExp.$3 + RegExp.$4;

        //Luhn algorithm here

    } else {
        return false;
    }
}
```

The Luhn algorithm has four steps. The first step is to start at the last digit in the card number and go backwards digit by digit, adding together all the digits in odd positions (1, 3, and so on). To keep track of whether the digit is in an even position, it's easiest to use a Boolean flag (which is called `bIsOdd`). The flag starts out `true`, because the last position is number 15.

It's helpful to define the Luhn algorithm in a separate function so other functions access it easily:

```
function luhnCheckSum(sCardNum) {

    var iOddSum = 0;
    var bIsOdd = true;

    for (var i=sCardNum.length-1; i >= 0; i--) {

        var iNum = parseInt(sCardNum.charAt(i));

        if (bIsOdd) {
            iOddSum += iNum;
        }

        bIsOdd = !bIsOdd;
    }
}
```

The next step is to add the digits in even positions; but there's a twist: You must first multiply the digit by two and then, if the result has two digits, you must add them together before adding to the overall sum. That's a bit wordy, so consider the credit card number 5432-1234-5678-9012. You have already added together the digits in the odd positions, which is equal to 4 + 2 + 2 + 4 + 6 + 8 + 0 + 2 = 28. In this step, you start by multiplying digits by two, which means that 5, 3, 1, 3, 5, 7, 9, and 1 will all be multiplied by two, leaving you with 10, 6, 2, 6, 10, 14, 16, and 2. Because 10, 10, 14, and 16 each have two digits, these digits must be added, so you are now left with 1, 6, 2, 6, 1, 5, and 7. It is these numbers that you add and store, which equals 28.

Putting this algorithm into code, you get this:

```
function luhnCheckSum(sCardNum) {

    var iOddSum = 0;
    var iEvenSum = 0;
    var bIsOdd = true;

    for (var i=sCardNum.length-1; i >= 0; i--) {

        var iNum = parseInt(sCardNum.charAt(i));

        if (bIsOdd) {
            iOddSum += iNum;
        } else {
            iNum = iNum * 2;
            if (iNum > 9) {
                iNum = eval(iNum.toString().split("").join("+"));
            }
            iEvenSum += iNum;
```

```
            }

            bIsOdd = !bIsOdd;
        }
    }
```

Adding the `else` statement to `if (bIsOdd)` accomplishes adding the odd position digits together. If the number is greater than 9 (which means it has two digits), the number is transformed using a variety of methods talked about earlier in the book:

1. The number is transformed into a string using `toString()`.
2. The string is then split into an array of two characters using `split()`. For example, 12 would be split into an array of `"1"` and `"2"`.
3. The array is combined with a plus sign using `join()`, so `"1"` and `"2"` become `"1+2"`.
4. The resulting string is then passed in to `eval()`, which interprets it as literal code (so `"1+2"` is added as 1+2 and returns 3).

The very last step is to add the two sums (from the even and odd position digits) and perform a modulus (remainder) operation on the result. If the number is valid, the sum is equally divisible by 10 (so it will be equal to 20, 30, 40, and so on).

```
function luhnCheckSum(sCardNum) {

    var iOddSum = 0;
    var iEvenSum = 0;
    var bIsOdd = true;

    for (var i=sCardNum.length-1; i >= 0; i--) {

        var iNum = parseInt(sCardNum.charAt(i));

        if (bIsOdd) {
            iOddSum += iNum;
        } else {
            iNum = iNum * 2;
            if (iNum > 9) {
                iNum = eval(iNum.toString().split("").join("+"));
            }
            iEvenSum += iNum;
        }

        bIsOdd = !bIsOdd;
    }

    return ((iEvenSum + iOddSum) % 10 == 0);
}
```

Add this method back into the `isValidMasterCard()` method, and you're done:

```
function isValidMasterCard(sText) {
    var reMasterCard = /^(5[1-5]\d{2})[\s\-]?(\d{4})[\s\-]?(\d{4})[\s\-]?(\d{4})$/;
```

```
        if (reMasterCard.test(sText)) {

            var sCardNum = RegExp.$1 + RegExp.$2 + RegExp.$3 + RegExp.$4;

            return luhnCheckSum(sCardNum);

        } else {
            return false;
        }
    }
```

You can now pass in MasterCard numbers like this:

```
alert(isValidMasterCard("5432 1234 5678 9012"));  //outputs "false"
alert(isValidMasterCard("5432-1234-5678-9012"));  //outputs "false"
alert(isValidMasterCard("5432123456789012"));     //outputs "false"
```

For other types of credit cards, you must know the rules governing their credit card numbers.

Visa card numbers can have either 13 or 16 digits and the first digit must always be 4, therefore, the pattern to match a Visa number (with no spaces) is:

```
var reVisa = /^(4\d{12}(?:\d{3})?)$/;
```

A couple of things to note in this pattern:

- A non-capturing group surrounds the final three digits of the card number because these three digits alone aren't of much use.
- The question mark after the non-capturing group indicates that there should be either three more digits or no more digits.

With the regular expression complete, you just extract the number and apply the Luhn algorithm:

```
function isValidVisa(sText) {
    var reVisa = /^(4\d{12}(?:\d{3})?)$/;

    if (reVisa.test(sText)) {
        return luhnCheckSum(RegExp.$1);
    } else {
        return false;
    }
}
```

> **For more on credit card number patterns and using Luhn's algorithm, see `http://www.beachnet.com/~hstiles/cardtype.html`.**

Validating e-mail addresses

Creating a pattern to match all valid e-mail addresses is quite an undertaking. The specification that defines what a valid e-mail address is, RFC 2822, defines all the following patterns as valid:

- john@somewhere.com
- john.doe@somewhere.com
- John Doe <john.doe@somewhere.com>
- "john.doe"@somewhere.com
- john@[10.1.3.1]

Realistically, however, you will probably only see the first three variations and only the first two would ever be entered by a user into a text box on your Web site (or Web application). For this reason, this section focuses on validating these two patterns.

You already know the basic format for an e-mail address is a bunch of characters (which can be numbers, letters, dashes, dots—pretty much anything but spaces), followed by an *at* (@) symbol, followed by more characters. You also know (perhaps only subconsciously), that at least one character must precede the @ and at least three must come after it, the second of which must be a period (a@a.b is a valid e-mail address, a@a and a@a. are not).

The text before and after the @ follows the same two rules: It cannot begin or end with a period, and it cannot have two periods in a row. Therefore, the regular expression is the following:

```
var reEmail = /^(?:\w+\.?)*\w+@(?:\w+\.?)*\w+$/;
```

The expression begins with a non-capturing group `(?:\w+\.?)`, which tells you that any number of word characters can be followed by zero or one periods. This can happen zero or more times (such as *a.b.c.d*), so the asterisk is used for that group.

The next part of the expression is `\w+@`, which ensures that a word character is always before the @. Immediately after that is the same non-capturing group, `(?:\w+\.?)`, which can also appear zero or more times, so the asterisk is used. The last part of the regular expression is `\w+$`, which states that a word character must be the last character on the line, disallowing e-mail addresses such as "john@doe.".

Just wrap this pattern in a function and you're ready to go:

```
function isValidEmail(sText) {
    var reEmail = /^(?:\w+\.?)*\w+@(?:\w+\.?)*\w+$/;
    return reEmail.test(sText);
}
```

This function can be called like so:

```
alert("john.doe@somewhere.com");    //outputs "true"
alert("john.doe@somewhere.");       //outputs "false"
```

Summary

This chapter introduced the JavaScript/ECMAScript implementation of regular expressions. It covered the two ways of declaring regular expressions, Perl-style and with the `RegExp` constructor, as well as the various properties and methods that can be used with them.

You learned how to create many different types of regular expressions, ranging from simply using character literals to using character classes, quantifiers, and groups. Additionally, you learned advanced regular expression techniques such as alternation, lookaheads, boundaries, and multiline mode.

Finally, the chapter showed you how to use regular expressions to solve a variety of problems, including validating dates, credit card numbers, and e-mail addresses, as well as how to remove excess white space and superfluous HTML tags from text.

8

Browser and Operating System Detection

A big part of Web programming is identifying target browsers and operating systems. Whether you are building a simple Web site or a complex Web application, this important information must be determined before any work begins. Because browsers support different levels of HTML and JavaScript, often differing across operating systems, you can save time and money by knowing your targets. This ensures that you won't include features that aren't available to your users.

Today, the challenge is even greater with the vast number of Web browsers available on so many different platforms. Windows users can use Internet Explorer, Mozilla, and Opera; Macintosh users have Internet Explorer, Mozilla, and now, Safari; Unix users can use Mozilla as well as Konqueror. Developing for all of them requires a great deal of forethought and a well-planned approach to dealing with their similarities and differences.

This chapter gives you an in-depth look at JavaScript browser and operating system detection to prepare you to develop cross-browser solutions.

The Navigator Object

The most important object in client-side browser detection is the `navigator` object. The `navigator` object is one of the earliest BOM objects implemented (beginning in Netscape Navigator 2.0 and Internet Explorer 3.0). As I mentioned in Chapter 5, "JavaScript in the Browser," it contains a number of properties that can give you information about the browser, such as the name, version, and platform.

*Although Microsoft objected to the term **`navigator`** as being specific to Netscape's browser, the **`navigator`** object has become a sort of de facto standard for providing information about a Web browser. (Microsoft does have its own object called **`clientInformation`** in addition to the **`navigator`** object, but they both provide similar data.)*

Methods of Browser Detection

Like most things in JavaScript, a few different forms of browser detection are available. Presently, two approaches to browser detection are used: object/feature detection and user-agent string detection. Each approach has its advantages and disadvantages, and you should understand proper usage of each when you are deploying your Web solution.

Object/feature detection

Object detection (also called feature detection) is a generic way of determining a browser's capabilities rather than the exact make and model of a target browser. Most JavaScript experts point to this method as the most appropriate one to use because they believe it *future proofs* scripts against changes that might make it difficult to determine the exact browser being used.

Object detection involves checking to see if a given object exists before using it. For instance, suppose you want to use the DOM method `document.getElementById()`, but you aren't sure if the browser supports it. You can use the following code:

```
if (document.getElementById) {
    //the method exists, so use it here
} else {
    //do something else
}
```

The previous code checks whether the method exists. You have learned that a property (or method) that doesn't exist returns a value of `undefined`. You may also remember that the value `undefined`, when translated into a Boolean, is equal to `false`. So, if `document.getElementById()` doesn't exist, the code skips to the `else` clause; otherwise the first set of code is executed.

> **Note that to check for the existence of a function, you must omit the parentheses. If you include the parentheses, the interpreter tries to call the function, which causes an error if the function doesn't exist.**

This method of detection should be used when you are more concerned with the capabilities of the browser than you are with its actual identity. Throughout the book, you see examples of object detection used in specific instances, whereas in other instances another method, user-agent string detection is most appropriate.

User-agent string detection

User-agent string detection is the oldest browser detection method there is. Every program that accesses a Web site is required to provide a user-agent string identifying itself to the server. Traditionally, this information was only accessible from the server in the CGI environment variable HTTP_USER_AGENT (accessed by `$ENV{'HTTP_USER_AGENT'}`). However, JavaScript introduced the `userAgent` property of the `navigator` object to provide client-side access to the user-agent string:

```
var sUserAgent = navigator.userAgent;
```

The user-agent string provides a lot of information about a Web browser, including the browser name and version. This is why Web site traffic evaluation software uses the user-agent string to determine how many of your visitors are using a particular browser or operating system. The following table displays some common browsers and their user-agent strings

Browser	User-Agent String
Internet Explorer 6.0 (Windows XP)	`Mozilla/4.0 (compatible; MSIE 6.0; Windows NT 5.1)`
Mozilla 1.5 (Windows XP)	`Mozilla/5.0 (Windows; U; Windows NT 5.1; en-US; rv:1.5) Gecko/20031007`
Firefox 0.92 (Windows XP)	`Mozilla/5.0 (Windows; U; Windows NT 5.1; en-US; rv:1.7) Gecko/20040707 Firefox/0.8`
Opera 7.54 (Windows XP)	`Opera/7.54 (Windows NT 5.1; U)`
Safari 1.25 (MacOS X)	`Mozilla/5.0 (Macintosh; U; PPC Mac OS X; en) Apple-WebKit/124 (KHTML, like Gecko) Safari/125.1`

Just a quick look at these user-agent strings reveals a lot about the browsers that are generating them. Also, you may notice just how different each browser's user-agent string is. Opera's user-agent string is pretty short whereas Safari's is extremely long. You may also notice that Internet Explorer's user-agent string looks suspiciously like Mozilla's, and Safari's says `like Gecko`. The history of how user-agent strings developed is a very revealing journey into how browsers have developed over the years.

A (Not So) Brief History of the User-Agent String

Before you delve into user-agent detection, you should understand why the detection script looks for certain parts of a user-agent string. Understanding user-agent strings can be very difficult without understanding why and how they developed. This section takes a look into the evolution of user-agent strings from early browser, such as Netscape Navigator 3.0, through modern-day browsers, such as Safari.

Netscape Navigator 3.0 and Internet Explorer 3.0

The browser that spearheaded the popularity of the Web was Netscape Navigator 3.0, which was released around 1996. The code name of the Netscape engine was *Mozilla*, and the user-agent string had a very simple format:

```
Mozilla/AppVersion (Platform; Security [; OS-or-CPU-Description])
```

For example, Netscape Navigator 3.0 running on Windows 95 would have the following user-agent string:

```
Mozilla/3.0 (Win95; I)
```

The *I* indicates that this browser has weak security, as opposed to *N* for no security or *U* for strong 128-bit security (most modern browsers have 128-bit security in the United States). When running on Windows, Netscape left off the last section that contained the operating system or CPU description.

Shortly thereafter, Microsoft introduced Internet Explorer (IE) 3.0 with a user-agent string designed to indicate full compatibility with Netscape Navigator. To accomplish this, IE's user-agent string began with the string `"Mozilla"`, so any server checking for this (as was standard at the time when checking for Netscape) would allow IE to view the page.

The user-agent string for Internet Explorer 3.0 had the following format:

```
Mozilla/2.0 (compatible; MSIE [IEVersion]; [OS])
```

For example, IE 3.02 running on Windows 95 had the following user-agent string:

```
Mozilla/2.0 (compatible; MSIE 3.02; Windows 95)
```

In this example, IEVersion is `3.02` and *OS* is `Windows 95`. For some reason, Microsoft put in `Mozilla/2.0` instead of `Mozilla/3.0`. History hasn't determined why this happened, although it was most likely an oversight. Unfortunately, this error was responsible for a long sequence of user-agent string confusion.

To understand the problem, consider the `appVersion` property of the `navigator` object, which returns everything after the first forward slash in a user-agent string. For Netscape Navigator 3.0, `appVersion` returns `3.0 (Win95; I)`. This value could be passed right into `parseFloat()` to get the browser version. However, for IE 3.0, `appVersion` returns `2.0 (compatible; MSIE 3.02; Windows 95)`. Passing that into `parseFloat()` returns 2.0, which is incorrect.

Essentially, developers wanted to be able to use one algorithm to check for 3.0-level browsers, such as this:

```
if (parseFloat(navigator.appVersion) >= 3) {
    //do 3.0-level stuff here
}
```

Because of IE's user-agent string format, this algorithm had to change:

```
if (navigator.userAgent.indexOf("MSIE") > -1) {

    //IE, now check the version
    if (navigator.userAgent.indexOf("MSIE 3.") > -1) {
        //do IE 3.0 browser stuff here
    }

} else if (parseFloat(navigator.appVersion) >= 3) {
    //do other 3.0 browser stuff here
}
```

Another problem occurs when you try to determine the operating system from the user-agent string. Because Netscape and Microsoft decided to represent the same operating system with different strings, two checks must be used for each operating system, like so:

```
var isWin95 = navigator.userAgent.indexOf("Win95") > -1 ||
navigator.userAgent.indexOf("Windows 95") > -1;
```

But this was only the beginning.

Netscape Communicator 4.0 and Internet Explorer 4.0

Netscape Communicator 4.0 was released in August of 1997 (the name changed from *Navigator* to *Communicator* for this version). Netscape remained true to its original user-agent string format:

```
Mozilla/AppVersion (Platform; Security [; OS-or-CPU-Description])
```

With version 4.0 on a Windows 98 machine, the user-agent string looked like this:

```
Mozilla/4.0 (Win98; I)
```

And as Netscape released patches and fixes for its browser, the AppVersion (accessible through `navigator.appVersion`) was incremented accordingly, as a user-agent string from version 4.79 indicates:

```
Mozilla/4.79 (Win98; I)
```

To Netscape's credit, the method for detecting the version of Netscape Communicator being used remained the same.

When Internet Explorer 4.0 was released a short time later, Microsoft did developers a favor by updating the user-agent string, changing the Mozilla version to 4.0 (which matched Netscape's latest browser). Except for this minor modification, IE remained with its original user-agent string format of:

```
Mozilla/4.0 (compatible; MSIE [IEVersion]; [OS])
```

For example, IE 4.0 running on Windows 98 returned the following user-agent string:

```
Mozilla/4.0 (compatible; MSIE 4.0; Windows 98)
```

This change allowed a very simple algorithm to be used when determining if a browser was 4.0-level:

```
if (parseFloat(navigator.appVersion) >= 4) {
    //do 4.0-level stuff here
}
```

Although IE 4.0 was the only one of the 4.0 family to be released on the Windows platform, IE 4.5 was released for MacOS shortly thereafter. This gave a glimpse into the future of IE's user-agent string format.

IE 4.5 for the MacOS stayed true to the IE 4.0 format for user-agent strings, but updated the IE version number:

```
Mozilla/4.0 (compatible; MSIE 4.5; Mac_PPC)
```

The browser version is 4.5, but the Mozilla version is 4.0, forcing developers to adjust their algorithms when detecting IE/Mac. This is important to keep in mind.

Internet Explorer 5.0 and higher

Microsoft released the next version of IE, 5.0, in 1999. As expected, the user-agent string once again presented problems. For example, IE 5.0 running on Windows NT 4.0 returned this user-agent string:

```
Mozilla/4.0 (compatible; MSIE 5.0; Windows NT)
```

Once again, the IE version was updated, but the Mozilla version was left at 4.0.

This pattern continued as versions 5.5 and 6.0 were released, ultimately leading to a 6.0 user-agent string similar to this:

```
Mozilla/4.0 (compatible; MSIE 6.0; Windows NT)
```

Because of this, it's still necessary to do a separate check for IE.

Mozilla

As part of the development of Netscape 6 (Mozilla), a short document was written up as a specification for the user-agent string. The new format represented the first departure from Netscape's original user-agent string format:

```
Mozilla/MozillaVersion ( Platform ; Security ; OS-or-CPU ; Localization information
?[; PrereleaseVersion] *[; Optional Other Comments] ) Gecko/GeckoVersion
[ApplicationProduct/ApplicationProductVersion]
```

Obviously, a lot of thought went into the user-agent string format. The individual pieces of the user-agent string are listed in the following table.

String	Required?	Description
MozillaVersion	Yes	The version of Mozilla
Platform	Yes	The type of computer system being used. Possible values: Windows, Macintosh, X11 (for Unix).
Security	Yes	The security of the browser. Possible values: N (for no security), U (for strong security), I (for weak security).
OS-or-CPU	Yes	Either the operating system the browser is being run on or the processor type of the computer running the browser. If the *Platform* is Windows, this is the version of Windows (such as WinNT, Win95, and so on). If the *Platform* is Macintosh, then this is the CPU (either 68k or PPC for PowerPC). If the *Platform* is X11, this is the Unix operating system name as obtained by the Unix command uname -sm.
Localization information	Yes	The language for the browser. Typically en-US in America.

String	Required?	Description
Prerelease Version	No	The version of the open source Mozilla code base being used in this browser. **Note:** This was not used until Mozilla 0.9.2 (Netscape 6.1).
Optional Other Comments	No	This is space for custom implementations of Mozilla to add in additional information.
GeckoVersion	Yes	The version of the Gecko rendering engine being used. This is a date in the format *yyyymmdd*.
Application Product	No	The name of the branded browser using the Mozilla code. In Netscape 6 releases, this is Netscape6; Netscape 7 changed it to just Netscape.
Application Product Version	No	The version of the branded browser using the Mozilla code.

In order to fully understand exactly what is going on, take a look at an example from Netscape 6.2.1 running on Windows XP:

```
Mozilla/5.0 (Windows; U; Windows NT 5.1; en-US; rv:0.9.4) Gecko/20011128
Netscape6/6.2.1
```

Matching up the various pieces of information:

- MozillaVersion is `5.0`.
- Platform is `Windows`.
- Security is `U`.
- OS-or-CPU is `Windows NT 5.1`
- Localization information is `en-US`.
- PrereleaseVersion is `rv:0.9.4`.
- GeckoVersion is `20011128`.
- ApplicationProduct is `Netscape 6`
- ApplicationProductVersion is `6.2.1`.

It all seems pretty straightforward, right? Then why is MozillaVersion described as *5.0* for Netscape 6.0? Although no one seems to be sure why this happened, it's safe to assume that this is a holdover from when the next planned version of Netscape was 5.0.

Netscape 7.1 was the last version of the Netscape-branded browser. AOL renewed its license agreement with Microsoft to use Internet Explorer as the AOL software's built-in browser and then it disbanded the Netscape team. The Mozilla project still releases new versions of the browser on its own, along with a friendlier version of Mozilla called Firefox.

Opera

The strongest alternative to IE and Mozilla on most operating systems is Opera.

Opera has a unique approach to its user-agent string. The basic user-agent string has the following format:

```
Opera/AppVersion (OS; Security) [Language]
```

Using Opera 7.54 on a Windows XP computer, the user-agent string is the following:

```
Opera/7.54 (Windows NT 5.1; U) [en]
```

To its credit, Opera came up with a unique user-agent string to correctly (and simply) identify its Web browser. The problem comes with another unique browser feature: the capability to disguise itself as another browser.

> **Before version 7.0, Opera could interpret the meaning of Windows operating system strings. For example, Windows NT 5.1 actually means Windows XP, so in Opera 6.0, the user agent included *Windows XP* instead of *Windows NT 5.1*. In an effort to be more standards-compliant, version 7.0 started including the officially reported operating system version instead of an interpreted one.**

Just by using a menu, Opera users can choose to identify the browser as Opera or as one of the various versions of Internet Explorer and Mozilla, including older Netscape versions. To do this, Opera changes the user-agent string it reports, as well as adapts some of its other features (including values of the `navigator` object) to try to emulate the other browsers. However, it doesn't fully emulate the browsers it disguises itself as, so it is still important to determine if a browser is actually Opera in disguise.

When Opera is being disguised as Mozilla 5.0, it returns a user-agent string that looks like this:

```
Mozilla/5.0 (Windows NT 5.1; U) Opera 7.54
```

As you can see, the application name has changed to Mozilla, and the version is now 5.0, just like Mozilla's user-agent string. Note that the string `"Opera 7.54"` is added towards the end, which still allows identification of the browser as Opera.

If Opera is disguised as Mozilla 4.78, the user-agent string looks like the following:

```
Mozilla/4.78 (Windows NT 5.1; U) Opera 7.54
```

This isn't too different from the Mozilla 5.0 identification because only the Mozilla version has changed. The same is true for Mozilla 3.0, which looks like this:

```
Mozilla/3.0 (Windows NT 5.1; U) Opera 7.54
```

If Opera is disguised as IE 6.0, the user-agent string changes to this:

```
Mozilla/4.0 (compatible; MSIE 6.0; Windows NT 5.1) Opera 7.54
```

tring are the following:

› 4.0, just like IE 6.0.

is present.

5.0's user-agent string.

er called Safari. Safari is based on another open source project nent of the Unix-based Konqueror Web browser. Apple created ng Macintosh developers with their first official Web technol- plication of the Apple Web Kit and now ships as the default By doing this, Apple instantly created a segment of the market come.

ring is the following:

```
OS-or-CPU; Language)
HTML, like Gecko) Safari/SafariVersion
```

```
OS X; en) AppleWebKit/124 (KHTML, like Gecko)
```

string. It takes into account not only the version of the oint of contention over whether to identify the browser as bility reasons. Now, all Safari browsers identify them- owsers. The Safari version has typically been the build entation of the release version number. So although nt string, there may not always be a one-to-one match.

is user-agent string is the addition of the string pre-1.0 version of Safari. Apple got a lot of pushback from developers w... as a blatant attempt to trick clients and servers into thinking Safari was actually Mozilla (as if adding Mozilla/5.0 wasn't enough). Apple's response was similar to Microsoft's when the IE user-agent string came under fire: Safari is compatible with Mozilla, and Web sites shouldn't block out Safari users because they appear to be using an unsupported browser.

Epilogue

Even though user-agent string detection can be highly effective in identifying the browser being used, it does require some research in order to get accurate results. It is because of this tumultuous history that many developers favor object/feature detection instead of user-agent string detection. However, user-agent string detection has enough practical uses to warrant learning how to use it effectively.

The Browser Detection Script

The browser detection script described in this section uses the user-agent string detection to identify the following browsers:

- Opera 4.0 and higher
- Internet Explorer 4.0 and higher
- Mozilla 0.9.2 and higher
- Safari 1.0 and higher
- Netscape Navigator 4.0 – 4.8x

In addition, the methods developed in this chapter fail gracefully and do not cause JavaScript errors in older browsers that perhaps don't support ECMAScript Edition 3 fully.

Methodology

To be practical, it is necessary to detect minimal versions of browsers instead of exact versions. For instance, this code detects exact versions:

```
if (isIE5 || isIE6) {
    //code
}
```

It may not seem like a problem now, but what if IE gets up to version 10? You would be required to keep adding to this code:

```
if (isIE5 || isIE6 || isIE7 || isIE8 || isIE9 || isIE10) {
    //code
}
```

This obviously is not optimal. However, if you test for minimal versions of browsers, the test remains the same regardless of how many future versions are released:

```
if (isMinIE5) {
    //code
}
```

This algorithm never changes, and it represents the way that the browser detection code in this chapter is developed.

First Steps

The first two steps necessary for browser detection are storing the user-agent string in a local variable and getting the reported browser version:

```
var sUserAgent = navigator.userAgent;
var fAppVersion = parseFloat(navigator.appVersion);
```

A common occurrence in user-agent strings is a version number with multiple decimal points (for example, Mozilla 0.9.2). This causes a problem when you are trying to compare browser versions. You already know that the `parseFloat()` function is used to convert a string into a floating-point number. In addition, `parseFloat()` works by going character-by-character through a string, stopping when it finds a *non-number* character. In the case of a version number with multiple decimal points, the non-number character is the second decimal point. That means using `parseFloat()` on the string `"0.9.2"` yields a floating-point value of `0.9`, completely losing `.2`. That's not good.

The best method for comparing two versions of this type of string is to compare the value after the decimal point in each. For instance, suppose you want to determine whether 0.9.2 is greater than 0.9.1. The correct way to do this is to compare 0 to 0, 9 to 9, and 2 to 1. Because 2 is greater than 1, version 0.9.2 is greater than 0.9.1. Because you perform this operation so often when detecting browser and operating system versions, it's logical to encapsulate this logic in a function.

The function `compareVersions()` accept two string versions as arguments and returns 0 if they are equal, 1 if the first version is greater than the second, and –1 if the first version is less than the second. (As you saw earlier in this book, this is a very common way of representing the relationship between two versions.)

The first step in the function is to convert each version into an array of values. This fastest way to do this is to use the `split()` method and pass in the decimal point as the character separator:

```
function compareVersions(sVersion1, sVersion2) {

    var aVersion1 = sVersion1.split(".");
    var aVersion2 = sVersion2.split(".");

}
```

At this point, `aVersion1` contains the numbers for the first version passed in, and `aVersion2` contains the number of the last version passed in. Next, it is necessary to assure that the arrays have the same number of digits; otherwise, it is very difficult to compare 0.8.4 to 0.9. To do this, first determine which array has more digits, and then add zeroes to the other array. This results in 0.9 becoming 0.9.0.

```
function compareVersions(sVersion1, sVersion2) {

    var aVersion1 = sVersion1.split(".");
    var aVersion2 = sVersion2.split(".");

    if (aVersion1.length > aVersion2.length) {
        for (var i=0; i < aVersion1.length - aVersion2.length; i++) {
            aVersion2.push("0");
        }
    } else if (aVersion1.length < aVersion2.length) {
        for (var i=0; i < aVersion2.length - aVersion1.length; i++) {
            aVersion1.push("0");
        }
    }

}
```

The highlighted block of code contains an `if` statement testing which array has more items (if they are equal, no changes are necessary). Both branches of the `if` statement do the same thing on different arrays: The first adds zeroes to `aVersion2`, whereas the second adds zeroes to `aVersion1`. After this point, both arrays have an equal number of digits.

The final step is to iterate through the arrays and compare the corresponding digits in each array:

```
function compareVersions(sVersion1, sVersion2) {

    var aVersion1 = sVersion1.split(".");
    var aVersion2 = sVersion2.split(".");

    if (aVersion1.length > aVersion2.length) {
        for (var i=0; i < aVersion1.length - aVersion2.length; i++) {
            aVersion2.push("0");
        }
    } else if (aVersion1.length < aVersion2.length) {
        for (var i=0; i < aVersion2.length - aVersion1.length; i++) {
            aVersion1.push("0");
        }
    }

    for (var i=0; i < aVersion1.length; i++) {

        if (aVersion1[i] < aVersion2[i]) {
            return -1;
        } else if (aVersion1[i] > aVersion2[i]) {
            return 1;
        }
    }

    return 0;

}
```

In this section, a `for` loop is used to compare the arrays. If a digit in `aVersion1` is less than the corresponding digit in `aVersion2`, the function automatically exits and returns –1. Likewise, if the digit in `aVersion1` is greater than the one from `aVersion2`, the function exits and returns 1. If all digits are tested and no value has been returned, the function returns 0, meaning that the two versions are equal.

This function is used like this:

```
alert(compareVersions("0.9.2", "0.9"));       //returns 1
alert(compareVersions("1.13.2", "1.14"));     //returns -1
alert(compareVersions("5.5", "5.5"));         //returns 0
```

The first line returns 1 because 0.9.2 is greater than 0.9; the second line returns –1, because 1.13.2 is less than 1.14; the third line returns 0 because the two versions are equal. This function is used extensively in this chapter.

Detecting Opera

The simplest and best way to begin browser detection is to start with the *problem* browsers, such as Opera and Safari. If you determine that a browser is not one of these, it is much easier to determine when a browser is legitimately IE or Mozilla.

To begin, consider the possible Opera user-agent strings:

```
Opera/7.54 (Windows NT 5.1; U)
Mozilla/5.0 (Windows NT 5.1; U) Opera 7.54
Mozilla/4.78 (Windows NT 5.1; U) Opera 7.54
Mozilla/3.0 (Windows NT 5.1; U) Opera 7.54
Mozilla/4.0 (compatible; MSIE 6.0; Windows NT 5.1) Opera 7.54
```

One thing that jumps out right away is that each of these strings has the word `"Opera"`. So the easiest way to determine if the browser is Opera is just to search for that string:

```
var isOpera = sUserAgent.indexOf("Opera") > -1;
```

> **You could also use a regular expression to do this check; however, regular expressions aren't supported by some earlier browsers and could cause an error when the line is executing. Using `indexOf()` ensures that this line works because the method has been included since the very first version of JavaScript.**

When you know you have an Opera browser, you can go ahead and determine the actual version. The first step is to define several variables to test for the various versions of Opera.

To determine what version of Opera is being used, you can define some variables:

```
var isMinOpera4 = isMinOpera5 = isMinOpera6 = isMinOpera7 = isMinOpera7_5 = false;
```

This code uses compound assignment to set each variable to an initial value of `false`, ensuring that if the browser is Netscape, these variables return the correct value.

Naturally, you shouldn't even bother setting these variables unless the browser has been identified as Opera, so any further evaluation of the browser version needs to take place inside of an `if` statement:

```
if (isOpera) {
    //version detection here
}
```

Because of Opera's disguises, you have two different ways to determine the browser version. If Opera is using its own user-agent string, the version is contained in `fAppVersion`, which was defined earlier. You can check to see if Opera is using a disguise by checking `navigator.appName`; if it equals `"Opera"`, then the browser isn't using a disguise.

The first step is to define a variable to hold the Opera version called `fOperaVersion`. Then, you can test to see if Opera is using a disguise. If it isn't, then just assign `fAppVersion` to `fOperaVersion`:

```
if (isOpera) {
    var fOperaVersion;
    if(navigator.appName == "Opera") {
        fOperaVersion = fAppVersion;
    }
}
```

The more difficult case is when Opera is using a disguise. For this, you need to use the user-agent string and extract the version by using a regular expression:

```
var reOperaVersion = new RegExp("Opera (\\d+\\.\\d+)");
```

This regular expression captures the Opera version, which is one or more numbers, followed by a decimal point, followed by one or more numbers. Note that this regular expression uses the constructor method and so `\d` and `\.` must be double escaped. The constructor method is used for backwards compatibility. Even if the browser proves not to be Opera and this code isn't executed, it may not support the regular expression literal style (which breaks ECMAScript Edition 1 syntax). This may cause an error.

Using this regular expression with the `test()` method stores the version in `RegExp.$1`, which is represented as `RegExp["$1"]` to ensure it won't break old-style JavaScript syntax.

```
if (isOpera) {
    var fOperaVersion;
    if(navigator.appName == "Opera") {
        fOperaVersion = fAppVersion;
    } else {
        var reOperaVersion = new RegExp("Opera (\\d+\\.\\d+)");
        reOperaVersion.test(sUserAgent);
        fOperaVersion = parseFloat(RegExp["$1"]);
    }
}
```

It's okay to use regular expressions inside this if statement because Opera has supported regular expressions almost before 4.0, the earliest version this script will detect.

At this point, the version of Opera is contained in `fOperaVersion`. The only thing left is to fill in the variables:

```
if (isOpera) {
    var fOperaVersion;
    if(navigator.appName == "Opera") {
        fOperaVersion = fAppVersion;
    } else {
        var reOperaVersion = new RegExp("Opera (\\d+\\.\\d+)");
        reOperaVersion.test(sUserAgent);
        fOperaVersion = parseFloat(RegExp["$1"]);
    }
```

```
        isMinOpera4 = fOperaVersion >= 4;
        isMinOpera5 = fOperaVersion >= 5;
        isMinOpera6 = fOperaVersion >= 6;
        isMinOpera7 = fOperaVersion >= 7;
        isMinOpera7_5 = fOperaVersion >= 7.5;
    }
```

This completes the first section of the browser detection code. With just this section, it is possible to determine if a browser is Opera; and if it is, which version. Next up is the other *problem* browser: Safari.

Detecting Konqueror/Safari

Both Konqueror and Safari are based on the KHTML project and so can be considered the same. The problem is that you have no way to tell what version of KHTML the browser is using. Therefore, you can detect whether KHTML is in use, but you still need to rely on the browser version numbers to indicate browser capabilities.

To start, take a look at a few KHTML-based user agent strings:

```
Mozilla/5.0 (compatible; Konqueror/2.2.2; SunOS)
Mozilla/5.0 (compatible; Konqueror/3; Linux; de, en_US, de_DE)
Mozilla/5.0 (compatible; Konqueror/3.1; Linux 2.4.20)
Mozilla/5.0 (compatible; Konqueror/3.2; FreeBSD) (KHTML, like Gecko)
Mozilla/5.0 (Macintosh; U; PPC Mac OS X; en) AppleWebKit/51 (like Gecko) Safari/51
Mozilla/5.0 (Macintosh; U; PPC Mac OS X; es-es) AppleWebKit/106.2 (KHTML, like
Gecko) Safari/100.1
Mozilla/5.0 (Macintosh; U; PPC Mac OS X; en) AppleWebKit/124 (KHTML, like Gecko)
Safari/125.1
```

The first four strings are from Konqueror; the last two are from Safari. Notice a few things in this mixture. First, not all the user-agent strings contain the string `"KHTML"`, so it is necessary to search for `"Konqueror"` and `"AppleWebKit"` or `"Safari"` as well as `"KHTML"`. Apple suggests that you look for `"AppleWebKit"` instead of `"Safari"` because other developers may embed the Apple Web Kit to create other browsers. Second, the Konqueror version number has no relation to either the Apple Web Kit or Safari version numbers.

So to start, you should determine if the browser is KHTML based:

```
var isKHTML = sUserAgent.indexOf("KHTML") > -1
              || sUserAgent.indexOf("Konqueror") > -1
              || sUserAgent.indexOf("AppleWebKit") > -1;
```

After `isKHTML` is set, you can then determine which KHTML browser is being used.

```
if (isKHTML) {
    isSafari = sUserAgent.indexOf("AppleWebKit") > -1;
    isKonq = sUserAgent.indexOf("Konqueror") > -1;
}
```

Next, set up the variables for the different versions of the browsers:

```
var isMinSafari1 = isMinSafari1_2 = false;
var isMinKonq2_2 = isMinKonq3 = isMinKonq3_1 = isMinKonq3_2 = false;
```

To determine the version of Safari, you can either interpret the build number or the Apple Web Kit version. As mentioned previously, Apple suggests you only use the Apple Web Kit information. Safari 1.0 uses Apple Web Kit version 85 whereas Safari 1.2 uses version 124. To extract this information, it is again necessary to use a regular expression.

Looking at the user-agent strings at the beginning of this section, you see that the Apple Web Kit version can have decimals, but doesn't always. This makes the regular expression a little bit more complicated than others in this chapter:

```
var reAppleWebKit = new RegExp("AppleWebKit\\/(\\d+(?:\\.\\d*)?)");
```

This expression uses a non-capturing group to include the decimal point and numbers after it. Other than that bit of trickery, the capturing group returns the version:

```
if (isKHTML) {
    isSafari = sUserAgent.indexOf("AppleWebKit") > -1;
    isKonq = sUserAgent.indexOf("Konqueror") > -1;

    if (isSafari) {
        var reAppleWebKit = new RegExp("AppleWebKit\\/(\\d+(?:\\.\\d*)?)");
        reAppleWebKit.test(sUserAgent);
        var fAppleWebKitVersion = parseFloat(RegExp["$1"]);

        isMinSafari1 = fAppleWebKitVersion >= 85;
        isMinSafari1_2 = fAppleWebKitVersion >= 124;
    }
}
```

To determine the version of Konqueror, the regular expression is also a little bit complicated because Konqueror uses version numbers with zero, one, or two decimal points. Because of this, multiple non-capturing groups are necessary to capture all the variations.

```
var reKonq = new RegExp("Konqueror\\/(\\d+(?:\\.\\d+(?:\\.\\d)?)?)");
```

This regular expression says to match the string `"Konqueror"`, followed by a forward slash, followed by at least one digit, which may or may not be followed by a decimal point and one or more digits, which may or may not be followed by another decimal point and one or more digits.

After this value is extracted, it must be tested using the `compareVersions()` function in order to determine the minimal browser versions:

```
if (isKHTML) {
    isSafari = sUserAgent.indexOf("AppleWebKit") > -1;
    isKonq = sUserAgent.indexOf("Konqueror") > -1;

    if (isSafari) {
```

```
            var reAppleWebKit = new RegExp("AppleWebKit\\/(\\d+(?:\\.\\d*)?)");
            reAppleWebKit.test(sUserAgent);
            var fAppleWebKitVersion = parseFloat(RegExp["$1"]);

            isMinSafari1 = fAppleWebKitVersion >= 85;
            isMinSafari1_2 = fAppleWebKitVersion >= 124;
        } else if (isKonq) {

            var reKonq = new RegExp("Konqueror\\/(\\d+(?:\\.\\d+(?:\\.\\d)?)?)");
            reKonq.test(sUserAgent);
            isMinKonq2_2 = compareVersions(RegExp["$1"], "2.2") >= 0;
            isMinKonq3 = compareVersions(RegExp["$1"], "3.0") >= 0;
            isMinKonq3_1 = compareVersions(RegExp["$1"], "3.1") >= 0;
            isMinKonq3_2 = compareVersions(RegExp["$1"], "3.2") >= 0;
        }
    }
```

In this section of the code, check whether the `compareVersions()` returns a value greater-than or equal to zero, which indicates that the versions are either equal (if it returns 0) or that the first version is greater than the second (if it returns 1).

The detection for KHTML-based browsers is complete. You can either just use `isKHTML` if you don't care which browser is being used, or use the more specific variables to determine the browser and version.

Detecting Internet Explorer

As discussed earlier, the IE user-agent string is quite unique. Recall the user-agent string for IE 6.0:

```
Mozilla/4.0 (compatible; MSIE 6.0; Windows NT)
```

When you compare this to other browsers, two parts stand out as unique: `"compatible"` and `"MSIE"`. This is the basis for detecting IE:

```
var isIE = sUserAgent.indexOf("compatible") > -1
           && sUserAgent.indexOf("MSIE") > -1;
```

This seems to be straightforward, but there is a problem. Take a second look at the Opera user-agent string when it is disguised as IE 6.0:

```
Mozilla/4.0 (compatible; MSIE 6.0; Windows NT 5.1) Opera 7.54
```

See the problem? If you check for only `"compatible"` and `"MSIE"`, then Opera disguised as IE also returns `true`. The solution is to use the `isOpera` variable (explained previously) to ensure proper detection:

```
var isIE = sUserAgent.indexOf("compatible") > -1
           && sUserAgent.indexOf("MSIE") > -1
           && !isOpera;
```

Next, define variables for the different IE versions:

```
var isMinIE4 = isMinIE5 = isMinIE5_5 = isMinIE6 = false;
```

Just as when you are determining the version of a disguised Opera, using a regular expression is the easiest way to extract IE's version from the user-agent string:

```
var reIE = new RegExp("MSIE (\\d+\\.\\d+)");
```

Once again, the pattern looks for one or more numbers, followed by a decimal point, followed by one or more numbers. Putting that expression into practice, you end up with this code:

```
if (isIE) {
    var reIE = new RegExp("MSIE (\\d+\\.\\d+);");
    reIE.test(sUserAgent);
    var fIEVersion = parseFloat(RegExp["$1"]);

    isMinIE4 = fIEVersion >= 4;
    isMinIE5 = fIEVersion >= 5;
    isMinIE5_5 = fIEVersion >= 5.5;
    isMinIE6 = fIEVersion >= 6.0;
}
```

And that's all it takes to detect Internet Explorer. This code works equally well on Windows and Macintosh. Next up is IE's main competitor, Mozilla.

Detecting Mozilla

By now, you should be familiar with how this works. Refresh your memory with the Mozilla user-agent string:

```
Mozilla/5.0 (Windows; U; Windows NT 5.1; en-US; rv:0.9.4) Gecko/20011128
Netscape6/6.2.1
```

To be thorough, take a look at the Opera user-agent string when it is disguised as Mozilla 5.0:

```
Mozilla/5.0 (Windows NT 5.1; U) Opera 7.54
```

Fortunately, you have plenty of ways to determine that this is Mozilla. The glaring item that is clearly visible is that the Mozilla user-agent string says `"Gecko"`. If you a look at the Opera Mozilla 5.0 `disguise`, the string does not appear there. Eureka! That makes this easy:

```
var isMoz = sUserAgent.indexOf("Gecko") > -1;
```

Up until recently, this was enough to determine if the browser was indeed Mozilla. However, as you saw earlier, KHTML-based browsers have a user-agent string containing the phrase `"like Gecko"`, which would also return `true` for this test. So it is necessary to make sure that the browser contains `"Gecko"` but is not KHTML-based:

```
var isMoz = sUserAgent.indexOf("Gecko") > -1
            && !isKHTML;
```

The `isMoz` variable is now accurate, so it's time to move on to the specific versions.

Depending on which browsers you plan on supporting, you may have different Mozilla versions. For instance, Netscape 7 is based on Mozilla 1.0 whereas Netscape 7.1 is based on Mozilla 1.4. So, it makes sense to test for these versions in case some users still have the Netscape-branded browsers. Mozilla 1.5 also is fairly popular, so that would be a good one to include as well:

```
var isMinMoz1 = sMinMoz1_4 = isMinMoz1_5 = false;
```

Once again, it is necessary to pull out the actual version number from the user-agent string. In Mozilla's case, the Mozilla version is located after the text `"rv:"` and can contain either one or two decimal points, so a non-capturing group is also necessary here:

```
var reMoz = new RegExp("rv:(\\d+\\.\\d+(?:\\.\\d+)?)");
```

It is easy to detect the Mozilla version if you use this value and the `compareVersions()` function:

```
if (isMoz) {
    var reMoz = new RegExp("rv:(\\d+\\.\\d+(?:\\.\\d+)?)");
    reMoz.test(sUserAgent);
    isMinMoz1 = compareVersions(RegExp["$1"], "1.0") >= 0;
    isMinMoz1_4 = compareVersions(RegExp["$1"], "1.4") >= 0;
    isMinMoz1_5 = compareVersions(RegExp["$1"], "1.5") >= 0;
}
```

The last task is to properly detect Mozilla's predecessor: the original Netscape browser.

Detecting Netscape Communicator 4.x

Although Netscape Communicator is a dinosaur in the light of today's standards-compliant browsers, it still has a pretty significant user base around the world.

To start, remember the user-agent string from Netscape Communicator 4.79:

```
Mozilla/4.79 (Win98; I)
```

As you can see, the user-agent string doesn't specifically say that this is Netscape Communicator. All other browsers include the string `"Mozilla"` in their user-agent strings, so you can't just check for that. The method for detecting Netscape Communicator 4.x is the same one used by Sherlock Holmes: If you eliminate the impossible, whatever remains, however implausible, must be true. For the purposes of browser detection, this means you must first determine all the browsers that the user isn't using:

```
var isNS4 = !isIE && !isOpera && !isMoz && !isKHTML;
```

So far so good. Next, there are three additional things to check:

1. That the string "Mozilla" is at the beginning of the user-agent string (at position 0).
2. That the value of `navigator.appName` is `"Netscape"`.
3. That the value of `navigator.appVersion` is greater-than or equal to 4.0, but less than 5.0 (this value has already been stored in the variable `fAppVersion`, created way back at the beginning of the code).

Adding these checks to the code, you get the following:

```
var isNS4 = !isIE && !isOpera && !isMoz && !isKHTML
            && (sUserAgent.indexOf("Mozilla") == 0)
            && (navigator.appName == "Netscape")
            && (fAppVersion >= 4.0 && fAppVersion < 5.0);
```

This variable accurately determines if the browser is Netscape Communicator. Next you want to determine the minimal versions. For this, you should check for version 4.0, 4.5 (which was a major release with lots of code improvements), 4.7 (another major release), and 4.8 (the last release).

```
var isMinNS4 = isMinNS4_5 = isMinNS4_7 = isMinNS4_8 = false;
```

And because Netscape Communicator stores its version number in a logical way, it is very easy to determine the values for these variables:

```
if (isNS4) {
    isMinNS4 = true;
    isMinNS4_5 = fAppVersion >= 4.5;
    isMinNS4_7 = fAppVersion >= 4.7;
    isMinNS4_8 = fAppVersion >= 4.8;
}
```

The first variable, `isMinNS4`, is automatically set to `true` because this was one of the tests performed when calculating `isNS4`. All the other minimal versions must be checked for in the normal way.

This completes the browser detection portion of the script. Next up is platform and operating system detection.

The Platform/Operating System Detection Script

Now that you have delved into the world of browser detection at great length, you must meet another challenge: figuring out the operating system on the client's machine. Even though the browser companies say that their browsers act the same across different platforms and operating systems, it is not so.

Take the case of Internet Explorer. On Windows, a powerful interface allows Microsoft ActiveX controls to be embedded in pages or used in JavaScript. The problem is that these ActiveX controls require Windows to work. So even though Microsoft says that IE on Unix and Macintosh works the same as IE on Windows, you know that this is impossible. Therefore, you must, at least, be able to tell which operating system you are dealing with in order to determine if special accommodations must be made.

Methodology

The method for determining the operating system is to start by looking for the platform. For the purposes of this book, the platforms are divided into three groups: Windows, Macintosh, and Unix.

After the platform is determined, it is then possible to determine some operating system information. For Windows or Unix, you can actually pull out the operating system version. For Macintosh, however, you cannot. The Macintosh platform provides information only if the processor is a 68000 chip or a PowerPC, although Safari includes the string `"MacOS X"` (but then again, Safari runs only on MacOS X, so is that really helpful?).

Typically, determining the platform alone is good enough for making appropriate JavaScript branches. However, sometimes additional operating system information is important, and this script provides for that.

First steps

So how does one go about determining the platform of the client user? Once again, the `navigator` object comes to the rescue with its `platform` property. But as usual, things aren't as easy as they seem. Indeed, each browser provides different information to `navigator.platform`. For instance, IE and Netscape Communicator return `"Win32"` for Windows 32-bit systems, `"Mac68k"` or `"MacPPC"` (depending on the processor) for Macintosh systems. It returns the actual name of the operating system for Unix systems. On the other hand, Mozilla returns `"Windows"` for all Windows systems, `"Macintosh"` for all Macintosh systems, and `"X11"` for all Unix systems. So you have a lot of options to check for when checking the client platform.

Checking for Windows and Macintosh systems is pretty straightforward; you just need to check for the various strings:

```
var isWin = (navigator.platform == "Win32") || (navigator.platform == "Windows");
var isMac = (navigator.platform == "Mac68K") || (navigator.platform == "MacPPC")
            || (navigator.platform == "Macintosh");
```

Because browsers return such varying values when a Unix platform is in use, it is necessary to make sure that the platform isn't Windows or Macintosh, and then check for `"X11"` as well:

```
var isUnix = (navigator.platform == "X11") && !isWin && !isMac;
```

After you know what platform you are dealing with, you can try to determine which operating system is being used.

Detecting Windows operating systems

It seems like every other year a new version of the Windows operating system is released. For a long time, Microsoft has had two separate versions of Windows: one for home use and one for business use. The home use version was called simply called Windows. The business version was called Windows NT. Little overlap occurred between the two versions. The one exception, however, was the user interface. In 2001, Microsoft decided to merge the home and business versions into a new product, Windows XP. This new operating system combines the stability and security of Windows NT with the user-friendliness of traditional Windows.

With that brief history lesson out of the way, many different versions of Windows are out there to detect:

- Windows 95
- Windows 98
- Windows NT 4.0
- Windows 2000
- Windows ME
- Windows XP

Luckily, the operating system information is included in the user-agent string, meaning that the browser gets to decide exactly what is displayed. The following table shows the different strings that are included in the user-agent string depending on the operating system being used:

	IE4+	NS4x	Mozilla	Opera pre-6	Opera 7+
Windows 95	"Windows 95"	"Win95"	"Win95"	"Windows 95"	"Windows 95"
Windows 98	"Windows 98"	"Win98"	"Win98"	"Windows 98"	"Windows 98"
Windows NT 4.0	"Windows NT"	"WinNT"	"WinNT4.0"	"Windows NT 4.0"	"Windows NT 4.0"
Windows 2000	"Windows NT 5.0"	"Windows NT 5.0"	"Windows NT 5.0"	"Windows 2000"	"Windows NT 5.0"
Windows ME	"Win 9x 4.90"	"Win 9x 4.90"	"Win 9x 4.90"	"Windows ME"	"Win 9x 4.90"
Windows XP	"Windows NT 5.1"	"Windows NT 5.1"	"Windows NT 5.1"	"Windows XP"	"Windows NT 5.1"

This task begins just like the task of detecting browser versions, by defining some variables:

```
var isWin95 = isWin98 = isWinNT4 = isWin2K = isWinME = isWinXP = false;
```

In order to determine each version of Windows, you must check the user-agent string for each value in a row from the previous table. For example, if you want to check for Windows 98, you must check the user-agent string for `"Windows 98"` and `"Win98"`, which covers all four browsers.

The easiest checks are for the Windows 95, 98, ME, 2000, and XP because they have only two values:

```
if (isWin) {
    isWin95 = sUserAgent.indexOf("Win95") > -1
              || sUserAgent.indexOf("Windows 95") > -1;
    isWin98 = sUserAgent.indexOf("Win98") > -1
              || sUserAgent.indexOf("Windows 98") > -1;
    isWinME = sUserAgent.indexOf("Win 9x 4.90") > -1
```

```
                || sUserAgent.indexOf("Windows ME") > -1;
    isWin2K = sUserAgent.indexOf("Windows NT 5.0") > -1
                || sUserAgent.indexOf("Windows 2000") > -1;
    isWinXP = sUserAgent.indexOf("Windows NT 5.1") > -1
                || sUserAgent.indexOf("Windows XP") > -1;
}
```

Windows NT 4.0 is a bit more complicated, and it is IE's fault. It includes the string `"Windows NT"` only in its user-agent string, which means that you cannot search on it alone. Why? Because IE identifies Windows 2000 as `"Windows NT 5.0"` and Windows XP as `"Windows NT 5.1"`. If you simply searched for `"Windows NT"`, the result would be true for all three, and that is not preferred behavior. So for Windows NT 4.0, you have to search for `"Windows NT"`, `"WinNT"`, `"WinNT4.0"`, and `"Windows NT 4.0"` and then make sure that it isn't the other versions of Windows:

```
if (isWin) {
    isWin95 = sUserAgent.indexOf("Win95") > -1
                || sUserAgent.indexOf("Windows 95") > -1;
    isWin98 = sUserAgent.indexOf("Win98") > -1
                || sUserAgent.indexOf("Windows 98") > -1;
    isWinME = sUserAgent.indexOf("Win 9x 4.90") > -1
                || sUserAgent.indexOf("Windows ME") > -1;
    isWin2K = sUserAgent.indexOf("Windows NT 5.0") > -1
                || sUserAgent.indexOf("Windows 2000") > -1;
    isWinXP = sUserAgent.indexOf("Windows NT 5.1") > -1
                || sUserAgent.indexOf("Windows XP") > -1;
    isWinNT4 = sUserAgent.indexOf("WinNT") > -1
                || sUserAgent.indexOf("Windows NT") > -1
                || sUserAgent.indexOf("WinNT4.0") > -1
                || sUserAgent.indexOf("Windows NT 4.0") > -1
                && (!isWinME && !isWin2K && !isWinXP);
}
```

And there you have it. You have successfully detected the various Windows operating systems.

Detecting Macintosh operating systems

Believe it or not, this is actually an easy part of the trek into the client's machine. Traditionally, Macintosh browsers would not tell you the operating system being used; the only information they provided was whether the Macintosh was using a 68000 processor or a PowerPC processor. Only recently have browsers begun to report the MacOS X as the operating system, meaning that testing for MacOS X is trustworthy if you find "MacOS X" in the user-agent string. If it's not there, however, the user could still be using MacOS X but not have a browser that reports it. For this reason, it's best to stick to the old method of checking the processor.

The following table shows the strings that each browser includes in its user-agent string to indicate the processor being used:

	IE	NS4	Mozilla	Opera
MacOS (68k)	"Mac_68000"	"68K"	"68K"	N/A
MacOS (PPC)	"Mac_PowerPC"	"PPC"	"PPC"	"Mac_PowerPC"

First step, of course, is to define the variables:

```
var isMac68K = isMacPPC = false;
```

Next, check for the various strings in the user-agent string:

```
if (isMac) {
    isMac68K = sUserAgent.indexOf("Mac_68000") > -1
               || sUserAgent.indexOf("68K") > -1;
    isMacPPC = sUserAgent.indexOf("Mac_PowerPC") > -1
               || sUserAgent.indexOf("PPC") > -1;
}
```

With this, you have covered how to determine the Macintosh platform. The only platform left is Unix.

Detecting Unix operating systems

In some ways this is the simplest of the platforms to deal with; in other ways, it is the most difficult. As you are well aware, Unix comes in many shapes and sizes. There's SunOS, HP-UX, AIX, Linux, IRIX, and many more. With each new flavor comes new versioning and different representations in a user-agent string. In order to avoid being redundant, this section focuses on specifically detecting SunOS and a few SunOS versions. Using this and the previous information you have been given, you should have sufficient knowledge to adapt this script to detect any other Unix platforms.

To determine a specific Unix platform, such as SunOS, search the user-agent string for the appropriate substring. This is actually much easier on Unix, because browsers use the Unix command `uname -sm` to include in the user-agent string. Thus, every browser shows the same string for the same operating system. Here are some examples for SunOS:

```
Mozilla/4.0 (compatible; MSIE 6.0; SunOS 5.6 sun4u)
Mozilla/5.0 (X11; U; SunOS 5.6 sun4u; en-US; rv:0.9.4) Gecko/20011128 Netscape6/6.2
Mozilla/4.7 [en] (X11; U; SunOS 5.6 sun4u)
Opera/6.0 (SunOS 5.6 sun4u; U) [en]
```

Begin by defining a few variables representing the various versions you're looking for:

```
var isSunOS = isMinSunOS4 = isMinSunOS5 = isMinSunOS5_5 = false;
```

For the SunOS, the string to search for is `"SunOS"`:

```
if (isUnix) {
    isSunOS = sUserAgent.indexOf("SunOS") > -1;
}
```

Next, extract the operating system version by using a regular expression. Because SunOS uses the two-decimal approach, the expression looks similar to the one used with Mozilla:

```
var reSunOS = new RegExp("SunOS (\\d+\\.\\d+(?:\\.\\d+)?)");
```

After the version is extracted, you must use the `compareVersions()` function (explained in a previous section) to determine the minimum operating system versions:

```
if (isUnix) {
    isSunOS = sUserAgent.indexOf("SunOS") > -1;

    if (isSunOS) {
        var reSunOS = new RegExp("SunOS (\\d+\\.\\d+(?:\\.\\d+)?)");
        reSunOS.test(sUserAgent);
        isMinSunOS4 = compareVersions(RegExp["$1"], "4.0") >= 0;
        isMinSunOS5 = compareVersions(RegExp["$1"], "5.0") >= 0;
        isMinSunOS5_5 = compareVersions(RegExp["$1"], "5.5") >= 0;
    }
}
```

With that, you can now use `isSunOS`, `isMinSunOS4`, `isMinSunOS5`, and `isMinSunOS5_5`.

Of course, all this knowledge of browsers and operating systems is useless unless you can come up with a practical way to use it.

The Full Script

The entire script is listed here for your convenience. Note that the order in which the various checks appear is very important. The complete script should be stored in a JavaScript such as detect.js.

```
var sUserAgent = navigator.userAgent;
var fAppVersion = parseFloat(navigator.appVersion);

function compareVersions(sVersion1, sVersion2) {

    var aVersion1 = sVersion1.split(".");
    var aVersion2 = sVersion2.split(".");

    if (aVersion1.length > aVersion2.length) {
        for (var i=0; i < aVersion1.length - aVersion2.length; i++) {
            aVersion2.push("0");
        }
    } else if (aVersion1.length < aVersion2.length) {
        for (var i=0; i < aVersion2.length - aVersion1.length; i++) {
            aVersion1.push("0");
        }
    }

    for (var i=0; i < aVersion1.length; i++) {

        if (aVersion1[i] < aVersion2[i]) {
            return -1;
        } else if (aVersion1[i] > aVersion2[i]) {
            return 1;
        }
```

```
    }

    return 0;

}

var isOpera = sUserAgent.indexOf("Opera") > -1;
var isMinOpera4 = isMinOpera5 = isMinOpera6 = isMinOpera7 = isMinOpera7_5 = false;

if (isOpera) {
    var fOperaVersion;
    if(navigator.appName == "Opera") {
        fOperaVersion = fAppVersion;
    } else {
        var reOperaVersion = new RegExp("Opera (\\d+\\.\\d+)");
        reOperaVersion.test(sUserAgent);
        fOperaVersion = parseFloat(RegExp["$1"]);
    }

    isMinOpera4 = fOperaVersion >= 4;
    isMinOpera5 = fOperaVersion >= 5;
    isMinOpera6 = fOperaVersion >= 6;
    isMinOpera7 = fOperaVersion >= 7;
    isMinOpera7_5 = fOperaVersion >= 7.5;
}

var isKHTML = sUserAgent.indexOf("KHTML") > -1
              || sUserAgent.indexOf("Konqueror") > -1
              || sUserAgent.indexOf("AppleWebKit") > -1;

var isMinSafari1 = isMinSafari1_2 = false;
var isMinKonq2_2 = isMinKonq3 = isMinKonq3_1 = isMinKonq3_2 = false;

if (isKHTML) {
    isSafari = sUserAgent.indexOf("AppleWebKit") > -1;
    isKonq = sUserAgent.indexOf("Konqueror") > -1;

    if (isSafari) {
        var reAppleWebKit = new RegExp("AppleWebKit\\/(\\d+(?:\\.\\d*)?)");
        reAppleWebKit.test(sUserAgent);
        var fAppleWebKitVersion = parseFloat(RegExp["$1"]);

        isMinSafari1 = fAppleWebKitVersion >= 85;
        isMinSafari1_2 = fAppleWebKitVersion >= 124;
    } else if (isKonq) {

        var reKonq = new RegExp("Konqueror\\/(\\d+(?:\\.\\d+(?:\\.\\d)?)?)");
        reKonq.test(sUserAgent);
        isMinKonq2_2 = compareVersions(RegExp["$1"], "2.2") >= 0;
        isMinKonq3 = compareVersions(RegExp["$1"], "3.0") >= 0;
        isMinKonq3_1 = compareVersions(RegExp["$1"], "3.1") >= 0;
        isMinKonq3_2 = compareVersions(RegExp["$1"], "3.2") >= 0;
    }

}
```

```
var isIE = sUserAgent.indexOf("compatible") > -1
           && sUserAgent.indexOf("MSIE") > -1
           && !isOpera;

var isMinIE4 = isMinIE5 = isMinIE5_5 = isMinIE6 = false;

if (isIE) {
    var reIE = new RegExp("MSIE (\\d+\\.\\d+);");
    reIE.test(sUserAgent);
    var fIEVersion = parseFloat(RegExp["$1"]);

    isMinIE4 = fIEVersion >= 4;
    isMinIE5 = fIEVersion >= 5;
    isMinIE5_5 = fIEVersion >= 5.5;
    isMinIE6 = fIEVersion >= 6.0;
}

var isMoz = sUserAgent.indexOf("Gecko") > -1
            && !isKHTML;

var isMinMoz1 = sMinMoz1_4 = isMinMoz1_5 = false;

if (isMoz) {
    var reMoz = new RegExp("rv:(\\d+\\.\\d+(?:\\.\\d+)?)");
    reMoz.test(sUserAgent);
    isMinMoz1 = compareVersions(RegExp["$1"], "1.0") >= 0;
    isMinMoz1_4 = compareVersions(RegExp["$1"], "1.4") >= 0;
    isMinMoz1_5 = compareVersions(RegExp["$1"], "1.5") >= 0;
}

var isNS4 = !isIE && !isOpera && !isMoz && !isKHTML
            && (sUserAgent.indexOf("Mozilla") == 0)
            && (navigator.appName == "Netscape")
            && (fAppVersion >= 4.0 && fAppVersion < 5.0);

var isMinNS4 = isMinNS4_5 = isMinNS4_7 = isMinNS4_8 = false;

if (isNS4) {
    isMinNS4 = true;
    isMinNS4_5 = fAppVersion >= 4.5;
    isMinNS4_7 = fAppVersion >= 4.7;
    isMinNS4_8 = fAppVersion >= 4.8;
}

var isWin = (navigator.platform == "Win32") || (navigator.platform == "Windows");
var isMac = (navigator.platform == "Mac68K") || (navigator.platform == "MacPPC")
            || (navigator.platform == "Macintosh");

var isUnix = (navigator.platform == "X11") && !isWin && !isMac;

var isWin95 = isWin98 = isWinNT4 = isWin2K = isWinME = isWinXP = false;
var isMac68K = isMacPPC = false;
var isSunOS = isMinSunOS4 = isMinSunOS5 = isMinSunOS5_5 = false;
```

```
if (isWin) {
    isWin95 = sUserAgent.indexOf("Win95") > -1
              || sUserAgent.indexOf("Windows 95") > -1;
    isWin98 = sUserAgent.indexOf("Win98") > -1
              || sUserAgent.indexOf("Windows 98") > -1;
    isWinME = sUserAgent.indexOf("Win 9x 4.90") > -1
              || sUserAgent.indexOf("Windows ME") > -1;
    isWin2K = sUserAgent.indexOf("Windows NT 5.0") > -1
              || sUserAgent.indexOf("Windows 2000") > -1;
    isWinXP = sUserAgent.indexOf("Windows NT 5.1") > -1
              || sUserAgent.indexOf("Windows XP") > -1;
    isWinNT4 = sUserAgent.indexOf("WinNT") > -1
              || sUserAgent.indexOf("Windows NT") > -1
              || sUserAgent.indexOf("WinNT4.0") > -1
              || sUserAgent.indexOf("Windows NT 4.0") > -1
              && (!isWinME && !isWin2K && !isWinXP);
}

if (isMac) {
    isMac68K = sUserAgent.indexOf("Mac_68000") > -1
               || sUserAgent.indexOf("68K") > -1;
    isMacPPC = sUserAgent.indexOf("Mac_PowerPC") > -1
               || sUserAgent.indexOf("PPC") > -1;
}

if (isUnix) {
    isSunOS = sUserAgent.indexOf("SunOS") > -1;

    if (isSunOS) {
        var reSunOS = new RegExp("SunOS (\\d+\\.\\d+(?:\\.\\d+)?)");
        reSunOS.test(sUserAgent);
        isMinSunOS4 = compareVersions(RegExp["$1"], "4.0") >= 0;
        isMinSunOS5 = compareVersions(RegExp["$1"], "5.0") >= 0;
        isMinSunOS5_5 = compareVersions(RegExp["$1"], "5.5") >= 0;
    }
}
```

Example: A Login Page

When creating Web applications, the first page a user sees is the login page. Most login pages have at least two fields: username and password. The purpose, of course, is to keep unauthorized users out. But what about those users who don't meet the minimum browser and system requirements for the application? They really should not be allowed to log in. The solution that many developers choose is to make a login page that does browser detection before the user is even able to enter a username, password, or any other information. For this purpose, the browser and operating system detection script works beautifully.

The first step is to decide the minimum requirements for the Web application. For example, suppose that the Web application is limited to working on Internet Explorer 5.5 and higher on Windows, Mozilla 1.0 or higher on Unix, and Safari 1.0 or higher on Macintosh (these requirements aren't exactly realistic, but make for a good example). Keep in mind a certain unspoken requirement: The browser must support JavaScript; this must also be checked.

Because you are only be scripting for two browsers, by default you should have an error message telling users that they are using the wrong browser. This displays if there is no JavaScript support, as well as if the wrong browser or wrong operating system is being used. Here's a sample:

```
<html>
    <head>
        <title>Login</title>
        <script type="text/javascript" src="detect.js"></script>
    </head>
    <body>
        <form method="post" action="DoLogin.jsp">
            <div style="border: 2px dashed blue; background-color: #dedede; height:
300px; padding: 10px">
                <div id="divError" style="position: absolute; left: 20px; top:
100px; ">
                    This Web application requires one of the following:
                    <ul>
                        <li>Internet Explorer 5.5 or higher for Windows</li>
                        <li>Mozilla 1.0 or higher for Unix</li>
                        <li>Safari 1.0 or higher for Macintosh</li>
                    </ul>
                </div>
            </div>
        </form>
    </body>
</html>
```

The highlighted section of code contains the actual error message. Note that the entire error message is contained within a `<div/>` named `divError`. Also note that `divError` has an absolute position. This is important because the login form lies directly over the error message. However, the login form is invisible at load time and is only shown if appropriate. Before getting to that, add the code for the login form right after the error message:

```
<html>
    <head>
        <title>Login</title>
        <script type="text/javascript" src="detect.js"></script>
    </head>
    <body>
        <form method="post" action="DoLogin.jsp">
            <div style="border: 2px dashed blue; background-color: #dedede; height:
300px; padding: 10px">
                <div id="divError" style="position: absolute; left: 20px; top:
100px; ">
                    This Web application requires one of the following:
                    <ul>
                        <li>Internet Explorer 5.5 or higher for Windows</li>
                        <li>Mozilla 1.0 or higher for Unix</li>
                        <li>Safari 1.0 or higher for Macintosh</li>
                    </ul>
                </div>
```

```
            <div id="divLogin" style="position: absolute; left: 20px; top:
100px; visibility: hidden">
                <table border="0" width="100%" height="100%"><tr><td
align="center">
                <table border="0">
                    <tr>
                        <td>Username:</td><td><input type="text"
name="txtUsername" /></td>
                    </tr>
                    <tr>
                        <td>Password:</td><td><input type="password"
name="txtPassword" /></td>
                    </tr>
                    <tr>
                        <td> </td><td><input type="Submit" value="Login"
/></td>
                    </tr>
                </table>
            </td></tr></table>
            </div>
        </div>
    </form>
  </body>
</html>
```

Now that the pieces are in place, you can use the detection script to check for the appropriate browsers and operating systems. The code should show the login form and hide the error message if the user has fulfilled the requirements:

```
if ((isMinIE5_5 && isWin) || (isMinMoz1 && isUnix) || (isMinSafari1 && isMac)) {
    document.getElementById("divLogin").style.visibility = "visible";
    document.getElementById("divError").style.visibility = "hidden"
}
```

This code snippet uses the style extensions of the DOM to set the CSS visibility property of each `<div/>`. Accessing the CSS style of elements using script is covered fully in Chapter 10, "Advanced DOM Techniques."

This code should be executed when the document is loaded, so it should be assigned to the `window.onload` event handler. (Don't worry too much about this now; events and event handlers are discussed in the next chapter.)

```
<html>
    <head>
        <title>Login</title>
        <script type="text/javascript" src="detect.js"></script>
        <script type="text/javascript">
            window.onload = function () {
                if ((isMinIE5_5 && isWin) || (isMinMoz1 && isUnix)
                   || (isMinSafari1 && isMac)) {

                    document.getElementById("divLogin").style.visibility = "visible";
                    document.getElementById("divError").style.visibility = "hidden"
```

```
                }
            };
        </script>
    </head>
    <body>
        <form method="post" action="DoLogin.jsp">
            <div style="border: 2px dashed blue; background-color: #dedede; height:
300px; padding: 10px">
                <div id="divError" style="position: absolute; left: 20px; top:
100px; ">
                    This Web application requires one of the following:
                    <ul>
                        <li>Internet Explorer 5.5 or higher for Windows</li>
                        <li>Mozilla 1.0 or higher for Unix</li>
                        <li>Safari 1.0 or higher for Macintosh</li>
                    </ul>
                </div>
                <div id="divLogin" style="position: absolute; left: 20px; top:
100px; visibility: hidden">
                    <table border="0" width="100%" height="100%"><tr><td
align="center">
                    <table border="0">
                        <tr>
                            <td>Username:</td><td><input type="text"
name="txtUsername" /></td>
                        </tr>
                        <tr>
                            <td>Password:</td><td><input type="password"
name="txtPassword" /></td>
                        </tr>
                        <tr>
                            <td> </td><td><input type="Submit" value="Login"
/></td>
                        </tr>
                    </table>
                </td></tr></table>
                </div>
            </div>
        </form>
    </body>
</html>
```

As a final step, you can include a special notice just in case the user doesn't have JavaScript or has disabled it. To do this, you use the `<noscript/>` tag. Any text within the `<noscript/>` tag is ignored if the browser supports JavaScript. If the browser doesn't support it (or has it disabled), then the text is displayed normally. This should be place in `divError` just after the `<ul/>` element:

```
<html>
    <head>
        <title>Login</title>
        <script type="text/javascript" src="detect.js"></script>
        <script type="text/javascript">
            window.onload = function () {
                if ((isMinIE5_5 && isWin) || (isMinMoz1 && isUnix)
```

```
                || (isMinSafari1 && isMac)) {

                document.getElementById("divLogin").style.visibility = "visible";
                document.getElementById("divError").style.visibility = "hidden"
            }
        };
    </script>
</head>
<body>
    <form method="post" action="DoLogin.jsp">
        <div style="border: 2px dashed blue; background-color: #dedede; height:
300px; padding: 10px">
            <div id="divError" style="position: absolute; left: 20px; top:
100px; ">
                This Web application requires one of the following:
                <ul>
                    <li>Internet Explorer 5.5 or higher for Windows</li>
                    <li>Mozilla 1.0 or higher for Unix</li>
                    <li>Safari 1.0 or higher for Macintosh</li>
                </ul>
                <noscript>
                  <p>This Web application also requires JavaScript (if you are
using one of the above browsers, make sure that JavaScript is enabled).</p>
                </noscript>
            </div>
            <div id="divLogin" style="position: absolute; left: 20px; top:
100px; visibility: hidden">
                <table border="0" width="100%" height="100%"><tr><td
align="center">
                <table border="0">
                    <tr>
                        <td>Username:</td><td><input type="text"
name="txtUsername" /></td>
                    </tr>
                    <tr>
                        <td>Password:</td><td><input type="password"
name="txtPassword" /></td>
                    </tr>
                    <tr>
                        <td> </td><td><input type="Submit" value="Login"
/></td>
                    </tr>
                </table>
            </td></tr></table>
            </div>
        </div>
    </form>
</body>
</html>
```

Now, all cases are covered. If the user is accessing the page with an incorrect browser, the error message is displayed (Figure 8-1) because the script will not hide it to show the login form.

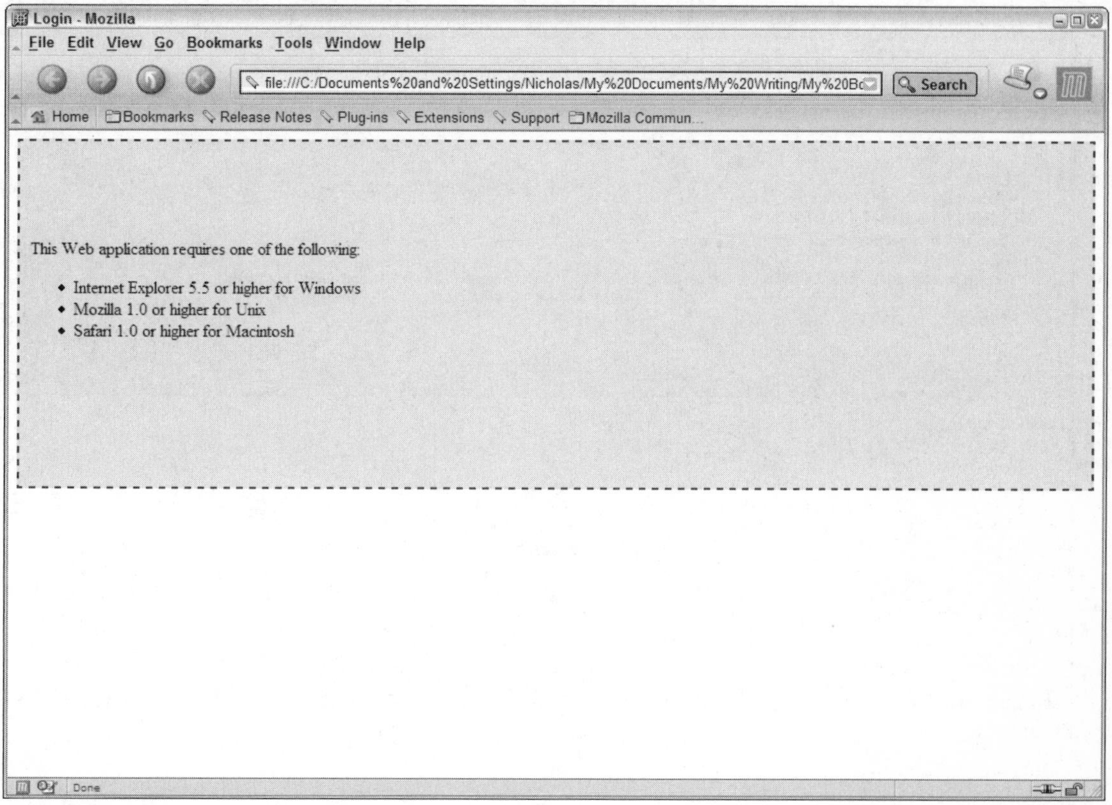

Figure 8-1

If the browser being used does not support JavaScript, the code isn't run and the additional message is displayed (Figure 8-2).

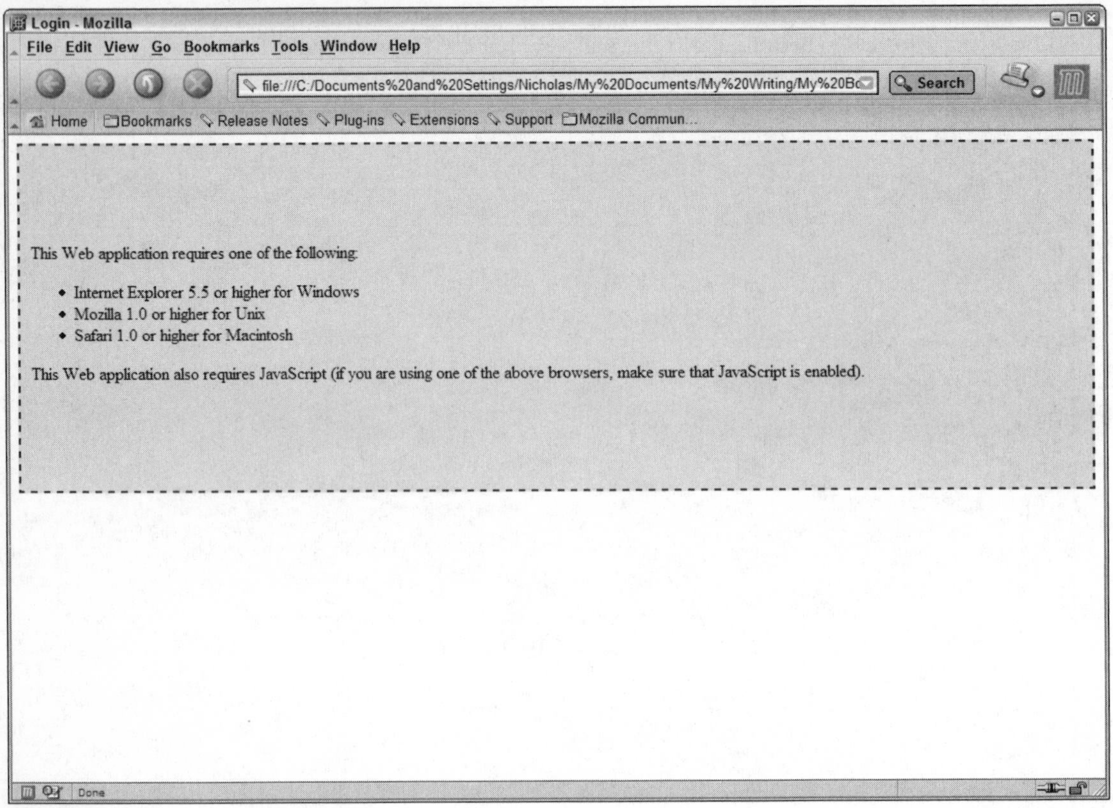
Login - Mozilla
File Edit View Go Bookmarks Tools Window Help
file:///C:/Documents%20and%20Settings/Nicholas/My%20Documents/My%20Writing/My%20Bo
Search
Home Bookmarks Release Notes Plug-ins Extensions Support Mozilla Commun...
This Web application requires one of the following:
Internet Explorer 5.5 or higher for Windows
Mozilla 1.0 or higher for Unix
Safari 1.0 or higher for Macintosh
This Web application also requires JavaScript (if you are using one of the above browsers, make sure that JavaScript is enabled).
Done

Figure 8-2

If the correct browser and platform are being used, the script is executed when the page is loaded, hiding the error message (so the user never sees it) and displaying the login form (Figure 8-3).

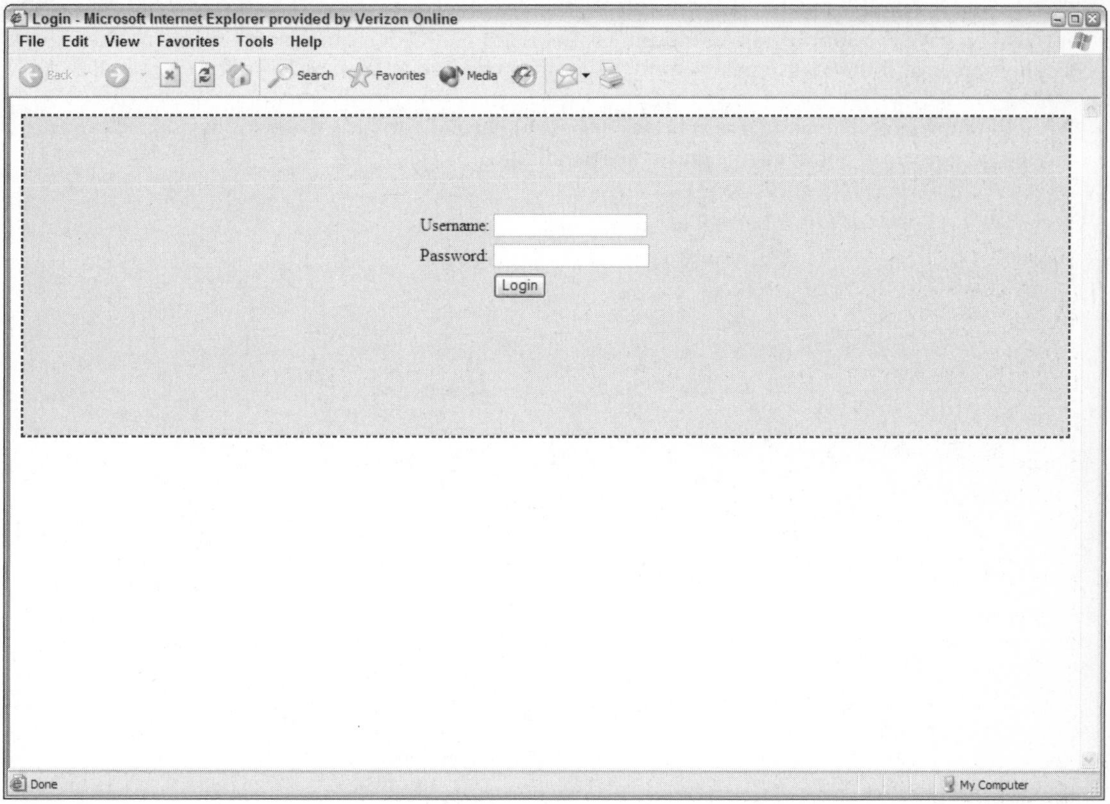

Figure 8-3

This is an important part of Web application usability. Many sites provide a generic login form that any browser can use even though the internal functionality requires a specific browser. This login page ensures that users of the Web application have the minimum requirements necessary to access all its features without making a trip back to the server.

Summary

In this chapter, you've learned how to detect browsers, platforms, and operating systems using the navigator object, and more specifically, the browser user-agent string. You built a browser and operating system detection script that accurately detects the most common Web browsers and operating systems. The detection script makes use of skills you've learned earlier in the book, such as string manipulation and regular expressions.

The chapter finished up with a practical application of the detection script: ensuring that users of a Web application have the appropriate minimum browser and platform requirements to log in. The login form displays an error if the requirements aren't met; otherwise, it displays the login form normally.

The login form example made use of JavaScript event handling to hide the error message. In the next chapter, you learn all about events and event handling.

9

All about Events

JavaScript's interaction with HTML is handled through *events* that occur when the user or browser manipulates a page. When the page loads, that's an event. When the user clicks a button, that click, too, is an event. Developers can use these events to execute coded responses, which cause buttons to close windows, messages to be displayed to users, data to be validated, and virtually any other type of response imaginable to occur.

When events first appeared in browsers (IE 3.0 and Netscape Navigator 3.0), they focused on moving some server functionality to the client. At that time, the standard method for accessing the Internet was through a dial-up connection and modem. With speeds topping out at 56 kbps, each trip to the server could turn into minutes of down time.

JavaScript is designed to solve this problem by allowing such functionality to take place on the client, saving a trip to the server. As such, most of the early events centered on the use of forms and form elements, where simple validation could be more efficiently carried out. Through the years and browser versions, events continued to grow to support more of the page.

Events Today

As discussed earlier, events are a part of the Document Object Model (DOM). Unfortunately, as also discussed previously, no events are defined in DOM Level 1 and only in a subset in DOM Level 2. The full development of events occurred in DOM Level 3, which was finalized in 2004.

With few standards to guide them early on, browsers developers were left to invent their own event models. Internet Explorer first created and implemented its own event model in version 4.0 (circa 1995) and hasn't altered it significantly since that time. Of course, no DOM standards existed at that point, which means Internet Explorer still uses what can be considered a proprietary event model. Some of its design, however, was eventually folded in the DOM.

When Netscape released its source code into the open source community under the name Mozilla, a key aim of the developers was to adhere to as many of the standards as possible. When there were gaps in the standards, the Mozilla group looked at working drafts of the standards to fill them. Because of this, Mozilla's event model closely follows the DOM standards.

Latecomers Opera and Safari have also recently embraced the DOM standard event model, leaving Internet Explorer as the main browser without proper support for the DOM event model.

But even with different DOM implementations between browsers, some basic characteristics remain the same.

Event Flow

Both the development teams for Internet Explorer 4.0 and Netscape Navigator 4.0 decided that supporting events was not enough, so each came up with its own form of *event flow*. Event flow means that more than one element on the page can respond to the same event. What happens when you click a button on the page? In reality, you are clicking the button, its container, and the page as a whole. Logically, each of the elements should be able to respond to that event in a specific order. The order of events (the event flow) is the main difference between event support in IE 4.0 and Netscape 4.0.

Event bubbling

For Internet Explorer, the solution was answered by a technique dubbed *bubbling*. The basic idea of event bubbling is that the event fires sequentially from the most specific event target to the least specific (the `document` object). For instance, you have the following page:

```
<html>
    <head>
        <title>Example</title>
    </head>
    <body onclick="handleClick()">
        <div onclick="handleClick()">Click Me</div>
    </body>
</html>
```

If a user clicks the `<div/>` element using IE 5.5, the event bubbles in the following order:

1. `<div/>`
2. `<body/>`
3. `document`

Logically, you can think of the event bubbling in this example as it is mapped in Figure 9-1.

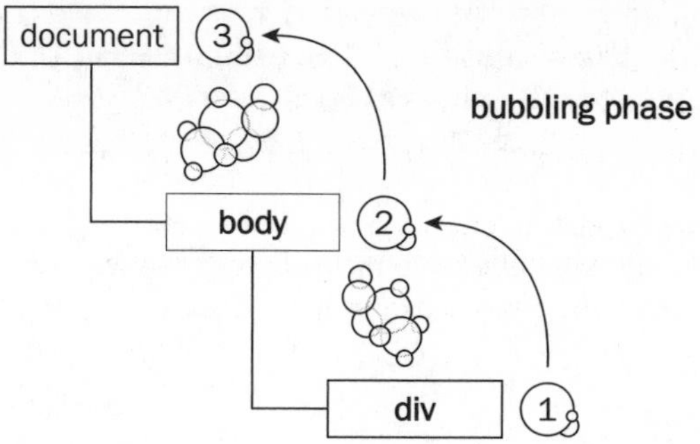

Figure 9-1

This manner of flow is called *bubbling* because, as displayed in the diagram, the event *bubbles up* the DOM hierarchy until it reaches the top.

IE changed event bubbling slightly in version 6.0 so that the `<html/>` element also receives the bubbled events, allowing for code such as this:

```
<html onclick="handleClick()">
    <head>
        <title>Example</title>
    </head>
    <body onclick="handleClick()">
        <div onclick="handleClick()">Click Me</div>
    </body>
</html>
```

In this example, a click on the page bubbles back up to the `<html/>` element, causing the previous diagram to change as shown in Figure 9-2.

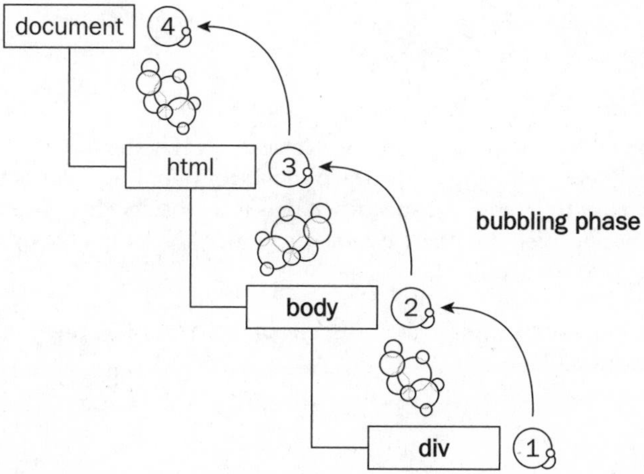

Figure 9-2

> **If you are unsure whether your users will be using IE 5.5 or IE 6.0, it is best to avoid handling events at the `<html/>` element level.**

Mozilla 1.0 and higher also supports event bubbling, but to another level. Just like IE 6.0, it supports events on the `<html/>` element. However, events bubble all the way up to the window object (which is not a part of the DOM). Using the previous example in Mozilla, clicking the `<div/>` element causes the event bubbling displayed in Figure 9-3.

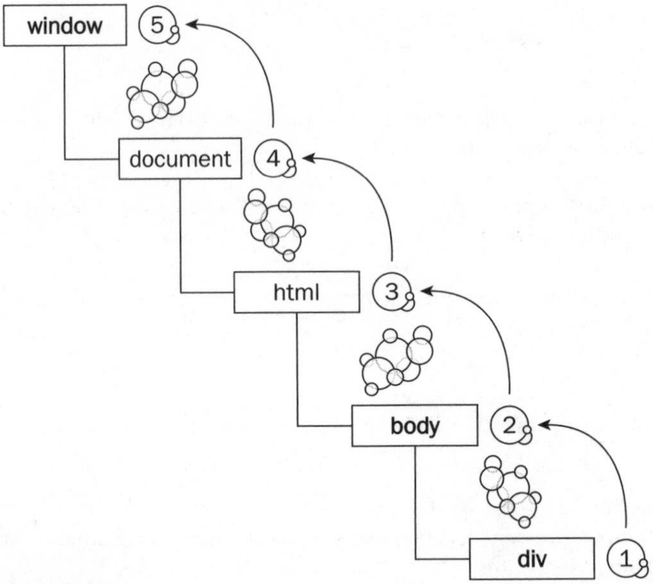

Figure 9-3

Event capturing

While Internet Explorer 4.0 used event bubbling, Netscape Navigator 4.0 used an alternate solution called *event capturing*. Event capturing is just the opposite of bubbling; events fire from the least-specific object (the `document` object) to the most specific (it was also possible to capture events at the window level, but that has to be specified explicitly by the developer). Netscape Navigator also doesn't expose many elements on the page to events.

Referring again to the previous example, if a user clicks the `<div/>` element using Netscape 4.x, the event takes the following path:

1. `document`
2. `<div/>`

Some have also called this the *top-down event model* because it works from the top of the DOM hierarchy to the bottom (see Figure 9-4).

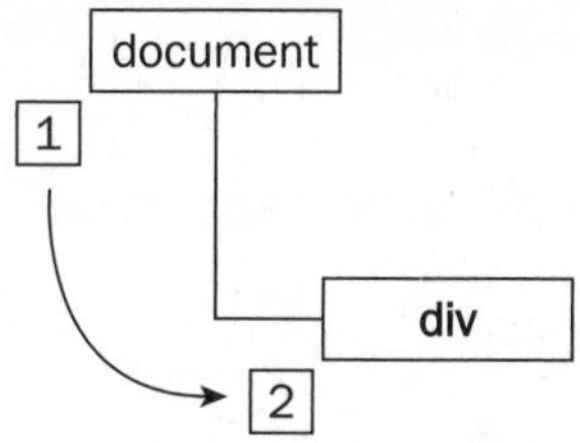

Figure 9-4

DOM event flow

The DOM supports both event capturing and event bubbling, but event capturing occurs first. Both event flows hit all the objects in the DOM, beginning and ending with the `document` object (most standards-compliant browsers continue capturing/bubbling up to the `window` object).

Consider once again the simple example shown earlier. When the `<div/>` element is clicked in a DOM-compliant browser, the event flow proceeds as shown in Figure 9-5.

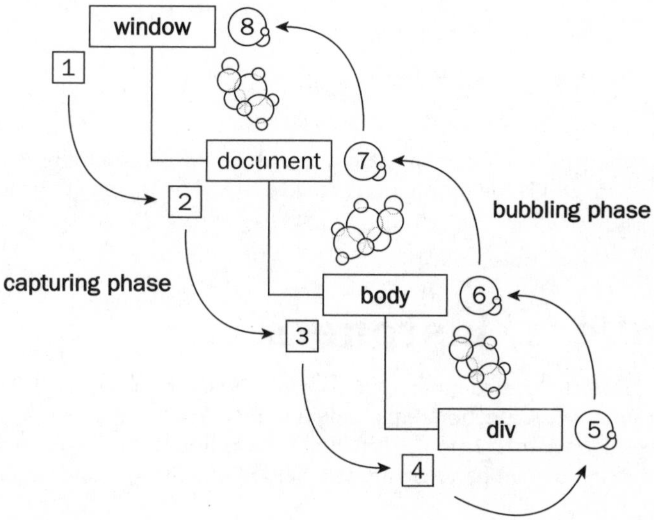

Figure 9-5

Note that because the target of the event (the `<div/>` element) is the most specific element (and therefore, deepest in the DOM tree), it actually receives the event two times in a row, once in the capturing phase and once in the bubbling phase.

A unique feature of the DOM event model is that text nodes fire events as well (this is not so in Internet Explorer). So if you click the text *Click Me* in the example, the event flow actually looks like Figure 9-6.

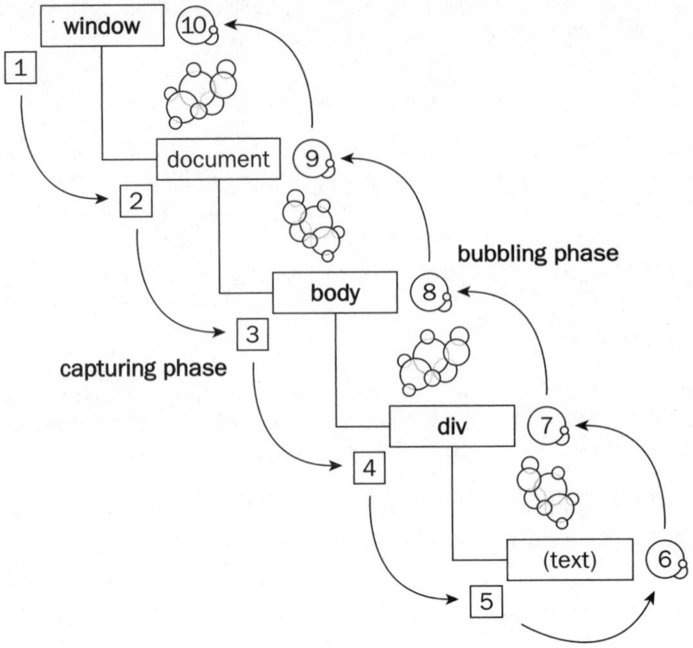

Figure 9-6

This is an important concept when you are working with DOM-compliant browsers. Forgetting that text nodes fire events in the DOM is the number one reason why developers get headaches working with newer browsers.

Event Handlers/Listeners

Events are certain actions performed either by the user or by the browser itself. These events have names like *click*, *load*, and *mouseover*. A function that is called in response to an event is called an *event handler* (or, as the DOM describes it, an *event listener*). A function responding to a `click` event is considered an *onclick* event handler. Traditionally, event handlers are assigned in one of two ways: in JavaScript or in HTML.

To assign an event handler in JavaScript, you have to get a reference to the object in question and then assign a function to the corresponding event handler property like this:

```
var oDiv = document.getElementById("div1");
oDiv.onclick = function () {
    alert("I was clicked");
};
```

Using this method of assignment, the event handler name must be represented in all lowercase letters to properly respond to the event.

To assign an event handler in HTML, you simply add an event handler attribute to the HTML tag and include the appropriate script as the attribute value, like so:

```
<div onclick="alert('I was clicked')"></div>
```

With this method, the event handler can have any case, so `onclick` is equal to `onClick`, `OnClick`, and `ONCLICK`. (However, if you are using valid XHTML code, event handlers should be defined using all lowercase letters.)

When you are assigning event handlers in HTML, remember that the code contained in the attribute value (between the quotes) is wrapped in an anonymous function, so the HTML code actually executes the following JavaScript:

```
oDiv.onclick = function () {
    alert("I was clicked");
};
```

Look familiar? Yes, it is the same code as the JavaScript example.

These methods both work in all modern browsers, but additional methods can make more than one event handler per event available. Once again, Internet Explorer contains a proprietary method whereas the DOM prescribes another.

Internet Explorer

In IE, every element and `window` object has two methods: `attachEvent()` and `detachEvent()`. As the names indicates, `attachEvent()` is used to attach an event handler to an event and `detachEvent()` is used to detach an event handler. Each method takes two arguments: the name of the event handler to assign to (for example: *onclick*) and a function.

```
[Object].attachEvent("name_of_event_handler", fnHandler);
[Object].detachEvent("name_of_event_handler", fnHandler);
```

In the case of `attachEvent()`, the function is added as an event handler; for `detachEvent()`, it looks for the given function in the event handler list and removes it. For example:

```
var fnClick = function () {
    alert("Clicked!");
};

var oDiv = document.getElementById("div");
oDiv.attachEvent("onclick", fnClick);          //add the event handler
//do some other stuff here
oDiv.detachEvent("onclick", fnClick);         //remove the event handler
```

As previously stated, this method can be used to attach more than one event handler:

```
var fnClick1 = function () {
    alert("Clicked!");
};

var fnClick2 = function () {
    alert("Also clicked! ");
};

var oDiv = document.getElementById("div");
oDiv.attachEvent("onclick", fnClick1);
oDiv.attachEvent("onclick", fnClick2);
```

This code segment causes two alerts to be displayed when you click the `<div/>` element. The first is `"Clicked!"`, followed by `"Also clicked!"`. The event handlers always execute in the order in which they are added.

You can also use the traditional JavaScript method of assigning event handlers:

```
var fnClick1 = function () {
    alert("Clicked!");
};

var fnClick2 = function () {
    alert("Also clicked! ");
};

var oDiv = document.getElementById("div");
oDiv.onclick = fnClick1;
oDiv.attachEvent("onclick", fnClick2);
```

This code is exactly equal to the previous example, and the alerts are displayed in the same order. Assigning an event handler in the traditional way is considered just another call to `attachEvent()`, so the event handlers are still executed in the order in which they are defined.

DOM

The DOM methods `addEventListener()` and `removeEventListener()` accomplish the assignment and removal of event handlers. These methods, unlike IE, take three parameters: the event name, the function to assign, and whether the handler should be used for the bubbling or capture phase. If the handler is to be used in the capture phase, the third parameter is `true`; for the bubbling phase, it is `false`. Here's the general syntax:

```
[Object].addEventListener("name_of_event", fnHandler, bCapture);
[Object].removeEventListener("name_of_event", fnHandler, bCapture);
```

To use these methods, you must first get a reference to the object in question and then assign or remove the event handlers:

```
var fnClick = function () {
    alert("Clicked!");
};
```

```
var oDiv = document.getElementById("div1");
oDiv.addEventListener("click", fnClick, false);             //add the event handler
//do some other stuff here
oDiv.removeEventListener("click", fnClick, false);           //remove the event
handler
```

And just as in IE, you can attach more than one event handler:

```
var fnClick1 = function () {
    alert("Clicked!");
};

var fnClick2 = function () {
    alert("Also clicked!");
};

var oDiv = document.getElementById("div1");
oDiv.addEventListener("onclick", fnClick1);
oDiv.addEventListener("onclick", fnClick2);
```

This code displays `"Clicked!"` and then `"Also clicked!"` when the user clicks on the `<div/>`. Similar to IE, the event handlers are executed in the order in which they are defined.

If an event handler is added in the capturing phase using `addEventListener()`, the capturing phase must be specified in `removeEventListener()` for it to be properly removed. For instance, don't do this:

```
var fnClick = function () {
    alert("Clicked!");
};

var oDiv = document.getElementById("div1");

//add the event handler in the bubbling phase
oDiv.addEventListener("click", fnClick, false);

//do some other stuff here

//try to remove the event handler, but the third parameter is true
//instead false...this will fail, though it won't cause an error.
oDiv.removeEventListener("click", fnClick, true);
```

Here, the function `fnClick` is added in the bubbling phase, and then an attempt is made to remove it from the capture phase. This won't cause an error, but the function won't be removed.

If you use the traditional way of assigning a function directly to the event handler property, the event handler is added in the bubbling phase of the event. For example, the following two lines achieve the same effect:

```
oDiv.onclick = fnClick;
oDiv.addEventListener("click", fnClick, false);
```

The direct assignment of an event handler is considered to be just another call to `addEventListener()`, so the event handlers are used in the order in which they are specified.

One important difference in direct assignment is that subsequent assignments to the event handler wipe out the previous assignment:

```
oDiv.onclick = fnClick;
oDiv.onclick = fnDifferentClick;
```

In this example, `fnClick` is assigned as the `onclick` event handler first, but is then replaced by `fnDifferentClick`.

The Event Object

Developers for both browsers knew that it was important to pass information about an event to the developer. The result was to create an event object that contained information specific to the event that had just occurred such as:

- The object that caused the event
- Information about the mouse at the time of the event
- Information about the keyboard at the time of the event

Event objects are only created when an event occurs and are made accessible to the event handlers. After all event handlers have been executed, the event object is destroyed.

As you can probably guess, Internet Explorer and the DOM implement the event object in two different ways.

Locating

In Internet Explorer, the `event` object is a property of the `window` object. This means that an event handler must access the event object in this way:

```
oDiv.onclick = function () {
    var oEvent = window.event;
}
```

Even though it is a property of the `window` object, the `event` object is only accessible when an event occurs. After all event handlers have been executed, the `event` object is destroyed.

The DOM standard says that the `event` object must be passed in as the sole argument of the event handler. So, to access the event object in a DOM-compliant browser (such as Mozilla, Safari, or Opera), you do the following:

```
oDiv.onclick = function () {
    var oEvent = arguments[0];
}
```

Of course, you can also name the argument for easier access:

```
oDiv.onclick = function (oEvent) {
}
```

Properties/methods

Internet Explorer

Here are the event properties and methods for Internet Explorer (please note: properties and methods that apply to IE-only technologies and features are not listed):

Property/Method	Type	R/W	Description
altKey	Boolean	R/W	True indicates the ALT key is pressed; false indicates it is not.
button	Integer	R/W	The mouse button has been clicked for certain mouse events. Values: 0 – No button is pressed. 1 – Left button is pressed. 2 – Right button is pressed. 3 – Left and right buttons are both pressed. 4 – Middle button is pressed. 5 – Left and middle buttons are both pressed. 6 – Right and middle buttons are both pressed. 7 – Left, middle, and right buttons are all pressed.
cancelBubble	Boolean	R/W	The developer sets this to true to stop the bubbling up of an event.
clientX	Integer	R/W	The x-coordinate of the mouse pointer within the client area (excludes toolbars, scrollbars, and so on) when the event occurs
clientY	Integer	R/W	The y-coordinate of the mouse pointer within the client area (excludes toolbars, scrollbars, and so on) when the event occurs
ctrlKey	Boolean	R/W	True indicates the CTRL key is pressed; false indicates it is not.
fromElement	Element	R/W	The element that the mouse is leaving during some mouse events
keyCode	Integer	R/W	For the `keypress` event, indicates the Unicode character of the key that was pressed; for the `keydown/keyup` events, numeric indicator as to the key that was pressed.
offsetX	Integer	R/W	The x-coordinate of the mouse pointer relative to the object that caused the event
offsetY	Integer	R/W	The y-coordinate of the mouse pointer relative to the object that caused the event
repeat	Boolean	R	True if the `keydown` event is being fired repeatedly; false if not

Table continued on following page

Property/Method	Type	R/W	Description
`returnValue`	Boolean	R/W	The developer sets this to false in order to cancel the default action for the event.
`screenX`	Integer	R/W	The x-coordinate of the mouse pointer relative to the entire computer screen
`screenY`	Integer	R/W	The y-coordinate of the mouse pointer relative to the entire computer screen
`shiftKey`	Boolean	R/W	True indicates the Shift key is pressed; false indicates it is not.
`srcElement`	Element	R/W	The element that caused the event.
`toElement`	Element	R/W	The element that the mouse is entering during some mouse events.
`type`	String	R/W	The name of the event.
`x`	Integer	R/W	The x-coordinate of the mouse pointer relative to the parent element of the element that caused the event
`y`	Integer	R/W	The y-coordinate of the mouse pointer relative to the parent element of the element that caused the event

DOM

The DOM event object contains similar core properties and methods with some important differences. The following table enumerates them.

Property/Method	Type	R/W	Description
`altKey`	Boolean	R/W	True indicates the ALT key is pressed; false indicates it is not.
`bubbles`	Boolean	R	Indicates if the event bubbles.
`button`	Integer	R/W	The mouse button that has been pressed for certain mouse events. Values: 0 – No button is pressed. 1 – Left button is pressed. 2 – Right button is pressed. 3 – Left and right buttons are both pressed. 4 – Middle button is pressed. 5 – Left and middle buttons are both pressed. 6 – Right and middle buttons are both pressed. 7 – Left, middle, and right buttons are all pressed.
`cancelable`	Boolean	R	Indicates if the event can be cancelled.
`cancelBubble`	Boolean	R	Indicates whether event bubbling has been cancelled

Property/Method	Type	R/W	Description
`charCode`	Integer	R	The Unicode value of the character for the key that was pressed
`clientX`	Integer	R	The x-coordinate of the mouse pointer within the client area (excludes toolbars, scrollbars, and so on) when the event occurs
`clientY`	Integer	R	The y-coordinate of the mouse pointer within the client area (excludes toolbars, scrollbars, and so on) when the event occurs
`ctrlKey`	Boolean	R	True indicates the CTRL key is pressed; false indicates it is not.
`currentTarget`	Element	R	The element that is currently the event target
`detail`	Integer	R	The number of times the mouse button has been clicked
`eventPhase`	Integer	R	The phase of the event, which is one of the following values: 0 – capturing phase 1 – at target 2 – bubbling phase
`isChar`	Boolean	R	Indicates if the key that was pressed has a character associated with it
`keyCode`	Integer	R/W	Numeric indicator as to the key that was pressed
`metaKey`	Integer	R	Indicates if the META key has been pressed
`pageX`	Integer	R	The x-coordinate of the mouse pointer relative to the page
`pageX`	Integer	R	The y-coordinate of the mouse pointer relative to the page
`prevent Default()`	Function	N/A	You can call this method to prevent the default behavior for the event.
`relatedTarget`	Element	R	The secondary target of the event, most often used in mouse events
`screenX`	Integer	R	The x-coordinate of the mouse pointer relative to the entire computer screen
`screenY`	Integer	R	The y-coordinate of the mouse pointer relative to the entire computer screen
`shiftKey`	Boolean	R	True indicates the Shift key is pressed; false indicates it is not.

Table continued on following page

Property/Method	Type	R/W	Description
`stopPropagation()`	Function	N/A	You can call this method to prevent the further propagation (bubbling) of the event.
`target`	Element	R	The element/object that caused the event
`timeStamp`	Long	R	The time that this event occurred in milliseconds after midnight on January 1, 1970
`type`	String	R	The name of the event

Similarities

Here is a brief roundup of the similarities between the two event objects.

Getting the event type

In order to get the event type in either browser, use the following:

```
var sType = oEvent.type;
```

This returns a value such as `"click"` or `"mouseover"` and is useful when one function is used as an event handler for two different events. For example:

```
function handleEvent(oEvent) {
    if (oEvent.type == "click") {
        alert("Clicked!");
    } else if (oEvent.type == "mouseover") {
        alert("Mouse Over!");
    }
}

oDiv.onclick = handleEvent;
oDiv.onmouseover = handleEvent;
```

In this code, the function `handleEvent()` is assigned as an event handler for both the `click` and `mouseover` events. Inside of the function, the `type` property is used to determine which course of action should be taken.

Note that this example uses the DOM method of passing in the event object, but the code inside the function can also be used in Internet Explorer after the `event` object has been assigned to `oEvent`.

Getting the key code (keydown/keyup events)

During a `keydown` or `keyup` event, you can retrieve the code for the key that was pressed by using the `keyCode` property:

```
var iKeyCode = oEvent.keyCode;
```

The `keyCode` property always contains a code the represents the key pressed, which may or may not represent a character. For example, the Enter (or Return) key has a `keyCode` of 13, the space bar has a `keyCode` of 32, and the BackSpace key has a `keyCode` of 8.

Detecting Shift, Alt, Ctrl

To detect if the Shift, Alt, or Ctrl keys are pressed, both IE and the DOM can do the following:

```
var bShift = oEvent.shiftKey;
var bAlt = oEvent.altKey;
var bCtrl = oEvent.ctrlKey;
```

Each of these properties contains a Boolean value indicating whether the key is being pressed (each of these keys also fires a `keydown` event enabling you to retrieve its `keyCode`).

Getting the client coordinates

During mouse events, you can retrieve the location of the mouse cursor in relation to the client area by using the `clientX` and `clientY` properties:

```
var iClientX = oEvent.clientX;
var iClientY = oEvent.clientY;
```

The client area is the part of the window that displays the Web page (see Figure 9-7). These properties tell you how far from the edge (in pixels) of that area the mouse is located.

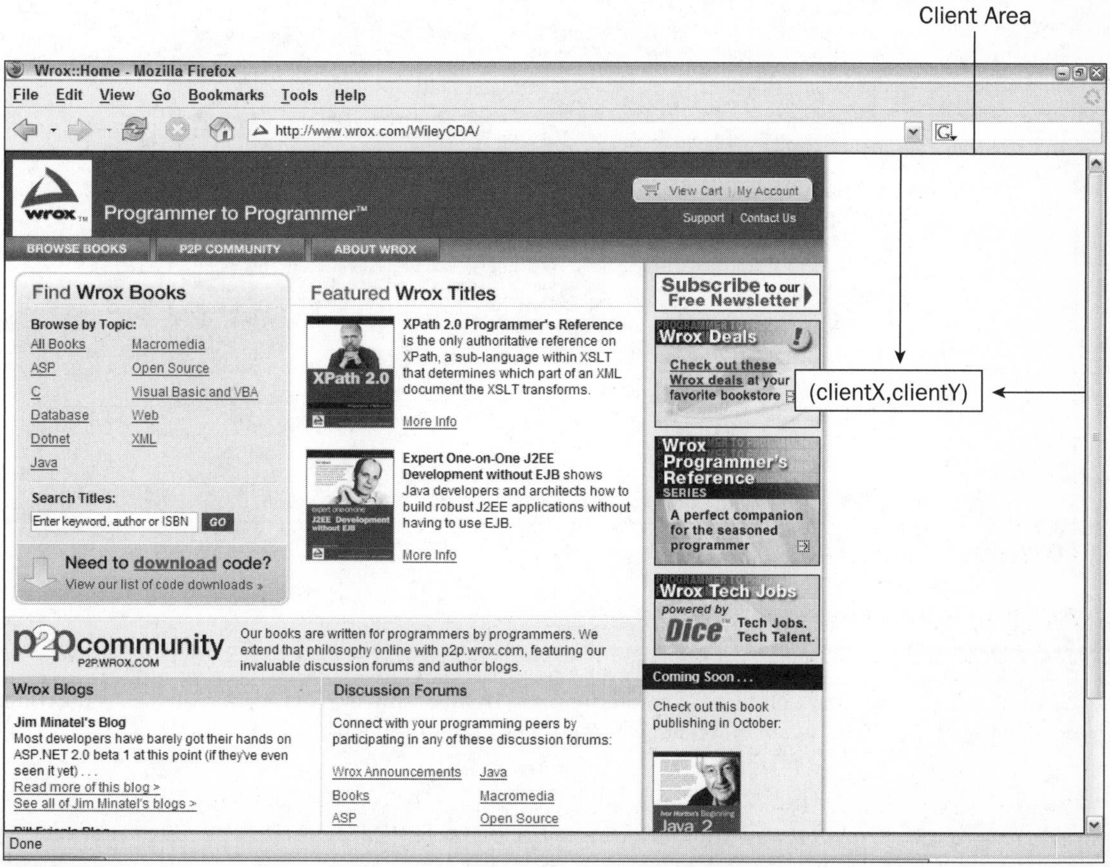

Figure 9-7

Getting the screen coordinates

During mouse events, you can retrieve the location of the mouse cursor in relation to the computer screen by using the `screenX` and `screenY` properties:

```
var iScreenX = oEvent.screenX;
var iScreenY = oEvent.screenY;
```

Each of these properties returns an integer representing the number of pixels from the edge of the user's screen (see Figure 9-8).

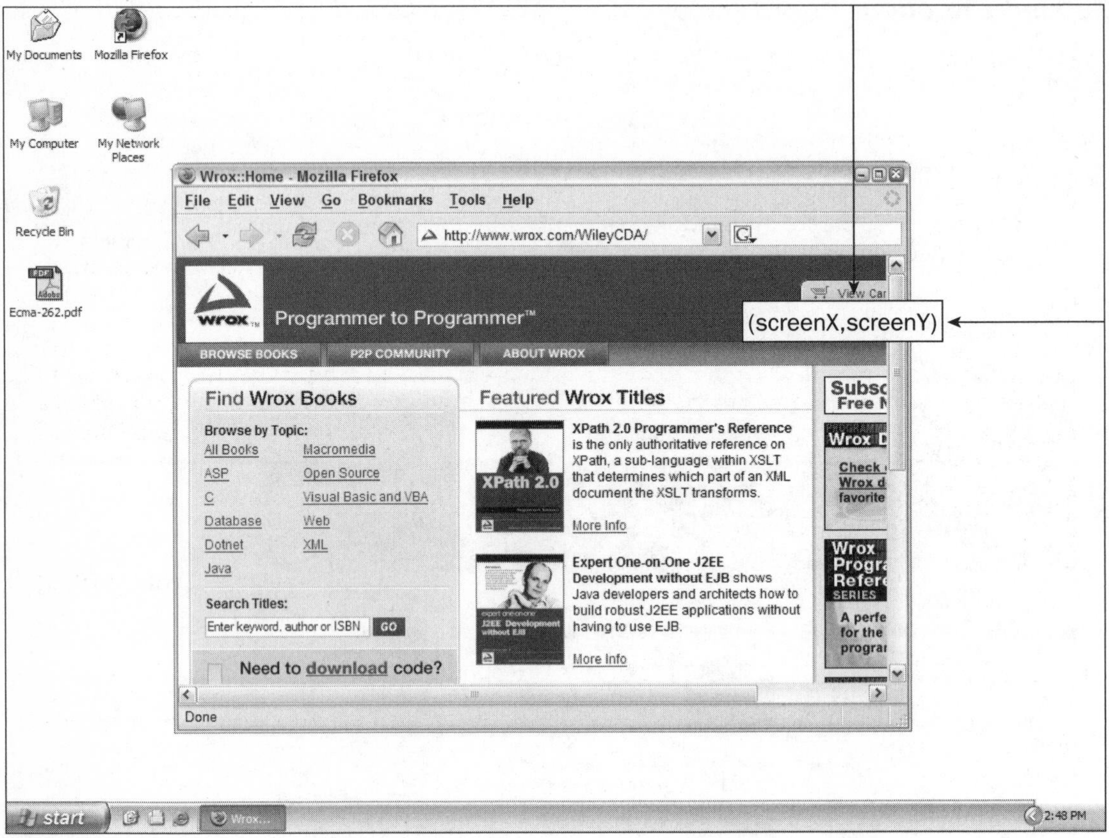

Figure 9-8

Differences

Of course, not everything in Internet Explorer and the DOM is similar. This section describes the difference that you should be aware of when scripting for cross-browser support.

Getting the target

The object at the center of an event is called the *target*. Suppose that you assigned an `onclick` event handler to a `<div/>` element. When the `click` events fires, the `<div/>` element is considered the target.

In IE, the target is contained in the `srcElement` property of the `event` object:

```
var oTarget = oEvent.srcElement;
```

IE on Macintosh also supports both the `srcElement` and `target` attributes.

In DOM-compliant browsers, the target is contained in the `target` property:

```
var oTarget = oEvent.target;
```

IE targets can only be elements, `document`, or `window`; DOM-compliant browsers also allow text nodes to be targets.

Getting the character code

Earlier you saw that both IE and the DOM support an `event` object property called `keyCode`, which returns a numeric code for the key that was pressed. If the key represents a character (unlike Shift, Ctrl, and so on), IE's `keyCode` property returns the character code of the character (which is its Unicode equivalent):

```
var iCharCode = oEvent.keyCode;
```

In DOM-compliant browsers, a separation occurs between the code of the key that was pressed and the character code. To get the character code, use the `charCode` property:

```
var iCharCode = oEvent.charCode;
```

You can then use this value to get the actual character by passing it to the `String.fromCharCode()` method:

```
var sChar = String.fromCharCode(oEvent.charCode);
```

If you are unsure as to whether the key that was pressed contains a character, you can use the `isChar` property:

```
if (oEvent.isChar) {
    var iCharCode = oEvent.charCode;
}
```

Preventing the default behavior for an event

To prevent the default behavior for an event in IE, you must set the `returnValue` property to `false`:

```
oEvent.returnValue = false;
```

In Mozilla, you just call the `preventDefault()` method:

```
oEvent.preventDefault();
```

You may think, "When would I ever want to prevent the default behavior of an event?" Actually preventing the default behavior can be helpful in several situations.

First, use it when you want to prevent the user from using the context menu that appears when he or she right-clicks the page. To do this, you prevent the default behavior of the `contextmenu` event, by doing this:

```
document.body.oncontextmenu = function (oEvent) {
    if (isIE) {
        oEvent = window.event;
        oEvent.returnValue = false;
    } else {
        oEvent.preventDefault();
    }
};
```

In addition, you may want to prevent the default behavior of text boxes when a key is pressed to reject a certain character, or forestall a button's action unless certain criteria are met. This is a very powerful feature and I discuss it further later in the book.

Stopping event propagation (bubbling)

To prevent the event from propagating/bubbling in IE, you must set the `cancelBubble` property to `true`:

```
oEvent.cancelBubble = true;
```

In Mozilla, you just call the `stopPropagation()` method:

```
oEvent.stopPropagation ();
```

Stopping the event propagation prevents the event handlers for the other objects in the event flow from being executed. Consider this example:

```
<html onclick="alert('html')">
    <head>
        <title>Event Propagation Example</title>
    </head>
    <body onclick="alert('body')">
        <input type="button" value="Click Me" onclick="alert('input')" />
    </body>
</html>
```

When the button is clicked on this page, three alerts are displayed one after another: `"input"`, `"body"`, and `"html"`. This happens, of course, because the event bubbles up from the `<input/>` element to `<body/>` and then to `<html/>`. If, however, you stop the event propagation at the button, things change:

```
<html onclick="alert('html')">
    <head>
        <title>Stopping Event Propagation Example</title>
        <script type="text/javascript" src="detect.js"></script>
        <script type="text/javascript">
            function handleClick(oEvent) {
                alert("input");
                if (isIE) {
                    oEvent.cancelBubble = true;
                } else {
                    oEvent.stopPropagation();
                }
            }
        </script>
    </head>
    <body onclick="alert('body')">
        <input type="button" value="Click Me" onclick="handleClick(event)" />
    </body>
</html>
```

When this example is executed and the button is clicked, you only see the `"input"` alert and none of the others because the propagation has been stopped. In order to do this correctly, you make use of the browser detection code from the last chapter.

You may also notice that the `<input/>` element passes in the `event` object as an argument to the `handleClick()` function. This works in all browsers because the `event` object is created as soon as the event happens and is a global variable at this point.

Types of Events

The events that occur in a browser can be grouped into several specific types, depending on the object the event is fired from and what triggered the event to fire. The DOM specification defines the following event groups:

- Mouse Events are fired when the user uses the mouse to perform certain actions.
- Keyboard Events are fired when the user types on the keyboard.
- HTML Events are fired when certain changes occur to the browser window or specific client-server interaction occurs.
- Mutation Events are fired when a change occurs to the underlying DOM structure.

Mouse events

Mouse events are the most commonly used group of events on the Web. They include the following:

- `click` — Occurs when the user clicks the left mouse button (not if the right mouse button is used). Also occurs when focus is on a button and the user presses the Enter key.
- `dblclick` — Occurs when the user double clicks the left mouse button (not if the right mouse button is used).
- `mousedown` — Occurs when the user pushes any mouse button down.
- `mouseout` — Occurs when the cursor is over an element and the user moves it outside the boundaries of the element.
- `mouseover` — Occurs when the cursor is outside of an element and the user moves it over the element.
- `mouseup` — Occurs when the user releases any mouse button.
- `mousemove` — Occurs repeatedly when the cursor is over an element.

All elements on a page support the mouse events. This simple example illustrates all the mouse events:

```
<html>
    <head>
        <title>Mouse Events Example</title>
        <script type="text/javascript">
            function handleEvent(oEvent) {
                var oTextbox = document.getElementById("txt1");
                oTextbox.value += "\n" + oEvent.type;
            }
        </script>
    </head>
    <body>
        <p>Use your mouse to click and double click the red square.</p>
        <div style="width: 100px; height: 100px; background-color: red"
             onmouseover="handleEvent(event)"
             onmouseout="handleEvent(event)"
             onmousedown="handleEvent(event)"
             onmouseup="handleEvent(event)"
             onclick="handleEvent(event)"
             ondblclick="handleEvent(event)" id="div1"></div>
        <p><textarea id="txt1" rows="15" cols="50"></textarea></p>
    </body>
</html>
```

This code displays a red square and a text box. When you interact with the red square using your mouse, the text box displays the events that are fired. Note that just one function is used as an event handler for all events. It simply outputs the type of event into the text box.

Using the mouseover and mouseout events is a popular way to change the appearance of something on the page, such as an image. This is a very simple technique, but is still very frequently used:

```
<img src="image1.gif" onmouseover="this.src='image2.gif'"
onmouseout="this.src='image1'.gif" />
```

In this code snippet, the onmouseover and onmouseout event handlers are filled with just a single line. Notice the use of the this object to change the src property of the image? This is one of the hidden truths of event handlers: An event handler is considered a method of the object on which it is assigned. Therefore, the this object can be used to access the event target (which is helpful, in this instance, because it avoids a browser detect). When the mouseover event fires, the image's src property is set to image2.gif, which presumably is different from image1.gif; when the mouseout event fires, the src property is set back to image1.gif.

Event properties

For each mouse event, the following properties are filled in on the event object:

- Coordinate properties (such as clientX and clientY, and so on)
- The type property
- The target (DOM) or srcElement (IE) property
- The shiftKey, ctrlKey, altKey, and metaKey (DOM) properties
- The button property (only on mousedown, mousemove, mouseout, mouseover, and mouseup events)

Each of these properties gives some information about the mouse event that just occurred. You are already familiar with the type property, but if the other properties are added into event handling, you begin to get a more complete picture of the event that occurred:

```
<html>
    <head>
        <title>Mouse Events Example</title>
        <script type="text/javascript">
            function handleEvent(oEvent) {
                var oTextbox = document.getElementById("txt1");
                oTextbox.value += "\n>" + oEvent.type;
                oTextbox.value += "\n    target is " + (oEvent.target ||
oEvent.srcElement).id;
                oTextbox.value += "\n    at (" + oEvent.clientX + "," +
oEvent.clientY + ") in the client";
                oTextbox.value += "\n    at (" + oEvent.screenX + "," +
oEvent.screenY + ") on the screen";
                oTextbox.value += "\n    button down is " + oEvent.button;

                var arrKeys = [];
                if (oEvent.shiftKey) {
                    arrKeys.push("Shift");
                }
```

```
                if (oEvent.ctrlKey) {
                    arrKeys.push("Ctrl");
                }

                if (oEvent.altKey) {
                    arrKeys.push("Alt");
                }

                oTextbox.value += "\n    keys down are " + arrKeys;

            }
        </script>
    </head>
    <body>
        <p>Use your mouse to click and double click the red square.</p>
        <div style="width: 100px; height: 100px; background-color: red"
             onmouseover="handleEvent(event)"
             onmouseout="handleEvent(event)"
             onmousedown="handleEvent(event)"
             onmouseup="handleEvent(event)"
             onclick="handleEvent(event)"
             ondblclick="handleEvent(event)" id="div1"></div>
        <p><textarea id="txt1" rows="15" cols="50"></textarea></p>
    </body>
</html>
```

This example is an update of the previous one with more information displayed in the text box. Here, the properties just mentioned are output in addition to the event type. One line to take note of is where the code `(oEvent.target || oEvent.srcElement).id` appears. Remember that when the logical OR operator is used with two objects, it always returns either the first or the non-`null` object. In this case, it is used to determine which property holds the event target and then to return the `id` attribute.

Opera 7.5 has a bug when detecting the various keys (Shift, Ctrl, and Alt). It incorrectly reports a Shift key as a Ctrl key and vice versa. Additionally, it doesn't detect the Alt key at all. Use these properties with caution if you plan on supporting Opera.

For `mouseover` and `mouseout` events have additional properties. In IE, the property `fromElement` contains the element the cursor moved from and `toElement` contains the element that the cursor moved to. For `mouseover`, `toElement` is always equal to `srcElement` whereas on `mouseout`, `fromElement` is always equal to `srcElement`. You can test this for yourself:

```
<html>
    <head>
        <title>IE Mouse Events Example</title>
        <script type="text/javascript">
            function handleEvent(oEvent) {
                var oTextbox = document.getElementById("txt1");
                oTextbox.value += "\n>" + oEvent.type;
                oTextbox.value += "\n    target is " + oEvent.srcElement.tagName;
```

```
                if (oEvent.fromElement) {
                    oTextbox.value += "\n    fromElement is " +
oEvent.fromElement.tagName;
                }

                if (oEvent.toElement) {
                    oTextbox.value += "\n    toElement is " +
oEvent.toElement.tagName;
                }            }
        </script>
    </head>
    <body>
        <p>Use your mouse to click and double click the red square.</p>
        <div style="width: 100px; height: 100px; background-color: red"
             onmouseover="handleEvent(event)"
             onmouseout="handleEvent(event)"
             onmousedown="handleEvent(event)"
             onmouseup="handleEvent(event)"
             onclick="handleEvent(event)"
             ondblclick="handleEvent(event)" id="div1"></div>
        <p><textarea id="txt1" rows="15" cols="50"></textarea></p>
    </body>
</html>
```

Because of this redundancy, the DOM supports only one `event` property called `relatedTarget` for both `mouseover` and `mouseout`. On a `mouseover` event, `relatedTarget` points to the element that cursor moved from; on a `mouseout` event, `relatedTarget` points to the element that cursor moved to. You can modify the previous example to test this:

```
<html>
    <head>
        <title>DOM Mouse Events Example</title>
        <script type="text/javascript">
            function handleEvent(oEvent) {
                var oTextbox = document.getElementById("txt1");
                oTextbox.value += "\n>" + oEvent.type;
                oTextbox.value += "\n    target is " + oEvent.target.tagName;
                oTextbox.value += "\n    relatedTarget is " +
oEvent.relatedTarget.tagName;
            }
        </script>
    </head>
    <body>
        <p>Use your mouse to click and double click the red square.</p>
        <div style="width: 100px; height: 100px; background-color: red"
             onmouseover="handleEvent(event)"
             onmouseout="handleEvent(event)"
             onmousedown="handleEvent(event)"
             onmouseup="handleEvent(event)"
             onclick="handleEvent(event)"
             ondblclick="handleEvent(event)" id="div1"></div>
        <p><textarea id="txt1" rows="15" cols="50"></textarea></p>
    </body>
</html>
```

Sequencing

It takes a `mousedown` event followed by a `mouseup` event on the same target before a `click` event fires. Likewise, to get a `dblclick` event to fire, it takes the following sequence of events on the same target:

1. `mousedown`
2. `mouseup`
3. `click`
4. `mousedown`
5. `mouseup`
6. `click`
7. `dblclick`

When moving the mouse from one object to another, the first event to fire is `mouseout` (on the object that the mouse is moving away from). Next, the `mousemove` event fires on the object between these two. Finally, the `mouseover` event fires on the object the mouse is moving to.

Keyboard events

Keyboard events are caused by user action on the keyboard. The keyboard events are the following:

- `keydown` — Occurs when the user presses a key on the keyboard. It also occurs repeatedly as the key is being held down.
- `keypress` — Occurs when the user presses a key on the keyboard that results in a character (disregards keys like Shift and Alt). It also occurs repeatedly as the key is being held down.
- `keyup` — Occurs when the user releases a key that was down.

These events are most easily seen as you type in a text box, although all elements support keyboard events:

```
<html>
    <head>
        <title>Key Events Example</title>
        <script type="text/javascript">
            function handleEvent(oEvent) {
                var oTextbox = document.getElementById("txt1");
                oTextbox.value += "\n>" + oEvent.type;
            }
        </script>
    </head>
    <body>
        <p>Type some characters into the first textbox.</p>
        <p><textarea id="txtInput" rows="15" cols="50"
            onkeydown="handleEvent(event)"
            onkeyup="handleEvent(event)"
            onkeypress="handleEvent(event)"></textarea></p>
        <p><textarea id="txt1" rows="15" cols="50"></textarea></p>
    </body>
</html>
```

Event properties

For each keyboard event, the following event properties are filled in:

- The keyCode property
- The charCode property (DOM only)
- The target (DOM) or srcElement (IE) property
- The shiftKey, ctrlKey, altKey, and metaKey (DOM) properties

Note that pressing the Shift, Ctrl, Alt, or Meta keys causes a keydown event in addition to setting the appropriate property to true. The following example tests these properties:

```
<html>
    <head>
        <title>Key Events Example</title>
        <script type="text/javascript">
            function handleEvent(oEvent) {
                var oTextbox = document.getElementById("txt1");
                oTextbox.value += "\n>" + oEvent.type;
                oTextbox.value += "\n    target is " + (oEvent.target ||
oEvent.srcElement).id;
                oTextbox.value += "\n    keyCode is " + oEvent.keyCode;
                oTextbox.value += "\n    charCode is " + oEvent.charCode;

                var arrKeys = [];
                if (oEvent.shiftKey) {
                    arrKeys.push("Shift");
                }

                if (oEvent.ctrlKey) {
                    arrKeys.push("Ctrl");
                }

                if (oEvent.altKey) {
                    arrKeys.push("Alt");
                }

                oTextbox.value += "\n    keys down are " + arrKeys;
            }
        </script>
    </head>
    <body>
        <p>Type some characters into the first textbox.</p>
        <p><textarea id="txtInput" rows="15" cols="50"
            onkeydown="handleEvent(event)"
            onkeyup="handleEvent(event)"
            onkeypress="handleEvent(event)"></textarea></p>
        <p><textarea id="txt1" rows="15" cols="50"></textarea></p>
    </body>
</html>
```

Sequencing

When the user presses a character key once, the following sequence of events occurs:

1. keydown
1. keypress
2. keyup

If the user presses a non-character key once, such as Shift, the following event sequence takes place:

1. keydown
2. keyup

If the user presses a character key and holds it down, `keydown` and `keypress` are fired repeatedly, one after the other, until the key is released; if the user presses and holds down a non-character key, only the `keydown` event fires repeatedly. You can test this out using the previous example.

HTML events

The HTML events group makes up a large number of the remaining events from the original event model created by developers of IE 4.0 and Netscape 4.0. It includes the following:

- The `load` event, which fires on a `window` when the page has been completely loaded, on a frameset when all frames have been completely loaded, on an `<img/>` element when it has been completely loaded, or on an `<object />` element when it has been completely loaded.
- The `unload` event, which fires on a `window` when the page has been completely unloaded, on a frameset when all frames have been completely unloaded, or on an `<object/>` element when it has been completely unloaded.
- The `abort` event, which fires on an `<object/>` element if it is not fully loaded before the user stops the download process.
- The `error` event, which fires on a `window` when a JavaScript error occurs, on an `<img/>` element if the image specified cannot be loaded, on an `<object/>` element if it cannot be loaded, or on frameset if one or more frames cannot be loaded. This event is discussed in Chapter 14, "Error Handling."
- The `select` event, which fires when the user selects one or more characters in a text box (either `<input/>` or `<textarea/>`). This event is discussed further in Chapter 11, "Forms and Data Integrity."
- The `change` event, which fires on a text box (either `<input/>` or `<textarea/>`) when it loses focus and the value has changed since the textbox got focus, and on a `<select/>` element when its value is changed. This event is discussed further in Chapter 11.
- The `submit` event, which fires on a `<form/>` when a Submit button (`<input type="submit"/>`) is clicked. This event is discussed further in Chapter 11.
- The `reset` event, which fires on a `<form/>` when a Reset button (`<input type="reset"/>`) is clicked. This event is discussed further in Chapter 11.

- The `resize` event, which fires on a `window` or frame when it is resized.
- The `scroll` event, which fires on any element with a scrollbar when the user scrolls it. The `<body/>` element contains the scrollbar for a loaded page.
- The `focus` event, which fires on any element or on the `window` itself when it gets focus (the user clicks on it, tabs to it, or otherwise interacts with it).
- The `blur` event, which fires on any element or on the `window` itself when it loses focus.

The load and unload events

The `load` event is probably used most often because DOM manipulation can't take place until the entire page has been loaded. Two methods define an `onload` event handler for a `window`. First, you can use JavaScript and assign it to the `window` object:

```
<html>
    <head>
        <title>Onload Example</title>
        <script type="text/javascript">
            window.onload = function () {
                alert("Loaded");
            };
        </script>
        <body>
        </body>
</html>
```

The second way is to assign it in the HTML on the `<body/>` element:

```
<html>
    <head>
        <title>Onload Example</title>
        <body onload="alert('Loaded')">
        </body>
</html>
```

Confused? The problem here is that the `load` event actually happens on the window, which is why the event handler is defined on the `window` object using JavaScript. In HTML, however, there is no code representation of the `window` object, so the HTML gurus decided that the handler should be assigned on the `<body/>` element and then placed on the `window` object behind the scenes. So, if you set the `onload` event handler on the `<body/>` element and then check the `window.onload` property, you see the following code has been placed there:

```
<html>
    <head>
        <title>Onload Example</title>
        <script type="text/javascript">
            function handleLoad() {
                alert(window.onload);
            }
        </script>
        <body onload="handleLoad()">
        </body>
</html>
```

Can you still assign an event handler to `document.body.onload`? Yes, you can. The problem is that `document.body` doesn't exist until the page has loaded the `<body/>` tag. This means that if you try to assign the event handler in the `<head/>` element, where it should be done, you get an error. Try it for yourself:

```
<html>
    <head>
        <title>Onload Example</title>
        <script type="text/javascript">
            document.body.onload = function () {
                alert("loaded");
            }
        </script>
        <body>
        </body>
</html>
```

If you run this code, you get an error saying that `document.body` isn't defined. So, it is always best to assign the `onload` event handler to the `window` object.

The `unload` event can be handled the same way, either by assigning the event handler to the `window` object or by assigning it in the `<body/>` element. The unload event fires when you navigate from one page to another (by clicking a link or using the Back/Forward buttons) or when you close the browser window:

```
<html>
    <head>
        <title>OnUnload Example</title>
    </head>
    <body onunload="alert('Goodbye')">
    </body>
</html>
```

> **You have very short amount of time in which to execute the event handler code before the window is closed or the next page takes control, so it's usually best to avoid using an `onunload` event handler. The best reason to use onunload is to dereference objects that were used on the page; any functionality more complicated than this should be avoided.**

The resize event

At times your Web page may change depending on the size of the browser window. For this case, you can use the `resize` event to determine when to change these dynamic elements.

Similar to the load and unload events, the event handler for the resize event must be assigned either to the `window` object using JavaScript code or to the `<body/>` element in HTML:

```
<html>
    <head>
        <title>OnResize Example</title>
```

```
        </head>
        <body onresize="alert('Resizing')">
        </body>
</html>
```

The actual `resize` event occurs at different times depending on the browser being used. In Internet Explorer and Opera, the `resize` event occurs as soon as a change occurs in the size of the browser. As soon as the window border is moved one pixel, the event fires. In Mozilla, the `resize` event fires only after you have stopped resizing the window. Try out the previous example in a few different browsers.

The `resize` event also fires when you maximize or minimize the window.

The scroll event

You may also want to keep track of when a user scrolls the window (or another element) in order to ensure something remains visible on the screen at all times. By using the `scroll` event, this is easy:

```
<html>
    <head>
        <title>OnScroll Example</title>
    </head>
    <body onscroll="alert('Scrolling')">
         <p>Try scrolling this window.</p>
         <p> </p>
         <p> </p>
         <p> </p>
         <p> </p>
         <p> </p>
         <p> </p>
         <p> </p>
         <p> </p>
         <p> </p>
         <p> </p>
         <p> </p>
         <p> </p>
    </body>
</html>
```

You can also assign the event handler to the `window.onscroll` property:

```
<html>
    <head>
        <title>OnScroll Example</title>
        <script type="text/javascript">
            window.onscroll = function () {
                alert("scrolling");
            }
        </script>
    </head>
    <body>
         <p>Try scrolling this window.</p>
         <p> </p>
         <p> </p>
```

```
            <p> </p>
            <p> </p>
            <p> </p>
            <p> </p>
            <p> </p>
            <p> </p>
            <p> </p>
            <p> </p>
            <p> </p>
            <p> </p>
        </body>
    </html>
```

You can also use this event in conjunction with several properties of the `<body/>` element, namely `scrollLeft`, which tells you how far the window has scrolled horizontally, and `scrollTop`, which tells you how far the window has scrolled vertically:

```
<html>
    <head>
        <title>OnScroll Example</title>
        <script type="text/javascript">
            window.onscroll = function () {
                var oTextbox = document.getElementById("txt1");
                oTextbox.value += "\nscroll is at " + document.body.scrollLeft + "
horizontally and " + document.body.scrollTop + " vertically.";
            }
        </script>
    </head>
    <body>
        <p>Try scrolling this window.</p>
        <p><textarea rows="15" cols="50" id="txt1"></textarea>
        <p> </p>
        <p> </p>
        <p> </p>
        <p> </p>
        <p> </p>
        <p> </p>
        <p> </p>
        <p> </p>
        <p> </p>
        <p> </p>
        <p> </p>
        <p> </p>
    </body>
</html>
```

In this example, a text box is used to track the `scrollLeft` and `scrollTop` properties so you can see the changes accurately. This works on all major browsers and can be used to create cool effects like a watermark that always appears at the top of the page:

```
<html>
    <head>
        <title>OnScroll Example</title>
```

```
        <script type="text/javascript">
            window.onscroll = function () {
                var oWatermark = document.getElementById("divWatermark");
                oWatermark.style.top = document.body.scrollTop;
            }
        </script>
    </head>
    <body>
         <p>Try scrolling this window.</p>
         <div id="divWatermark" style="position: absolute; top: 0px; right: 0px;
color: #cccccc; width: 150px; height: 30px; background-color: navy">Watermark</div>
         <p>Line 1</p>
         <p>Line 2</p>
         <p>Line 3</p>
         <p>Line 4</p>
         <p>Line 5</p>
         <p>Line 6</p>
         <p>Line 7</p>
         <p>Line 8</p>
         <p>Line 9</p>
         <p>Line 10</p>
         <p>Line 11</p>
         <p>Line 12</p>
    </body>
</html>
```

In this example, a `<div/>` specified with absolute positioning is the watermark. It starts out at the top of the page, and as the window scrolls, it must stay there. To handle this, a simple piece of code is added to the `onscroll` event handler that moves the watermark equal to the `scrollTop` property, which has the effect of always keeping it in the upper-right corner of the window.

Mutation events

Mutation events, although part of the DOM standard, have yet to be implemented in any major browser. As such, the following information is intended to provide a brief look into what the standard defines and not to discuss how these events might be used.

The mutation events include the following:

- `DOMSubtreeModified` — fires when the subtree of a document or element is modified by either adding or removing nodes
- `DOMNodeInserted` — fires when a node is inserted as a child of another node
- `DOMNodeRemoved` — fires when a node is removed as a child of another node
- `DOMNodeRemovedFromDocument` — fires when a node is removed from a document
- `DOMNodeInsertedIntoDocument` — fires when a new node is inserted into a document

The purpose of these events is to provide a language-independent event paradigm for use in all XML-based languages (such as XHTML, SVG, and newer languages like MathML).

Cross-Browser Events

Up until this point, you have seen many different types of browser and feature detection used in each example. In actual code, you want to try to minimize the number of times you use such detection in the main section of code. To achieve this, most developers come up with a cross-browser approach to events so that all the browser and feature detection is done behind the scenes. This section guides you through the creation of such an approach.

The purpose of the cross-browser code in this section is to equalize, as much as possible, the differences between the IE event model and the DOM event model, allowing one set of code to run across all major browsers almost identically. Of course, some limitations exist, such as IE's lack of support for bi-directional event flow, but it is still possible to cover 80 to 90% of all cases.

The EventUtil object

Whenever you are planning on creating multiple functions that are used in the same task, it's always best to create a container object to manage them. Doing so makes it easy to figure out where the function is defined when debugging.

In this case, the `EventUtil` object is the container for all the event-related functions defined in this section. Because there are no properties and you only need one instance of this object, there's no need to define a class:

```
var EventUtil = new Object;
```

Adding/removing event handlers

As you saw earlier, IE uses the `attachEvent()` method to assign any number of event handlers to an element, whereas the DOM uses `addEventListener()`. The first method of the `EventUtil` object creates a common way to assign event handlers and is called `addEventHandler()` (so as not to be confused with either browser's implementation). This method accepts three arguments: the object to assign the event handler to, the name of the event to handle, and the function to assign. Because IE doesn't support event capturing, this method assigns event handlers during bubbling only. Inside the body of the method is a simple detection algorithm designed to use the correct functionality at the correct time:

```
EventUtil.addEventHandler = function (oTarget, sEventType, fnHandler) {
    if (oTarget.addEventListener) {    //for DOM-compliant browsers
        oTarget.addEventListener(sEventType, fnHandler, false);
    } else if (oTarget.attachEvent) {    //for IE
        oTarget.attachEvent("on" + sEventType, fnHandler);
    } else {  //for all others
        oTarget["on" + sEventType] = fnHandler;
    }
};
```

The code in this method uses feature detection to determine which way to add an event handler. The first branch of the `if` statement is for DOM-compliant browsers that support the `addEventListener()` method. When the browser is DOM-compliant, the event handler is added using `addEventListener()` with the last parameter equal to `false`, specifying the bubbling phase.

In the second part of the `if` statement, another feature detect is done for IE's `attachEvent()` method. Note that in order to work properly, you must prepend the string `"on"` in front of the event type (remember, the `attachEvent()` method accepts the name of the event handler, not the name of the event, as the first parameter).

The `else` clause is simply used for all browsers that are neither DOM- nor IE-compliant. There aren't too many browsers that fit these criteria, so chances are this branch won't be used very much.

Of course, you can't just add event handlers; you must also create a way to remove them. To this end, the `EventUtil` object gets another method called `removeEventHandler()`. As you may expect, this method accepts the same parameters as `addEventHandler()` and uses pretty much the same algorithm:

```
EventUtil.removeEventHandler = function (oTarget, sEventType, fnHandler) {
    if (oTarget.removeEventListener) {   //for DOM-compliant browsers
        oTarget.removeEventListener(sEventType, fnHandler, false);
    } else if (oTarget.detachEvent) {   //for IE
        oTarget.detachEvent("on" + sEventType, fnHandler);
    } else {  //for all others
        oTarget["on" + sEventType] = null;
    }
};
```

As you can see, this code mirrors the `addEventHandler()` code almost exactly, complete with corresponding feature detects. The only big difference is in the final `else` statement, where the event handler is set to `null` and doesn't use the `fnHandler` argument at all.

These methods can be used as shown in the following example:

```
<html>
    <head>
        <title>Add/Remove Event Handlers Example</title>
        <script type="text/javascript">
                var EventUtil = new Object;
                EventUtil.addEventHandler = function (oTarget, sEventType, 
fnHandler) {
                    if (oTarget.addEventListener) {
                        oTarget.addEventListener(sEventType, fnHandler, false);
                    } else if (oTarget.attachEvent) {
                        oTarget.attachEvent("on" + sEventType, fnHandler);
                    } else {
                        oTarget["on" + sEventType] = fnHandler;
                    }
                };

                EventUtil.removeEventHandler = function (oTarget, sEventType, 
fnHandler) {
                    if (oTarget.removeEventListener) {
                        oTarget.removeEventListener(sEventType, fnHandler, false);
                    } else if (oTarget.detachEvent) {
                        oTarget.detachEvent("on" + sEventType, fnHandler);
                    } else {
                        oTarget["on" + sEventType] = null;
```

```
                }
            };

            function handleClick() {
                alert("Click!");
                var oDiv = document.getElementById("div1");
                EventUtil.removeEventHandler(oDiv, "click", handleClick);
            }

            window.onload = function() {
                var oDiv = document.getElementById("div1");
                EventUtil.addEventHandler(oDiv, "click", handleClick);
            }
        </script>
    </head>
    <body>
        <div id="div1" style="background-color: red; width: 100px; height:
100px"></div>
    </body>
</html>
```

In this code, the `onload` event handler assigns an `onclick` event handler to the `<div/>` with the ID `"div1"`. When you click on the `<div/>`, you get the alert that says `"Click!"`, and then the event handler is removed. Any time that you click the `<div/>` after that, there will be no alert.

Formatting the event object

One of the best ways to deal with the discrepancies between event objects in IE and the DOM is to make them behave as similarly as possible. Because more browsers use the DOM event model, it only makes sense to make the IE event model match the DOM event model more closely.

The following table is a comparison of DOM and IE `event` object properties and methods. Often, the event objects and methods are capable of doing the same thing (such as blocking default behaviors), but they are implemented in different ways. This table shows the IE way of doing some of the DOM behaviors. Although you cannot accurately copy all the properties into IE (such as `bubbles` or `cancelable`), it is possible to come up with an equivalent method for most.

DOM Property/Method	IE Property/Method
altKey	altKey
bubbles	-
button	button
cancelBubble	cancelBubble
cancelable	-
charCode	keyCode
clientX	clientX

DOM Property/Method	IE Property/Method
clientY	clientY
ctrlKey	ctrlKey
currentTarget	-
detail	-
eventPhase	-
isChar	-
keyCode	keyCode
metaKey	-
pageX	-
pageX	-
preventDefault()	returnValue = false;
relatedTarget	fromElement
	toElement
screenX	screenX
screenY	screenY
shiftKey	shiftKey
stopPropagation()	cancelBubble = true;
target	srcElement
timeStamp	-
type	type

To start, define a new method for `EventUtil` called `formatEvent()`, which accepts one parameter, the `event` object:

```
EventUtil.formatEvent = function (oEvent) {
    return oEvent;
}
```

The first thing to do is check for IE on Windows using the browser detection script from the previous chapter. In this case, you must check for the specific browser because this script is targeted at fixing a problem only in IE on Windows:

```
EventUtil.formatEvent = function (oEvent) {
    if (isIE && isWin) {

    }
    return oEvent;
};
```

To make this easy, just go straight down the table of properties and methods and try to make IE comply with the DOM model. The `altKey` property is already there, the `bubbles` property cannot be recreated, the `button` property is there, the `cancelBubble` property is there, and the `cancelable` property cannot recreated — that brings up the `charCode` property.

As mentioned earlier, in IE the character code is contained in the `keyCode` property on the `keypress` event; otherwise it's the correct value. So, if the type of event is `keypress`, it's logical to create a `charCode` property that is equal to `keyCode`; otherwise, the `charCode` property should be set to `0`:

```
EventUtil.formatEvent = function (oEvent) {
    if (isIE && isWin) {
        oEvent.charCode = (oEvent.type == "keypress") ? oEvent.keyCode : 0;
    }
    return oEvent;
};
```

Continuing down the table, the `clientX`, `clientY`, and `ctrlKey` properties are all the same in IE as in the DOM. We can't accurately recreate `currentTarget` or `detail`, so leave those off. However, you can put a value for `eventPhase`. This property is always equal to `2` for the bubbling phase because that is all IE supports:

```
EventUtil.formatEvent = function (oEvent) {
    if (isIE && isWin) {
        oEvent.charCode = (oEvent.type == "keypress") ? oEvent.keyCode : 0;
        oEvent.eventPhase = 2;
    }
    return oEvent;
};
```

Next in the table is the `isChar` property, which is `true` if the `charCode` property is not `0`:

```
EventUtil.formatEvent = function (oEvent) {
    if (isIE && isWin) {
        oEvent.charCode = (oEvent.type == "keypress") ? oEvent.keyCode : 0;
        oEvent.eventPhase = 2;
        oEvent.isChar = (oEvent.charCode > 0);
    }
    return oEvent;
};
```

The `keyCode` property is the same in both browsers, and the `metaKey` property cannot be recreated in IE, so that brings up `pageX` and `pageY`. Although the IE `event` object doesn't have equivalent properties, these properties can be calculated by taking the `clientX` and `clientY` values and augmenting them with the `scrollLeft` and `scrollTop` values of the document body:

```
EventUtil.formatEvent = function (oEvent) {
    if (isIE && isWin) {
        oEvent.charCode = (oEvent.type == "keypress") ? oEvent.keyCode : 0;
        oEvent.eventPhase = 2;
        oEvent.isChar = (oEvent.charCode > 0);
        oEvent.pageX = oEvent.clientX + document.body.scrollLeft;
        oEvent.pageY = oEvent.clientY + document.body.scrollTop;
```

```
    }
    return oEvent;
};
```

The `preventDefault()` method is next. Just define a method for the `event` object that sets its `returnValue` to `false`:

```
EventUtil.formatEvent = function (oEvent) {
    if (isIE && isWin) {
        oEvent.charCode = (oEvent.type == "keypress") ? oEvent.keyCode : 0;
        oEvent.eventPhase = 2;
        oEvent.isChar = (oEvent.charCode > 0);
        oEvent.pageX = oEvent.clientX + document.body.scrollLeft;
        oEvent.pageY = oEvent.clientY + document.body.scrollTop;
        oEvent.preventDefault = function () {
            this.returnvalue = false;
        };
    }
    return oEvent;
};
```

Note the use of the `this` object. In the context of an `event` object method, `this` refers to the `event` object.

The `relatedTarget` property can be either the `fromElement` or `toElement` property depending on the event type:

```
EventUtil.formatEvent = function (oEvent) {
    if (isIE && isWin) {
        oEvent.charCode = (oEvent.type == "keypress") ? oEvent.keyCode : 0;
        oEvent.eventPhase = 2;
        oEvent.isChar = (oEvent.charCode > 0);
        oEvent.pageX = oEvent.clientX + document.body.scrollLeft;
        oEvent.pageY = oEvent.clientY + document.body.scrollTop;
        oEvent.preventDefault = function () {
            this.returnValue = false;
        };

        if (oEvent.type == "mouseout") {
            oEvent.relatedTarget = oEvent.toElement;
        } else if (oEvent.type == "mouseover") {
            oEvent.relatedTarget = oEvent.fromElement;
        }
    }
    return oEvent;
};
```

The `screenX`, `screenY`, and `shiftKey` properties are all the same, so no work there. That brings up the `stopPropagation()` method, which simply involves setting `cancelBubble` to `true`:

```
EventUtil.formatEvent = function (oEvent) {
    if (isIE && isWin) {
        oEvent.charCode = (oEvent.type == "keypress") ? oEvent.keyCode : 0;
        oEvent.eventPhase = 2;
```

```
        oEvent.isChar = (oEvent.charCode > 0);
        oEvent.pageX = oEvent.clientX + document.body.scrollLeft;
        oEvent.pageY = oEvent.clientY + document.body.scrollTop;
        oEvent.preventDefault = function () {
            this.returnValue = false;
        };

        if (oEvent.type == "mouseout") {
            oEvent.relatedTarget = oEvent.toElement;
        } else if (oEvent.type == "mouseover") {
            oEvent.relatedTarget = oEvent.fromElement;
        }

        oEvent.stopPropagation = function () {
            this.cancelBubble = true;
        };
    }
    return oEvent;
};
```

Up next is the `target` property, which is exactly equivalent to IE's `srcElement` property:

```
EventUtil.formatEvent = function (oEvent) {
    if (isIE && isWin) {
        oEvent.charCode = (oEvent.type == "keypress") ? oEvent.keyCode : 0;
        oEvent.eventPhase = 2;
        oEvent.isChar = (oEvent.charCode > 0);
        oEvent.pageX = oEvent.clientX + document.body.scrollLeft;
        oEvent.pageY = oEvent.clientY + document.body.scrollTop;
        oEvent.preventDefault = function () {
            this.returnValue = false;
        };

        if (oEvent.type == "mouseout") {
            oEvent.relatedTarget = oEvent.toElement;
        } else if (oEvent.type == "mouseover") {
            oEvent.relatedTarget = oEvent.fromElement;
        }

        oEvent.stopPropagation = function () {
            this.cancelBubble = true;
        };

        oEvent.target = oEvent.srcElement;
    }
    return oEvent;
};
```

For the `time` property, you just create a `Date` object with the current date/time and get the milliseconds:

```
EventUtil.formatEvent = function (oEvent) {
    if (isIE && isWin) {
        oEvent.charCode = (oEvent.type == "keypress") ? oEvent.keyCode : 0;
```

```
            oEvent.eventPhase = 2;
            oEvent.isChar = (oEvent.charCode > 0);
            oEvent.pageX = oEvent.clientX + document.body.scrollLeft;
            oEvent.pageY = oEvent.clientY + document.body.scrollTop;
            oEvent.preventDefault = function () {
                this.returnValue = false;
            };

            if (oEvent.type == "mouseout") {
                oEvent.relatedTarget = oEvent.toElement;
            } else if (oEvent.type == "mouseover") {
                oEvent.relatedTarget = oEvent.fromElement;
            }

            oEvent.stopPropagation = function () {
                this.cancelBubble = true;
            };

            oEvent.target = oEvent.srcElement;
            oEvent.time = (new Date).getTime();
        }

        return oEvent;
    };
```

Because the `type` property is the same in both IE and the DOM, this is the end of the method. However, this method isn't intended to be used alone. Instead, it is intended to be used inside of another method that gets a reference to the `event` object.

Getting the event object

Unfortunately, IE and the DOM use very different methods to get the `event` object. In IE, the `event` object is tied to the `window` object although in the DOM it is independent of any other object and is passed in as an argument. Because of this, it is very difficult to make IE's event model act like Mozilla's, or vice versa. Instead of trying to make one like the other, you can create a new method that can be used by both browsers called `getEvent()`.

The `getEvent()` method accepts no arguments and its sole purpose is to return the event object. The first case it deals with is IE, checking for the existence of `window.event` and then using `formatEvent()` before returning the `event` object:

```
EventUtil.getEvent = function() {
    if (window.event) {
        return this.formatEvent(window.event);
    }
};
```

Next up is the DOM case. Remember, DOM-compliant browsers pass the `event` object as an argument to the event handler. This is when it pays to remember that a function is actually an object that has properties. In this case, the property of interest is called `caller`.

Every function has a `caller` property that contains a pointer to the method that is calling it. For instance, if `funcA()` calls `funcB()`, `funcB.caller` is equal to `funcA`. Assuming that an event handler calls `EventUtil.getEvent()`, then `EventUtil.getEvent.caller` points to the event handler itself.

Remember in Chapter 2, "ECMAScript Basics," you learned about the `arguments` property of a function. Because the `caller` property is a pointer to a `function`, you can access the `arguments` property of the event handler. The `event` object is always the first argument in an event handler, which means you can access `arguments[0]` in the event handler to get the `event` object:

```
EventUtil.getEvent = function() {
    if (window.event) {
        return this.formatEvent(window.event);
    } else {
        return EventUtil.getEvent.caller.arguments[0];
    }
};
```

This method can now be used inside of an event handler as shown here:

```
oDiv.onclick = function () {
         var oEvent = EventUtil.getEvent();
};
```

It's best to put all the `EventUtil` code defined in the last few sections into a separate file called `eventutil.js` to make it easy to include this script in any page.

Example

This code is rewritten from an example in the Mouse Events section:

```
<html>
    <head>
        <title>Mouse Events Example</title>
        <script type="text/javascript" src="detect.js"></script>
        <script type="text/javascript" src="eventutil.js"></script>
        <script type="text/javascript">

            EventUtil.addEventHandler(window, "load", function () {
                var oDiv = document.getElementById("div1");

                EventUtil.addEventHandler(oDiv, "mouseover", handleEvent);
                EventUtil.addEventHandler(oDiv, "mouseout", handleEvent);
                EventUtil.addEventHandler(oDiv, "mousedown", handleEvent);
                EventUtil.addEventHandler(oDiv, "mouseup", handleEvent);
                EventUtil.addEventHandler(oDiv, "click", handleEvent);
                EventUtil.addEventHandler(oDiv, "dblclick", handleEvent);

            });

            function handleEvent() {
                var oEvent = EventUtil.getEvent();
```

```
                var oTextbox = document.getElementById("txt1");
                oTextbox.value += "\n>" + oEvent.type;
                oTextbox.value += "\n    target is " + oEvent.target.tagName;
                if (oEvent.relatedTarget) {
                    oTextbox.value += "\n    relatedTarget is "
                                    + oEvent.relatedTarget.tagName;
                }
            }

        </script>
    </head>
    <body>
        <p>Use your mouse to click and double click the red square.</p>
        <div style="width: 100px; height: 100px; background-color: red"
id="div1"></div>
        <p><textarea id="txt1" rows="15" cols="50"></textarea></p>
    </body>
</html>
```

This example works in all DOM-compliant browsers as well as those that are IE-compliant, making use of the `target` and `relatedTarget` attributes of the newly formatted event object.

Summary

This chapter introduced the concept of events in JavaScript. You learned the difference between an event, which is the occurrence of an action, and an event handler, which is a function assigned to execute when an event occurs. You learned about the different ways to assign event handlers as well as the different methods used by Internet Explorer and the DOM standard for assigning multiple event handlers to the same event.

The concept of event flow was introduced in this chapter and the two different event flows, bubbling and capturing, were explained.

You then explored the `event` object, which is used to give the developer information about a particular event. The chapter showed you how Internet Explorer and the DOM each support different `event` objects. You also learned the different categories of events: mouse events, keyboard events, HTML events, and mutation events.

The last section of the chapter walked you through the creation of a cross-browser library for events, enabling you to use one set of methods to access the `event` object and add/remove event handlers without the need for browser detection.

10

Advanced DOM Techniques

Although the basic DOM is pretty straightforward, you can manipulate a document's underlying DOM tree in several ways. First, you can make use of several nonstandard properties and methods available in modern browsers, as well as little-known and underused DOM standard interfaces.

This chapter highlights the browser features that make this possible. Some of the interfaces discussed in this chapter are defined by the DOM and some are not, but they all enhance your ability manipulate DOM documents and nodes.

Scripting Styles

When Cascading Style Sheets (CSS) were introduced 1996, they completely changed the way developers formatted their HTML pages. Instead of using HTML tags such as `<font/>` and `<b/>`, pages began using CSS to define the appearance of fonts and other items. The natural next step for CSS support was to make styles accessible from JavaScript.

Internet Explorer 4.0 introduced a `style` object for each element on a page to manage that element's CSS-defined styles. The DOM eventually adopted this approach as a standard way to access an element's style information.

Today, the `style` object contains a property for each CSS style, albeit with some different formatting. All one-word CSS styles are represented by a property with the same name (for example, the `color` style is represented by `style.color`); two-word styles are represented by the first word followed by the capitalized second word with no dashes (for example, the `background-color` style is represented as `style.backgroundColor`). The following table lists some popular CSS attributes and their JavaScript `style` object equivalents:

CSS Style Attribute	JavaScript Style Property
background-color	style.backgroundColor
color	style.color
font	style.font
font-family	style.fontFamily
font-weight	style.fontWeight

To change a style's value using JavaScript, simply assign a CSS string to the style object property. For example, the following code changes the CSS `border` attribute of a `<div/>` to `"1px solid black"`:

```
var oDiv = document.getElementById("div1");
oDiv.style.border = "1px solid black";
```

It is possible to retrieve the value of any inline styles (those assigned by using the HTML `style` attribute) by using the `style` object as well. For example, the following page displays the background color of a `<div/>` by clicking a button:

```
<html>
    <head>
        <title>Style Example</title>
        <script type="text/javascript">
            function sayStyle() {
                var oDiv = document.getElementById("div1");
                alert(oDiv.style.backgroundColor);
            }
        </script>
    </head>
    <body>
        <div id="div1" style="background-color: red; height: 50px; width:
50px"></div><br />
        <input type="button" value="Get Background Color" onclick="sayStyle()" />
    </body>
</html>
```

This same technique can be used to apply *rollover* effects when the user moves the mouse over a given element on the page. Although CSS Level 2 provides the `:hover` pseudo-class to provide rollover effects on all elements, it is not supported by all browsers on all elements. To overcome this lack of support, just use the `style` object:

```
<html>
    <head>
        <title>Style Example</title>
    </head>
    <body>
        <div id="div1"
             style="background-color: red; height: 50px; width: 50px"
             onmouseover="this.style.backgroundColor = 'blue'"
```

```
                onmouseout="this.style.backgroundColor = 'red'"></div>
        </body>
    </html>
```

When you move the mouse over the red `<div/>`, it changes to blue; when you mouse out, it returns to red. Note that the event handlers use the `this` keyword to refer to the `<div/>` itself and gain access to its `style` object.

The style object also has a property called `cssText` that contains the CSS string describing the style of the element:

```
<html>
    <head>
        <title>Style Example</title>
    </head>
    <body>
        <div id="div1"
             style="background-color: red; height: 50px; width: 50px"
             onclick="alert(this.style.cssText)"></div>
    </body>
</html>
```

When you click on the `<div/>` in this example, the text `"background-color: red; height: 50px; width: 50px"` displays.

DOM style methods

The DOM also described several methods for the style object, all designed to interact with individual parts of the CSS style definition:

- `getPropertyValue(`*`propertyName`*`)` — Returns the string value of the CSS property *`propertyName`*. The property must be specified in CSS style, such as `"background-color"` instead of `"backgroundColor"`.
- `getPropertyPriority()` — Returns the string `"important"` if the CSS property `"!important"` is specified in the rule; otherwise it returns an empty string
- `item(`*`index`*`)` — Returns the name of the CSS property at the given *`index`*, such as `"background-color"`
- `removeProperty(`*`propertyName`*`)` — Removes *`propertyName`* from the CSS definition
- `setProperty(`*`propertyName, value, priority`*`)` — Sets the CSS property *`propertyName`* to *`value`* with the given *`priority`* (either `"important"` or an empty string)

Here's a simple example:

```
<html>
    <head>
        <title>Style Example</title>
        <script type="text/javascript">
            function useMethods() {
```

```
                var oDiv = document.getElementById("div1");
                alert(oDiv.style.item(0));    //outputs "background-color"
                alert(oDiv.style.getPropertyValue("background-color"));
                alert(oDiv.style.removeProperty("background-color");
            }
        </script>
    </head>
    <body>
        <div id="div1" style="background-color: red; height: 50px; width:
50px"></div><br />
        <input type="button" value="Use Methods" onclick="useMethods()" />
    </body>
</html>
```

When the button is clicked on this page, three things happen. First, the item in the first position (position 0) is displayed, which is `"background-color"` because it comes first in the `style` attribute of the `<div/>`. Second, the current value of `background-color` (red) is displayed. Finally, the `background-color` property is removed altogether, effectively making the `<div/>` invisible.

These methods can be used in place of the various `style` object properties to accomplish the same thing. For example, this returns the background color of the `<div/>`:

```
<html>
    <head>
        <title>Style Example</title>
        <script type="text/javascript">
            function sayStyle() {
                var oDiv = document.getElementById("div1");
                alert(oDiv.style.getPropertyValue("background-color"));
            }
        </script>
    </head>
    <body>
        <div id="div1" style="background-color: red; height: 50px; width:
50px"></div><br />
        <input type="button" value="Get Background Color" onclick="sayStyle()" />
    </body>
</html>
```

This is a rewrite of the rollover effect using the `style` methods:

```
<html>
    <head>
        <title>Style Example</title>
    </head>
    <body>
        <div id="div1"
            style="background-color: red; height: 50px; width: 50px"
            onmouseover="this.style.setProperty('background-color', 'blue', '')"
            onmouseout="this.style.setProperty('background-color', 'red', '')">
        </div>
    </body>
</html>
```

The DOM style methods are not supported by Internet Explorer. For this reason, it is best to use properties of the `style` object to get and set CSS properties.

Custom tooltips

Another interesting use of the `style` object is to create custom tooltips, which are those helpful yellow boxes that appear when you move a mouse over an image button. By using the `title` attribute, HTML elements can provide plain text tooltips, such as this:

```
<a href="http://www.wrox.com" title="Wrox Site">Wrox</a>
```

However, these plain text tooltips may not be enough. Suppose you want to create a tooltip with bold or italic text, or maybe even an image, you can do so by creating a hidden `<div/>` that is displayed only when the mouse moves over its designated target. This is essentially the same as the rollover code, with one extra step: moving the `<div/>` into a position close to the mouse. To correctly position the `<div/>`, you can make use of the `clientX` and `clientY` properties of the `event` object. Note that because these properties are available in all instances of the `event` object, you don't need to use the `EventUtil` object created earlier in the book:

```
<html>
    <head>
        <title>Style Example</title>
        <script type="text/javascript">
            function showTip(oEvent) {
                var oDiv = document.getElementById("divTip1");
                oDiv.style.visibility = "visible";
                oDiv.style.left = oEvent.clientX + 5;
                oDiv.style.top = oEvent.clientY + 5;
            }

            function hideTip(oEvent) {
                var oDiv = document.getElementById("divTip1");
                oDiv.style.visibility = "hidden";
            }
        </script>
    </head>
    <body>
        <p>Move your mouse over the red square.</p>
        <div id="div1"
             style="background-color: red; height: 50px; width: 50px"
             onmouseover="showTip(event)" onmouseout="hideTip(event)"></div>

         <div id="divTip1"
              style="background-color: yellow; position: absolute; visibility:
hidden; padding: 5px">
            <span style="font-weight: bold">Custom Tooltip</span><br />
            More details can go here.
         </div>
    </body>
</html>
```

This example passes the event object into the showTip() and hideTip() methods directly (as discussed in the previous chapter). When showTip() is called, divTip1 is first made visible by setting style.visibility to "visible". Then, the function moves divTip1 into position by setting style.left and style.top equal to event.clientX and event.clientY. To ensure that the tip doesn't appear directly under the cursor, five pixels are added to both the left and top coordinates. The hideTip() function simply sets style.visibility back to "hidden" so that the tip is no longer visible.

Collapsible sections

Using a similar technique, it's possible to create collapsible sections on a Web page. This type of functionality has become increasingly popular over the past few years to hide certain settings and fields until needed. The popularity of this user interface paradigm continues to grow, and it is now added to the Windows XP file system shell.

The basic idea of collapsible sections is that you can click somewhere to either display or hide a section of the screen. When one section collapses, all others shift their position to move into the empty space. Using the CSS display attribute can accomplish the same thing. When display is set to none, the element is effectively removed from the flow of the page and the page is redrawn as if the element doesn't exist. This is different from setting visibility to hidden, which simply hides the element, creating an empty space where the element resides.

Typically, collapsible sections are arranged into a title bar, which always remains visible, and a content section, which is expanded or collapsed. To mimic this on the Web, you can use a couple of <div/> elements: one for the header and one for the content. You also need a small function to toggle the expand/collapse of the content. Throw this all together and you get the following example:

```
<html>
    <head>
        <title>Style Example</title>
        <script type="text/javascript">
            function toggle(sDivId) {
                var oDiv = document.getElementById(sDivId);
                oDiv.style.display = (oDiv.style.display == "none") ? "block" :
"none";
            }
        </script>
    </head>
    <body>
        <div style="background-color: blue; color: white; font-weight: bold;
padding: 10px; cursor: pointer"
             onclick="toggle('divContent1')">Click Here</div>
        <div style="border: 3px solid blue; height: 100px; padding: 10px"
             id="divContent1">This is some content
        to show and hide.</div>
        <p> </p>
        <div style="background-color: blue; color: white; font-weight: bold;
padding: 10px; cursor: pointer"
             onclick="toggle('divContent2')">Click Here</div>
        <div style="border: 3px solid blue; height: 100px; padding: 10px"
             id="divContent2">This is some content
        to show and hide.</div>
    </body>
</html>
```

This page displays two collapsible sections. The two `<div/>` elements that are displayed or hidden are named `divContent1` and `divContent2`. When the `toggle()` function is called, the ID of the `<div/>` to act on is passed in as an argument. If the `<div/>` has `style.display` equal to `none` (meaning that it is not displayed), the value is switched to `block` (the default for `<div/>` elements); otherwise, `style.display` is set to `none`. This effectively creates collapsible sections on a Web page.

Accessing style sheets

The `style` object is useful for getting the CSS style of an element using the `style` attribute. What it cannot do is represent the CSS style of an element as defined by a CSS rule or class defined outside of the `style` attribute, such as in a `<style/>` element or an external style sheet. The following example illustrates the problem:

```
<html>
    <head>
        <title>Runtime Style Example</title>
        <style type="text/css">
            div.special {
                background-color: red;
                height: 10px;
                width: 10px;
                margin: 10px;
            }
        </style>
        <script type="text/javascript">
            function getBackgroundColor() {
                var oDiv = document.getElementById("div1");
                alert(oDiv.style.backgroundColor);
            }
        </script>
    </head>
    <body>
        <div id="div1" class="special"></div>
        <input type="button" value="Get Background Color"
onclick="getBackgroundColor()" />
    </body>
</html>
```

In this code, the style for the `<div/>` is defined in the class `special`. When you click the button and `getBackgroundColor()` is called, the alert displays an empty string because the CSS data isn't stored there; it is stored in the class. So the question becomes, how do you access the CSS class?

The first step is to get a reference to the style sheet in which the class is defined. To do this, use the `document.styleSheets` collection, which contains references to all the style sheets in an HTML page, including all `<style/>` elements (which are considered to be full-fledged style sheets by JavaScript). The DOM specifies a style sheet object as having the following properties:

- `disabled` — Indicates whether the style sheet is disabled.
- `href` — The URL of the style sheet for externally referenced files; for `<style/>` elements this should be `null`, although Mozilla returns the URL of the HTML page.

- `media` — A list of media types that can use the style sheet, as specified by the HTML `media` attribute. Internet Explorer incorrectly implements this property as a string containing the exact contents of the `media` attribute.
- `ownerNode` — The DOM node specifying the style sheet (either a `<link/>` or `<style/>` element). Internet Explorer doesn't support this property.
- `parentStyleSheet` — If the style sheet is included by the CSS `@import` statement, this points to the style sheet in which the statement occurs.
- `title` — The title assigned to the style sheet by the HTML title attribute, which can be used on both `<link/>` and `<style/>`.
- `type` — The mime type of the style sheet; usually this is `text/css` for CSS.

> **Opera doesn't support JavaScript style sheet access or manipulation. Safari provides limited support, but can't access disabled style sheets those with the `rel` attribute set to `"alternate stylesheet"`.**

Accessing the individual rules in a style sheet is a little bit tricky because of browser differences. The DOM specifies a collection called `cssRules` for each style sheet, which contains all the CSS rules defined in the style sheet. Mozilla and Safari correctly implement this standard, although Internet Explorer has named the collection `rules`. Consequently, before working with rules in style sheets, you must use an object detect to determine which collection name to use:

```
var oCSSRules = document.styleSheets[0].cssRules || document.styleSheets[0].rules;
```

Each rule contains a `selectorText` property that returns all the text for a CSS rule before an opening curly brace. Recall the CSS rule from the previous example:

```
div.special {
    background-color: red;
    height: 10px;
    width: 10px;
    margin: 10px;
}
```

The `selectorText` property for this rule is `div.special` (although Internet Explorer actually capitalizes all tag names, so it would be `DIV.special`).

Rules also contain a `style` property, which is a `style` object just like those found on elements. Therefore, the previous example can be updated to report the correct background color by using the `style` object on the CSS rule instead of the one on the `<div/>` itself:

```
<html>
    <head>
        <title>Accessing Style Sheets Example</title>
        <style type="text/css">
            div.special {
                background-color: red;
```

```
                height: 10px;
                width: 10px;
                margin: 10px;
            }
        </style>
        <script type="text/javascript">
            function getBackgroundColor() {
                var oCSSRules = document.styleSheets[0].cssRules ||
document.styleSheets[0].rules;
                alert(oCSSRules[0].style.backgroundColor);
            }
        </script>

    </head>
    <body>
        <div id="div1" class="special"></div>
        <input type="button" value="Get Background Color"
onclick="getBackgroundColor()" />
    </body>
</html>
```

When the button is clicked for this example, an alert correctly displays the background color based on the rule defined as `div.special`.

The `style` object on a rule isn't read-only; you can modify it as well. But this is where you must be careful, because modifying a CSS rule affects all elements using it on that page. Consider this example:

```
<html>
    <head>
        <title>Accessing Style Sheets Example</title>
        <style type="text/css">
            div.special {
                background-color: red;
                height: 10px;
                width: 10px;
                margin: 10px;
            }
        </style>
        <script type="text/javascript">
            function changeBackgroundColor() {
                var oCSSRules = document.styleSheets[0].cssRules ||
document.styleSheets[0].rules;
                oCSSRules[0].style.backgroundColor = "blue";
            }
        </script>
    </head>
    <body>
        <div id="div1" class="special"></div>
        <div id="div2" class="special"></div>
        <div id="div3" class="special"></div>
        <input type="button" value="Change Background Color"
onclick="changeBackgroundColor()" />
    </body>
</html>
```

In this example, three `<div/>` elements have a CSS class of `"special"`. When the button is clicked, `style.backgroundColor` is set to `"blue"`, thus changing the background color of all three elements. Because of this side effect, it is always better to modify the `style` object of an individual element instead of the one on a CSS rule. Changes to an element's `style` object override the corresponding setting on the CSS rule:

```
<html>
    <head>
        <title>Accessing Style Sheets Example</title>
        <style type="text/css">
            div.special {
                background-color: red;
                height: 10px;
                width: 10px;
                margin: 10px;
            }
        </style>
        <script type="text/javascript">
            function changeBackgroundColor() {
                var oDiv = document.getElementById("div1");
                oDiv.style.backgroundColor = "blue";
            }
        </script>
    </head>
    <body>
        <div id="div1" class="special"></div>
        <div id="div2" class="special"></div>
        <div id="div3" class="special"></div>

        <input type="button" value="Change Background Color"
onclick="changeBackgroundColor()" />
    </body>
</html>
```

This example changes the background color of only the first `<div/>` by modifying its `style` object; the other `<div/>` elements are unaffected by the change.

Computed styles

In addition to the `style` object of elements and CSS rules is the *computed style* of an element. The *computed style* is made up of all the style information from inline styles and CSS rules to give a true indication of how the element is being represented on the screen. As usual, Internet Explorer and the DOM differ in their implementations.

Computed styles in IE

Microsoft offers a `currentStyle` object on each element that includes all properties from the element `background-color` object as well the properties from any relevant CSS rule's `style` object. The `currentStyle` object works in the exact same way as the `style` object, with all the same properties and methods. This means that even if a background color is defined in a CSS rule, `currentStyle.backgroundColor` still contains the correct value:

```
<html>
    <head>
        <title>Computed Style Example</title>
        <style type="text/css">
            div.special {
                background-color: red;
                height: 10px;
                width: 10px;
                margin: 10px;
            }
        </style>
        <script type="text/javascript">
            function getBackgroundColor() {
                var oDiv = document.getElementById("div1");
                alert(oDiv.currentStyle.backgroundColor);
            }
        </script>

    </head>
    <body>
        <div id="div1" class="special"></div>
        <input type="button" value="Get Background Color"
onclick="getBackgroundColor()" />
    </body>
</html>
```

In this example, clicking the button displays the computed background color (red) even though the background color is defined in the `div.special` rule.

Keep in mind that all properties of the `currentStyle` object are read-only, and you cause an error if you try to assign a value. This happens because the `currentStyle` object is a summation of all applicable styles from the element and CSS rules; it is not a living, breathing object. To make style changes dynamically, you must use the `style` object as discussed previously.

Computed styles in the DOM

The DOM provides a method called `getComputedStyle()` that creates a `style`-like object based on a given element. The method accepts two parameters, the element to get the style for and a pseudo-element, such as `:hover` or `:first-letter` (it can also be `null` if not needed). You can access this method from the `document.defaultView` object, which is used to represent the currently rendered view of the document (`document.defaultView` is not supported in Internet Explorer or Safari).

You can rewrite the previous example using DOM methods like this:

```
<html>
    <head>
        <title>Computed Style Example</title>
        <style type="text/css">
            div.special {
                background-color: red;
                height: 10px;
                width: 10px;
                margin: 10px;
```

```
            }
        </style>
        <script type="text/javascript">
            function getBackgroundColor() {
                var oDiv = document.getElementById("div1");
                alert(document.defaultView.getComputedStyle(oDiv,
null).backgroundColor);
            }
        </script>

    </head>
    <body>
        <div id="div1" class="special"></div>
        <input type="button" value="Get Background Color"
onclick="getBackgroundColor()" />
    </body>
</html>
```

DOM-compliant browsers running this example display the background color in an alert when the button is clicked.

> **Note that although some browsers support this functionality, the manner in which values are represented can differ. For example, Mozilla translates all colors into RGB form (`rgb(255,0,0)` for red), whereas Opera translates all colors into their hexadecimal representations (`#ff0000` for red). It's always best to test your functionality on a number of browsers when using `getComputedStyle()`.**

innerText and innerHTML

Despite the advantages that the DOM brought to dynamically modifying documents, it wasn't enough for the developers at Microsoft. Internet Explorer 4.0 introduced two properties on all elements designed to ease the manipulation of the document called `innerText` and `innerHTML`.

The `innerText` property is designed to modify text between a starting and ending tag. For example, suppose you have an empty `<div/>` element that you wanted to change to `<div>New text for the div.</div>`. Using the DOM, you do this:

```
oDiv.appendChild(document.createTextNode("New text for the div."));
```

This code isn't difficult, but it is a bit verbose. Using `innerText`, you can just do this:

```
oDiv.innerText = "New text for the div.";
```

Using `innerText`, the code is much simpler and easier to understand. Additionally, `innerText` automatically HTML-encodes any less-than, greater-than, quote, and ampersand characters so you never have to worry about them:

```
oDiv.innerText = "New text for the <div/>.";
```

This line of code results in <div>New text for the <div/>.</div>. But what if you want to include HTML tags inside of the element as well? That's where innerHTML comes in.

The innerHTML property enables you to assign HTML strings to an element without worrying about creating elements using the DOM methods. For example, suppose an empty <div/> needs to become <div><strong>Hello</strong> <em>World</em></div>. Using the DOM, this is the code you use:

```
var oStrong = document.createElement("strong");
oStrong.appendChild(document.createTextNode("Hello"));
var oEm = document.createElement("em");
oEm.appendChild(document.createTextNode("World"));
oDiv.appendChild(oStrong);
oDiv.appendChild(document.createTextNode("")); //space between "Hello" and "World"
oDiv.appendChild(oEm);
```

Using innerHTML, the code becomes this:

```
oDiv.innerHTML = "<strong>Hello</strong> <em>World</em>";
```

Seven lines of code down to one line of code, that's the power of innerHTML!

You can also use innerText and innerHTML to get the contents of an element. If an element has only text, innerText and innerHTML return the exact same value. If, however, it has elements and text, innerText returns only the text portions, and innerHTML returns the HTML code for all elements and text. The following table lists the different values for innerText and innerHTML based on certain code.

Code	innerText	innerHTML
<div>Hello world</div>	"Hello world"	"Hello world"
<div><b>Hello</b> world</div>	"Hello world"	"<b>Hello</b> world"
<div><span></span></div>	""	"<span></span>"

Ultimately, this means that you can strip out all HTML tags from a given element by setting innerText to equal itself:

```
oDiv.innerText = oDiv.innerText;
```

Even though they are not part of the DOM standard, most modern browsers, including Internet Explorer, Opera, and Safari, support innerText and innerHTML; Mozilla supports only innerHTML.

outerText and outerHTML

Along with innerText and innerHTML, Internet Explorer 4.0 also introduced outerText and outerHTML, which do exactly the same thing as their inner counterparts except that they replace the node in question. For example, setting `outerText` on a `<div/>` removes it and replaces it with a text node. Consider the following line of code:

```
oDiv.outerText = "Hello world!";
```

This single line of code is the same as this set of DOM manipulations:

```
var oText = document.createTextNode("Hello world! ");
var oDivParent = oDiv.parentNode;
oDivParent.replaceChild(oText, oDiv);
```

The `outerText` property has the same rules as the `innerText` property in that it replaces all less-than, greater-than, quote, and ampersand characters with their HTML entities. Similarly, `outerHTML` behaves the same as `innerHTML`, creating all the necessary DOM nodes represented by the HTML string:

```
oDiv.outerHTML = "<p>This is a paragraph.</p>";
```

This line of code performs the following DOM modifications:

```
var oP = document.createElement("p");
oP.appendChild(document.createTextNode("This is a paragraph. "));
var oDivParent = oDiv.parentNode;
oDivParent.replaceChild(oP, oDiv);
```

Whereas `outerText` and `outerHTML` provide developers with a lot of power, they don't clearly indicate exactly what is happening (the code doesn't *read*). Many developers shy away from using `outerText` and `outerHTML` because they can lead to bigger headaches down the road if something goes wrong. Generally speaking, you're safer using the DOM methods, whose meanings are much clearer.

Both these properties can also be used to get the contents of an element. The `outerText` property always returns the same value as `innerText`, regardless of the element contents. On the other hand, `outerHTML` returns the full HTML code for the element, including the element itself. The following table lists the different values for `outerText` and `outerHTML` based on certain code.

Code	outerText	outerHTML
`<div>Hello world</div>`	`"Hello world"`	`"<div>Hello world</div>"`
`<div><b>Hello</b> world</div>`	`"Hello world"`	`"<div><b>Hello</b> world</div>"`
`<div><span></span></div>`	`""`	`"<div><span></span></div>"`

Similar to `innerText`, you can use `outerText` in a unique way. By setting `outerText` equal to itself, you actually remove the element and replace it with a text node containing all the text inside the element:

```
<html>
    <head>
        <title>OuterText Example</title>
        <style type="text/css">
            div.special {
```

```
                background-color: red;
                padding: 10px;
            }
        </style>
        <script type="text/javascript">
            function useOuterText() {
                var oDiv = document.getElementById("div1");
                oDiv.outerText = oDiv.outerText;
                alert(document.getElementById("div1"));
            }
        </script>

    </head>
    <body>
        <div id="div1" class="special">This is my original text</div>
        <input type="button" value="Use OuterText" onclick="useOuterText()" />
    </body>
</html>
```

When you click the button in this example, the `<div/>` is replaced with a text node containing `This is my original text`. You can tell that the `<div/>` no longer exists by using `document.getElementById()` to look for `div1` again. In this example, the result of the function (`null`) is displayed in an alert.

> **The `outerText` and `outerHTML` properties are supported in Internet Explorer and Opera only.**

Ranges

To allow an even greater measure of control over a page, you can use something called a *range*. A range can be used to select a section of a document regardless of node boundaries (note that the selection occurs behind the scenes and cannot be seen by the user).

Ranges are helpful when regular DOM manipulation isn't specific enough to change a document. And as usual, there are two different implementations of ranges: one from the DOM and one from Internet Explorer.

Ranges in the DOM

DOM Level 2 defines a method called `createRange()` to, well, create ranges. In DOM-compliant browsers, this method belongs to the `document` object, so a new range can be created like this:

```
var oRange = document.createRange();
```

Just like nodes, a range is tied directly to a document. To determine if the document supports DOM-style ranges, you can use the `hasFeature()` method discussed in Chapter 6, "DOM Basics."

```
var supportsDOMRanges = document.implementation.hasFeature("Range", "2.0");
```

If you plan to use DOM ranges, it is always best to make this check first and wrap your code in an `if` statement:

```
if (supportsDOMRange) {
    var oRange = document.createRange();

    //range code here
}
```

Simple selection in DOM ranges

The simplest way to select a part of the document using a range is to use either `selectNode()` or `selectNodeContents()`. These methods each accept one argument, a DOM node, and fill a range with information from that node.

The `selectNode()` method selects the entire node, including its children, whereas `selectNodeContents()` selects all of the node's children. For example, consider the following:

```
<p id="p1"><b>Hello</b> World</p>
```

This code can be accessed using the following JavaScript:

```
var oRange1 = document.createRange();
var oRange2 = document.createRange();
var oP1 = document.getElementById("p1");
oRange1.selectNode(oP1);
oRange2.selectNodeContents(oP1);
```

The two ranges in this example contain different sections of the document: oRange1 contains the `<p>` element and all its children, whereas oRange2 contains the `<b/>` element and the text node `World` (see Figure 10-1).

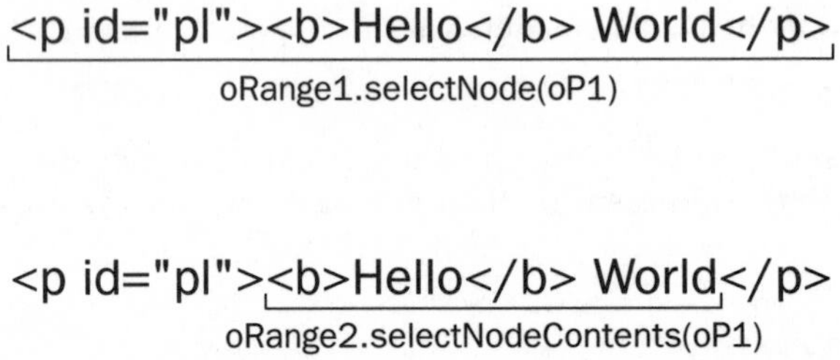
<p id="pl"><b>Hello</b> World</p>
oRange1.selectNode(oP1)
<p id="pl"><b>Hello</b> World</p>
oRange2.selectNodeContents(oP1)

Figure 10-1

Whenever you create a range, a number of properties are assigned to it:

- `startContainer` — The node within which the range starts (the parent of the first node in the selection)
- `startOffset` — The offset within the `startContainer` where the range starts. If `startContainer` is a text node, comment node, or CData node, the `startOffset` is the number of characters skipped before the range starts; otherwise, the offset is the index of the first child node in the range.

- `endContainer` — The node within which the range ends (the parent of the last node in the selection)
- `endOffset` — The offset within the `endContainer` where the range ends (follows the same rules as `startOffset`)
- `commonAncestorContainer` — The first node within which both `startContainer` and `endContainer` exist

These properties are all read-only and are designed to give you additional information about the range.

When you use `selectNode()`, the `startContainer`, `endContainer`, and `commonAncestorContainer` are all equal to the parent node of the node that was passed in; `startOffset` is equal to the index of the given node within the parent's `childNodes` collection, whereas `endOffset` is equal to the `startOffset` plus one (because only one node is selected).

When you use `selectNodeContents()`, `startContainer`, `endContainer`, and `commonAncestorContainer` are equal to the node that was passed in; `startOffset` is equal to 0; `endOffset` is equal to the number of child nodes (`node.childNodes.length`).

The following example illustrates these properties:

```
<html>
    <head>
        <title>DOM Range Example</title>
        <script type="text/javascript">
            function useRanges() {
                var oRange1 = document.createRange();
                var oRange2 = document.createRange();
                var oP1 = document.getElementById("p1");
                oRange1.selectNode(oP1);
                oRange2.selectNodeContents(oP1);

                document.getElementById("txtStartContainer1").value =
oRange1.startContainer.tagName;
                document.getElementById("txtStartOffset1").value =
oRange1.startOffset;
                document.getElementById("txtEndContainer1").value =
oRange1.endContainer.tagName;
                document.getElementById("txtEndOffset1").value = oRange1.endOffset;
                document.getElementById("txtCommonAncestor1").value =
oRange1.commonAncestorContainer.tagName;

                document.getElementById("txtStartContainer2").value =
oRange2.startContainer.tagName;
                document.getElementById("txtStartOffset2").value =
oRange2.startOffset;
                document.getElementById("txtEndContainer2").value =
oRange2.endContainer.tagName;
                document.getElementById("txtEndOffset2").value = oRange2.endOffset;
                document.getElementById("txtCommonAncestor2").value =
oRange2.commonAncestorContainer.tagName;
            }
        </script>
```

```
    </head>
    <body><p id="p1"><b>Hello</b> World</p>
        <input type="button" value="Use Ranges" onclick="useRanges()" />
        <table border="0">
        <tr>
            <td>
                <fieldset>
                    <legend>oRange1</legend>
                    Start Container: <input type="text" id="txtStartContainer1"
/><br />
                    Start Offset: <input type="text" id="txtStartOffset1" /><br />
                    End Container: <input type="text" id="txtEndContainer1" /><br
/>
                    End Offset: <input type="text" id="txtEndOffset1" /><br />
                    Common Ancestor: <input type="text" id="txtCommonAncestor1"
/><br />
                </fieldset>
            </td>
            <td>
                <fieldset>
                    <legend>oRange2</legend>
                    Start Container: <input type="text" id="txtStartContainer2"
/><br />
                    Start Offset: <input type="text" id="txtStartOffset2" /><br />
                    End Container: <input type="text" id="txtEndContainer2" /><br
/>
                    End Offset: <input type="text" id="txtEndOffset2" /><br />
                    Common Ancestor: <input type="text" id="txtCommonAncestor2"
/><br />
                </fieldset>
            </td>
        </tr>
        </table>
    </body>
</html>
```

Figure 10-2 displays the result when this example is run in a DOM-compliant browser, such as Mozilla.

As you can see, `oRange1`'s `startContainer`, `endContainer`, and `commonAncestorContainer` are equal to the `<body/>` element because the `<p/>` element is wholly contained within it. Also, `startOffset` is equal to 0, because the `<p/>` element is the first child of `<p/>`, and `endOffset` is equal to 1, meaning that the range is over before the second child node (which is index 1).

Looking over at `oRange2`'s information gathered by `selectNodeContents()`, `startContainer`, `endContainer`, and `commonAncestorContainer` are equal to the `<p/>` element itself because you are selecting its children. The `startOffset` is equal to 0, because the selection begins with the first child node of `<p/>`. The `endOffset` is equal to 2 because there are two child nodes of `<p/>`: `<b/>` and the text node `World`.

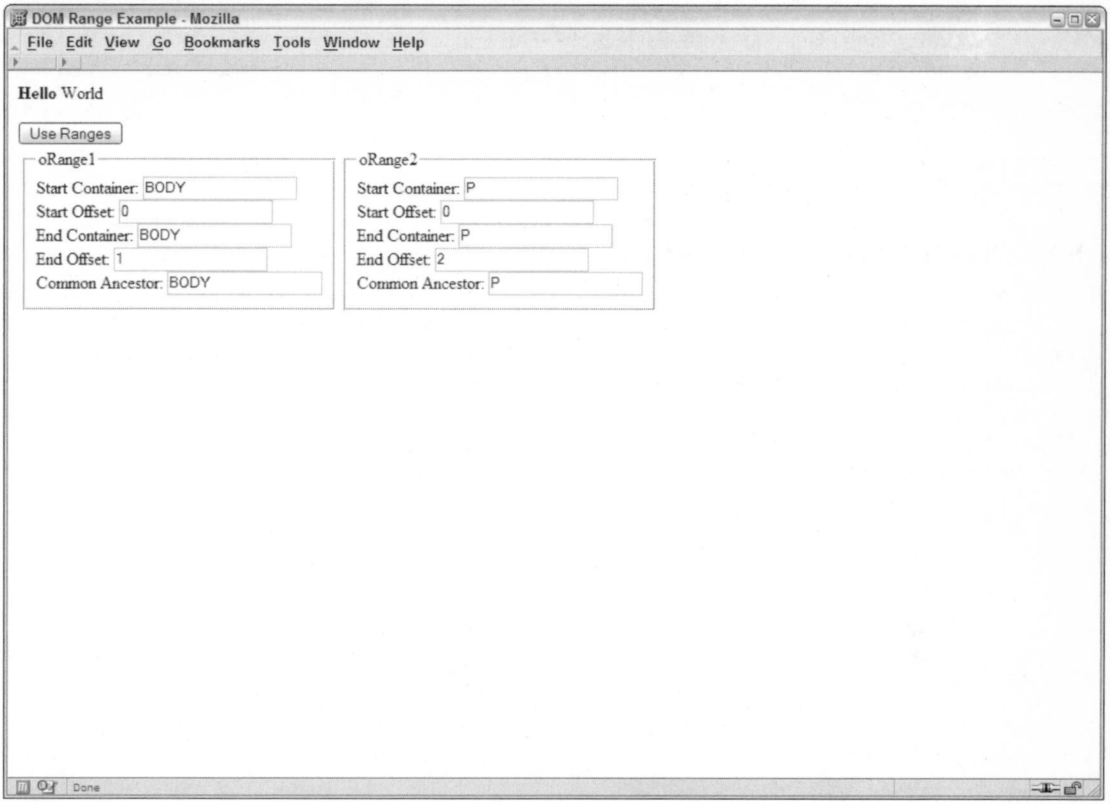

Figure 10-2

Several methods help you get more specific with selections while still setting these properties for you. These are the following:

- `setStartBefore(`*`refNode`*`)` — Sets the starting point of the range to begin before *`refNode`* (so *`refNode`* is the first node in the selection). The `startContainer` property is set to *`refNode`*'s parent and the `startOffset` property is set to the index of *`refNode`* within its parent's `childNodes` collection.
- `setStartAfter(`*`refNode`*`)` — Sets the starting point of the range to begin after *`refNode`* (so *`refNode`* is not part of the selection; rather, its next sibling is the first node in the selection). The `startContainer` property is set to *`refNode`*'s parent and the `startOffset` property is set to the index of *`refNode`* within its parent's `childNodes` collection plus one.
- `setEndBefore(`*`refNode`*`)` — Sets the ending point of the range to begin before *`refNode`* (so *`refNode`* is not part of the selection; its previous sibling is the last node in the selection). The `endContainer` property is set to *`refNode`*'s parent and the `endOffset` property is set to the index of *`refNode`* within its parent's `childNodes` collection.

- `setEndAfter(refNode)` — Sets the ending point of the range to begin before *refNode* (so *refNode* is the last node in the selection). The `endContainer` property is set to *refNode*'s parent and the `endOffset` property is set to the index of *refNode* within its parent's `childNodes` collection plus one.

Using any of these methods, all properties are assigned for you. However, it is possible to assign these values directly in order to make complex range selections.

Complex selection in DOM ranges

Creating complex ranges requires the use of range `setStart()` and `setEnd()` methods. Both methods accept two arguments: a reference node and an offset. For `setStart()`, the reference node becomes the `startContainer`, and the offset becomes the `startOffset`; for `setEnd()`, the reference node becomes the `endContainer`, and the offset becomes the `endOffset`.

Using these methods, it is possible to mimic `selectNode()` and `selectNodeContents()`. For example, the `useRanges()` function in the previous example can be rewritten using `setStart()` and `setEnd()`:

```
function useRanges() {
    var oRange1 = document.createRange();
    var oRange2 = document.createRange();
    var oP1 = document.getElementById("p1");

    var iP1Index = -1;
    for (var i=0; i < oP1.parentNode.childNodes.length; i++) {
        if (oP1.parentNode.childNodes[i] == oP1) {
            iP1Index = i;
            break;
        }
    }

    oRange1.setStart(oP1.parentNode, iP1Index);
    oRange1.setEnd(oP1.parentNode, iP1Index + 1);
    oRange2.setStart(oP1, 0);
    oRange2.setEnd(oP1, oP1.childNodes.length);

    //textbox assignments here
}
```

Note that to select the node (using `oRange1`), you must first determine the index of the given node (`oP1`) in its parent node's `childNodes` collection. To select the node contents (using `oRange2`), no calculations are necessary. But you already know easier ways to select the node and node contents; the real power here is to be able to select only parts of nodes.

Recall the very first example mentioned in this section, selecting `llo` from `Hello` and `Wo` from `World` in the HTML code `<p id="p1"><b>Hello</b> World</p>`. Using `setStart()` and `setEnd()`, this is quite easy to accomplish.

The first step in the process is to get references to the text nodes containing `Hello` and `World` using the regular DOM methods:

```
var oP1 = document.getElementById("p1");
var oHello = oP1.firstChild.firstChild;
var oWorld = oP1.lastChild;
```

The `Hello` text node is actually a grandchild of `<p/>` because it's apparently `<b/>`, so you can use `oP1.firstChild` to get `<b/>` and `oP1.firstChild.firstChild` to get the text node. The `World` text node is the second (and the last) child of `<p/>`, so you can use `oP1.lastChild` to retrieve it.

Next, create the range and set the appropriate offsets:

```
var oP1 = document.getElementById("p1");
var oHello = oP1.firstChild.firstChild;
var oWorld = oP1.lastChild;
var oRange = document.createRange();

oRange.setStart(oHello, 2);
oRange.setEnd(oWorld, 3);
```

For `setStart()`, the offset is 2, because the first `l` in `Hello` is in position `2` (starting from `H` in position 0). For `setEnd()`, the offset is 3, indicating the first character that *should not* be selected, which is `r` in position 3. (There is actually a space in position 0. See Figure 10-3.)

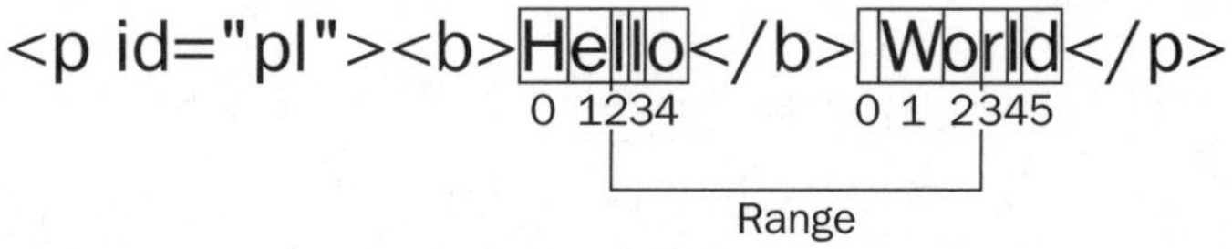

Figure 10-3

Because both `oHello` and `oWorld` are text nodes, they become the `startContainer` and `endContainer` for the range so that the `startOffset` and `endOffset` accurately look at the text contained within each node instead of looking for child nodes, which is what happens when an element is passed in. The `commonAncestorContainer` is the `<p/>` element, which is the first ancestor that contains both nodes.

Of course, just selecting sections of the document isn't very useful unless you can interact with the selection.

> **There is a bug in Mozilla's implementation of the DOM Range (bug #135928) that causes an error to occur when you try to use `setStart()` and `setEnd()` with the same text node. This bug has been resolved and this fix is included in a future Mozilla release.**

Interacting with DOM range content

When a range is created, internally it creates a document fragment node onto which all the nodes in the selection are attached. Before this can happen, however, the range must make sure that the selection is well-formed.

You just learned that it is possible to select the entire area from the first letter `l` in `Hello` to the `o` in `World`, including the `</b>` end tag (see Figure 10-4). This would be impossible using the normal DOM methods described earlier in the book.

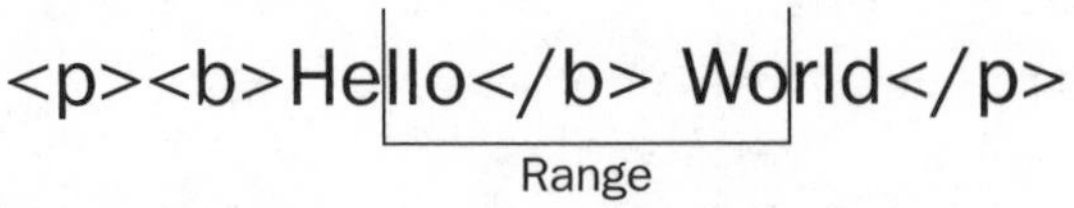

Figure 10-4

The reason a range can get away with this trick is that it recognizes missing opening and closing tags. In the previous example, the range calculates that a `<b>` start tag is missing inside the selection, so the range dynamically adds it behind the scenes, along with a new `</b>` end tag to enclose `He`, thus altering the DOM to the following:

```
<p><b>He</b><b>llo</b> World</p>
```

The document fragment contained within the range is displayed in Figure 10-5.

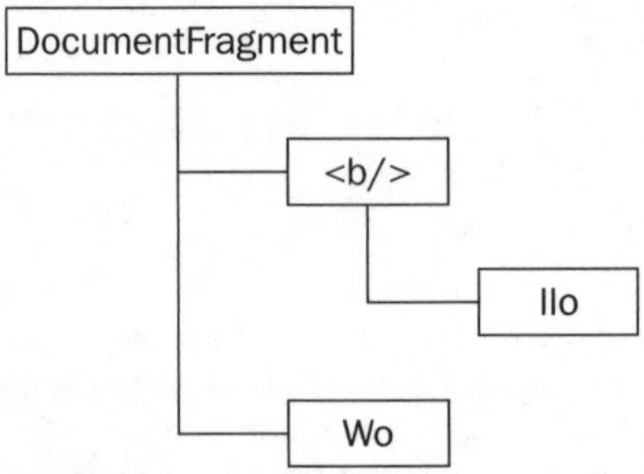

Figure 10-5

With the document fragment created, you can manipulate the contents of the range using a variety of methods.

The first method is the simplest to understand and use: `deleteContents()`. This method simply deletes the contents of the range from the document. In the previous example, calling `deleteContents()` on the range leaves this HTML in the page:

```
<p><b>He</b>rld</p>
```

Because the entire document fragment is removed, the range is kind enough to place the missing `</b>` tag into the document so it remains well-formed.

extractContents() is similar to deleteContents(). It also removes the range selection from the document and returns the range's document fragment as the function value. This allows you to insert the contents of the range somewhere else:

```
var oP1 = document.getElementById("p1");
var oHello = oP1.firstChild.firstChild;
var oWorld = oP1.lastChild;
var oRange = document.createRange();

oRange.setStart(oHello, 2);
oRange.setEnd(oWorld, 3);
var oFragment = oRange.extractContents();

document.body.appendChild(oFragment);
```

In this example, the fragment is extracted and added to the end of the document's <body/> element (remember, when a document fragment is passed into appendChild(), only the fragment's children are added, not the fragment itself). What you see in this example is the code <b>He</b>rld at the top of the page, and <b>llo</b> Wo at the bottom of the page.

Another option is to leave the fragment in place, but create a clone of it that can be inserted elsewhere in the document by using cloneContents():

```
var oP1 = document.getElementById("p1");
var oHello = oP1.firstChild.firstChild;
var oWorld = oP1.lastChild;
var oRange = document.createRange();

oRange.setStart(oHello, 2);
oRange.setEnd(oWorld, 3);
var oFragment = oRange.cloneContents();

document.body.appendChild(oFragment);
```

This method is very similar to deleteContents() because both return the range's document fragment. This results in <b>llo</> Wo being added to the end of the page; the original HTML code remains intact.

The document fragment and accompanying changes to the range selection do not happen until one of these methods is called. The original HTML remains intact right up until that point.

Inserting DOM range content

The previous three methods all dealt with removing information from the range in one way or another. It is also possible to add content to the range using a couple of different methods.

The insertNode() method enables you to insert a node at the beginning of the selection. Suppose you wanted to insert the following HTML code into the range defined in the previous section:

```
<span style="color: red">Inserted text</span>
```

The following code accomplishes this:

```
var oP1 = document.getElementById("p1");
var oHello = oP1.firstChild.firstChild;
var oWorld = oP1.lastChild;
var oRange = document.createRange();

var oSpan = document.createElement("span");
oSpan.style.color = "red";
oSpan.appendChild(document.createTextNode("Inserted text"));

oRange.setStart(oHello, 2);
oRange.setEnd(oWorld, 3);
oRange.insertNode(oSpan);
```

Running this JavaScript effectively creates the following HTML code:

```
<p id="p1"><b>He<span style="color: red">Inserted text</span>llo</b> World</p>
```

Note that the `<span/>` is inserted just before the `llo` in `Hello`, which is the first part of the range selection. Also note that the original HTML didn't add or remove `<b/>` elements because none of the methods introduced in the previous section were used. You can use this technique to insert helpful information, such as an image next to links that open in a new window.

Along with inserting into the range, it is possible to insert content surrounding the range by using the `surroundContents()` method. This method accepts one parameter, which is the node that surrounds the range contents. Behind the scenes, the following steps are taken:

1. The contents of the range are extracted (similar to `extractContents()`).
2. The given node is inserted into the position in the original document where the range was.
3. The contents of the document fragment is added to the given node.

This sort of functionality is useful online to highlight certain words in a Web page, like this:

```
var oP1 = document.getElementById("p1");
var oHello = oP1.firstChild.firstChild;
var oWorld = oP1.lastChild;
var oRange = document.createRange();

var oSpan = document.createElement("span");
oSpan.style.backgroundColor = "yellow";

oRange.setStart(oHello, 2);
oRange.setEnd(oWorld, 3);
oRange.surroundContents(oSpan);
```

The previous code highlights the range selection with a yellow background.

Collapsing a DOM Range

To empty a range, (that is, to have it select no part of the document), you *collapse* it. Collapsing a range resembles the behavior of a text box. When you have text in a text box, you can highlight an entire word using the mouse. However, if you left-click the mouse again, the selection is removed and the cursor is located between two letters. When you collapse a range, you are setting its locations between parts of a document, either at the beginning of the range selection or at the end. Figure 10-6 illustrates what happens when a range is collapsed.

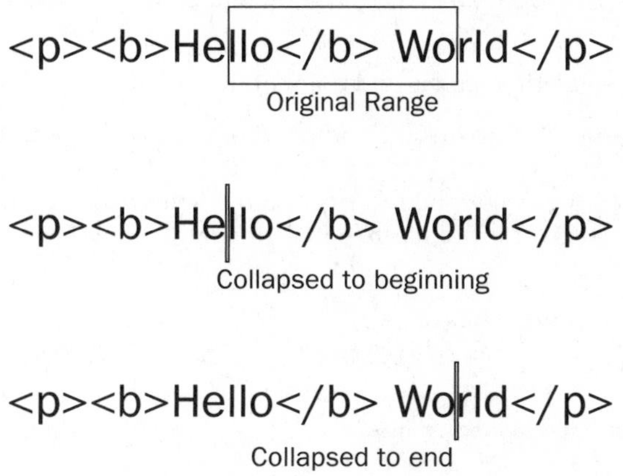

Figure 10-6

You can collapse a range by using the `collapse()` method, which accepts a single argument: a Boolean value indicating which end of the range to collapse to. If the argument is `true`, then the range is collapsed to its starting point; if `false`, the range is collapsed to its ending point. To determine if a range is collapsed, you can use the `collapsed` property:

```
oRange.collapse(true);       //collapse to the starting point
alert(oRange.collapsed);     //outputs "true"
```

Testing whether a range is collapsed is helpful if you aren't sure if two nodes in the range are next to each other. For example, consider this HTML code:

```
<p id="p1">Paragraph 1</p><p id="p2">Paragraph 2</p>
```

If you don't know the exact makeup of this code (because, perhaps, it is automatically generated), you might try creating a range like this:

```
var oP1 = document.getElementById("p1");
var oP2 = document.getElementById("p2");
var oRange = document.createRange();
oRange.setStartAfter(oP1);
oRange.setStartBefore(oP2);
alert(oRange.collapsed);     //outputs "true"
```

In this case, the created range is collapsed because there is nothing between the end of `p1` and the beginning of `p2`.

Comparing DOM ranges

If you have more than one range, you can use the `compareBoundaryPoints()` method to determine if the ranges have any boundaries (start or end) in common. The method accepts two arguments: the range to compare to and how to compare, which is a constant value:

- `START_TO_START` (0) — Compares the starting point of the first range to the starting point of the second
- `START_TO_END` (1) — Compares the starting point of the first range to the end point of the second
- `END_TO_END` (2) — Compares the end point of the first range to the end point of the second.
- `END_TO_START` (3) — Compares the end point of the first range to the start point of the second

The `compareBoundaryPoints()` method returns –1 if the point from the first range comes before the point from the second range, 0 if the points are equal, or 1 if the point from the first range comes after the point from the second range.

For example:

```
var oRange1 = document.createRange();
var oRange2 = document.createRange();
var oP1 = document.getElementById("p1");
oRange1.selectNodeContents(oP1);
oRange2.selectNodeContents(oP1);
oRange2.setEndBefore(oP1.lastChild);
alert(oRange1.compareBoundaryPoints(Range.START_TO_START, oRange2));   //outputs 0
alert(oRange1.compareBoundaryPoints(Range.END_TO_END, oRange2));       //outputs 1;
```

In this code, the starting points of the two ranges are exactly the same because both use the default value from `selectNodeContents()`; therefore, the method returns 0. For `oRange2`, however, the end point is changed using `setEndBefore()`, making the end point of `oRange1` come after the end point of `oRange2` (see Figure 10-7), so the method returns 1.

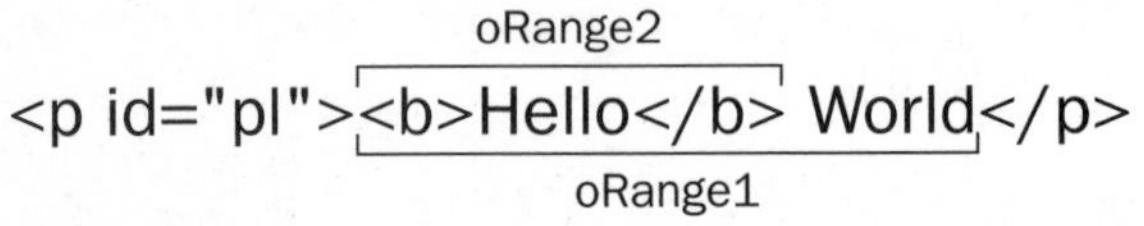

Figure 10-7

Cloning DOM ranges

If you find the need, you can duplicate any range by calling the `cloneRange()` method. This method creates an exact duplicate of the range on which it is called:

```
var oNewRange = oRange.cloneRange();
```

The new range contains all of the same properties as the original and can be modified without affecting the original in any way.

Clean up

When you are done using a range, it is best to call the `detach()` method to free up system resources. This isn't required because dereferenced ranges are picked up by the garbage collector eventually. If, however, the range is used initially and then no longer required, calling `detach()` ensures that it isn't taking up any more memory than necessary:

```
oRange.detach();
```

Ranges in Internet Explorer

Internet Explorer has a non-standard way of dealing with ranges, which can nonetheless be very effective as long as you understand the differences.

To begin, ranges in IE are called *text ranges* because they are intended primarily to deal with text (not specifically DOM nodes). To create a range, you must call `createTextRange()` on a `<body/>`, `<button/>`, `<input/>`, or `<textarea/>` element (not on the `document` itself):

```
var oRange = document.body.createTextRange();
```

Creating a range in this way allows it to be used anywhere on the page (creating a range on one of the other specified elements limits the range to working on that element).

Simple selection in IE ranges

The simplest way to select an area of the page is to use the `findText()` method of the range. This method finds the first instance of a given text string and moves the range to surround it. Once again, consider the following HTML code:

```
<p id="p1"><b>Hello</b> World</p>
```

To select `Hello`, you can use the following code:

```
var oRange = document.body.createTextRange();
var bFound = oRange.findText("Hello");
```

After the second line of code, the text `Hello` is contained within the range. You can test this by using the range's `text` property (which returns the text contained in the range) or checking the returned value of `findText()`, which is true if the text was found:

```
alert(bFound);
alert(oRange.text);
```

To move the range through the document, you can use the second parameter of the `findText()` method, which is a number indicating the direction to continue searching: A negative number indicates that the search should go backwards, whereas a positive number indicates that the search should go forward. So, to find the first two instances of `Hello` in a document, you could use this code:

```
var bFound = oRange.findText("Hello");
var bFoundAgain = oRange.findText("Hello", 1);
```

The closest thing to the DOM's `selectNode()` is IE's `moveToElementText()`, which accepts a DOM element as an argument and selects all the element's text, including HTML tags:

```
var oRange = document.body.createTextRange();
var oP1 = document.getElementById("p1");
oRange.moveToElementText(oP1);
```

To test that this works, you can use the `htmlText` property, which returns all the HTML contained within the range:

```
alert(oRange.htmlText);
```

Ranges in IE don't have any other properties that are dynamically updated as the range selection changes, although a `parentElement()` method behaves the same as the DOM's `commonAncestorContainer` property:

```
var oCommonAncestor = oRange.parentElement();
```

Complex selection in IE ranges

One of the complex parts of complex range selection in IE is that you must use one of the simple methods of selection first. After the range is in a relatively correct position, you can use `move()`, `moveStart()`, `moveEnd()`, and `expand()` to further position the range.

Each of these methods accepts two arguments: the type of units to move and the number of units to move. The type of units to move is one of the following string values:

- "character" — Moves a point by one character
- "word" — Moves a point by one word (a sequence of non-whitespace characters)
- "sentence" — Moves a point by one sentence (a sequence of characters ending with a period, question mark, or exclamation point)
- "textedit" — Moves a point to the start or end of the current range selection

The `moveStart()` method moves the starting point of the range by the given number of units, whereas the `moveEnd()` method moves the endpoint of the range by the given number of units:

```
oRange.moveStart("word", 2);        //move the start point by two words
oRange.moveEnd("character", 1);     //move the ending point by two words
```

You can also use the `expand()` method to normalize the range. The `expand()` method makes sure that any partially selected units become fully selected. For example, if you selected only the middle two characters of a word, you can call `expand("word")` to ensure that the entire word is enclosed by the range.

The `move()` method first collapses the range (making the start and end point equal) and then moves the range by the specified number of units:

```
oRange.move("character", 5);    //move over five characters
```

After using `move()`, you must use either `moveEnd()` to once again make a selection.

Interacting with IE range content

Interacting with a range's content in IE is done through either the `text` property or the `pasteHTML()` method.

The `text` property, which you used previously to retrieve the text content of the range, can also be used to set the text content of the range. For example:

```
var oRange = document.body.createTextRange();
oRange.findText("Hello");
oRange.text = "Howdy";
```

If you run this code against the same `Hello World` code shown earlier, the resulting code is the following:

```
<p id="p1"><b>Howdy</b> World</p>
```

Note that all the HTML tags remained intact when setting the `text` property. If you want to insert more content than just plain text, you can use `pasteHTML()` to insert HTML code. For instance:

```
var oRange = document.body.createTextRange();
oRange.findText("Hello");
oRange.pasteHTML("<em>Howdy</em>");
```

If you run this code, the following is the resulting HTML :

```
<p id="p1"><b><em>Howdy</em></b> World</p>
```

> **It is not recommended to use `pasteHTML()` when the range contains HTML code because this causes unpredictable results and often results in improperly formed HTML.**

Collapsing an IE range

Ranges in IE have a `collapse()` method that works exactly the same as the DOM method: Pass in `true` to collapse the range to the beginning and `false` to collapse the range to the end.

```
oRange.collapse(true);
```

Unfortunately, no corresponding `collapsed` property tells you whether a range is already collapsed. Instead, you must use the `boundingWidth` property, which returns the width (in pixels) of the range. If `boundingWidth` is equal to 0, the range is collapsed:

```
var bIsCollapsed = (oRange.boundingWidth == 0);
```

The `boundingHeight`, `boundingLeft`, and `boundingTop` properties also give information about the range location, although these are less helpful than `boundingWidth`.

Comparing IE ranges

Ranges in IE have a similar capability to the DOM range's `compareBoundaryPoints()` method called `compareEndPoints()`. This method accepts two arguments: the type of comparison and the range to compare to. Unlike the DOM implementation, the type of comparison in IE is one of the following strings: "StartToStart", "StartToEnd", "EndToEnd", and "EndToStart". These comparisons are identically equal to the comparable ones in DOM ranges.

Also similar to the DOM, `compareEndPoints()` returns –1 if the first range boundary occurs before the second range's boundary, 0 if they are equal, and 1 if the first range boundary occurs after the second range boundary. Once again, consider using the Hello World HTML code from the previous example. The following code creates two ranges, one that selects `"Hello World"` (including the `<b/>` tags) and one that selects `"Hello"` (also including the `<b/>` tags, see Figure 10-7):

```
var oRange1 = document.body.createTextRange();
var oRange2 = document.body.createTextRange();
oRange1.findText("Hello World");
oRange2.findText("Hello");
alert(oRange1.compareEndPoints("StartToStart", oRange2));   //outputs 0
alert(oRange1.compareEndPoints("EndToEnd", oRange2));       //outputs 1;
```

Similar to the example in "Comparing DOM Ranges," the first and second range share the same starting point, so `compareEndPoints()` returns 1; `oRange1`'s end point occurs after `oRange2`'s endpoint, so `compareEndPoints()` returns 1.

IE also has two additional methods for comparing ranges: `isEqual()`, which determines if two ranges are identically equal, and `inRange()`, which determines if a range occurs inside of another range:

```
var oRange1 = document.body.createTextRange();
var oRange2 = document.body.createTextRange();
oRange1.findText("Hello World");
oRange2.findText("Hello");
alert("oRange1.isEqual(oRange2): " + oRange1.isEqual(oRange2));  //outputs "false"
alert("oRange1.inRange(oRange2): " + oRange1.inRange(oRange2));  //outputs "true"
```

This example uses the same ranges as in the previous example to illustrate these methods. You already know that the ranges are not equal because the end points are different; to be equal, the ranges must share both start and end points. So the first alert displays `"false"`. However, `oRange2` is actually inside of `oRange1`, because its end point occurs before `oRange1`'s end point but after `oRange1`'s start point. For this reason, the second alert displays `"true"`, telling you `oRange2` is in `oRange1`.

Cloning an IE range

Similar to the DOM, it is possible to create exact duplicates (clones) of a given range by calling the `duplicate()` method:

```
var oNewRange = oRange.duplicate();
```

All properties from the original range are carried over into the newly created one.

How practical are ranges?

The dissimilarities between the DOM and IE range implementations make it difficult to create cross-browser solutions, which is perhaps why many developers shy away from using ranges at all. When evaluating your own usage, it's important to understand your target audience, what browsers they will be using, and if there is a nonrange way to create the same effect.

Ranges can provide very useful functionality on Web pages. Some pages use ranges to highlight certain words on a page based on a series of search terms, so the user can easily find the words he or she is searching for. Another use, popular among advertisers, is to turn certain words into links (for instance, turning the word *computer* into a link to a computer manufacturer or the word *JavaScript* to a description of the language).

Summary

This chapter introduced several new ways to manipulate a document's DOM tree.

First, you learned how to affect the CSS style of elements on a Web page. Several examples were discussed, including hover effects and custom tooltips. You learned how to access the style definitions of elements as well as CSS rules, and in doing so, saw their difference from computed styles.

The next section introduced `innerText`, `innerHTML`, `outerText`, and `outerHTML`. You learned how `innerText` can be used to change the text content of a DOM element and how `innerHTML` can be used to change the HTML content of a DOM element. Likewise, you learned how `outerText` and `outerHTML` can be used to replace a DOM element altogether (either with plain text or HTML code, respectively).

Lastly, you learned about ranges. The differences between DOM ranges and ranges in Internet Explorer were discussed, and several examples were given to show the similarities between the two.

11

Forms and Data Integrity

Form elements were created to address the need for the user to send data back to the server. The answer they provided came in the form (no pun intended) of Web forms, using the HTML `<form/>`, `<input/>`, `<select/>`, and `<textarea/>` elements. Using these elements, browsers can render text boxes, combo boxes, and other user input controls to allow communication from the client to the server.

Although the Web has developed at a rapid pace, Web forms have remained virtually unchanged. Although a new standard called XForms looms on the horizon, no browser has made a move to adopt it natively, and so Web forms today rely on JavaScript to augment the built-in behavior.

In this chapter, you learn how to use JavaScript to extend the behavior and usability of common Web forms to include the functionality that today's users expect.

Form Basics

An HTML form is defined by using the `<form/>` element, which has several attributes:

- `method` — Indicates whether the browser should sent a GET request or a POST request
- `action` — Indicates the URL to which the form should be submitted
- `enctype` — The way the data should be encoded when sent to the server. The default is `application/x-www-url-encoded`, but it may be set to `multipart/form-data` if the form is uploading a file.
- `accept` — Lists the mime types the server will handle correctly when a file is uploaded
- `accept-charset` — Lists the character encodings that are accepted by the server when data is submitted

A form can contain any number of input elements:

- `<input/>` —The main HTML input element. The type attribute determines what type of input control is displayed:
  - `"text"` — A single-line text box
  - `"radio"` — A radio button
  - `"checkbox"` — A check box
  - `"file"` — A file upload text box
  - `"password"` – A password text box (where characters are not displayed as you type)
  - `"button"` — A generic button that can be used to cause a custom action
  - `"submit"` — A button whose sole purpose is to submit the form
  - `"reset"` — A button whose sole purpose is to reset all fields in the form to their default values
  - `"hidden"` — An input field that isn't displayed on screen
  - `"image"` — An image that is used just like a Submit button
- `<select/>` — Renders either a combo box or a list box composed of values defined by `<option/>` elements
- `<textarea/>` — Renders a multiline text box in a size determined by the `rows` and `cols` attributes.

Here is a simple form using the various input elements:

```
<html>
    <head>
        <title>Sample Form</title>
    </head>
    <body>
        <form method="post" action="handlepost.jsp">
            <!-- regular textbox -->
            <label for="txtName">Name:</label><br />
            <input type="text" id="txtName" name="txtName" /><br />

            <!-- password textbox -->
            <label for="txtPassword">Password:</label><br />
            <input type="password" id="txtPassword" name="txtPassword" /><br />

            <!-- age comboxbox (drop-down) -->
            <label for="selAge">Age:</label><br />
            <select name="selAge" id="selAge">
                <option>18-21</option>
                <option>22-25</option>
                <option>26-29</option>
                <option>30-35</option>
                <option>Over 35</option>
            </select><br />
```

```
            <!-- multiline textbox -->
            <label for="txtComments">Comments:</label><br />
            <textarea rows="10" cols="50" id="txtComments"
name="txtComments"></textarea><br />

            <!-- submit button -->
            <input type="submit" value="Submit Form" />

        </form>
    </body>
</html>
```

In this example, five form fields are described: a regular text box, a password text box, a combo box, a multiline text box, and a Submit button. Note that with the exception of the Submit button, each field is preceded by a `<label/>` element. This element is used behind the scenes to logically tie a label to a particular form field. This feature is very useful for screen readers used by visually impaired users. The `for` attribute indicates the ID of the form field it identifies. Because of this, each form field should have `name` and `id` equal to the same value (`name` is submitted to the server; `id` identifies the element on the client).

Each type of form field can be manipulated using JavaScript. The `<form/>` element itself can also be controlled using JavaScript to provide further control over transmission of data.

Scripting the <form/> Element

Using JavaScript with the `<form/>` element is different from using other HTML elements. You aren't limited to just using the core DOM methods to access forms; you can access both the `<form/>` element itself and the form fields in a few different ways. This section covers the basic information you need to begin scripting forms.

Getting form references

Before scripting a form, you first must get a reference to the `<form/>` element. This can be done in a number of different ways.

First, you can use the typical method of locating an element in a DOM tree, that is, use `getElementById()` and pass in the form's ID:

```
var oForm = document.getElementById("form1");
```

Alternately, you can use the `document`'s `forms` collection and reference the form either by its position in the `forms` collection or by its `name` attribute:

```
var oForm = document.forms[0];                //get the first form
var oOtherForm = document.forms["formZ"];     //get the form whose name is "formZ"
```

Any of these methods for retrieving a form reference is acceptable (they all return the same thing, after all).

Accessing form fields

Every form field, whether it is a button, text box, or other, is contained in the form's `elements` collection. You can access the various fields in the collection by using their `name` attributes or their positions in the collection:

```
var oFirstField = oForm.elements[0];     //get the first form field
var oTextbox1 = oForm.elements["textbox1"];//get the field with the name "textbox1"
```

In the shorthand version for accessing an element by its name, every form field becomes a property of the form itself and can be accessed directly by using its `name`:

```
var oTextbox1 = oForm.textbox1; //get the field with the name "textbox1"
```

If the name has a space in it, use bracket notation instead:

```
var oTextbox1 = oForm["text box 1"]; //get the field with the name "text box 1"
```

> **Of course, you can still use `document.getElementById()` with a form field's ID to retrieve it directly. The methods discussed in this section are most useful when you need to iterate over all the fields in a single form.**

Form field commonalities

All form fields (except for hidden fields) contain common properties, methods, and events:

- The `disabled` property is used both to indicate whether the control is disabled as well as to actually disable the control (a disabled control doesn't allow any user input, but gives no visual indication that the control is disabled).
- The `form` property is a pointer back to the form of which the field is a part.
- The `blur()` method causes the form field to lose focus (by shifting the focus elsewhere).
- The `focus()` method causes the form field to gain focus (the control is selected for keyboard interaction).
- The `blur` event occurs when the field loses focus; the `onblur` event handler is then executed.
- The `focus` event occurs when the field gains focus; the `onfocus` event handler is then executed.

For example:

```
var oField1 = oForm.elements[0];
var oField2 = oForm.elements[1];

//set the first field to be disabled
oField1.disabled = true;

//set the focus to the second field
oField2.focus();
```

```
//is the form property equal to oForm?
alert(oField1.form == oForm);    //outputs "true"
```

These properties, methods, and events can come in handy when advanced functionality is needed, such as when you want to move the focus to the first field.

> **Hidden fields only support the `form` property, but none of the methods or events common to form fields.**

Focus on the first field

When a form is displayed on a Web page, the focus is typically not on the first control. It's easy to change this with a generic script that can be used on any form page.

Many developers just put the following in the page's `onload` event handler:

```
document.forms[0].elements[0].focus();
```

This works in most situations, but consider the problem when the first element in the form is a hidden field, an element that doesn't support the `focus()` method. In this case, you'd be greeted with a JavaScript error. The key is to set the focus to the first visible form field, and you can write a short method for that.

All the methods pertaining to forms in this chapter are written to an object called `FormUtil` for easy encapsulation:

```
var FormUtil = new Object;
```

*The **`FormUtil`** object is only intended to keep similar functions grouped together; you may choose to provide these methods in a separate object or on their own.*

The method to set the focus on the first field first checks to ensure that a form exists on the page. It does this by checking the value of `document.forms.length`:

```
FormUtil.focusOnFirst = function () {
    if (document.forms.length > 0) {
        //...
    }
};
```

After you know at least one form is present, you can start to iterate through the form fields until you find the first one that isn't hidden.

```
FormUtil.focusOnFirst = function () {
    if (document.forms.length > 0) {
        for (var i=0; i < document.forms[0].elements.length; i++) {
            var oField = document.forms[0].elements[i];
            if (oField.type != "hidden") {
                oField.focus();
```

```
                    return;
                }
            }
        }
    };
```

This method can then be called in the onload event handler:

```
<body onload="FormUtil.focusOnFirst()">
```

Be careful when using this method. In slow-loading pages, it is possible that the user may start typing into a field before the page has been fully loaded. When the focus is then set to the first field, it disrupts the user's input. To prepare for this issue, first check for a value in the first field; if one is there, don't set the focus to it.

Submitting forms

In regular HTML, you submit the form by using a Submit button or an image that acts like a Submit button:

```
<input type="submit" value="Submit" />      <!-- submit button -->
<input type="image" src="submit.gif" />    <!-- image button -->
```

When the user clicks either one of these buttons, the form is submitted without requiring any additional coding. If you press Enter on the keyboard when one of these types of buttons is present, the browser submits the form as if the button were clicked.

You can test to see if a form is submitting by providing an alert for the action attribute:

```
<form method="post" action="javascript:alert('Submitted')">
```

This submits the form to the JavaScript function, which just pops up an alert with the word "Submitted" in it. This is helpful to test form submission because it doesn't actually involve going back to the server.

If you want to submit the form without using one of the previously mentioned buttons, you can use the submit() method. The submit() method is part of the DOM definition of a <form/> element and can be used anywhere on a page. To use this method, you must first get a reference to the <form/> element either by using getElementById() or by using the document.forms collection. Each of the following three lines is an acceptable way to reference a form:

```
oForm = document.getElementById("form1");
oForm = document.forms["form1"];
oForm = document.forms[0];
```

After getting the form reference, you can just call the submit() method directly:

```
oForm.submit();
```

You can actually mimic the behavior of a Submit button by creating a generic button and assigning its `onclick` event handler to submit the form:

```
<input type="button" value="Submit Form" onclick="document.forms[0].submit()" />
```

Before the form is submitted, but after a Submit button is clicked, the `submit` event is fired and the `onsubmit` event handler is executed. Using the `onsubmit` event handler, it is possible to stop form submission, which is especially useful if client-side validation is necessary before the form can be submitted. Using the event methods mentioned earlier in the book, you can cancel the event and prevent the form submission:

```
function handleSubmit() {
    var oEvent = EventUtil.getEvent();
    oEvent.preventDefault();
}
```

This method can then be called from a form's `onsubmit` event handler:

```
<form method="post" action="javascript:alert('Submitted')"
onsubmit="handleSubmit()">
```

When you try to submit a form using the Submit button or the Image button, the form is not submitted.

> **The `onsubmit` event handler enables you to validate a form before submission, but only if you use one of the two types of buttons mentioned previously. When using the `submit()` method, the `submit` event isn't fired, so all validation should be done prior to making the call.**

Submit only once

A constant problem in Web forms is that users get very impatient when submitting a form. If the form doesn't disappear right away when they click the Submit button, users often click multiple times. The problems this causes vary from creating duplicate requests to charging a credit card more than once. The solution is a very simple one: After the user clicks the Submit button, you disable it. Here's how: Use a regular button, not a Submit button, and disable the button after the user clicks it. So instead of using this code:

```
<input type="submit" value="Submit" />
```

use this code:

```
<input type="button" value="Submit"
       onclick="this.disabled=true; this.form.submit()" />
```

When this button is clicked, it is disabled by setting the `disabled` property to `true`. Then, the form is submitted (note that the code uses the `this` keyword to reference the button and the `form` property to reference the form that it's a part of). This code can also be encapsulated in a function, if you so desire.

> **You may be wondering why you can't just use a Submit button and disable it using `onclick`. The answer is that the button actually disables before the form is submitted, which then prevents the form from being submitted at all.**

Resetting forms

If you want to provide the user a way to reset all form fields to their default values, you can use an HTML Reset button:

```
<input type="reset" value="Reset Values" />
```

Similar to a Submit button, a Reset button requires no scripting for the browser to know what to do when it is clicked. Also similar to the Submit button, a `reset` event fires when the button is clicked:

```
<form method="post" action="javascript:alert('Submitted')" onreset="alert('I am
resetting')">
```

Of course, you can also use the `onreset` event handler to cancel the form reset.

The form does have a `reset()` method that can reset the form directly from script without using a Reset button:

```
<input type="button" value="Reset" onclick="document.forms[0].reset()" />
```

Unlike `submit()`, using `reset()` still fires the `reset` event and the `onreset` event handler is still executed.

> **Resetting a form has fallen out of favor among Web developers because an increasing number of users have mistakenly reset the form instead of submitting it (often the Submit and Reset buttons are next to each other). If a form contains information in form fields when it is first loaded, a Reset button can be helpful because it resets the fields to their initial values. For forms that initially load without any information in form fields, it is recommended to avoid using a Reset button.**

Text boxes

Two flavors of text boxes are used in HTML: a single-line version, `<input type="text"/>`, and a multiline version, `<textarea/>`.

The `<input/>` element must have its `type` attribute set to `"text"` in order to display a text box. You then use the `size` attribute to specify how wide the text box should be in terms of visible characters (for instance, setting `size` to `"10"` means that only 10 characters are visible at one time). The value attribute specifies the initial `value` of the text box and the `maxlength` attribute specifies how many characters are allowed in the text box. So to create a text box that can display 25 characters at a time but has a maximum length of 50, the following code can be used:

```
<input type="text" size="25" maxlength="50" value="initial value" />
```

The `<textarea/>` element always renders a multiline text box. To specify how large the text box should be, you can use the `rows` attribute, which specifies the height of the text box in number of characters, and the `cols` attribute, which specifies the width in number of characters (similar to `size` for an `<input/>` element). Unlike `<input/>`, the initial value of a `<textarea/>` must be enclosed between `<textarea>` and `</textarea>`, as shown here:

```
<textarea rows="25" cols="5">initial value</textarea>
```

Also unlike the `<input/>` element, a `<textarea/>` cannot specify the maximum number of characters allowed.

Retrieving/changing a text box value

Even though they are different elements, both `<input type="text"/>` and `<textarea/>` support the same property, `value`, to retrieve the text contained in the text box. Consider the following example:

```
<html>
    <head>
        <title>Retrieving a Textbox Value Example</title>
        <script type="text/javascript">
            function getValues() {
                var oTextbox1 = document.getElementById("txt1");
                var oTextbox2 = document.getElementById("txt2");
                alert("The value of txt1 is \"" + oTextbox1.value + "\"\n" +
                      "The value of txt2 is \"" + oTextbox2.value + "\"");

            }
        </script>
    </head>
    <body>
        <input type="text" size="12" id="txt1" /><br />
        <textarea rows="5" cols="25" id="txt2"></textarea><br />
        <input type="button" value="Get Values" onclick="getValues()" />
    </body>
</html>
```

This example displays two text boxes, a single-line and a multiline, as well as a button. When you click the button, an alert is displayed showing the values contained in each text box. Try typing into each text box a couple of times and then click the button.

Because the value property is a string, you can use all the properties and methods of a string. For example, you can get the length of text inside a text box by using the `length` property:

```
<html>
    <head>
        <title>Retrieving a Textbox Length Example</title>
```

```
        <script type="text/javascript">
            function getLengths() {
                var oTextbox1 = document.getElementById("txt1");
                var oTextbox2 = document.getElementById("txt2");
                alert("The length of txt1 is " + oTextbox1.value.length + "\n"
                     + "The length of txt2 is " + oTextbox2.value.length);

            }
        </script>
    </head>
    <body>
        <input type="text" size="12" id="txt1" /><br />
        <textarea rows="5" cols="25" id="txt2"></textarea><br />
        <input type="button" value="Get Lengths" onclick="getLengths()" />
    </body>
</html>
```

This example uses the `length` property of the `value` to determine how many characters are in each text box.

The `value` property can also be used to assign a new value to a text box:

```
<html>
    <head>
        <title>Changing a Textbox Value Example</title>
        <script type="text/javascript">
            function setValues() {
                var oTextbox1 = document.getElementById("txt1");
                var oTextbox2 = document.getElementById("txt2");
                oTextbox1.value = "first textbox";
                oTextbox2.value = "second textbox";

            }
        </script>
    </head>
    <body>
        <input type="text" size="12" id="txt1" /><br />
        <textarea rows="5" cols="25" id="txt2"></textarea><br />
        <input type="button" value="Set Values" onclick="setValues()" />
    </body>
</html>
```

In this example, clicking the button sets the first text box to `"first textbox"` and the second text box to `"second textbox"`.

Selecting text

Both text box types support a method called `select()`, which selects all the text in the text box. In order to work, the text box must have focus. To ensure that the text box has focus, you should always call another method, `focus()`, before calling `select()`. (This isn't required in all browsers, but it's safer to always call `focus()` first.) For example:

```
<html>
    <head>
        <title>Select Text Example</title>
        <script type="text/javascript">
            function selectText() {
                var oTextbox1 = document.getElementById("txt1");
                oTextbox1.focus();
                oTextbox1.select();
            }
        </script>
    </head>
    <body>
        <input type="text" size="12" id="txt1" value="initial value" /><br />
        <input type="button" value="Select Text" onclick="selectText()" />
    </body>
</html>
```

This example displays a text box and a button. When you click the button, the text in the text box is selected.

Text box events

Both text box types support the previously mentioned form-field `blur` and `focus` events along with two others: `change` and `select`.

- `change` — Occurs when the text box loses focus after the user changed the value (does not fire if you change the value setting the `value` property).
- `select` — Occurs when one or more characters have been selected, either manually or by using the `select()` method.

Note the difference between the `change` event and the `blur` event. The `blur` event fires whenever the text box loses focus; the `change` event fires when the text box loses focus as well, but only if the text in the text box has changed. If the text is the same and the text box loses focus, only the `blur` event is fired; if the text has changed, the `change` event fires first, followed by the `blur` event. Try it out to better get the hang of it:

```
<input type="text" name="textbox1" value=""
       onblur="alert('Blur')" onchange="alert('Change')"/>
```

The `select` event, on the other hand, has nothing to do with the focus of the text box. This event fires when one or more characters are selected by the user or when the `select()` method is called. You can experiment with it:

```
<input type="text" name="textbox1" value="" onselect="alert('Select')"/>
```

Select text automatically

When a user is entering information into a traditional desktop application, it is not uncommon for the entire contents of a text box to be highlighted when the user tabs into it. This can be accomplished on both an input-style text box and a textarea in HTML very easily: Just add the code `"this.select()"` to the control's `onfocus` event handler:

```
<input type="text" onfocus="this.select()" />
<textarea onfocus="this.select()"></textarea>
```

It's a small change, but it can provide big usability gains for users. If you want to apply this behavior automatically to all text boxes on a screen, you can use the following function:

```
FormUtil.setTextboxes = function() {
    var colInputs = document.getElementsByTagName("input");
    var colTextAreas = document.getElementsByTagName("textarea");

    for (var i=0; i < colInputs.length; i++){
        if (colInputs[i].type == "text" || colInputs [i].type == "password") {
            colInputs[i].onfocus = function () { this.select(); };
        }
    }

    for (var i=0; i < colTextAreas.length; i++){
        colTextAreas[i].onfocus = function () { this.select(); };
    }
};
```

This function starts by getting all instances of `<input/>` and `<textarea/>` in the document. The first `for` loop iterates through all the `<input/>` tags to find the text box and password fields (password fields are text boxes, too). The function then adds an anonymous function containing the select code to the field's `onfocus` event handler (optionally, you can use the `EventUtil.addEventHandler()` method). The second `for` loop does the same `onfocus` assignment for all textareas on the page.

Tab forward automatically

When a text box can only accept a certain number of characters, wouldn't it make sense to automatically tab to the next field? This is done quite frequently when entering data such as social security numbers or product ID numbers. This behavior is easy to mimic in JavaScript. This script requires that the `maxlength` attribute of the text box be used, such as:

```
<input type="text" maxlength="4" />
```

The basic idea is to determine when the maximum number of characters is entered into a text box and then call the `focus()` method on the next field. To do this, another method is necessary:

```
FormUtil.tabForward = function(oTextbox) {

    var oForm = oTextbox.form;

    //make sure the textbox is not the last field in the form
    if (oForm.elements[oForm.elements.length-1] != oTextbox
        && oTextbox.value.length == oTextbox.getAttribute("maxlength")) {

        for (var i=0; i < oForm.elements.length; i++) {
            if (oForm.elements[i] == oTextbox) {
                 for(var j=i+1; j < oForm.elements.length; j++) {
                     if (oForm.elements[j].type != "hidden") {
                         oForm.elements[j].focus();
                         return;
```

```
                        }
                    }
                    return;
                }
            }
        }
    };
```

The `FormUtil.tabForward()` method takes one argument, the text box to check. Inside the method, a reference to the owning form is extracted by using the text box's `form` property. Next, the method checks to see if the text box is the last element in the form by comparing it to the element in the last position. If the text box passes this test, it is then tested to see if it has reached the maximum number of allowable characters by using the text box's `maxlength` attribute. If the text box doesn't have the maximum number of characters yet, the method exits quietly; otherwise, the first loop is entered.

The first `for` loop's sole purpose is to locate the text box in the `form.elements` collection. When it is found, a problem similar to the one encountered in the previous section pops up: What if the next element is a hidden field? That's where the second loop comes in, as it iterates up through the remaining form elements until it finds the first non-hidden field. When that field is found, the user focus is set to it, and the method is exited via the `return` statement.

This method must be called after each character has been entered into the text box, so you need to use the `onkeyup` event handler (the `keyup` event, you may recall, fires after the character has been placed into the text box; the `keypress` event fires before):

```
<input type="text" maxlength="4" onkeyup="FormUtil.tabForward(this) " />
```

Note that the `this` keyword is being used to pass into the method a pointer to the text box. Suppose you want the user to enter a U.S.-format phone number (three digits, three digits, four digits). You could create three text boxes like this:

```
<input type="text" id="txtAreaCode" maxlength="3"
       onkeyup="FormUtil.tabForward(this)" />

<input type="text" id="txtExchange" maxlength="3"
       onkeyup="FormUtil.tabForward(this)" />

<input type="text" id="txtNumber" maxlength="4"
       onkeyup="FormUtil.tabForward(this)" />
```

As soon as the user finishes entering the numbers in one text box, the focus moves to the next, so the user never has to use the Tab key or the mouse to move between fields.

Limit textarea characters

Although the `<input/>` element text boxes can easily limit the number of characters allowed, the `<textarea/>` elements cannot do this because they do not have a `maxlength` property. The solution is to create some JavaScript to mimic the `maxlength` property. Ultimately, you want to be able to do the following:

```
<textarea rows="10" cols="25" maxlength="150"></textarea>
```

You add extra attributes frequently in this chapter; however, if you are using the strict implementation of XHTML, the page is considered invalid if it contains an unexpected attribute. Depending on your specific requirements, it may be necessary to add a JavaScript property to the element's DOM node or to pass in the extra information directly to a function instead of using the attribute in HTML.

This is the first method of the chapter dealing directly with text boxes (the previous sections have had methods that work between text boxes and the rest of the form), and so it is time for a new wrapper object to encapsulate the coming methods:

```
var TextUtil = new Object();
```

The first method for this object is called `isNotMax()`, which returns `true` when the maximum number of characters hasn't yet been reached or `false` if it has. The reasoning for this is explained in a moment. First, take a look at the code:

```
TextUtil.isNotMax = function(oTextArea) {
    return oTextArea.value.length != oTextArea.getAttribute("maxlength");
}
```

As you can see, this method is very simple: just an equality comparison between the length of the text in the text box and the `maxlength` attribute. Note that even though `maxlength` isn't a valid HTML attribute for the `<textarea/>` element, you can still retrieve its value by using `getAttribute()`.

Next, the method call must be inserted into the text box's `onkeypress` event handler. Remember, the `keypress` event fires before a character is inserted into the text box, which is exactly what you must stop to enforce the maximum character limit. Here's what the code looks like:

```
<textarea rows="10" cols="25" maxlength="150"
          onkeypress="return TextUtil.isNotMax(this)"></textarea>
```

Notice that the return value of `isNotMax()` is being returned to the event handler. This is an older way of preventing the default behavior for an event. When the text length is less than the `maxlength` attribute, the method returns `true`, indicating that the `keypress` event should continue normally. As soon as the maximum length has been reached, the method returns `false`, preventing the character from being added to the text box.

This method can be used in conjunction with `FormUtil.tabForward()` to allow the same *skip ahead* functionality using `<textarea/>` elements.

You may be wondering why the code doesn't use the standard `preventDefault()` method of the event object to block the `keypress` event. The simple answer is that a bug in Mozilla's handling of the `keypress` events causes `preventDefault()` to malfunction. In order to make this a truly cross-browser solution, the faulty functionality had to be eliminated. The code in this example works in all DOM-compliant browsers, including Internet Explorer, Safari, Opera, as well as Mozilla.

Allowing/blocking characters in text boxes

In handling data entry, you must limit the data that a user can enter. For instance, if a field requires a number and a user enters a letter, it should be recognized as invalid. Before JavaScript, a round trip to the server was necessary to do this type of validation. With JavaScript, not only can the client validate user data, it can also prevent the user from ever entering invalid data.

Blocking invalid characters

The first method is to block invalid characters only. Because many fields within one form require different types of characters to be entered, you must be able to specify the characters to block on a field-by-field basis. The ideal way to do this would be to add an attribute to the HTML `<input/>` element that specifies the invalid characters, such as this:

```
<input type="text" invalidchars="0123456789" />
```

The previous example would ideally block the numbers 0 through 9 from being entered into the text box. Of course, first you need a method to use for this purpose.

The `TextUtil.block()` method accepts two arguments: the text box to act on and the `event` object. Just like `TextUtil.isNotMax()`, this method is called in the `onkeypress` event handler, and it returns `true` when the character should be allowed or `false` if it should not. The body of the method contains only four lines of code:

```
TextUtil.blockChars = function (oTextbox, oEvent) {

    oEvent = EventUtil.formatEvent(oEvent);

    var sInvalidChars = oTextbox.getAttribute("invalidchars");
    var sChar = String.fromCharCode(oEvent.charCode);

    var bIsValidChar = sInvalidChars.indexOf(sChar) == -1;

    return bIsValidChar || oEvent.ctrlKey;
};
```

Notice the use of the `EventUtil.formatEvent()` method defined earlier in the book, which is necessary whenever the `event` object is passed directly into a method without using the `EventUtil.getEvent()` method. After the event object is properly formatted, the method stores the `invalidchars` attribute in a variable and then extracts the character to be entered in the text box using the `charCode` property and `String.fromCharCode()`. At that point, the invalid characters are stored in `sInvalidChars` and the character to be inserted is stored in `sChar`. The only thing left to do is to determine if that character exists inside the `sInvalidChars` string by using the `indexOf()` method. You'll recall that `indexOf()` returns –1 if the substring (or in this case, the character) doesn't exist in the string. So `bIsValidChar true` when the character doesn't exist in `sInvalidChars`. The return statement returns the logical OR of `bIsValidChar` and `oEvent.ctrlKey`. The OR condition is necessary because if the Ctrl key is down when a character is pressed (such as Ctrl + C for copy), this method would block it. So, if the character is valid, the method returns `true`, and if the Ctrl key is down, it returns `true`.

To use this method, insert it into the HTML code for a text box (either `<input/>` or `<textarea/>`) along with the `invalidchars` attribute:

```
<input type="text" invalidchars="0123456789"
       onkeypress="return TextUtil.blockChars(this, event) " />

<textarea rows="10" cols="25" invalidchars="0123456789"
       onkeypress="return TextUtil.blockChars(this, event)" />
```

This one function can be used to block characters in a variety of useful ways:

```
<!-- block all numbers -->
<input type="text" onkeypress="return FormUtil.block(this, event)"
    invalidchars="0123456789" />

<!-- block all uppercase letters -->
<input type="text" onkeypress="return FormUtil.block(this, event) "
    invalidchars="ABCDEFGHIJKLMNOPQRSTUVWXYZ" />

<!-- block all lowercase letters -->
<input type="text" onkeypress="return FormUtil.block(this, event)"
    invalidchars="abcdefghijklmnopqrstuvwxyz" />

<!-- block spaces -->
<input type="text" onkeypress="return FormUtil.block(this, event)"
    invalidchars=" " />
```

Allowing valid characters

Naturally, the other method of restricting user input is to only allow certain characters in a text box. Once again, the easiest way to accomplish this is to add an HTML attribute to a text box:

```
<input type="text" validchars="0123456789" />
```

This example would allow the numbers 0 through 9 only, and no other characters. Naturally, you'll need to have an `allowChars()` method that does the opposite of the `blockChars()` method:

```
TextUtil.allowChars = function (oTextbox, oEvent) {

    oEvent = EventUtil.formatEvent(oEvent);

    var sValidChars = oTextbox.getAttribute("validchars");
    var sChar = String.fromCharCode(oEvent.charCode);

    var bIsValidChar = sValidChars.indexOf(sChar) > -1;

    return bIsValidChar || oEvent.ctrlKey;
};
```

As you can see, the `allowChars()` has a lot in common with `blockChars()`: It accepts the text box and the event object as arguments; it formats the event object using `EventUtil.formatEvent()`; it stores the character that will be entered into the text box in a variable using `String.fromCharCode()`. The main difference between the two is that `allowChars()` is looking for the `validchars` attribute and returns `true` only if `sChar` is contained in `sValidChars`. Once again, keep in mind that, if the Ctrl key is down, the user is performing some sort of function on the text box, so the method has to return `true`. The method is even used in a similar manner, by returning a value to the `onkeypress` event handler:

```
<input type="text" validchars="0123456789"
       onkeypress="return TextUtil.allowChars(this, event)" />

<textarea rows="10" cols="25" validchars="0123456789"
       onkeypress="return TextUtil.allowChars(this, event)" />
```

The previous text boxes only allow numerals to be entered (no spaces, letters, or anything else). This functionality can also be used in a number of creative ways:

```
<!-- only allow positive integers -->
<input type="text" validchars="0123456789"
    onkeypress="return FormUtil.allow(this, event)" />

<!-- only allow "Y" or "N" -->
<input type="text" validchars="YN"
    onkeypress="return FormUtil.allow(this, event)" />
```

Don't forget the paste

One aspect of text validation that most developers forget about is that the user can paste a value into the text box. In the `blockCars()` and `allowChars()` methods, it is assumed that the user is typing in the characters one by one, so they check each character as it comes in. When a user pastes a value, an entire string is being placed in the text box. You have two ways to deal with validating pasted values: Either don't allow pasting or validate the text box when it loses focus.

Blocking paste

Blocking the user's capability to paste is very easy to accomplish, but you must cover all bases. A user can paste in two ways: by clicking Paste on the text box context menu (when right-clicking on it) or by holding the Ctrl key and pressing V.

In Internet Explorer, the solution is very simple because there is a `paste` event. If the `onpaste` event handler prevents the default behavior, no paste works no matter how the user tries to do it:

```
<input type="text" onkeypress="return allow(this, event) " validchars="0123456789"
    onpaste="return false" />
```

For other browsers, the process is a little more involved. The first thing to do is block the context menu, which can be accomplished by returning `false` from the `oncontextmenu` event handler.

```
<input type="text" onkeypress="return allow(this, event) " validchars="0123456789"
    onpaste="return false" oncontextmenu="return false" />
```

Next, you need to block pasting when the user presses Ctrl and V. The part that makes this easy is that pressing Ctrl and V causes the `keypress` event to fire, so its possible to use the `allowChars()` and `blockChars()` methods with some modifications:

```
TextUtil.blockChars = function (oTextbox, oEvent, bBlockPaste) {

    oEvent = EventUtil.formatEvent(oEvent);

    var sInvalidChars = oTextbox.getAttribute("invalidchars");
    var sChar = String.fromCharCode(oEvent.charCode);

    var bIsValidChar = sInvalidChars.indexOf(sChar) == -1;

    if (bBlockPaste) {
        return bIsValidChar && !(oEvent.ctrlKey && sChar == "v");
    } else {
        return bIsValidChar || oEvent.ctrlKey;
    }
};

TextUtil.allowChars = function (oTextbox, oEvent, bBlockPaste) {

    oEvent = EventUtil.formatEvent(oEvent);

    var sValidChars = oTextbox.getAttribute("validchars");
    var sChar = String.fromCharCode(oEvent.charCode);

    var bIsValidChar = sValidChars.indexOf(sChar) > -1;

    if (bBlockPaste) {
        return bIsValidChar && !(oEvent.ctrlKey && sChar == "v");
    } else {
        return bIsValidChar || oEvent.ctrlKey;
    }
};
```

Notice that the same code is added to both methods. First, a third argument is added, `bBlockPaste`, which must be set to `true` if you want to block pasting in a text box. Then, an `if` statement is added at the end of each method, to check whether pasting should be blocked. If so, the return value is `true` only if the character is valid and Ctrl + V hasn't been pressed. If pasting shouldn't be blocked, the `return` statement from the original method is used.

To use the new methods, just add the third argument:

```
<input type="text" validchars="0123456789"
       onpaste="return false" oncontextmenu="return false"
       onkeypress="return TextUtil.allowChars(this, event, true)" />

<textarea rows="10" cols="25" validchars="0123456789"
       onpaste="return false" oncontextmenu="return false"
       onkeypress="return TextUtil.allowChars(this, event, true)" />
```

Even though the third argument is defined, you can still use these methods with only the first two arguments, because an `undefined` value is considered `false` when used in the `if` statement and won't block pasting.

> **You must use `onpaste="return false"` as well as the `allowChars()` and `blockChars()` methods because you cannot block the Ctrl + V keystroke in Internet Explorer.**

Validating onblur

If you don't want to block the user's capability to paste, you must validate the input in another way. The easiest way to do this is to create an `onblur` event handler that won't let the user move to another field until the value in the text box is valid. This necessitates two additional methods: one to use with `blockChars()` and one to use with `allowChars()`.

The companion function for `blockChars()` is called `blurBlock()`, and it accepts the text box as its only argument. Here's the code:

```
TextUtil.blurBlock = function(oTextbox) {

    var sInvalidChars = oTextbox.getAttribute("invalidchars");
    var arrInvalidChars = sInvalidChars.split("");

    for (var i=0; i< arrInvalidChars.length; i++){
        if (oTextbox.value.indexOf(arrInvalidChars[i]) > -1) {
            alert("Character '" + arrInvalidChars[i] + "' not allowed.");
            oTextbox.focus();
            oTextbox.select();
            return;
        }
    }
};
```

The first step in this method is the same as in `blockChars()`: You must get the invalid characters from the `invalidchars` attribute. Because all the text in the text box must be validated (not just a single character), it's necessary to test for each invalid character individually, so the next step in the method splits the invalid character string into an array of characters (you'll recall that using `split()` with an empty string argument returns an array of the characters). Then, the method loops through each invalid character to see if it exists in the text box. When an invalid character is found, an alert is displayed telling the user that the given character is invalid. The focus is then set back to the text box and its contents are selected. The method exits at that point, because so long as there is one invalid character, there's no need to check for any others (you may also choose to look for all invalid characters before exiting).

This method is inserted into the `onblur` event handler like this:

```
<input type="text" onkeypress="return TextUtil.blockChars(this, event)"
    invalidchars="0123456789" onblur="TextUtil.blurBlock(this)" />
```

A similar method is needed to use with `allowChars()`. This method, called `blurAllow()`, is almost exactly the same as `blurBlock()`, only it makes sure that every character in the text box is valid:

```
TextUtil.blurAllow = function(oTextbox) {

    var sValidChars = oTextbox.getAttribute("validchars");
    var arrTextChars = oTextbox.value.split("");

    for (var i=0; i< arrTextChars.length; i++){
        if (sValidChars.indexOf(arrTextChars[i]) == -1) {
            alert("Character '" + arrTextChars[i] + "' not allowed.");
            oTextbox.focus();
            oTextbox.select();
            return;
        }
    }
};
```

Notice this method begins by retrieving the valid characters from the `validchars` attribute, just as in `allowChars()`. The next step is to split the text in the text box into an array of characters because each character must be checked for validity. The method loops through the array, checking to see if each character is contained in the `sValidChars` string. When it encounters a character that isn't valid (meaning that `indexOf()` returns –1, indicating that the given character doesn't exist in `sValidChars`), an alert is displayed showing the illegal character. Then, just as in `blurBlock()`, focus is shifted to the text box, text is selected, and the method exits. This method is used like this:

```
<input type="text" onkeypress="return TextUtil.allowChars(this, event)"
    validchars="0123456789" onblur="TextUtil.blurAllow(this)" />
```

The end result of this is a way that does not prevent a user from pasting illegal values, but it ensures that if an illegal value is pasted in, the user is notified right away.

> **You may be wondering why this code uses the `onblur` event handler instead of `onchange`. Logically, because the `change` event fires when the value in a text box changes and then the text box loses focus, this would seem to be the perfect way to check for pasted values. Consider what happens as this code is executed. First, the user pastes an illegal value into the text box and tries to tab to the next field. The `change` event fires here, as will `blur`. The user is presented with an alert saying that an illegal character has been found, and focus is shifted back to the text box. For some reason, the user doesn't fix the illegal character, but instead tabs forward once again. This time, the `change` event doesn't fire because the value in the text box hasn't changed since it got focus. The `blur` event, however, still fires.**

Numeric text boxes with the up/down arrow keys

Suppose you've implemented a numbers-only text box using the `TextUtil.allowChars()` method, but that still isn't enough to make your users happy. What they really want is the capability to press the up arrow and down arrow keys in order to increment and decrement the number. To address this, use the `onkeydown` event handler.

You may ask, why not just use the `onkeypress` event handler again? The answer is that the `keypress` event only fires for those keys that represent characters in a text box. Because the arrow keys don't cause a character to be put into the text box, the `keypress` event won't fire. The `keydown` event, however, fires no matter what kind of key is pressed.

To make sure you're only dealing with the up and down arrow keys, use the `keyCode` property of `event`. The code for the up arrow is 38 and the code for the down arrow is 40. All other keys can be ignored:

```
TextUtil.numericScroll = function (oTextbox, oEvent) {

    oEvent = EventUtil.formatEvent(oEvent);
    var iValue = oTextbox.value.length == 0 ? 0 :parseInt(oTextbox.value);

    if (oEvent.keyCode == 38) {
        oTextbox.value = (iValue + 1);
    } else if (oEvent.keyCode == 40){
        oTextbox.value = (iValue - 1);
    }
};
```

Once again, the `EventUtil.formatEvent()` method is used to ensure the `event` object is properly formatted. The next step is to determine the integer value of the text. If there is some text in the text box, the `parseInt()` function is used to convert the value; otherwise, the value is assumed to be zero. Then, the `keyCode` property of the event is tested to see whether it's the up arrow or down arrow. Depending on the `keyCode`, the integer value is either incremented or decremented and then placed in the text box. The method must be used in conjunction with the `allowChars()` (and either way of dealing with pasted values) to ensure that only numeric values are present in the text box.

The method is used like this:

```
<input type="text" onkeypress="return TextUtil.allowChars(this, event)"
    validchars="0123456789" onblur="TextUtil.blurAllow(this)"
    onkeydown="TextUtil.numericScroll(this, event)" />
```

This simple addition now enables the up and down keys to change the numeric value of the text box. What else could you possibly want? How about a minimum value and a maximum value? By adding two custom attributes, `min` and `max`, and updating the method, you can add the capability to specify a minimum and maximum value to scroll to:

```
TextUtil.numericScroll = function (oTextbox, oEvent) {

    oEvent = EventUtil.formatEvent(oEvent);
    var iValue = oTextbox.value.length == 0 ? 0 :parseInt(oTextbox.value);

    var iMax = oTextbox.getAttribute("max");
    var iMin = oTextbox.getAttribute("min");

    if (oEvent.keyCode == 38) {
        if (iMax == null || iValue < parseInt(iMax)) {
            oTextbox.value = (iValue + 1);
        }
    } else if (oEvent.keyCode == 40){
```

```
            if (iMin == null || iValue > parseInt(iMin)) {
                oTextbox.value = (iValue - 1);
            }
        }
    };
```

The few lines added to the method do some very specific things. First, the minimum and maximum values are retrieved from the custom attributes. Then, when each key is tested, a test checks whether the minimum and maximum values have been specified. If the attributes haven't been specified, `iMax` and `iMin` are equal to `null`. If they aren't `null`, `parseInt()` is called to get the integer value of the attributes. This value is then compared with the value in the text box to determine it is should be changed (incremented or decremented) or not.

To use this functionality, just add either the `min` attribute or the `max` attribute (or both) to the `<input/>` tag:

```
<input type="text" onkeypress="return TextUtil.allowChars(this, event)"
    validchars="0123456789" onblur="TextUtil.blurAllow(this)"
    onkeydown="TextUtil.numericScroll(this, event)"
    max="100" min="0" />
```

Using this code, the values will stop incrementing and decrementing when either of these limits is hit.

List Boxes and Combo Boxes

List boxes and combo boxes are created using the HTML `<select/>` element. By default, the browser renders the `<select/>` element as a combo box:

```
<select name="selAge" id="selAge">
    <option value="1">18-21</option>
    <option value="2">22-25</option>
    <option value="3">26-29</option>
    <option value="4">30-35</option>
    <option value="5">Over 35</option>
</select>
```

The `value` attribute of each `<option/>` is used to determine the value for the control as a whole; the selected option gives its `value` to the control (so it can be sent to the server).

To render this same code as a list box, you need only add the `size` attribute and indicate how many items you want visible at the same time. For example, the following displays a list box with three items visible at once.

```
<select name="selAge" id="selAge" size="3">
    <option value="1">18-21</option>
    <option value="2">22-25</option>
    <option value="3">26-29</option>
    <option value="4">30-35</option>
    <option value="5">Over 35</option>
</select>
```

Because both controls use the same HTML code, it's possible to manipulate them using the same JavaScript code. Naturally, the first step to manipulating either is to get a reference from the document either by using `document.getElementById()` or accessing it in the `document.forms` collection:

```
oListbox = document.getElementById("selAge");
oListbox = document.forms["form1"].selAge;
oListbox = document.forms[0].selAge;
```

For this section, the methods you create are all attached to a common object called `ListUtil`, in order to keep them straight (similar to the `EventUtil` object created earlier in the book). `ListUtil` is just a simple object to which the methods are attached:

```
var ListUtil = new Object();
```

Accessing options

The HTML DOM defines each `<select/>` element to have a collection called `options`, which is the list of all `<option/>` elements for the control. To get the display text and value of an `<option/>`, you can use normal DOM functionality:

```
alert(oListbox.options[1].firstChild.nodeValue);     //output display text
alert(oListbox.options[1].getAttribute("value"));    //output value
```

However, it is easier to use two special `<option/>` properties that are defined in the HTML DOM: `text`, which returns the display text, and `value`, which returns the value attribute. These two properties are provided for backwards compatibility with older BOM functionality used to manipulate options.

```
alert(oListbox.options[1].text);     //output display text
alert(oListbox.options[1].value);    //output value
```

Each `<option/>` also has an `index` property, indicating its position in the `options` collection:

```
alert(oListbox.options[1].index);     //outputs "1"
```

Of course, because `options` is a collection, you can use its length property to determine how many options exist:

```
alert("There are " + oListbox.options.length + " in the list.");
```

But how do you know which option is currently selected?

Retrieving/changing the selected option(s)

The `<select/>` element has an attribute, `selectedIndex`, which always contains the index of the currently selected option (or –1 if no options are selected).

```
alert("The index of the selected option is " + oListbox.selectedIndex);
```

It is possible, however, to select more than one option in a list box (but not in a combo box) by setting the `multiple` attribute of the `<select/>` element to `"multiple"`:

```
<select name="selAge" id="selAge" size="3" multiple="multiple">
    <option value="1">18-21</option>
    <option value="2">22-25</option>
    <option value="3">26-29</option>
    <option value="4">30-35</option>
    <option value="5">Over 35</option>
</select>
```

If multiple options are selected, `selectedIndex` contains the index of the first selected item, but that really doesn't help. What you need is a way to get the indexes of all the selected options. For this, you need a custom method, which is the first for the `ListUtil` object.

The `getSelectedIndexes()` method takes advantage of another special property of the `<option/>` element: the `selected` property. The HTML DOM defines the `selected` property as a Boolean value indicating whether the individual option is selected. So, all that is necessary is to loop through the options of a list box and test to see if they are selected or not. If so, you need to save that index into an array that will ultimately hold the indices of all selected options.

This method needs only one argument, the list box to check:

```
ListUtil.getSelectedIndexes = function (oListbox) {
    var arrIndexes = new Array;

    for (var i=0; i < oListbox.options.length; i++) {
        if (oListbox.options[i].selected) {
            arrIndexes.push(i);
        }
    }

    return arrIndexes;
};
```

The `getSelectedIndexes()` method can then be used to either retrieve the indexes of the selected options or, using the length of the returned array, to determine how many options are selected:

```
var oListbox = document.getElementById("selListbox");
var arrIndexes = ListUtil.getSelectedIndexes(oListbox);

alert("There are " + arrIndexes.length + " option selected."
      + "The options have the indexes " + arrIndexes + ".");
```

This code first gets a reference to the list box with the ID `"selListbox"` and then retrieves the selected indexes and stores them in `arrIndexes`. The alert displays the a message indicating the number of selected options as well as displaying their indexes (remember, the `toString()` method of an `Array` object returns all items in a comma-separated string).

Even though intended for multiple-selection list boxes, the `getSelectedIndexes()` method works in both single-selection list boxes and combo boxes, returning an array with only one item: the value of `selectedIndex`.

Adding options

If you don't load any options into a list box or combo box using HTML, you can do so using JavaScript.

To start, define a method with three arguments: the list box to work on, the name of the option to add, and the value of the option to add.

```
ListUtil.add = function (oListbox, sName, sValue) {
    //...
}
```

Next, create an `<option/>` element using the DOM methods and assign the option name by creating a text node:

```
ListUtil.add = function (oListbox, sName, sValue) {

    var oOption = document.createElement("option");
    oOption.appendChild(document.createTextNode(sName));

    //...
}
```

The option value is actually not required, so you should only add it if the argument has been passed in. To do this, ensure that `arguments.length` is equal to 3, and if so, set the `value` attribute:

```
ListUtil.add = function (oListbox, sName, sValue) {

    var oOption = document.createElement("option");
    oOption.appendChild(document.createTextNode(sName));

    if (arguments.length == 3) {
        oOption.setAttribute("value", sValue);
    }

    //...
}
```

The last step is to add the new option to the list box by using the `appendChild()` method:

```
ListUtil.add = function (oListbox, sName, sValue) {

    var oOption = document.createElement("option");
    oOption.appendChild(document.createTextNode(sName));

    if (arguments.length == 3) {
```

```
        oOption.setAttribute("value", sValue);
    }

    oListbox.appendChild(oOption);

}
```

This method can be used like this:

```
var oListbox = document.getElementById("selListbox");

ListUtil.add(oListbox, "New Display Text");  //add option with no value
ListUtil.add(oListbox, "New Display Text 2", "New value");  //add option with value
```

Removing options

JavaScript provides the capability to not only add options, but to remove them as well. There is an old way of removing an option from a list box, which is simply to use the `options` collection and set the option in question to be equal to `null`:

```
oListbox.options[1] = null;
```

Once again, this is BOM functionality; things can be done in a much more logical sense using the HTML DOM, which provides a `remove()` method for the `<select/>` element. You just pass in the index of the option to remove:

```
var oListbox = document.getElementById("selListbox");
oListbox.remove(0);    //remove the first option
```

If you are so inclined, you may choose to wrap this into a `ListUtil` method so that you can do both add and remove the same way:

```
ListUtil.remove = function (oListbox, iIndex) {
    oListbox.remove(iIndex);
}
```

The code can then be rewritten like this:

```
var oListbox = document.getElementById("selListbox");
ListUtil.remove(oListbox, 0);    //remove the first option
```

If you want to remove all the options in a list box, you can just call `remove()` on each option:

```
ListUtil.clear = function (oListbox) {
    for (var i=oListbox.options.length-1; i >= 0; i--) {
        ListUtil.remove(oListbox, i);
    }
};
```

This method removes all options by iterating in reverse order. This is necessary because every time an option is removed, the `index` property of each option is reset to the proper position. For this reason, it is always best to remove the option with the highest index first and work your way back to the option with the lowest index. Otherwise, you must keep track of multiple changing indexes.

Moving Options

In early JavaScript, moving options from one list box to another was a rather arduous process that involved removing the option from the first list box, creating a new option with the same name and value, then adding that new option to the second list box. Fortunately, the DOM provides a much more concise way of doing things. Using DOM methods, it's possible to literally move an option from the first list box into the second list box by using the `appendChild()` method. If you pass an element that is already in the document into this method, the element is removed from its parent and put into the position specified.

The method to execute this functionality accepts three arguments: the list box that the option currently resides in, the list box to move the option to, and the index of the option to move. The method can then take the option in the given index (assuming it exists) and move it to the second list box:

```
ListUtil.move = function (oListboxFrom, oListboxTo, iIndex) {
    var oOption = oListboxFrom.options[iIndex];

    if (oOption != null) {
        oListboxTo.appendChild(oOption);
    }
}
```

It is then possible to move a given option from one list box to another by using code such as the following:

```
var oListbox1 = document.getElementById("selListbox1");
var oListbox2 = document.getElementById("selListbox2");
ListUtil.move(oListbox1, oListbox2, 0);    //move the first option
```

This code moves the first option from `oListbox1` into `oListbox2` (the new option appears at the bottom of `oListbox2`).

> **Moving options is the same as removing them in that the `index` property of each option is reset into the proper position, so you should always move the option with the highest index first.**

Reordering options

To reorder options in a list box, moving a particular option either up or down, two methods are necessary, one to shift an option up and one to shift an option down. Each method takes two arguments: the list box to act on and the index of the option to move. Both also make use of the DOM `insertBefore()` method to reorder the `<option/>` elements.

Start with the `shiftUp()` method, which moves an option up one spot in the list box:

```
ListUtil.shiftUp = function (oListbox, iIndex) {
    if (iIndex > 0) {
        var oOption = oListbox.options[iIndex];
        var oPrevOption = oListbox.options[iIndex-1];
        oListbox.insertBefore(oOption, oPrevOption);
    }
};
```

This method first checks to make sure the index of the option to move is greater than 0 because, of course, you cannot move the first option up one spot. The option with the given index is stored in the variable `oOption` and the option before it is stored in `oPrevOption`. Last, the `insertBefore()` method is called to move `oOption` before `oPrevOption`. The method to move an option down one spot is very similar:

```
ListUtil.shiftDown = function (oListbox, iIndex) {
    if (iIndex < oListbox.options.length - 1) {
        var oOption = oListbox.options[iIndex];
        var oNextOption = oListbox.options[iIndex+1];
        oListbox.insertBefore(oNextOption, oOption);
    }
};
```

In this case, you must first get the collection of options in order to make sure that `iIndex` isn't the last position in the list (because you can't move the last option down any further). The option in position `iIndex` is stored in `oOption`; the option in the next position is stored in `oNextOption`. Using `insertBefore()`, `oNextOption` is placed before `oOption` in the list box.

These two methods can be used as in the following example:

```
var oListbox = document.getElementById("selListbox");
ListUtil.shiftUp(oListbox,1);   //move the option in position 1 up one spot
ListUtil.shiftDown(oListbox,2); //move the option in position 2 down one spot
```

Creating an Autosuggest Text Box

Let's face it, people really don't enjoy filling out forms, especially when values need to be typed in. That's why applications like Microsoft Outlook incorporate autosuggest text boxes, which are text boxes that examine the first few characters a user has typed and then suggests a word (or multiple words) from a given list that may complete his entry. Web browsers also work in this way when you are typing a Web address. With a little bit of JavaScript trickery, it's possible to create the same type of behavior in Web forms.

Matching

The first step in the process is to write a method to search an array of strings and return all values that begin with a certain set of letters (for example, if you pass in `a`, the method returns all values in the array beginning with the letter *a*). This method is called `TextUtil.autosuggestMatch()` and takes two arguments: the text to match and the array of values to match against.

```
TextUtil.autosuggestMatch = function (sText, arrValues) {

    var arrResult = new Array;

    if (sText != "") {
        for (var i=0; i < arrValues.length; i++) {
            if (arrValues[i].indexOf(sText) == 0) {
                arrResult.push(arrValues[i]);
            }
        }
    }

   return arrResult;

};
```

The first step in this method is to create an array to return all matching values. Next, the method checks to ensure that the string to match isn't empty (an empty string is always considered to be present in any string). If the string isn't empty, a simple `for` loop is used to check each value to see if it begins with the string. To determine this, the `indexOf()` method is used. When `indexOf()` returns 0, it means that the string is present at the beginning of the value, so it should be added to the result array. Finally, the array of matching values is returned.

The guts

With the matching method complete, it's time to create the most important part of the script: the `TextUtil.autosuggest()` method. This method takes three arguments: the text box to act on, an array of possible values, and the ID of a list box in which the suggestions should be displayed. Assuming that the array of values is called `arrValues`, the call looks like this:

```
<input type="text"
    onkeyup="TextUtil.autosuggest(this, arrValues, 'lstSuggestions')" />
```

The `onkeyup` event handler is used because the `keyup` event fires after a character has been entered into the text box, allowing the suggestions to be made on the most recent change to the text box. The method is defined as follows:

```
TextUtil.autosuggest = function (oTextbox, arrValues, sListboxId) {

    var oListbox = document.getElementById(sListboxId);
    ListUtil.clear(oListbox);

    var arrMatches = TextUtil.autosuggestMatch(oTextbox.value, arrValues);

    for (var i=0; i < arrMatches.length; i++) {
        ListUtil.add(oListbox, arrMatches[i]);
    }

};
```

This method begins by getting a reference to the list box with the ID of `sListboxId`. The list box is then cleared of all prior options by using the `ListUtil.clear()` method explained earlier in the chapter.

Next, the method calls `TextUtil.autosuggestMatch()` to get the matching values for the string in the text box. The last step is to iterate through the matching values and add them to the list box by using the `ListUtil.add()` method.

To use this method, you must set up a text box and list box on a page along with an array of values to use. The values should be in alphabetical order so that they appear in alphabetical order when suggested to the user. Here's an example page:

```
<html>
    <head>
        <title>Autosuggest Textbox Example</title>
        <script type="text/javascript" src="listutil.js"></script>
        <script type="text/javascript" src="textutil.js"></script>
        <script type="text/javascript">
            var arrColors = ["red", "orange", "yellow", "green", "blue", "indigo",
                             "violet", "brown", "black", "tan", "ivory", "navy",
                             "aqua", "white", "purple", "pink", "gray", "silver"];
            arrColors.sort();

            function setText(oListbox, sTextboxId) {
                var oTextbox = document.getElementById(sTextboxId);
                if (oListbox.selectedIndex > -1) {
                    oTextbox.value =
                       oListbox.options[oListbox.selectedIndex].text;
                }
            }
        </script>
    </head>
    <body>
        <p>Type in a color in lowercase:<br />

        <input type="text" value="" id="txtColor"
            onkeyup="TextUtil.autosuggest(this, arrColors, 'lstColors')" /><br />

        <select id="lstColors" size="5" style="width: 200px"
            onclick="setText(this, 'txtColor')"></select>
        </p>
    </body>
</html>
```

In this example, an array of colors called `arrColors` is defined. Because the values aren't in alphabetical order, the `sort()` method is called after the array is created. It is this array that is referenced by `TextUtil.autosuggest()`. The list box with the ID `"lstColors"` contains the suggestions for what the user may want to type. This list box also has an `onclick` event handler that simply sets the text box value to the currently selected option (this is for convenience, although it isn't a necessary part of the autosuggest functionality). The `setText()` method takes two arguments: the list box and the ID of the text box. The method then gets a reference to the text box and sets its value to the currently selected value in the list box.

The autosuggest functionality described in this section is case-sensitive. To make a case-insensitive version, you should convert all values in the array to lowercase and then compare these values against the value of the text box (which should also be converted to all lowercase).

Summary

In this chapter you explored many ways to enhance Web forms. You learned how to use JavaScript to reset and submit a form. This included ensuring that the form is submitted only one time. You also explored different ways to access elements in a form.

You learned a great deal about text boxes, including how to allow or disallow certain characters. Further, you discovered how to prevent a user from pasting invalid values into a text box and how to validate a text box value using the `onblur` event handler.

List boxes and combo boxes were introduced and various methods of manipulation were discussed, including how to add new options, remove existing options, and move options within a single list box and between two list boxes.

Finally, all this knowledge is used to create an autosuggest text box that presents the user with a number of suggestions after he has typed in a few characters. In the next few chapters, you'll learn more about how to enhance the usability of Web pages using JavaScript.

12

Sorting Tables

In most applications, sorting lists and tables is a normal procedure that you might use on a daily basis. When you checking your e-mail, you probably have the table set up to sort by descending order on the date column, placing the most recent e-mails at the top. It was only a matter of time before this paradigm made its way onto the Web.

Traditionally, sorting on the Web involves a round-trip to the server with the request indicating which column should be sorted and in what direction. However, JavaScript enables you to create the same functionality on the client. Using JavaScript, it's possible to use sortable tables and also eliminate the need for costly server-side processing.

The Starting Point — Arrays

Back in Chapter 3, "Object Basics," you were introduced to the `Array` object and its `sort()` method. You may remember that the `sort()` method sorts in ascending order by the ASCII character code of each item, meaning that numbers are also sorted by their string equivalents:

```
var arr = [3, 32, 2, 5]
arr.sort();
alert(arr.toString());     //outputs "2,3,32,5"
```

The previous example displays `"2,3,32,5"` when the array is output. Luckily, JavaScript doesn't leave you stranded. The `sort()` method can also be given a single argument: a comparison function to tell the sorting algorithm when one value is greater than, less than, or equal to another value.

A *comparison function* is a function with a specific algorithm. It's helpful to take a look at a basic comparison function before continuing with the explanation:

```
function comparison_function(value1, value2) {
    if (value1 < value 2) {
```

```
        return -1;
    } else if (value1 > value2) {
        return 1;
    } else {
        return 0;
    }
};
```

As you can see, a comparison function compares two values, which is why a comparison function always has two arguments. If the first argument should come before the second argument, the function returns –1. If the first argument should come *after* the second argument, the function returns 1. If, however, the arguments are equal, the function returns 0. The comparison function is used in the `sort()` method like this:

```
arr.sort(comparison_function);
```

The basic comparison function pattern described previously sorts an array in ascending order. To sort in descending order, you just reverse 1 and –1:

```
function comparison_function_desc(value1, value2) {
    if (value1 < value 2) {
        return 1;
    } else if (value1 > value2) {
        return -1;
    } else {
        return 0;
    }
};
```

If this pattern sounds familiar, that's because the `String`'s `localeCompare()` method works the same way. So if you are sorting an array of strings, you can use this method directly:

```
function compareStrings(string1, string2) {
    return string1.localeCompare(string2);
}
```

This function causes an array of strings to be sorted in ascending order. To sort an array in descending order, just put a negative sign in front of the call:

```
function compareStringsDesc(string1, string2) {
    return -string1.localeCompare(string2);
}
```

By adding the negation operator, 1 becomes –1, –1 becomes 1, and 0 remains unchanged.

Now, go back to the previous example, in which numbers are sorted incorrectly. You can easily remedy the problem by writing a comparison function that transforms the arguments into numbers first and then compares them:

```
function compareIntegers(vNum1, vNum2) {
    var iNum1 = parseInt(vNum1);
    var iNum2 = parseInt(vNum2);
```

```
        if (iNum1 < iNum2) {
            return -1;
        } else if (iNum1 > iNum2) {
            return 1;
        } else {
            return 0;
        }
    }
```

If you apply this comparison function to the earlier example, the correct result is returned:

```
    var arr = [3, 32, 2, 5]
    arr.sort(compareIntegers);
    alert(arr.toString());     //outputs "2,3,5,32"
```

This example now outputs the numbers in correct order (2, 3, 5, 32).

The reverse() method

You were introduced to the `reverse()` method, which simply reverses the order of the items in an array, in Chapter 3, "Object Basics." In this chapter, you learn that the `reverse()` method is an essential part of sorting.

So, if you use a comparison function that sorts in ascending order, you can easily change the sort to descending order by using the `reverse()` method after the `sort()` method:

```
    var arr = [3, 32, 2, 5]
    arr.sort(compareIntegers);
    alert(arr.toString());     //outputs "2,3,5,32"
    arr.reverse();
    alert(arr.toString());     //outputs "32,5,3,2"
```

Of course, this is an extra step added to the sorting process, and there is certainly nothing wrong with creating two comparison functions whenever sorting is necessary. Just keep in mind that whenever an array is already sorted in one direction, it is much faster to use `reverse()` to sort it in the opposite direction than it is to call `sort()` once again.

Sorting a One-Column Table

Now you begin the task at hand, sorting a table. The simplest case is to sort a table with just one column and, therefore, just one data type. The best way to set up a table for sorting is to create a `<thead/>` element for the table header rows and a `<tbody/>` element for the rows that contain data:

```
    <table border="1" id="tblSort">
        <thead>
            <tr>
                <th>Last Name</th>
            </tr>
        </thead>
```

```
        <tbody>
            <tr>
                <td>Smith</td>
            </tr>
            <tr>
                <td>Johnson</td>
            </tr>
            <tr>
                <td>Henderson</td>
            </tr>
            <tr>
                <td>Williams</td>
            </tr>
            <tr>
                <td>Gilliam</td>
            </tr>
            <tr>
                <td>Walker</td>
            </tr>
        </tbody>
    </table>
```

With this setup, it's easy to distinguish between the header rows and the data rows (obviously, you don't want to sort the header rows along with the data, so this is an important distinction). Using the table's `tBodies` collection (which you may remember from earlier in the book), you can get a reference to the `<tbody/>` element as well as to the rows it contains:

```
var oTBody = oTable.tBodies[0];
var colDataRows = oTBody.rows;
```

To get the value in a table cell using the DOM is a bit involved, although not necessarily difficult. Each of the `<tr/>` elements contained in the `rows` collection contains a child `<td/>` element. Each <td/> element has a child text node that contains the actual value to be sorted on. Figure 12-1 shows this DOM hierarchy.

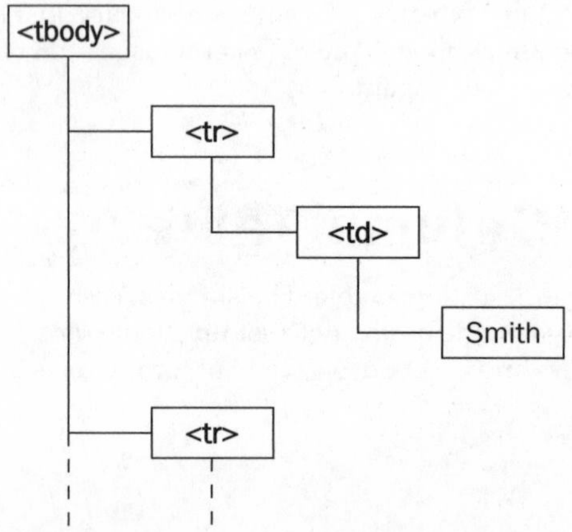

Figure 12-1

In order to retrieve the value `Smith` from the table defined previously, you use this code:

```
var sSmith = colDataRows[0].cells[0].firstChild.nodeValue;
```

This methodology can be used to retrieve the value contained in each row, which is what you need in order to create a comparison function for sorting.

The comparison function

The interesting thing about this comparison function is that it sorts `<tr/>` elements by using a value contained within the row, meaning that you must retrieve that value from within the function. After these values are retrieved, you can just use `localeCompare()` to compare them:

```
function compareTRs(oTR1, oTR2) {
    var sValue1 = oTR1.cells[0].firstChild.nodeValue;
    var sValue2 = oTR2.cells[0].firstChild.nodeValue;

    return sValue1.localeCompare(sValue2);
}
```

This comparison function sorts the table rows by the value in the first cell (index 0). Next, you use this comparison function with the table.

The sortTable() function

The `sortTable()` function does most of the heavy lifting. It accepts one argument, which is the ID of the table to sort. Naturally, this means the first step in the function must be to retrieve a DOM reference to the table as well as to locate the data rows:

```
function sortTable(sTableID) {
    var oTable = document.getElementById(sTableID);
    var oTBody = oTable.tBodies[0];
    var colDataRows = oTBody.rows;
    //...
}
```

The problem at this point is how to sort the rows in `colDataRows`. Remember, `rows` is a DOM collection, not an array and, therefore, it doesn't have the `sort()` method. The only solution is to create an array and fill it with the `<tr/>` elements, sort that array, and finally place the rows in order using the DOM. So first, you iterate through the `<tr/>` elements and add them to an array:

```
function sortTable(sTableID) {
    var oTable = document.getElementById(sTableID);
    var oTBody = oTable.tBodies[0];
    var colDataRows = oTBody.rows;
    var aTRs = new Array;

    for (var i=0; i < colDataRows.length; i++) {
        aTRs.push(colDataRows[i]);
    }

    //...
}
```

This section of code creates an array called aTRs and fills it with references to the <tr/> elements. Doing this doesn't remove the <tr/> elements from the table because you are only storing pointers, not the actual elements.

The next step is to sort the array using the compareTRs() function:

```
function sortTable(sTableID) {
    var oTable = document.getElementById(sTableID);
    var oTBody = oTable.tBodies[0];
    var colDataRows = oTBody.rows;
    var aTRs = new Array;

    for (var i=0; i < colDataRows.length; i++) {
        aTRs.push(colDataRows[i]);
    }

    aTRs.sort(compareTRs);

    //...
}
```

After this, all the <tr/> elements are in order in the array, but the order on the page hasn't changed. To actually change the order on the page, you add each row back in order. The fastest way to do this is to create a document fragment and add all <tr/> elements to it in the correct order. Then, you can use appendChild() to add all the child nodes from the document fragment back into the <tbody/> element.

```
function sortTable(sTableID) {
    var oTable = document.getElementById(sTableID);
    var oTBody = oTable.tBodies[0];
    var colDataRows = oTBody.rows;
    var aTRs = new Array;

    for (var i=0; i < colDataRows.length; i++) {
        aTRs[i] = colDataRows[i];
    }

    aTRs.sort(compareTRs);

    var oFragment = document.createDocumentFragment();
    for (var i=0; i < aTRs.length; i++) {
        oFragment.appendChild(aTRs[i]);
    }

    oTBody.appendChild(oFragment);
}
```

This code creates a document fragment and adds all the <tr/> elements to it, which effectively removes them from the table (Figure 12-2). Then, the children of the fragment are added back to the <tbody/> element. Remember, when you use appendChild() and pass it a document fragment, all the child nodes of the fragment are appended, not the fragment itself.

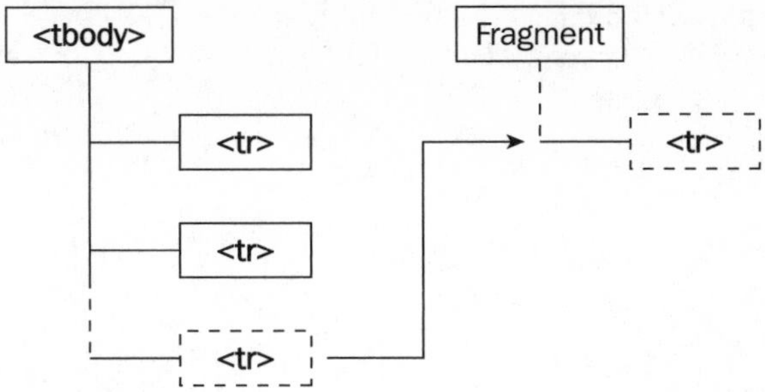

Figure 12-2

All that's left to do is to call the function when the user clicks on the column header. You can do this in any number of ways, but the simplest is just to add the function call as the `<th/>` element's `onclick` event handler:

```
<table border="1" id="tblSort">
    <thead>
        <tr>
            <th onclick="sortTable('tblSort')"
                style="cursor:pointer">Last Name</th>
        </tr>
    </thead>
    <tbody>
        <!-- data rows -->
    </tbody>
</table>
```

Also note the `style` attribute has been set to `cursor:pointer`, which ensures that the cursor turns into the hand pointer when the user mouses over the column header.

At this point, you just click on the column header to sort all the last names in alphabetical order.

Sorting a Multicolumn Table

In practice, it's very rare to have a single-column table, which is why the next task is to sort a table with more than one column. Suppose you added a second column to the table in the previous example, perhaps to display the first name of a person in addition to the last name:

```
<table border="1" id="tblSort">
    <thead>
        <tr>
            <th>Last Name</th>
            <th>First Name</th>
        </tr>
    </thead>
    <tbody>
        <tr>
```

```
                <td>Smith</td>
                <td>John</td>
            </tr>
            <tr>
                <td>Johnson</td>
                <td>Betty</td>
            </tr>
            <tr>
                <td>Henderson</td>
                <td>Nathan</td>
            </tr>
            <tr>
                <td>Williams</td>
                <td>James</td>
            </tr>
            <tr>
                <td>Gilliam</td>
                <td>Michael</td>
            </tr>
            <tr>
                <td>Walker</td>
                <td>Matthew</td>
            </tr>
        </tbody>
    </table>
```

Of course, the functions from the previous section only worked with one column, so modifications are needed.

The comparison function generator

Earlier in the book, it was mentioned that functions are just like any other type in JavaScript, meaning that they can be passed as arguments to other functions or returned as a function value. In this chapter, you have already seen a function passed to another function (the `sort()` method); now it's time to look at a function that returns a function.

The major limitation of the comparison function is its acceptance of two — and only two — arguments, meaning that additional information can't be passed in. To get around this, you can create a comparison function generator, which is a separate function that returns a comparison function.

Because the `compareTRs()` must know which the column's values to compare, it is necessary to pass in an additional argument: the index of the column to act on. Using a comparison function generator, it's possible to pass this extra value into the comparison function:

```
function generateCompareTRs(iCol) {

    return  function compareTRs(oTR1, oTR2) {
                var sValue1 = oTR1.cells[iCol].firstChild.nodeValue;
                var sValue2 = oTR2.cells[iCol].firstChild.nodeValue;

                return sValue1.localeCompare(sValue2);
            };
}
```

The `generateCompareTRs()` function takes only one argument, which is the index of the column to act on. It returns as its function value another function that looks suspiciously like `compareTRs()`. Note that the `iCol` argument, even though it isn't defined within the comparison function, is used within the comparison function. You may recognize this as a closure (discussed back in Chapter 2, "ECMAScript Basics"). The variable `iCol` is *captured* by the comparison function and, therefore, can be used when it is returned by `generateCompareTRs()`.

With the function defined, you can generate any comparison function necessary to sort a column:

```
var compareTRs = generateCompareTRs(0);
var compareTRs1 = generateCompareTRs(1);
var compareTRs2 = generateCompareTRs(2);
```

The first line in the previous code generates the exact same `compareTRs()` function you first defined in the previous section. The second and third lines generate a comparison function that compares the second and third columns, respectively. Of course, you don't need to assign the comparison function to a variable; it can just be passed directly into the `sort()` method:

```
aTRs.sort(generateCompareTRs(0));
```

In fact, this is how the `sortTable()` function must be modified to work with multiple columns.

Modifying the sortTable() function

Because there are multiple columns to deal with, the `sortTable()` function must now accept another argument indicating the index of the column to sort. Then, it can pass that value into the `generateCompareTRs()` function to sort the appropriate column:

```
function sortTable(sTableID, iCol) {
    var oTable = document.getElementById(sTableID);
    var oTBody = oTable.tBodies[0];
    var colDataRows = oTBody.rows;
    var aTRs = new Array;

    for (var i=0; i < colDataRows.length; i++) {
        aTRs[i] = colDataRows[i];
    }

    aTRs.sort(generateCompareTRs(iCol));

    var oFragment = document.createDocumentFragment();
    for (var i=0; i < aTRs.length; i++) {
        oFragment.appendChild(aTRs[i]);
    }

    oTBody.appendChild(oFragment);
}
```

With these two changes, it's now possible to pass in which column to sort. Don't forget, this change also needs to be included on the column headers in the table:

```
<table border="1" id="tblSort">
    <thead>
        <tr>
            <th onclick="sortTable('tblSort', 0)"
                style="cursor:pointer">Last Name</th>
            <th onclick="sortTable('tblSort', 1)"
                style="cursor:pointer">First Name</th>
        </tr>
    </thead>
    <tbody>
        <!-- data rows -->
    </tbody>
</table>
```

Of course, this function isn't limited to tables with just two columns. Any table with any number of columns can take advantage of it, just so long as you remember to pass in the correct column index to the function.

Sorting in descending order

In the first two examples, you learned how to sort single column and multicolumn tables in ascending order. Now, it's time to learn how to sort the table columns in descending order.

First and foremost, consider the expected behavior of a sortable table. When you sort a column in, say, Microsoft Outlook, you click on the column header. When you do this, the column is sorted in ascending order. If you then click on the column header a second time, the column sorts into descending order. This functionality is pretty standard in user interface design, so you really want to mimic it in your tables.

You can already sort each column in ascending order, so you're halfway there. The crux of this problem is that, on the *second* click, you want to sort in descending order. This means that in order to sort in descending order, you must already have clicked on the column header once (so the column is already sorted in ascending order). You can simply reverse the order (using the `reverse()` method) of the column to sort in descending order.

To make this change, it's necessary to once again modify the `sortTable()` function.

Modifying the sortTable() function

In order to create a descending sort, it is necessary to store the column index passed into the function for later reference. To do this, you can create an *expando* property on the table. An expando property is an extra JavaScript property that is added to an object during runtime. The expando property in this example is called `sortCol`, and it simply stores the index of the column that was sorted last:

```
function sortTable(sTableID, iCol) {
    var oTable = document.getElementById(sTableID);
    var oTBody = oTable.tBodies[0];
    var colDataRows = oTBody.rows;
    var aTRs = new Array;

    for (var i=0; i < colDataRows.length; i++) {
        aTRs[i] = colDataRows[i];
    }
```

```
        aTRs.sort(generateCompareTRs(iCol));

        var oFragment = document.createDocumentFragment();
        for (var i=0; i < aTRs.length; i++) {
            oFragment.appendChild(aTRs[i]);
        }

        oTBody.appendChild(oFragment);
        oTable.sortCol = iCol;
    }
```

Next, code must be added to check whether the column index being passed in is the same as the last sorted column index. If they are equal, the array should just be reversed instead of sorted:

```
    function sortTable(sTableID, iCol) {
        var oTable = document.getElementById(sTableID);
        var oTBody = oTable.tBodies[0];
        var colDataRows = oTBody.rows;
        var aTRs = new Array;

        for (var i=0; i < colDataRows.length; i++) {
            aTRs[i] = colDataRows[i];
        }

        if (oTable.sortCol == iCol) {
            aTRs.reverse();
        } else {
            aTRs.sort(generateCompareTRs(iCol));
        }

        var oFragment = document.createDocumentFragment();
        for (var i=0; i < aTRs.length; i++) {
            oFragment.appendChild(aTRs[i]);
        }

        oTBody.appendChild(oFragment);
        oTable.sortCol = iCol;
}
```

The best thing about this change is that it doesn't require any changes in the HTML. So now when the user clicks a column header once, it sorts into ascending order as always. When the user clicks the column header a second time, it is sorted in descending order. If the user clicks it a third time, the order reverses once again, sorting in ascending order. But so far this only works with strings. What about other data types?

Sorting with different data types

Although sorting strings is a good start, many times you may want to sort a column that contains other data types. Because the DOM text nodes always contain string values, that means the data must be converted before any sorting can be done. To do this, it's necessary to create a conversion function.

Creating a conversion function

A conversion function is relatively simple: You need two arguments, one for the value to be converted and one indicating what type of conversion should take place. Generally speaking, three conversions are frequently used: convert to integer, convert to float, and convert to date. Of course, if you need a string, no conversion is necessary.

For this conversion function, the second argument is a string indicating the type of conversion to do:

- "int" to convert to an integer
- "float" to convert to a float
- "date" to convert to a date
- Any other value always returns a string

Here's the function:

```
function convert(sValue, sDataType) {
    switch(sDataType) {
        case "int":
            return parseInt(sValue);
        case "float":
            return parseFloat(sValue);
        case "date":
            return new Date(Date.parse(sValue));
        default:
            return sValue.toString();

    }
}
```

This function uses the `switch` statement to determine the value of `sDataType` (remember, the `switch` statement works on all types in JavaScript). When `sDataType` is `"int"`, `parseInt()` is called on `sValue` and the result is returned; when `sDataType` is `"float"`, `parseFloat()` is called and the result is returned. If `sDataType` is `"date"`, then `Date.parse()` is used in conjunction with the `Date` constructor to create and return a new `Date` object. If `sDataType` is any other value, the function returns `sValue.toString()`, to ensure that a string value is returned. This means that if `sDataType` is `"string"`, `null`, or any other value, `convert()` always returns a string. For example:

```
var sValue = "25";
var iValue = convert(sValue, "int");
alert(typeof iValue);     //outputs "number"
var sValue2 = convert(sValue, "string");
alert(typeof sValue2);     //outputs "string"
var sValue3 = convert(sValue);
alert(typeof sValue3);     //outputs "string"
var sValue4 = convert(sValue, "football");
alert(typeof sValue4);     //outputs "string"
```

In this example, `convert()` is used to convert the string `"25"` into an integer, meaning that when `typeof` is called against it, the value returned is `"number"`. If, however, the second argument is `"string"`, the returned value is a string and `typeof` returns `"string"`. A string is also returned when the second argument is omitted and when the second argument is `"football"`.

With the conversion function complete, you must modify the rest of the code to use it.

> **It may not always be necessary to distinguish between integer and floating-point values when sorting. Most of the time, simply converting all numbers to floating-point is sufficient. The code in this chapter uses both types of numbers for illustrative purposes only.**

Modifying the code

The first step is to modify the `generateCompareTRs()` function, which now must accept an additional argument indicating the data type to use when comparing values. Then, the values from the table must be converted into the appropriate data type within the comparison function:

```
function generateCompareTRs(iCol, sDataType) {

    return  function compareTRs(oTR1, oTR2) {
                var vValue1 = convert(oTR1.cells[iCol].firstChild.nodeValue,
                                      sDataType);
                var vValue2 = convert(oTR2.cells[iCol].firstChild.nodeValue,
                                      sDataType);

                //...
            };
}
```

This change to `generateCompareTRs()` once again takes advantage of JavaScript's support of closures, passing the `sDataType` argument directly into the comparison function. Unfortunately, you can no longer use the `localeCompare()` method to return the appropriate function value because numbers and dates don't support it. Because you can't be sure which type of value is being stored, and it doesn't make sense to handle each data type's comparisons differently, it's best just to use less-than and greater-than to determine which value to return:

```
function generateCompareTRs(iCol, sDataType) {

    return  function compareTRs(oTR1, oTR2) {
                var vValue1 = convert(oTR1.cells[iCol].firstChild.nodeValue,
                                      sDataType);
                var vValue2 = convert(oTR2.cells[iCol].firstChild.nodeValue,
                                      sDataType);

                if (vValue1 < vValue2) {
                    return -1;
                } else if (vValue1 > vValue2) {
                    return 1;
                } else {
                    return 0;
                }
            };
}
```

Using this methodology, the comparison function returns the correct value no matter which data type is being used.

> **It's important not to use the equality operator (==) in this case. Although it works for strings and numbers (both integer and float), it won't work for dates. Remember, dates are objects, not primitive values. This means that the equality operator compares the objects to see if they are the same; it does not compare the values of the `Date` objects. However, the less-than and greater-than symbols use the `valueOf()` method of the `Date` objects to compare their milliseconds representation.**

Next, you modify the `sortTable()` function to use the new comparison function generator. To do so, this function also must accept an additional argument indicating the data type to use for the comparison. Then, this data type must be passed into the `generateCompareTRs()` function.

```
function sortTable(sTableID, iCol, sDataType) {
    var oTable = document.getElementById(sTableID);
    var oTBody = oTable.tBodies[0];
    var colDataRows = oTBody.rows;
    var aTRs = new Array;

    for (var i=0; i < colDataRows.length; i++) {
        aTRs[i] = colDataRows[i];
    }

    aTRs.sort(generateCompareTRs(iCol, sDataType));

    var oFragment = document.createDocumentFragment();
    for (var i=0; i < aTRs.length; i++) {
        oFragment.appendChild(aTRs[i]);
    }

    oTBody.appendChild(oFragment);
    oTable.sortCol = iCol;
}
```

With the JavaScript code all done, it's time to add extra data to the table for the various data types:

```
<table border="1" id="tblSort">
    <thead>
        <tr>
            <th onclick="sortTable('tblSort', 0)"
                style="cursor:pointer">Last Name</th>
            <th onclick="sortTable('tblSort', 1)"
                style="cursor:pointer">First Name</th>
            <th onclick="sortTable('tblSort', 2, 'date')"
                style="cursor:pointer">Birthday</th>
            <th onclick="sortTable('tblSort', 3, 'int')"
                style="cursor:pointer">Siblings</th>
        </tr>
    </thead>
    <tbody>
```

```
            <tr>
                <td>Smith</td>
                <td>John</td>
                <td>7/12/1978</td>
                <td>2</td>
            </tr>
            <tr>
                <td>Johnson</td>
                <td>Betty</td>
                <td>10/15/1977</td>
                <td>4</td>
            </tr>
            <tr>
                <td>Henderson</td>
                <td>Nathan</td>
                <td>2/25/1949</td>
                <td>1</td>
            </tr>
            <tr>
                <td>Williams</td>
                <td>James</td>
                <td>7/8/1980</td>
                <td>4</td>
            </tr>
            <tr>
                <td>Gilliam</td>
                <td>Michael</td>
                <td>7/22/1949</td>
                <td>1</td>
            </tr>
            <tr>
                <td>Walker</td>
                <td>Matthew</td>
                <td>1/14/2000</td>
                <td>3</td>
            </tr>
        </tbody>
    </table>
```

Note that the code in the column headers has also been updated to include the new data type argument. For the first two columns, you don't have to change the function call because both columns contain strings. The third and fourth columns, however, contain dates and integers, respectively. For each of these column headers, you must include the data type argument.

Advanced sorting

At this point, you've already learned how to sort different data types in the same table in both ascending and descending order. Unfortunately, it's very rare that a table contains only regular data types. The truth is that you will always end up with links, images, or some other sort of HTML in tables; and users will still want to sort. The most common situation is probably a column that contains icons. Whether the icon is indicative of something (for instance, an attachment on an e-mail) or just decorative, people want to be able to sort by it. The previous code does not support such a thing, but that can be fixed.

The concept

Keep in mind is that each cell in a table must have a sortable value, meaning a value that is a string, integer, float, or date. Because all HTML code can't be converted directly into one of these data types, you need to specify an alternate value to sort by. This can be accomplished by adding an extra attribute on each `<td/>` that contains HTML, like this:

```
<td value="blue"><img src="blueimage.gif" /></td>
```

Because this table cell contains an image, you normally wouldn't be able to sort it. However, the addition of the `value` attribute specifies that the value to sort is `"blue"`, not the contents of the `<td/>` element.

And as you learned earlier, it is possible to access this new attribute using the DOM `getAttribute()` method:

```
var sValue = oTD.getAttribute("value");
```

Now, it isn't necessary to add a `value` attribute to every cell in a table, because this gives you a lot of redundant information. You should only add the attribute to those table cells containing HTML code. For example, the following table lists filenames along with their associated icons. Note that only the first column uses the extra `value` attribute:

```
<table border="1" id="tblSort">
    <thead>
        <tr>
            <th>Type</th>
            <th>Filename</th>
        </tr>
    </thead>
    <tbody>
        <tr>
            <td value="doc"><img src="images/wordicon.gif"/></td>
            <td>My Resume.doc</td>
        </tr>
        <tr>
            <td value="xls"><img src="images/excelicon.gif"/></td>
            <td>Fall Budget.xls</td>
        </tr>
        <tr>
            <td value="pdf"><img src="images/acrobaticon.gif"/></td>
            <td>How to be a better programmer.pdf</td>
        </tr>
        <tr>
            <td value="doc"><img src="images/wordicon.gif"/></td>
            <td>My Old Resume.doc</td>
        </tr>
        <tr>
            <td value="txt"><img src="images/notepadicon.gif"/></td>
            <td>Notes from Meeting.txt</td>
        </tr>
        <tr>
            <td value="zip"><img src="images/zippedfoldericon.gif"/></td>
            <td>Backups.zip</td>
```

```
        </tr>
        <tr>
            <td value="xls"><img src="images/excelicon.gif"/></td>
            <td>Spring Budget.xls</td>
        </tr>
        <tr>
            <td value="doc"><img src="images/wordicon.gif"/></td>
            <td>Job Description - Web Designer.doc</td>
        </tr>
        <tr>
            <td value="pdf"><img src="images/acrobaticon.gif"/></td>
            <td>Saved Web Page.pdf</td>
        </tr>
        <tr>
            <td value="doc"><img src="images/wordicon.gif"/></td>
            <td>Chapter 1.doc</td>
        </tr>
    </tbody>
</table>
```

However, this new attribute alone doesn't solve the problem. You must also update the JavaScript code to take advantage of the `value` attribute.

> **As mentioned earlier in the book, adding custom attributes to HTML tags is not allowed using the strict representation of XHTML. You may alternately want to provide the value for a table cell using the `title` attribute (if the value will make sense to the user) or by providing an invisible `<div/>` inside the table cell that contains the value.**

Modifying the code

This final modification to the code determines whether to get the sortable value from the `<td/>` element's text or from the `value` attribute. Here's the updated code:

```
function generateCompareTRs(iCol, sDataType) {

    return  function compareTRs(oTR1, oTR2) {

                var vValue1, vValue2;

                if (oTR1.cells[iCol].getAttribute("value")) {
                    vValue1 = convert(oTR1.cells[iCol].getAttribute("value"),
                                      sDataType);
                    vValue2 = convert(oTR2.cells[iCol].getAttribute("value"),
                                      sDataType);
                } else {
                    vValue1 = convert(oTR1.cells[iCol].firstChild.nodeValue,
                                      sDataType);
                    vValue2 = convert(oTR2.cells[iCol].firstChild.nodeValue,
                                      sDataType);
                }
```

```
                if (vValue1 < vValue2) {
                    return -1;
                } else if (vValue1 > vValue2) {
                    return 1;
                } else {
                    return 0;
                }
            };
        }
```

Basically, `vValue1` and `vValue2` are defined to have no initial value. Then, you check to see if the cell in the first row has a `value` attribute defined by using `getAttribute()`, which will return `null` when the attribute doesn't exist. When placed in the `if` statement, `null` is evaluated as `false` and a non-`null` value is evaluated as `true`. Therefore, if the `value` attribute exists, both `vValue1` and `vValue2` are assigned the value of the attribute for `oTR1` and `oTR2`, respectively. If the `value` attribute doesn't exist, then `vValue1` and `vValue2` are assigned the value contained inside the table cell.

The only thing left to do is to add the sorting calls to the HTML code:

```
<table border="1" id="tblSort">
    <thead>
        <tr>
            <th onclick="sortTable('tblSort', 0)"
                style="cursor:pointer">Type</th>
            <th onclick="sortTable('tblSort', 1)"
                style="cursor:pointer">Filename</th>
        </tr>
    </thead>
    <tbody>
        <tr>
            <td value="doc"><img src="images/wordicon.gif"/></td>
            <td>My Resume.doc</td>
        </tr>
        <tr>
            <td value="xls"><img src="images/excelicon.gif"/></td>
            <td>Fall Budget.xls</td>
        </tr>
        <tr>
            <td value="pdf"><img src="images/acrobaticon.gif"/></td>
            <td>How to be a better programmer.pdf</td>
        </tr>
        <tr>
            <td value="doc"><img src="images/wordicon.gif"/></td>
            <td>My Old Resume.doc</td>
        </tr>
        <tr>
            <td value="txt"><img src="images/notepadicon.gif"/></td>
            <td>Notes from Meeting.txt</td>
        </tr>
        <tr>
            <td value="zip"><img src="images/zippedfoldericon.gif"/></td>
            <td>Backups.zip</td>
        </tr>
```

```
            <tr>
                <td value="xls"><img src="images/excelicon.gif"/></td>
                <td>Spring Budget.xls</td>
            </tr>
            <tr>
                <td value="doc"><img src="images/wordicon.gif"/></td>
                <td>Job Description - Web Designer.doc</td>
            </tr>
            <tr>
                <td value="pdf"><img src="images/acrobaticon.gif"/></td>
                <td>Saved Web Page.pdf</td>
            </tr>
            <tr>
                <td value="doc"><img src="images/wordicon.gif"/></td>
                <td>Chapter 1.doc</td>
            </tr>
        </tbody>
    </table>
```

This HTML code sorts both columns by using strings; therefore, the third argument isn't necessary when calling `sortTable()`. Even though the first column contains images, the code uses the value attribute to sort it in both ascending and descending order.

Summary

This chapter explored using JavaScript to move more server-based functionality onto the client: sorting HTML tables. You learned about using comparison functions along with the `Array`'s `sort()` method to define custom sort order. With this knowledge, you went on to sort columns with string values in ascending order.

Next, you learned how to sort in descending order by using the `reverse()` method of the `Array`. Then, columns with different values were introduced for sorting as well. After you wrote a small conversion function, you were able to sort integers, floats, and dates in table columns. Lastly, you learned how to account for table cells that contained HTML instead of simple text values.

Along the way, you learned about closures in JavaScript, which allow generated functions to contain references to variables that are seemingly out of scope. Using closures, you saw how the seemingly limited definition of comparison functions could be extended to allow the usage of additional data to determine which of two values should occur first.

13

Drag and Drop

One of the biggest improvements in computer usability was the proliferation of drag-and-drop behavior, allowing users to drag something from one spot on the screen and drop it somewhere else to either create an action or simply move the item. This paradigm, developed by XEROX, was first incorporated into consumer technology in Mac OS 1.0 and since that time has been incorporated in most personal computer operating systems (including Windows). When Dynamic HTML was first introduced, developers around the world starting experimenting with drag-and-drop functionality using JavaScript.

Drag and drop is a buzzword in usability, so adding this functionality to your Web site or Web application can win major points with customers and clients. At present time, you can accomplish drag and drop in two ways using JavaScript: system drag and drop and simulated drag and drop.

System Drag and Drop

System drag and drop is what you probably do on a daily basis when using your Windows, Macintosh, or other graphical operation system: You drag something from one area of the screen and drop it somewhere else. To delete a file, you drag it to the trash (Macintosh) or the recycle bin (Windows); to move a file from one folder to another, you just drag the file from where it is and drop it into its new home. System drag and drop works because it has help from the operating system to complete its task. Currently, only one Web browser on one platform supports system drag and drop in Web pages, and that is Internet Explorer on Windows (although Mozilla supports it in XUL-based pages).

A system drag and drop can move in between windows and frames because the drag action is handled by the operating system. You can drag an image from a Web browser onto your desktop or into another browser. When you drag it onto your desktop, you download the image; when you drag it into another browser, the browser displays the image. The communication between the browser and the desktop (or other browser) is handled by the operating system.

In Internet Explorer version 4.0, only two items on a Web page could initiate a system drag: an image or some text. When dragging an image, you just simply held the mouse button down and then moved it; with text, you first highlighted some text and then you could drag it the same way as you would drag an image. In IE 4.0, the only valid drop target was a text box.

In version 5.0, Internet Explorer extended its drag-and-drop capabilities by adding new events and allowing nearly anything on a Web page to become a drop target. Version 5.5 went a little bit further by allowing nearly anything to become draggable (IE 6.0 supports this functionality as well).

> **The system drag-and-drop functionality discussed in this section pertains to Internet Explorer for Windows only; the Macintosh version of IE never developed the drag-and-drop functionality to this extent because of its separation from the operating system.**

Drag-and-drop events

The drag-and-drop events Microsoft added to Internet Explorer enable you to control nearly every aspect of a system drag-and-drop operation. The tricky part is determining where each event is fired: Some fire on the dragged item; others fire on the drop target.

Dragged item events

When an item is dragged, the following events fire (in this order):

1. `dragstart`
2. `drag`
3. `dragend`

At the moment you hold a mouse button down and begin to move the mouse, the `dragstart` event fires on the item that is being dragged. By default, this event fires on an image or text selection being dragged. The cursor changes to the *no-drop* symbol (a circle with a line through it) indicating that the item cannot be dropped on itself. You can use the `ondragstart` event handler to run JavaScript code as the dragging begins.

After the `dragstart` event fires, the `drag` event fires and continues firing so long as the object is being dragged. You can think of this event as similar to `mousemove` (which also fires repeatedly as the mouse is moved). When the dragging stops (because you drop the item onto either a valid or invalid drop target) the `dragend` event fires.

The following example shows how to use the `ondragstart`, `ondrag`, and `ondragend` event handlers:

```
<html>
    <head>
        <title>System Drag And Drop Example</title>
        <script type="text/javascript">
            function handleDragDropEvent(oEvent) {
                var oTextbox = document.getElementById("txt1");
                oTextbox.value +=  oEvent.type + "\n";
```

```
            }
        </script>
    </head>
    <body>
        <form>
        <p>Try dragging the image.</p>
        <p><img src="images/smiley.gif" alt=""
                ondragstart="handleDragDropEvent(event)"
                ondrag="handleDragDropEvent(event)"
                ondragend="handleDragDropEvent(event)" /></p>
        <p><textarea rows="10" cols="25" readonly="readonly"
                     id="txt1"></textarea></p>
        </form>
    </body>
</html>
```

This example assigns `ondragstart`, `ondrag`, and `ondragend` event handlers to an image. When you drag the image, the following text box displays the events each time one occurs. You end up seeing something like this in the text box:

```
dragstart
drag
drag
drag
drag
drag
drag
dragend
```

Play around with this example for a while until you get the hang of these events.

> **On any browsers other than IE on Windows, the event handlers in the previous example are ignored. Keep this in mind if you plan on implementing a system drag-and-drop solution.**

Drop Target Events

When an item is dragged over a valid drop target, the `dragenter` event (similar to the `mouseover` event) fires. Immediately after the `dragenter` event fires, the `dragover` event fires and continues to fire as the item is being dragged within the boundaries of the drop target. When the item is dragged outside of the drop target, `dragover` stops firing and the `dragleave` event is fired (similar to `mouseout`). If the dragged item is actually dropped on the target, the `drop` event fires instead of `dragleave`.

This example explores the drop target events:

```
<html>
    <head>
        <title>System Drag And Drop Example</title>
        <script type="text/javascript">
            function handleDragDropEvent(oEvent) {
                var oTextbox = document.getElementById("txt1");
```

```
                oTextbox.value +=  oEvent.type + "\n";
            }
        </script>
    </head>
    <body>
        <form>
        <p>Try dragging the text from the left textbox to the right one.</p>
        <p><input type="text" value="drag this text" />
        <input type="text" ondragenter="handleDragDropEvent(event)"
               ondragover="handleDragDropEvent(event)"
               ondragleave="handleDragDropEvent(event)"
               ondrop="handleDragDropEvent(event)" /></p>
        <p><textarea rows="10" cols="25" readonly="readonly"
id="txt1"></textarea></p>
         </form>
    </body>
</html>
```

The previous example provides two text boxes to work with the events and one to announce the events as they occur. When you drag the text from the text box on the left to the one on the right, the `<textarea/>` fills up with events as they fire. If you drag the text over the text box and then drag it back out, you see events like this:

```
dragenter
dragover
dragover
dragover
dragover
dragover
dragleave
```

Otherwise, if you drop the text into the second text box, you see something like this:

```
dragenter
dragover
dragover
dragover
dragover
dragover
drop
```

Note that when you drop the text into the second text box, the highlighted text actually moves into it.

Using all drag-and-drop events

The tricky part of handling system drag and drop is understanding the relationship between the dragged item events and the drop target events. Generally speaking, the dragged item events always fire first, except in the case of the `drop` event, which fires before `dragend`. The following example allows you to explore the relationship between these sets of events:

```
<html>
    <head>
        <title>System Drag And Drop Example</title>
        <script type="text/javascript">
```

```
            function handleDragDropEvent(oEvent) {
                var oTextbox = document.getElementById("txt1");
                oTextbox.value +=  oEvent.type + "\n";
            }
        </script>
    </head>
    <body>
        <p>Try dragging the text from the left textbox to the right one.</p>
        <form>
        <p><input type="text" value="drag this text"
                  ondragstart="handleDragDropEvent(event)"
                  ondrag="handleDragDropEvent(event)"
                  ondragend="handleDragDropEvent(event)" />
        <input type="text" ondragenter="handleDragDropEvent(event)"
               ondragover="handleDragDropEvent(event)"
               ondragleave="handleDragDropEvent(event)"
               ondrop="handleDragDropEvent(event)" /></p>
        <p><textarea rows="10" cols="25" readonly="readonly"
                     id="txt1"></textarea></p>
        </form>
    </body>
</html>
```

As you can tell, this example combines the functionality of the previous two examples, monitoring both the dragged item events and the drop target events. When you drag text into the right text box from the left, you see an event listing like this:

```
dragstart
drag
drag
drag
dragenter
drag
dragover
drag
dragover
drag
drop
dragend
```

Note that because you start dragging away from the drop target, only the dragged item events fire initially. When you drag the text over the drop target, the `dragenter` event fires, followed by `drag` and then `dragover`. These two events fires repeatedly while you are still dragging over the drop target. When you drop onto the target, the `drop` event fires and is immediately followed by `dragend`. This completes the drag and drop sequence.

If you don't drop onto the target, you see a series of events more like this:

```
dragstart
drag
drag
drag
dragenter
```

```
drag
dragover
drag
dragover
drag
dragleave
drag
drag
drag
dragend
```

In this case, you dragged the text over the right text box, and then dragged it back out, so the `dragleave` event fires, followed by the `drag` event. When you finally stop dragging the text, the `dragend` event fires.

By default, text boxes (`<input/>` or `<textarea/>`) are the only valid drop targets on a Web page, although it is possible to create a drop target from any item by altering the behavior of the `dragover` and `dragenter` events.

Creating your own drop target

When you try to drag some text (or an image) over an invalid drop target, you see a special cursor (a circle with a line through it) indicating that you cannot drop. Even though all elements support the drop target events, by default, their behavior is to not allow dropping. For example:

```
<html>
    <head>
        <title>System Drag And Drop Example</title>
        <script type="text/javascript">
            function handleDragDropEvent(oEvent) {
                var oTextbox = document.getElementById("txt1");
                oTextbox.value +=  oEvent.type + "\n";
            }
        </script>
    </head>
    <body>
        <p>Try dragging the text from the textbox to the red square.
        No drop target events fire.</p>
        <form>
        <p><input type="text" value="drag this text"
                ondragstart="handleDragDropEvent(event)"
                ondrag="handleDragDropEvent(event)"
                ondragend="handleDragDropEvent(event)" />
        <div style="background-color: red; height: 100px; width: 100px"
             ondragenter="handleDragDropEvent(event)"
             ondragover="handleDragDropEvent(event)"
             ondragleave="handleDragDropEvent(event)"
             ondrop="handleDragDropEvent(event)"></div></p>
        <p><textarea rows="10" cols="25" readonly="readonly"
                    id="txt1"></textarea></p>
        </form>
    </body>
</html>
```

In this example, all the dragged item events fire, but no drop target event fires when you drag the text over the red `<div/>`. In order to turn the `<div/>` into a valid drop target, you must override the default behavior of `dragenter` and `dragover`. Because this is IE-specific, you can just set the `oEvent.returnValue` attribute to `false`:

```
<html>
    <head>
        <title>System Drag And Drop Example</title>
        <script type="text/javascript">
            function handleDragDropEvent(oEvent) {
                var oTextbox = document.getElementById("txt1");
                oTextbox.value +=  oEvent.type + "\n";

                switch(oEvent.type) {
                    case "dragover":
                    case "dragenter":
                        oEvent.returnValue = false;
                }
            }
        </script>
    </head>
    <body>
        <p>Try dragging the text from the textbox to the red square.
        Drop target events fire now.</p>
        <form>
        <p><input type="text" value="drag this text"
                  ondragstart="handleDragDropEvent(event)"
                  ondrag="handleDragDropEvent(event)"
                  ondragend="handleDragDropEvent(event)" />
        <div style="background-color: red; height: 100px; width: 100px"
             ondragenter="handleDragDropEvent(event)"
             ondragover="handleDragDropEvent(event)"
             ondragleave="handleDragDropEvent(event)"
             ondrop="handleDragDropEvent(event)"></div></p>
        <p><textarea rows="10" cols="25" readonly="readonly"
                     id="txt1"></textarea></p>
        </form>
    </body>
</html>
```

In this example, when you drag the text over the red `<div/>`, the cursor changes to a pointer with a plus sign next to it, indicating that this is a valid drop target. By default, the `dragenter` and `dragover` events for the `<div/>` don't allow dropping, so if you prevent the default behavior you allow the `<div/>` to become a drop target. After `dragenter` and `dragover` are fired, `dragleave` and `drop` are also enabled.

The dataTransfer object

Simply dragging and dropping isn't of any use unless data is actually being affected. To aid in the transmission of data via drag and drop, Internet Explorer 5.0 introduced the `dataTransfer` object, which exists as a property of `event` and is used to transfer string data from the dragged item to the drop target (the `dataTransfer` object is still used in IE 6.0).

Because it is a property of `event`, the `dataTransfer` object doesn't exist except within the scope of an event handler, specifically, an event handler for a drag-and-drop event. Within an event handler, you can use the object's properties and methods to work with your drag-and-drop functionality.

Methods

The `dataTransfer` object has two methods: `getData()` and `setData()`. As you might expect, `getData()` is capable of retrieving a value stored by `setData()`. Two types of data can be set: plain text and URLs. The first argument for `setData()`, and the only argument of `getData()`, is a string indicating which type of data is being set, either `"text"` or `"URL"`. For example:

```
oEvent.dataTransfer.setData("text", "some text");
var sData = oEvent.dataTransfer.getData("text");
oEvent.dataTransfer.setData("URL", "http://www.wrox.com/");
var sURL = oEvent.dataTransfer.getData("URL");
```

It should be noted that two spaces can be used to store data: one for text and one for a URL. If you make repeated calls to `setData()`, you are always overwriting the data stored in the space specified.

The data stored in the `dataTransfer` object is only available up until the `drop` event. If you do not retrieve the data in the `ondrop` event handler, the `dataTransfer` object is destroyed and the data is lost.

When you drag text from a text box, the operating system calls `setData()` and stores the dragged text in the `"text"` format. It is possible to retrieve this value when it is dropped on a target. Consider the following example:

```
<html>
    <head>
        <title>System Drag And Drop Example</title>
        <script type="text/javascript">
            function handleDragDropEvent(oEvent) {

                switch(oEvent.type) {
                    case "dragover":
                    case "dragenter":
                        oEvent.returnValue = false;
                        break;
                    case "drop":
                        alert(oEvent.dataTransfer.getData("text"));
                }
            }
        </script>
    </head>
    <body>
        <p>Try dragging the text from the textbox to the red square.
        It will show you the selected text when dropped.</p>
        <p><input type="text" value="drag this text" />
        <div style="background-color: red; height: 100px; width: 100px"
             ondragenter="handleDragDropEvent(event)"
             ondragover="handleDragDropEvent(event)"
             ondrop="handleDragDropEvent(event)"></div></p>

    </body>
</html>
```

This is essentially the same as the last example, with the exception that the call to the `dataTransfer.getData()` method retrieves the text that was being dragged. When you drop that text onto the red `<div/>`, this example pops up an alert displaying the text you were dragging.

You may be wondering, what would happen if you used `getData()` with the argument `"URL"` instead of `"text"`? In this example, it would return a `null` value because the data is stored as text and, therefore, must be retrieved as text.

If instead you were to drag a link onto the red `<div/>`, you could use `getData()` with the `"URL"` format to retrieve the link:

```
<html>
    <head>
        <title>System Drag And Drop Example</title>
        <script type="text/javascript">
            function handleDragDropEvent(oEvent) {

                switch(oEvent.type) {
                    case "dragover":
                    case "dragenter":
                        oEvent.returnValue = false;
                        break;
                    case "drop":
                        alert(oEvent.dataTransfer.getData("URL"));
                }
            }
        </script>
    </head>
    <body>
        <p>Try dragging the link to the red square.
        It will show you the URL when dropped.</p>
        <p><a href="http://www.wrox.com" target="_blank">Wrox Home Page</a>
        <div style="background-color: red; height: 100px; width: 100px"
             ondragenter="handleDragDropEvent(event)"
             ondragover="handleDragDropEvent(event)"
             ondrop="handleDragDropEvent(event)"></div></p>

    </body>
</html>
```

When you begin dragging a link, the browser calls `setData()` and stores the `href` attribute as a URL. Using `getData()` and asking for the URL format, you can retrieve this value. So what is really the difference between the text and URL format?

When you specify data to be stored as text, it gets no special treatment whatsoever. In a manner of speaking, "it's just dumb text." When you specify data to be stored as a URL, however, it is treated just like a link on a Web page, meaning that if you drop it onto another browser window, the browser will navigate to that URL. This is discussed further later on.

dropEffect and effectAllowed

The `dataTransfer` object can be used to do more than simply transport data to and fro; it can also be used to determine what type of actions can be done with the dragged item and the drop target. You accomplish this by using two properties: `dropEffect` and `effectAllowed`.

The `dropEffect` property is set on the drop target to determine which type of drop behavior is allowed. These are four possible values:

- `"none"` — A dragged item cannot be dropped here. This is the default value for everything but text boxes.
- `"move"` — Indicates that the dragged item should be moved to the drop target.
- `"copy"` — Indicates that the dragged item should be copied to the drop target.
- `"link"` — Indicates that the drop target will navigate to the dragged item (but only if it is a URL).

Each of these values causes a different cursor to be displayed when an item is dragged over the drop target. It is up to you, however, to actually cause the actions indicated by the cursor. In other words, nothing is automatically moved, copied, or linked without your direction intervention. The only thing you get for free is the cursor change. In order to use the `dropEffect` property, it must be set in the `ondragenter` event handler for the drop target.

The `dropEffect` property is useless unless you also set the `effectAllowed` property on the dragged item. This property indicates which `dropEffect` is allowed for the dragged item. The possible values are the following:

- `"uninitialized"` — No action has been set for the dragged item.
- `"none"` — No action is allowed on the dragged item.
- `"copy"` — Only `dropEffect "copy"` is allowed.
- `"link"` — Only `dropEffect "link"` is allowed.
- `"move"` — Only `dropEffect "move"` is allowed.
- `"copyLink"` — `dropEffects "copy"` and `"link"` are allowed.
- `"copyMove"` — `dropEffects "copy"` and `"move"` are allowed.
- `"linkMove"` — `dropEffects "link"` and `"move"` are allowed.
- `"all"` — All `dropEffects` are allowed.

This property must be set inside the `ondragstart` event handler.

Suppose you want to allow a user to move text from a text box into a `<div/>`. You must set both `dropEffect` and `effectAllowed` to `"move"`. But alas, the text won't automatically move itself because the default behavior for the drop event on a `<div/>` is to do nothing. If you override the default behavior, the text is automatically removed from the text box. It is then up to you to insert it into the `<div/>` using the `innerHTML` property:

```
<html>
    <head>
        <title>System Drag And Drop Example</title>
        <script type="text/javascript">
            function handleDragDropEvent(oEvent) {

                switch(oEvent.type) {
                    case "dragstart":
```

```
                        oEvent.dataTransfer.effectAllowed = "move";
                        break;

                    case "dragenter":
                        oEvent.dataTransfer.dropEffect = "move";
                        oEvent.returnValue = false;
                        break;

                    case "dragover":
                        oEvent.returnValue = false;
                        break;

                    case "drop":
                        oEvent.returnValue = false;
                        oEvent.srcElement.innerHTML =
                                     oEvent.dataTransfer.getData("text");
                }
            }
        </script>
    </head>
    <body>
        <p>Try dragging the text in the textbox to the red square.
        The text will be "moved" to the red square.</p>
        <p><input type="text" value="drag this text"
                  ondragstart="handleDragDropEvent(event)" />
        <div style="background-color: red; height: 100px; width: 100px"
             ondragenter="handleDragDropEvent(event)"
             ondragover="handleDragDropEvent(event)"
             ondrop="handleDragDropEvent(event)"></div>
        </p>

    </body>
</html>
```

In this example, you can drag text from the text box and drop it onto the red `<div/>`. The text is removed from the text box because the default behavior of the drop event is overridden. The text is then inserted into the `<div/>` by using the `innerHTML` property.

If you were to change `dropEffect` and `effectAllowed` to `"copy"`, the text in the text box would remain and would be duplicated in the `<div/>`.

The dragDrop() method

You already know how to create your own drop targets, so now it's time to learn about creating your own draggable items. In IE 5.5, the `dragDrop()` method can be applied to almost any HTML element. You can initiate a system drag event by calling `dragDrop()` and, therefore, allow normally undraggable items to fire `dragstart`, `drag`, and `dragend` events.

The trick is to call `dragDrop()` at the correct time. To do this, it is best to use the `onmousemove` event handler to initiate the drag, like this:

```
oElement.onmousemove = function (oEvent) {
    if (oEvent.button == 1) {
```

```
            oElement.dragDrop();
        }
    };
```

By using the `event.button` property, you're making sure that the left mouse button is down while the mouse is moving, which is typically when an object begins to be dragged.

The next step is to use the `dataTransfer` object in the element's `ondragstart` event handler to determine the action of the dragged item. For example, you could make a `<div/>` that, when dragged into a text box, inserts text:

```
<html>
    <head>
        <title>System Drag And Drop Example</title>
        <script type="text/javascript">
            function handleMouseMove(oEvent) {
                if (oEvent.button == 1) {
                    oEvent.srcElement.dragDrop();
                }
            }

            function handleDragDropEvent(oEvent) {
                oEvent.dataTransfer.setData("text", "This is a red square");
            }
        </script>
    </head>
    <body>
        <p>Try dragging the red square into the textbox.</p>
        <p><div style="background-color: red; height: 100px; width: 100px"
                onmousemove="handleMouseMove(event)"
                ondragstart="handleDragDropEvent(event)">This is a red square</div>
        </p>
        <form>
        <p><input type="text" value="" /></p>
        </form>
    </body>
</html>
```

When you drag the red `<div/>` in this example, the text "This is a red square" is set to the `dataTransfer` object. So if you drop the square into the text box, that text is instantly inserted as if it had been dragged from another text box. You could even drag the red `<div/>` into another browser window's text box and the same thing would occur.

If you choose to store a URL instead of just text, it's possible to drag the red square into another browser window and have the browser navigate to the page specified:

```
<html>
    <head>
        <title>System Drag And Drop Example</title>
        <script type="text/javascript">

            function handleMouseMove(oEvent) {
                if (oEvent.button == 1) {
```

```
                    oEvent.srcElement.dragDrop();
                }
            }

            function handleDragDropEvent(oEvent) {
                oEvent.dataTransfer.setData("URL", "http://www.wrox.com/");
            }
        </script>
    </head>
    <body>
        <p>Try dragging the red square into another browser window.</p>
        <p><div style="background-color: red; height: 100px; width: 100px"
                onmousemove="handleMouseMove(event)"
                ondragstart="handleDragDropEvent(event)">http://www.wrox.com</div>
        </p>
    </body>
</html>
```

In this example, dragging the red `<div/>` into another browser window causes the browser to navigate to the Wrox home page, `http://www.wrox.com`.

Advantages and disadvantages

Obviously, system drag and drop in Internet Explorer is a very powerful piece of functionality, enabling you to tap into what is truly an operating-system function. The power to drag information across frames, as well as across browser windows, opens up a whole new world of possibilities for JavaScript developers. You must, however, be using Internet Explorer 5.0 or higher on Windows.

If you need to develop a drag-and-drop solution that works across multiple browsers, then system drag and drop is not the way to go. Despite the fact that this solution is so easy to use, no other browsers have made any moves to include such functionality, and that is not likely to change anytime in the near future. For those who only develop for Internet Explorer, this solution works pretty well; for others, the answer is to simulate drag-and-drop functionality.

Simulated Drag and Drop

Simulated drag and drop has been around since Internet Explorer 4.0 and Netscape Navigator 4.0 introduced support for Dynamic HTML. The basic idea is simple: You create an absolutely positioned layer that can be moved along with the mouse. In practice, it's a bit more complicated to get the true drag-and-drop feel to come across to users.

The method for this type of drag and drop is an extension of the classic cursor trail script. You may remember coming across a Web page where your cursor was followed by an image. This is quite easy to do:

```
<html>
    <head>
        <title>Simulated Drag And Drop Example</title>
        <script type="text/javascript">
```

```
            function handleMouseMove(oEvent) {
                var oDiv = document.getElementById("div1");
                oDiv.style.left = oEvent.clientX;
                oDiv.style.top = oEvent.clientY;
            }

        </script>
        <style type="text/css">
            #div1 {
                background-color: red;
                height: 100px;
                width: 100px;
                position: absolute;
            }
        </style>
    </head>
    <body onmousemove="handleMouseMove(event)">
        <p>Try moving your mouse around.</p>
        <p><div id="div1"></div> </p>
    </body>
</html>
```

In this example, a red `<div/>` follows the cursor around. Every time the cursor moves, the `<div/>` is positioned at the same position, making its upper-left corner equal to the point of the cursor. Note that the `onmousemove` event handler is assigned for the `<body/>` element, not for the `<div/>`. This is because you must track the mouse movement over the entire page, not just within the `<div/>`.

To simulate drag and drop, the `<div/>` shouldn't just move around on its own; the drag must be initiated and stopped. This is where the code gets a little bit tricky and requires the use of the `EventUtil` object from earlier in the book.

The code

The first step is to create three functions: one to handle each of three mouse events (`mousemove`, `mousedown`, and `mouseup`). The function that handles `mousedown` is assigned to the `<div/>` (or the element to be dragged). When the user's mouse button is pushed down over the `<div/>`, this function assigns the event handlers for `mousemove` and `mouseup` on `document.body`. When the user releases the mouse button, the dragging stops and the event handlers for `mousemove` and `mouseup` are removed. Here's the code:

```
<html>
    <head>
        <title>Simulated Drag And Drop Example</title>
        <script type="text/javascript" src="eventutil.js"></script>
        <script type="text/javascript">

            function handleMouseMove() {
                var oEvent = EventUtil.getEvent();
                var oDiv = document.getElementById("div1");
                oDiv.style.left = oEvent.clientX;
                oDiv.style.top = oEvent.clientY;
            }
```

```
            function handleMouseDown() {
                EventUtil.addEventHandler(document.body, "mousemove",
                                          handleMouseMove);
                EventUtil.addEventHandler(document.body, "mouseup",
                                          handleMouseUp);
            }

            function handleMouseUp() {
                EventUtil.removeEventHandler(document.body, "mousemove",
                                             handleMouseMove);
                EventUtil.removeEventHandler(document.body, "mouseup",
                                             handleMouseUp);
            }

        </script>
        <style type="text/css">
            #div1 {
                background-color: red;
                height: 100px;
                width: 100px;
                position: absolute;
            }
        </style>
    </head>
    <body>
        <p>Try dragging the red square.</p>
        <p><div id="div1" onmousedown="handleMouseDown()"></div> </p>
    </body>
</html>
```

As you can see, `handleMouseDown()` simply adds the `onmousemove` and `onmouseup` event handlers whereas `handleMouseUp()` removes the event handlers. Doing this prevents the dragging functionality from working by mistake. In this example, the only thing that can initiate the drag is the user holding the mouse button down on the `<div/>`.

When you try this out, note that the upper-left corner of the `<div/>` always lines up with the cursor, which is okay, but it's a little jarring to users. Ideally, the `<div/>` should look like it was *picked up* by the cursor, meaning that the point where the user clicked should be where the cursor appears to remain, even though the `<div/>` is moving (see Figure 13-1).

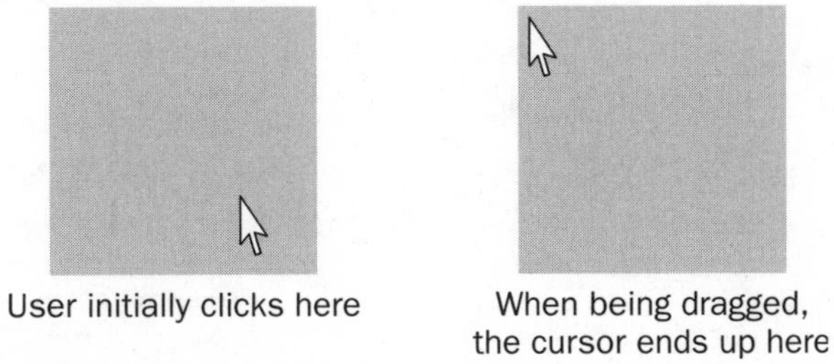

Figure 13-1

Some calculations can be done to make the cursor appear in the proper position. To do this, you capture the difference between where the <div/> is located and where the cursor is located when it is initially clicked (in the handleMouseDown() function). You compare the clientX and clientY properties of the event object to the offsetLeft and offsetTop properties of the <div/> (see Figure 13-2).

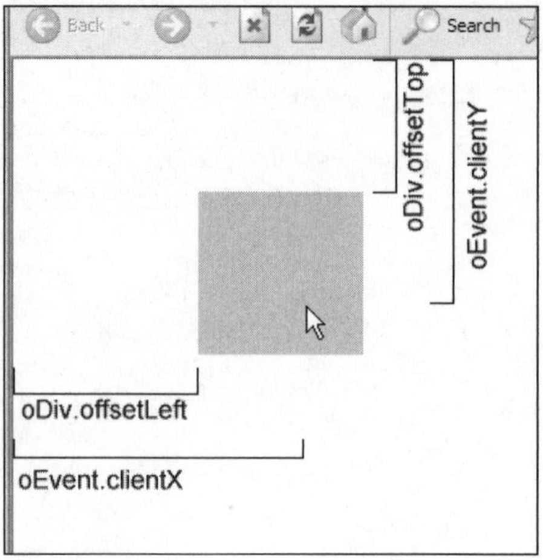

Figure 13-2

The differences between the x and y coordinates must be stored outside of the functions so that each function can have access to the values. The variables to store these differences are called iDiffX and iDiffY, and they are initialized in the handleMouseDown() function before the event handlers are added to document.body. Then, in handleMouseMove(), these values are subtracted from clientX and clientY, respectively, to move the <div/> into the correct position:

```
var iDiffX = 0;
var iDiffY = 0;

function handleMouseMove() {
    var oEvent = EventUtil.getEvent();
    var oDiv = document.getElementById("div1");
    oDiv.style.left = oEvent.clientX - iDiffX;
    oDiv.style.top = oEvent.clientY - iDiffY;
}

function handleMouseDown() {
    var oEvent = EventUtil.getEvent();
    var oDiv = document.getElementById("div1");
    iDiffX = oEvent.clientX - oDiv.offsetLeft;
    iDiffY = oEvent.clientY - oDiv.offsetTop;

    EventUtil.addEventHandler(document.body, "mousemove", handleMouseMove);
    EventUtil.addEventHandler(document.body, "mouseup", handleMouseUp);
}
```

```
function handleMouseUp() {
    EventUtil.removeEventHandler(document.body, "mousemove", handleMouseMove);
    EventUtil.removeEventHandler(document.body, "mouseup", handleMouseUp);
}
```

Making these changes allows the `<div/>` to be dragged in a nicer-looking way.

Creating drop targets

Now that you know how to drag an element around the screen, all you need is a place to drop it. Creating a drop target for simulated drag and drop involves checking the coordinates of the mouse to see if it is located inside the boundaries of the drop target.

Like the dragged item, the drop target is also absolutely positioned so you can use the element's `offsetLeft`, `offsetTop`, `offsetHeight`, and `offsetWidth` properties to determine the x and y coordinates of each corner. The function `isOverDropTarget()` is designed to encapsulate this evaluation by taking a set of coordinates as arguments and returning `true` if the coordinates are within the drop target.

```
function isOverDropTarget(iX, iY) {
    var oTarget = document.getElementById("divDropTarget");
    var iX1 = oTarget.offsetLeft;
    var iX2 = iX1 + oTarget.offsetWidth;
    var iY1 = oTarget.offsetTop;
    var iY2 = iY1 + oTarget.offsetHeight;

    return (iX >= iX1 && iX <= iX2 && iY >= iY1 && iY <= iY2);
}
```

The first line in the function gets a reference to the element with the ID of `"divDropTarget"`. The following lines determine the two x coordinates and two y coordinates. The last line tests to see if the coordinate arguments are located within the drop target, returning `true` if so or `false` if not.

```
function handleMouseUp() {
    var oEvent = EventUtil.getEvent();
    EventUtil.removeEventHandler(document.body, "mousemove", handleMouseMove);
    EventUtil.removeEventHandler(document.body, "mouseup", handleMouseUp);

    if (isOverDropTarget(oEvent.clientX,oEvent.clientY)) {
        alert("dropped!");
        var oDiv = document.getElementById("divDropTarget");
        var oTarget = document.getElementById("div2");
        oDiv.style.left = oTarget.offsetLeft;
        oDiv.style.top = oTarget.offsetTop;
    }
}
```

The highlighted section of code shows an alert if the cursor is over the designated drop target. Then, the dragged element is positioned into the upper-left corner of the drop target so it appears to *snap* into place. Of course, if you have more than one item to drag onto a drop target, you must create some sort of logic to ensure that each item is arranged appropriately, but this is enough to get you started. Here is how all the code looks when put together:

```
<html>
    <head>
        <title>Simulated Drag And Drop Example</title>
        <script type="text/javascript" src="eventutil.js"></script>
        <script type="text/javascript">

            var iDiffX = 0;
            var iDiffY = 0;

            function handleMouseMove() {
                var oEvent = EventUtil.getEvent();
                var oDiv = document.getElementById("div1");
                oDiv.style.left = oEvent.clientX - iDiffX;
                oDiv.style.top = oEvent.clientY - iDiffY;
            }

            function handleMouseDown() {
                var oEvent = EventUtil.getEvent();
                var oDiv = document.getElementById("div1");
                iDiffX = oEvent.clientX - oDiv.offsetLeft;
                iDiffY = oEvent.clientY - oDiv.offsetTop;

                EventUtil.addEventHandler(document.body, "mousemove",
handleMouseMove);
                EventUtil.addEventHandler(document.body, "mouseup", handleMouseUp);
            }

            function handleMouseUp() {
                var oEvent = EventUtil.getEvent();
                EventUtil.removeEventHandler(document.body, "mousemove",
handleMouseMove);
                EventUtil.removeEventHandler(document.body, "mouseup",
handleMouseUp);

                if (isOverDropTarget(oEvent.clientX,oEvent.clientY)) {
                    alert("dropped!");
                    var oDiv = document.getElementById("div1");
                    var oTarget = document.getElementById("divDropTarget");
                    oDiv.style.left = oTarget.offsetLeft;
                    oDiv.style.top = oTarget.offsetTop;
                }
            }

            function isOverDropTarget(iX, iY) {
                var oTarget = document.getElementById("divDropTarget");
                var iX1 = oTarget.offsetLeft;
                var iX2 = iX1 + oTarget.offsetWidth;
                var iY1 = oTarget.offsetTop;
                var iY2 = iY1 + oTarget.offsetHeight;
```

```
                return (iX >= iX1 && iX <= iX2 && iY >= iY1 && iY <= iY2);
            }
        </script>
        <style type="text/css">
            #div1 {
                background-color: red;
                height: 100px;
                width: 100px;
                position: absolute;
                z-index: 10;
            }

            #divDropTarget {
                background-color: blue;
                height: 200px;
                width: 200px;
                position: absolute;
                left: 300px;
            }
        </style>
    </head>
    <body>
        <p>Try dragging the red square onto the blue square.</p>
        <div id="div1" onmousedown="handleMouseDown(event)"></div>
        <div id="divDropTarget"></div>
    </body>
</html>
```

Advantages and disadvantages

The major advantage of simulated drag and drop is that it works across DOM-compliant browsers, such as Internet Explorer 5.0+, Mozilla 1.0+, Safari 1.0+, and Opera 7.0+. This strategy is known to work across multiple platforms, as well, because it uses basic DOM functionality.

Of course, simulated drag and drop doesn't give you the hooks into the operating system that system drag and drop provides. You can't affect text or links being dragged by the user, and the dragged elements can only be dragged within a given window or frame. However, for most use cases, simulated drag and drop gets the job done.

zDragDrop

You've seen that simulating drag and drop takes a fair amount of JavaScript. You may be wondering, "Isn't there some sort of JavaScript library that handles all this for me?" The answer is the zDragDrop library, freely available from `http://www.nczonline.net/downloads/`. This library provides a set of objects that encapsulate much of the simulated drag-and-drop process. You need only include the file zdragdroplib.js in your page to take advantage of the functionality.

Creating a draggable element

The `zDraggable` class can be used to make any absolutely-positioned DOM element draggable. The constructor takes two arguments, the DOM element to make draggable and a set of constraints determining how the element can be dragged. The second argument is made up of one or more special values.

To make an element draggable horizontally only, use `zDraggable.DRAG_X` as the second argument:

```
var oDiv = document.getElementById("divToDrag");
var oDraggable = new zDraggable(oDiv, zDraggable.DRAG_X);
```

To make an element draggable vertically only, use `zDraggable.DRAG_Y` as the second argument:

```
var oDiv = document.getElementById("divToDrag");
var oDraggable = new zDraggable(oDiv, zDraggable.DRAG_Y);
```

If the element must be dragged in both directions, use the bitwise OR operator to combine the two values:

```
var oDiv = document.getElementById("divToDrag");
var oDraggable = new zDraggable(oDiv, zDraggable.DRAG_X | zDraggable.DRAG_Y);
```

Because the `zDraggable` constructor expects a DOM element as an argument, you can use this code only after the page has completely loaded.

Creating a drop target

Using the zDragDrop library, you must explicitly set a drop target for a draggable element. To start, create a `zDropTarget` object like this:

```
var oDivTarget = document.getElementById("divDropTarget");
var oDropTarget = new zDropTarget(oDiv);
```

After you have created the drop target, you can add it to the draggable element by using the `addDropTarget()` method. For example:

```
var oDivToDrag = document.getElementById("divToDrag");
var oDivTarget = document.getElementById("divDropTarget");

var oDraggable = new zDraggable(oDiv, zDraggable.DRAG_X | zDraggable.DRAG_Y);
var oDropTarget = new zDropTarget(oDiv);

oDraggable.addDropTarget(oDropTarget);
```

With this code set up, it's now possible to use the zDragDrop library's built-in events to manage the dragging and dropping.

Events

Although not as robust as Internet Explorer's drag-and-drop events, the zDragDrop library does offer a few basic events that can make dealing with simulated drag and drop a little bit easier.

The `zDraggable` object supports three events:

- `dragstart` — Occurs immediately before beginning to drag the element.
- `drag` — Fires continuously while the element is being dragged.
- `dragend` —Fires after the element has stopped being dragged, regardless of whether it has been dropped on a valid drop target.

The `zDropTarget` object supports only one event, `drop`, which occurs when a draggable item is dropped onto it.

To make use of these events, the zDragDrop library uses DOM-style event handlers that can be assigned using the `addEventListener()` method. Unlike the DOM, it has only two arguments: the type of event to handle and the event-handling function. For example, the following code assigns an event handler to a `zDropTarget` object that will display the message `"dropped"` when an item is dropped:

```
oDropTarget.addEventListener("drop", function () {
    alert("dropped");
});
```

It's also possible to remove event handlers by using `removeEventListener()` with the same arguments:

```
function handleDragEnd() {
    alert("drag end");
}

oDraggable.addEventListener("dragend", handleDragEnd);

//other code here

oDraggable.removeEventListner("dragend", handleDragEnd);
```

The zDragDrop library also supports an `event` object that contains extra information about a given event. The properties of this `event` object are:

- `type` – The type of event that occurred (such as `"drag"` or `"dragend"`).
- `target` — The object that caused the event (a `zDraggable` or `zDropTarget`).
- `timeStamp` — The date and time, in milliseconds, when the event occurred.
- `relatedTarget` — The other object related to the event. When the drop event fires on a `zDropTarget`, this is always equal to the `zDraggable` object that was dropped on it.
- `cancelable` — Indicates whether the event can be cancelled.

Additionally, the `event` object supports one method, `preventDefault()`, which can be used to prevent the default behavior of an event. Currently, the only event that can be prevented is `dragstart`.

The event object is passed into an event-handler function as the only argument, so you can access it this way:

```
oDraggable.addEventListener("dragstart", function (oEvent) {
    alert(oEvent.type + " occurred at " + oEvent.timeStamp);
    oEvent.preventDefault();
});
```

Example

To recreate the effect of the drop target example from the previous section, you can make use of several other methods built in to the zDragDrop library:

- `zDraggable.moveTo(x, y)` — Moves the `zDraggable` element to the position x,y.
- `zDropTarget.getLeft()` — Returns the left coordinate of the drop target.
- `zDropTarget.getTop()` — Returns the top coordinate of the drop target.

If you use these methods along with the event handling functionality of zDragDrop, the code becomes much cleaner:

```
<html>
    <head>
        <title>Simulated Drag And Drop Example</title>
        <script type="text/javascript" src="zdragdroplib.js"></script>
        <script type="text/javascript">

            function doLoad() {
                var oDraggable = new zDraggable(document.getElementById("div1"),
                                            zDraggable.DRAG_X | zDraggable.DRAG_Y);
                var oDropTarget =
                        new zDropTarget(document.getElementById("divDropTarget"));

                oDraggable.addDropTarget(oDropTarget);

                oDropTarget.addEventListener("drop", function (oEvent) {
                    oEvent.relatedTarget.moveTo(oDropTarget.getLeft(),
                                                oDropTarget.getTop());
                });
            }

        </script>
        <style type="text/css">
            #div1 {
                background-color: red;
                height: 100px;
                width: 100px;
                position: absolute;
                z-index: 10;
            }

            #divDropTarget {
                background-color: blue;
                height: 200px;
                width: 200px;
```

```
                position: absolute;
                left: 300px;
            }
        </style>
    </head>
    <body onload="doLoad()">
        <p>Try dragging the red square onto the blue square.</p>
        <div id="div1"></div>
        <div id="divDropTarget"></div>
    </body>
</html>
```

As you can see, the JavaScript section of this code is markedly smaller than that of the example in the previous section. The first two lines of JavaScript create the `zDraggable` and `zDropTarget` objects. Then, the drop target is registered to the `zDraggable` object by using `addDropTarget()`. Finally, an event handler for the `drop` event is added to the drop target. That event handler moves the draggable element to the upper-left corner of the drop target by making use of the previously mentioned methods. Remember, the `relatedTarget` property of the `event` object is equal to the draggable element when used in a `drop` event.

Of course, all this code must be called after the page has been loaded, so the `onload` event handler is used for that purpose.

Summary

This chapter introduced the concept of drag and drop in a Web browser and explained the difference between system drag and drop and simulated drag and drop.

You learned about Internet Explorer's built-in system drag-and-drop functionality, and that it is the only browser that supports system drag and drop from Web pages. The various events and methods provided by IE to work with system drag and drop were also discussed, as well as strategies for dragging text and links.

Next you learned about simulated drag and drop, a way to use the DOM to move elements around that gives the appearance of drag-and-drop functionality. You were shown how to build a simple drag-and-drop example.

Lastly, you were introduced to the zDragDrop library, a free JavaScript library that encapsulates a great deal of simulated drag-and-drop functionality. Using this library, you learned how to create a drag-and-drop example making use of the custom objects, methods, and events.

14

Error Handling

Traditionally, JavaScript has been known as a language filled with confusing error messages such as *Object Expected* and *Illegal Syntax* with nothing more than a line number to identify its origin. Debugging such messages was a painful experience at best, which is why the version 4 browsers (Internet Explorer 4.0 and Netscape Navigator 4.0) included some basic error-handling functionality. Shortly thereafter, an answer came from the ECMA in the form of ECMAScript, third edition.

This latest edition of ECMAScript added exception handling capabilities modeled after its big brother, Java. Using some of the reserved words from the second edition of ECMAScript, the third edition implements the `try...catch...finally` construct as well as the `throw` operator.

This chapter explores both the browser-based error-handling capabilities as well as ECMAScript's exception-handling features.

The Importance of Error Handling

In early browsers (such as Internet Explorer 3.0 and Netscape Navigator 3.0), there was no error handling. Typically, functions return an *invalid* value (often `null`, `false`, or –1, depending on the use case) to indicate that an error has occurred. Consider the following code:

```
var iLoc = findItem(colorarray, "blue");
if (iLoc == -1) {
    alert("The item doesn't exist. ");
} else {
    alert("The item is in location " + iLoc + ".");
}
```

In this case, the function `findItem()` returns a –1 (an invalid value) when the given string doesn't exist. Presumably, a valid value is a number greater than or equal to 0. But why did the function return the invalid value? Does the string `"blue"` simply not exist in `colorarray`? Or is there some other reason, perhaps, that the array has no items in it? There is no way to know why the invalid value was returned. Errors and error handling help eliminate this conundrum.

With the incorporation of error handling into JavaScript, Web developers now have the ability to better control code. Good error-handling techniques allow smooth developing, debugging, and deploying of scripts. In many ways, such techniques are actually more important in JavaScript than other programming languages because it lacks a standard development environment, such as Visual Studio.NET for the .NET Framework or NetBeans for Java development, to guide developers.

Errors versus Exceptions

When talking about errors in programming, you really have only two categories of primary concern: syntax errors and runtime errors.

Syntax errors, also called parsing errors, occur at compile time for traditional programming languages and at interpret time for JavaScript. These errors are a direct result of an unexpected character in the code and thus prevent it from being fully compiled/interpreted. For example, the following line causes a syntax error because it is missing a closing parenthesis:

```
document.write("test";
```

When a syntax error occurs, the code cannot be executed. In JavaScript, only the code contained within the same thread as the syntax error is affected. Code in other threads and other externally referenced files still execute appropriately assuming nothing in them depends on the code containing the error.

Runtime errors, also called exceptions, occur during execution (after compilation/interpretation). In this case, the problems are not with the syntax of the code. Rather, an operation attempting to complete is illegal in some way. Example:

```
window.openMySpecialWindow();
```

In the previous code, an attempt is made to access a method of the `window` object named `openMySpecialWindow`. Syntactically this line is correct, however, no such method exists. This causes the browser to return an exception.

Exceptions only affect the thread in which they occur, allowing other JavaScript threads to continue normal execution. Consider the following HTML page:

```
<html>
    <head>
        <title>Exception Test</title>
       <script type="text/javascript">
            function handleLoad() {
                 window.openMySpecialWindow();
                 alert("Loaded");
            }

            function handleClick() {
                alert("Clicked");
            }
```

```
        </script>
    </head>
    <body onload="handleLoad()">
        <input type="button" value="Click Me" onclick="handleClick()" />
    </body>
</html>
```

When this page loads, the `handleLoad()` function is called and an exception occurs when trying to call a non-existent method of the window object. That thread is then exited so the `alert("Loaded");` line is never executed. When the user clicks on the button, however, the `handleClick()` function is still called and an alert displays the text `"Clicked."`

Error Reporting

Because each browser has its own built-in JavaScript interpreter (including its own mechanisms for tracking down errors while interpreting), each reports errors in different ways: Some pop up an error message; others simply log the message to a JavaScript console. Regardless of the method used, be aware of where this data is located on your target browsers. Browsers such as Internet Explorer, Mozilla, Safari, and Opera each have their own unique ways of presenting this data. This section guides you to the error message information for each of them.

Internet Explorer (Windows)

Microsoft's flagship browser, Internet Explorer for Windows, is capable of reporting errors in a couple of different ways. By default, Internet Explorer pops up a dialog with the error details (Figure 14-1) and asks if you want to continue running scripts on the page. This is misleading, because clicking either Yes or No allows other scripts to continue running.

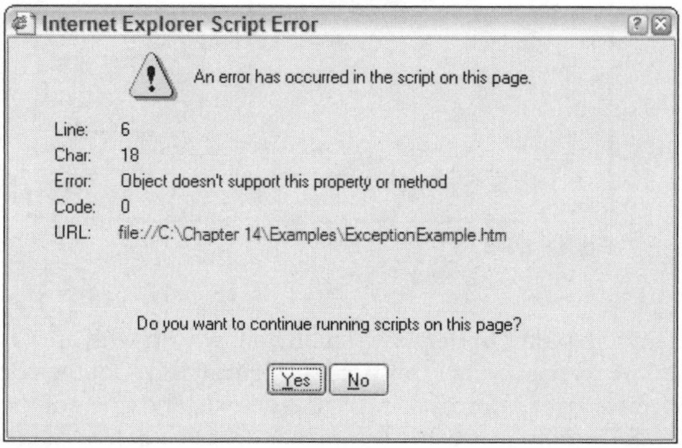

Figure 14-1

If the browser has a debugger (such as Microsoft Script Debugger, which is discussed later in this chapter), the dialog offers the option to debug the script or ignore it (Figure 14-2). Clicking Yes on this dialog brings you into the debugger; clicking No simply closes the dialog.

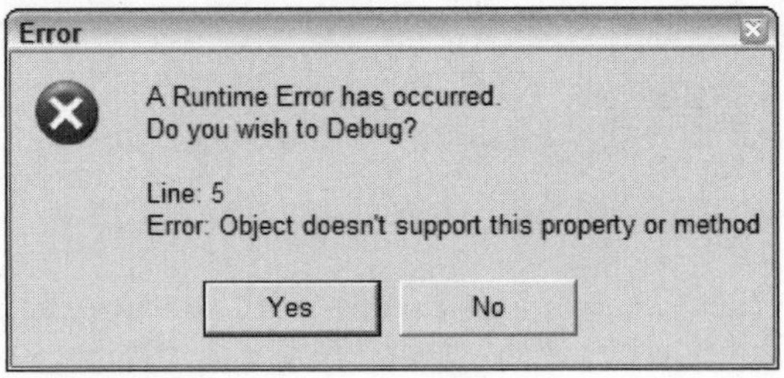

Figure 14-2

The other option is to *not* pop up an error dialog. This setting can be enabled by going to Internet Options, clicking on the Advanced tab, and unchecking "Display a notification about every script error" (Figure 14-3).

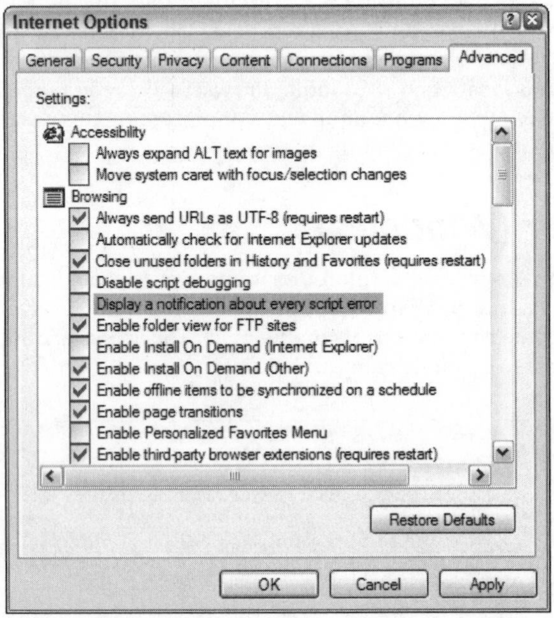

Figure 14-3

This setting causes Internet Explorer to display a small yellow icon with an X over it in the lower-left corner of the browser window whenever an error occurs (Figure 14-4). Double-clicking the icon brings up a dialog displaying the typical error information (message, URL, and line number). This dialog also enables you (by using the Previous button) to see any errors that occurred before the one being displayed.

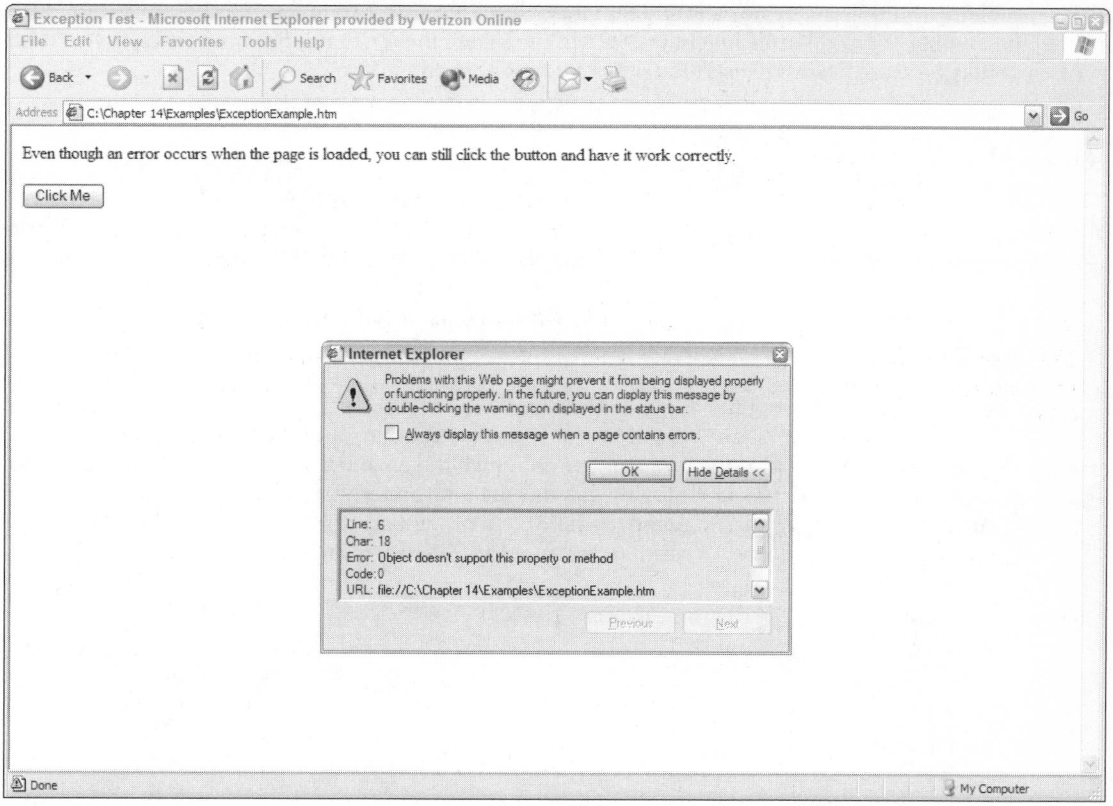

Figure 14-4

Be aware that the line number given isn't always accurate. If the code causing the error is inline, then the line number correctly identifies the line number in the HTML file where the error occurs; if the code causing the error is in an external file, the line number is typically off by one line, so an error that is purported to have occurred on line 5 actually occurred on line 4.

Internet Explorer (MacOS)

By default, Internet Explorer on the Macintosh doesn't show JavaScript errors. To turn on this feature, go to the Preferences dialog (available under Edit ➪ Preferences). Under the Web Browser section on the left side of the window, click Web Content. In the lower part of the window, you see a check box labeled Enable Scripting; immediately underneath is a check box labeled Show Scripting Error Alerts. Checking this box causes the browser to pop up an error message when a JavaScript error occurs.

The problem with IE/Mac's error alerts is that it doesn't give an accurate line number for external scripts (the line number is typically the line in the HTML file where the script has been referenced). In extreme cases, it may be more useful to insert the script inline for testing purposes.

Mozilla (all platforms)

Mozilla features a JavaScript console that logs not only errors, but warnings as well. To access the JavaScript console, look under Tools ➪ Web Development ➪ JavaScript Console in Mozilla 1.0+ (prior to 1.0, the JavaScript console was located under Tasks ➪ Tools ➪ JavaScript Console).

Just like its predecessor Netscape Navigator, Mozilla allows you to type ***javascript:*** *into the address box to open the JavaScript console instead of accessing it from the menu.*

The JavaScript console reports three types of messages: errors, strict warnings, and messages. Errors are either syntax or runtime errors (anything that stops script execution), and they are reported with the error message, the filename, and the line number on which the error occurred (Figure 14-5). Strict warnings occur when the code does something illegal, but the interpreter works around it allowing the script to continue running (such problems include redefining a previously defined variable). Messages are purely informational and often are a result of internal Mozilla processing, not JavaScript.

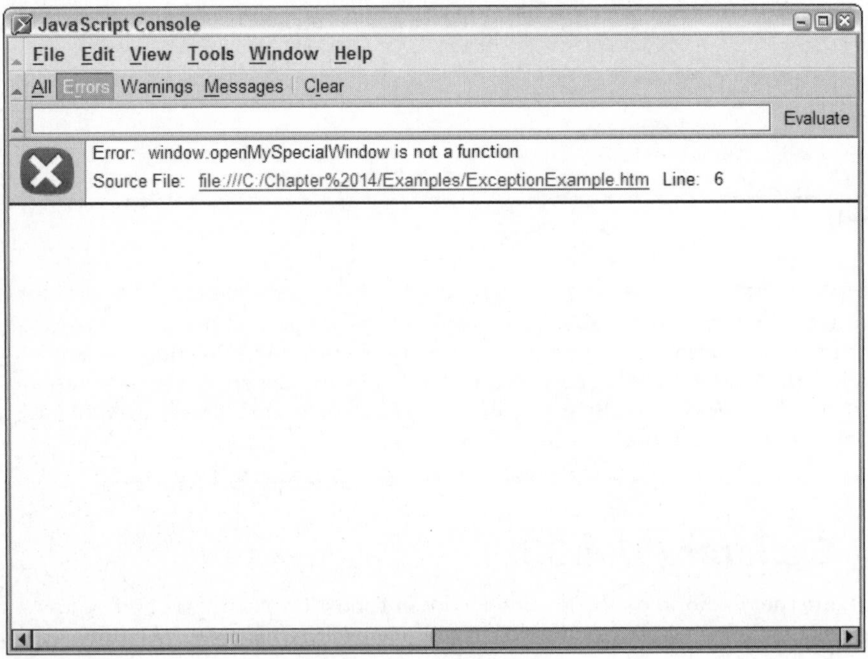

Figure 14-5

Safari (MacOS X)

Macintosh's Safari browser has perhaps the worst support for JavaScript errors and debugging. By default, it offers no JavaScript error reporting to the end user. In order to enable error reporting, follow these steps:

1. Open a command line shell.
2. Execute the following: `defaults write com.apple.Safari IncludeDebugMenu 1`.
3. Restart Safari.
4. Under the Debug menu, check Log JavaScript Exceptions (Figure 14-6).
5. Start Console.app under Application/Utilities.

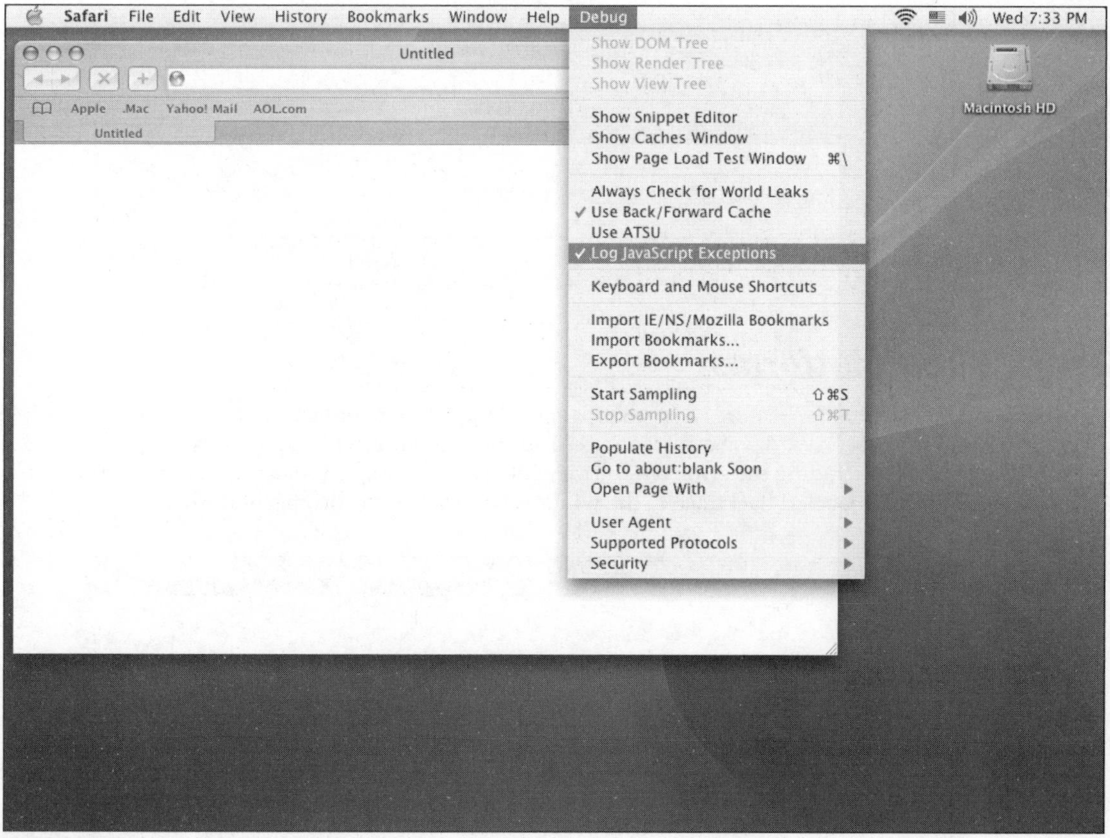

Figure 14-6

After completing these steps, JavaScript errors are logged to the Console.app window (Figure 14-7). Unfortunately, the messages are less than useful without a URL or line number to help locate the cause of any given error. However, it is the best Safari can offer at this point.

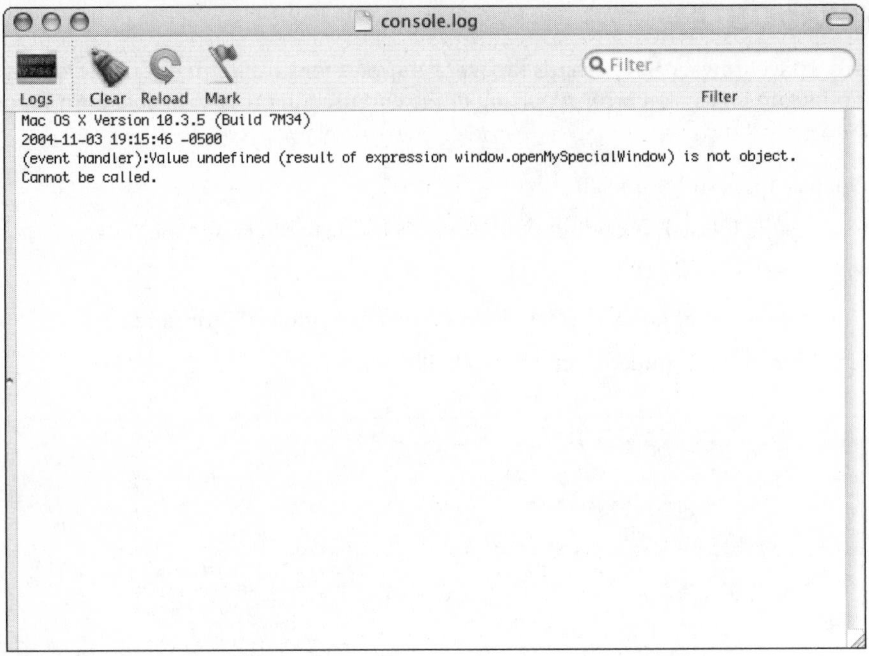

Figure 14-7

Opera 7 (all platforms)

Similar to Mozilla, Opera 7 features a JavaScript console to aid in debugging. The console is accessible under Window ➪ Special ➪ JavaScript Console. The console (Figure 14-8) provides the most data out of available browsers including the error type, error code, error message, the thread that the error occurred in, and a stack trace (labeled Backtrace in the window) indicating the origins of the error.

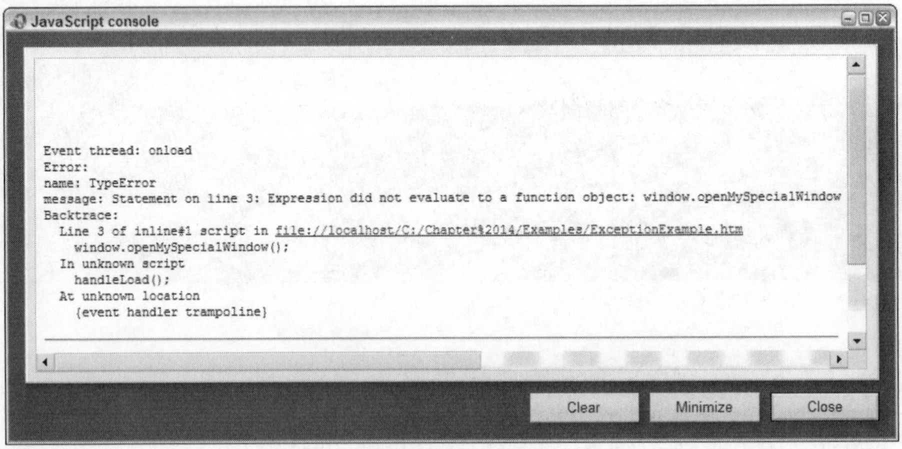

Figure 14-8

It is possible to have the JavaScript console come up whenever there is an error by going into Tools ➪ Preferences, and then clicking on Multimedia. You'll see a check box titled Enabled JavaScript, along with a button labeled JavaScript Options..... If you click the button, a new dialog pops up (see Figure 14-9), one of the options is Open JavaScript Console on Error. When this check box is checked (it is unchecked by default), the JavaScript console pops up whenever there is an error.

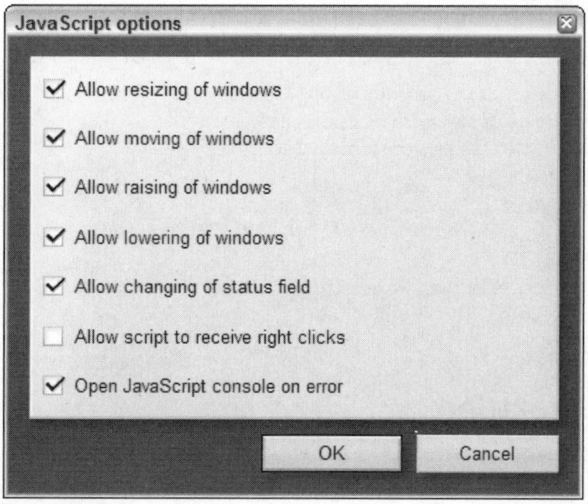

Figure 14-9

Handling Errors

Understanding errors is just part of the solution; understanding how to handle those errors is the other part. Instead of using multiple `if..else` statements, JavaScript offers two specific ways to handle errors. The Browser Object Model includes the `onerror` event handler on both the window object and on images, whereas ECMAScript defines the `try...catch` construct, another statement borrowed from Java, to deal with exceptions. This section outlines the advantages and disadvantages of each approach.

The onerror event handler

The `onerror` event handler was the first feature to facilitate error handling for JavaScript. The `error` event is fired on the `window` object whenever an exception occurs on the page. Example:

```
<html>
    <head>
        <title>OnError Example</title>
        <script type="text/javascript">
            window.onerror = function () {
                alert("An error occurred. ");
            }
        </script>
    </head>
    <body onload="nonExistentFunction()">
    </body>
</html>
```

In this example, an exception occurs when an attempt is made to call `nonExistentFunction()`, which doesn't exist. When this happens, the alert is displayed containing the message, `"An error occurred."` Unfortunately, the browser's error message is also displayed. To hide the error from the browser (and thus prevent it from reporting the error), the `onerror` event handler must return a value of `true`:

```
<html>
    <head>
        <title>OnError Example</title>
        <script type="text/javascript">
            window.onerror = function () {
                alert("An error occurred. ");
                return true;
            }
        </script>
    </head>
    <body onload="nonExistentFunction()">
    </body>
</html>
```

Extracting error information

Simply knowing that an error occurred is of little use to a programmer without the error details. Fortunately, the `onerror` event handler provides three pieces of information to identify the exact nature of the error:

- Error message — The same message that the browser would display for the given error
- URL — The file in which the error occurred
- Line number — The line number in the given URL that caused the error

This information is passed as three parameters into the `onerror` event handler and can be accessed like this:

```
<html>
    <head>
        <title>OnError Example</title>
        <script type="text/javascript">
            window.onerror = function (sMessage, sUrl, sLine) {
                alert("An error occurred:\n" + sMessage + "\nURL: " + sUrl +
"\nLine Number: " + sLine);
                return true;
            }
        </script>
    </head>
    <body onload="nonExistentFunction()">
    </body>
</html>
```

Using this code, it is possible to create custom JavaScript error dialogs that mimic the functionality of browser-error dialogs.

Image loading errors

The `window` object isn't the only one that supports the `onerror` event handler; images do too. When an image fails to load for any reason (for example, the file does not exist), the `error` event fires on the images. You can set the `onerror` event handler for an image either in HTML or through script. For example:

```
<html>
    <head>
        <title>Image Error Test</title>
    </head>
    <body>
        <p>The image below attempts to load a file that doesn't exist.</p>
        <img src="blue.gif"
             onerror="alert('An error occurred loading the image.')" />
    </body>
</html>
```

This example assigns the `onerror` event handler directly in the HTML. Because the image `"blue.gif"` doesn't exist, the alert is displayed letting the user know the image didn't load completely. In order to assign the event handler using a script, you must wait until after the page has loaded before setting the image's `src` attribute:

```
<html>
    <head>
        <title>Image Error Test</title>
        <script type="text/javascript">
            function handleLoad() {
                document.images[0].onerror = function () {
                    alert("An error occurred loading the image.");
                };

                document.images[0].src = "blue.gif";
            }
        </script>
    </head>
    <body onload="handleLoad()">
        <p>The image below attempts to load a file that doesn't exist.</p>
        <img />
    </body>
</html>
```

In this example, the first image isn't assigned an `src` attribute in the HTML. When the page is loaded, however, the image is first assigned an `onerror` event handler and then has its `src` property set to `"blue.gif"`, which doesn't exist. The alert displays once again, indicating the image didn't load.

> **Unlike the `onerror` event handler for the window object, the image's `onerror` event handler doesn't pass any arguments for extra information.**

Handling syntax errors

The `onerror` event handler isn't just good for dealing with exceptions; it is also the only way to deal with syntax errors.

To do so, the event handler must be the first code that appears in the page. Why the first? If a syntax error occurs before the event handler has been set up, that event handler will never be set up. Remember, a syntax error completely stops code execution. Consider the following example:

```
<html>
    <head>
        <title>OnError Example</title>
        <script type="text/javascript">
            alert("Syntax error. ";
            window.onerror = function (sMessage, sUrl, sLine) {
                alert("An error occurred:\n" + sMessage + "\nURL: " + sUrl +
"\nLine Number: " + sLine);
                return true;
            }
        </script>
    </head>
    <body onload="nonExistentFunction()">
    </body>
</html>
```

Because the highlighted line (which is a syntax error) occurs before the `onerror` event handler is assigned, the browser reports the error directly. The code immediately following the error is not interpreted (because the thread is exited) so when the `load` event fires and the `nonExistentFunction()` is called, the browser reports that error as well. If this page is rewritten to place the `onerror` event-handler assignment before the syntax error, two alerts are displayed: one showing the syntax error and one showing the exception.

```
<html>
    <head>
        <title>OnError Example</title>
        <script type="text/javascript">
            window.onerror = function (sMessage, sUrl, sLine) {
                alert("An error occurred:\n" + sMessage + "\nURL: " + sUrl +
"\nLine Number: " + sLine);
                return true;
            }
            alert("Syntax error. ";
        </script>
    </head>
    <body onload="nonExistentFunction()">
    </body>
</html>
```

The major problem with using the `onerror` event handler is that it is part of the BOM, and as such, has no standards governing its behavior. To this end, there is a pretty significant difference between the way browsers handle errors using this event. For example, when the `error` event occurs in Internet Explorer, normal code execution continues: All variables and data are retained and remain accessible from within the `onerror` event handler. In Mozilla, however, normal code execution ends, and all variables and data existing prior to the error occurring are destroyed, making it difficult to truly evaluate the error.

Safari and Konqueror do not support the `onerror` event handler on the `window` object but they do support it on images.

The try...catch statement

ECMAScript, third edition, introduced another feature from Java, the `try...catch` statement for browsers that support ECMAScript 3 (see Chapter 1, "What Is JavaScript?"). The basic syntax is the following:

```
try {
    //code to run
    [break;]
} catch ([exception]) {
    //code to run if an exception occurs and the expression is matched
    [break;]
} [finally {
    //code that is always executed regardless of an exception occurring
}]
```

For example:

```
try {
    window.nonExistentFunction();
    alert("Method completed. ");
} catch (exception) {
    alert("An exception occurred.");
} finally {
    alert("End of try...catch test.");
}
```

While running a `try...catch` statement, the interpreter first enters the code block immediately after the `try` keyword. In the previous example, the line `window.nonExistantFunction();` is executed, which causes an error (because no method named *nonExistantFunction* exists for the `window` object). At that point, execution immediately exits the `try` clause and goes into the `catch` clause, completely skipping over any further lines of code (the `alert("Method completed.");` line is skipped). The `alert` in the catch clause is displayed, and then execution moves into the `finally` clause to display that alert.

Unlike Java, the ECMAScript standard specifies only one catch clause per `try...catch` statement. Because JavaScript is only loosely typed, you have no way to specify a particular type of exception in the `catch` clause. All errors, regardless of type, are handled by a single `catch` clause.

> **Mozilla's extensions to ECMAScript include the capability to add more than one catch clause per `try...catch` statement. However, because this extension exists only in Mozilla, it is not recommended.**

The code in the `finally` clause behaves the same way as the `finally` clause in Java, containing code that should be executed whether or not an exception occurs. This is useful for closing open connections and freeing up resources. For instance:

```
connection.open();
try {
    connection.send(data);
} catch (exception) {
    alert("An exception occurred.");
} finally {
    connection.close();
}
```

Nested try...catch statements

It is possible for an error to occur inside the `catch` clause of a `try...catch` statement. In this case, using nested `try...catch` statements is the answer. Consider the following example

```
try {
    eval("a ++ b");         //causes error
} catch (oException) {
    alert("An exception occurred. ");
    try {
        var aErrors = new Array(1000000000000000000000);  //causes error
        aErrors.push(exception);
    } catch (oException2) {
        alert("Another exception occurred.");
    }
} finally {
    alert("All done.");
}
```

In this example, an error is thrown immediately and the first alert is displayed. When execution continues in the first `catch` clause, another error is thrown because of the attempt to create an array with too many elements. Execution goes to the second `catch` clause and displays the second alert before continuing on into the `finally` clause.

The Error object

So what exactly is it that the `catch` statement catches? Just as Java has a base class `Exception` to throw, JavaScript has a base class called `Error` to throw. An `Error` object has the following properties:

- `name` — A string indicating the type of error
- `message` — The actual error message

The name of the Error object corresponds to its class (because Error is just a base class), which is one of the following:

Class	Occurs When
EvalError	An error occurs in the eval() function.
RangeError	A number value is greater than or less than the numbers that can be represented in JavaScript (Number.MAX_VALUE and Number.MIN_VALUE).
ReferenceError	An illegal reference is used.
SyntaxError	A syntax error occurs inside of an eval() function call. All other syntax errors are reported by the browser and cannot be handled with a try...catch statement.
TypeError	A variable's type is unexpected.
URIError	An error occurs in the encodeURI() or the decodeURI() function.

The message property of an Error object is the browser-generated error message indicating the nature of the error. Because this property is browser-specific, the same error can generate a different error message in different browsers. Consider the following line of code:

```
eval("a ++ b");
```

This line alone causes a SyntaxError to be thrown because the ++ symbol isn't valid in this context. The error message from Internet Explorer 6 is "Expected ';'" whereas Mozilla 1.5 provides "missing ; before statement."

The message property can be used to display a more meaningful message to users while preventing the browser from reporting the error directly:

```
try {
    window.nonExistentFunction();
    alert("Method completed.");
} catch (oException) {
    alert("An exception occurred: " + oException.message);
} finally {
    alert("End of try...catch test.");
}
```

Both Mozilla and Internet Explorer have extended the `Error` object to suit their own needs. Mozilla provides a `fileName` property to indicate which file the error occurred in, a `lineNumber` property indicating the line that the error occurred on, and a stack property containing the call stack up to the point of the error; Internet Explorer provides a `number` property to indicate the error number.

Determining the type of error

Despite being limited to only one `catch` clause per `try...catch` statement, you have a couple of easy ways to determine the type of error that was thrown. The first is to use the `name` property of the `Error` object:

```
try {
    eval("a ++ b");          //causes SyntaxError
} catch (oException) {
    if (oException.name == "SyntaxError") {
        alert("Syntax Error: " + oException.message);
    } else {
        alert("An unexpected error occurred: " + oException.message);
    }
}
```

The second way is to use the `instanceof` operator and use the class name of different errors:

```
try {
    eval("a ++ b");          //causes SyntaxError
} catch (oException) {
    if (oException instanceof SyntaxError) {
        alert("Syntax Error: " + oException.message);
    } else {
        alert("An unexpected error occurred: " + oException.message);
    }
}
```

Raising exceptions

The third edition of ECMAScript also introduced the `throw` statement to raise exceptions purposely. The syntax is the following:

```
throw error_object;
```

The `error_object` can be a string, a number, a Boolean value, or an actual object. All the following lines are valid:

```
throw "An error occurred.";
throw 50067;
throw true;
throw new Object();
```

It is also possible to throw an actual `Error` object. The constructor for the `Error` object takes only one parameter, the error message, making it possible to do the following:

```
throw new Error("You tried to do something bad.");
```

All the other classes of `Error` are also available to developers:

```
throw new SyntaxError("I don't like your syntax.");
throw new TypeError("What type of variable do you take me for?");
throw new RangeError("Sorry, you just don't have the range.");
throw new EvalError("That doesn't evaluate.");
```

```
throw new URIError("Uri, is that you?");
throw new ReferenceError("You didn't cite your references properly.");
```

Practically speaking, an error would be thrown in a situation where normal execution could not continue, such as this:

```
function addTwoNumbers(a, b) {
    if (arguments.length < 2) {
        throw new Error("Two numbers are required.");
    } else {
        return a + b;
    }
}
```

In the previous code, the function requires two numbers to execute properly. If two arguments are not passed in, the function throws an error indicating that the calculation cannot be completed.

Developer-thrown exceptions are caught inside of `try...catch` statements just like an error thrown by the browser itself. Consider the following code, which catches a developer-thrown exception:

```
function addTwoNumbers(a, b) {
    if (arguments.length < 2) {
        throw new Error("Two numbers are required.");
    } else {
        return a + b;
    }
}

try {
    result = addTwoNumbers(90);
} catch (oException) {
    alert(oException.message);      //outputs "Two numbers are required."
}
```

Additionally, because browsers don't generate `Error` objects (they always generate one of the more specific `Error` objects, such as `RangeError`), it is easy to differentiate between an error thrown by the developer and one thrown by the browser using either one of the techniques discussed earlier:

```
function addTwoNumbers(a, b) {
    if (arguments.length < 2) {
        throw new Error("Two numbers are required.");
    } else {
        return a + b;
    }
}

try {
    result = addTwoNumbers(90, parseInt("z"));
} catch (oException) {
    if (oException instanceof SyntaxError) {
        alert("Syntax Error: " + oException.message);
    } else if (oException instanceof Error) {
        alert(oException.message);
    }
}
```

Note that the check for the `instanceof Error` must be the last condition in the `if` statement because all the other error classes inherit from it (so a `SyntaxError` returns `true` when testing `instanceof Error`).

> **All browsers report a developer-thrown error, but the way the error message is displayed may differ slightly. Internet Explorer 6 only displays the error messages when throwing the `Error` object; otherwise, it simply says `Exception thrown and not caught` without giving any of the details specified; Mozilla, however, reports `Error: uncaught exception:` and then calls the `toString()` method of the object that was thrown.**

Debugging Techniques

Before JavaScript debuggers were readily available, developers had to use creative methods to debug their code. This led to the placement of strategically placed alerts, using LiveConnect to access the Java console, using the JavaScript console, and throwing custom errors. Each of these techniques has its advantages and disadvantages. Which one should you use? This section explains which debugging technique is right for you.

Using alerts

The most popular (although the most unwieldy) method of debugging is the placement of alerts strategically throughout code. For example:

```
function test_function() {
    alert("Entering function.");

    var iNumber1 = 5;
    var iNumber2 = 10;

    alert("Before calculation.");
    var iResult = iNumber1 + iNumber2;
    alert("After calculation.");

    alert("Leaving function.");
}
```

JavaScript developers around the world turn to alerts as a quick and dirty approach for debugging. The most popular way is to show alerts with descriptive text, as in the previous example. Some also use a numbering method, starting the first alert at 0, the second at 1, and so on, to see where the code breaks.

This approach requires a lot of cleanup because you must remove the extra alerts when your debugging is complete. Another problem occurs when dealing with infinite loops: If your script is causing an infinite or long-running loop, alerts could keep popping up and prevent you from closing the browser. For this reason, using alerts for debugging is best kept to small code segments.

Using the Java console

In browsers that support LiveConnect (interaction between Java and JavaScript, discussed later in the book), you can use the Java console to log messages to yourself just as you can in Java.

For example, in Java you can log messages to the console window by doing this:

```
System.out.println("Message");
```

In JavaScript, you can do the same by expanding the `System` variable into its full `java.lang.System` notation:

```
java.lang.System.out.println("Message");
```

Placing calls like this into a function is a great way to track code execution:

```
function test_function() {
    java.lang.System.out.println("Entering function.");

    var iNumber1 = 5;
    var iNumber2 = 10;

    java.lang.System.out.println("Before calculation.");
    var iResult = iNumber1 + iNumber2;
    java.lang.System.out.println("After calculation.");

    java.lang.System.out.println("Leaving function.");
}
```

To see the output, select Tools ➪ Java Console. You see the output after the default Java console output (Figure 14-10).

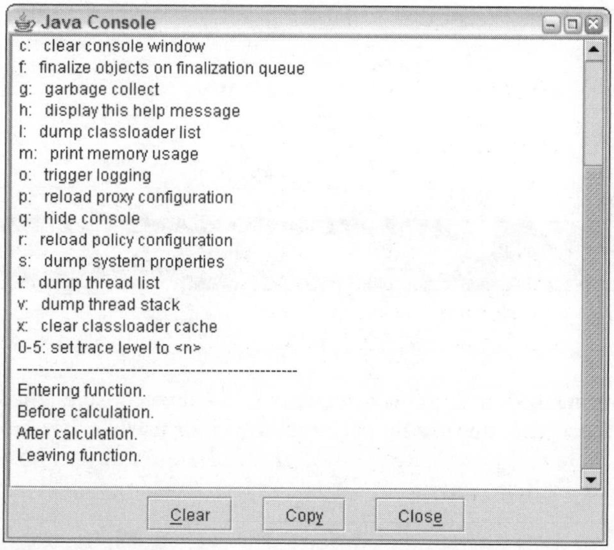

Figure 14-10

Mozilla, Safari, and Opera all support LiveConnect; Internet Explorer does not.

Posting messages to the JavaScript console (Opera 7+ only)

In Opera 7+, it's possible to write message directly to the JavaScript console by using the `opera.postError()` method:

```
function test_function() {
    opera.postError("Entering function.");

    var iNumber1 = 5;
    var iNumber2 = 10;

    opera.postError ("Before calculation.");
    var iResult = iNumber1 + iNumber2;
    opera.postError ("After calculation.");

    opera.postError ("Leaving function.");
}
```

Even though the method is called *postError,* it can be used to post any message to the JavaScript console (see Figure 14-11).

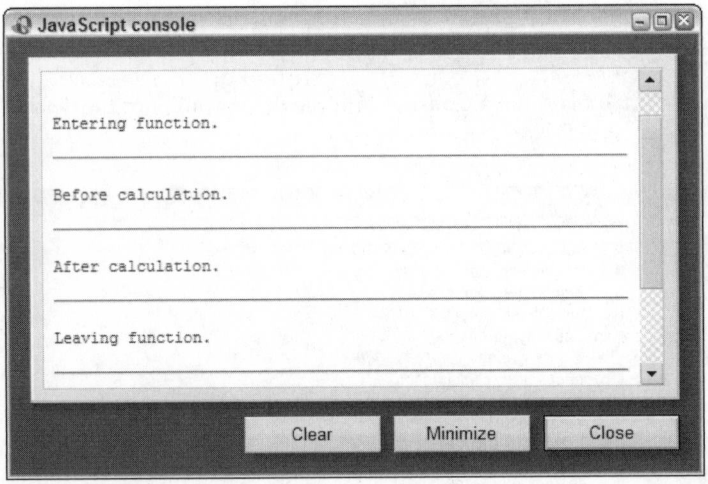

Figure 14-11

The Opera JavaScript console works in the same way as the Java console when used for debugging. The only problem is, of course, that this code must be removed for use in other browsers.

Throwing your own errors

One of the best ways to manage debugging and errors in JavaScript code is to throw your own errors. Now, you may be thinking, "How do I reduce errors by causing errors?" The idea is that you throw specific errors that tell you exactly what error occurred instead of relying on JavaScript's cryptic `object expected` error messages. Doing so can cut down debugging time dramatically. Consider a function designed to divide one number by another:

```
function divide(iNum1, iNum2) {
    return iNum1.valueOf() / iNum2.valueOf();
}
```

This function assumes several things. First, it assumes that two arguments are passed in; second, it assumes that both arguments are numbers. But if you make a call that breaks these assumptions, such as `divide("a")`, you end up with an error message like `undefined' is not an object` or `iNum2 has no properties`. Add some specific error messages, and the problem becomes clear:

```
function divide(iNum1, iNum2) {
    if (arguments.length != 2) {
        throw new Error("divide() requires two arguments.");
    } else if (typeof iNum1 != "number" || typeof iNum2 != "number") {
        throw new Error("divide() requires two numbers for arguments.");
    }

    return iNum1.valueOf() / iNum2.valueOf();
}
```

In this case, if you call `divide("a")`, you'll get an error saying `divide() requires two arguments`; if you call `divide("a", "b")`, you get an error saying `divide() requires two numbers for arguments`. In both cases, these messages give you much more information than the default JavaScript error messages and make debugging much easier.

Because of the amount of code required to check for errors and throw messages, many developers create their own `assert()` function. Many programming languages have an `assert()` method built-in, and it's also easy to create your own:

```
function assert(bCondition, sErrorMessage) {
    if (!bCondition) {
        throw new Error(sErrorMessage);
    }
}
```

The `assert()` function simply tests to see if the first argument evaluates to `false` and, if so, throws an error with the given error message. You can then use `assert()` like this:

```
function divide(iNum1, iNum2) {
    assert(arguments.length == 2, "divide() requires two arguments.");
    assert(typeof iNum1 == "number" && typeof iNum2 == "number",
                    "divide() requires two numbers for arguments.");

    return iNum1.valueOf() / iNum2.valueOf();
}
```

As you can see, this reduces the amount of code contained in the `divide()` function and also makes it clearer what the developer was thinking when writing this function.

The JavaScript Verifier

Douglas Crockford, a software engineer, wrote a small tool called jslint — The JavaScript Verifier. The purpose of jslint is to point out unprofessional JavaScript syntax and possible syntax errors. You simply paste your JavaScript code (either pure JavaScript code or code enclosed in a `<script/>` tag) into a text box and click the jslint button. The tool then outputs warnings and errors about your code underneath.

The types of warnings provided by jslint are in line with the professional standards mentioned throughout this book. You receive a warning if the code contains an inappropriate coding technique, such as the following:

- A statement (`if`, `for`, `while`, and so on) that doesn't use block notation (see Chapter 2, "ECMAScript Basics")
- A line that doesn't end with a semicolon
- A `var` statement declaring a variable name that is already in use
- The `with` statement (for reasons to avoid `with`, see Chapter 2)

The JavaScript Verifier is available online at `http://www.crockford.com/javascript/jslint.html`, and it can also be downloaded in its original source code for your own use.

Debuggers

Programmers used to developing in languages such as C, C++, Java, and Perl know that debugging is an important part of the development process. These developers rely heavily on debuggers for such programming languages to aid in tracking down errors in their code. Most languages offer some type of debugger, from simple command line programs to exhaustive GUI layouts. Although JavaScript itself doesn't have a debugger, both Internet Explorer and Mozilla have debuggers available.

Microsoft Script Debugger

The Microsoft Script Debugger is a free utility available from Microsoft's Web site. To download it, go to `http://www.microsoft.com/downloads/search.aspx?categoryid=10` and type **script debugger** into the Search box. The results list comes up with Script Debugger for Windows NT, 2000, XP. Click that link and click the Download button. Run the installation program and then restart Internet Explorer. Notice a new menu item that appears under the View menu called Script Debugger. This provides options for running the debugger.

Running

You can run the Microsoft Script Debugger in a number of ways. First, you can open it directly by selecting View ⇨ Script Debugger ⇨ Open, which opens the debugger with no information loaded. The second method is to select View ⇨ Script Debugger ⇨ Break at Next Statement, which opens the debugger before the next JavaScript command on the page is executed. The debugger is brought up with the file that contains the executing JavaScript. Using this method, the line about to be run is highlighted in yellow. Lastly, you can use the JavaScript `debugger` command to bring up the debugger from anywhere in your code:

```
var iSum = 1 + 2;
debugger;
var iProduct = iSum * 10;
```

When the code encounters the `debugger` command, code execution is halted and the debugger is opened (making it very similar to the Break At Next Statement option).

The Window

The Microsoft Script Debugger is actually made up of a single window with three smaller utility windows (see Figure 14-12).

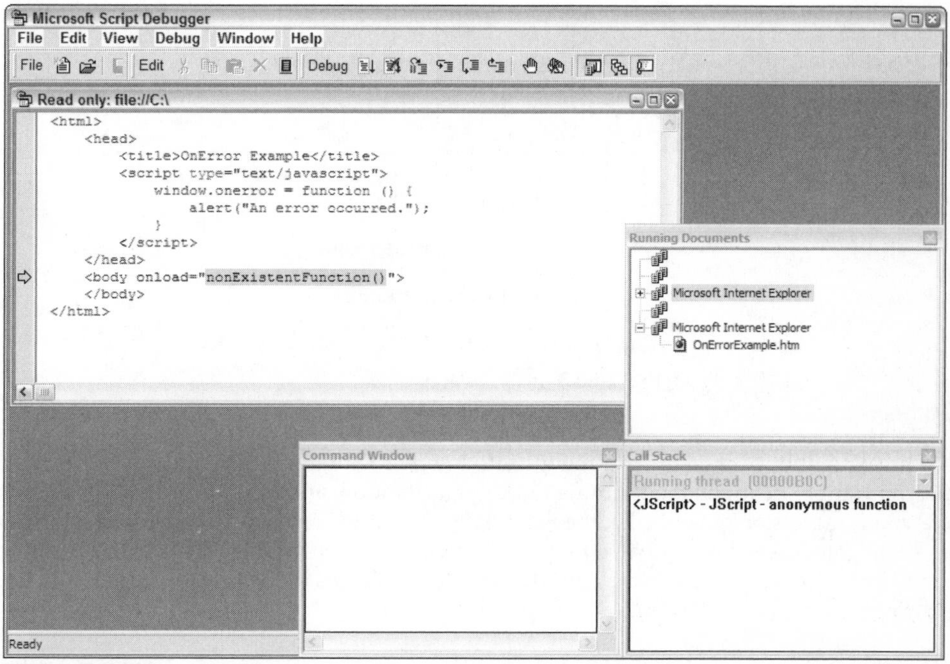

Figure 14-12

The first utility window is labeled Running Documents. This window displays all instances of Internet Explorer that are currently running, as well as all the documents that are loaded into each instance. By clicking on the plus sign next to an icon, you can see not only the HTML file that is loaded, but also all its associated JavaScript files. You can then bring up the source of any file by double-clicking on it in the window.

The second utility window is labeled Call Stack and, as you might assume, this displays the call stack up to the current breakpoint in the code. Double-clicking on an entry in the Call Stack window brings up the source code for the function.

The last utility window is labeled Command Window and is very similar to the Immediate window in Visual Studio. Here, you can type in JavaScript commands in the context of the executed code to check the values of variables. To do this, simply type the variable whose value you want to see followed by a semicolon. For instance, to get the URL of the window, type:

```
window.location.href;
```

When you hit the Enter key, the line of code is evaluated and the value displayed.

Breakpoints and stepping

The Debug toolbar (Figure 14-13) contains all the options you need to step through JavaScript code and set breakpoints.

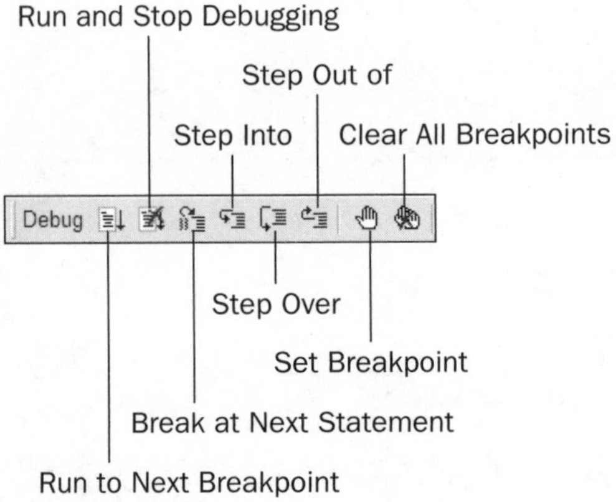

Figure 14-13

To set a breakpoint in your code, load the file into Internet Explorer and then open the debugger. Find the file you want to debug in the Running Documents window and double-click it. Then, go to the line of code you want to stop on and click the Set Breakpoint button (the white hand) in the toolbar. The line is then highlighted in yellow, and a yellow arrow is placed in the margin. Then, go back and reload the page in Internet Explorer and run the command; execution stops at the specified point and the debugger takes over.

At that point, you can do several things. If you want to step through the code, you can use the Step Into (which executes the code line by line, stopping after each one), Step Over (which doesn't follow code execution into functions), and Step Out (which moves execution outside of the function to the place where the function was called).

If you want to continue normal execution of the code until the next breakpoint, click the Run button; if you want to stop debugging altogether, click the Stop Debugging button to prevent any further stoppage in the code's execution.

The Microsoft Script Debugger is, ironically enough, buggy. On machines using Windows 2000 and later, the Script Debugger seems to have problems staying activated. It's not uncommon to use the debugger during one Windows session, shut down the computer, and return only to find that the menu items in Internet Explorer have disappeared. If this happens, go into Internet Options and click on the Advanced Tab. Select the check box labeled Disable Script Debugging and click the Apply button. Then, uncheck the check box and click the OK button. Most of the time, this re-enables the debugger.

Venkman – Mozilla's debugger

The Mozilla debugger, Venkman (named after the character Peter Venkman of the *Ghostbusters* movies), is a free utility for Mozilla-based browsers (including Firefox). To install, open up your Mozilla browser and go to `http://www.hacksrus.com/~ginda/venkman/`. At this address, you find a list of all the Venkman builds. Click the Install link next to the latest version. You are prompted to continue the installation because Venkman is an unsigned Mozilla plugin. Click Install Now. Restart the browser and you notice a new entry under the Tools ➪ Web Development menu.

Running

To run Venkman, click Tools ➪ Web Development ➪ JavaScript Debugger to manually open the window. When you do so, the Venkman window automatically loads all the files containing JavaScript into the debugger.

You can also use the `debugger` command in your code. It works with Microsoft's Script Debugger. Any time you include the `debugger` command, the debugger opens up at that line of code and stops execution.

Unlike Internet Explorer, Mozilla never asks you if you'd like to debug an error.

The Window

The Venkman window (Figure 14-14) is much more complicated than the Microsoft Script Debugger, but also a lot more powerful.

The window is made up of several smaller windows (or views) containing various information about the scripts you are inspecting. Each view is made up of several common components, as illustrated in Figure 14-15.

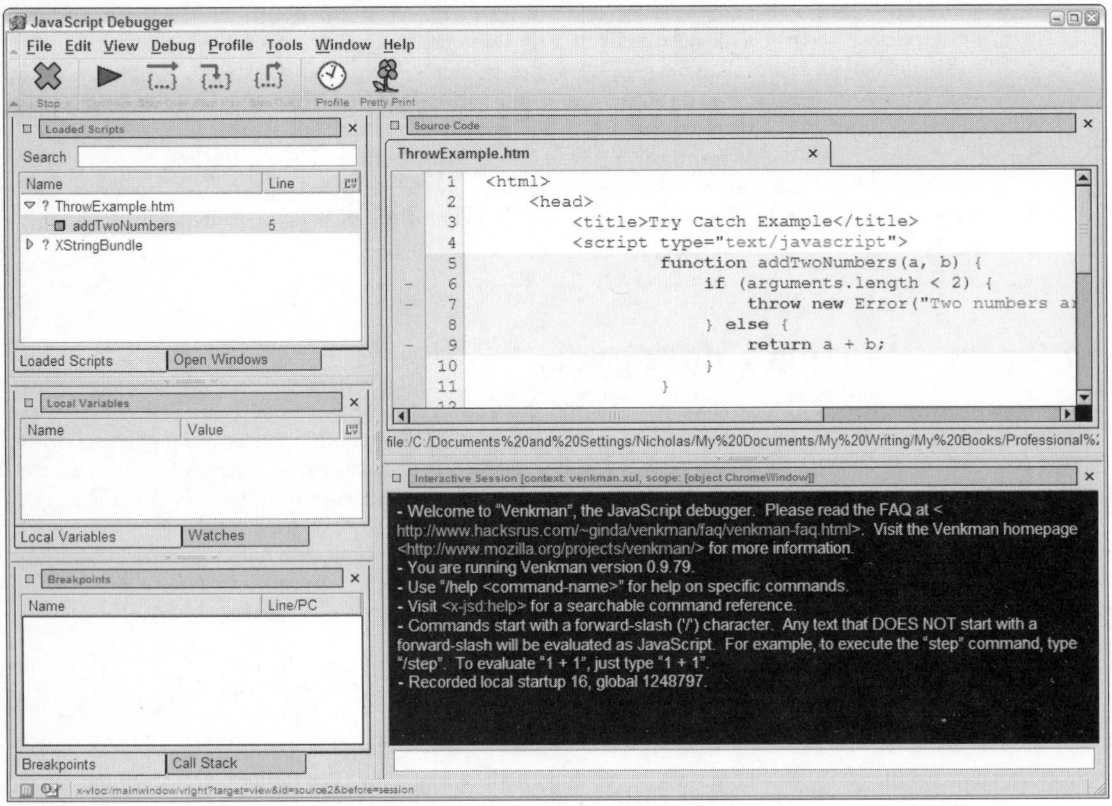

Figure 14-14

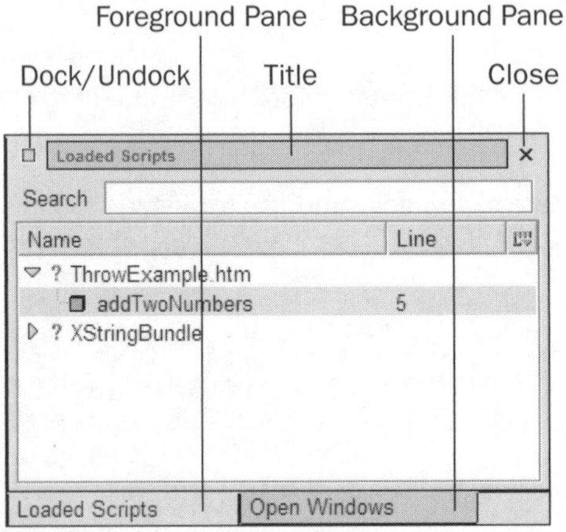

Figure 14-15

Each view consists of the following:

- A small square in the upper-left corner. Clicking this square causes the view to dock or undock from the main window. You can also drag this square into another view's square to combine views into one tabbed view.
- A title for the view
- An X in the upper-right corner, used to close the view. (You can always bring the view back by choosing View ➪ Show/Hide and then the appropriate view.)
- A content area, displaying a list or other information about the script
- An optional tabset. If more than one view exists in the same area, the debugger adds a tabset to allow you to switch back and forth between the views.

The entire interface is completely configurable to allow you to rearrange, resize, and otherwise manipulate the Venkman window to best suite your needs.

Eight views are available in Venkman, and each is just as powerful as the last:

1. Loaded Scripts— Displays the files that contain JavaScript, whether they are HTML or external JavaScript files. Each file can then be expanded to show the functions contained within, complete with the function name and the line on which the function begins.
2. Open Windows — Displays all browser windows (and tabs) Mozilla has open. Under each window is the HTML file that is loaded, and under that is a list of JavaScript files. You can shift the focus of the debugger to a particular window by right-clicking on a given file and selecting Set As Evaluation Object.
3. Local Variables — When a breakpoint is encountered, this view fills up with all the variables available in the scope of the executing code. If a variable contains an object, you can expand the variable name to see all the object's properties as well. To change a value of a variable while stopped at a breakpoint, just double-click the variable name and enter a new value.
4. Watches — Displays a list of watches for the debugger session. Watches work by *watching* variables to see when their values change. When a value changes, it's updated in the Watches view (Watches will be discussed further later on).
5. Breakpoints — Displays a list of breakpoints registered for the debugger session.
6. Call Stack — When a breakpoint is encountered, this view shows the call stack (the sequence of function calls that led to the breakpoint).
7. Source Code — Displays the source code for any file containing JavaScript code.
8. Interactive — A traditional-style command line interface to the debugger. In this view, you can control nearly every part of the debugger with text commands.

The Loaded Scripts pane

By default, the Loaded Scripts pane is displayed in the upper-left corner of the debugger window. It displays the location of the scripts currently loaded into the debugger. This includes any scripts contained in HTML pages as well as external JavaScript files.

Under each file (JavaScript or HTML) is a list of functions that exist within that file. In Figure 14-16, the example using the throw operator is loaded, so you can see the function `addTwoNumbers()` as well as the line number that the function begins on within the file. If you double-click on the file (or right-click and select Find File), the source code of the file is displayed in the Source Code pane. If you double-click on a function (or right-click and select Find Function), that function becomes highlighted in the source code pane.

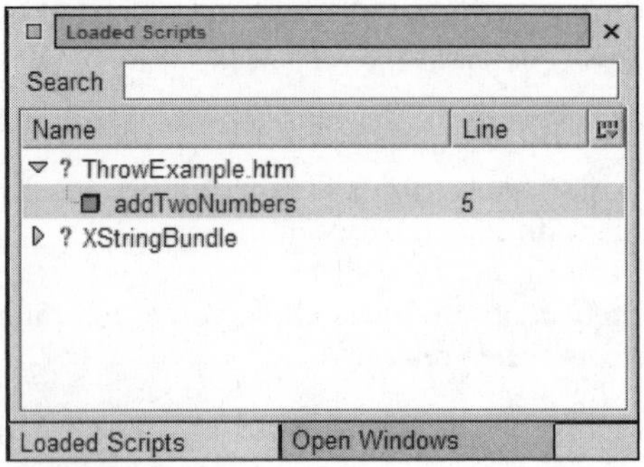

Figure 14-16

For each file in the Loaded Scripts pane, you can determine whether the script contained within it should be debugged or not. Just right-click on the file and select File Options. A submenu appears (Figure 14-17) giving you complete control over debugging and profiling (discussed later in the chapter).

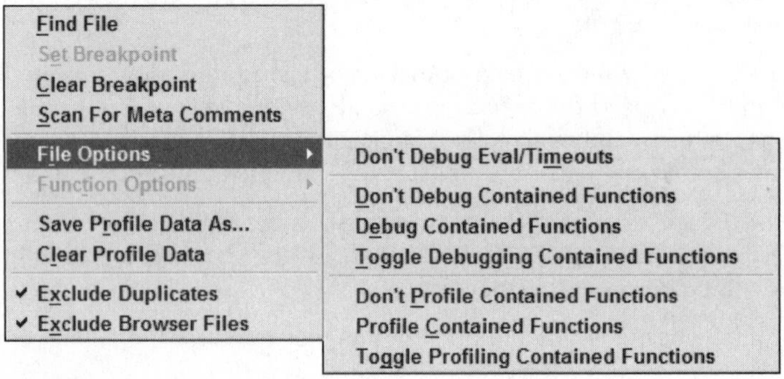

Figure 14-17

If you don't want to debug any code in the file, click Don't Debug Contained Functions (by default, all functions are debugged). This menu also allows you to prevent debugging of `eval()` or timeout code by selecting Don't Debug Eval/Timeout.

By default, Venkman tries to show only the files you have loaded into the browser; however, it is capable of loading all files that the browser loaded behind the scenes in addition to your own. You see all the loaded browser files by unchecking Exclude Browser Files on the context menu. Also by default, the pane only shows one instance of each file that is loaded; you can override this by unchecking Exclude Duplicates on the context menu.

Each function in the Loaded Scripts pane also has a certain level of control. By right-clicking on the function, a context menu similar to that of the file is presented. Under Function Options, you can click Don't Debug to force the debugger to ignore that one function instead of the entire file. This gives you an optimal level of control over the debugging process.

Breakpoints

Among the several ways to set up breakpoints in Venkman, the fastest and easiest way is to double-click on the file containing the script to debug. When that code shows up in the Source Code view, scroll down to the line on which you want to set the breakpoint on and click the left margin next to the line (a dash is next to any line where a breakpoint can be set). You see a `B`, meaning that a hard breakpoint has been set, or an `F`, meaning that the debugger could only set a future breakpoint (see Figure 14-18). A future breakpoint is created when the script has already been unloaded from memory, but it becomes a hard breakpoint the next time the script is loaded (if you reload the browser, for example).

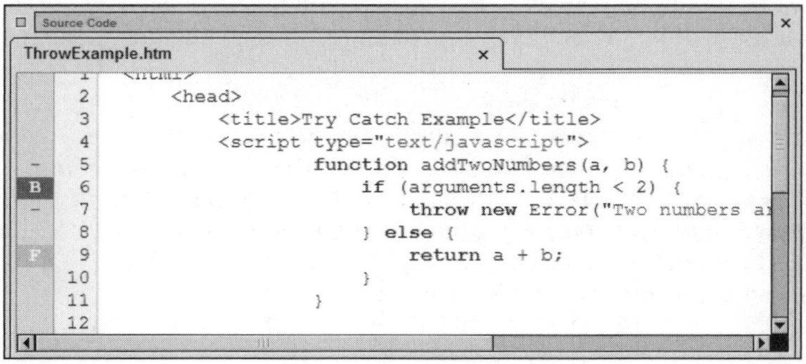

Figure 14-18

You can always create a future breakpoint by double-clicking in the left margin instead of single clicking, but you cannot force a hard breakpoint if, after one click, a future breakpoint is set.

The second way to set a breakpoint or future breakpoint is to use the command-line interface and the `/break` command (to set a hard breakpoint) or `/fbreak` command (to set a future breakpoint). Both commands take two arguments: the filename to set the breakpoint in and the line number to set the breakpoint on. For example:

```
/break ThrowExample.htm 7
```

This command sets a breakpoint on line 7 in the file matching ThrowExample.htm. For the filename, you don't need to type in the full path or even the full filename. Just a few characters are needed to uniquely identify the file among all the files that are loaded into Venkman. Just the first few letters of the filename are usually enough:

```
/break Thr 7
```

After a breakpoint has been created (using either method), it is stored in the Breakpoints view under the filename. Hard and future breakpoints are stored separately, so you may see two different entries for the same file (as in Figure 14-19). Only hard breakpoints can be viewed by function name and line; future breakpoints are listed only as filename and line number.

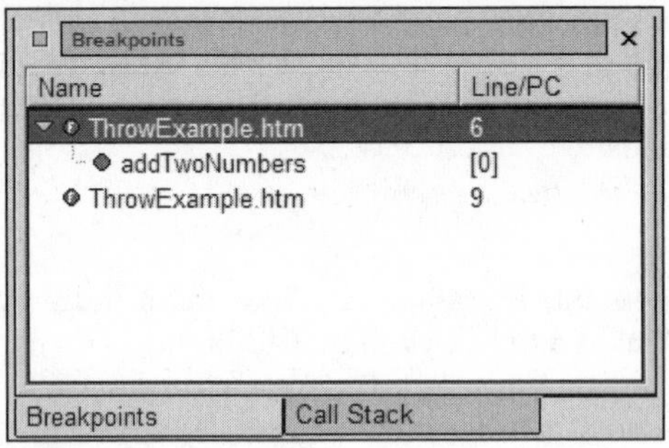

Figure 14-19

You also have many options to clear a breakpoint. First, you can click on the `B` or `F` in the left margin until it turns back to a dash. You can also right-click on the Breakpoints view to call up a context menu where you can select whether to clear a hard breakpoint, a future breakpoint, all hard breakpoints, or all future breakpoints.

The last method is to use the command line interface again and use the `/clear` command (to clear hard breakpoints) or the `/fclear` command (to clear future breakpoints). These commands accept the same arguments as `/break` and `/fbreak`: the filename and the line number to clear. Once again, the full filename isn't necessary, so the following two lines accomplish the same thing:

```
/clear ThrowExample.htm 7
/clear Thr 7
```

You can clear all hard breakpoints using the `/clear-all` command and all future breakpoints using the `/fclear-all` command.

When you clear a hard breakpoint, it automatically becomes a future breakpoint. That means you must first clear all hard breakpoints and then all future breakpoints to effectively eliminate all breakpoints.

Stepping through the code

As with breakpoints, you have numerous ways to step through your source code. The simplest way is to use the debug toolbar (Figure 14-20), which is prominently displayed at the top of the Venkman window.

Figure 14-20

The debug toolbar is made up of five buttons: Stop, Continue, Step Over, Step Into, and Step Out. The Stop button stops the currently active script without executing any further lines of code. If no code is being executed, three white dots appear over the Stop button to indicate that the debugger is not currently running any code. The Continue button resumes executing the script and continues until the natural end of the script or a breakpoint is encountered. The last three buttons are standard Step Over, Step Into, and Step Out commands.

All these actions can also be performed in the Interactive view by using the commands in the following table.

Debug Button	Text Command
Stop	`/stop`
Continue	`/cont`
Step Over	`/next`
Step Into	`/step`
Step Out	`/finish`

When code execution is stopped on a particular line, that line is highlighted in yellow in the Source Code view. Additionally, the function containing that line is displayed with a yellow arrow in the Call Stack view (Figure 14-21).

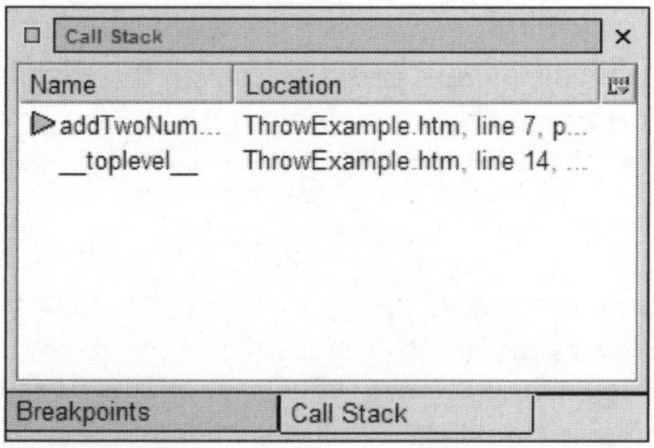

Figure 14-21

The Call Stack view always has a generic `__toplevel__` item to represent the global scope from which the first function was called.

Watches

One of the unique features of Venkman is its capability to set up variable watches. Watches literally *watch* variables for changes in their values and display them in the Watches view.

To add watches, you can select a variable in the Local Variables view, right-click, and select Add Watch Expression. You can also use the `/watch-expr` command in the Interactive view to do the same thing:

```
/watch-expr variable_name
```

Adding a watch adds a variable into the Watches view. The Watches view behaves in the exact same way as the Local Variables view, displaying the value of each variable when available and enumerating all properties of each object.

> **Watches in Venkman are tied to variable names, not directly to variables, so if you have two variables with the same name in different scopes, both of their values are displayed in the Watches view when appropriate.**

Profiling

One of the unique features of Venkman is its profiling capability. If you turn on profiling, Venkman begins keeping track of each function, how many times it's called, and how long each call takes.

You can turn profiling on and off by clicking the Profile button on the toolbar. A green checkmark appears on the Profile button when Venkman is profiling; no checkmark appears when it is not profiling. After Venkman is in profiling mode, run your script. When you are satisfied with your tests, select Profile ➪ Save Profile Data As. You are presented with a Save File dialog where you can save the profile data to view later.

By default, the dialog suggests you save the file in HTML format. This is a bug; you should save the file as plain text.

When you profile your script, each function gets a section in the file that looks like this:

```
<file:/C:/Chapter%2014/Examples/ThrowExample.htm>

  ThrowExample.htm: 1000 - 5000 milliseconds

    Function Name: addTwoNumbers  (Lines 5 - 10)
    Total Calls: 1 (max recurse 0)
    Total Time: 4696.75 (min/max/avg 4696.75/4696.75/4696.75)
```

Each section begins with the location of the file containing the function and is followed by each function contained in the file. Each function is displayed with the following:

- The lines it appears on
- The total number of calls to the function and the maximum recursion level reached (identified by `max recurse`)
- The total amount of time (in milliseconds) it took to run the function along with the minimum time for a call, the maximum time for a call, and the average time for a call

This information is incredibly useful for detecting bottlenecks in your code.

Unfortunately, the profile data includes data about the browser and debugger itself, so you need to read through it all to get to the information you want.

You can also determine which functions are profiled. To set an entire file so that it won't be profiled, right-click on the file in the Loaded Scripts view and select File Options ➪ Don't Profile Contained Functions. If you want to disable profiling for a single function, right-click on the function in the Loaded Scripts view and select Function Options ➪ Don't Profile.

Summary

This chapter introduced the many aspects of errors and error handling in JavaScript. The `onerror` event handler was covered, including the creation of your own error-message windows. You also learned how to use the `try...catch` statement to trap errors in progress. An in-depth discussion of the `Error` object followed, introducing you to how you can throw your own JavaScript errors.

Next, several debugging techniques were discussed, ranging from using alerts and Java console messages to throwing your own errors. You also learned how to create your own `assert()` function to make throwing your own errors easier.

Finally, you were introduced to the JavaScript debuggers for Internet Explorer and Mozilla. You learned how to download, install, and run each debugger in its browser, as well as how to use the debugger to set breakpoints and step through code.

15

XML in JavaScript

With the rising popularity of XML, JavaScript developers were clamoring for a way to make use of it in client-side Web development. When the fourth-generation browsers were released, many developers began writing their own objects for the manipulation of XML using JavaScript. Hearing the call, some browser developers boldly pushed toward adding support for XML and XML-related language on the client side.

XML DOM Support in Browsers

Even though XML and the DOM have become an important part of Web development, there are still only two browsers that support client-side XML manipulation. Not surprisingly, they are the two most popular browsers in the world: Internet Explorer and Mozilla.

XML DOM support in IE

When looking to add XML support to Internet Explorer, Microsoft looked outside of JavaScript to their ActiveX-based library called MSXML. MSXML was developed to provide developers with the first DOM implementation for Windows. As an ActiveX control, MSXML could be used in conjunction with Visual Basic, C++, and other Windows-based development environments. It made sense to use what the company was already offering as the basis for client-side XML support.

To create an ActiveX object using JavaScript, Microsoft introduced a class called `ActiveXObject`. The constructor for `ActiveXObject` takes one argument, which is the string identifying the ActiveX object to instantiate. For example, the first version of the XML DOM object was called *Microsoft.XmlDom*. To create a new instance of this object, you would do this:

```
var oXmlDom = new ActiveXObject("Microsoft.XmlDom");
```

After this line is executed, the `oXmlDom` object behaves like any other DOM Document, complete with all the properties and methods discussed earlier in the book.

When developers first started using this method of XML manipulation, it was problematic because the user often did not have MSXML installed. Most of the time, developers had to download the library from Microsoft directly. However, Internet Explorer 5.0 fixed this problem by shipping with MSXML, thus ensuring anyone using IE 5.0 or higher could make use of this functionality.

DOM creation

With each new version of MSXML, a new version of the XML DOM object was created, each with its own unique name. The most recent and final version of MSXML is 5.0, meaning that the following XML DOM implementations now exist:

- Microsoft.XmlDom (original)
- MSXML2.DOMDocument
- MSXML2.DOMDocument.3.0
- MSXML2.DOMDocument.4.0
- MSXML2.DOMDocument.5.0

Naturally, you want the most recent version of the XML DOM whenever possible because of improvements in speed and enhanced support for features such as validation. However, if you try to create an ActiveX object that doesn't exist on the client machine, IE throws an error and stops all processing. So, to be sure you are using the correct version of the XML DOM and to avoid any unsightly errors, create a function that tries each XML DOM string and captures any errors that occur:

```
function createXMLDOM() {

    var arrSignatures = ["MSXML2.DOMDocument.5.0", "MSXML2.DOMDocument.4.0",
                         "MSXML2.DOMDocument.3.0", "MSXML2.DOMDocument",
                         "Microsoft.XmlDom"];

    for (var i=0; i < arrSignatures.length; i++) {
        try {

            var oXmlDom = new ActiveXObject(arrSignatures[i]);

            return oXmlDom;

        } catch (oError) {
            //ignore
        }
    }

    throw new Error("MSXML is not installed on your system.");
}
```

This function contains an array of all the possible XML DOM strings, called `arrSignatures`, sorted in descending order from most recent to least recent. The `for` loop tries to create an XML DOM object by using the string in position `i` and assigned it to the variable `oXmlDom`. If that version of the XML DOM isn't present on the user's machine, it causes an error, which is caught by the `try...catch` statement and ignored. When that error occurs, the line `return oXmlDom` is completely skipped, and the `for` loop starts again. Only if the XML DOM object is successfully created is it returned as the function value. If, on the other hand, each version of the XML DOM is tested and no version is available, the function throws its own error telling the user that MSXML isn't installed on the system and processing cannot continue.

By using this function, you can be sure that the XML DOM version you are using is the most recent:

```
var oXmlDom = createXMLDOM();
```

> **The code to create an XML DOM in Internet Explorer causes an error in any other browser. Therefore, you must do a browser detect before attempting to create the XML DOM in this way.**

Loading XML

Now that you have an XML DOM object, you load some XML into it. Microsoft's XML DOM comes with two methods for loading XML: `loadXML()` and `load()`.

The `loadXML()` method enables you to enter an XML string directly into the XML DOM:

```
oXmlDom.loadXML("<root><child/></root>");
```

The `load()` method is used to load an XML file from the server. Rather, the `load()` method can load an XML file stored on the same server as the page that contains the JavaScript, meaning that you can't load XML from someone else's server.

There are two modes of loading a file: synchronous and asynchronous. When you load a file in synchronous mode, the JavaScript code waits for the file to be fully loaded before executing the next line of code; a file loaded in asynchronous mode won't wait, so you need to use an event handler to determine when the file has been fully loaded.

By default, files are loaded asynchronously. To set files to load synchronously, just set the `async` property to `false`:

```
oXmlDom.async = false;
```

You can then use the `load()` method by passing in the name of the file to load:

```
oXmlDom.load("test.xml");
```

After this line executes, `oXmlDom` contains a DOM Document representing the XML file, so you can use all the DOM properties and methods:

```
alert("Tag name of the root element is " + oXmlDom.documentElement.tagName);
alert("The root element has this many children: " +
      oXmlDom.documentElement.childNodes.length);
```

To load the file asynchronously, use the `readyState` property and the `onreadystatechange` event handler.

The `readyState` property has five possible values:

- 0 — The DOM hasn't been initialized with any information.
- 1 — The DOM is loading data.
- 2 — The DOM has completed loading the data.
- 3 — The DOM may be used although some sections may not be available.
- 4 — The DOM is completely loaded and ready to be used.

Whenever the `readyState` property changes from one value to another, the `readystatechange` event is fired. If you use the `onreadystatechange` event handler, you are notified when the DOM has been fully loaded:

```
oXmlDom.onreadystatechange = function () {
    if (oXmlDom.readyState == 4) {
        alert("Done");
    }
};
```

You must assign the `onreadystatechange` event handler *before* you call the `load()` method, as shown in the following:

```
oXmlDom.onreadystatechange = function () {
    if (oXmlDom.readyState == 4) {
        alert("Done");
    }
};

oXmlDom.load("test.xml");
```

Now when the file is completely loaded, you see the alert `Done`.

> **You may note that the event handler code uses `oXmlDom` instead of the `this` keyword. This is a peculiarity of ActiveX objects in JavaScript: The `this` keyword doesn't always work as expected. To avoid any problems, it's best to use the full variable name in the event handler.**

Whether you choose to load files synchronously or asynchronously, the `load()` method can be used with a partial, relative, or full path to the XML file, such as in the following:

```
oXmlDom.load("test.xml");
oXmlDom.load("../test.xml");
oXmlDom.load("http://www.mydomain.com/test.xml");
```

The partial and relative paths are always calculated from the page using the XML DOM object, just as a link or image would be.

Retrieving XML

After you've gotten XML into a DOM, it's logical to assume you must be able to get that XML back out. Microsoft made this easy by adding an `xml` property for every node, including a document node, which returns its representative XML code as a string. So to retrieve the XML that you just loaded is simple:

```
oXmlDom.load("test.xml");
alert(oXmlDom.xml);
```

You can also retrieve the XML for a particular node:

```
var oNode = oXmlDom.documentElements.childNodes[1];
alert(oNode.xml);
```

The `xml` property is read-only and causes an error if you try to assign a value to it.

Parsing errors

When you try to load XML into an XML DOM object, whether by using `loadXML()` or `load()`, there's the possibility that the XML isn't well-formed. To provide for this, the Microsoft XML DOM has a property called `parseError` that contains all the information about any errors encountered while parsing XML code.

The `parseError` property is actually an object with the following properties:

- `errorCode` — Numeric code indicating the type of error that occurred (0 when there's no error)
- `filePos` — Position within the file where the error occurred
- `line` — The line on which the error occurred
- `linepos` – The character on the line where the error occurred
- `reason` — A plain text explanation of the error
- `srcText` — The code that caused the error
- `url` — The URL of the file that caused the error (if available)

When the `parseError` property is used by itself, it returns the value of `errorCode`, meaning that you can check for errors by doing this:

```
if (oXmlDom.parseError != 0) {
    //there were errors, do something about it here
}
```

Always check that the error code is not equal to 0, rather than if it's greater than or less than 0, because error codes can be either positive or negative.

You can use the `parseError` object to create your own error dialogs:

```
if (oXmlDom.parseError != 0) {
    var oError = oXmlDom.parseError;

    alert("An error occurred:\nError Code: "
```

```
            + oError.errorCode + "\n"
            + "Line: " + oError.line + "\n"
            + "Line Pos: " + oError.linepos + "\n"
            + "Reason: " + oError.reason);

}
```

Another option is to throw your own errors:

```
if (oXmlDom.parseError != 0) {
    var oError = oXmlDom.parseError;

    throw new Error(oError.reason + " (at line " + oError.line
                    + ", position " + oError.linepos + ")");

}
```

Regardless of how you end up representing errors, it's always best to check the XML DOM for errors immediately after it's loaded.

The MSXML ActiveX controls are available only on Windows; therefore, Internet Explorer on the Macintosh cannot make use of this functionality. Windows XP Service Pack 2 introduces new security restrictions on many ActiveX controls, but MSXML is not one of them (all controls in MSXML are considered to be secure).

XML DOM support in Mozilla

As with many other things, Mozilla supports a more standard version of the XML DOM than Internet Explorer. The XML DOM in Mozilla is actually part of its JavaScript implementation, meaning that it not only evolves with the browser, but it is also readily available on all platforms that Mozilla supports. Unlike Internet Explorer, which has no XML DOM support on the Macintosh or Unix, Mozilla's support crosses all platform boundaries. Additionally, Mozilla's XML DOM implementation supports DOM Level 2 functionality, unlike Microsoft's, which supports only DOM Level 1.

DOM creation

The DOM standard specifies that a method called `createDocument()` be available as part of the `document.implementation` object. Mozilla follows this specification exactly, enabling you to create an XML DOM like this:

```
var oXmlDom = document.implementation.createDocument("","", null);
```

The three arguments for `createDocument()` are the namespace URL for the document, the tag name for the document element, and a document type object (always `null`, because no support exists for the document type object in Mozilla). The previous line of code creates an empty XML DOM. To create an XML DOM with a document element, just specify the tag name as the second argument:

```
var oXmlDom = document.implementation.createDocument("","root", null);
```

This line of code creates an XML DOM that represents the XML code `<root/>`. If you specify a namespace URL in the first argument, you can further define the document element:

```
var oXmlDom = document.implementation.createDocument("http://www.wrox.com",
                                                      "root", null);
```

This line of code creates an XML DOM representing `<a0:root xmlns:a0="http://www.wrox.com" />`. Mozilla automatically creates a namespace named `a0` to represent the URL you entered for the namespace.

Loading XML

Unlike Microsoft's XML DOM, Mozilla's only supports one method for loading data: `load()`. The `load()` method in Mozilla works exactly the same as the `load()` method in Internet Explorer. All you need is to specify the XML file to load and whether to load it synchronously or asynchronously (default).

To load the XML file synchronously, the code is essentially the same as in IE:

```
oXmlDom.async = false;
oXmlDom.load("test.xml");
```

If you want to load a file asynchronously, things are a little bit different.

Mozilla doesn't support Microsoft's `readyState` property on the XML DOM (indeed, `readyState` isn't part of the DOM Level 3 Load and Save specification upon which Mozilla's implementation is based). Instead, Mozilla's XML DOM fires a `load` event when the file has been fully loaded, meaning that you must use the `onload` event handler to determine when DOM is ready:

```
oXmlDom.onload = function () {
    alert("Done");
};

oXmlDom.load("test.xml");
```

> **Prior to version 1.4, Mozilla only supported asynchronous loading of external files. In 1.4, Mozilla introduced the `async` property and the capability to load files synchronously.**

Unfortunately, Mozilla's XML DOM doesn't support the `loadXML()` method. To parse an XML string into a DOM, you must use the `DOMParser` object:

```
var oParser = new DOMParser();
var oXmlDom = oParser.parseFromString("<root/>", "text/xml");
```

This code creates an XML DOM that represents `<root/>`. The `DOMParser` object is created in the first line, and the second line uses its only method, `parseFromString()`, to create the XML DOM. This method accepts two arguments, the XML string to parse and the content type of the string. To parse XML code, the content type can be `"text/xml"` or `"application/xml"`; any other content type is ignored (although it is possible to parse XHTML code using the content type `"application/xhtml+xml"`).

Because the XML DOM is part of Mozilla's JavaScript implementation, it is possible to add a `loadXML()` method. The actual class for the XML DOM is called `Document`, so adding a new method is as easy as using the `prototype` object:

```
Document.prototype.loadXML = function (sXml) {
   //function body
};
```

Then, use the `DOMParser` to create a new XML DOM:

```
Document.prototype.loadXML = function (sXml) {

    var oParser = new DOMParser();
    var oXmlDom = oParser.parseFromString(sXml, "text/xml");

    //...

};
```

Next, the original document must be emptied of its contents. You can do this by using a `while` loop and removing all the document's child nodes:

```
Document.prototype.loadXML = function (sXml) {

    var oParser = new DOMParser();
    var oXmlDom = oParser.parseFromString(sXml, "text/xml");

    while (this.firstChild) {
        this.removeChild(this.firstChild);
    }

    //...

};
```

Remember, because this function is a method, the `this` keyword refers to the XML DOM object. After all the children have been removed, all the children of `oXmlDom` must be imported into the document (using `importNode()`) and added as children (using `appendChild()`):

```
Document.prototype.loadXML = function (sXml) {

    var oParser = new DOMParser();
    var oXmlDom = oParser.parseFromString(sXml, "text/xml");

    while (this.firstChild) {
        this.removeChild(this.firstChild);
    }

    for (var i=0; i < oXmlDom.childNodes.length; i++) {
        var oNewNode = this.importNode(oXmlDom.childNodes[i], true);
        this.appendChild(oNewNode);
    }

};
```

As long as you include this code, you can use the `loadXML()` method in Mozilla the same way as in IE.

> **This code will cause an error in IE, where no `Document` object exists. To prevent this, use a browser detect around the code.**

Retrieving XML

Remember that Microsoft's XML DOM provides an `xml` property that allows easy access to the underlying XML code. Because this property is not part of the standard, Mozilla doesn't support it. Instead, Mozilla has the `XMLSerializer` object, which is used for the same purpose:

```
var oSerializer = new XMLSerializer();
var sXml = oSerializer.serializeToString(oXmlDom, "text/xml");
```

This simple code snippet creates the XML code for `oXmlDom` by using the `XMLSerializer`'s only method: `serializeToString()`. The `serializeToString()` method accepts the node to serialize and the content type as arguments. Once again, the content type can be `"text/xml"` or `"application/xml"`. Using this object, it's possible to synthesize the `xml` property for Mozilla using a little-known method called `defineGetter()`.

The `defineGetter()` method exists only in Mozilla and is used to define a *getter function* for a property, meaning that when the property is accessed in read mode, this function is called and the return value is assigned to the property. For example:

```
var sValue = oXmlNode.nodeValue;        //read mode
oXmlNode.nodeValue = "New value";       //write mode
```

The first line of code uses the `nodeValue` property in read mode, meaning that the interpreter is reading the value from the property. If a getter function is defined, it is run and its value returned. The second line of code uses `nodeValue` in write mode, meaning that a value is being assigned to it. If a *setter function* is defined (the opposite of a getter function), then it is called with `New value` as an argument. Yes, there is also a `defineSetter()` method, but it's unnecessary here.

This method, `defineGetter()`, is hidden by using the JavaScript standard for private properties and methods — using double underscores before and after the name:

```
oObject.__defineGetter__("propertyName", function() { return "propertyValue"; });
```

As you can see, `defineGetter()` takes two arguments: the name of the property and the function to call. Whatever you specify as the property name cannot be used as a regular property. For example, you should never do this:

```
oObject.propertyName = "blue";
oObject.__defineGetter__("propertyName", function() { return "propertyValue"; });
```

Typically getter and setter functions are defined in pairs, although you can effectively create a read-only property by assigning just a getter. This is way to create the `xml` property.

Because the `xml` property needs to be available on every type of node in a document, it's best to add it to the `Node` class itself (remember, all other node types inherit from `Node`):

```
Node.prototype.__defineGetter__("xml", function () {
    var oSerializer = new XMLSerializer();
    return oSerializer.serializeToString(this, "text/xml");
});
```

The function assigned to the `xml` property is very simple, and the only change from the earlier example is that `this` is the first argument for the `serializeToString()` method (remember, in this context `this` refers to the node). If you include this code in a page, it's possible to use this custom `xml` property in the same manner as Microsoft's `xml` property:

```
oXmlDom.load("test.xml");
alert(oXmlDom.xml);

var oNode = oXmlDom.documentElements.childNodes[1];
alert(oNode.xml);
```

> **This code must also be surrounded by a browser detect because it only works in Mozilla.**

Parsing errors

When an error occurs in the parsing of an XML file, the XML DOM creates a document explaining the error. Suppose you ran the following code:

```
var oParser = new DOMParser()
var oXmlDom = oParser.parseFromString("<root><child></root>");
```

Although no error is thrown, `oXmlDom` shows you the error. In this case, it presents this code:

```
<parsererror xmlns="http://www.mozilla.org/newlayout/xml/parsererror.xml">
XML Parsing Error: not well-formed
Location: file://c:/Chapter 15/examples/MozillaXmlDomExample.htm
Line Number 5, Column 1:<sourcetext>&lt;root&gt;&lt;child&gt;&lt;/root&gt;
--------------^</sourcetext>
</parsererror>
```

So to determine if there's an error in the parsing of XML code, you must test the tag name of the document element:

```
if (oXmlDom.documentElement.tagName != "parsererror") {
    //continue on, no errors
} else {
    //do something else, there was an error
}
```

Unfortunately, the only way to get specific error information is to parse the error message text. The easiest way to do this is to use a regular expression:

```
var reError = />([\s\S]*?)Location:([\s\S]*?)Line Number (\d+), Column
(\d+):<sourcetext>([\s\S]*?)(?:\-*\^)/;
```

This rather long regular expression pulls all the relevant information out of the XML code. The first capturing group retrieves the error message, the second retrieves the filename, the third retrieves the line number, the fourth retrieves the column number, and the fifth retrieves the source code that caused the error (without the trailing dashes and caret). To use this to create an error message, just use the `test()` method:

```
var reError = />([\s\S]*?)Location:([\s\S]*?)Line Number (\d+), Column
(\d+):<sourcetext>([\s\S]*?)(?:\-*\^)/;

if (oXmlDom.documentElement.tagName == "parsererror") {
    reError.test(oXmlDom.xml);
    alert("An error occurred:\nDescription: "
          + RegExp.$1 + "\n"
          + "File: " + RegExp.$2 + "\n"
          + "Line: " + RegExp.$3 + "\n"
          + "Line Pos: " + RegExp.$4 + "\n"
          + "Source: " + RegExp.$5);
}
```

Making interfaces play together

Developing with the XML DOM is only useful if you have a cross-browser solution. As you can see, the IE and Mozilla implementations differ enough to cause significant problems for you when you are developing. The only solution is to come up with a common way to use the XML DOM that works in both browsers.

Modifying DOM creation

The first step is to create a common way for IE and Mozilla to create an XML DOM object. The easiest way to do this is to create a pseudo-class that enables you to create an XML DOM like this:

```
var oXmlDom = new XmlDom();
```

Of course, to make this work, you need browser detection going on inside the constructor for XmlDom:

```
function XmlDom() {
    if (window.ActiveXObject) {
        //IE-specific code
    } else if (document.implementation && document.implementation.createDocument) {
        //DOM-specific code
    } else {
        throw new Error("Your browser doesn't support an XML DOM object.");
    }
}
```

This code uses object/feature detection to determine which way to go. Because Internet Explorer on Windows is the only browser that supports the `ActiveXObject` class, that is a fair way to test for IE. The second test is a generic one determining if the browser supports the DOM standard `createDocument()` method. Even though Mozilla is the only browser that currently supports this, it's conceivable that other browsers may adopt this functionality in the future, so testing in this way makes the code future-proof. If neither statement evaluates to `true`, then the constructor throws an error indicating no XML DOM object is available.

The IE branch

For the IE section of the constructor, just insert the code from the `createXMLDOM()` function earlier in the chapter:

```
function XmlDom() {
    if (window.ActiveXObject) {
        var arrSignatures = ["MSXML2.DOMDocument.5.0", "MSXML2.DOMDocument.4.0",
                             "MSXML2.DOMDocument.3.0", "MSXML2.DOMDocument",
                             "Microsoft.XmlDom"];

        for (var i=0; i < arrSignatures.length; i++) {
            try {

                var oXmlDom = new ActiveXObject(arrSignatures[i]);

                return oXmlDom;

            } catch (oError) {
                //ignore
            }
        }

        throw new Error("MSXML is not installed on your system.");

    } else if (document.implementation && document.implementation.createDocument) {
        //DOM-specific code
    } else {
        throw new Error("Your browser doesn't support an XML DOM object.");
    }
}
```

That's all you do for this to work in IE. The more complicated part has to do with Mozilla.

The Mozilla branch

The first step in the Mozilla branch is to create the XML DOM object using `createDocument()`:

```
function XmlDom() {
    if (window.ActiveXObject) {
        var arrSignatures = ["MSXML2.DOMDocument.5.0", "MSXML2.DOMDocument.4.0",
                             "MSXML2.DOMDocument.3.0", "MSXML2.DOMDocument",
                             "Microsoft.XmlDom"];

        for (var i=0; i < arrSignatures.length; i++) {
```

```
                try {

                    var oXmlDom = new ActiveXObject(arrSignatures[i]);

                    return oXmlDom;

                } catch (oError) {
                    //ignore
                }
            }

            throw new Error("MSXML is not installed on your system.");

        } else if (document.implementation && document.implementation.createDocument) {

            var oXmlDom = document.implementation.createDocument("","",null);
            return oXmlDom;

        } else {
            throw new Error("Your browser doesn't support an XML DOM object.");
        }
    }
```

The next task is to make Mozilla support the `readyState` property and the `onreadystatechange` event handler. This requires you to make some additional changes to the `Document` class.

First, add a `readyState` property and initialize it to 0.

```
Document.prototype.readyState = 0;
```

Next, create an `onreadystatechange` property and assign it the value of `null`:

```
Document.prototype.onreadystatechange = null;
```

Whenever the `readyState` property changes, the `onreadystatechange` function must be called. To facilitate this, it's best to create a method:

```
Document.prototype.__changeReadyState__ = function (iReadyState) {
    this.readyState = iReadyState;

    if (typeof this.onreadystatechange == "function") {
        this.onreadystatechange();
    }
};
```

This method takes the new ready state as an argument and assigns it to the `readyState` property. Be sure you check that `onreadystatechange` is actually a function before calling it (otherwise, this causes an error). Because this method shouldn't be called outside of the `Document` object, it uses the JavaScript notation for a private method (leading and trailing double underscores).

Internet Explorer's XML DOM supports five ready states, but there is no way to mimic all of them for Mozilla. Really, the only important value for `readyState` is 4, which indicates that the XML DOM is completely loaded and ready for use. This value is easy to mimic by assigning an `onload` event handler. It's also easy to simulate `readyState 1`, which indicates that the XML DOM has just started loading. The other ready states aren't as important and even more difficult — if not impossible — to simulate.

The two methods that affect the `readyState` property are `loadXML()` and `load()`. The `loadXML()` method is easy to update because it's your creation. Just add two lines of code:

```
Document.prototype.loadXML = function (sXml) {

    this.__changeReadyState__(1);

    var oParser = new DOMParser();
    var oXmlDom = oParser.parseFromString(sXml, "text/xml");

    while (this.firstChild) {
        this.removeChild(this.firstChild);
    }

    for (var i=0; i < oXmlDom.childNodes.length; i++) {
        var oNewNode = this.importNode(oXmlDom.childNodes[i], true);
        this.appendChild(oNewNode);
    }

    this.__changeReadyState__(4);
};
```

The updated `loadXML()` method sets the `readyState` to `1` at the beginning and `4` at the end.

To update the `load()` method, start by creating a pointer to the original load method:

```
Document.prototype.__load__ = Document.prototype.load;
```

Next, define a new `load()` method that sets the `readyState` property to `1` and then calls the original `load()` method:

```
Document.prototype.load = function (sURL) {
    this.__changeReadyState__(1);
    this.__load__(sURL);
};
```

In order to set the `readyState` property to `4` at the right time, use the `onload` event handler. Because you can only assign an event handler after the XML DOM object has been instantiated, this must take place back in the `XmlDom` constructor:

```
function XmlDom() {
    if (window.ActiveXObject) {
        var arrSignatures = ["MSXML2.DOMDocument.5.0", "MSXML2.DOMDocument.4.0",
                             "MSXML2.DOMDocument.3.0", "MSXML2.DOMDocument",
                             "Microsoft.XmlDom"];

        for (var i=0; i < arrSignatures.length; i++) {
            try {
```

```
                var oXmlDom = new ActiveXObject(arrSignatures[i]);

                return oXmlDom;

            } catch (oError) {
                //ignore
            }
        }

        throw new Error("MSXML is not installed on your system.");

    } else if (document.implementation && document.implementation.createDocument) {

        var oXmlDom = document.implementation.createDocument("","",null);

        oXmlDom.addEventListener("load", function () {
            this.__changeReadyState__(4);
        }, false);

        return oXmlDom;

    } else {
        throw new Error("Your browser doesn't support an XML DOM object.");
    }
}
```

Now the Mozilla XML DOM properly supports the `readyState` property (for values of `0`, `1`, and `4`), the `onreadystatechange` event handler, the `loadXML()` method, and the `xml` property. The following example works in both IE and Mozilla:

```
var oXmlDom = new XmlDom();
oXmlDom.onreadystatechange = function () {
    if (oXmlDom.readyState == 4) {
        alert(oXmlDom.xml);
    }
};

oXmlDom.load("test.xml");
```

The main difference between the two is how the two XML DOMs handle errors. But this can be remedied.

Error handling

The last step is to create a `parseError` object for Mozilla. Once again, it's not possible to provide every IE property, but you have enough information in the Mozilla parser error XML to mimic most of them.

To begin, this object must be created in the `XmlDom` constructor with all its initial values set:

```
function XmlDom() {
    if (window.ActiveXObject) {
        var arrSignatures = ["MSXML2.DOMDocument.5.0", "MSXML2.DOMDocument.4.0",
                             "MSXML2.DOMDocument.3.0", "MSXML2.DOMDocument",
                             "Microsoft.XmlDom"];
```

```
        for (var i=0; i < arrSignatures.length; i++) {
            try {

                var oXmlDom = new ActiveXObject(arrSignatures[i]);

                return oXmlDom;

            } catch (oError) {
                //ignore
            }
        }

        throw new Error("MSXML is not installed on your system.");

    } else if (document.implementation && document.implementation.createDocument) {

        var oXmlDom = document.implementation.createDocument("","",null);

        oXmlDom.parseError = {
            valueOf: function () { return this.errorCode; },
            toString: function () { return this.errorCode.toString() }
        };

        oXmlDom.__initError__();

        oXmlDom.addEventListener("load", function () {
            this.__changeReadyState__(4);
        }, false);

        return oXmlDom;

    } else {
        throw new Error("Your browser doesn't support an XML DOM object.");
    }
}
```

This code uses object literal notation to create the `parseError` object in order to save space. The `valueOf()` method is defined to return the `errorCode` property, which is the same as IE's implementation; the `toString()` method also returns the `errorCode` property, but as a string primitive. The `initError()` method initializes all the `parseError` object's properties. Here's the code:

```
Document.prototype.__initError__ = function () {
    this.parseError.errorCode = 0;
    this.parseError.filepos = -1;
    this.parseError.line = -1;
    this.parseError.linepos = -1;
    this.parseError.reason = null;
    this.parseError.srcText = null;
    this.parseError.url = null;
};
```

The next step is to check for a parsing error. This must be done in both the `load()` and `loadXML()` methods because a parsing error can occur in either one. Because it's bad coding practice to have the same code in two places, it's best to create a new method to handle parsing errors:

```
Document.prototype.__checkForErrors__ = function () {

    if (this.documentElement.tagName == "parsererror") {

        var reError = />([\s\S]*?)Location:([\s\S]*?)Line Number (\d+), Column
(\d+):<sourcetext>([\s\S]*?)(?:\-*\^)/;

        reError.test(this.xml);

        this.parseError.errorCode = -999999;
        this.parseError.reason = RegExp.$1;
        this.parseError.url = RegExp.$2;
        this.parseError.line = parseInt(RegExp.$3);
        this.parseError.linepos = parseInt(RegExp.$4);
        this.parseError.srcText = RegExp.$5;

    }
};
```

Note that the `errorCode` is set to `-999999` no matter what error occurs. Trying to map all of Microsoft's error codes would be a tedious and unnecessary task. Most of the time, you just check to see if `parseError` is anything other than `0`, not necessarily a particular number.

Next, the `load()` and `loadXML()` methods must be updated to use `initError()` (to clear all error values before parsing begins) and `checkForErrors()` (to check for any parsing errors when the parsing has completed):

```
function XmlDom() {
    if (window.ActiveXObject) {
        var arrSignatures = ["MSXML2.DOMDocument.5.0", "MSXML2.DOMDocument.4.0",
                            "MSXML2.DOMDocument.3.0", "MSXML2.DOMDocument",
                            "Microsoft.XmlDom"];

        for (var i=0; i < arrSignatures.length; i++) {
            try {

                var oXmlDom = new ActiveXObject(arrSignatures[i]);

                return oXmlDom;

            } catch (oError) {
                //ignore
            }
        }

        throw new Error("MSXML is not installed on your system.");

    } else if (document.implementation && document.implementation.createDocument) {

        var oXmlDom = document.implementation.createDocument("","",null);

        oXmlDom.parseError = {
            valueOf: function () { return this.errorCode; },
```

```
            toString: function () { return this.errorCode.toString() }
        };

        oXmlDom.__initError__();

        oXmlDom.addEventListener("load", function () {
            this.__initError__();
            this.__changeReadyState__(4);
        }, false);

        return oXmlDom;

    } else {
        throw new Error("Your browser doesn't support an XML DOM object.");
    }
}

Document.prototype.load = function (sURL) {
    this.__initError__();
    this.__changeReadyState__(1);
    this.__load__(sURL);
};

Document.prototype.loadXML = function (sXml) {

    this.__initError__();
    this.__changeReadyState__(1);

    var oParser = new DOMParser();
    var oXmlDom = oParser.parseFromString(sXml, "text/xml");

    while (this.firstChild) {
        this.removeChild(this.firstChild);
    }

    for (var i=0; i < oXmlDom.childNodes.length; i++) {
        var oNewNode = this.importNode(oXmlDom.childNodes[i], true);
        this.appendChild(oNewNode);
    }

    this.__checkForErrors__();
    this.__changeReadyState__(4);
};
```

Notice that `initError()` is always called before the `readyState` is set to `1`. Likewise, `checkForErrors()` is always called just before `readyState` is set to `4` (which is why it must be called in the `onload` event handler). These methods must called in order because `onreadystatechange` is called each time the `readyState` changes. If there is old data in the `parseError` object, it must be reset before `onreadystate-change` is called, otherwise the old data could cause confusion. Along the same lines, the `parseError` object must contain the right data after `readyState` changes to `4` because all processing should be done by then.

With this code added, it's now possible to write one set of code that runs in both Internet Explorer and Mozilla to handle parsing errors:

```
var oXmlDom = new XmlDom();
oXmlDom.onreadystatechange = function () {
    if (oXmlDom.readyState == 4) {

        if (oXmlDom.parseError != 0) {
            var oError = oXmlDom.parseError;
            alert("An error occurred:\nError Code: "
                  + oError.errorCode + "\n"
                  + "Line: " + oError.line + "\n"
                  + "Line Pos: " + oError.linepos + "\n"
                  + "Reason: " + oError.reason);

        }
    }
};

oXmlDom.load("errors.xml");
```

This example loads an XML file with errors in it. When the `readyState` property is set to `4` (the file is loaded and parsed), the value of `parseError` is checked to see if it isn't equal to zero (which indicates an error). If an error has occurred, an alert is displayed with the error code, line number, line position (column number), and reason for the error.

The complete code

In this chapter, I jumped around a lot as I developed the code. Here's a look at the complete code (note that it makes use of the browser detection code created earlier in the book):

```
function XmlDom() {
    if (window.ActiveXObject) {
        var arrSignatures = ["MSXML2.DOMDocument.5.0", "MSXML2.DOMDocument.4.0",
                             "MSXML2.DOMDocument.3.0", "MSXML2.DOMDocument",
                             "Microsoft.XmlDom"];

        for (var i=0; i < arrSignatures.length; i++) {
            try {

                var oXmlDom = new ActiveXObject(arrSignatures[i]);

                return oXmlDom;

            } catch (oError) {
                //ignore
            }
        }

        throw new Error("MSXML is not installed on your system.");

    } else if (document.implementation && document.implementation.createDocument) {
```

```
            var oXmlDom = document.implementation.createDocument("","",null);

            oXmlDom.parseError = {
                valueOf: function () { return this.errorCode; },
                toString: function () { return this.errorCode.toString() }
            };

            oXmlDom.__initError__();

            oXmlDom.addEventListener("load", function () {
                this.__checkForErrors__();
                this.__changeReadyState__(4);
            }, false);

            return oXmlDom;

        } else {
            throw new Error("Your browser doesn't support an XML DOM object.");
        }
    }

    if (isMoz) {

        Document.prototype.readyState = 0;
        Document.prototype.onreadystatechange = null;

        Document.prototype.__changeReadyState__ = function (iReadyState) {
            this.readyState = iReadyState;

            if (typeof this.onreadystatechange == "function") {
                this.onreadystatechange();
            }
        };

        Document.prototype.__initError__ = function () {
            this.parseError.errorCode = 0;
            this.parseError.filepos = -1;
            this.parseError.line = -1;
            this.parseError.linepos = -1;
            this.parseError.reason = null;
            this.parseError.srcText = null;
            this.parseError.url = null;
        };

        Document.prototype.__checkForErrors__ = function () {

            if (this.documentElement.tagName == "parsererror") {

                var reError = />([\s\S]*?)Location:([\s\S]*?)Line Number (\d+), Column
    (\d+):<sourcetext>([\s\S]*?)(?:\-*\^)/;

                reError.test(this.xml);

                this.parseError.errorCode = -999999;
                this.parseError.reason = RegExp.$1;
```

```
            this.parseError.url = RegExp.$2;
            this.parseError.line = parseInt(RegExp.$3);
            this.parseError.linepos = parseInt(RegExp.$4);
            this.parseError.srcText = RegExp.$5;
        }
    };


    Document.prototype.loadXML = function (sXml) {

        this.__initError__();

        this.__changeReadyState__(1);

        var oParser = new DOMParser();
        var oXmlDom = oParser.parseFromString(sXml, "text/xml");

        while (this.firstChild) {
            this.removeChild(this.firstChild);
        }

        for (var i=0; i < oXmlDom.childNodes.length; i++) {
            var oNewNode = this.importNode(oXmlDom.childNodes[i], true);
            this.appendChild(oNewNode);
        }

        this.__checkForErrors__();

        this.__changeReadyState__(4);

    };

    Document.prototype.__load__ = Document.prototype.load;

    Document.prototype.load = function (sURL) {
        this.__initError__();
        this.__changeReadyState__(1);
        this.__load__(sURL);
    };

    Node.prototype.__defineGetter__("xml", function () {
        var oSerializer = new XMLSerializer();
        return oSerializer.serializeToString(this, "text/xml");
    });

}
```

XPath Support in Browsers

Because XML was being used for so many kinds of data, it became necessary to create a means to locate data inside of XML code. The answer to this problem is XPath, which is a small language used specifically to locate a single node or multiple nodes that match a particular pattern. Although an in-depth discussion of XPath is beyond the scope of this book, a brief introduction is in order.

Introduction to XPath

Every XPath expression has two parts: a context node and a node pattern. The context node provides the context from which the node pattern should begin. The node pattern is a string made up of one or more node selectors.

For instance, consider the following XML document:

```
<?xml version="1.0"?>
<employees>
    <employee title="Software Engineer">
        <name>Nicholas C. Zakas</name>
    </employee>
    <employee title="Salesperson">
        <name>Jim Smith</name>
    </employee>
</employees>
```

And consider this XPath expression:

```
employee/name
```

If the context node is `<employees/>`, then the previous XPath expression matches both `<name>Nicholas C. Zakas</name>` and `<name>Jim Smith</name>`. In the expression, both `employee` and `name` refer to tag names of XML elements in the order in which they appear from the context node; the slash indicates a parent-to-child relationship. In essence, the XPath expression says, "Starting from `<employees/>`, match any `<name/>` elements located under any `<employee/>` element that is a child of the reference node."

To select only the first `<employee/>` element's `<name/>` element, the XPath expression is the following:

```
employee[position() = 1]/name
```

In XPath, the square brackets notation is used to provide more specific information about an element. This example uses the XPath `position()` function, which returns the element's position under its parent element. The first child node is in position `1`, so comparing `position()` to `1` matches only the first `<employee/>` element. Then, the slash and `name` match the `<name/>` element under that first `<employee/>` element.

You can use a variety of ways to match elements in addition to their names and positions. Suppose you want to select all `<employee/>` elements with the `title` attribute equal to `"Salesperson"`, the XPath expression would be the following:

```
employee[@title = "Salesperson"]
```

In this expression, the `@` symbol is short for `attribute`.

XPath is a very powerful expression that can make finding specific nodes within a DOM Document much easier. Because of this, both IE and Mozilla made sure to include XPath support in their DOM implementations.

If you'd like to learn more about XPath, consider picking up XPath 2.0: Programmer's Reference (Wiley Publishing, Inc., ISBN 0-7645-6910-4).

XPath support in IE

Microsoft saw fit to build XPath support right into the XML DOM object. Each node has two methods that can be used to retrieve nodes matching an XPath pattern: `selectNodes()`, which returns a collection of nodes matching a pattern, and `selectSingleNode()`, which returns the first node that matches a given pattern.

Using the same data as the previous section, you can select all `<name/>` elements that are children of an `<employee/>` element by using the following code:

```
var lstNodes = oXmlDom.documentElement.selectNodes("employee/name");
```

Because `selectNodes()` is called as a method of `oXmlDom.documentElement`, the document element is considered the context node for the XPath expression. The method returns a `NodeList` containing all elements that match the given pattern, meaning that you can iterate through the elements like so:

```
for (var i=0; i < lstNodes.length; i++) {
    alert(lstNodes[i]);
}
```

Even if there are no matches to a given pattern, a `NodeList` is still returned. If it is empty, its `length` property is equal to `0`.

> **The result of `selectNodes()` is a *living* list. So, if you update the document with another element that matches the XPath expression, that element is automatically added to the `NodeList` in the appropriate position.**

If you want only the first element matching the pattern, then `selectSingleNode()` is the method to use:

```
var oElement = oXmlDom.documentElement.selectSingleNode("employee/name");
```

The `selectSingleNode()` method returns an `Element` as the function value if found, otherwise it returns `null`.

XPath support in Mozilla

As you may have guessed, Mozilla supports the XPath according to the DOM standard. A DOM Level 3 addition called DOM Level 3 XPath defines interfaces to use for evaluating XPath expressions in the DOM. Unfortunately, this standard is more complicated than Microsoft's fairly straightforward approach.

Although a handful of XPath-related objects exist, the two most important ones are `XPathEvaluator` and `XPathResult`. An `XPathEvaluator` is used to evaluate an XPath expression with a method named, appropriately enough, `evaluate()`.

The `evaluate()` method takes five arguments: the XPath expression, the context node, a namespace resolver, the type of result to return, and an `XPathResult` object to fill with the result (usually `null`).

The third argument, the namespace resolver, is necessary only when the XML code uses an XML namespace, and so typically is left as `null`. The fourth argument, the type of result to return, is one of 10 constants values:

- `XPathResult.ANY_TYPE` — Returns the type of data appropriate for the XPath expression
- `XPathResult.ANY_UNORDERED_NODE_TYPE` — Returns a node set of matching nodes, although the order may not match the order of the nodes within the document
- `XPathResult.BOOLEAN_TYPE` — Returns a Boolean value
- `XPathResult.FIRST_ORDERED_NODE_TYPE` — Returns a node set with only one node, which is the first matching node in the document
- `XPathResult.NUMBER_TYPE` — Returns a number value
- `XPathResult.ORDERED_NODE_ITERATOR_TYPE` — Returns a node set of matching nodes in the order in which they appear in the document. This is the most commonly used result type.
- `XPathResult.ORDERED_NODE_SNAPSHOT_TYPE` — Returns a *node set snapshot*, capturing the nodes outside of the document so that any further document modification doesn't affect the node list. The nodes in the node set are in the same order as they appear in the document.
- `XPathResult.STRING_TYPE` — Returns a string value
- `XPathResult.UNORDERED_NODE_ITERATOR_TYPE` — Returns a node set of matching nodes, although the order may not match the order of the nodes within the document
- `XPathResult.UNORDERED_NODE_SNAPSHOT_TYPE` — Returns a node set snapshot, capturing the nodes outside of the document so that any further document modification doesn't affect the node set. The nodes in the node set are not necessarily in the same order as they appear in the document.

The type of result you specify determines how to retrieve the value of the result. Here's a typical example:

```
var oEvaluator = new XPathEvaluator();
var oResult = oEvaluator.evaluate("employee/name", oXmlDom.documentElement, null,
                                  XPathResult.ORDERED_NODE_ITERATOR_TYPE, null);

if (oResult != null) {
    var oElement = oResult.iterateNext();
    while(oElement) {
        alert(oElement.tagName);
        oElement = oResult.iterateNext();
    }
}
```

This example uses the `XPathResult.ORDERED_NODE_ITERATOR_TYPE` result, which is the most commonly used result type. If no nodes match the XPath expression, `evaluate()` returns `null`; otherwise, it returns an `XPathResult` object. If the result is a node iterator, whether it be ordered or unordered, you use the `iterateNext()` method repeatedly to retrieve each matching node in the result. When there are no further matching nodes, `iterateNext()` returns `null`. Using a node iterator, it's possible to create a `selectNodes()` method for Mozilla:

```
Element.prototype.selectNodes = function (sXPath) [
    var oEvaluator = new XPathEvaluator();
    var oResult = oEvaluator.evaluate(sXPath, this, null,
```

```
                                            XPathResult.ORDERED_NODE_ITERATOR_TYPE,
                                            null);

        var aNodes = new Array;

        if (oResult != null) {
            var oElement = oResult.iterateNext();
            while(oElement) {
                aNodes.push(oElement);
                oElement = oResult.iterateNext();
            }
        }

        return aNodes;

    };
```

The `selectNodes()` method is added to the `Element` class to mimic the behavior in IE. When `evaluate()` is called, it uses the `this` keyword as the context node (which is also how IE works). Then, a result array (`aNodes`) is filled with all the matching nodes. You can use this new method like so:

```
var aNodes = oXmlDom.documentElement.selectNodes("employee/name");
for (var i=0; i < aNodes.length; i++) {
    alert(aNodes[i].xml);
}
```

If you specify a snapshot result type (either ordered or unordered), you must use the `snapshotItem()` and `snapshotLength()` methods, as in the following example:

```
var oEvaluator = new XPathEvaluator();
var oResult = oEvaluator.evaluate("employee/name", oXmlDom.documentElement, null,
                                  XPathResult.ORDERED_NODE_SNAPSHOT_TYPE, null);

if (oResult != null) {
    for (var i=0; i < oResult.snapshotLength; i++) {
        alert(oResult.snapshotItem(i).tagName);
    }
}
```

In this example, `snapshotLength` returns the number of nodes in the snapshot and `snapshotItem()` returns the node in a given position in the snapshot (similar to `length` and `item()` in a `NodeList`).

The `XPathResult.FIRST_ORDERED_NODE_TYPE` result returns the first matching node, which is accessible through the `singleNodeValue` property:

```
var oEvaluator = new XPathEvaluator();
var oResult = oEvaluator.evaluate("employee/name", oXmlDom.documentElement, null,
                                  XPathResult.FIRST_ORDERED_NODE_TYPE, null);

alert(oResult.singleNodeValue.xml);
```

As you may have guessed, this code can be used to mimic the IE `selectSingleNode()` method:

```
Element.prototype.selectSingleNode = function (sXPath) {
    var oEvaluator = new XPathEvaluator();
    var oResult = oEvaluator.evaluate(sXPath, this, null,
                                      XPathResult.FIRST_ORDERED_NODE_TYPE, null);

    if (oResult != null) {
        return oResult.singleNodeValue;
    } else {
        return null;
    }
}
```

This method can then be used the same as the one in IE:

```
var oNode = oXmlDom.documentElement.selectSingleNode("employee/name");
alert(oNode);
```

The last section of `XPathResult` types are the Boolean type, number type, and string type. Each of these result types returns a single value using the `booleanValue`, `numberValue`, and `stringValue` properties, respectively. For the Boolean type, the evaluation typically returns `true` if at least one node matches the XPath expression and returns `false` otherwise:

```
var oEvaluator = new XPathEvaluator();
var oResult = oEvaluator.evaluate("employee/name", oXmlDom.documentElement, null,
                                  XPathResult.BOOLEAN_TYPE, null);
alert(oResult.booleanValue);
```

In this example, if any nodes match `"employee/name"`, the `booleanValue` property is equal to `true`.

For the number type, the XPath expression must use an XPath function that returns a number, such as `count()`, which counts all the nodes that match a given pattern:

```
var oEvaluator = new XPathEvaluator();
var oResult = oEvaluator.evaluate("count(employee/name)", oXmlDom.documentElement,
                                  null, XPathResult.BOOLEAN_TYPE, null);
alert(oResult.numberValue);
```

This code outputs the number of nodes that match `"employee/name"` (which is 2). If you try using this method without one of the special XPath functions, `numberValue` is equal to `NaN`.

For the string type, the `evaluate()` method finds the first node matching the XPath expression, then returns the value of the first child node, assuming the first child node is a text node. If not, the result is an empty string. Here's an example:

```
var oEvaluator = new XPathEvaluator();
var oResult = oEvaluator.evaluate("employee/name", oXmlDom.documentElement, null,
                                  XPathResult.STRING_TYPE, null);

alert(oResult.stringValue);
```

The previous code outputs `"Nicholas C. Zakas"`, because that is the first text node in the first `<name/>` element under an `<employee/>` element.

If you feel like living dangerously, you can use the `XPathResult.ANY_TYPE`. By specifying this result type, `evaluate()` returns the most appropriate result type based on the XPath expression. Typically, this result type is a Boolean value, number value, string value, or an unordered node iterator. To determine which result type has been returned use the `resultType` property:

```
var oEvaluator = new XPathEvaluator();
var oResult = oEvaluator.evaluate("employee/name", oXmlDom.documentElement, null,
                                  XPathResult.STRING_TYPE, null);

if (oResult != null) {
    switch(oResult.resultType) {
        case XPath.STRING_TYPE:
            //handle string type
            break;
        case XPath.NUMBER_TYPE:
            //handle number type
            break;
        case XPath.BOOLEAN_TYPE:
            //handle boolean type
            break;
        case XPath.UNORDERED_NODE_ITERATOR_TYPE:
            //handle unordered node iterator type
            break;
        default:
            //handle other possible result types

    }
}
```

As you can tell, XPath evaluation in Mozilla is much more complicated than IE, but also much more powerful. By using the custom `selectNodes()` and `selectSingleNode()` methods, you can perform XPath evaluation in both browsers using the same code.

XSLT Support in Browsers

A sibling language to XML, eXtensible Stylesheet Language Transformations (XSLT) allows the manipulation and transformation of XML code into almost any other text-based form. Presently, many developers use XSLT to transform XML into HTML, but this is just one use (see Figure 15-1).

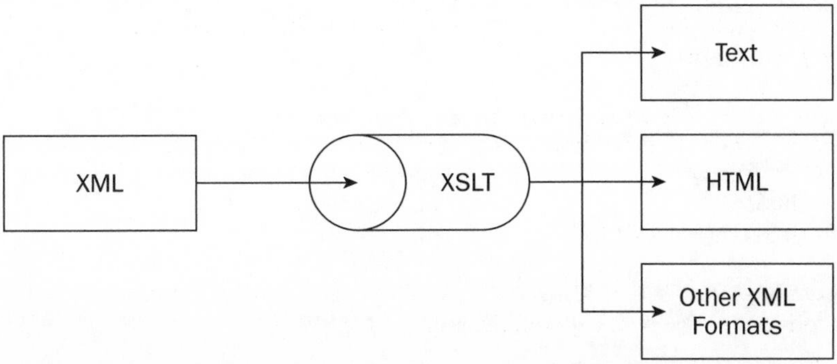

Figure 15-1

XSLT files are called style sheets and are made up of a number of *templates*. A template pertains to a specific part of an XML file (using XPath) and determines what text is output for that section. By defining templates for various elements and conditions, and XSLT style sheet becomes a sort of XML parser. For example, consider the XML used earlier:

```
<?xml version="1.0"?>
<employees>
    <employee title="Software Engineer">
        <name>Nicholas C. Zakas</name>
    </employee>
    <employee title="Salesperson">
        <name>Jim Smith</name>
    </employee>
</employees>
```

Now suppose you'd like to display the list of employees in the following HTML format:

```
<html>
    <head>
        <title>Employees</title>
    </head>
    <body>
        <ul>
            <li>Nicholas C. Zakas, <em>Software Engineer</em></li>
            <li>Jim Smith, <em>Salesperson</em></li>
        </ul>
    </body>
</html>
```

Essentially, you just want to pull the contents of the `<name/>` element out and put it into an unordered list. Then you want to pull out the title attribute of `<employee/>` and place it next to the name inside of a `<em/>` element. To make this happen, you can create an XSLT style sheet:

```
<?xml version="1.0"?>
<xsl:stylesheet version="1.0" xmlns:xsl="http://www.w3.org/1999/XSL/Transform">

    <xsl:output method="html" />

    <xsl:template match="/">
        <html>
            <head>
                <title>Employees</title>
            </head>
            <body>
                <ul>
                    <xsl:apply-templates select="*" />
                </ul>
            </body>
        </html>
    </xsl:template>

    <xsl:template match="employee">
        <li><xsl:value-of select="name" />, <em><xsl:value-of select="@title"
/></em></li>
```

```
    </xsl:template>

</xsl:stylesheet>
```

As you can see, XSLT is actually another language based on XML. The document element is `<xsl:stylesheet/>`, which also specifies the version of XSLT being used (1.0) and the namespace URL. Without this information, an XSLT processor can't properly use the style sheet.

The next line contains the `<xsl:output/>` element, which specifies the rules by which the output should be handled. For the `method` attribute, three possible values exist: html, xml, and text. When you use `"html"`, the parser treats the output as HTML, meaning that the strict XML rules are not applied; `"xml"` forces all XML rules to be applied to the output, whereas `"text"` only outputs the content contained outside of elements.

Next come the templates. The first template matches the document element, as indicated by `match="/".`; the `/` XPath expression always refers to the document element. There is HTML code inside the template, right up until the `<xsl:apply-templates/>` element, which tells the parser to apply any matching templates to the child nodes (which is an XPath expression for any child node). Because a template is defined that matches that pattern, processing continues.

Inside the second template, notice the `<li>` element. Immediately following is the `<xsl:value-of/>` element, which is used to output a value from the source XML. The `select` attribute is another XPath expression, `"name"`, which tells the transformer to output the text value of the `<name/>` element (which is the text contained inside of it). After that, there's a comma, then the opening `<em>` tag, followed by another `<xsl:value-of/>` element. This time, the `select` attribute points to the `title` attribute of `<employee/>` and so the transformer outputs that value.

When this XSLT style sheet is run against the XML file, the result is the HTML shown previously. Although this is a simple example, it does show some of the unique capabilities of XSLT.

If you'd like to learn more about XSLT, consider picking up XSLT 2.0: Programmer's Reference, 3rd Edition (Wiley Publishing, Inc., ISBN 0-7645-6909-0).

XSLT support in IE

Beginning with MSXML 3.0, Internet Explorer fully supports XSLT 1.0. If you are still using Internet Explorer 5.0 or 5.5, you should install a new version of MSXML manually; if you are using IE 6.0, then you already have at least MSXML 3.0.

The simplest way to conduct an XSLT transformation is to load the source XML and the XSLT file each into their own DOMs and then use the proprietary `transformNode()` method:

```
oXmlDom.load("employees.xml");
oXslDom.load("employees.xslt");
var sResult = oXmlDom.transformNode(oXslDom);
```

This example loads a DOM with XML and a DOM with the XSLT style sheet (note that you can load XSLT into an XML DOM because it is just another form of XML). Then, the third line calls the `transformNode()` method on the document, passing in the DOM containing the XSLT code as its only argument. The variable `sResult` is then filled with a string resulting from the transformation.

You don't need to start the transformation from the document level; every node has the `transformNode()` method. The following are all valid:

```
sResult = oXmlDom.documentElement.transformNode(oXslDom);
sResult = oXmlDom.documentElement.childNodes[1].transformNode(oXslDom);
sResult = oXmlDom.getElementsByTagName("name")[0].transformNode(oXslDom);
sResult = oXmlDom.documentElement.firstChild.lastChild.transformnode(oXslDom);
```

If you call `transformNode()` from anywhere other than the document element, you start the transformation at that spot. The XSLT style sheet, however, still has access to the full XML document from which that node came.

The more complicated way to use XSLT in IE is to use an XSL template and processor. To do so, you must use a few more ActiveX controls from the MSXML library. First, the XSLT file must be loaded into a free-threaded DOM document, which behaves just like a regular DOM document but is thread-safe:

```
var oXslDom = new ActiveXObject("MSXML2.FreeThreadedDOMDocument");
oXslDom.async = false;
oXslDom.load("employees.xsl");
```

After the free-threaded DOM document is created and loaded, it must be assigned to an XSL template, which is another ActiveX object:

```
var oTemplate = new ActiveXObject("MSXML2.XSLTemplate");
oTemplate.stylesheet = oXslDom;
```

The XSL template is then used to create an XSL processor (you guessed it, another ActiveX object):

```
var oProcessor = oTemplate.createProcessor();
```

With the processor created, you set the `input` property equal to the XML DOM node to transform and then call the `transform()` method:

```
oProcessor.input = oXmlDom;
oProcessor.transform();
```

The resulting string is then accessible from the output property:

```
var sResult = oProcessor.output;
```

All this code mimics the functionality of `transformNode()`. You may be wondering why anyone would use the XSL template/processor methodology if it does the same thing as `transformNode()`. The answer is that the processor allows you more control over XSLT.

For example, XSLT style sheets accept parameters that can be passed in and used as local variables. Consider the following style sheet:

```
<?xml version="1.0"?>
<xsl:stylesheet version="1.0" xmlns:xsl="http://www.w3.org/1999/XSL/Transform">

    <xsl:output method="html" />
```

```
    <xsl:param name="message" />

    <xsl:template match="/">
        <html>
            <head>
                <title>Employees</title>
            </head>
            <body>
               <ul>
                   <xsl:apply-templates select="*" />
               </ul>
               <p>Message: <xsl:value-of select="$message" /></p>
            </body>
        </html>
    </xsl:template>

    <xsl:template match="employee">
        <li><xsl:value-of select="name" />, <em><xsl:value-of select="@title"
/></em></li>
    </xsl:template>

</xsl:stylesheet>
```

This style sheet adds two lines of code. The first is an `<xsl:param/>` element that defines a parameter named `message`. The second line outputs the `message` by using the `<xsl:value-of/>` element (the dollar sign indicates that this is a local variable, not an element or an attribute).

To set the value of `message`, you use the `addParameter()` method before calling `transform()`. The `addParameter()` method takes two arguments, the name of the parameter to set (as specified in `<xsl:param/>`'s name attribute) and the value to assign it (most often a string, but can be a number or Boolean as well):

```
oProcessor.input = oXmlDom.documentElement;
oProcessor.addParameter("message", "Hello World!");
oProcessor.transform();
```

By setting a value for the parameter, the output now becomes the following:

```
<html>
    <head>
        <title>Employees</title>
    </head>
    <body>
        <ul>
            <li>Nicholas C. Zakas, <em>Software Engineer</em></li>
            <li>Jim Smith, <em>Salesperson</em></li>
        </ul>
        <p>Message: Hello World!</p>
    </body>
</html>
```

As you can see, the value passed in through JavaScript is correctly output to the HTML result. If you use parameters in this way, you can make style sheets more extensible by incorporating different behaviors based on parameters.

Another advanced feature of the XSL processor is the capability to set a mode of operation. In XSLT, it's possible to define a mode for a template. When a `mode` is defined, the template isn't run unless `<xsl:apply-templates />` is specifically called with its `mode` attribute. For example:

```
<xsl:stylesheet version="1.0" xmlns:xsl="http://www.w3.org/1999/XSL/Transform">

    <xsl:output method="html" />

    <xsl:param name="message" />

    <xsl:template match="/">
        <html>
            <head>
                <title>Employees</title>
            </head>
            <body>
                <ul>
                    <xsl:apply-templates select="*" />
                </ul>
                <p>Message: <xsl:value-of select="$message" /></p>
            </body>
        </html>
    </xsl:template>

    <xsl:template match="employee">
        <li><xsl:value-of select="name" />, <em><xsl:value-of select="@title"
/></em></li>
    </xsl:template>

    <xsl:template match="employee" mode="position-first">
        <li><em><xsl:value-of select="@title" /></em>, <xsl:value-of select="name"
/></li>
    </xsl:template>

</xsl:stylesheet>
```

This style sheet defines a template with its `mode` attribute set to `"position-first"` (note that you can name a mode whatever you want; there are no predefined modes). Inside of this template, the employee's position is output first, and the employee name is output second. In order to use this template, the `<xsl:apply-templates/>` element must have its `mode` set to `"position-first"` as well. If you use this style sheet, it has the same output as the previous one, displaying the employee name first and the position second. If, however, you use this style sheet and set the mode to `"position-first"` using JavaScript, it outputs the employee's position first:

```
oProcessor.input = oXmlDom;
oProcessor.addParameter("message", "Hello World!");
oProcessor.setStartMode("position-first");
oProcessor.transform();
```

The `setStartMode()` method accepts only one argument, which is the mode to set to. Just like `addParameter()`, this must be called before `transform()`.

If you are going to do multiple transformations using the same style sheet, you can reset the processor after each transformation. When you call the `reset()` method, the input and output properties are cleared and the processor is ready to be used again:

```
oProcessor.reset();
```

Because the processor has compiled the XSLT style sheet, it is faster to make repeat transformations versus using `transformNode()`.

> **MSXML only supports XSLT 1.0. Development on MSXML has stopped since the movement to the .NET framework. It is expected that, at some point in the future, JavaScript will have access to the XML and XSLT .NET objects.**

XSLT support in Mozilla

Beginning in Mozilla 1.2, a new object called `XSLTProcessor` has been available to JavaScript developers in order to enable client-side XSLT transformations. This object uses Mozilla's built-in XSLT processor, Transformiix, to enable this functionality.

The first step in the transformation is to load both the XML and XSLT into DOMs:

```
oXmlDom.load("employees.xml");
oXslDom.load("employees.xslt");
```

Then, create the `XSLTProcessor` and use the `importStylesheet()` method to assign the XSLT DOM:

```
var oProcessor = new XSLTProcessor()
oProcessor.importStylesheet(oXslDom);
```

The last step is to call either `transformToDocument()` or `transformToFragment()` with the XML DOM as an argument to produce a result. As you may have guessed, `transformToDocument()` returns a new DOM document as its result and `transformToFragment()` returns a new document fragment as its result. Generally speaking, you should use `transformToDocument()` unless you intend to add the result directly to an existing document; then you should use `transformToFragment()`.

When using `transformToDocument()`, just pass in the XML DOM and use the result as another completely different DOM:

```
var oResultDom = oProcessor.transformToDocument(oXmlDom);
alert(oResultDom.xml);
```

When using `transformToFragment()`, pass in the XML DOM as well as the document you intend to add the result to. This ensures that the new document fragment is valid in the destination document:

```
var oResultFragment = oProcessor.transformToDocument(oXmlDom, document);
var oDiv = document.getElementById("divResult");
oDiv.appendChild(oResultFragment);
```

In the previous example, the processor creates a fragment owned by the `document` object. This enables the fragment to be added to a `<div/>` element existing in the page.

This all makes perfect sense when the output method for XSLT is either HTML or XML, but what about when the output is text? To solve this problem, Mozilla creates an XML document with a single element, `<transformiix:result/>`, that contains all the text output. So, using text output from an XSLT file still results in a valid document or document fragment.

Keeping this in mind, it's possible to create a `transformNode()` method for Mozilla:

```
Node.prototype.transformNode = function (oXslDom) {

    var oProcessor = new XSLTProcessor();
    oProcessor.importStylesheet(oXslDom);

    var oResultDom = oProcessor.transformToDocument(this);
    var sResult = oResultDom.xml;

    if (sResult.indexOf("<transformiix:result") > -1) {
        sResult = sResult.substring(sResult.indexOf(">") + 1,
                                    sResult.lastIndexOf("<"));
    }

    return sResult;
};
```

This method creates a result document using the given XSLT DOM. The resulting XML code is then stored in `sResult` using the `xml` property defined earlier in the chapter. That code is then checked to see if it contains `<transformiix:result/>`. If it does, then the XML part is stripped out (by taking only the string between the first greater-than symbol and the last less-than symbol). Lastly, `sResult` is returned. Using this method, you can create code to run in both Mozilla and IE:

```
var oXmlDom = new XmlDom();
var oXslDom = new XmlDom();

oXmlDom.async = false;
oXslDom.async = false;

oXmlDom.load("employees.xml");
oXslDom.load("employees.xslt");

alert(oXmlDom.transformNode(oXslDom));
```

The `XSLTProcessor` in Mozilla also allows you to set XSLT parameters. The `setParameter()` method accepts three arguments: the namespace URI, the parameter local name, and the value to set. Typically, the namespace URI is `null` and the local name is simply the parameter's name. This method must be called prior to `transformToDocument()` or `transformToFragment()`:

```
var oProcessor = new XSLTProcessor()
oProcessor.importStylesheet(oXslDom);
oProcessor.setParameter(null, "message", "Hello World!");
var oResultDom = oProcessor.transformToDocument(oXmlDom);
```

Two other methods are related to parameters, `getParameter()` and `removeParameter()`, which are used to get the current value of a parameter and remove the parameter value, respectively. Each method takes the namespace URI (once again, typically `null`) and the local name of the parameter:

```
var oProcessor = new XSLTProcessor()
oProcessor.importStylesheet(oXslDom);
oProcessor.setParameter(null, "message", "Hello World! ");

alert(oProcessor.getParameter(null, "message");    //outputs "Hello World!"
oProcessor.removeParameter(null, "message");

var oResultDom = oProcessor.transformToDocument(oXmlDom);
```

These methods aren't used often and are provided mostly for convenience.

Summary

This chapter introduced you to the client-side XML capabilities of Internet Explorer and Mozilla. The first topic covered was the use of an XML DOM model on the client side using the MSXML library in IE and a native, DOM-compliant interface in Mozilla. You learned the differences between the two models, as well as a way to bridge that gap to make your code more straightforward.

Next, you learned about each browser's support for XPath, a language designed to locate specific parts of an XML document. This section included discussion on the different implementations in IE and Mozilla. You learned that IE chose a non-standard API, whereas Mozilla chose to follow the DOM Level 3 XPath specification. Again, methods of creating a standard cross-browser approach were discussed.

The last topic discussed was the concept of JavaScript XML manipulation and transformation using XSLT. You learned about the two ways to accomplish XSLT transformations using JavaScript in IE, through the `transformNode()` method and the `XSLProcessor` object. You also learned about Mozilla's `XSLTProcessor` object and how it compares to IE's implementation. Using `XSLTProcessor`, you learned how to create a `transformNode()` method for use in Mozilla.

Remember, the material covered in this chapter only works in Internet Explorer and Mozilla because other browsers have not yet implemented any JavaScript support for XML, XPath, and XSLT.

16

Client-Server Communication

Traditionally, JavaScript had no interaction with the server at all; it merely performed operations on the client and then got out of the way to allow the server to do its job. As the Web progressed, however, JavaScript was required to send data back to the server and/or receive a response. This need led to several methods of establishing such communication.

Cookies

Despite reports in newspapers and magazines citing security issues, a cookie is nothing more than a small amount of information that a Web page places on a user's machine. Cookies have traditionally been used to store login information so that users aren't required to log in each time they access a restricted page from the same machine (the ubiquitous Remember Me check box on many login pages).

Because a cookie is unique to a user, Web sites can determine when a user has returned to the site, as well as what pages he visits; this is where the privacy concerns arise. Yes, a cookie can be used to track where you go on an individual Web site, but it cannot be used to grab personal information (such as credit card numbers, e-mail addresses, and so on), as many novices think.

Cookies were the first method of client-server interaction that JavaScript took advantage of. Every time the browser makes a request to a server, the cookies for that server are sent along with any other information. This enables JavaScript to set a cookie on the client that a server can read later.

Cookie ingredients

No chocolate chips and sugar here! These cookies are made up of small pieces of information:

- Name — Each cookie is represented by a unique name. This name can be made up of letters, numbers, and underscores. Unlike JavaScript variables, cookie names are not case-sensitive, so *myCookie* and *MyCookie* are considered to be the same. In reality, however, it's always best to treat the cookie names as case-sensitive because some server software may treat them as such.
- Value — The string value stored in the cookie. This value must be encoded using `encodeURIComponent()` before being stored in order to avoid losing data or corrupting the cookie. The total number of bytes stored in the name and value combined cannot exceed 4095 bytes, or roughly 4 KB.
- Domain — For security purposes, Web sites cannot access cookies created by other domains. When a cookie is created, the domain is stored as a part of the cookie. It is possible to override this setting, however, to allow a different Web site to access the cookie, although that is typically not the case.
- Path — Another security feature of cookies, paths restrict access of a cookie to a particular directory on a Web server. For example, you can specify that the cookie only accessible from `http://www.wrox.com/books` so pages at `http://www.wrox.com` can't access it even though the request comes from the same domain.
- Expiration — When the cookie should be deleted. By default, all cookies are deleted when the browser closes; however, it is possible to set another time for the deletion. This value is set as a date in GMT format (using the `toGMTString()` method of the `Date` object) and specifies an exact time when the cookie should be deleted. Because of this, a cookie can remain on a user's machine even after the browser is closed. When you set an expiration time that has already occurred, the cookie is deleted immediately.
- Secure Flag — A true/false value indicating whether the cookie can be accessed only from secure sites (those using SSL and the `https` protocol). Setting this value to `true` provides another layer of protection to ensure the cookie isn't accessible by other Web sites.

Other security restrictions

To ensure that cookies aren't used maliciously, browsers place certain restrictions on cookie usage:

- Each domain can only store up to 20 cookies on a user's machine.
- The total size of the cookie cannot exceed 4096 bytes.
- The total number of cookies allowed on a user's machine is 300.

In addition, newer browsers place strict control on cookies, allowing the user to block all cookies, block cookies from unknown sites, or be alerted every time a cookie is being created.

Cookies in JavaScript

Dealing with cookies in JavaScript is a little complicated because of a notoriously poor interface. The `document` object has a property called `cookie`, which is a single string containing all cookies accessible by the given page. The `cookie` property is also unique in that setting it to a specific value only alters the cookies available to the page; it doesn't actually change the value of `cookie` itself. This functionality is part of the BOM and, as such, isn't guided by any sort of specifications (which explains its lack of logic).

To create a cookie, you must create a string in the following format:

```
cookie_name=cookie_value; expires=expiration_time; path=domain_path;
domain=domain_name; secure
```

Only the first part of the string, specifying the name and value, is mandatory to set a cookie; all other parts are optional. This string is then set to the `document.cookie` property to create the cookie. For example, to set a simple cookie, use the following:

```
document.cookie = "name=Nicholas";
document.cookie = "book=" + encodeURIComponent("Professional JavaScript");
```

Reading the value of `document.cookie` gives access to these cookies, along with all others accessible from the given page. If you display the value of `document.cookie` after running the two lines of the previous code, it equals `"name=Nicholas; book=Professional%20JavaScript"`. Even if other cookie attributes are specified, such as an expiration time, `document.cookie` only returns the name and value of each cookie with a semicolon separating the cookies.

Because creating and reading cookies requires remembering this format, most developers use functions to handle the details. The function to create a cookie is the easiest:

```
function setCookie(sName, sValue, oExpires, sPath, sDomain, bSecure) {
    var sCookie = sName + "=" + encodeURIComponent(sValue);

    if (oExpires) {
        sCookie += "; expires=" + oExpires.toGMTString();
    }

    if (sPath) {
        sCookie += "; path=" + sPath;
    }

    if (sDomain) {
        sCookie += "; domain=" + sDomain;
    }

    if (bSecure) {
        sCookie += "; secure";
    }

    document.cookie = sCookie;
}
```

The `setCookie()` function systematically builds up a cookie string based on the arguments passed in. Only the first two arguments are required, so the function checks to make sure that each argument exists before it's added to the cookie string. The third argument is expected to be a `Date` object so the `toGMTString()` method can be called. At the end of the function, the `document.cookie` is set with the cookie string. This function is used as follows:

```
setCookie("name", "Nicholas");
setCookie("book", "Professional JavaScript", new Date(Date.parse("Jan 1, 2006")));
setCookie("message", "Hello World! ", new Date(Date.parse("Jan 1, 2006")),
         "/books", "http://www.wrox.com", true);
```

The next function, `getCookie()`, retrieves the value of a cookie when the name is passed in:

```
function getCookie(sName) {

    var sRE = "(?:; )?" + sName + "=([^;]*);?";
    var oRE = new RegExp(sRE);

    if (oRE.test(document.cookie)) {
        return decodeURIComponent(RegExp["$1"]);
    } else {
        return null;
    }

}
```

This function uses a regular expression built out of the name of the cookie. Regular expressions are the easiest way to extract a particular value from `document.cookie` because of the cookie string format. If there's only one cookie, then the string is a simple name and value pair, and the value is all the characters after the equal sign up to the end of the string. If more cookies follow, they are separated by semicolons. This means that the value for any cookie (other than the last one) comprises all characters after the equal sign but before the next semicolon. The regular expression makes it easy to take all this into account, setting up a capturing group to retrieve the cookie value. You can then get the values of cookies like so:

```
var sName = getCookie("name");
var sBook = getCookie("book");
var sMessage = getCookie("message");
```

The last function is `deleteCookie()`, which immediately removes a cookie from the system. As mentioned previously, setting its expiration time to a past date can accomplish this. In order have this work, however, the path and domain information must be the same as when you created the cookie, so these must also be arguments:

```
function deleteCookie(sName, sPath, sDomain) {
    setCookie(sName, "", new Date(0), sPath, sDomain);
}
```

Because `setCookie()` sets all the same information as `deleteCookie()`, it makes sense just to use it and pass in an expiration date that already occurred (in this case, January 1, 1970).

Using these functions, it's easy to manipulate cookies using JavaScript. Even if the server creates cookies, JavaScript can still read them, which is where the real power lies.

Cookies on the server

Of course, using cookies for client-server communication requires additional logic on the server. Server-side technologies such as JSP, ASP.NET, and PHP provide built-in functionality to read, write, and otherwise manipulate cookies. Using JavaScript and one of these server-side languages, you can pass data back and forth using cookies.

JSP

Java Server Pages (JSP) provides a very easy interface for handling cookies. The `request` object, which is instantiated automatically when a JSP is executed, has a method called `getCookies()` that returns an array of `Cookie` objects. Each `Cookie` object has the following methods (from the Javadoc documentation):

- `getComment()` — Returns the comment describing the purpose of this cookie, or `null` if the cookie has no comment
- `getDomain()` — Returns the domain name set for this cookie
- `getMaxAge()` —Returns the maximum age of the cookie, specified in seconds; by default, -1 indicates the cookie will persist until browser shutdown.
- `getName()` — Returns the name of the cookie
- `getPath()` — Returns the path on the server to which the browser returns this cookie
- `getSecure()` — Returns `true` if the browser is sending cookies only over a secure protocol, or `false` if the browser can send cookies using any protocol.
- `getValue()` — Returns the value of the cookie
- `getVersion()` — Returns the version of the protocol this cookie complies with
- `setComment(String purpose)` — Specifies a comment that describes a cookie's purpose.
- `setDomain(String pattern)` — Specifies the domain within which this cookie should be presented
- `setMaxAge(int expiry)` — Sets the maximum age of the cookie in seconds
- `setPath(String uri)` - Specifies a path for the cookie to which the client should return the cookie
- `setSecure(boolean flag)` — Indicates to the browser whether the cookie should only be sent using a secure protocol, such as HTTPS or SSL
- `setValue(String newValue)` — Assigns a new value to a cookie after the cookie is created
- `setVersion(int v)` — Sets the version of the cookie protocol this cookie complies with

To get a specific cookie, it's also necessary to create a function to iterate through each cookie to determine which one you want:

```
<%!
public static Cookie getCookie(HttpServletRequest request, String name) {
    Cookie[] cookies = request.getCookies();

    if (cookies != null) {
```

```
            for (int i=0; i < cookies.length; i++) {
                if (cookies[i].getName().equals(name)) {
                    return cookies[i];
                }
            }
        } else {
            return null;
        }
    }
    %>
```

When this code is inserted into a JSP, you can retrieve the value of a cookie by doing the following:

```
<%
Cookie nameCookie = getCookie(request, "name");
System.out.println("Name is " + nameCookie.getValue());
%>
```

Creating a cookie is equally easy in the JSP world. To create a new cookie, simply instantiate a new `Cookie` object and pass in the name and value. Then, add it to the user's system by using the `addCookie()` method of the response object:

```
<%
    Cookie nameCookie = new Cookie("name", "Nicholas");
    response.addCookie(nameCookie);
%>
```

Alternately, you can add additional data to the cookie before storing it:

```
<%
    Cookie nameCookie = new Cookie("name", "Nicholas");
    nameCookie.setDomain("http://www.wrox.com");
    nameCookie.setPath("/books");
    response.addCookie(nameCookie);
%>
```

To delete a specific cookie, you must first retrieve it and then set its expiration to `0` (JSP cookies use the number of milliseconds as the expiration value):

```
<%
    Cookie cookieToDelete = getCookie("name");
    cookieToDelete.setMaxAge(0);
    response.addCookie(cookieToDelete);
%>
```

ASP.NET

ASP.NET handles cookies in a very similar way to JSP. The `Request` object (automatically created for each ASP.NET page) contains a `Cookies` collection from which all cookies can be read. Each cookie is an instance of `HttpCookie`, which has the following properties:

- `Name` — The name of the cookie
- `Value` — The value of the cookie
- `Expires` — The date when the cookie expires
- `Path` — The path for the cookie
- `Domain` — The domain for the cookie
- `Secure` — A Boolean indicating whether the cookie is secure

Other properties of `HttpCookie` are used when cookies store multiple values, but since those cookies won't work in concert with the JavaScript code in this chapter, they are not listed here.

To read a cookie, you can access it by its name in the `Cookies` collection:

```
Dim cookie as HttpCookie
Dim cookieValue as String
cookie = Request.Cookies("name")
cookieValue = cookie.Value
```

This example reads a cookie with the name `"name"` and assigns the value to the variable `cookieValue`.

To create a new cookie, create a new instance of `HttpCookie` and pass the name and value to the constructor. Then, you set any other properties for the cookie before saving it with a call to `Response.SetCookie()`:

```
Dim cookie as HttpCookie = New HttpCookie("name", "Nicholas");
cookie.Expires = #1/1/2006#;
Response.SetCookie(cookie);
```

Note that the `Expires` property expects a `DateTime` object, not a numeric value as in JSP.

To delete a cookie, just set the `Expires` property to a date in the past:

```
cookie.Expires = DateTime.Now.addDays(-1);
```

PHP

PHP's cookie functions are very straightforward, as is most of the PHP language. To create a cookie, PHP provides a `setcookie()` function that takes the same arguments as the JavaScript `setCookie()` function described in this chapter. The main difference is that the expiration date is specified as a number, just as it is in JSP:

```
bool setcookie ( string name [, string value [, int expire [, string path
                [, string domain [, bool secure]]]]])
```

Calling the function is very easy:

```
<?php
    setcookie("name", "Nicholas");
    setcookie("book", "Professional JavaScript");
?>
```

The one restriction on setting cookies in PHP is that it must be done before anything is output to the client. This is similar to the way the `header()` function works. For instance, this code won't work:

```
<html>
    <head>
<?php
    setcookie("name", "Nicholas");
    setcookie("book", "Professional JavaScript");
?>
```

To retrieve the value of a cookie in PHP, use the `$_COOKIE` associative array with the name of the cookie as the key:

```
<?php
    $name = $_COOKIE["name"];
    $book = $_COOKIE["book"];
?>
```

Note that you cannot retrieve the value of a cookie created with `setcookie()` until the next page loads, meaning that is the following code is impossible:

```
<?php
    setcookie("name", "Nicholas");
    setcookie("book", "Professional JavaScript");
    $name = $_COOKIE["name"];
    $book = $_COOKIE["book"];
?>
```

To delete a cookie in PHP, just use the `setcookie()` method and set the expiration time to `0`:

```
<?php
    setcookie("name", "", 0);
?>
```

Passing cookies between client and server

To communicate to JavaScript, often the server creates a cookie (perhaps in a servlet or other application running on the server) just before a response is sent out. The page that is loaded now has JavaScript designed to retrieve the cookie value.

For example, suppose you are creating a feedback form on a Web site where the user is required to enter a name, e-mail address, and the feedback message. You can make this more user-friendly by allowing the users to save their names and e-mail addresses so the next time they visit and want to leave feedback, both fields are already filled in. Typically, you do this with a Remember Me check box, as in the following form:

```
<form name="feedbackForm" method="post" action="submitfeedback.php">
        <p>Name: <input type="text" name="personName" /><br />
        E-mail Address: <input type="text" name="personEmail" /><br />
```

```
        Feedback: <textarea rows="10" cols="50" name="feedbackText">
                  </textarea><br />
        <input type="checkbox" name="rememberMe" value="yes" /> Remember Me<br />
        <input type="submit" value="Submit Feedback" />
</form>
```

The server-side code (in this case, written in PHP) looks something like this:

```
<?php
    //send e-mail
    mail("you@yourdomain.com", "User Feedback", $feedbackText,
         "From: feedback@{$_SERVER['SERVER_NAME']}");

    //if flag is set, set cookies
    if ($rememberMe == "yes") {
        setcookie("personName", $personName, time() + 1000 * 60 * 60 * 24 * 365);
        setcookie("personEmail", $personEmail, time() + 1000* 60 * 60 * 24 * 365);
    }
?>
<!-- thank you message goes here -->
```

This PHP code first sends the feedback e-mail using PHP's `mail()` function and then checks to see if the user wants to be remembered, meaning that the value of `$rememberMe` equals `yes`. If so, cookies are used to store the user's name and e-mail address. Both cookies are set to expire a year after the current day by using the PHP `time()` function and adding the value of 365 days in milliseconds (1000 milliseconds x 60 seconds x 60 minutes x 24 hours x 365 days).

In PHP, the values of form fields are made accessible as variables with the same name as the form field, so the value in the text box named personName is accessible as a string variable ***`$personName`***.

Remember to include at least the `getCookie()` function on the feedback form page to retrieve the value of each cookie. Then, in the `onload` event handler, look for a cookie containing user information and, if you find it, assign that information back into the form.

```
window.onload = function () {

    var sName = getCookie("personName");
    var sEmail = getCookie("personEmail");

    if (sName && sEmail) {
        var oForm = document.forms["feedbackForm"];
        oForm.personName.value = sName;
        oForm.personEmail.value = sEmail;
    }
};
```

This JavaScript code checks to see if both the person's name and e-mail address have been stored in cookies. If they have, the values are assigned to the appropriate fields in the form. Now, your users won't have to type in the same contact information each time they send feedback (well, at least for a year).

Hidden Frames

A trick that developers have used for a long time is the *hidden frame method*. The basic idea is to create a frame that is 0 pixels high (thus, it's hidden) that can be used by JavaScript to communicate with the server. This type of communication requires two parts: a JavaScript object to handle the communication on the client side and a special page that handles the communication on the server side.

As a very simple example, start out with a frameset:

```
<html>
    <head>
        <title>Hidden Frame Example</title>
    </head>
    <frameset rows="*,0">
        <frame src="HiddenFrameExampleMain.htm" name="mainFrame" />
        <frame src="HiddenFrameExampleBlank.htm" name="hiddenFrame" />
    </frameset>
</html>
```

This frameset is made up of two rows, the second of which has a height of 0 (in Netscape 4.x, frames can't be 0 pixels high, so the frame is still visible). The first frame is where the user is interacting; the second is the hidden frame used to communicate with the server. By default, the second frame is loaded with a blank HTML page.

In the first frame, two functions are defined: one to send the request to the server and one to handle the response. The function that sends the request, called getServerInfo(), just assigns a URL to the hidden frame:

```
function getServerInfo() {
        parent.frames["hiddenFrame"].location.href = "HiddenFrameExampleCom.htm"'
}
```

This function is capable, of course, of attaching extra parameters to the request's query string.

The second function, called handleResponse(), is called when the hidden frame returns from the server. This function can do anything you want to deal with the data that is returned, but for this example, the data is just displayed in an alert:

```
function handleResponse(sResponseText) {
    alert("The server returned: " + sResponseText);
}
```

The page that handles the hidden requests must output a normal HTML page with a <textarea/> element enclosing the returned data. Using <textarea/> makes it easy to deal with multiple lines of data, which is difficult to do when outputting the data directly into JavaScript. This page must also call the handleResponse() function in the main frame with the data that was returned:

```
<html>
    <head>
        <title>Hidden Frame Example (Response)</title>
        <script type="text/javascript">
```

```
            window.onload = function () {
                parent.frames[0].handleResponse(
                                      document.forms["formResponse"].result.value);
            };
        </script>

    </head>
    <body>
        <form name="formResponse">
            <textarea name="result">This is some data coming from the
server.</textarea>
        </form>
    </body>
</html>
```

The important part about this window is the `onload` event handler, which calls the `handleResponse()` function from the first frame, passing in the value contained in the `<textarea/>` element. It's very important that the `handleResponse()` function be called no matter what, even if there is an error, to prevent the JavaScript in the main frame from hanging while waiting for a response.

> *The previous code shows data already inserted into the* **`<textarea/>`** *for illustrative purposes; in reality, this data would be output by some server-side logic.*

When the `getServerInfo()` function is called in the main frame, the request is sent through the hidden frame, and the data is passed back through the `handleResponse()` function and is displayed in an alert. This is obviously a very simplistic example, but it illustrates the basic idea. The added bonus is that this form of client-server communication works in any browser that supports framesets and JavaScript (including older browsers like Netscape Navigator 4.x).

Using iframes

The hidden frame method evolved with the introduction of iframes into HTML. An *iframe* is a frame that can be inserted anywhere in an HTML document, completely disconnected from any frameset. With this innovation, developers changed the hidden frame method to create hidden iframes on the fly for the purpose of communicating with the server.

To make use of iframes, you must make some changes to the `getServerInfo()` function:

```
var oHiddenFrame = null;

function getServerInfo() {
    if (oHiddenFrame == null) {
        oHiddenFrame = document.createElement("iframe");
        oHiddenFrame.name = "hiddenFrame";
        oHiddenFrame.id = "hiddenFrame";
        oHiddenFrame.style.height = "0px";
        oHiddenFrame.style.width = "0px";
        oHiddenFrame.style.position = "absolute";
        oHiddenFrame.style.visibility = "hidden";
        document.body.appendChild(oHiddenFrame);
    }
```

```
        setTimeout(function () {
            frames["hiddenFrame"].location.href = "HiddenFrameExampleCom2.htm";
        }, 10);
    }
```

The first change is the addition of a global variable names `oHiddenFrame`. Because the same frame can be used repeatedly for requests, there's no reason to keep creating new iframes for each request. Instead, this global variable holds a reference to the iframe when it's created. When `getServerInfo()` is called, it first checks to see if an iframe already exists by checking the value of `oHiddenFrame`. If it doesn't exist, the frame is created using the DOM `createElement()` method.

Creating the iframe using the DOM is very specific. Both the `name` and `id` attribute must be set to equal `"hiddenFrame"` in order for this to work in most browsers (some require `name` to be set, others require `id`). Next, the appearance of the frame is specified to have a height and width of `0`, an absolute position, and visibility set to `"hidden"`. All these changes are necessary to ensure that this new addition to the document doesn't disrupt the display. Lastly, the iframe is added to the document body.

When the iframe has been created and added, it takes most browsers (notably Mozilla and Opera) a couple of milliseconds to recognize it as a new frame in the `frames` collection. To take this into account, the `setTimeout()` function is used to create a wait of 10 milliseconds before the request is sent. By the time the request executes, the browsers recognizes the new frame, and it's sent off without a hitch.

The only modification necessary to the page providing the response is to use `parent` instead of `parent.frames[0]` to call `handleResponse()`:

```
<html>
    <head>
        <title>Hidden Frame Example (Response)</title>
        <script type="text/javascript">
            window.onload = function () {
                parent.handleResponse(document.forms["formResponse"].result.value);
            };
        </script>

    </head>
    <body>
        <form name="formResponse">
            <textarea name="result">This is some data coming from the
server.</textarea>
        </form>
    </body>
</html>
```

Now calling `getServerInfo()` has the exact same effect as the previous example using the traditional hidden frame technique. This technique requires, of course, that the browser support iframes in the first place, which leaves older browsers like Netscape Navigator 4.x out of the loop.

HTTP Requests

In many modern browsers, it's possible to initiate HTTP requests directly from JavaScript and get the result back in JavaScript, completely eliminating the need for hidden frames and other such trickery.

At the center of this exciting new capability is an object Microsoft created called the XML HTTP request. This object came along with MSXML but wasn't fully explored until recently. Essentially, an XML HTTP request is a regular HTTP request with added functionality for sending and receiving XML code.

To create a new XML HTTP request in Internet Explorer, you must once again use an `ActiveXObject`:

```
var oRequest = new ActiveXObject("Microsoft.XMLHTTP");
```

Like the XML DOM in IE, the XML HTTP request object has multiple versions, so a function is necessary to make sure you're using the most recent one:

```
function createXMLHTTP() {

    var arrSignatures = ["MSXML2.XMLHTTP.5.0", "MSXML2.XMLHTTP.4.0",
                         "MSXML2.XMLHTTP.3.0", "MSXML2.XMLHTTP",
                         "Microsoft.XMLHTTP"];

    for (var i=0; i < arrSignatures.length; i++) {
        try {

            var oRequest = new ActiveXObject(arrSignatures[i]);

            return oRequest;

        } catch (oError) {
            //ignore
        }
    }

    throw new Error("MSXML is not installed on your system.");
}
```

After you have created it, you can use the `open()` method to specify the request to send. This method takes three arguments: the type of request to send (GET, POST, or any other HTTP method supported by the server); the URL of the request; and a Boolean indicating whether the request should be sent asynchronously or not (the same as you do with the XML DOM `load()` method). For example:

```
oRequest.open("get", "example.txt", false);
```

After opening the request, you must send it by using the `send()` method. This method always requires an argument, which can be `null` most of the time:

```
oRequest.send(null);
```

If you choose to make the request synchronously (setting the third argument to `false`), the JavaScript interpreter waits for the request to return. When the response comes back, it fills the `status` property with the HTTP status of the request (200 is good, 404 means the page wasn't found, and so on). It also fills the `statusText` property with a message describing the status and the `responseText` property with the text received back from the server. Additionally, if the text is XML, it fills the `responseXML` property, which is an XML DOM object constructed from the returned text. For example:

```
var oRequest = createXMLHTTP();
oRequest.open("get", "example.txt", false);
oRequest.send(null);
alert("Status is " + oRequest.status + " (" + oRequest.statusText + ")");
alert("Response text is: " + oRequest.responseText);
```

This example gets a plain text file and displays its contents. The `status` and `statusText` are also displayed.

> **If you run this example locally, the `status` is `0` and the `statusText` is `"Unknown"` because a local file read isn't an actual HTTP request.**

Requesting an XML file also fills the `responseXML` property:

```
var oRequest = createXMLHTTP();
oRequest.open("get", "example.xml", false);
oRequest.send(null);
alert("Status is " + oRequest.status + " (" + oRequest.statusText + ")");
alert("Response text is: " + oRequest.responseText);
alert("Tag name of document element is: " +
      oRequest.responseXML.documentElement.tagname);
```

This example shows the tag name of the document element loaded into the `responseXML` property.

> **This example doesn't work when run locally: It must be run on a server because the XML HTTP object relies on the server-reported mime type to determine if the requested file is an XML document.**

If you decide to send an asynchronous request, you must use the `onreadystatechange` event handler to see when the `readyState` property is equal to `4` (the same as with the XML DOM). All the same properties and methods are used, with the slight alteration that the response properties can't be used until the request has completed:

```
var oRequest = createXMLHTTP();
oRequest.open("get", "example.txt", true);
oRequest.onreadystatechange = function () {
    if (oRequest.readyState == 4) {
        alert("Status is " + oRequest.status + " (" + oRequest.statusText + ")");
        alert("Response text is: " + oRequest.responseText);
    }
}
oRequest.send(null);
```

As in the synchronous calls, the `status`, `statusText`, and `responseText` properties are filled with data.

With asynchronous calls, it's possible to cancel the request altogether by calling the `abort()` method before the `readyState` reaches 4:

```
var oRequest = createXMLHTTP();
oRequest.open("get", "example.txt", true);
oRequest.onreadystatechange = function () {
    if (oRequest.readyState == 3) {
        oRequest.abort();
    } else if (oRequest.readyState == 4) {
        alert("Status is " + oRequest.status + " (" + oRequest.statusText + ")");
        alert("Response text is: " + oRequest.responseText);
    }
}
oRequest.send(null);
```

In this example, the alerts are never displayed because the request is aborted when `readyState` is 3.

Using headers

Every HTTP request sends along with it a group of headers with additional information. In everyday browser use, these headers are hidden because they aren't needed by the end user. However, these headers can be quite necessary to developers, and so the XML HTTP request object provides methods to get and set them.

The first is a method called `getAllResponseHeaders()`, which returns a string containing all the headers attached to the response. Here's a sample of the type of information returned by `getAllResponseHeaders()`:

```
Date: Sun, 14 Nov 2004 18:04:03 GMT
Server: Apache/1.3.29 (Unix)
Vary: Accept
X-Powered-By: PHP/4.3.8
Connection: close
Content-Type: text/html; charset=iso-8859-1
```

From this header information, you can tell that the server is running Apache on Unix with PHP support and the file being returned is an HTML file. If you want to retrieve only one of the headers, you can use the `getResponseHeader()` method with the name of header to retrieve. For example, to retrieve the value of the `"Server"` header, you can do this:

```
var sValue = oRequest.getResponseHeader("Server");
```

Reading request headers is just part of the equation; the other part is setting your own headers on the request before it's sent.

Using the `setRequestHeader()` method, you can set headers on the XML HTTP request before it's sent out. For example:

```
oRequest.setRequestHeader("myheader", "yippee");
oRequest.setRequestheader("weather", "warm");
```

Assuming that you have some server-side logic designed to take these headers into account, you can provide some additional functionality and/or evaluation of requests.

Copycat implementations

This object proved to be so popular among Web developers that other browser makers copied the implementation. Mozilla was the first of the copycats, creating a JavaScript object called `XMLHttpRequest` that behaves exactly the same as Microsoft's version. Both Safari (as of 1.2) and Opera (as of 7.6) copied Mozilla's implementation, creating their own `XMLHttpRequest` objects.

To allow creation of an XML HTTP request in a common way, just add this simple wrapper class to your pages:

```
if (typeof XMLHttpRequest == "undefined" && window.ActiveXObject) {
    function XMLHttpRequest() {

        var arrSignatures = ["MSXML2.XMLHTTP.5.0", "MSXML2.XMLHTTP.4.0",
                             "MSXML2.XMLHTTP.3.0", "MSXML2.XMLHTTP",
                             "Microsoft.XMLHTTP"];

        for (var i=0; i < arrSignatures.length; i++) {
            try {

                var oRequest = new ActiveXObject(arrSignatures[i]);

                return oRequest;

            } catch (oError) {
                //ignore
            }
        }

        throw new Error("MSXML is not installed on your system.");
    }
}
```

This code allows you to use the following line to create an XML HTTP request in all browsers that support it:

```
var oRequest = new XMLHttpRequest();
```

After this point, the XML HTTP request can be used in all supporting browsers as described in the previous sections.

Performing a GET request

The most common type of request on the Web is a GET request. Every time you enter a URL into your browser and click Go, you are sending a GET request to a server.

Parameters to a GET request are attached to the end of the URL with a question mark, followed by name/value pairs separated by an ampersand. For example:

```
http://www.somewhere.com/page.php?name1=value1&name2=value2&name3=value3
```

Each name and value must be encoded for use in a URL (in JavaScript, this can be done using `encodeURIComponent()`). The URL has a maximum size of 2048 characters (2 MB). Everything after the question mark is referred to as the query string, and these parameters are accessible by server-side pages.

To send a GET request using the XML HTTP request object, just place the URL (with all parameters) into the `open()` method and make sure this first argument is `"get"`:

```
oRequest.open("get", "http://www.somewhere.com/page.php?name1=value1", false);
```

Because the parameters must be added to the end of an existing URL, it's helpful to have a function that handles all the details:

```
function addURLParam(sURL, sParamName, sParamValue) {
    sURL += (sURL.indexOf("?") == -1 ? "?" : "&");
    sURL += encodeURIComponent(sParamName) + "=" + encodeURIComponent(sParamValue);
    return sURL;
}
```

The `addURLParam()` function takes three arguments: the URL to add the parameters to, the parameter name, and the parameter value. First, the function checks to see if the URL already contains a question mark (to determine if other parameters already exist). If it doesn't, then the function appends a question mark; otherwise, it adds an ampersand. Next, the name and value are encoded and appended to the end of the URL. The last step is to return the updated URL.

This function can be used to build up a URL for a request:

```
var sURL = "http://www.somwhere.com/page.php";
sURL = addURLParam(sURL, "name", "Nicholas");
sURL = addURLParam(sURL, "book", "Professional JavaScript");
oRequest.open("get", sURL, false);
```

You can then handle the response as usual.

Performing a POST request

The second most common type of HTTP request is a POST. Typically, POST requests are used when entering data into a Web form because they are capable of sending much more data (around 2 GB) than GET requests.

Just like a GET request, the parameters for a POST request must be encoded for use in a URL and separated with an ampersand, although the parameters aren't attached to the URL. When sending a POST request, you pass in the parameters as an argument to the `send()` method:

```
oRequest.open("post", "page.php", false);
oRequest.send("name1=value1&name2=value2");
```

It also helps to have a function for formatting the parameters for a POST request:

```
function addPostParam(sParams, sParamName, sParamValue) {
    if (sParams.length > 0) {
        sParams += "&";
    }
    return sParams + encodeURIComponent(sParamName) + "="
                   + encodeURIComponent(sParamValue);
}
```

This function is similar to the `addURLParam()` function, although `addPostParam()` deals with a string of parameters instead of a URL. The first argument is the existing list of parameters, the second argument is the parameter name, and the third is the parameter value. The function checks whether the length of the parameters string is longer than `0`. If so, then it adds an ampersand to separate the new parameter. Otherwise, it returns the parameter string with the new name and value added. Here's a brief example of its use:

```
var sParams = "";
sParams = addPostParam(sParams, "name", "Nicholas");
sParams = addPostParam(sParams, "book", "Professional JavaScript");
oRequest.open("post", "page.php", false);
oRequest.send(sParams);
```

Even though this looks like a valid POST request, a server-side page expecting a POST actually won't interpret this code correctly. That's because all POST requests sent by a browser have the `"Content-Type"` header set to `"application/x-www-form-urlencoded"`. Fortunately, that can be easily corrected using the `setRequestHeader()` method:

```
var sParams = "";
sParams = addPostParam(sParams, "name", "Nicholas");
sParams = addPostParam(sParams, "book", "Professional JavaScript");
oRequest.open("post", "page.php", false);
oRequest.setRequestHeader("Content-Type", "application/x-www-form-urlencoded");
oRequest.send(sParams);
```

Now this example works just like a form POSTed from a Web browser.

LiveConnect Requests

Netscape Navigator introduced a concept called *LiveConnect*, a capability that enables JavaScript to interact with and use Java classes. To work, the user must have a Java Runtime Environment (JRE) installed, and Java must be enabled in the browser. Almost all modern browsers (with Internet Explorer being the major exception) support LiveConnect, which provides access to all the HTTP-related libraries that Java offers.

Performing a GET request

If you know how to perform a GET request using Java, it's very easy to convert the request into a LiveConnect script. The first step is to create a new instance of `java.net.URL`:

```
function httpGet(sURL) {

    var oURL = new java.net.URL(sURL);

    //...
}
```

Note that when you use LiveConnect, you must furnish the complete name of the class, including the package, to instantiate a Java object. After the URL is created, you open up an input stream and create a reader to get the data back. The preferred way to do this is to create an `InputStreamReader` and then a `BufferedReader` based on it:

```
function httpGet(sURL) {

    var oURL = new java.net.URL(sURL);
    var oStream = oURL.openStream();
    var oReader = new java.io.BufferedReader(new
java.io.InputStreamReader(oStream));

    //...
}
```

With the buffered reader created, all that's left to do is read the data back from the server. A buffered reader gets data line-by-line, so you create a variable to build up the response into the full text. This response text variable (named `sResponseText`) must start out as an empty string, not null, so that string concatenation can be used to build the result:

```
function httpGet(sURL) {

    var oURL = new java.net.URL(sURL);
    var oStream = oURL.openStream();
    var oReader = new java.io.BufferedReader(new
java.io.InputStreamReader(oStream));
    var sResponseText = "";

    var sLine = oReader.readLine();
    while (sLine != null) {
        sResponseText += sLine + "\n";
        sLine = oReader.readLine();
    }

    //...
}
```

Because the buffered reader returns lines, each line must be appended with a new line character to ensure that it remains in the same form, as it should. The last steps are to close the reader and return the response text:

```
function httpGet(sURL) {

    var oURL = new java.net.URL(sURL);
    var oStream = oURL.openStream();
```

```
        var oReader = new java.io.BufferedReader(new
    java.io.InputStreamReader(oStream));
        var sResponseText = "";

        var sLine = oReader.readLine();
        while (sLine != null) {
            sResponseText += sLine + "\n";
            sLine = oReader.readLine();
        }

        oReader.close();
        return sResponseText;
    }
```

Now this function can be used to send a GET request using the same `addURLParam()` function defined earlier:

```
var sURL = "http://www.somwhere.com/page.php";
sURL = addURLParam(sURL, "name", "Nicholas");
sURL = addURLParam(sURL, "book", "Professional JavaScript");
var sData = httpGet(sURL);
```

Unfortunately, you don't get all the same information, such as status, when using LiveConnect. Also, this function creates a synchronous call without the option of creating an asynchronous one. But the advantage is that this works in Netscape Navigator 4.x and most versions of Opera, as well as any other browser that supports LiveConnect.

> **Unlike the XML HTTP request object, LiveConnect requires you to enter the complete URL for the request, starting with `http://`. This is because the Java objects don't have any sort of context for resolving relative URLs.**

Performing a POST request

As discussed earlier, POST requests are slightly different from GET requests in their format and behavior. However, it's possible to send a POST request just as easily as a GET request using LiveConnect. To start, you provide a URL and a parameters string (using `addPostParam()` from earlier in the chapter). Then, you create another `java.net.URL` instance. Unlike last time, this code uses a `Connection` object to facilitate the request:

```
function httpPost(sURL, sParams) {

    var oURL = new java.net.URL(sURL);
    var oConnection = oURL.openConnection();

    //...
}
```

Next, you must determine the settings on the connection. Because a POST request is considered bi-directional, the connection must be set up to accept input and output by using the `setDoInput()`

and `setDoOutput()` methods. Additionally, the connection shouldn't use any cached data, so `setUseCaches()` is given an argument of `false`. Just as with the XML HTTP request object, you must set the `"Content-Type"` header to the appropriate value using the `setRequestProperty()` method:

```
function httpPost(sURL, sParams) {

    var oURL = new java.net.URL(sURL);
    var oConnection = oURL.openConnection();

    oConnection.setDoInput(true);
    oConnection.setDoOutput(true);
    oConnection.setUseCaches(false);
    oConnection.setRequestProperty("Content-Type",
                                   "application/x-www-form-urlencoded");

    //...
}
```

After the connection has been set up, it's possible to get an output stream for the request. It's on the output stream that you place the parameter string using the `writeBytes()` method. After that, a call to `flush()` sends the data along, and the stream can be closed:

```
function httpPost(sURL, sParams) {

    var oURL = new java.net.URL(sURL);
    var oConnection = oURL.openConnection();

    oConnection.setDoInput(true);
    oConnection.setDoOutput(true);
    oConnection.setUseCaches(false);
    oConnection.setRequestProperty("Content-Type",
                                   "application/x-www-form-urlencoded");

    var oOutput = new java.io.DataOutputStream(oConnection.getOutputStream());
    oOutput.writeBytes(sParams);
    oOutput.flush();
    oOutput.close();

    //...
}
```

The next part of the function gets the input stream for the connection and reads the data in, line-by-line, similar to the `httpGet()` function. Then, the input stream is closed, and the response text returned as the function value:

```
function httpPost(sURL, sParams) {

    var oURL = new java.net.URL(sURL);
    var oConnection = oURL.openConnection();

    oConnection.setDoInput(true);
    oConnection.setDoOutput(true);
    oConnection.setUseCaches(false);
```

```
        oConnection.setRequestProperty("Content-Type",
                                       "application/x-www-form-urlencoded");

        var oOutput = new java.io.DataOutputStream(oConnection.getOutputStream());
        oOutput.writeBytes(sParams);
        oOutput.flush();
        oOutput.close();

        var sLine = "", sResponseText = "";

        var oInput = new java.io.DataInputStream(oConnection.getInputStream());
        sLine = oInput.readLine();

        while (sLine != null){
            sResponseText += sLine + "\n";
            sLine = oInput.readLine();
        }

        oInput.close();

        return sResponseText;
    }
```

Using this function, you can submit a POST request like the following:

```
var sParams = "";
sParams = addPostParam(sParams, "name", "Nicholas");
sParams = addPostParam(sParams, "book", "Professional JavaScript");
var sData = httpPost("http://www.somewere.com/reflectpost.php",sParams);
```

Intelligent HTTP Requests

With two completely different ways of doing HTTP requests, it's helpful to have a common set of functions to avoid headaches. First, you determine whether you can use the XML HTTP request object or not. To check, see if the type of `XMLHttpRequest` is equal to `"object"` or if `window.ActiveXObject` is valid:

```
var bXmlHttpSupport = (typeof XMLHttpRequest == "object" || window.ActiveXObject);
```

Next, create a placeholder object named `Http` to contain the methods:

```
var Http = new Object;
```

The get() method

The first method is called, simply, `get()`, and its purpose is to perform a GET request on a specific URL. This method has two arguments: the URL to send the request to and a callback function. Callback functions are used in many programming languages to notify the developer when a request has concluded. For the `get()` method, the callback function has the following format:

```
function callback_function(sData) {
    //interpret data here
}
```

The callback function is passed the data retrieved from the HTTP request as its only argument, `sData`. You are then free to do as you please with the result. In order to use the callback function, you must consider a couple of details.

First, when using the XML HTTP request object to perform a GET, it's easy to set up a callback function by using an asynchronous request and calling the function when the `readyState` is equal to `4`:

```
Http.get = function (sURL, fnCallback) {

    if (bXmlHttpSupport) {

        var oRequest = new XMLHttpRequest();
        oRequest.open("get", sURL, true);
        oRequest.onreadystatechange = function () {
            if (oRequest.readyState == 4) {
                fnCallback(oRequest.responseText);
            }
        }
        oRequest.send(null);

    }

    //...

};
```

This section of code uses JavaScript closures to allow the callback function, `fnCallback`, to be used in the `onreadystatechange` event handler. Because `fnCallback` is just a function, it's called like any other function and passed the `responseText` of the request when `readyState` is `4`.

If there is no support for the XML HTTP request, you must check whether LiveConnect is enabled. Unfortunately, no property or setting indicates whether LiveConnect can be used. The only way to tell is to ensure that Java is enabled in the browser by using the `navigator.javaEnabled()` method and determine whether the type of `java` and `java.net` are not undefined:

```
Http.get = function (sURL, fnCallback) {

    if (bXmlHttpSupport) {

        var oRequest = new XMLHttpRequest();
        oRequest.open("get", sURL, true);
        oRequest.onreadystatechange = function () {
            if (oRequest.readyState == 4) {
                fnCallback(oRequest.responseText);
            }
        }
        oRequest.send(null);
```

```
        } else if (navigator.javaEnabled() && typeof java != "undefined"
                && typeof java.net != "undefined") {

            //LiveConnect code here
        }

    };
```

After you have determined if LiveConnect can be used, it's time to use the `httpGet()` function. To make the call almost asynchronous, use the `setTimeout()` function to delay its start for a short time; then call the callback function with the `httpGet()` call as its argument.

```
    Http.get = function (sURL, fnCallback) {

        if (bXmlHttpSupport) {

            var oRequest = new XMLHttpRequest();
            oRequest.open("get", sURL, true);
            oRequest.onreadystatechange = function () {
                if (oRequest.readyState == 4) {
                    fnCallback(oRequest.responseText);
                }
            }
            oRequest.send(null);

        } else if (navigator.javaEnabled() && typeof java != "undefined"
                && typeof java.net != "undefined") {

            setTimeout(function () {
                fnCallback(httpGet(sURL));
            }, 10);
        }
        //...
    };
```

The only thing left to do is to provide a message for those unfortunate users whose browsers can't make HTTP requests from JavaScript:

```
    Http.get = function (sURL, fnCallback) {

        if (bXmlHttpSupport) {

            var oRequest = new XMLHttpRequest();
            oRequest.open("get", sURL, true);
            oRequest.onreadystatechange = function () {
                if (oRequest.readyState == 4) {
                    fnCallback(oRequest.responseText);
                }
            }
            oRequest.send(null);

        } else if (navigator.javaEnabled() && typeof java != "undefined"
                && typeof java.net != "undefined") {
```

```
        setTimeout(function () {
            fnCallback(httpGet(sURL));
        }, 10);
    } else {
        alert("Your browser doesn't support HTTP requests.");
    }

};
```

With this completed, it's now possible to send a GET request using common code in a variety of browsers:

```
var sURL = "http://www.somewhere.com/page.php";
sURL = addURLParam(sURL, "name", "Nicholas");
sURL = addURLParam(sURL, "book", "Professional JavaScript");
Http.get(sURL, function(sData) {
    alert("Server sent back: " + sData);
});
```

Remember, because LiveConnect requires you to enter the full URL for the request, you must always supply the full URL with the `Http.get()` method, just in case the browser uses LiveConnect.

The post() method

The `post()` method works similarly to the `get()` method, except it needs three arguments: the URL, the parameters string, and the callback function. For simplicity's sake, a callback function for `post()` uses the same format as the one used for `get()`.

The method itself is also remarkably similar to `get()`, using the same `if..else` statements. The only differences are the setting of the request header, the number of arguments, and the fact that the method sends a POST request instead of a GET. Here's the method:

```
Http.post = function (sURL, sParams, fnCallback) {

    if (bXmlHttpSupport) {

        var oRequest = new XMLHttpRequest();
        oRequest.open("post", sURL, true);
        oRequest.setRequestHeader("Content-Type",
                                  "application/x-www-form-urlencoded");
        oRequest.onreadystatechange = function () {
            if (oRequest.readyState == 4) {
                fnCallback(oRequest.responseText);
            }
        }
        oRequest.send(sParams);

    } else if (navigator.javaEnabled() && typeof java != "undefined"
            && typeof java.net != "undefined") {

        setTimeout(function () {
            fnCallback(httpPost(sURL, sParams));
```

```
        }, 10);
    } else {
        alert("Your browser doesn't support HTTP requests.");
    }

};
```

Using this method, it's now possible to perform POST requests in a variety of browsers using the same code:

```
var sURL = "http://www.somewhere.com/page.php";
var sParams = "";
sParams = addPostParam(sParams, "name", "Nicholas");
sParams = addPostParam(sParams, "book", "Professional JavaScript");
oHttp.post(sURL, function(sData) {
    alert("Server sent back: " + sData);
});
```

Once again, always supply the full URL when using this method.

Practical Uses

Although all this client-server communication stuff is really cool, it also has some practical applications. You can, for example, create a search page that never unloads. It simply makes a request to get new data for each new search you submit. This is the model used by Amazon.com's new Web search engine, A9 (`http://www.a9.com`).

After your first A9 search, you can choose to add images, movies, books, and other information to your search results by clicking on the various options on the right of the screen. As you do, a new area in the page opens up, and new search results are loaded using the hidden iframe technique discussed earlier in the chapter.

Several Web sites use JavaScript client-server communication to provide search results. One such site, the Bitflux blog (`http://blog.bitflux.ch/`), uses a XML HTTP request objects for its *LiveSearch* capability. This cool technique uses the `onkeypress` event handler to detect what the user types into the search box. For each new letter entered into the text box, the site does a search and displays its results in a layer directly on the page, without ever reloading the page.

Another good use for this type of communication is to provide functionality that isn't available in JavaScript. For instance, you may want to validate some data the user has entered against a database. Using the `onblur` event handler, you can make a request back to the database to determine if the value is valid, and then present an error message to the user if is the data is not valid. The possibilities really are endless.

Summary

In this chapter you learned all about JavaScript client-server communication. The chapter began with a discussion of the oldest form of client-server communication involving JavaScript: cookies. You learned that cookies are small pieces of data stored on the user's machine that can be used for a variety of purposes. Because cookies are accessible to both the server and through JavaScript, this provides a unique way for the two to communicate.

The chapter then moved on to make requests back to the server using hidden frames. The implementation of this technique using both hidden frames and iframes was discussed.

You then learned how newer browsers enable you to make HTTP requests directly back to the server from JavaScript without the need for hidden frames. The XML HTTP request object was introduced, and you learned how to send both GET and POST requests to the server. For those browsers that don't support XML HTTP requests, you learned about using LiveConnect, the capability to interface with Java from JavaScript, to send GET and POST requests.

Lastly, you learned how to create a cross-browser method of executing both GET and POST requests. This method takes advantage of the browser's built-in capabilities, whether these use the XML HTTP request or LiveConnect to make the requests.

17

Web Services

In the past two years, Web services have become a hot topic. Thanks to Microsoft's .NET initiative, developers are now able to create, deploy, and access Web services quickly and easily. The idea is simple: Servers can provide (*publish*) Web services over the Internet. Any developer can access this functionality from a program, seamlessly providing the functionality encapsulated by the Web service. But Web services aren't available only to compiled programs; they are also available to Web pages using JavaScript.

A Quick Web Service Primer

Understanding what Web services are is the key to understanding how to use them. This section covers some of the basics.

What is a Web service?

Think of a Web service as a function call, only this function exists on a server while being called from the client. This necessitates that messages be sent back and forth between the client (called the consumer) and the server. These messages are in a format called SOAP (Simple Object Access Protocol), which is an XML-based wrapper for Web service messages. The SOAP message is transferred using a standard HTTP request (although other protocols can be used as well) with a couple of special request headers:

- `SOAPAction` — Gives a specific SOAP action to take if there are multiple possible actions. If only one action is possible, this is typically left as an empty string.
- `Content-Type` — Set to text/xml

The SOAP message itself is contained inside an *envelope*, which is used to transfer the Web service call to and from the server. A typical SOAP message looks like this:

```
<soap:Envelope xmlns:n="custom namespace goes here"
     xmlns:soap="http://schemas.xmlsoap.org/soap/envelope/"
     xmlns:soapenc="http://schemas.xmlsoap.org/soap/encoding/"
     xmlns:xs="http://www.w3.org/2001/XMLSchema"
     xmlns:xsi="http://www.w3.org/2001/XMLSchema-instance">

   <soap:Body soap:encodingStyle="http://schemas.xmlsoap.org/soap/encoding/">
      <!-- method-specific XML goes here -->
   </soap:Body>

</soap:Envelope>
```

In the case of the client sending the message, the XML in `<soap:Body/>` includes a method to call and parameters. When the server sends the message, `<soap:Body/>` includes the result(s) of the call. The result can be a single value or a complex data type with multiple values.

Naturally, it is important that the client sends the SOAP message in the correct format, but how does a developer know how to format the message? This is where WSDL comes in.

WSDL

Web Services Description Language (WSDL, pronounced wizdel) is used to describe the capabilities, format, and other important information about Web services. WSDL files define the various operations a Web service provides. *Operations* are specific remote functions that can be called for a given service (a Web service can have one or more operations). It helps to think of a Web service as an object with one or more methods; the object itself represents the service whereas the operations are considered the methods.

The basic sections of a WSDL file are the following:

- Types — Defines the types used for the Web service calls. These types are based on XML Schema data types and can represent simple types — such as numbers or strings — or complex types, similar to objects that have properties.
- Messages — Defines the input arguments and the output value for a given operation. Each operation gets two message definitions, one for the operation request and one for the response.
- Port Type — Defines the operations that are available from the Web service.
- Bindings — Defines the format of the messages sent and received with each operation.
- Service — Defines how to access the Web service operations.

A standard WSDL file has the following format:

```
<definitions name="name_of_service"
    targetNamespace="target_namespace"
    xmlns:tns="location_of_wsdl"
    xmlns:xsd="http://www.w3.org/2001/XMLSchema"
    xmlns:soap="http://schemas.xmlsoap.org/wsdl/soap/"
```

```
    xmlns="http://schemas.xmlsoap.org/wsdl/">
    <types>
        <!-- custom types defined here -->
    </types>
    <message name="request_name">
        <!-- parameters -->
    </message>
    <message name="response_name">
        <!-- return value(s) -->
    </message>
    <portType name="porttype_name">
      <operation name="method_name">
         <input message="tns:request_name" />
         <output message="tns:response_name" />
       </operation>
    </portType>
    <binding name="binding_name" type="tns:porttype_name">
        <soap:binding style="rpc" transport="http://schemas.xmlsoap.org/soap/http"
/>
        <operation name="method_name">
             <soap:operation soapAction="soap_action" />
             <input>
                 <soap:body use="encoded" namespace="urn_string"
encodingStyle="http://schemas.xmlsoap.org/soap/encoding/" />
             </input>
             <output>
                <soap:body use="encoded" namespace="urn_string"
encodingStyle="http://schemas.xmlsoap.org/soap/encoding/" />
            </output>
        </operation>
    </binding>
    <service name="service_name">
        <documentation><!-- description of service --></documentation>
        <port name="port_name" binding="tns:binding_name">
            <soap:address location="webservice_url" />
        </port>
    </service>
</definitions>
```

As you can tell, WSDL files can be very complex and actually aren't intended for the human eye. The intended use of these files is to provide programs (and their components) with enough information to call the Web service operations on their own. With most Web service toolkits, you never have to write a WSDL file; it is automatically generated for you.

Sometimes, however, you must locate certain pieces of information within a WSDL file in order to access a Web service (depending on the type of development you are doing). The important pieces of information in a WSDL file are the following:

- The name of the method you want to call (`method_name`)
- The SOAP action (`soap_action`)
- The target namespace for the input of the method you want call (`urn_string`)

- The port name (`port_name`)
- The location of the service (`webservice_url`)

To understand how to find this information, it's best to look at a real WSDL file.

The Temperature Service is a Web service provided by XMethods (`http://www.xmethods.net`), a public Web service publisher as well as a directory of publicly accessible Web services. This service accepts a five-digit U.S. zip code and then returns the current temperature for that area. The WSDL file for the Temperature Service looks like this:

```
<definitions name="TemperatureService"
   targetNamespace="http://www.xmethods.net/sd/TemperatureService.wsdl"
   xmlns:tns="http://www.xmethods.net/sd/TemperatureService.wsdl"
   xmlns:xsd="http://www.w3.org/2001/XMLSchema"
   xmlns:soap="http://schemas.xmlsoap.org/wsdl/soap/"
   xmlns="http://schemas.xmlsoap.org/wsdl/">

    <message name="getTempRequest">
        <part name="zipcode" type="xsd:string" />
    </message>
    <message name="getTempResponse">
        <part name="return" type="xsd:float" />
    </message>
    <portType name="TemperaturePortType">
        <operation name="getTemp">
            <input message="tns:getTempRequest" />
            <output message="tns:getTempResponse" />
        </operation>
    </portType>
    <binding name="TemperatureBinding" type="tns:TemperaturePortType">
        <soap:binding style="rpc" transport="http://schemas.xmlsoap.org/soap/http"
/>
        <operation name="getTemp">
            <soap:operation soapAction="" />
            <input>
                <soap:body use="encoded" namespace="urn:xmethods-Temperature"
encodingStyle="http://schemas.xmlsoap.org/soap/encoding/" />
            </input>
            <output>
                <soap:body use="encoded" namespace="urn:xmethods-Temperature"
encodingStyle="http://schemas.xmlsoap.org/soap/encoding/" />
            </output>
        </operation>
    </binding>
    <service name="TemperatureService">
        <documentation>Returns current temperature in a given U.S.
zipcode</documentation>
        <port name="TemperaturePort" binding="tns:TemperatureBinding">
            <soap:address
location="http://services.xmethods.net:80/soap/servlet/rpcrouter" />
        </port>
    </service>
</definitions>
```

The pertinent information (highlighted previously) from this file is the following:

- The only operation is called `getTemp`.
- The SOAP action for `getTemp` is "" (an empty string).
- The target namespace for the input to `getTemp` is `urn:xmethods-Temperature`.
- The name of the port is `TemperaturePort`.
- The service location is `http://services.xmethods.net:80/soap/servlet/rpcrouter`.

Depending on the type of consumer used to access Web services, you may need to know some or all the previous information.

Web Services in Internet Explorer

The folks over at Microsoft were kind enough to create an HTML component (also called a behavior) that hides a lot of the ugly details from developers who wish to consume Web services. An HTML component is essentially a COM component defined using XML and JavaScript. HTML components can have properties, methods, and support custom events, making them ideal for creating functionality that doesn't exist in the browser by default. The downside is that only Internet Explorer supports HTML components, and thus Microsoft's `WebService` component does not work in other browsers. The `WebService` component is available for free from Microsoft's Web site (`http://msdn.microsoft.com/library/default.asp?url=/workshop/author/webservice/webservice.asp`).

Using the WebService component

After the `webservice.htc` file is downloaded, place it in the directory with your JavaScript files. You can then access the functionality by applying it to an HTML element. To do this, use the `style` attribute and the custom `behavior` CSS attribute:

```
<div style="behavior(webservice.htc)"></div>
```

After doing this, the HTML element takes on all the properties, methods, and events of the `WebService` component. To use the component as a JavaScript object, just assign an ID to the element:

```
<div id="service" style="behavior(webservice.htc)"></div>
```

Then use the `document.getElementById()` method to retrieve a reference:

```
var oService = document.getElementById("service");
```

Next, you need to specify a Web service to use by calling `useService()`. The `useService()` method accepts two parameters: the WSDL file describing the service and a friendly name for the service. A typical call looks like this:

```
oService.useService(sUrl, "FriendlyName");
```

When this method is called, the component downloads the WSDL file and uses it to create JavaScript objects and methods to access the Web service. This functionality is available through an object identified by the friendly name specified in the `useService()` method:

```
var oSpecificService = oService.FriendlyName;
```

This object has a method, `callService()`, that makes the actual request to the server. The method accepts a function name to call and any number of parameters to pass to that function. When executed, `callService()` returns a call ID that is necessary when you want to retrieve a value from the result. The format for this method call is as follows:

```
iCallID = oService.FriendlyName.callService(sFuncName, sParam0, sParam1..sParamN);
```

The Web service call is then made asynchronously, so JavaScript execution won't stop and wait for the response from the server. Instead, you must use the `onresult` event handler to handle the response. You can either assign the event handler right in the HTML or by using JavaScript. Using HTML, just treat `onresult` as if it were any other event handler:

```
<div id="service" style="behavior(webservice.htc)" onresult="alert('Done') "></div>
```

To assign the event handler using JavaScript, assign the function directly to the `onresult` property:

```
oService.onresult = function () {
    alert("Done");
};
```

When the `result` event is fired, it creates an `event` object with a special property called `result`. This property contains an object with all the details about the response. The properties of `result` are listed in the following table:

Property Name	Data Type	Description
`error`	`Boolean`	True if an error occurred during the call
`errorDetail`	`Object`	An object that contains all the information about an error, if one occurs. The two properties of interest are the code that returns the error code and the string that returns a human-readable error message.
`id`	`Number`	The call ID created by `callService()`
`raw`	`String`	The raw SOAP code being sent back from the server
`SOAPHeader`	`Array`	An array of headers used for the call
`value`	`Variant`	The value returned by the call. This may be a simple data type, like a number or string, or it could be an object.

So how do you use this object? Here's a simple example:

```
var iCallID = -1;

oService.onresult = function () {
```

```
        var oResult = window.event.result;

        if (oResult.id == iCallID) {
            if (oResult.error) {
                alert("An error occurred: " + oResult.errorDetail.string);
            } else {
                alert("Received back: " + oResult.value);
            }
        }
    };

    iCallID = oService.FriendlyName.callService(...);
```

In this code, the `onresult` event handler first checks whether the result it's handling is the response for the appropriate request (in this way, a single `WebService` object can handle multiple requests). If the ID of the result matches the call ID, the result is processed. The function ensures that there are no errors; if an error occurs, the detailed error message is returned; otherwise the returned value is displayed.

Of course, it is up to you if you want to use the `value` property directly or use the `raw` property to parse the returned SOAP code on your own.

WebService component example

This example uses the Temperature Service described in the sample WSDL earlier in the chapter. Because the Microsoft `WebService` component requires you to know only the WSDL location and the name of the operation you want to call, you don't need the WSDL to get this working.

The Web page for this example consists of a text box (with the ID `"txtZip"`) and a button (labeled `"Get Temperature"`). The user enters a zip code into the text box and then clicks the button to get the temperature in that zip code (he calls the Web service). Of course, you also need an element to which you can assign the `WebService` component. Here is the HTML:

```
<html>
    <head>
        <title>IE Web Service Example</title>
        <script type="text/javascript">
            //...
        </script>
    </head>
    <body>
        <p><input type="text" id="txtZip" size="10" /><input type="button"
value="Get Temperature" onclick="callWebService()" />
        <div id="service" style="behavior:url(webservice.htc)"
onresult="onWebServiceResult()"></div>
    </body>
</html>
```

The JavaScript to run this page is fairly simple:

```
var iCallID = null;
var sWSDL = "http://www.xmethods.net/sd/2001/TemperatureService.wsdl";
```

```
function callWebService() {

    var sZip = document.getElementById("txtZip").value;
    var oService = document.getElementById("service");

    oService.useService(sWSDL, "Temperature");
    iCallID = oService.Temperature.callService("getTemp", sZip);
}

function onWebServiceResult() {
    var oResult = event.result;

    if (oResult.id == iCallID) {

        var oDiv = document.getElementById("divResult");

        if (oResult.error) {
            alert("An error occurred:" + oResult.errorDetail.string);
        } else {
            alert("It is currently " + oResult.value
                  + " degrees in that zip code.");
        }
    }
}
```

The first function, `callWebService()`, gets the zip code from the text box and calls the Web service. It first loads the WSDL file with the friendly name `Temperature`. The next line uses the `callService()` method, passing in the operation name and the zip code.

The other function, `onWebServiceResult()`, displays the result of the call. This function uses the same basic algorithm as the example earlier to check whether the result ID is equal to the call ID. It then reports either an error or the returned value.

> **Windows XP Service Pack 2 has some significant effects on the WebService component. First, you must specify that files ending with .htc are served with a mime type of `text/x-component` (this must be done on the server). Second, the WebService component is forbidden access to external Web sites, meaning that you can only access Web services hosted on the same server as the page attempting to call them.**

Web Services in Mozilla

Beginning in Mozilla 1.0, Web developers have had access to Web services. Mozilla currently supports two ways of handling Web services: using a low-level SOAP API or using WSDL proxy objects (introduced in Mozilla 1.4). Before exploring the WSDL-based functionality, it's important to understand the basic SOAP API.

Enhanced privileges

Contacting a different server using JavaScript is expressly prohibited in Mozilla for security reasons. This is certainly troublesome given that the very nature of Web services requires contacting different servers. There is the capability, however, to have the user approve a script and allow it cross-domain access. By default, Mozilla installations don't allow this type of advanced privilege (once again, for security reasons). You can, however, override this setting in the `all.js` configuration file (which is located in `Program Files\Mozilla\defaults\pref` on Windows-based machines).

Open up `all.js` in any text editor and find the following line:

```
pref("signed.applets.codebase_principal_support", false);
```

Change this line to:

```
pref("signed.applets.codebase_principal_support", true);
```

After setting this preference, you must close all running Mozilla instances and restart the browser. This is only the first step. The second step is to request the Universal Browser Read privilege, which allows cross-domain communication. Here's how:

```
try {
        netscape.security.PrivilegeManager.enablePrivilege("UniversalBrowserRead");
} catch (e) {
      alert("Script not signed.");
}
```

When the second line is executed, the user is presented with a dialog box explaining that the script would like enhanced privileges. The user can then click Yes to allow the privileges, or No to deny them (Figure 17-1).

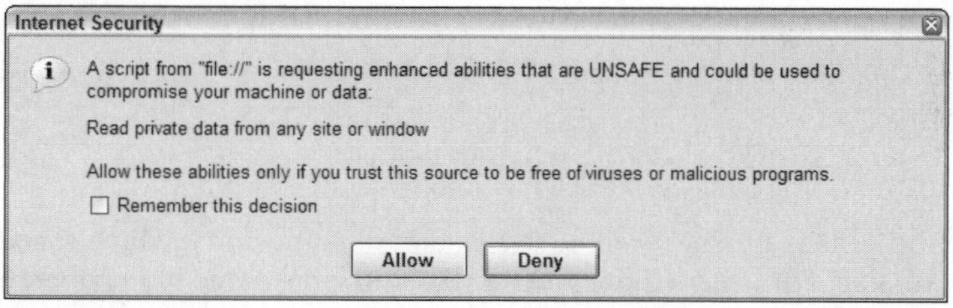

Figure 17-1

If the user clicks Yes, the code continues on; if the user clicks No, an error occurs and, in the previous example, the alert indicates to the script that the privilege has been denied.

> **Note that you cannot assume that users have their browsers set up to allow the UniversalBrowserRead privilege. If you plan on using this method of Web service invocation, you must create a signed script (explained more fully in Chapter 19, "Deployment Issues"). Also note that this is Mozilla-specific code that does not run properly in IE, so it is important to do a browser detect before requesting a signature for your script.**

Using the SOAP methods

Mozilla provides a very large amount of SOAP functionality, but because this is an older API, only the most common usage is discussed here.

The basis of Mozilla's SOAP functionality is the `SOAPCall` object. This object embodies the entire Web service request and response. The `SOAPCall` object is created just like any other object:

```
var oSoapCall = new SOAPCall();
```

The next step is to set the location of the Web service by assigning it to the `SOAPCall` object's `transportURI` property:

```
oSoapCall.transportURI = "http://address_of_service";
```

This address is *not* the address of the WSDL, as it is in Internet Explorer. Instead, this is the actual URL for the Web service itself (as defined in the WSDL element `<soap:address location="http://address_of_service" />` element).

After setting the location of the service, you create an array to handle the SOAP parameters. This is just a regular array filled with `SOAPParameter` objects. The `SOAPParameter` constructor takes two arguments: the value of the parameter, and the name (in that order). The array can contain any number of parameters and is created like this:

```
var arrParams = new Array;
arrParams[0] = new SOAPParameter("value", "name");
```

Next you create the `SOAPCall` object's `encode()` method on the array, which encodes the parameters for proper transmission. For this method, you need to know the name of the operation and the target namespace:

```
oSOAPCall.encode(0, "operation_name", "target_namespace", 0, null,
arrParams.length, arrParams);
```

The arguments are:

- The version of SOAP used:
    - 0 for version 1.1
    - 1 for version 1.2
    - 65535 if the version is unknown

- The operation name (such as "getTemp")
- The target namespace.
- The number of header blocks provided for the request
- An array of SOAPHeaderBlock objects (not required for most Web services)
- The number of parameters being passed
- Any array of SOAPParameter objects

Lastly, use the asyncInvoke() method to make the call to the server. This method takes only one argument, a function that is called when the Web service returns a result. If you have a function named onWebServiceResult, the code looks like this:

```
oSoapCall.asyncInvoke(onWebServiceResult);
```

The callback function itself has the following format:

```
function onWebServiceResult(oResponse, oSoapCall, iError) {
    //...
}
```

Callback functions accept three arguments: a SOAPResponse object, the SOAPCall object, and an error code. The SOAPResponse object contains all the information about a successful request. The properties are listed in the following table.

Property	Description
actionURI	The SOAPAction header string (may be an empty string)
body	The <Body/> element of the SOAP response
encoding	A SOAPEncoding object indicating the encoding of the response
envelope	The <Envelope/> element of the SOAP response
fault	A SOAPFault object if a fault occurs; null otherwise
header	The <Header/> element of the SOAP response or null if it doesn't exist
message	A DOM document for the SOAP response
methodName	The name of the method invoked. Most of the time, this is the tag name of the element represented by the body property (typically "Body").
targetObjectURI	The target namespace of the response
version	The SOAP version number (if it can be obtained from the envelope). One of the following constants: 0 for version 1.1, 1 for version 1.2, and 65535 if the version is unknown.

The second argument of the callback function is the same instance of SOAPCall that was used to make the request. The third argument is an error code that indicates a problem with the client-server communication;

when there is no error, this is equal to 0. If the Web service itself causes the error, a `SOAPFault` object is created and stored in the `fault` property of the `SOAPResponse`.

If there is a communication error, the error code is a number other than `0`. If the Web service itself causes an error, then the `oResponse.fault` object is not `null`. This object has `faultString` and `faultCode` properties that provide additional details about the fault.

> **It is also possible to call the service synchronously by using the `invoke()` method, which returns a `SOAPResponse` object as its function value.**

If there isn't an error or a fault, you must get the data from the SOAP response. To do this, use the `getParameters()` method of the `SOAPResponse` object, which returns an array of the parameters returned by the Web service:

```
var oParamCount = null;
var arrParams = oResponse.getParameters(false, oParamCount);
```

The first parameter of the `getParameters()` method indicates whether the response is in RPC format or not. It is `false` for non-RPC and `true` for RPC (although using `false` works most of the time). The second parameter is just an object that is filled with the number of parameters returned. In many cases, the parameter count isn't necessary because the number of parameters can be determined by using the `length` property on the returned array, and so typically the call is made like this:

```
var arrParams = oResponse.getParameters(false, {});
```

Note that, in this case, the second parameter is an object literal without a reference. The second parameter must be included even if it isn't used, so this is acceptable.

Each parameter has an `element` property that gives you access to the corresponding element in the SOAP response. This is an XML element with all the methods and attributes of any XML element. To get the string value of a parameter, you typically do something like this:

```
var sValue = arrParams[0].element.firstChild.nodeValue;
```

What you do with the value after that point, of course, is up to you.

To use the Temperature Service with the Mozilla SOAP objects, you need several pieces of information: the Web service URL and the target namespace. Remember that this information is located in the WSDL file:

```
var sURL = "http://services.xmethods.net:80/soap/servlet/rpcrouter";
var sTargetNamespace = "urn:xmethods-Temperature";
```

The HTML for this example is the same as the IE example, with the exclusion of the extra `<div/>` element needed for the `WebService` component.

Once again, the first function is named `callWebService()`. The first step must be a request for enhanced privileges as described previously. If the privileges aren't given, there's no point in the function continuing, so it returns. If the privileges are enabled, then the zip code is retrieved and placed in a `SOAPParameter` array. Lastly, the SOAP call is created and made asynchronously:

```
function callWebService() {

    try {
        netscape.security.PrivilegeManager.enablePrivilege("UniversalBrowserRead");
    } catch (e) {
        alert(e);
        return false;
    }

    var sZip = document.getElementById("txtZip").value;

    var arrParams = new Array;
    arrParams[0] = new SOAPParameter(sZip, "zipcode");

    var oSoapCall = new SOAPCall();
    oSoapCall.transportURI = sURL;
    oSoapCall.encode(0, "getTemp", sTargetNamespace, 0, null,
                     arrParams.length, arrParams);
    oSoapCall.asyncInvoke(onWebServiceResult);
}
```

Next, the `onWebServiceResult()` function handles the response. Most of the function is dedicated to determining if an error occurred during the Web service call:

```
function onWebServiceResult(oResponse,oSoapCall,iError) {

    if (iError != 0) {
        alert("An unspecified error occurred.");
    } else if (oResponse.fault != null) {
        alert("An error occurred (code=" + oResponse.fault.faultCode
              + ", string=" + oResponse.fault.faultString + ")");
    } else {
        var oParams = oResponse.getParameters(false, {});
        alert("It is currently " + oParams[0].element.firstChild.nodeValue
              + " degrees in that zip code.");
    }
}
```

The first step in this function is to check the error code `iError`. If it's not equal to `0`, that means there isn't a response to evaluate, so an error message is displayed. If the error code is `0`, the next step is to determine that there wasn't a SOAP error. This ensures that the `fault` property is `null` (if it's not, a detailed error message is displayed).

When the two other conditions fail, the response must be valid. So, the value of the first parameter is displayed in a user-friendly message.

Using WSDL proxies

As you can tell, using the Mozilla SOAP functionality is quite a process and requires a bit of research (looking at the WSDL file) to use properly. Additionally, the hassle of signing a script for cross-domain communication isn't something developers really want to deal with. Being a forward-looking organization, Mozilla realized this and came up with an answer: WSDL proxies.

The basic idea of WSDL proxies is that SOAP requests should be allowed to go through provided that they are valid. In the case of Web services, the server is only vulnerable insofar as it's vulnerable to any Web service consumer. Presumably, each server publishes only functionality that can't hurt itself. With this in mind, it was decided that if the Web service request could be flagged as such, it should be allowed to communicate with other servers. This resulted in the WSDL proxies introduced in Mozilla 1.4.

A WSDL proxy is essentially an object that represents a Web service by creating operations as methods of the proxy. You can specify the methods to make calls either synchronously or asynchronously, but all methods of a proxy must use the same synchronicity (all are synchronous or all are asynchronous — you can't pick and choose).

Unfortunately, using WSDL proxies isn't as straightforward as using the low-level SOAP functionality or the Microsoft `WebService` component.

To begin, you create a `WebServiceProxyFactory`:

```
var oFactory = new WebServiceProxyFactory();
```

The factory's only implemented method (there are others in the documentation) is `createProxyAsync()`, which creates a proxy asynchronously, so as not to interfere with regular JavaScript processing. The method accepts the following arguments:

- The location of the WSDL file
- The port name
- A qualifier, which is always set to an empty string (this argument is only used when the object is used at the C++ level of Mozilla)
- A Boolean value indicating whether the methods of the created proxy should be called asynchronously
- A callback object whose methods are notified when certain events occur during proxy creation

That last argument, the callback object, must have two methods: `onLoad()`, which is called when the proxy has been loaded completely, and `onError()`, which is called if an error occurs during proxy creation. Each method accepts one argument. The `onLoad()` method is passed the created proxy object; the `onError()` method is passed an error message.

Typically, the callback object is created using object literal notation, such as the following:

```
var oCallbackObject = {
    onLoad: function (oCreatedProxy) {
        //...
    },
```

```
        onError: function (sMessage) {
            //...
        }
    }
```

This object is passed into the `createProxyAsync()` method as in the following:

```
oFactory.createProxyAsync("wsdl_location", "port_name", "", true, oCallbackObject);
```

The `createProxyAsync()` method should always be called within a `try..catch` statement because it throws an error if the method fails for any reason.

After this method is called, a new thread is started to load the WSDL proxy. When loaded, the `onLoad()` method is called and the new proxy is passed in. If you are only making a single Web service call, you may want to have this method call the specific operation. Otherwise, you'll probably want to store a reference to the proxy, such as this one, for later use:

```
var oProxy = null;

var oCallbackObject = {
    onLoad: function (oCreatedProxy) {
        oProxy = oCreatedProxy;
    },

    onError: function (sMessage) {
        alert(sMessage);
    }
}
```

In this example, a global variable named `oProxy` is created that stores the created proxy. In the `onLoad()` method, the created proxy is assigned into `oProxy` so it can be accessed in other functions.

Even though you can specify whether the proxy operations are called synchronously or asynchronously, the synchronous calls don't always work. It's always best to use asynchronous calls.

To call an operation asynchronously requires yet another callback object. This object must have a callback method for each operation you intend to call. The name of the callback method is always the name of the operation followed by *Callback* (for instance, the callback method for `getTemp` is called `getTempCallback`). This method receives as its arguments the response data from the Web service call. To understand this better, it's best to take a look at an example.

This example once again uses the Temperature Service. The important pieces of information are the WSDL file location and the port name. Here are the global variables:

```
var oProxy = null;
var sWSDL = "http://www.xmethods.net/sd/2001/TemperatureService.wsdl";
var sPort = "TemperaturePort";
```

Next, you need a callback object for creation of the proxy. This simply assigns the created proxy to the `oProxy` variable and assigns a callback object for the operations using the `setListener()` method:

```
var oProxyCreateCallback = {
    onLoad: function(oCreatedProxy) {
        oProxy = oCreatedProxy;
        oProxy.setListener(oGetTempCallback);
    },

    onError: function(sError) {
        alert(sError);
    }
};
```

The callback object for operations is called `oGetTempCallback`, and looks like this:

```
var oGetTempCallback = {
    getTempCallback: function (iDegrees) {
            alert("It is currently " + iDegrees + " degrees in that zip code.");
        }
}
```

As you can see, the only method is `getTempCallback()`. Because the Web service simply returns a number, the first (and only) argument contains a simple number. The argument is named `iDegrees`, but, in practice, it doesn't matter what you name the argument. This method is called as soon as `getTemp` returns a value and displays the temperature in a user-friendly message.

Next, a function is needed to create the WSDL proxy. In many cases, it's best to create the proxy during the page's `onload` event handler because of the asynchronous nature of proxy creation, so this example assigns the function directly to `window.onload`:

```
function createProxy() {
   try {
        var oFactory = new WebServiceProxyFactory();
        oFactory.createProxyAsync(sWSDL, sPort, "", true, oProxyCreateCallback);
    } catch (oError) {
        alert(oError.message);
    }
}

window.onload = createProxy;
```

This function creates a `WebServiceProxyFactory` and uses it to create a proxy, assigning the location of the WSDL file, the port name, and the callback object. It also specifies all methods to be called asynchronously.

Last is the `callWebService()` function. The function first checks that the proxy has been created before attempting to make the call. If the proxy has been created, then `getTemp()` is called as a method of the proxy and the zip code is passed in:

```
function callWebService() {

    if (oProxy) {
        var sZip = document.getElementById("txtZip").value;
        oProxy.getTemp(sZip);
```

```
        } else {
            alert("Proxy not available.");
        }

    }
```

When `getTemp()` is called in this function, another thread is started to make the Web service call. The result is passed into the `oGetTempCallback` object. This function is called when the user clicks the Get Temperature button (this example uses the same HTML page as the previous examples).

The way this code executes is very non-linear (see Figure 17-2), but it gets the job done.

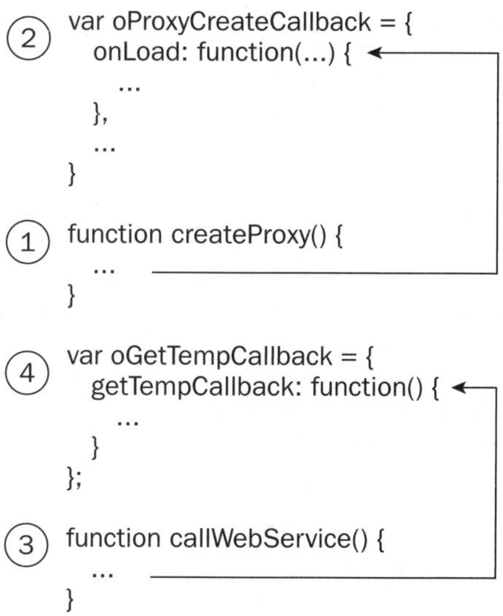

Figure 17-2

A Cross-Browser Approach

Once again, the differences in how browsers access Web services are so vast that you can't create a cross-browser method using the current browser functionality. But because Web services are nothing more than standard HTTP requests with a special format, it's possible to create a cross-browser approach using the XML HTTP request object. For this to work, you use the browser detection script and the script creating a `XMLHttpRequest` constructor for Internet Explorer explained earlier in the book.

The WebService object

Each Web service is unique, so how can you possibly develop a standard way to use them? The answer is to create a generalized template object definition that can be overridden to make it more specific. This template object is called `WebService` and is defined this way:

```
function WebService() {
    this.action = "";
    this.url = "";
}

WebService.prototype.buildRequest = function () {
    return "";
};

WebService.prototype.handleResponse = function (sSOAP) {
};

WebService.prototype.send = function () {

    if (isMoz) {
        try {
        netscape.security.PrivilegeManager.enablePrivilege("UniversalBrowserRead");
        } catch (oError) {
            alert(oError);
            return false;
        }
    }

    var oRequest = new XMLHttpRequest;
    oRequest.open("post", this.url, false);
    oRequest.setRequestHeader("Content-Type", "text/xml");
    oRequest.setRequestHeader("SOAPAction", this.action);
    oRequest.send(this.buildRequest());

    if (oRequest.status == 200) {
        return this.handleResponse(oRequest.responseText);
    } else {
        throw new Error("Request did not complete, code " + oRequest.status);
    }
};
```

The `WebService` object is the basis of cross-browser Web service support. It has two properties: the URL for the SOAP request (`url`) and the SOAP action (`action`). Both properties are initialized to `null`; subclasses fill these in as needed. The `buildRequest()` method is intended to build the SOAP message string; but in this case, it just returns an empty string. The `handleResponse()` method receives the SOAP message from the response and returns the appropriate value.

The `send()` method does the heavy lifting for this functionality. First, if the browser is Mozilla, you must request the `UniversalBrowserRead` privilege. Then, an `XMLHttpRequest` object is created (remember, this code uses the wrapper for IE), and the SOAP request is built up. This request includes opening a request to the specified URL, setting the content type to `"text/xml"` and setting the SOAP action. Then, the `buildRequest()` method is called to get the SOAP message and send it using the `XMLHttpRequest`'s `send()` method.

Lastly, if the request returns a status of 200, the text returned is interpreted by the `handleResponse()` and that value is returned. Otherwise, an error is thrown. The intent is to allow you to use a `WebService` object like this:

```
var oService = new WebService();
var vResult = oService.send();
alert("Service returned " + vResult);
```

This object, of course, doesn't have enough information to be used on its own. However, it can be used to create a wrapper for any other Web service.

The Temperature Service

Once again, it's time to take a look at the Temperature Service. To do this, the `TemperatureService` object inherits from `WebService` and defines both the `url` and `action` properties:

```
function TemperatureService() {
        WebService.apply(this);
        this.url = "http://services.xmethods.net:80/soap/servlet/rpcrouter";
        this.zipcode = "";
}

TemperatureService.prototype = new WebService();
```

Remember that the SOAP action for the Temperature Service is actually an empty string, so the default value (inherited from `WebService`) is fine. A new property, zipcode, is used to store the zip code to check.

For the `buildRequest()` method, you first determine the format for the SOAP request. This can easily be done for any Web service by using the WSDL analyzer tool available at XMethods (`http://www.xmethods.net/ve2/Tools.po`). These methods enable you to see the request and response formats for any Web service with a WSDL file.

The SOAP request for the Temperature Service looks like this:

```
<soap:Envelope xmlns:n="urn:xmethods-Temperature"
   xmlns:soap="http://schemas.xmlsoap.org/soap/envelope/"
   xmlns:soapenc="http://schemas.xmlsoap.org/soap/encoding/"
   xmlns:xs="http://www.w3.org/2001/XMLSchema"
   xmlns:xsi="http://www.w3.org/2001/XMLSchema-instance">
   <soap:Body soap:encodingStyle="http://schemas.xmlsoap.org/soap/encoding/">
      <n:getTemp>
         <zipcode xsi:type="xs:string"><!-- zipcode here --></zipcode>
      </n:getTemp>
   </soap:Body>
</soap:Envelope>
```

A whole lot of information is contained in this simple SOAP request, but the important line (which is highlighted) is where the zip code should be entered. The `buildRequest()` method must create this SOAP string with the zip code inserted:

```
TemperatureService.prototype.buildRequest = function () {
    var oBuffer = new StringBuffer();

    oBuffer.append("<soap:Envelope xmlns:n=\"urn:xmethods-Temperature\" ");
    oBuffer.append("xmlns:soap=\"http://schemas.xmlsoap.org/soap/envelope/\" ");
```

```
        oBuffer.append("xmlns:soapenc=\"http://schemas.xmlsoap.org/soap/encoding/\" ");
        oBuffer.append("xmlns:xs=\"http://www.w3.org/2001/XMLSchema\" ");
        oBuffer.append("xmlns:xsi=\"http://www.w3.org/2001/XMLSchema-instance\">");
        oBuffer.append("<soap:Body soap:encodingStyle=");
        oBuffer.append("\"http://schemas.xmlsoap.org/soap/encoding/\">");
        oBuffer.append("<n:getTemp><zipcode xsi:type=\"xs:string\">");
        oBuffer.append(this.zipcode);
        oBuffer.append("</zipcode></n:getTemp></soap:Body></soap:Envelope>");

        return oBuffer.toString();
    };
```

Because the SOAP request string is so long, this method uses the `StringBuffer()` object created earlier in the book to build up the string. Note that the `zipcode` property is used here to insert the zip code in question instead of passing it in as an argument. If the zip code is passed in as an argument, you must rewrite the `send()` method to take this into account; this way, the `send()` method can be used as-is.

The `handleResponse()` method expects to receive a SOAP response string as its only argument. Once again, this format can be determined by using the WSDL analyzer tool from XMethods:

```
<SOAP-ENV:Envelope
    xmlns:SOAP-ENV="http://schemas.xmlsoap.org/soap/envelope/"
    xmlns:xsi="http://www.w3.org/2001/XMLSchema-instance"
    xmlns:xsd="http://www.w3.org/2001/XMLSchema">

   <SOAP-ENV:Body>
      <ns1:getTempResponse
           SOAP-ENV:encodingStyle="http://schemas.xmlsoap.org/soap/encoding/"
           xmlns:ns1="urn:xmethods-Temperature">
         <return xsi:type="xsd:float"><!--returned value--></return>
      </ns1:getTempResponse>
   </SOAP-ENV:Body>
</SOAP-ENV:Envelope>
```

Despite all the extra code, the only part of interest is what is contained within the `<return/>` element. The easiest way to extract that data from the string is to use a regular expression; there's no need for expensive DOM parsing and operations in this case (for more complicated Web services, however, that may be an option). After the value is extracted, the `parseFloat()` function can be used to get the floating-point value:

```
TemperatureService.prototype.handleResponse = function (sResponse) {
    var oRE = /<return .*?>(.*)<\/return>/gi;
    oRE.test(sResponse);
    return parseFloat(RegExp["$1"]);
};
```

The only thing left to do is modify the `send()` method to accept an argument (the zip code) because the `zipcode` property must be assigned for the method to function properly (remember, the `send()` method calls `buildRequest()`, which uses the `zipcode` property to create the SOAP string).

To accomplish this, you first must create a pointer to the original `send()` method:

```
TemperatureService.prototype.webServiceSend = TemperatureService.prototype.send;
```

This line of code creates a property called `webServiceSend` that points to the `send()` function. This procedure makes it possible to redefine `send()` without losing the original functionality:

```
TemperatureService.prototype.send = function (sZipcode) {
        this.zipcode = sZipcode;
        return this.webServiceSend();
};
```

The first thing the new `send()` method does is assign the `zipcode` property. Then, it returns the result of the `webServiceSend()` method (which is a call to the original `send()` method). The `TemperatureService` object can be used like this:

```
var oService = new TemperatureService();
var fResult = oService.send("90210");
alert("Temperature is " + fResult + "degrees");
```

Using the TemperatureService object

To recreate the temperature example one more time, the code is much simpler:

```
<html>
    <head>
       <title>Cross-Browser Web Service Example</title>
        <script type="text/javascript" src="detect.js"></script>
        <script type="text/javascript" src="stringbuffer.js"></script>
        <script type="text/javascript" src="http.js"></script>
        <script type="text/javascript" src="webservice.js"></script>
        <script>
            function callWebService() {
                var sZip = document.getElementById("txtZip").value;
                var oService = new TemperatureService();
                var fResult = oService.send(sZip);

                alert("It is currently " + fResult + " degrees in that zip code.");
            }

        </script>
    </head>
    <body>
        <p><input type="text" id="txtZip" size="10" />
        <input type="button" value="Get Temperature" onclick="callWebService()" />
        </p>
    </body>
</html>
```

As you can see, the `callWebService()` function is greatly simplified in this example. The zip code is obtained from the text box; then the `TemperatureService` object is created, and the zip code is passed into the `send()` method, which returns the temperature in degrees. An alert is then displayed indicating the temperature.

Summary

Web services are a new technology and, indeed, a new technology for JavaScript. In this chapter, you learned how two browsers, Internet Explorer and Mozilla, are trying to give JavaScript developers access to Web service functionality.

You learned how Microsoft created an HTML component to encapsulate Web service calls. This `WebService` component reads Web service information from a WSDL file and develops a friendly object to handle the requests and responses.

You also learned how Mozilla is still developing its Web service functionality. It provides a low-level SOAP API and also WSDL proxies. Issues of cross-domain security and advanced privileges are also discussed as they relate to Web services.

Lastly, you were introduced to a cross-browser Web service solution that, although not pretty, can provide a common interface for use in both Internet Explorer and Mozilla.

18

Interacting with Plugins

The Web is much more than HTML and images. Today, Web sites across the world make use of many different types of plugins. Plugins give Web browsers the capability to embed small (and sometimes large) programs or objects into a page without interfering with the underlying HTML. When a browser encounters content inside of an `<object/>` element, it hands over rendering responsibility to the associated plugin.

Originally, the plugin of choice was a Java applet. Applets allowed Web developers to include Java functionality directly in a Web page. Since that time, many more plugins have been developed. This chapter focuses on the most popular plugins used today and how you can use JavaScript to interact with them.

Why Use Plugins?

In the beginning, Web pages were fairly static creations. Before the advent of the DOM, after a page was loaded its appearance remained the same until it was unloaded. Traditional developers lived in a world of dynamic interfaces, where everything the user did caused a change on the screen, but when they turned to the Web, they found the environment severely lacking in dynamism. Then came Java.

Java originally wasn't designed for use in Web browsers because, at the time of its inception, the World Wide Web was nothing but a concept. However, as the Internet and the Web gained popularity, the original Java developers saw the opportunity to enrich the Web browsing experience by using Java. The result was an experimental browser called HotJava, which was written by Sun Microsystems as a proof of concept for how Java applets could be embedded into Web pages. For the first time ever, Web pages were no longer static; instead, there was movement, user interaction without page reloading, and a bright new future for the Web.

Around the same time, Netscape began developing an architecture for *helper applications*. The basic idea was to enable the browser to recognize the mime type of information and then launch the appropriate application to view the content. When Netscape 2.0 was introduced, it featured a new plugin architecture, essentially providing the capability to embed these helper applications directly into Web pages.

Since that time, Web browsers have come a long way. All browsers today allow Java applets to be embedded in pages, along with a whole host of other plugins. Of course, dynamic pages can be created today using the DOM, so is there really any reason to use plugins? The answer is yes.

Plugins continue to push the envelope for Web page interaction, offering a whole host of advantages over built-in browser technology. Although many browsers have built-in HTTP request capabilities for JavaScript, the only way to have true bi-directional client-server communication using sockets is through plugins. Likewise, the only way to embed and animate vector graphics is through the use of plugins. As an added bonus, most plugins work across browsers without any problem.

The bottom line is that plugins are able to provide functionality that the browsers either can't or won't provide natively. Because companies don't have to wait for a browser to be updated in order to update a plugin, plugins are an attractive option for many developers.

Popular Plugins

Many plugins are popular today on the World Wide Web. The most notable are the following:

- **Macromedia Flash Player** — Macromedia Flash provides vector graphic-based animation and an ever-increasing amount of complex functionality that can be embedded in Web pages using the Flash Player. Flash has arguably become the most popular use of a plugin. Some Web sites are written entirely in Flash. The Flash Player is shipped with almost every Web browser and works on Windows, MacOS, Linux, and most Unix systems.
- **Java Plugin** — Still one of the leaders in plugin technology, the Java plugin enables you to embed Java applets in Web pages. It works on almost all platforms.
- **Apple Quicktime** — Enables the embedding of Apple Quicktime videos in Web pages. Quicktime videos can be standard, start-to-finish videos or Quicktime VR (Virtual Reality) movies that allow the user to pan around a 3D room. Quicktime is available for Windows and MacOS.
- **Real Player** — Real Player was the early leader in delivering streaming audio and video over the Internet. Today, it's in a tight race with Quicktime and Windows Media Player (see following) for control of streaming media. It does a good job — with support for almost every computing platform.
- **Windows Media Player** — Not to be outdone, Microsoft offers its own embeddable movie player featuring the Windows Media Player. Although it is capable of handling Quicktime movies and its own format, the Windows Media Player is available only on Windows operating systems.
- **Adobe SVG Viewer** —Scalable Vector Graphics (SVG) is a new XML-based language for creating vector graphics. Although browsers still don't support the language natively, Adobe has taken up the battle and introduced the SVG Viewer, which can be used to embed SVG images in Web pages. The SVG Viewer is currently available on most platforms, with support for Internet Explorer and Netscape 4.x; Mozilla support is not yet available.

- **ActiveX Objects** — ActiveX objects are everywhere in Internet Explorer. You can use them from JavaScript and you can embed them in Web pages. Although not technically a plugin, because ActiveX support exists in Internet Explorer itself, ActiveX objects are embedded into a Web page the same way as other plugins.
- **Macromedia Shockwave** — Before there was Flash, there was Shockwave. Shockwave plays files created in Macromedia Director, a multimedia programming environment allowing developers to create interactive demos, games, and other advanced content. Although not as popular since Flash gained notoriety, Shockwave is still available on both Windows and MacOS.

MIME Types

When talking about plugins, the concept of MIME types is central. MIME stands for Multipurpose Internet Mail Extension, a simple text string originally designed to determine the format of e-mail attachments. From that humble beginning, MIME types (also called content types) have grown into the de facto standard for identifying file formats on the Internet.

Each MIME type is made up of a media type and a subtype. The media type can be application, image, audio, video, text, message, model, and multipart. The subtype is typically a more unique identifier, specifying anything from the type of compression scheme used to the file extension. The media type and subtype are separated by a forward-slash (/), such as `text/css`, which tells the browser (or other Internet application) that the file is plain text and is also a CSS style sheet. Browser plugins work by mapping themselves to specific MIME types, telling the browser that when this specific type of file has to be handled, it should be done by the plugin.

Naturally, several MIME types are handled by the browser itself, such as `text/javascript` (JavaScript files), `text/css` (CSS style sheets), `image/gif` (GIF-encoded images), `image/jpeg` (JPEG-encoded images), `text/xml` (XML files), and `text/html` (HTML files). Many others, however, are handled by plugins.

Embedding Plugins

To embed a plugin into a Web page, HTML offers the `<object/>` element. At the very least, `<object/>` requires four attributes:

- `type` — The MIME type of the file or object being embedded
- `data` — The URL of a file to load into the object
- `width` — The horizontal space the object should take up in the page
- `height` — The vertical space the object should take up in the page

The browser internally equates the MIME type of a file with a particular plugin, so setting the `type` attribute is enough to tell the browser which plugin to load. For example, the content type for a Flash file is `application/x-shockwave-flash`, so the following code is all you need to embed a Flash movie:

```
<object type="application/x-shockwave-flash" data="myflashmovie.swf"
        width="100" height="100"></object>
```

If there is no registered plugin for the MIME type, the browser may (depending on which one you are using) offer to install the correct plugin for the file. Many browsers also look for the `pluginspage` attribute, which is an unofficial attribute of `<object/>` (it doesn't exist in the HTML specification). This attribute specifies where to find the plugin for the embedded object if it isn't already on the user's machine. Example:

```
<object type="application/x-shockwave-flash" data="myflashmovie.swf"
pluginspage="http://www.macromedia.com/shockwave/download/download.cgi?P1_Prod_Vers
ion=ShockwaveFlash"
        width="100" height="100"></object>
```

Including parameters

Sometimes an object requires additional parameters before it can start running. To specify parameters for an embedded object, use the `<param/>` element with its `name` and `value` attributes:

```
<object type="application/x-shockwave-flash" data="myflashmovie.swf"
        width="100" height="100">
    <param name="message" value="Hello World!" />
</object>
```

Each object can have any number of parameters. Including parameters that aren't necessary doesn't have any negative effect.

Netscape 4.x

The old Netscape 4.x browsers don't support the `<object/>` element, so you use the old Netscape proprietary `<embed/>` element. The `<embed/>` element accepts most of the same attributes as `<object/>` (indeed, `<object/>` was modeled after `<embed/>`), except the `src` attribute is used instead of `data`:

```
<embed type="application/x-shockwave-flash" src="myflashmovie.swf"
        width="100" height="100">
    <param name="message" value="Hello World!" />
</embed>
```

As you can see, this approach is very similar to using `<object/>`. The problem is that newer browsers don't support this element (it has officially been deprecated). So if you plan on supporting Netscape 4.x, the preferred solution is to use `<object/>` with an `<embed/>` element inside of it, such as in the following:

```
<object type="application/x-shockwave-flash" data="myflashmovie.swf"
        width="100" height="100">
    <param name="message" value="Hello World!" />
    <embed type="application/x-shockwave-flash" src="myflashmovie.swf"
            width="100" height="100">
        <param name="message" value="Hello World!" />
    </embed>
</object>
```

Using this approach, the newer browsers ignore the `<embed/>` element and use `<object/>` to embed the file; Netscape 4.x ignores `<object/>` and uses `<embed/>` to embed the file.

Detecting Plugins

As with most Web technology, two types of plugins are available: those from Microsoft and those from others. The Microsoft way uses ActiveX technology, which you may remember as the way to create XML-related objects; the other way has been called *Netscape-style plugins* because Netscape Navigator introduced the concept of plugins to the Web. Until recently, Internet Explorer supported Netscape-style plugins in addition to ActiveX controls. Beginning with Internet Explorer 5.5 Service Pack 2 (Windows only), however, Microsoft eliminated support for the Netscape-style plugins.

The main difference between the two types of plugins is the architecture. ActiveX plugins are built on Microsoft's ActiveX platform whereas Netscape-style plugins are built on top of the Netscape Plugin API. Originally, every browser (including Internet Explorer) was forced to support the Netscape-style plugins because Netscape was the dominant browser and only compatible browsers could compete. Although many will speculate why Microsoft ended support for Netscape-style plugins, it has created a clear rift in the world of plugins. Many plugin developers are required to create both Netscape-style plugins and ActiveX wrappers for these plugins in order to support Internet Explorer.

Today, browsers are separated into those that don't support Netscape-style plugins (such as Internet Explorer on Windows) and those that do (such as Mozilla, Opera, Safari, and many other browsers).

Because of these differences, you have different ways of detecting whether a plugin is installed on a given browser.

Detecting Netscape-style plugins

Since Netscape 3.0, many browsers (notably those based on Mozilla) allow JavaScript to determine which MIME types are mapped to plugins, ultimately enabling you to determine if a given plugin is installed. This is determined through the help of the `window.mimeTypes` collection.

> *Two types of Netscape-style plugins exist: the style used in Netscape 4.x and the newer Gecko style used in Mozilla. The details of the differences are of no consequence to JavaScript developers because both styles are accessed the same way.*

Each MIME type registered to a plugin is present in `window.mimeTypes`, indexed both by number and by MIME type, allowing you to access a MIME type directly or to iterate through the collection. An object with four properties represents each MIME type:

- `description` — A description of the type of file represented by the MIME type
- `enabledPlugin` — Reference to a plugin object with information about the specific plugin
- `suffixes` —The file suffixes associated with this MIME type (such as mapping `.gif` to `image/gif`)
- `type` — The MIME type

You can print out a list of all visible MIME types and their descriptions by running a simple script:

```
<html>
    <head>
        <title>MIME Types Example</title>
```

```
    </head>
    <body>
        <script type="text/javascript">

            if (navigator.mimeTypes) {
                document.writeln("<h3>Supported MIME Types:</h3>");
                document.writeln("<ul>");
                for (var i=0; i < navigator.mimeTypes.length; i++) {
                    document.writeln("<li>" + navigator.mimeTypes[i].type + " ("
                        + navigator.mimeTypes[i].description + ", "
                        + navigator.mimeTypes[i].suffixes + ")</li>");

                }
                document.writeln("</ul>");
            }
        </script>
    </body>
</html>
```

This example doesn't print out any information about `enabledPlugin`, which is another object with another set of properties:

- `description` — A description of the plugin
- `filename` — The plugin filename
- `length` — The number of MIME types associated with the plugin
- `name` — The name of the plugin

It's worth noting that not every MIME type has a plugin associated with it, meaning that `enabledPlugin` can be `null`. The example can be updated to include plugin information keeping this in mind:

```
<html>
    <head>
        <title>MIME Types Example</title>
    </head>
    <body>
        <script type="text/javascript">

            if (navigator.mimeTypes) {
                document.writeln("<h3>Supported MIME Types:</h3>");
                document.writeln("<ul>");
                for (var i=0; i < navigator.mimeTypes.length; i++) {
                    document.writeln("<li>" + navigator.mimeTypes[i].type + " ("
                        + navigator.mimeTypes[i].description + ", "
                        + navigator.mimeTypes[i].suffixes + ")</li>");

                    if (navigator.mimeTypes[i].enabledPlugin) {
                        var oPlugin = navigator.mimeTypes[i].enabledPlugin;
                        document.writeln("<ul>");
                        document.writeln("<li>Name: " + oPlugin.name + "</li>");
                        document.writeln("<li>" + oPlugin.description + "</li>");
                        document.writeln("<li>MIME types supported: "
                                 + oPlugin.length + "</li>");
```

```
                        document.writeln("<li>Filename: " + oPlugin.filename
                                        + "</li>");
                        document.writeln("</ul>");
                    }

                }
                document.writeln("</ul>");
            }
        </script>
    </body>
</html>
```

This example outputs each MIME type complete with its plugin information (if one is available).

Just like the previous example, this page prints out the MIME types that are numerically indexed. Some MIME types are indexed only by the MIME type string, and these are not accessible using this approach. For instance, `text/html` is a registered MIME type with the browser, but it does not appear in the list generated from the previous code. However, you can explicitly test for it:

```
alert( navigator.mimeTypes["text/html"] != null);
```

These *invisible* MIME types are typically those handled by the browser itself and usually don't have a plugin registered to them. A simple page can be used to test any MIME type you can dream up:

```
<html>
    <head>
        <title>MIME Types Example</title>
        <script type="text/javascript">

            function findPlugin() {
                var sType = document.getElementById("txtMimeType").value;

                if (navigator.mimeTypes) {
                    if (navigator.mimeTypes[sType]) {
                        if (navigator.mimeTypes[sType].enabledPlugin) {
                            alert("The MIME type \"" + sType
                                   + "\" uses the plugin \""
                                   + navigator.mimeTypes[sType].enabledPlugin.name
                                   + "\".");
                        } else {
                            alert("The MIME type \"" + sType
                                   + "\" has no registered plugin.");
                        }
                    } else {
                        alert("The MIME type \"" + sType
                               + "\" is not registered.");
                    }
                } else {
                    alert("Browser doesn't support navigator.mimeTypes.");
                }
            }

        </script>
```

```
    </head>
    <body>
        <p>Type the name of the <acronym title="Multipurpose Internet Mail
Extension">MIME</acronym>
        you want to check and click the Find Plugin button.</p>
        <p><input type="text" id="txtMimeType" />
        <input type="button" value="Find Plugin" onclick="findPlugin()" /></p>
    </body>
</html>
```

The HTML page listed previously allows you to enter a MIME type into a text box and click a button to determine if a MIME type is registered. If so, you can tell whether it has a browser plugin. The `findPlugin()` function retrieves the value from the text box and first checks to see if the `navigator.mimeTypes` collection exists. If it does, then the function continues on to see if the MIME type is defined. If it is, you can tell whether it has a plugin installed.

You can extract the methodology to test for a plugin that handles a particular MIME type into a separate function:

```
function hasPluginForMimeType(sMimeType) {
    if (navigator.mimeTypes) {
        return navigator.mimeTypes[sMimeType].enabledPlugin != null;
    } else {
        return false;
    }
}
```

Then, you can check for the existence of a given plugin like so:

```
if (hasPluginForMimeType("application/x-shockwave-flash")) {
    alert("The Flash plugin is installed.");
} else {
    alert("The Flash plugin is not installed.");
}
```

It's also possible to retrieve a list of all registered plugins without using the MIME types. The `navigator.plugins` collection contains all plugins, indexed by name and by number, available for the given browser. Each entry in the collection is a plugin object equivalent to the one referenced by `enabledPlugin` for each MIME type. So, if you know the name of a plugin (equivalent to its `name` property), you can access it directly:

```
var oFlashPlugin = navigator.plugins["Shockwave Flash"];
```

Otherwise, you can iterate through the plugins to print out the information about each one. A simple page can also be used to do this:

```
<html>
    <head>
        <title>Plugins Example</title>
    </head>
    <body>
        <script type="text/javascript">
```

```
            if (navigator.mimeTypes) {
                document.writeln("<h3>Loaded Plugins:</h3>");
                document.writeln("<ul>");
                for (var i=0; i < navigator.plugins.length; i++) {
                    document.writeln("<li>" + navigator.plugins[i].name + " ("
                        + navigator.plugins[i].description + ")</li>");

                }
                document.writeln("</ul>");
            }
        </script>
    </body>
</html>
```

This page prints out a list of all registered plugins and their descriptions. But the plugin object holds a secret; it is actually a collection of MIME types, meaning that MIME types for the plugin can be accessed like this:

```
var oMimeType = navigator.plugins[0][0];
```

This line of code accesses the first MIME type supported by the first plugin. So now, you can update the previous example to include the registered MIME types for each plugin:

```
<html>
    <head>
        <title>Plugins Example</title>
    </head>
    <body>
        <script type="text/javascript">

            if (navigator.mimeTypes) {
                document.writeln("<h3>Loaded Plugins:</h3>");
                document.writeln("<ul>");
                for (var i=0; i < navigator.plugins.length; i++) {
                    document.writeln("<li>" + navigator.plugins[i].name + " ("
                        + navigator.plugins[i].description + ")</li>");

                    document.writeln("<ul>");

                    for (var j=0; j < navigator.plugins[i].length; j++) {
                        document.writeln("<li>" + navigator.plugins[i][j].type +
"</li>");
                    }

                    document.writeln("</ul>");
                }
                document.writeln("</ul>");
            }
        </script>
    </body>
</html>
```

Now this example displays each plugin's name and description, followed by a list of supported MIME types.

The last thing to be aware of is that the `navigator.plugins` collection can sometimes become out of date, or *stale*, as the user is downloading a plugin required for viewing your page. To prepare for this possibility, you should always start out by refreshing `navigator.plugins` by calling the `refresh()` method. This method accepts one argument, a Boolean value, indicating whether the browser should reload the page (or pages) using an embedded object; to reload the pages, pass in `true`, otherwise, pass in `false`. For example:

```
navigator.plugins.refresh(true);     //reload all pages using plugins
```

Making this simple call could save you some heartache later on.

> **Presently, Netscape Navigator 3.0+, Opera 5.0+, Safari 1.0, Internet Explorer 5.0+ (Macintosh only), Internet Explorer 3.0-5.5 SP 1 (Windows), and all Mozilla-based Web browsers support this functionality; Internet Explorer 5.5 SP 2+ on Windows does not, even though it creates both `navigator.plugins` and `navigator.mimeTypes` (each is a collection with zero items).**

Detecting ActiveX plugins

Because Internet Explorer plugins are just ActiveX controls, all you need to know is the name of the control to detect if it is installed. Earlier in this book, you saw some code to detect the latest version of the Microsoft XML DOM. This same methodology can be used for any IE plugin. But how do you find the name of the ActiveX control you're interested in?

Microsoft has a tool called the OLE/COM Object Viewer that can be used to find the ActiveX control name for all ActiveX controls installed on your computer. You can download this tool for free from `http://www.microsoft.com/downloads/details.aspx?FamilyID=5233b70d-d9b2-4cb5-aeb6-45664be858b6&displaylang=en`. After it is installed, it provides a list of all OLE, COM, and ActiveX objects installed on your machine as well as important information about each one. It may take some time to look through all of the installed objects, but once you find the one you're looking for, all the pertinent information is displayed (Figure 18-1).

The important piece of information is listed as `VersionIndependentProgID`, which gives you the name of the generic ActiveX control that creates the most recent version of the control. The `ProgID` listed typically gives you a version-specific control name, which helps to determine if a specific version is installed (although it doesn't always list the highest version available). The following table lists the version-independent and version-specific ActiveX control names for several popular plugins.

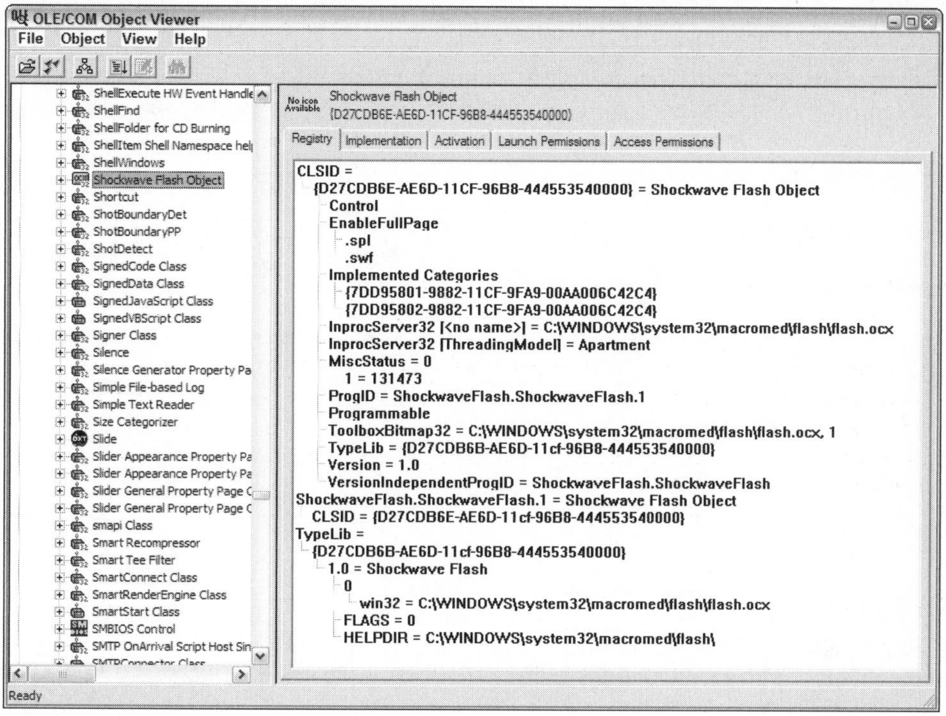

Figure 18-1

Plugin	Version-Independent Name	Version-Specific Names
Adobe (Acrobat) Reader	`PDF.PdfCtrl`	`PDF.PdfCtrl.5` `PDF.PdfCtrl.6`
Adobe SVG Viewer	`Adobe.SVGCtl`	`Adobe.SVGCtl.2` `Adobe.SVGCtl.3`

Macromedia Flash Player	`ShockwaveFlash.ShockwaveFlash`	`ShockwaveFlash.ShockwaveFlash.6`
		`ShockwaveFlash.ShockwaveFlash.7`
		`ShockwaveFlash.ShockwaveFlash.8`
		`ShockwaveFlash.ShockwaveFlash.9`

Real Player 5	`RealPlayer.RealPlayer(tm) ActiveX Control (32-bit)`	(none)
Real Video 5	`RealVideo.RealVideo(tm) ActiveX Control (32-bit)`	(none)

Table continued on following page

Plugin	Version-Independent Name	Version-Specific Names
Real Player G2	`rmocx.RealPlayer G2 Control`	`rmocx.RealPlayer G2 Control.1`
Quicktime	`Quicktime.Quicktime`	`Quicktime.Quicktime.1`
Windows Media Player	`WMPlayer.OCX`	`WMPlayer.OCX.7` `WMPlayer.OCX.8`

To make use of the ActiveX control name, try to create the given object using an `ActiveXObject`. For example:

```
function detectFlashInIE() {
    try {
        new ActiveXObject("ShockwaveFlash.ShockwaveFlash");
        return true;
    } catch (oError) {
        return false;
    }
}
```

This function's purpose is to determine if the Flash Player is installed. To do so, it tries to create the `ActiveXObject` with the name `ShockwaveFlash.ShockwaveFlash`. If this is successful, the next line executes and the function returns `true`. If the object can't be created, the error is caught and the function returns `false`. This same basic algorithm can be used for any plugin with an ActiveX wrapper.

> **This method of plugin detection works only in Internet Explorer 5.0 and higher for Windows.**

Cross-browser detection

Unfortunately, you have no easy way to establish cross-browser plugin detection in a generic way. In order to accurately detect if a plugin is available, you must know both the MIME type and the ActiveX control name. Most of the time, developers just create specific detection functions that include both pieces of information, such as the following:

```
function detectFlash() {
    if (navigator.mimeTypes.length > 0) {
        return navigator.mimeTypes["application/x-shockwave-flash"].enabledPlugin
!= null;
    } else if (window.ActiveXObject) {
        try {
            new ActiveXObject("ShockwaveFlash.ShockwaveFlash");
            return true;
        } catch (oError) {
            return false;
        }
```

```
        } else {
            //no way to detect!
            return false;
        }
    }
```

This function uses object detection to determine which methodology to use. If `navigator.mimeTypes` is available, then the function checks for an installed plugin using Netscape-style plugin detection. If, on the other hand, it's possible to create `ActiveXObject` objects, it uses the IE-style of detection. If neither of these options is available (which isn't very likely), the function just returns `false`.

To detect specific plugins, you can customize this algorithm and create a whole host of plugin detection functions.

> **Macromedia provides a Flash Detection Kit, available at `http://www.macromedia.com/software/flash/download/detection_kit/`, which can be used to produce cross-browser HTML and JavaScript for embedding Flash movies.**

Java Applets

The oldest form of plugin, the Java applet has recently been redefined to work with the generic browser plugin framework. Previously, applets had to be loaded using the `<applet/>` element. HTML 4.0 deprecated `<applet/>`, favoring `<object/>` as the sole means for embedding plugins. To aid in this move, Sun Microsystems created the Java Plugin, which is included as part of the Java Runtime Environment (JRE) and is available at `http://java.sun.com/`.

Embedding applets

Embedding an applet requires you to use the nonstandard `code` property of `<object/>` to specify the class to load. Although all browsers should work when using `data` for the same purpose, the reality is that support isn't yet universal. So, in the interest of cross-browser compatibility, it's best to use `code` in this way:

```
<object type="application/x-java-applet"
        code="ExampleApplet.class" width="100" height="100" id="ExampleApplet">
</object>
```

Note the mime type for Java applets is `application/x-java-applet`. By specifying this, you are sure that the browser will use the most appropriate (and available) version of the Java plugin. You can optionally specify the exact version required by adding it to the end of the mime type. For example, to specify version 1.4.2 (from JRE 1.4.2), add `"jpi-version=1.4.2"`:

```
<object type="application/x-java-applet;jpi-version=1.4.2"
        code="ExampleApplet.class" width="100" height="100" id="ExampleApplet">
</object>
```

In this mime type, JPI is short for *Java PlugIn* and it ensures that the applet is not run unless the plugin on the user's computer is exactly equal to version 1.4.2. So even if the user has version 1.4.3, the applet does not run. For this reason, it's best to omit the plugin version to avoid any annoyance for your users.

The applet class can be contained within a JAR (Java Archive) file. In that case, specify the JAR file by using the `archive` attribute:

```
<object type="application/x-java-applet"
        archive="ExampleArchive.jar"
        code="ExampleApplet.class" width="100" height="100" id="ExampleApplet">
</object>
```

To support Netscape Navigator 4.x, you use the original `<applet/>` element. To ensure that the code works in all browsers, you can embed `<applet/>` inside of `<object/>` (similar to the way you can place `<embed/>` inside of `<object/>`). However, doing so requires the use of the IE-proprietary `<comment/>` element. Although Mozilla and other browsers ignore content inside of `<object/>`, IE doesn't, and could end up rendering two copies of the same applet. Inserting the `<comment/>` element tells IE to ignore the extra content:

```
<object type="application/x-java-applet"
        code="ExampleApplet.class" width="100" height="100" id="ExampleApplet">
    <comment>
        <applet code="ExampleApplet.class" width="100" height="100"
                name="ExampleApplet"></applet>
    </comment>
</object>
```

Referencing applets in JavaScript

After an applet has been included in an HTML page, you need a way to access it via JavaScript. Traditionally, applets were referenced through the `document.applets` collection, which indexed all `<applet/>` elements by their name attribute and position in the document (similar to `document.forms` and `document.frames`). For example, to get a reference to an applet with the `name` attribute set to `"ExampleApplet"`, you could do the following:

```
var oApplet = document.applets["ExampleApplet"];
```

However, if you use the `<object/>` element to embed applets, the `document.applets` collection doesn't include it. When using `<object/>`, you can access the applet using `document.getElementById()`:

```
var oApplet = document.getElementById("ExampleApplet");
```

If you are using both `<object/>` and `<applet/>` for compatibility with older browsers, you should use a function to determine the appropriate method:

```
function getApplet(sName) {
    if (document.getElementById) {
        return document.getElementById(sName);
    } else {
        return document.applets[sName];
    }
```

```
}

var oApplet = getApplet("ExampleApplet");
```

After you have a reference to the applet, you can actually access all the applet's public methods directly from JavaScript, such as:

```
oApplet.appletPublicMethod();
```

This opens up all kinds of functionality to JavaScript by using a Java applet as a host environment; JavaScript can control anything that can be done within the applet.

Writing applets

To write a Java applet, you must first download the Java Development Kit (JDK) from Sun's Web site (`http://java.sun.com/j2se/`). It is up to you whether you use a development environment or a plain text editor to write the applet, but all applets have one thing in common: they must inherit from `java.applet.Applet`. (You can, however, create a Swing-based Java applet by inheriting from `javax.swing.JApplet`, which inherits from `java.applet.Applet`).

Here's a small example applet:

```
import java.applet.Applet;
import java.awt.Graphics;
import java.awt.HeadlessException;

public class ExampleApplet extends Applet {

    private String message = "Hello World!";

     public ExampleApplet() throws HeadlessException {
         super();
     }

     public void paint(Graphics g) {
         g.drawString(message, 20, 20);
     }

     public void setMessage(String message) {
         this.message = message;
         repaint();
     }
}
```

This applet simply displays the text `"Hello World!"` on the applet. The `paint()` method controls what is displayed when the applet is first loaded, and it receives a `Graphics` object as its sole argument. The `Graphics` object is a representation of the visual area of the applet with methods to draw onto the applet, such as `drawString()`, which draws the given text at the x and y coordinates specified.

The applet defined previously also has a private property called `message`, which is initialized to `"Hello World!"` This property can be changed by calling `setMessage()`, which is accessible from JavaScript because it is a public method. The method simply assigns the specified string to the `message` property, then calls `repaint()`, which clears the display of the applet and calls the `paint()` method again.

Applets only require a default constructor (which throws a `HeadlessException` if the operating system doesn't have a graphical interface). If the applet's purpose is solely to provide Java functionality to JavaScript, you can just add public methods and set the applet to a width and height of 0 in the HTML. If, however, the applet is to display something, you most likely need to defined a `paint()` method.

After the applet is defined and saved in a file with a `.java` extension, compile the file using the `javac` utility from the command line:

```
javac ExampleApplet.java
```

This command creates a file with a `.class` extension (the previous example creates `ExampleApplet.class`). The `.class` file must be placed in a Web server directory to allow HTML pages to access it.

JavaScript-to-Java communication

Now that you have an applet with a public method, you can include it in a Web page and access it via JavaScript. The following example uses `ExampleApplet` from the previous section and shows how JavaScript can be used to change the message displayed in the applet:

```
<html>
    <head>
        <title>Applet Example</title>
        <script>
            function changeAppletMessage() {
                var oApplet = document.getElementById("ExampleApplet");
                var oTextbox = document.getElementById("txtMessage");
                oApplet.setMessage(oTextbox.value);
            }
        </script>
    </head>
    <body>
        <p>Enter the message you want to see in the applet.</p>
        <p><input type="text" id="txtMessage" size="10" />
        <input type="button" value="Set Message" onclick="changeAppletMessage()" />
        </p>

        <object type="application/x-java-applet" code="ExampleApplet.class"
                width="100" height="100" border="1" id="ExampleApplet">
            <comment>
                <applet code="ExampleApplet.class" width="100" height="100"
                        name="ExampleApplet"></applet>
            </comment>
        </object>
    </body>
</html>
```

This example presents the user with a text box where a new message can be entered. When the user clicks the Set Message button, it calls the `changeAppletMessage()` function, which gets a reference to the applet and retrieves the text from the text box. Then, the function calls the applet's `setMessage()` method, passing in the entered text. The message displayed in the applet changes from `"Hello World!"` to whatever the user enters (sometimes this happens quickly, sometimes slowly).

Type conversion

Although JavaScript-to-Java communication is a powerful tool for developers, it is not without its issues. In the previous example, a string was passed from JavaScript to a Java method without issue. That's because the JavaScript `String` object maps directly to the Java `String` object. The same is true for any primitive value in JavaScript because they all have equivalent primitive types in Java. You can run into trouble when trying to pass objects into a Java method because no equivalent class exists. For this reason, it's always best that any method you create for use with JavaScript accept only primitive values.

Handling Java exceptions

Exceptions are much more common in Java than in JavaScript, so you must be aware when they could possibly occur. When accessing an applet method that could cause an error, you can prepare by wrapping the call in `try..catch` statement. Yes, the JavaScript `try..catch` statement catches exceptions thrown by an applet.

Suppose you change the `ExampleApplet` to throw an error if `setMessage()` is passed a zero-length string, such as:

```
import java.applet.Applet;
import java.awt.Graphics;
import java.awt.HeadlessException;

public class ExampleApplet2 extends Applet {

    private String message = "Hello World!";

    public ExampleApplet2() throws HeadlessException {
        super();
    }

    public void paint(Graphics g) {
        g.drawString(message, 20, 20);
    }

    public void setMessage(String message) throws Exception {
        if (message.length()== 0) {
            throw new Exception("Message must have at least one character.");
        }

        this.message = message;
        repaint();
    }
}
```

It would then be possible to catch a thrown error using the JavaScript `try..catch` statement:

```
var oApplet = document.getElementById("ExampleApplet");
var oTextbox = document.getElementById("txtMessage");

try {
    oApplet.setMessage(oTextbox.value);
} catch (oError) {
    alert("Error caught!");
}
```

Because of differences in browsers, it's not easy to say what will be returned by `oError`. Internet Explorer returns a JavaScript object representing the Java exception, whereas Mozilla returns the Java exception object itself. The two browsers have different ways to access the error information: In IE, the `oError.message` property displays the Java exception message; in Mozilla, the `toString()` method returns a string of Java exceptions, but doesn't contain the original exception method. In most cases, however, it's enough to know that an error occurred.

Security restrictions

Although Java is more powerful than JavaScript, it doesn't have free reign over the browser when included in a Web page. Java applets must follow a strict set of rules set out by the browser. (The rules are different in every browser, although several rules are fairly common.) This behavior is called *sandboxing*.

First, applets are not allowed access to the user's file system. This prevents a major security problem if a malicious applet writer gets an unsuspecting user to open a page containing the applet. By default, this isn't possible.

Second, applets aren't allowed to access resources across domains. This is the same security restriction placed on the XML HTTP requests discussed earlier in the book.

It is possible to get around these restrictions by digitally *signing* the applet. When an applet is signed, a dialog is presented to the user asking whether the signature is valid and, in turn, whether the applet should be allowed enhanced privileges not available otherwise. If the signature is accepted, the restrictions mentioned previously are lifted.

You can read more about applet security and signing at `http://java.sun.com/developer/technicalArticles/Security/Signed/`.

Java-to-JavaScript communication

Not only can JavaScript access methods contained in a Java applet, an applet can actually access JavaScript objects and functions as well by using LiveConnect. LiveConnect was mentioned earlier as a way for JavaScript to access Java objects, but it can also be used to more closely integrate applets and JavaScript using a special Java package: `netscape.javascript`.

This package contains two classes: `JSObject`, which is a Java representation of a JavaScript object, and `JSException`, which represents a JavaScript error. However, the `JSObject` is really the focus of Java-to-JavaScript communication.

The `JSObject` class has the following methods:

- `getMember(String name)` — Retrieves a named property of an object. Equivalent to `oObject.property` or `oObject["property"]` in JavaScript. The returned value is a Java `Object`.
- `getSlot(int index)` — Retrieves a numbered property of an object (mostly for use with JavaScript arrays). Equivalent to `oObject[index]`. The returned value is a Java `Object`.
- `setMember(String name, Object value)` — Sets the value of a named property.
- `setSlot(int index, Object value)` — Sets the value of a numbered property.
- `removeMember(String name)` — Removes the value of a named property.
- `call(String methodName, Object args[])` — Calls the method with the given name and passes in the arguments contained in the array of `Object`s. The returned value is a Java `Object`.
- `eval(String code)` — Evaluates a string of JavaScript code in the context of the object; similar to JavaScript's `eval()` function. The returned value is a Java `Object`.
- `equals(Object object)` — Determines if the object is equal to another.

One static method for `JSObject`, called `getWindow()`, accepts a Java `Applet` object as an argument and returns a `JSObject` representation of the JavaScript `window` object.

Using `JSObject` and LiveConnect takes a little getting used to. Suppose you want to retrieve the currently loaded URL. In JavaScript, this simply requires one line of code:

```
var sURL = window.location.href
```

In Java, it becomes a bit more involved:

```
JSObject window = JSObject.getWindow(this);
JSObject location = (JSObject) window.getMember("location");
String sURL = location.getMember("href").toString();
```

The first line gets a reference to the JavaScript `window` object (the argument, `this`, represents the applet from which the function is being called). The second line retrieves a pointer to the `location` object by using `getMember()`. Because `getMember()` returns an `Object`, it has to be cast as a `JSObject` in order to get access to the `JSObject` methods. The last line uses `getMember()` to get the value of `href`, which is also returned as an `Object`, meaning that `toString()` must be called to get the string value. Obviously, the Java code for accessing JavaScript objects is a bit verbose, but it gets the job done.

To use LiveConnect in an applet, you must import the package `netscape.javascript`. It's not necessary to distribute the package with your applet because it is built in to the Java plugin. So, just add the following line to your `.java` file and begin coding:

```
import netscape.javascript.*;
```

Here's an example applet that makes use of the LiveConnect package:

```
import java.applet.Applet;
import java.awt.Graphics;
import java.awt.HeadlessException;
import netscape.javascript.*;

public class ExampleApplet3 extends Applet {

    public ExampleApplet3() throws HeadlessException {
        super();
    }

    public void paint(Graphics g) {
        JSObject window = JSObject.getWindow(this);
        JSObject document = (JSObject) window.getMember("document");
        JSObject location = (JSObject) window.getMember("location");

        g.drawString("Title: " + document.getMember("title"), 10, 20);
        g.drawString("URL: " + location.getMember("href"), 10, 40);

        window.eval("getMessageFromApplet(\"Hello from the Java applet!\")");

    }
}
```

This applet uses the applet's `paint()` method to interact with the page's JavaScript. The method begins by getting references to the window, document, and location objects using the methodology discussed previously. Next, the applet draws the title of the page (retrieved from `document.title`) and the URL of the page (from `location.href`) onto the applet canvas.

Lastly, the `window`'s `eval()` method is used to evaluate a call to `getMessageFromApplet()`, which is a JavaScript function that must be defined in the HTML page containing the applet. If the function doesn't exist when the applet is initialized, then a `JSException` occurs.

When including an applet that uses the LiveConnect package, you must set a special parameter to allow it access to the HTML document. The parameter's name is `mayscript`, and it should be set to `true`:

```
<object type="application/x-java-applet" code="ExampleApplet3.class"
        width="100" height="100" id="ExampleApplet">
    <param name="mayscript" value="true" />
</object>
```

If you are using the old `<applet/>` element, then just include `mayscript` as an attribute:

```
<applet code="ExampleApplet3.class" mayscript="mayscript"
        width="100" height="100" name="ExampleApplet">
</applet>
```

Back to the example, the `getMessageFromApplet()` function does nothing more than display the argument that was passed. Here's the complete HTML code for the page:

```
<html>
    <head>
       <title>Applet Example</title>
        <script>
            function getMessageFromApplet(sMessage) {
                alert("Applet says: " + sMessage);
            }
        </script>
    </head>
    <body>
        <p>This page defines a function that is called by the applet once
        it is loaded.</p>
        <object type="application/x-java-applet" code="ExampleApplet3.class"
                width="400" height="50" id="ExampleApplet">
            <param name="mayscript" value="true" />
        </object>
    </body>
</html>
```

When this page is loaded, the applet displays the page title (`Applet Example`) and the URL you are viewing the example from. Then, you should see an alert displaying the message `"Applet says: Hello from the Java applet!"`

You can also use `call()` to execute `getMessageFromApplet()`:

```
Object[] args = new Object[1];
args[0] = "Hello from the Java applet!";
window.call("getMessageFromApplet", args);
```

Because `getMessageFromApplet()` is a global function, it's considered a method of `window` and, therefore, can be called using the `call()` method.

Flash Movies

What began as a way to embed small, vector-based animations on Web pages has grown into a development environment for entire Web sites and Web applications. Macromedia Flash has evolved into more than just a tool for animations, but an entire development environment designed for use on the Web.

Flash movies, as they are called, are created using Macromedia's proprietary Flash and Flash MX development environments (although many graphics programs now feature an Export to Flash feature based on Macromedia's Open SWF initiative). Because of its ubiquity, the Flash plugin now ships with most browsers, meaning that most users never have to download the plugin manually to enjoy the benefits (unless an upgrade is made available, of course).

Embedding Flash movies

To embed a Flash movie into an HTML page, use the `<object/>` element:

```
<object type="application/x-shockwave-flash" data="myflashmovie.swf"
        width="100" height="100" id="FlashMovie"></object>
```

Mozilla-based browsers won't display this properly, so you need to add a `movie` parameter set to the same URL as the `data` attribute:

```
<object type="application/x-shockwave-flash" data="myflashmovie.swf"
        width="100" height="100" id="FlashMovie">
    <param name="movie" value="myflashmovie.swf" />
</object>
```

Of course, if you want to support Netscape 4.x, include the `<embed/>` element:

```
<object type="application/x-shockwave-flash" data="myflashmovie.swf"
        width="100" height="100" id="FlashMovie">
    <param name="movie" value="myflashmovie.swf" />
    <embed type="application/x-shockwave-flash" src="myflashmovie.swf"
           width="100" height="100" quality="high" name="FlashMovie">
    </embed>
</object>
```

Referencing Flash movies

Just like Java applets, Flash movies can be referenced in a couple of different ways depending on how you embed them (using `document.getElementById()` for `<object/>` or `document.embeds` for `<embed/>`). The following function can be used to retrieve a reference to a Flash movie regardless of the embedding process used:

```
function getFlashMove(sName) {
    if (document.getElementById) {
        return document.getElementById(sName);
    } else {
        return document.embeds[sName];
    }
}
```

This function can be called like so:

```
var oFlashMovie = getFlashMovie("FlashMovie");
```

After you have a reference to the movie, it's possible to communicate back and forth using JavaScript.

JavaScript-to-Flash communication

Flash movies provide a number of standard methods that can be accessed by JavaScript:

- `GetVariable(variable_name)` — Retrieves the value of a Flash movie variable
- `GotoFrame(frame_number)` — Sets the current Flash frame to the given frame number
- `IsPlaying()` — Indicates whether the Flash movie is current playing
- `LoadMovie(layer_num, url)` — Loads a Flash movie at the given URL into the given Flash layer
- `Pan(x, y, mode)` — Pans a zoomed movie to the given coordinate. The mode argument is either 0, to consider the coordinates as pixel values, or 1, to consider the coordinates as percentages.
- `PercentLoaded()` — Returns the percent of the Flash movie that has been loaded (a number 0 to 100)
- `Play()` — Plays the movie from the current position
- `Rewind()` — Sets the movie back to the first frame
- `SetVariable(variable_name, value)` — Sets the value of a Flash movie variable
- `SetZoomRect(left, top, right, bottom)` — Sets the rectangle to zoom in on
- `StopPlay()` — Stops the Flash movie
- `TotalFrames()` — Returns the total number of frames in the Flash movie
- `Zoom(percent)` — Zooms in by a given percentage

These methods work directly on the movie object itself, so to stop a movie named *ExampleMovie*, you can do this:

```
var oFlashMovie = getFlashMovie("ExampleMovie");
oFlashMovie.StopPlay();
```

To get the total number of frames in the movie, use `TotalFrames()`. However, you must be aware of some cross-browser compatibility issues. In Internet Explorer on Windows, there is a bug where `TotalFrames` is an integer value instead of a function. It is necessary to check for this using `typeof` to determine if `TotalFrames` is a number or a function for cross-browser functionality:

```
function getTotalFrames(sName) {
    var oFlashMovie = document.getElementById(sName);

    if (typeof oFlashMovie == "function") {
        return oFlashMovie.TotalFrames();
    } else {
        return oFlashMovie.TotalFrames;
    }
}
```

Using `SetVariable()` and `GetVariable()`, it's possible to pass information to and get information from a Flash movie. For this to work, the Flash movie must have a variable that is watched for a value change. The simplest way to do this is to create a text field and tie its value to a variable (by selecting Dynamic Text from the Flash Properties panel and entering the name of the variable). Then, you can get the value of the variable using `GetVariable()` and change its value using `SetVariable()`. Both methods require the name of the variable in relation to its timeline. So, to access a variable named `message` in the main timeline, the first argument for both methods is `"/:message"`, where `"/"` represents the default timeline, the colon indicates a part of the timeline to access, and `message` is the variable name. For example:

```
var sOriginalMessage = oFlashMovie.GetVariable("/:message");
oFlashMovie.SetVariable("/:message", "my new message");
```

Some methods also work on a specific timeline in the movie:

- `TCallFrame(timeline, frame_number)` — Executes the action in the Eframe that is in the given position
- `TCallLabel(timeline, frame_label)` — Executes the action in the frame represented by the given label
- `TCurrentFrame(timeline)` — Returns the position of the current frame in the timeline
- `TCurrentLabel(timeline)` — Returns the label of the current frame in the timeline
- `TGetProperty(timeline, property_constant)` — Returns the value of the property indicated by the property constant (discussed later) as a string
- `TGetPropertyAsNumber(timeline, property_constant)` — Returns the value of the property indicated by the property constant as a number
- `TGotoFrame(timeline, frame_number)` — Sets the movie to the frame in the given position in the timeline
- `TGotoLabel(timeline, frame_label)` — Sets the movie to the frame with the given label in the timeline
- `TPlay(timeline)` — Plays the movie on the given timeline
- `TSetProperty(timeline, property_constant, value)` — Sets the value of the property indicated by the property constant as a string
- `TStopPlay(timeline)` — Stops the movie on the given timeline

The `TGetProperty()`, `TGetPropertyAsNumber()`, and `TSetProperty()` methods all use constants to indicate the property to get or set. Because the constants are only accessible from within Flash, JavaScript must always use the numeric value. The constants are listed in the following table:

Flash Constant	Value	Description
X_POS	0	The x-coordinate of the movie
Y_POS	1	The y-coordinate of the movie
X_SCALE	2	Horizontal scaling

Flash Constant	Value	Description
Y_SCALE	3	Vertical scaling
CURRENT_FRAME	4	The position of the current frame in the movie
TOTAL_FRAMES	5	The total number of frames in the movie
ALPHA	6	The opacity of the movie (number between 0 and 100)
VISIBLE	7	If the movie is visible or not
WIDTH	8	The width of the movie
HEIGHT	9	The height of the movie
ROTATION	10	The rotation of the movie in degrees
TARGET	11	The timeline name (same as first argument of any of the timeline-specific methods)
FRAMES_LOADED	12	The number of frames currently loaded
NAME	13	The name of the movie
DROP_TARGET	14	The name of the drop target inside the movie, if one exists
URL	15	The URL of the movie
HIGH_QUALITY	16	If the movie is in high-quality rendering mode or not (1 for true, 0 for false)
FOCUS_RECT	17	Whether or not a focus rectangle should be displayed (1 for true, 0 for false)
SOUND_BUF_TIME	18	The amount of time that sound should be buffered to produce uninterrupted playback

When using the timeline-specific methods, the first argument is always the name of the timeline to act on. The default timeline is represented by a single forward slash:

```
var iXPos = oFlashMovie.TGetProperty("/", 0);
```

The first argument is always mirrored by the `TARGET` property:

```
var sTarget = oFlashMovie.TGetProperty("/", 11);
alert(sTarget == "/");    //outputs true
```

Because Flash uses an ECMAScript-based scripting language called ActionScript, the interaction with JavaScript is seamless.

Flash-to-JavaScript communication

Flash also has the capability to interact with JavaScript that exists on the HTML page in which it is embedded. When using the `<object/>` element to embed the Flash movie, this capability is enabled by default. If you are using the <embed/> element, even for backwards compatibility, you must add a special attribute called swLiveConnect:

```
<object type="application/x-shockwave-flash" data="myflashmovie.swf"
        width="100" height="100">
    <param name="message" value="Hello World! " />
    <embed type="application/x-shockwave-flash" src="myflashmovie.swf"
           width="100" height="100" swLiveConnect="true">
        <param name="message" value="Hello World!" />
    </embed>
</object>
```

With the attribute set, you can be assured that the Flash-to-JavaScript communication channel is open.

Flash provides two different ways to achieve this interaction: getURL() and fsCommand(). Both can send only primitive values to JavaScript, and each has its own strengths and weaknesses.

getURL()

The getURL() function is a generic way of interacting with the browser. It can be used to open up a document in the browser window (or in a new window) similar to window.open() is JavaScript. For example, you can open www.wrox.com in a new browser window with the following code:

```
getURL("http://www.wrox.com", "_blank");
```

Because getURL() simply passed the given URL to the browser, it can accept javascript: URLs as well. For example, suppose you have a function, getMessageFromFlash(), that accepts a string as its only argument and then displays that string in an alert, such as in the following:

```
function getMessageFromFlash(sMessage) {
    alert("Flash says: \"" + sMessage + "\".");
}
```

Inside of the Flash movie, create a button and assign the following ActionScript to it:

```
on(release) {
    getURL("javascript:getMessageFromFlash(\"Hello from Flash!\")");
}
```

When you export the movie and embed it in the HTML page containing getMessageFromFlash(), clicking on the button pops up the JavaScript alert displaying the text "Hello from Flash!"

The getURL() function is the simplest way to call JavaScript from Flash, although you have another way to do this.

fscommand()

Using fscommand() in Flash is like sending a message to JavaScript. This message consists of a command (indicating the action the movie is expecting) and a single argument (although Flash allows you to enter more than one argument, this isn't handled correctly by JavaScript). A typical call from inside a Flash movie looks like this:

```
on(release) {
    fscommand("send_message", "the message");
}
```

In order for JavaScript to handle this command, a special function must be defined. This function must begin with the name (or ID) of the Flash movie object and be followed by `_DoFSCommand`, such as the following:

```
function ExampleMovie_DoFSCommand(sCommand, vArgument) {
    ...
}
```

The function always accepts two arguments, the command and an argument. The command is always a string, but the argument may be any primitive type. All calls to `fscommand()` are routed to this function, so, by providing different commands, you can determine what action should be taken with JavaScript. For example:

```
function ExampleMovie_DoFSCommand(sCommand, vArgument) {
    switch(sCommand) {
        case "change_color":
            //change the color of something
            break;

        case "change_height":
            //change the height of something
            break;

        //etc.
}
```

When using any browser other than Internet Explorer, this function is called when `fscommand()` is executed. For Internet Explorer, another function is needed.

For reasons unknown, the Flash Player routes `fscommand()` calls in Internet Explorer to VBScript, not JavaScript. VBScript is an IE-only technology that allows developers to use Visual Basic code to script Web pages. Originally intended to compete with JavaScript, VBScript never gained the popularity or support from other browsers that would have enabled it to be a true rival. Instead, it was remanded to niche developers working on IE-only solutions.

In order to avoid writing a lot of VBScript, you can just write a simple function that passes the command and the argument back to the JavaScript function. This code must be enclosed in its own `<script/>` element with the language attribute set to `"VBScript"`. The VBScript function takes the same form as the JavaScript function, although it ends with `_FSCommand` instead of `_DoFSCommand`:

```
<script language="VBScript">
    Sub ExampleMovie_FSCommand(ByVal sCommand, ByVal vArgument)
        call ExampleMovie_DoFSCommand(sCommand, vArgument)
    end sub
</script>
```

All non-IE browsers ignore this code block because `"VBScript"` is unrecognized as a scripting language; therefore, it's safe to include this in your cross-browser pages (although it is still recommended that this reside in the `<head/>` element to prevent rendering of the code as plain text). Another alternative is to place the VBScript into an external file (ending in .vbs) and load it into the page like this:

```
<script language="VBScript" src="example.vbs"></script>
```

Because of the intricate workings of `fscommand()`, many developers simply choose to use `getURL()` for JavaScript communication.

ActiveX Controls

In Internet Explorer on Windows, you can embed ActiveX controls in the page by using the `<object/>` element. To do this, you need to know the class ID of the ActiveX control you wish to embed (this information can be gleaned using the OLE/COM Object Viewer) and insert it as the `classid` attribute:

```
<object classid="activex_class_id" id="ActiveXControl"></object>
```

Not all ActiveX controls behave properly when embedded in a Web page. Indeed, some of them trigger security warnings in Internet Explorer and possibly in software such as antivirus programs. However, a few ActiveX controls were designed to work appropriately and safely in Web pages. One such component is the tabular data control.

> **ActiveX-based plugins do not work on any non-Windows browser because ActiveX is a Windows-specific technology. On Windows XP Service Pack 2, any ActiveX control that attempts to contact an outside server or is capable of accessing a local file triggers a warning.**

The tabular data control has no visual component to it, so it is an invisible object on your page. At first glance, it hardly looks exciting — especially when compared to what you can do with Java and Flash. At second glance, however, the tabular data control reveals some powerful functionality that allows JavaScript to use database-like functionality.

Specifically, the tabular data control allows you to use a flat text file as if it were a database table. You tell the control what the value delimiter character is, and it parses the text file into a series of rows and values.

To create a tabular data control on a page, you must use the class ID `"CLSID:333C7BC4-460F-11D0-BC04-0080C7055A83"` (retrieved using the OLE/COM Object Viewer) and give the object an ID:

```
<object classid="CLSID:333C7BC4-460F-11D0-BC04-0080C7055A83" id="TextData">
</object>
```

Next, you must specify the `DataURL` parameter, which indicates where the text file is located (this can be either a relative or complete URL), and the `FieldDelim` parameter, which indicates what the delimiter is between two values in the same row (most often this is a comma):

```
<object classid="CLSID:333C7BC4-460F-11D0-BC04-0080C7055A83" id="TextData">
    <param name="DataURL" value="Names.txt" />
    <param name="FieldDelim" value="," />
</object>
```

Lastly, if the file in question uses the first row as headers, you should set the `UseHeader` parameter to `true`, which doesn't include the first row in the data values and also enables you to reference columns by name as well as position:

```
<object classid="CLSID:333C7BC4-460F-11D0-BC04-0080C7055A83" id="TextData">
    <param name="DataURL" value="Names.txt" />
    <param name="FieldDelim" value="," />
    <param name="UseHeader" value="true" />
</object>
```

This code says to load the tabular data control with the data in `Names.txt` that has a field delimiter of `","` and use the headers as a key for each column.

Here's a sample `Names.txt` file:

```
first_name,last_name
Nicholas,Zakas
Michael,Smith
Joyce,Anderson
Benjamin,Johnson
Amy,Jones
```

The first column is named `first_name`, and the second column is named `last_name`. On each row, commas, as indicated by using the `FieldDelim` parameter, separate the values.

The page's `load` event does not fire until the tabular data control has fully loaded its data, so it's safe to use the `onload` event handler to determine when the data is available. At that point, you retrieve the recordset created by accessing the `recordset` property of the control:

```
window.onload = function () {
    oDataset = document.getElementById("TextData").recordset;
};
```

This code creates a global variable named `oDataset` that points to the recordset containing all the data.

You can iterate through the recordset by using the `moveFirst()`, `moveLast()`, `moveNext()`, and `movePrevious()` methods in combination with the `EOF` (end of file) and `BOF` (beginning of file) markers. For example, here's a basic code outline to iterate through the recordset starting from the first record and ending with the last:

```
oDataset.moveFirst();

while (!oDataset.EOF) {

    //do something with the data here

   oDataset.moveNext();
}
```

The first step in the previous code is to set the recordset to the first record. The `while` loop then tests EOF, which is `true` when the end of the file has been reached. Inside of the loop is where the data processing occurs before moving on to the next record.

It's also possible to move backwards through the recordset using the opposite methods:

```
oDataset.moveLast();

while (!oDataset.BOF) {

    //do something with the data here

    oDataset.movePrevious();
}
```

This code starts from the last record and works its way back to the first. The `BOF` property is equal to `true` when you reach the beginning of the file.

To get at the data, use the `fields()` method of the recordset with the column name (either `first_name` or `last_name` in the previous example) or the position of the column, starting at 0, in the table. This method returns an object representing the field that has a `value` property with the actual value. So to display the first name for each person in `Names.txt`, the following code can be used:

```
oDataset.moveFirst();

while (!oDataset.EOF) {

    alert(oDataset.fields(0).value);

    oDataset.moveNext();
}
```

You could also use `first_name` instead of `0`:

```
oDataset.moveFirst();

while (!oDataset.EOF) {

    alert(oDataset.fields("first_name").value);

    oDataset.moveNext();
}
```

In this way, you can move through the recordset and get all the data you need.

The tabular data control is a useful component if you have the luxury of developing only for Internet Explorer on Windows. It has a great many uses for it, many more than can be discussed in this context. Its tie to both Internet Explorer as a browser and Windows as a platform has, however, greatly inhibited its use and adoption in Web development. Presently, such solutions are best suited for Intranet applications where the user base can be kept to those using IE on Windows exclusively.

Summary

This chapter introduced the concept of plugins and how to use JavaScript to communicate with them. You learned about the two different styles of plugins, ActiveX and Netscape-style, as well as how to embed each into a Web page.

Next, Java applets and their use on the Web were discussed. You learned how JavaScript, via LiveConnect, can access public methods of Java applets and how Java applets can be programmed to call JavaScript directly.

From that point, you learned about Macromedia Flash and how to embed Flash movies in HTML pages. You learned about the large number of JavaScript methods capable of controlling Flash movies as well as how to pass data to and receive data from them. Additionally, you learned the two ways to call JavaScript from inside Flash movies using `getURL()` and `fscommand()`.

The chapter finished up by discussing embedded ActiveX controls and the tabular data control specifically. You learned how to load data from a flat text file into the tabular data control and how to access that data from within JavaScript.

19

Deployment Issues

So the JavaScript for your Web application or Web site has been coded, you've fully debugged it, and you've made sure that it works in each of your target browsers. The time is coming for deployment, and that introduces a whole host of new issues. Although you can test on various operating systems with various browsers, seemingly little things can cause unexpected browser behavior. It might be an operating system service pack; it could be a bug patch for a browser; or it could be a difference in cross-platform behavior. All these fall under the umbrella of deployment issues: things you need to worry about when setting up a system outside of your development environment.

Security

One of the biggest issues for any Web-based system, whether it be purely informational or an online storefront, is security. JavaScript is filled with security checks to prevent malicious scripts from attacking your computer, but specific security measures are also taken by each browser. Mozilla, for instance, has an entirely unique security model involving signed scripts and enhanced privileges. If you understand which security measures apply to all browsers and which are browser-specific you can create more secure JavaScript.

The Same Origin Policy

It was briefly mentioned earlier in the book that JavaScript can only communicate with pages from the same domain. For example, a script running on Wrox's home page (`www.wrox.com`) cannot interact with any browser window or frame containing a page from Mozilla's Web site (`www.mozilla.org`). This security measure is known as the Same Origin Policy.

Two scripts are considered to have the same origin if the containing pages:

- Use the same protocol (such as http://)
- Use the same port (typically port 80)
- Have the same domain name

If all three of these conditions aren't met, the two scripts are not allowed to interact. For instance, a script running on `www.wrox.com` cannot access a page from `p2p.wrox.com` because these are considered different domain names (even though `p2p.wrox.com` is technically a subdomain of `www.wrox.com`). This same script can't access pages from `www.wrox.com:8080` because it has a different port number or from `about:blank` because it's a different protocol (not `http://`).

The effect on BOM and DOM scripting

These rules affect the way you can interact with the BOM and the DOM. For instance, you cannot access the `document` object for any page from a different origin, meaning that you can't access any of the DOM structure. The following two lines illustrate the issue:

```
alert(frames[1].location.href);
alert(frames[1].document.location.href);     //fails
```

The previous code should output two alerts, each displaying the URL of the page in the second frame (the frame at index 1). You may recall from earlier in the book that both the `window` and `document` objects have a `location` object as a property. If the script using these two lines of code is from a different origin than the page contained in the frame, the second line of code fails because the script cannot access the `document.location` object or any of its properties. The script can, however, access the `window.location` object (represented by `frames[1].location`) and can still access all the other properties of the window.

You may also remember from earlier in the book that the XML HTTP Request object (in all browsers) and the Web Service functionality work only with resources from the same domain; this is yet another instance where the Same Origin Policy takes effect. It also applies to plugins.

The exception to the rule

Common logic dictates that `www.wrox.com` and `p2p.wrox.com` belong to the same domain, so they should be able to communicate with one another. As it turns out, the browser developers agree and have provided a way to allow such communication.

In the pages from each subdomain, a single line of script can be included to circumvent the Same Origin Policy. This is done by setting the `document.domain` property as shown here:

```
document.domain = "wrox.com";
```

This simple line of code then eliminates all the security blocks for JavaScript communication. Note, however, that you can set the domain only to a value already in the URL, so a page from `www.wrox.com` cannot set the domain to `mozilla.org`, because that is a violation of the Same Origin Policy.

Window object issues

A number of measures protect end users from malicious scripts attempting to use windows.

First and foremost, windows cannot be opened off screen or smaller than 100 x 100. If you specify coordinates that are off the screen, the window is automatically placed on the screen in a location close to where you specified, but with enough space to see the entire window. Likewise, if you try to open a window smaller than 100 x 100, the window automatically opens up to 100 x 100. These rules, although seemingly impractical, help to ensure that users are always aware of windows popped up from scripts.

You also can't open windows that are larger than the user's desktop. You can't, for instance, open a window that is 1600 x 1200 on a screen that is 1024 x 768.

> **Internet Explorer on Windows XP Service Pack 2 exhibits a slightly different behavior. It enables you to open windows off screen or at small sizes if the site you are visiting is listed as *trusted* in Internet Options. *Trusted sites* are typically those accessed using https://, but not necessarily. For any *untrusted* site, you receive a security warning if the site attempts to open the window. If you allow the pop-up, it has all the traditional limitations (can't be opened off screen, can't be opened to a very small size).**

These same window position and dimension rules apply after the window has been created. You cannot move a pop-up window off screen using `moveBy()` or `moveTo()`, nor can you resize the window to be smaller than 100 x 100 or to be larger than the desktop using `resizeBy()` and `resizeTo()`.

> **Some browsers (such as Mozilla) allow the end user to decide whether scripts should be allowed to move and resize windows.**

Also a window cannot be closed using the `close()` method unless the window was opened using `window.open()`. If you try to close a window that wasn't opened by script, a dialog is displayed asking for the user's permission to close to the window.

Most browsers now come with pop-up blockers built-in. Many non-technical users actually have no idea whether or not pop-up blocking is turned on. Keep this in mind when designing your Web solution.

Typically, pop-up blockers work by blocking all pop-up windows that occur without user interaction, meaning that you can't open up a new window during events such as `load` and `unload`; pop-up windows can only be opened during events such as `click` and `keypress`. However, some pop-up blockers that block all pop-up windows without regard for user interaction. So how can you tell if one of your pop-up windows has met with an untimely block?

The `window.open()` method typically returns a pointer to the newly created window. If the window was blocked, `window.open()` usually returns `null`:

```
var oWindow = window.open("page.htm", "mywindow");

if (oWindow == null) {
     alert("Your popup blocker won't allow you access to this window.");
} else {
     //continue on
}
```

The preceding code displays a message to the user when the window has been blocked. In general, it's always best to make sure the method returned doesn't return `null` whenever you open a window.

This method works well for Windows XP Service Pack 2's IE pop-up blocker, Mozilla's pop-up blocker, and the Google Toolbar pop-up blocker. For others, you may need to surround the `window.open()` call in a `try..catch` block (because some other pop-up blockers actually cause JavaScript errors instead of just returning `null`).

Mozilla-specific issues

As part of the Netscape Communicator code overhaul, Mozilla introduced several new security mechanisms for ensuring the authenticity and safety of scripts embedded in Web pages. The first involves activating enhanced privileges.

Privileges

Various security-related capabilities are arranged into privileges. In order to use these privileged functions, you must request permission from the user using `netscape.security.PrivilegeManager.enablePrivilege()`.

Mozilla provides guidance to developers regarding the proper use of privileges in a document entitled "JavaScript Security: Signed Scripts" (available at `http://www.mozilla.org/projects/security/components/signed-scripts.html`). In this document, Jesse Ruderman lists the following available privileges for Mozilla:

Privilege	Description
`UniversalBrowserRead`	Enables the browser to circumvent the Same Origin Policy and read resources outside of the current domain.
`UniversalBrowserWrite`	Enables the browser to circumvent the Same Origin Policy and write to resources outside of the current domain.
`UniversalXPConnect`	Allows access to the browser API using XPConnect.
`UniversalPreferencesRead`	Allows reading of user preferences using `navigator.preferences`.
`UniversalPreferencesWrite`	Allows setting of user preferences using `navigator.preferences`.
`CapabilityPreferencesAccess`	Allows reading/setting of preferences governing security. To read one of these preferences, you also need `UniversalBrowserRead`; to set one, you also need `UniversalBrowserWrite`.
`UniversalFileRead`	Allows opening of browser windows using the `file://` protocol.

In order to enable a privilege, you must pass in one of these values to the `enablePrivilege()` method:

```
netscape.security.PrivilegeManager.enablePrivilege("UniversalBrowserRead");
```

You may remember this line of code from Chapter 17, "Web Services." This privilege was necessary in order to complete the Web Service calls. The `UniversalBrowserRead` privilege also allows you to access the URLs in the browser's history, such as the following:

```
netscape.security.PrivilegeManager.enablePrivilege("UniversalBrowserRead");

for (var i=0; i < history.length; i++){
    alert(history[i]);
}
```

This script outputs the URL of each page in the browser's history, as stored in the `history` object.

As soon as you have completed the use of privileged actions, it's best to disable the privilege to ensure that no malicious scripts can use the privilege:

```
netscape.security.PrivilegeManager.enablePrivilege("UniversalBrowserRead");

for (var i=0; i < history.length; i++){
    alert(history[i]);
}

netscape.security.PrivilegeManager.disablePrivilege("UniversalBrowserRead");
```

The `UniversalBrowserWrite` privilege is perhaps the most interesting because it enables you to avoid the window restrictions mentioned earlier in this chapter. When this privilege is enabled, you can:

- Resize windows to be less than 100 x 100 or greater than the user's desktop size.
- Move windows off screen.
- Create windows without a window title.
- Close a window using `close()` regardless of how the window was opened.

If a privilege is requested and not accepted, then the JavaScript Console displays a message saying, `"User did not grant privilege"`.

Signed scripts

In order to use the extended privileges, your script must be signed. JavaScript files can be signed in the same manner as applets, and doing so allows access to these privileges. Signing a script involves obtaining a digital certificate from a security firm that authenticates the script's location, publisher, and usage. When a signed script is loaded, the browser displays a message asking if the signed script should be allowed to access the extended privileges it may use.

The Mozilla Foundation provides SignTool to aid in the signing of scripts. This small utility packages a script into a JAR file along with its digital certificate. In order to use signed scripts, the containing HTML page must be accessed using a URL with the following format:

```
jar:http://www.yourdomain.com/signedscripts.jar!/page.htm
```

When the script is properly signed and accessed with an appropriate URL, the user just accepts the digital certificate; he is not required to allow each privilege as it is enabled.

If the script isn't signed appropriately, it won't run. The JavaScript Console displays the same message the user sees when he doesn't allow an extended privilege (`"User did not grant privilege"`). For more information on signed scripts in Mozilla, see `http://www.mozilla.org/projects/security/components/signed-scripts.html`.

> **There is no way to sign scripts on Internet Explorer or on any other browser. Internet Explorer does offer some advanced security through the use of HyperText Applications (HTAs). For more information on using HTAs, refer to `http://msdn.microsoft.com/workshop/author/hta/overview/htaoverview.asp`.**

Codebase Principals

Another way to access the extended privileges is to enable Codebase Principals. This policy determines the safety of a given script based on where it's loaded from (its *codebase*). Presumably, a script is safe if it is being loaded from the same server as the HTML page. This is not exactly a safe assumption, which is why all Mozilla browsers come with Codebase Principals disabled. It is purposely difficult to enable so that the average user won't turn on Codebase Principals by mistake.

Codebase Principals should only be used for testing and debugging of a script that will eventually be signed.

Resource limitations

If you're a software developer or a software user, you're probably aware that some programs can end up overreaching their memory limit, making your machine run more slowly, become unstable, and sometimes crash. It was decided by browser companies that JavaScript would not affect the user's computer in this detrimental way. For this reason, browsers only run up to one million lines of JavaScript is any one call.

One million sounds like a lot of lines (probably more lines than you'll ever need), but every once in a while you may find yourself bumping up against this limit. When this happens, the browser notifies you in some way: Internet Explorer pops up a dialog box telling you that a script is causing the browser to run slowly and asks if you would like to continue running the script; Mozilla simply opts out of the current operation and places an error message in the JavaScript Console.

The one million lines aren't cumulative, so you don't need to worry if you have scripts that run when the user clicks on different parts of the page. This restriction exists only within a single function call to prevent problems such as infinite loops and infinite recursion.

Internationalization Concerns

If you are planning to create a Web site that can be accessed from anywhere in the world, or a Web application that can be installed anywhere in the world, internationalization is a concern. Entire libraries, available in numerous programming languages, help you with internationalization of software, ranging from typical C++ applications to Web-based systems. Companies spend hundreds of hours examining their Web sites and Web applications for internationalization purposes, but they often forget to examine JavaScript code.

Detecting language using JavaScript

In Chapter 5, "JavaScript in the Browser," you were introduced to the `navigator` object and its properties. One of the properties that has not been discussed in detail is the `language` property, which returns the language and country code in which the browser is currently operating (for example, "en-us" for United States English):

```
var sLang = navigator.language;  //won't work in IE
```

Mozilla, Opera, and Safari/Konqueror all support this property, but Internet Explorer does not.

Instead, Internet Explorer provides three properties: `browserLanguage` (indicates the language being used by the browser), `userLanguage` (essentially identical to `browserLanguage`), and `systemLanguage` (indicating the language of the operating system). The `userLanguage` property is essentially the same as `language`, so you can make a simple addition to the previous code to detect the language for all browsers:

```
var sLang = navigator.language || navigator.browserLanguage;
```

Using this code, you can determine if someone is viewing your page from a browser with an unsupported language setting and take appropriate action, such as redirecting the visitor to a more appropriate page:

```
if (sLang.toLowerCase() == "fr") {
    document.location.replace("index_fr.htm");
}
```

This code checks to see if the language is French (represented as `"fr"`), and if so, it redirects to another page.

> **You may have noticed that this code uses `toLowerCase()` on the language string. This is necessary because capitalization is not consistent across browsers. Some report United States English as `"en-us"`, whereas others use `"en-US"`.**

Strategies

The most important step in internationalizing your JavaScript is to avoid hard-coded strings. For example, don't do this:

```
alert("The date you entered is incorrect.");
```

In this example, the string `"The date you entered is incorrect."` is hard-coded. When a value is hard-coded, its value cannot be changed without directly editing the line that uses it. Compare this with the following example:

```
var sIncorrectDateMessage = "The date you entered is incorrect.";

//more code here

alert(sIncorrectDateMessage);
```

This example places the message string into a variable called `sIncorrectDateMessage`. All other internationalized strings should be stored alongside this variable so you can change any and all values in only one place.

The best way to handle internationalized strings is to separate all strings into a separate JavaScript file (similar to the way JSP applications use properties files). Each language you support should have its own JavaScript file. For example, suppose you have three languages to support: English (language code en), German (de), and French (fr). Each language should have its own JavaScript file containing any strings necessary for the Web site or Web application. The easiest way to do this is to give each file a filename that differs only in the language code. For example, these filenames make selecting the correct file easy:

- Strings_en.js
- Strings_de.js
- Strings_fr.js

Then, using a little server-side logic, you can ensure that the correct one is included. In PHP, you could do this:

```
$supported = array("en","de","fr");

if (in_array($lang, $supported)) {
    $filename = "Strings_$lang.js";
} else {
    $filename = "Strings_en.js";
}

<script type="text/javascript"
        src="scripts/<?php echo $filename ?>"></script>
```

This example assumes a variable named `$lang` contains the language to use and then matches it up against an array of supported languages (`$supported`). If the language is supported, the JavaScript file for that language is loaded; otherwise, the default (English) language script is loaded. This ensures that the correct JavaScript string values are used for the given language and that there is a default language to fall back on if an unsupported language is encountered.

String considerations

The first edition of ECMAScript introduced support for Unicode characters (which number upwards of 65,000 as compared to 128 ASCII characters), effectively assuring that ECMAScript can handle strings of any kind, including typically problematic double-byte characters.

What exactly is Unicode?

According to the official Unicode home page, "Unicode provides a unique number for every character, no matter what the platform, no matter what the program, no matter what the language."

Unicode was developed to provide a common encoding to handle all the characters that exist in the world. Prior to Unicode, each language had its own encoding, meaning that characters in different languages could be represented by the same code, so the letter *A* in English could use the same code as a different letter in a different language (obviously, not optimal).

Unicode represents characters as a 16-bit number, allowing for over 65,000 possible characters, making it an ideal solution to internationalization concerns. Additionally, the first 128 Unicode characters are, in fact, the 128 ASCII characters, making compatibility with older English-language applications much easier.

Representation in JavaScript

All Unicode characters, including ASCII, are represented in Unicode as a four-digit hexadecimal value prefixed with a `\u` to indicate a Unicode character. For example, `\u0045` is the Unicode form of the *E* (which can also be represented using ASCII syntax as `\x45`).

This representation of characters can be used in comments and strings in JavaScript just as you use special characters like `\n`. For example:

```
alert("\u0048\u0045\u004C\u004C\u004F \u0057\u004F\u0052\u004C\u0044");
```

Not sure what this line does? It presents an alert with the text `"HELLO WORLD"` to the user. Using the Unicode character set, you can create messages in any number of languages. Even though the plain text form of such messages isn't human readable, it's still the only way to deal with multibyte characters from other languages.

Browser versus operating system support

Just because JavaScript can display and understand Unicode characters doesn't necessarily mean the operating system can. Why should this concern Web developers who care only about what the browser supports, you may ask? The answer is because JavaScript uses some operating system functionality to do its job, although most developers never realize it. For internationalization, you must be aware of this very important boundary.

Any time you use `alert()`, `confirm()`, or `prompt()`, you are using an operating system dialog box. Unless the client operating system has foreign language support installed, you end up with a dialog full of gibberish. Most of the time, the browser reflects the language of the operating system, however you never can tell what individuals with do with their browsers.

When using operating system dialogs with internationalization, be aware that these problems can occur. When dealing with a distributed Web application, it may be enough to inform the customer of this limitation; on public Web sites, however, it may be best to avoid using these dialogs altogether.

Error-proofing strings

Oftentimes in internationalized Web pages, developers try to pass strings from a server-side variable into a JavaScript variable using a technique such as this:

```
<% String sJspHello = "Hello"; %>

<!-- more code here -->

<script type="text/javascript">
    var sJavaScriptHello = "<%= sJspHello %>";
```

```
    alert(sJavaScriptHello);
</script>
```

This example uses JSP with the intent of outputting the string `"Hello"` into a JavaScript variable. When this page gets to the browser, you can view the source:

```
<script type="text/javascript">
    var sJavaScriptHello = "Hello";
    alert(sJavaScriptHello);
</script>
```

The output looks correct and the JavaScript functions as expected. But now consider another example:

```
<% String sJspHeSaidHi = "He said, \"hi.\""; %>

<!-- more code here -->

<script type="text/javascript">
    var sJavaScriptHeSaidHi = "<%= sJspHeSaidHi %>";
    alert(sJavaScriptHeSaidHi);
</script>
```

The output to the browser now becomes this:

```
<script type="text/javascript">
    var sJavaScriptHeSaidHi = "He said, "hi."";
    alert(sJavaScriptHeSaidHi);
</script>
```

Do you see the problem? The string that was outputted from the JSP contained quotation marks, which creates a syntax error in JavaScript. This is the most common mistake made when internationalizing Web pages that use JavaScript to output strings. You must be aware of quotation marks contained within strings if the string is to be output into JavaScript code. The best way to deal with this is to replace the quotation marks in all strings before outputting to JavaScript, such as in the following:

```
<% String sJspHeSaidHi = "He said, \"hi.\""; %>

<!-- more code here -->

<script type="text/javascript">
    var sJavaScriptHeSaidHi = "<%= sJspHeSaidHi.replaceAll("\\\"", "\\\"")  %>";
    alert(sJavaScriptHeSaidHi);
</script>
```

This example converts all quotation marks to a backslash followed by a quotation mark using the Java `replaceAll()` method. The first argument is a string representation of a regular expression (you'll remember that regular expression strings must be double-escaped, so `\"` becomes `\\\"`); the second argument is identical, although this one is a string and not a regular expression. This effectively changes this string:

```
"He said, \"hi.\""
```

To this:

```
"He said, \\\"hi.\\\""
```

When this is output to JavaScript, you get a valid string:

```
<script type="text/javascript">
    var sJavaScriptHeSaidHi = "He said, \"hi.\"";
    alert(sJavaScriptHeSaidHi);
</script>
```

This JavaScript code is syntactically correct and runs without error.

Use double quotes

Another common mistake is to use apostrophes to indicate strings instead of quotation marks. As you remember, JavaScript allows either to represent strings, so the following two lines of code are equal:

```
sHello = "Hello";
sHello = 'Hello';
```

Just because JavaScript lets you use either syntax doesn't mean you can use them interchangeably when you want internationalization. In fact, because apostrophes are much more common than quotation marks in everyday language (especially in languages like French), you run into the same problem we just explored with quotation marks, but far more often. Because of this, it's considered best practice to only use quotation marks to represent strings.

Following the guidelines in this section ensures that your internationalized JavaScript code works seamlessly.

Optimizing JavaScript

When creating desktop applications, most developers don't need to think much about optimization. For the most part, programming languages are optimized when they are compiled: All variables, functions, objects, and so on, are replaced with symbolic pointers that are understood only by the processor. Macros are compiled to be faster than function calls. Templates are used to speed up object creation. But JavaScript is a very different animal because it's downloaded as source code and then interpreted (not compiled) by the browser. Because of this, the speed of JavaScript code is split into two categories: download time and speed of execution.

Download time

When using Java or other such programming languages, developers need not give any thought to having variable names that are 100 characters long because the names are all replaced; they need not worry about writing paragraphs of comments because these, too, are removed. As a JavaScript developer, you do not have this luxury.

Web browsers download JavaScript as source code, meaning that all long variable names and comments are included. These and other factors increase the download time and thus increase the overall time it takes for the script to run. The key factor in decreasing download time is the number of bytes that a script contains.

The key number to remember is 1160, which is the number of bytes that fit into a single TCP-IP packet. It's best to try to keep each JavaScript file to 1160 bytes or less for optimal download time.

Every character in a JavaScript file is a byte. Thus, every extra character (whether it be a variable name, function name, or comment) counts against the download speed. Before deploying any JavaScript code, the download time should be optimized as much as possible. Here are a handful of ways that you can decrease the overall number of bytes in a script.

Remove all comments

This should be a no-brainer, but many developers forget this because, once again, compilers have traditionally handled this.

Any comments in a script should be removed prior to deployment. Comments are important while you are developing so that all team members can understand the source code. However, when it comes time for deployment, those comments are slowing down your JavaScript code dramatically.

> **It may be legally necessary to leave in a copyright notice or other such comment in your file for deployment. If this is the case, ensure that all other comments are removed and the legal comments are as short as possible.**

Removing comments is the easiest way to cut down the number of bytes in a JavaScript file. Even if you don't follow any of the other suggestions I give, this alone can provide dramatic decreases in overall file size.

Remove tabs and spaces

Most good developers indent their code regularly in order to increase readability. This is good practice, but the browser doesn't need all those extra tabs and spaces; they must go. And don't forget about the spaces between function arguments, assignments, and comparisons: say goodbye to those as well. Consider the following two lines:

```
function doSomething ( arg1, arg2, arg3 ) { alert(arg1 + arg2 + arg3); }

function doSomething(arg1,arg2,arg3){alert(arg1+arg2+arg3);}
```

To a JavaScript interpreter, these two lines are exactly identical, although the first line contains 12 more bytes than the second. Removing the extra tabs and spaces between arguments, parentheses, and other language delimiters helps to decrease the overall file size and, in turn, decreases the download time.

> **Using semicolons at the end of each line helps to preserve the syntactical meaning of your code when extra tabs and spaces are removed.**

Remove all line breaks

The next most important (and simple) thing you can do to decrease the size of the script file is to remove all line breaks. As long as you program appropriately by including a semicolon at the end of each line, the line breaks are of no consequence.

Many schools of thought exist about line breaks in JavaScript, but the bottom line is that line breaks increase the readability of your code to prying eyes. Removing them is a fast, easy way to make it more difficult for anyone to reverse engineer your code.

> **If for some reason removing line breaks is not an option, then — at the very least — make sure that they are Unix format instead of Windows format. Windows uses two characters on a line break (carriage return and line feed, ASCII codes 13 and 10 respectively); Unix uses only one. So, translating the line breaks into Unix format from Windows still yields some byte savings.**

Replace variable names

This is the toughest optimization method to implement. Replacing variable names usually can't be done by hand because the process is not a standard find-and-replace text operation.

The basic idea is that any variable name (or private property of an object) should be replaced with a nonsense variable name that has no intuitive meaning when read in the code. After all, the name of the variable doesn't matter to the interpreter, only to the developer who wants his or her code to make sense. When it comes time to deploy the script, however, eliminate those descriptive variable names with simpler, shorter ones:

```
function doSomething(sName,sAge,sCity){alert(sName+sAge+sCity);}

function doSomething(a1,a2,a3){alert(a1+a2+a3);}
```

The first line of code above is the original; the second line has the argument names replaced. By doing this, the byte count was reduced by 16. Just imagine the savings if all the variable names in your entire script are replaced with two-character names.

> **Use extreme caution when trying to rename variables on your own. Using a standard *Find and Replace* method in a text editor is not recommended, as the editor can't tell the difference between a variable name and any other text that matches the given pattern. For example, you may have a variable named `on` (perhaps a Boolean indicating if a value is valid or not). If you try to replace `on` with another value, you also replace the `on` at the end of `function`, thus rendering your entire script useless.**

The ECMAScript cruncher

Following the four steps listed previously can be difficult. To help with the process, you can use an external program.

One of the best tools for JavaScript code minimizing and variable replacement is the ECMAScript Cruncher (ESC) by Thomas Loo (available from Saltstorm at `http://www.saltstorm.net/depo/esc/`). ESC is a small Windows Shell Script that can do all the optimizations mentioned in this section for you.

To run ESC, you must be using a Windows. Open up a console window and use the following format:

```
cscript ESC.wsf -l [0-4] -ow outputfile.js inputfile1.js [inputfile2.js]
```

The first part, `cscript`, is the Windows Shell Script interpreter. The filename `ESC.wsf` is the ESC program itself. After that is the crunch level, which is a number between `0` and `4`, indicating which optimizations should be applied. The `-ow` option indicates that the next argument is the output file for the optimization. Finally, all remaining arguments are the JavaScript files to optimize. You can specify only one file to optimize or multiple files (which are optimized and placed into the output file one after the other).

The four levels of optimization supported by ESC are explained in the following table:

Level	Description
0	Leaves the script as-is. This is valuable if you want to append multiple files into a single file.
1	Removes all comments.
2	Save as level 1, plus removes extra tabs and spaces.
3	Save as level 2, plus removes line breaks.
4	Save as level 3, plus replaces variable names.

ESC is very good at replacing variable names with nonsense names. It also is intelligent enough to replace private object properties and methods (those denoted with two underscores at the beginning and end of the name) with nonsense names, so your private properties and methods stay private.

ESC leaves your constructor names, public properties, and public methods intact, so no need to worry about those. The only thing to keep in mind when using ESC is that if the JavaScript file references a constructor in another file (such as the `StringBuffer` class from earlier in the book), crunching at level 4 replaces the references to this constructor with a nonsense name. The solution is to crunch both files into a single file, thus retaining the constructor name.

Other ways to decrease the byte count

The following are suggestions to optimize scripts for size using somewhat uncommon methods that save a lot of bytes. These suggestions aren't handled by ESC, so you must carry them out by hand.

Replace Boolean values

You learned early on that for comparison purposes, `true` is equal to `1` and `false` is equal to `0`. Therefore, anytime a script contains the literal value `true`, it can be replaced with a `1` and anytime a script contains `false`, it can be replaced with a `0`. This saves three bytes in the case of a `true` and four bytes in the case of a `false`, but it doesn't alter the meaning of any Boolean expression.

Consider this example:

```
var bFound = false;

for (var i=0; i < aTest.length && !bFound; i++) {
    if (aTest[i] == vTest) {
        bFound = true;
      }
}
```

You can replace the `true` and `false` without changing the meaning:

```
var bFound = 0;

for (var i=0; i < aTest.length && !bFound; i++) {
    if (aTest[i] == vTest) {
        bFound = 1;
      }
}
```

This code runs exactly the same way, and you've gained seven bytes.

Shorten negative tests

It's quite common to test whether a value is valid. The most these *negative tests* can do is determine if a variable is equal (or not equal) to `undefined`, `null`, or `false`, such as in the following:

```
if (oTest != undefined) {
    //do something
}

if (oTest != null) {
    //do something
}

if (oTest != false) {
    //do something
}
```

These are all fine, but they can all be rewritten using the logical NOT operator and have the exact same effect:

```
if (!oTest) {
    //do something
}
```

How is this possible? Remember way back at the beginning of the book when automatic type conversions were discussed? The NOT operator returns `true` when its operand is `undefined`, `null`, or `false` (it also returns `true` if the operand is `0`). Take a look at the byte savings anytime you replace one of these negative tests with the logical NOT operator.

Use array and object literals

The concept of array literals was touched on briefly earlier in the book. To review, the following two lines are equivalent:

```
var aTest = new Array;
var aTest = [];
```

The second line uses an array literal, which is just as valid as the first line. But as is very apparent, the second line uses fewer characters (and thus bytes). It's good practice to always use array literals when creating arrays.

Likewise, object literals can be used to save a lot of space as well. The following two lines are equivalent, but the one using an object literal uses fewer bytes:

```
var oTest = new Object;
var oTest = {};
```

This also works if you are creating a generic object with a few properties, such as this:

```
var oFruit = new Object;
oFruit.color = "red";
oFruit.name = "apple";
```

The previous code can be rewritten using an object literal as the following:

```
var oFruit = { color: "red", name: "apple" };
```

This example uses an object literal to assign the two properties `color` and `name`, and in doing so, saves a lot of bytes.

Execution time

The second part of overall JavaScript performance is the amount of time it takes a script to run. Because JavaScript is an interpreted language, the speed of execution is significantly slower than compiled languages.

Geoffrery Fox of Syracuse University wrote an online seminar entitled "JavaScript Performance Issues" (available at `http://www.npac.syr.edu/users/gcf/forcps616javascript/msrcobjectsapril99/tsld022.htm`), in which he described JavaScript's performance relative to other well-known programming languages. According to Fox, JavaScript is:

- 5000 times slower than compiled C
- 100 times slower than interpreted Java
- 10 times slower than interpreted Perl

Keeping this in mind, you can do some simple things to improve the performance of your JavaScript code.

Be scope aware

In JavaScript, scope is everything. A scope can be thought of as the space where certain variables exist. The default (or global) scope is the `window` in JavaScript. Variables created in the window scope aren't destroyed until the Web page is unloaded from the browser. Each function you define is another scope under that global scope. All variables created within the function exist only within the function scope and are destroyed when execution leaves the function.

You can think of scopes in JavaScript as a hierarchical tree. When a variable is referenced, the JavaScript interpreter looks to the most recent scope to see if it exists there. If not, it goes up to the next scope, and the next, and so on, until it reaches the `window` scope. If the variable is not found in the `window` scope, you receive an error during execution.

Every time the interpreter goes up to another scope in search of a variable, execution speed suffers. Variables that are local to a scope lead to faster script execution when compared to global variables. The less distance the interpreter has to travel up the tree, the faster your script runs. But what exactly does this mean? Consider the following example:

```
var sMyFirstName = "Nicholas";

function fn1() {
  alert(sMyFirstName);
}

function fn2() {
  var sMyLastName = "Zakas";
  fn1();
}

function fn3() {
  var sMyMiddleInitial = "C";
  fn2();
}

fn3();
```

When `fn3()` is called on the last line, a scope tree is created (see Figure 19-1).

The importance of understanding scopes becomes evident in this example as you travel down the scope tree. The function `fn3()` calls `fn2()`, which calls `fn1()`. The function `fn1()` then accesses the `window`-level variable `sMyFirstName`, but in order to locate this variable, the interpreter has to look back up the scope tree all the way to the window scope. This takes significant time. Finding ways to take advantage of JavaScript scoping is vital in optimizing execution time. You can do a few easy things to help the interpreter locate variables faster.

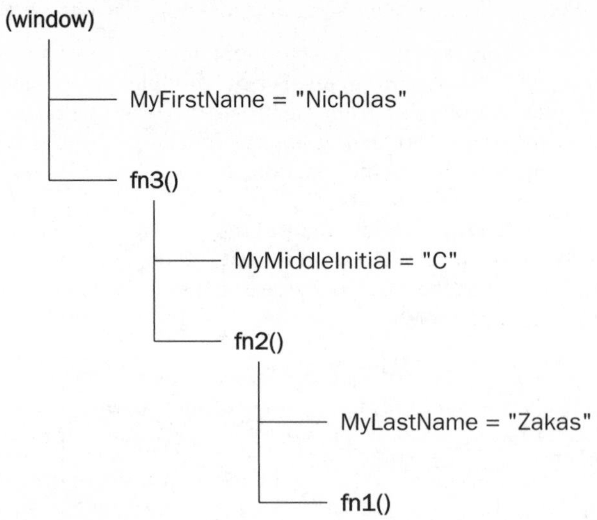

Figure 19-1

Use local variables

Always use the `var` statement to define variables inside functions. Whenever you used `var`, a local variable is created within the current scope. If you begin using a variable without first defining it with `var`, the variable is created at the `window` scope, meaning that every time you use that variable the interpreter has to search back up the scope tree to find it. For example, don't do this:

```
function sayFirstName() {
    sMyFirstName = "Nicholas";
    alert(sMyFirstName);
}
```

In this function, the variable `sMyFirstName` is assigned a value without using `var`; this variable is created at the `window` scope. You can prove this to yourself by defining another function that also uses this variable:

```
function sayFirstName() {
    sMyFirstName = "Nicholas";
    alert(sMyFirstName);
}

function sayFirstNameToo() {
    alert(sMyFirstName);
}

sayFirstName();
sayFirstNameToo();
```

In this example, you see two alerts displaying `"Nicholas"`. This happens because the first function call, `sayFirstName()`, creates the variable `sMyFirstName` at the window scope, which means the second function, `sayFirstNameToo()`, can also access it. Suppose you now change this example to use `var`, like this:

```
function sayFirstName() {
    var sMyFirstName = "Nicholas";
    alert(sMyFirstName);
}

function sayFirstNameToo() {
    alert(sMyFirstName);
}

sayFirstName();
sayFirstNameToo();
```

When you try to run this code, you get an error after the first alert is displayed because the second function has no knowledge of a variable named `sMyFirstName`. The variable was created within the `sayFirstName()` scope and was destroyed when the function finished executing.

Using local variables leads to faster execution because the interpreter doesn't have to leave the local scope in search of a variable. Local variables are also much more efficient because they are removed from memory long before the Web page is unloaded.

Avoid the with statement

You probably understand at this point that the fewer scopes you have, the better off you are. This is why it's important to avoid the `with` statement whenever possible.

As a quick refresher, the `with` statement enables you to access properties of objects as if they were variables, so instead of doing this:

```
alert(document.title);
alert(document.body.tagName);
alert(document.location);
```

You can do this:

```
with (document) {
    alert(title);
    alert(body.tagName);
    alert(location);
}
```

This saves bytes by eliminating the need to type `document` for each of the three lines contained in the `with` statement. But the `with` statement comes with a price: It is another scope. When you use the `with` statement, you are forcing the interpreter to not only look up the scope tree for local variables, but you are also forcing it to test each variable against the object specified to see if it's a property. After all, you could have a variable named `title` or `location` defined within the function as well.

Your best bet is to avoid using the `with` statement. The number of bytes saved doesn't outweigh the performance loss because of an added scope.

Remember Computer Science 101

A lot of the basics relating to optimization of code in other programming languages also apply to JavaScript. Because JavaScript borrows syntax and statements so heavily from C, Java, and Perl, the same techniques used to optimize code in those languages can also be used in JavaScript. The techniques presented in this section have been written about in books and articles such as Koushik Ghosh's "Writing Efficient C and C Code Optimization" (available online at `http://www.codeproject.com/cpp/C___Code_Optimization.asp`). In this article, Ghosh has compiled a list of the most popular code optimization techniques for C, many of which apply to JavaScript as well.

Choosing the right algorithm

When programming, choosing the right algorithm is as important as anything you do. The less complex the algorithm, the faster your code runs. To measure the complexity of algorithms, computer scientists use Big O notation. Big O notation consists of the letter *O* defined as a function with certain arguments.

The simplest algorithm is a constant value, represented as O(1). Retrieving a constant value is an extremely fast process. Constant values are made up of both true constants, such as the number 5, as well as values stored in variables. Consider the following example:

```
var iFive = 5;
var iSum = 10 + iFive;
alert(iSum);
```

This code retrieves three constant values. The first two are the number 10 and the variable `iFive` in the second line. Then, in Line 3, the value of `iSum` is retrieved; this is also a constant value. These three constant retrievals take very little time because of their simplicity.

All values stored in arrays are also constant values, so the following code uses only the constant value algorithm:

```
var aNumbers = [5,10];
var iSum = aNumbers[0] + aNumbers[1];
alert(iSum);
```

In this code the array `aNumbers` is used to store the numbers to be added. Both `aNumbers[0]` and `aNumbers[1]` are constant value retrievals, so the total number of O(1) algorithms in this code is also three.

The next algorithm is called linear, represented by O(*n*). This algorithm is used in simple searches, where an array is searched through, item by item, until a result is found. The following is an example of a linear algorithm:

```
for (var i=0; i < aNumbers.length; i++) {
    if (aNumbers[i] == 5) {
        alert("Found 5");
        break;
    }
}
```

This algorithm is fairly common because iterating over the values in an array is a very common technique. However, another linear algorithm is used commonly in JavaScript: the *named property lookup*.

Named properties are just basic properties of objects, such as `oDog.name`. Although this may look like a variable that is local to the given object, in reality, it's actually a search through the properties of the object looking for the one matching `name`. For this reason, it's always best to use local variables or numerically indexed array values instead of named properties.

Consider this example:

```
var aValues = [1, 2, 3, 4, 5, 6, 7, 8];

function testFunc() {
    for (var i=0; i < aValues.length; i++) {
        alert(i + "/" + aValues.length + "=" + aValues[i]);
    }
}
```

Here are the algorithms represented in this code:

- `i` in `i < aValues.length` — constant(O(1))
- `aValues.length` in `i < aValues.length` — linear(O(*n*))
- `i` in `alert(i + "/" + aValues.length + "=" + aValues[i]);` — constant(O(1))
- `aValues.length` in `alert(i + "/" + aValues.length + "=" + aValues[i]);` — linear(O(*n*))
- `aValues[i]` in `alert(i + "/" + aValues.length + "=" + aValues[i]);` — constant(O(1))

The linear algorithms are of particular interest here because they can easily be replaced with constant algorithms. All the linear algorithms are run twice every time the loop runs: once when the `i < aValues.length` test is run after each loop iteration, and once in the `alert()` call. That means the linear algorithms are executed 16 times throughout the function execution.

The following code does the exact same thing, but uses only one linear algorithm:

```
var aValues = [1, 2, 3, 4, 5, 6, 7, 8];

function testFunc() {
    for (var i=0, iCount=aValues.length; i < iCount; i++) {
        alert(i + "/" + iCount + "=" + aValues[i]);
    }
}
```

In this example, a second variable is initialized in the `for` loop, `iCount`, which is assigned the value of `aValues.length`. Then, the test after each iteration of the loop becomes a constant algorithm because it is accessing the variables `i` and `iCount` instead of `aValues.length`. Likewise, by replacing `aValues.length` with `iCount` in the `alert()` call, another linear algorithm is eliminated. Ultimately, this code executes with only one linear algorithm instead of 16, which decreases execution time.

Keep these algorithms in mind when trying to optimize your code. Here are a couple basic rules for using the correct algorithms:

- Whenever possible, use local variables or numerically indexed arrays instead of named properties.
- If a named property is going to be used more than once, store its value in a local variable to avoid running a linear algorithm each time the value is needed.

> **For further information on Big O Notation and computer science algorithms, please refer to "Big O Notation" from the Wikipedia, available at `http://en.wikipedia.org/wiki/Big_O_notation`.**

Reverse your loops

Loops account for a large amount of processing in most programming languages, so keeping them efficient can greatly decrease execution time. A well-known strategy in programming is to iterate through loops in reverse, starting at the last item and working back to the first. Here's a regular `for` loop:

```
for (var i=0; i < aValues.length; i++) {
    //do something here
}
```

To reverse this, start the iterator (`i`) at the last item in the array, which is in position `aValues.length-1`; then check to see if `i` greater than or equal to `0` and decrement `i` instead of incrementing it:

```
for (var i=aValues.length-1; i >= 0; i--) {
    //do something here
}
```

Reversing the loop helps by reducing the complexity of algorithms. It uses a constant value (0) as the control statement for the loop to reduce the execution time.

Flip your loops

You can replace `while` loops with `do..while` loops to further decrease execution time. Suppose you have the following `while` loop:

```
var i=0;

while (i < aValues.length) {
    //do something here

    i++;
}
```

The previous code can be rewritten using a `do..while` loop without changing its behavior:

```
var i=0;
```

```
do  {
    //do something here

    i++;
} while (i < aValues.length);
```

This code now runs faster than using the `while` loop, but it can be optimized further by reversing the loop:

```
var i=aValues.length-1;

do  {
    //do something here

    i--;
} while (i >= 0);
```

You can also eliminate an extra statement by putting the decrement into the control statement directly:

```
var i=aValues.length-1;

do  {
    //do something here

} while (i-- >= 0);
```

The loop has now been fully optimized for execution speed.

Unroll your loops

Instead of using loops that execute one statement each time through, you can *unroll* these loops to run multiple statements. Consider the following simple `for` loop:

```
var aValues = [1,2,3,4,5,6,7,8,9,10,11,12,13,14,15,16,17,18,19,20];
var iSum = 0;

for (var i=0; i < aValues.length; i++) {
    iSum += aValues[i];
}
```

This loop body executes 20 times, each time adding to the variable `iSum`. This is a fairly simple operation, so it's possible to unroll this operation and execute it several times within the `for` loop:

```
var aValues = [1,2,3,4,5,6,7,8,9,10,11,12,13,14,15,16,17,18,19,20];
var iSum = 0;

for (var i=0; i < aValues.length; i++) {
    iSum += aValues[i];
    i++;
    iSum += aValues[i];
    i++;
    iSum += aValues[i];
    i++;
```

```
        iSum += aValues[i];
        i++;
        iSum += aValues[i];
        i++;
    }
```

In this example, the addition is done five times within the body of the loop. After each addition, the variable `i` is incremented, so it moves along the array in the same way as the original `for` loop did. This way, the control statement is executed only four times; therefore the entire execution time decreases.

Of course, combining the variable increment with the additions can optimize this loop even further:

```
    var aValues = [1,2,3,4,5,6,7,8,9,10,11,12,13,14,15,16,17,18,19,20];
    var iSum = 0;

    for (var i=0; i < aValues.length; i++) {
        iSum += aValues[i++];
        iSum += aValues[i++];
        iSum += aValues[i++];
        iSum += aValues[i++];
        iSum += aValues[i++];
    }
```

This code eliminates five more statements, once again decreasing execution time. Is there a generic way to unroll loops? The answer is yes. Using a technique called Duff's Device (named after Tom Duff, the inventor), it's possible to unroll loops without knowing how much iteration is necessary beforehand.

The loop in the previous example executed 20 times, once for each item in an array. Because of this, the unrolled loop had to contain either ten, five, four, or two statements (all factors of 20) in order to work properly. Duff's Device uses the modulus operator to properly execute an unrolled loop containing eight identical statements. This technique allows any number of iterations to work properly.

Duff's Device was originally written in C, but has since been ported to JavaScript by Jeff Greenburg, who has done exhaustive tests on JavaScript optimization at his site, `http://home.earthlink.net/~kendrasg/info/js_opt/`. His algorithm is as follows:

```
    var iLoopCount = Math.ceil(iIterations / 8);
    var iTestValue = iIterations % 8;

    do {

        switch (iTestValue) {
            case 0: [execute statement];
            case 7: [execute statement];
            case 6: [execute statement];
            case 5: [execute statement];
            case 4: [execute statement];
            case 3: [execute statement];
            case 2: [execute statement];
            case 1: [execute statement];
        }
```

```
        iTestValue = 0;

    } while (--iLoopCount > 0);
```

The variable `iIterations` contains the number of times that the loop that should be executed. The variable `iLoopCount` contains the number of times it is necessary to repeat the `do..while` loop. The `iTestValue` variable represents which `case` in the `switch` statement should be executed the very first time the loop is entered; every other time, execution starts with `case 0` and runs through all the rest (notice that no `break` statements stop execution after a `case` statement is executed). If you apply Duff's Device to the previous example, this is the result:

```
var aValues = [1,2,3,4,5,6,7,8,9,10,11,12,13,14,15,16,17,18,19,20];

var iIterations = aValues.length;
var iLoopCount = Math.ceil(iIterations / 8);
var iTestValue = iIterations % 8;
var iSum = 0;
var i = 0;

do {

    switch (iTestValue) {
        case 0: iSum+= aValues[i++];
        case 7: iSum+= aValues[i++];
        case 6: iSum+= aValues[i++];
        case 5: iSum+= aValues[i++];
        case 4: iSum+= aValues[i++];
        case 3: iSum+= aValues[i++];
        case 2: iSum+= aValues[i++];
        case 1: iSum+= aValues[i++];
    }

    iTestValue = 0;

} while (--iLoopCount > 0);
```

Notice that `iIterations` has been set to the number of values in the array, and the `iSum` and `i` variables have been added. The `iSum` variable, of course, holds the result of adding all the numbers in the array; the `i` variable is used as an iterator to move through the array (just as with the `for` and `do..while` loops).

Before the loop is executed, `iLoopCount` is equal to `3`, meaning that the loop is executed three times. The value of `iTestValue` is equal to `4`, so when execution enters the first loop, it skips down to case 4 in the switch statement. After those four lines are executed, `iTestValue` is set back to `0`. From that point on, whenever the loop executes, all cases beginning at `case 0` are executed.

Greenburg further optimized his JavaScript version of Duff's Device by splitting the single `do..while` loop into two separate loops. The algorithm is as follows:

```
var iLoopCount = iIterations % 8;
while (iLoopCount--) {
    [execute statement]
}
```

```
iLoopCount = Math.floor(iIterations / 8);
while (iLoopCount--) {
    [execute statement]
    [execute statement]
    [execute statement]
    [execute statement]
    [execute statement]
    [execute statement]
    [execute statement]
    [execute statement]
}
```

The purpose of this algorithm is to account for all the *extra* iterations that must be done (that won't be included when the number of iterations is divided by 8) in the first loop. It then continues on into the second loop to iterate through the multiples of 8 remaining. Applying this algorithm to the previous example, you get the following:

```
var iIterations = aValues.length;
var iLoopCount = iIterations % 8;
var iSum = 0;
var i = 0;

while (iLoopCount--) {
    iSum += aValues[i++];
}

iLoopCount = Math.floor(iIterations / 8);

while (iLoopCount--) {
    iSum += aValues[i++];
    iSum += aValues[i++];
    iSum += aValues[i++];
    iSum += aValues[i++];
    iSum += aValues[i++];
    iSum += aValues[i++];
    iSum += aValues[i++];
    iSum += aValues[i++];
}
```

Once again, a few variables are added to make the example work, but it has the same result as the original Duff's Device port.

> **Yes, this algorithm can be optimized even further by switching the two `while` loops to `do..while` loops. However, this wasn't included in Greenburg's original algorithm.**

Whether to use an algorithm such as Duff's Device is entirely up to you. You must weigh the cost of adding extra bytes (increasing download time) against the speed optimization that doing so provides.

Optimize if statements

Whenever using `if` statements with multiple `else` statements, make sure you put the most likely condition first, followed by the second most likely condition, and so forth. For example, if you expect a number to typically be between 0 and 10, but you have specific functionality for other values, you can arrange the code like this:

```
if (iNum > 0 && iNum < 10) {
    alert("Between 0 and 10");
} else if (iNum > 9 && iNum < 20) {
    alert("Between 10 and 20");
} else if (iNum > 19 && iNum < 30) {
    alert("Between 20 and 30");
} else {
    alert("Less than or equal to 0 or greater than or equal to 30");
}
```

By always placing the most common conditions first, you can avoid running through multiple false conditions before getting to the true condition.

You should also try to minimize the number of `else if` statements and arrange the conditions so that they proceed in a binary search fashion. The previous example, for instance, can be rewritten this way:

```
if (iNum > 0) {
    if (iNum < 10) {
        alert("Between 0 and 10");
    } else {
        if (iNum < 20) {
            alert("Between 10 and 20");
        } else {
            if (iNum < 30) {
                alert("Between 20 and 30");
            } else {
                alert("Greater than or equal to 30");
            }
        }
    }
} else {
    alert("Less than or equal to 0");
}
```

This may look complicated, but it's more in line with how the underlying (interpreted) code is executed and so can result in faster execution. Always try to have a branch where the `if` condition tests if a value is greater than, less than, or equal another value; then let an `else` statement handle the other possibility.

Switch versus If

The classic question of whether to use a `switch` statement or an `if` statement applies to JavaScript as well. Generally speaking, anytime you have more than two conditions to test for, it's best to use a `switch` statement whenever possible. Often, using the `switch` statement instead of an `if` statement can result in execution that is up to 10 times faster. This is even easier to take advantage of in JavaScript because you can use any type of value in a `case` statement.

JavaScript gotchas

JavaScript, as you are well aware at this point, is unlike other programming languages in many ways. Therefore, it helps to keep in mind some of the *gotchas* of the language.

Avoid string concatenation

Earlier in the book, you learned about the hazards of string concatenation using the plus (+) operator. To work around this problem, you learned how to create a `StringBuffer` object to encapsulate string concatenations using an `Array` and the `join()` method.

Whenever you are doing more than five string concatenations in a row, it's best to use the `StringBuffer` object.

Use built-in methods first

Whenever possible, use built-in methods of JavaScript objects before making your own. The built-in methods are compiled in C++ and as such, run much faster than JavaScript that must be interpreted on the fly. For example, you could write a function that calculates the value of a number when raised to the power of *n* in this way:

```
function power(iNum, n) {
    var iResult = iNum;

    for (var i=1; i < n; i++) {
        iResult *= iNum;
    }

    return iResult;
}
```

Although this function works perfectly well, JavaScript already provides a way to calculate the power of a number by using `Math.pow()`:

```
alert(Math.pow(3, 4));     //raise 3 to the 4th power
```

The big difference is that `Math.pow()` is part of the browser, written and compiled in C++, and it is much faster than the custom `power()` function defined previously.

Numerous built-in methods are provided specifically to take care of these common tasks. It's always better for execution time to use built-in methods instead of functions you define.

Store commonly used values

Whenever you use the same value more than once, store it in a local variable for easy access. This is especially true for values that are normally accessed through a property of an object. Consider the following code:

```
oDiv1.style.left = document.body.clientWidth;
oDiv2.style.left = document.body.clientWidth;
```

In this example, the value `document.body.clientWidth` is used twice, but it's retrieved using named properties (an expensive operation compared to accessing a single variable). You can rewrite this code to use a local variable instead of accessing `document.body.clientWidth` twice:

```
var iClientWidth = document.body.clientWidth;
oDiv1.style.left = iClientWidth;
oDiv2.style.left = iClientWidth;
```

Note that this example also reduces the algorithmic complexity of the previous code by cutting two calls to linear algorithms down to one.

Minimize statement count

It stands to reason that the fewer statements a script has, the less time needed for it to execute. You can minimize the number of statements in JavaScript code in numerous ways when defining variables, dealing with iterating numbers, and using array and object literals.

Define multiple variables

As mentioned earlier in the book, you can use the `var` statement to define more than one variable at a time. Further, you can define variables of different types using the same `var` statement. For instance, the following code block uses four separate `var` statements to define four variables:

```
var iFive = 5;
var sColor = "blue";
var aValues = [1,2,3];
var oDate = new Date();
```

These four statements can be rewritten to use a single `var` statement:

```
var iFive = 5 , sColor = "blue", aValues = [1,2,3], oDate = new Date();
```

By eliminating three statements you make this code segment run faster.

Insert iterative values

Any time you are using an iterative value (that is, a value that is being incremented or decremented at various locations), combine statements whenever possible. Consider the following code snippet:

```
var sName = aValues[i];
i++;
```

The two preceding statements each have a single purpose: The first retrieves a value from `aValues` and stores it in `sName`; the second iterates the variable `i`. These can be combined into a single statement by inserting the iterative value into the first statement:

```
var sName = aValues[i++];
```

This single statement accomplishes the same thing as the previous two statements. Because the increment operator is postfix, the value of `i` isn't incremented until after the rest of the statement executes. Whenever you have a similar situation, try to insert the iterative value into the last statement that uses it.

Use array and object literals

I mentioned doing this to decrease byte count, but you can also replace array and object definitions with literals to decrease execution time. Consider the following object definition:

```
var oFruit = new Object;
oFruit.color = "red";
oFruit.name = "apple";
```

As mentioned previously, the previous code can be rewritten using an object literal:

```
var oFruit = { color: "red", name: "apple" };
```

Besides the decrease in byte count, the object literal is one statement whereas the extended syntax is three statements; one statement is always executed faster than three. The same effect can be achieved using array literals instead of the extended array syntax.

Use the DOM sparingly

One of the most time-intensive operations in JavaScript is DOM manipulation. Anytime you add, remove, or otherwise change the underlying DOM structure of a page, you are incurring a significant time penalty. This happens because every DOM manipulation alters the appearance of the page to a user, meaning that the entire page must be recalculated to ensure that the page is rendered properly. The way to get around this problem is to do as many DOM manipulations as possible with elements that aren't already in the DOM document.

Consider the following example that adds 10 items to a bulleted list:

```
var oUL = document.getElementById("ulItems");

for (var i=0; i < 10; i++) {
    var oLI = document.createElement("li");
    oUL.appendChild(oLI);
    oLI.appendChild(document.createTextNode("Item " + i));
}
```

Two problems arise with this code in terms of execution speed. The first is the `oUL.appendChild()` call at the middle of the loop. Each time through, this line executes and the entire page must be recalculated to allow for the item to be updated. The second problem is the following line that adds the text node to the list item, which also causes page recalculation. With these two problems, every trip through the loop causes two page recalculations for a total of 20.

To fix this problem, the list items should not be added until after the text nodes have been assigned. Additionally, you can use a document fragment to hold all the created list items until it's time to add them to the list:

```
var oUL = document.getElementById("ulItems");
var oFragment = document.createDocumentFragment();

for (var i=0; i < 10; i++) {
    var oLI = document.createElement("li");
    oLI.appendChild(document.createTextNode("Item " + i));
```

```
        oFragment.appendChild(oLI);
    }

    oUL.appendChild(oFragment);
```

In the rewritten code, a document fragment is created before the loop begins. Then, inside the loop, the list item is created and the text node is added to it. The last step in the loop is to add the list item to the document fragment. Because the fragment isn't a part of the DOM document, no recalculation is necessary. After the loop has executed, the list items are added to the list all at once by using the `appendChild()` method and passing in the document fragment (which, you'll remember, appends the children of fragment, not the fragment itself).

Keep this technique in mind whenever you are manipulating the DOM document. If you are going to be making more than one change, it's best to use a document fragment to store the changes before applying them to the document.

Intellectual Property Issues

After you've made all your size and speed improvements, you still must consider protecting your intellectual property. This is something traditional programmers don't need to worry about because the end product that is shipped to customers is compiled and fairly safe from reverse engineering. When shipping your JavaScript code, you are actually shipping source code, making it public. Although copyright notices and other legal wording can provide a small measure of protection in a court of law, it doesn't help you keep your code safe in the first place. So what's a developer to do?

Obfuscating

Obfuscating is the process of mixing up your source code to make it more difficult for prying eyes. ESC, described earlier, does a small amount of obfuscating by replacing variable and function names. This is the most basic form of obfuscating, but there are more.

The Dithered JavaScript compression utility (`http://www.dithered.com/javascript/compression/index.html`) provides an added amount of obfuscation in a unique way: It extracts sequences of characters from the JavaScript code and replaces them with special markers. When the code is executed, these markers are replaced using regular expressions and the entire code is evaluated. For example, consider the DOM code example from the previous section:

```
var oUL = document.getElementById("ulItems");
var oFragment = document.createDocumentFragment();

for (var i=0; i < 10; i++) {
    var oLI = document.createElement("li");
    oLI.appendChild(document.createTextNode("Item " + i));
    oFragment.appendChild(oLI);
}

oUL.appendChild(oFragment);
```

Using the JavaScript compression utility, the script becomes the following:

```
S="`4UL = docu`5.getEle`5ById(\"ulItems\");
`4`2`6Docu`5`2();
for (var i=0; i < 10; i++) {
`4LI`6Ele`5(\"li\"`3LI`1`0eTextNode(\"Item \" + i)`3`2`1oLI);
}oUL`1o`2);";for(I=6;I>=0;)S=S.replace(eval('/`'+I+'/g'),("document.creat~.appendCh
ild(~Fragment~);
    o~var o~ment~ = `0e~".split('~'))[I--]);eval(S);
```

This doesn't look smaller, but keep in mind that the original script didn't have tabs, spaces, or new line characters removed (the documentation suggests you use another tool for such optimization before using this utility).

The downside to this sort of obfuscation is that its startup time is slow because of the extra interpretation of the code. However, the overall file size can be cut significantly.

Microsoft Script Encoder (IE only)

If you are sure that your target audience will be using Internet Explorer on Windows, you can take advantage of the Microsoft Script Encoder to protect your code. The Microsoft Script Encoder is command-line program that encodes your JavaScript into completely unreadable code.

To begin, you download the utility from Microsoft (`http://www.microsoft.com/downloads/details.aspx?FamilyId=E7877F67-C447-4873-B1B0-21F0626A6329&displaylang=en`). After it is installed, open up a DOS command line window and use the following syntax:

```
screnc inputfile outputfile
```

The program accept numerous types of files as input, but for the purposes of encoding JavaScript the only ones of interest are HTML files and external JavaScript (.js) files. When you specify an HTML file for input, any code contained within an inline `<script/>` element is encoded; for .js files, the entire file is encoded.

For example, the code from the previous section gets encoded into this:

```
#@~^RAEAAA==-
mD~KjdP',NK^Es+UYconOAV+snxDAX&[cJ!V&Yn:dE*i@#@&7CD,Wo.mo:nUDPxP9G1Eh xDRmM+mO+GW^E
s+UOwDlTh+       Y`*I@#@&@#@&6W.Pc-
mD~k{Ti,k~@!,F!I~b_Q#,`@#@&~,P,\lMPKJq,'~NKm;h xYc^D lY 3s+s+
YcJsrr#I@#@&~P,PGJ&Rl22 x[Z4r^Nc9W1E: xD
mM+CY KnaD1W9n`rqY h~J,_,kb#I@#@&P~P,GsMlLh xY Cawnx9/4ks9`KSq*i@#@&8@#@&@#@&KjJ
mww UN;tk^[cWwDmoh+UO*i@#@&n18AAA==^#~@
```

If you specified an HTML file as input, the `<script/>` element is updated to have a `language` attribute equal to `"JScript.Encoded"`; if you specified a .js file as input, you must manually add the language attribute when referencing the file:

```
<script language="JScript.Encoded" src="encodedfile.js"></script>
```

Even if someone downloads your code, it's now impossible to reverse engineer or otherwise figure out. All your JavaScript calls from within an HTML file can be used in the exact same way (meaning you don't have to worry about encoding your JavaScript calls; just make them as you would normally).

The downside to this technique is that it works only on Internet Explorer on Windows. After it is encoded, the script is essentially useless to any other browsers on any other operating systems. If you are sure that your only users are running IE on Windows (such as in a corporate Intranet), this may be helpful to you. Otherwise it's best to go with an obfuscating utility that works across all browsers.

> **You can learn more about the Microsoft Script Encoder at `http://msdn.microsoft.com/library/default.asp?url=/library/en-us/script56/html/seusingscriptencoder.asp`.**

Summary

In this chapter, you've learned about several issues relating to the deployment of JavaScript to a public Web site or to a client via a Web application.

The first issue discussed was security. Various security issues, ranging from general concepts (such as the Same Origin Policy) to browser-specific issues (like Mozilla's signed scripts), were discussed. JavaScript's security limitations in regards to the BOM and the DOM were also covered.

Next, you learned how to optimize JavaScript code. The two ways to optimize JavaScript are to minimize the size of the code (by removing extra white space and comments) and to reduce the time it takes for the script to execute (by using common programming techniques). I discussed a variety of different methods to achieve optimization, and I also introduced several utilities that can aid in the process.

The last topic discussed was intellectual property. Code obfuscation and encoding were introduced as methods to prevent reverse engineering. You learned that obfuscation is a better solution for cross-browser compatibility than using the Windows Script Encoder, which works only for Internet Explorer on Windows. Ultimately, the method you use to protect your intellectual property is largely determined by the Web solution you are developing.

20

The Evolution of JavaScript

So far in this book, you have learned about the origins of JavaScript as well as about the implementations presently in use. This chapter talks about what lies ahead for JavaScript. Since its introduction and the standardization of ECMAScript, JavaScript and derivative languages have been used in many different programming environments. But JavaScript hasn't peaked: It's still growing and evolving with several interested parties (such as Microsoft and Mozilla) pushing it forward. In this chapter, you learn where the evolution of JavaScript is heading and what this means to your code.

ECMAScript 4

The future of JavaScript is inescapably tied to the fourth edition of ECMAScript, which has met with substantial problems since first being proposed.

Technical Committee 39 (TC39), which you may remember as the group inside of ECMA that first standardized ECMAScript, is still in charge of developing future editions. Like the first edition of ECMAScript, the fourth edition was first proposed by Netscape Communications, and TC39's schedule originally called for its release in 2002. However, issues arose surrounding the clout that Microsoft had gained on the Web since the first edition of ECMAScript had been standardized. Microsoft entered its own proposal to TC39 for the future direction of ECMAScript.

TC39 changed the planned release of ECMAScript Edition 4 to the first quarter of 2004, almost two years later than the originally scheduled release. However, March 2004 came and went without the release. As of the time of my writing, no indication has been given as to when the next edition of ECMAScript will be released. All schedules of record still indicate the Q1 2004 date.

Given this lack of direction from the ECMA, the only possible way to investigate the future of JavaScript is to take a look at the proposal that was sent to TC39 for consideration.

Netscape's proposal

When Netscape submitted its proposal to TC39, the future of Netscape Communications looked bleak. Since that time, Netscape was purchased by Time Warner (then AOL Time Warner) and then summarily disbanded, leaving the future of its Web browser strictly to the open-source Mozilla Foundation. The Mozilla Foundation still supports the Netscape proposal (which can be viewed at `http://www.mozilla.org/js/language/es4/`) and updates it periodically, although the last update noted was in June 2003.

Netscape's proposal for ECMAScript would turn ECMAScript into a lightweight version of the Java programming language. The goals listed in the proposal are the following:

- Making the language suitable for writing modular and object-oriented applications
- Making it possible and easy to write robust and secure applications
- Improving upon ECMAScript's facilities for interfacing with a variety of other languages and environments
- Improving ECMAScript's suitability for writing applications for which performance matters
- Simplifying the language where possible
- Keeping the language implementation compact and flexible

Although these goals seem pretty ambitious, the proposal is quick to point out that its authors do not see ECMAScript as a replacement for C++ or Java, nor do they intend to push it in that direction.

In order to accomplish the goals listed previously, the Netscape proposal suggests a number of changes to the language from the third edition. These changes include:

- **Optional strict typing and type checking of values.** As discussed throughout this book, ECMAScript is currently a loosely typed language. The proposal asks to change this in order to cut down on errors and bring ECMAScript more in line with other object-oriented languages.
- **More logical syntax for classes.** In the current edition of ECMAScript, a strict difference exists between defining a global function and defining a class. This proposal suggests the use of the reserved word `class` to make the syntax for defining classes more logical (and ultimately, more Java-like). This would include using the `extends` reserved word for more straightforward inheritance and the introduction of private and protected scopes.
- **Addition of more types.** Because one of the main goals of the proposal is to allow for easier interaction with other languages, it is suggested that the fourth edition of ECMAScript include more types, such as integer and long, that are supported in other languages.

Keywords and reserved words

Netscape proposes the following keywords:

```
as         break      case       catch      class      const      continue
default    delete     do         else       export     extends    false
finally    for        function   if         import     in         instanceof
is         namespace  new        null       package    private    public
return     super      switch     this       throw      true       try
typeof     use        var        void       while      with
```

You will probably recognize some of these keywords as reserved words in ECMAScript Edition 3, which is why they are reserved.

Additionally, the proposal asks for the following reserved words:

```
abstract    debugger     enum            goto      implements    interface
native      protected    synchronized    throws    transient     volatile
```

As you can see, this list of reserved words clearly shows the Netscape proposal moving ECMAScript more towards a Java-like syntax.

The following words were reserved in ECMAScript Edition 3, but are used as part of the language in Netscape's proposal:

```
boolean   byte   char   double   final   float   int   long   short   static
```

Finally, special meanings are attached to the words `get` and `set`, which cannot be used as variable names.

> **For compatibility with future ECMAScript implementations, you should avoid using these words as variable or function names.**

Variables

According to the Netscape proposal, variables can be defined with an explicit type by including a semi-colon and the type name when defining the variable, like this:

```
var color : String = "red";
```

In the previous code, a variable with name `color` is created as type `String`. Defining the type for a variable is optional under this proposal. This can also be used with classes you would define yourself:

```
var specialObject : MyClass = new MyClass();
```

A slight twist on variables is the capability to create true constant values that cannot be changed by using the `const` keyword:

```
const age = 32;
```

This code defines the variable `age` as a constant and assigns a value of `32`.

Functions

Functions also take advantage of this new type declaration by providing types for its arguments and return value. Consider the following example:

```
function sum(num1 : Integer, num2 : Integer) : Integer {
    return num1 + num2;
}
```

Here, the function named `sum()` takes two parameters of type `Integer` and returns an `Integer` (as indicated by the semicolon after the closing parenthesis). If the function doesn't return a value, it is defined as type `Void`:

```
function doNothing(num1 : Integer, num2 : Integer) : Void {
    num1 + num2;
}
```

Functions that have argument and return value types defined are type checked, although it is possible to leave off the types and have functions behave as they do in ECMAScript today.

Netscape's proposal would make overloading of functions work in a manner similar to overloading in Java: Just define as many functions as necessary with different argument lists. For example, you could make two different versions of the `sum()` function defined earlier, one to take two arguments and one to take three:

```
function sum(num1 : Integer, num2 : Integer) : Integer {
    return num1 + num2;
}

function sum(num1 : Integer, num2 : Integer, num3 : Integer) : Integer {
    return num1 + num2 + num3;
}
```

Another change to functions is the capability to define named arguments, which are optional and can be assigned in any order so long as the name of the argument is used. For example, the following function contains two named arguments:

```
function sum(num1 : Integer, num2: Integer, named num3 : Integer = 7, named num4 :
Integer = 10) {
    return num1 + num2 + num3 + num4;
}
```

To call this function, you can use only two arguments, three arguments, or all four:

```
result = sum(10, 20);
result = sum(10, 20, num3: 10);
result = sum(10, 20, num4: 10, num3: 20);
```

Note the last two lines where the named arguments are used; specifically notice the last line, where `num4` is used before `num3`.

Numeric literals

In order to support more types of numbers, the Netscape proposal introduces three new types of numbers: long, unsigned long (ulong), and float. You can indicate the type of number by including an `l` (or `L`) for long values, `ul` (or `uL`, `Ul`, `UL`) for ulong values, and `f` (or `F`) for float values. For example, `L25` is a long, `UL25` is a ulong, and `F25` is a float.

Types

Netscape's proposal introduces several new types:

- `Never` — Has no values
- `Void` — Replaces the Undefined type from ECMAScript Edition 3
- `Integer` — All integer values
- `char` — All single 16-bit Unicode characters
- `Type` — The supertype of all types

Unlike ECMAScript Edition 3, all types are considered objects and not primitive values.

New *machine types* represent primitive number values:

- `sbyte` — Signed byte integer, values between –128 and 127
- `byte` — Byte integer, values between 0 and 255
- `short` — Short integer, values between –32768 and 32767
- `ushort` — Unsigned short integer, values between 0 and 65535
- `int` — Integer, values between –2147483648 and 2147483647
- `uint` — Unsigned integer, values between 0 and 4294967295
- `long` — Long integer, values between –9223372036854775808 and 9223372036854775807
- `ulong` – Unsigned long integer, values between 0 and 18446744073709551615
- `float` — Floating-point number, all single precision IEEE floating-point numbers

The machine types can be used in place of regular types whenever a number must be represented. For example:

```
var b : byte = 10;
var longnum : long = L100;
```

Classes

A class in ECMAScript Edition 4 (per the Netscape proposal) takes a form like this:

```
class MyClass {
    private var color : String = "red";

    public function MyClass(color : String) {
        this.color = color;
    }

    public function sayColor() : Void {
        alert(this.color);
    }
}
```

As you can see, the `class` keyword is used to define `MyClass`. There is one private variable named `color`, one constructor, and one public method named `sayColor()`. In ECMAScript Edition 4, both `public` and `private` are considered *namespaces* that define the context in which variables and methods can be accessed. Classes defined in this manner are instantiated in the same way as in ECMAScript Edition 3, by using the `new` keyword:

```
var myObject : MyClass = new MyClass();
```

Along with variables and methods, it is possible to define getters and setters for properties. The getter is called when the variable is used for the value it contains, whereas a setter assigns a new value to a given variable.

```
class MyClass {
    private var color : String = "red";

    public function get myColor () {
        return this.color;
    }

    public function set myColor (value : String) : Void {
        this.color = value;
    }
}
```

The previous code creates a property named `myColor`, which can be used just like a regular property (such as `color`), but whose behavior is defined by the getter and setter functions. For instance:

```
var myObject : MyClass = new MyClass();
myObject.myColor = "blue";
```

Typically, this would be done when you want to perform some other action after a property value changes (such as changing the color of a UI element when the `myColor` property changes).

It is also possible to redefine the behavior of operators when they interact with classes. In ECMAScript Edition 3, all operators use an object's `valueOf()` or `toString()` method, but here it is possible for you to define exactly how a plus or minus should be used with an instance of a particular class.

```
class MyClass {
    private var value : Integer = 25;

    public function MyClass(value : Integer) {
        this.value = value;
    }

    public function getValue() : Integer {
        return this.value;
    }

    operator function "+" (anotherObject : MyClass) : MyClass {
        return new MyClass(this.value + anotherObject.getValue());
    }
}
```

This class defines a private property named value, which can be initialized using the class constructor. The last function defines what happens when a plus is used with a `MyClass` object. This particular function defines the behavior when the second operand is also a `MyClass` object: The values of the two objects are added and a new `MyClass` object is returned. With this definition, it is possible to use the following line:

```
var obj1 = new MyClass(20);
var obj2 = new MyClass(30);
var obj3 = obj1 + obj2;
alert(obj3.getValue());     //outputs "50"
```

Finally, classes can have true static properties and methods by using the `static` keyword:

```
class MyClass {
    public static var value : Integer = 25;
}
```

The static members of a class can then be accessed as you might expect:

```
var value : Integer = MyClass.value;
```

Inheritance

Inheritance in ECMAScript Edition 4 is done in the same way as in Java, by using the `extends` keyword. For example:

```
class ClassA {
    private var value : Integer = 0;

    public function ClassA(value : Integer) {
        this.value = value;
    }
    public function getValue() : Integer {
        return this.value;
    }
}


class ClassB extends ClassA {

    public function ClassB(value : Integer) {
        super(value);
    }

    public function sayValue() : Integer {
        alert(this.getValue());
    }

}
```

First, note that the `extends` keyword is used to inherit from `ClassA` to create `ClassB`. This is a much simpler and straightforward way to establish inheritance than the traditional ECMAScript method (although object masquerading and prototype chaining is still available for backwards compatibility).

The second thing to note is the use of the `super()` method to use `ClassA`'s constructor in `ClassB`. Once again, this is identical to Java.

Implementations

Although ECMAScript Edition 4 isn't an officially released standard, that hasn't stopped both Microsoft and Mozilla from implementing some of it.

Mozilla

Mozilla chose to implement some small features in the Web browser. For instance, it is possible to define constant values in Mozilla using the `const` keyword:

```
const message = "Hello World!";
```

This line causes an error in all other browsers because `const` is a reserved word in ECMAScript Edition 3. In Mozilla, however, this line defines a constant string named `message` that cannot have its value changed.

Mozilla also chose to implement getters and setters for object properties, albeit with a different syntax. You may remember getters and setters from earlier chapters of this book, but here is a brief example:

```
function MyClass() {
        this.__color__ = "red";
}

MyClass.prototype.color getter = function () {
    return this.__color__;
};

MyClass.prototype.color setter = function (value) {
    this.__color__ = value;
    alert("Color changed to " + value);
};

var obj = new MyClass();
alert(obj.color);       //outputs "red"
obj.color = "blue";     //outputs "Color change to blue"
```

This is an alternate syntax (so as not to break syntax in non-Mozilla browsers):

```
function MyClass() {
        this.__color__ = "red";
}

MyClass.prototype.__defineGetter__("color", function () {
    return this.__color__;
});

MyClass.prototype.__defineSetter__("color", function (value) {
    this.__color__ = value;
    alert("Color changed to " + value);
});

var obj = new MyClass();
alert(obj.color);       //outputs "red"
obj.color = "blue";     //outputs "Color change to blue"
```

Note that even though this example is syntactically correct, it causes an error in browsers other than Mozilla when it is executed because neither function (defineGetter() or `defineSetter()`) is defined.

Microsoft

Microsoft hasn't updated its browser-based implementation of JavaScript since Internet Explorer 5.5 was released. What it has done, however, is include a language called JScript.NET in the .NET Framework. JScript.NET is, for all intents and purposes, an implementation of ECMAScript Edition 4 with some Microsoft-specific additions added for good measure. However, it can't be used as a client-side scripting language in Internet Explorer, only as a server-side language in ASP.NET or as a standalone application (yes, JScript.NET can be compiled).

Unlike other versions of JavaScript, JScript.NET is a compiled language capable of becoming a standalone executable file. It is compiled down to the same .NET machine code and executed using the same Common Language Runtime (CLR) as both Visual Basic.NET and C#. Although it is beyond the scope of this book to discuss the full potential and scope of JScript.NET, more information is available on Microsoft's Web site at `http://msdn.microsoft.com/library/en-us/dnclinic/html/scripting07142000.asp?frame=true`.

ECMAScript for XML

In 2002, a group of companies led by BEA Systems proposed an extension to ECMAScript to add native XML support to the language. At that point, XML was starting to gain popularity, and the companies wanted to make sure that ECMAScript was in the forefront of this next technology wave. In June 2004, ECMAScript for XML (E4X) was released as ECMA-357. E4X is not its own language; rather, as originally intended, it is an optional extension to the ECMAScript language. As such, E4X introduces new syntax for dealing with XML, as well as for XML-specific objects.

Approach

E4X stays away from implementing the current XML standards, such as SAX, XPath, and DOM, and instead presents a unique way of creating and manipulating XML documents. The E4X approach takes aspects from technologies such as DOM, XPath, and XSLT, although it doesn't map specifically to either one.

For example, suppose you were dealing with the following XML code:

```
<employees>
    <employee position="Software Engineer">
        <name>Nicholas C. Zakas</name>
    </employee>
    <employee position="Salesperson">
        <name>Jim Smith</name>
    </employee>
</employees>
```

This XML could be assigned to an ECMAScript variable by using the following code:

```
var oXml = <employees>
    <employee position="Software Engineer">
        <name>Nicholas C. Zakas</name>
```

```
        </employee>
        <employee position="Salesperson">
            <name>Jim Smith</name>
        </employee>
    </employees>;
```

The data in this XML can then be referenced in a very logical, easy-to-understand way. In E4X, all XML elements become fully realized objects (based on the XML class, which is discussed later). So, to get a reference to the first employee, this code can be used:

```
var oFirstEmployee = oXml.employees.employee;
```

The name of the first employee can be returned by using this code:

```
var sName = oXml.employees.employee.name;
```

The position of the first employee can be returned using the @ symbol (which is also used in XPath to indicate an XML attribute):

```
var sPosition = oXml.employees.employee.@position;
```

To get a specific employee, use the same square bracket notation as used in arrays. The following code returns the second employee:

```
var oSecondEmployee = oXml.employees.employee[1];
```

It is possible to choose a descendant node by using the double-dot (..) notation. For instance, to go right to the first `<name/>` element, the following code can be used:

```
var oFirstEmployeeName = oXml..name;
```

It's also possible to use XPath-like expressions to return the correct object. Suppose you want to retrieve the first salesperson's name. This code accomplishes just that:

```
var oFirstSalesperson = oXml..employee.(@position="salesperson").name;
```

All values, aside from `XML` objects, are regular ECMAScript strings and can be manipulated in the same way. You can edit the preceding code to alter the first salesperson's name easily:

```
oXml..employee.(@position="salesperson").name = "Michael Anderson";
```

Executing this code automatically updates the XML representation being stored underneath.

Because its developers are always thinking ahead, E4X provides the capability to embed ECMAScript variables inside of XML to create new `XML` objects. To do this, curly braces must surround the variables. For example:

```
var tagname = "color";
var value = "blue";
var oXml = <{tagname}>{value}</{tagname}>;
```

In this example, the value of `oXml` becomes `<color>blue</color>`.

As you can see, E4X represents a radical departure from traditional ECMAScript to support XML in a simple yet powerful manner.

The for each..in Loop

Throughout the book, you have used the `for..in` loop to iterate over property names of an object. The `for each..in` loop, introduced in E4X, iterates the actual objects in an array. For example:

```
for each (var oItem in arrItems) {
    alert(oItem);
}
```

To accomplish the same thing using a `for..in` loop, you use code that looks like this:

```
for (var sProperty in arrItems) {
    alert(arrItems[sProperty]);
}
```

As you can see, the `for each..in` loop is a lot more useful and more like similar loops in other languages.

New classes

E4X introduces several new classes to deal specifically with XML:

- `Namespace` objects represent namespaces by using a URI and a prefix.
- `QName` objects represent XML qualified names composed of a local name and an optional namespace URI.
- `XML` objects represent individual XML elements.
- `XMLList` objects contain any number of XML objects.

The Namespace class

`Namespace` objects are a convenient way to reference namespaces in E4X. To create a `Namespace`, use its constructor with one or two arguments:

```
var oNamespace1 = new Namespace("http://www.wrox.com/");
var oNamespace2 = new Namespace("wrox", "http://www.wrox.com/");
```

In the first line, the constructor is called with just the URI of the namespace, which can be used when dealing with XML like this:

```
<root xmlns="http://www.wrox.com/">
    <message>Hello World!</message>
</root>
```

In the second line of the example, the constructor is being called with a namespace prefix and the URI, which is useful when dealing with XML code that looks like this:

```
<wrox:root xmlns:wrox="http://www.wrox.com/">
    <wrox:message>Hello World!</wrox:message>
</wrox:root>
```

A `Namespace` object can then be used in selection statements:

```
var oWroxNS = new Namespace("wrox", "http://www.wrox.com/");
var oXml = <wrox:root xmlns:wrox="http://www.wrox.com/">
    <wrox:message>Hello World!</wrox:message>
</wrox:root>;
var sMessage = oXml.oWroxNS::message;
```

The highlighted line uses the `oWroxNS` `Namespace` object to select the `<wrox:message>` text `Hello World!`. If the XML code specifies a namespace, this method must be used when selecting elements in E4X.

The QName class

The `QName` class represents a qualified name for XML elements and attributes. The qualified name is made up of a namespace prefix and a local name, such as the following:

```
<wrox:message xmlns:wrox="http://www.wrox.com/">Hello World!</wrox:message>
```

In this code, `wrox:message` is a qualified name, with `wrox` representing a namespace and `message` representing the local name (also called tag name). The prefix `wrox` points to a namespace URI of `http://www.wrox.com/`. A `QName` object can represent the `wrox:message` qualified name like this:

```
var oWroxNS = new Namespace("wrox", "http://www.wrox.com/");
var oQName = new QName(oWroxNS, "message");
```

Using this version of the constructor, a `Namespace` object must be provided to represent the qualified name. Alternately, a `QName` object can be created without any namespace if one isn't specified:

```
var oQName = new QName("message");
```

After the object is created, it has two properties that can be accessed: `uri` and `localName`. The `uri` property returns the URI of the namespace specified when the object is created (or an empty string if no namespace is specified); the `localName` property returns the local-name part of the qualified name. For example:

```
var oWroxNS = new Namespace("wrox", "http://www.wrox.com/");
var oQName = new QName(oWroxNS, "message");
alert(oQName.uri);          //outputs "http://www.wrox.com/"
alert(oQName.localName);  //outputs "message"
```

In this example, the `uri` property returns `"http://www.wrox/com/"` and `localName` returns `"message"`. These properties are read-only and cause an error if you try to change their values.

The `QName` object overrides the `toString()` object to return a string in the form `uri::localName`, such as `"http://www.wrox.com/::message"` in the previous example.

The XML class

As mentioned previously, an `XML` object represents an XML element, meaning that it represents an ordered list of properties with a name, a parent, a set of attributes, child nodes, and a set of namespaces.

An `XML` object can be created in one of two ways. The first way is to use its constructor and pass in an XML string like this:

```
var oXml = new XML("<person><name>Nicholas C. Zakas</name></person>");
```

The second way is to use the syntax extension mentioned earlier, allowing you to enter the XML directly into the code without using strings:

```
var oXml = <person>
               <name>Nicholas C. Zakas</name>
           </person>;
```

The XML is interpreted according to several flags on the `XML` constructor:

- `XML.ignoreComments` — If set to `true`, causes the parser to ignore comments
- `XML.ignoreProcessingInstructions` — If set to true, causes the parser to ignore processing instruction.
- `XML.ignoreWhitespace` — If set to true, causes the parser to ignore whitespace between elements

The `toString()` method is accompanied by the `toXMLString()` method, both of which returns string representations of the XML. The `toString()` method returns an XML-encoded string if the element contains complex children (that is, anything other than text); if the element contains only simple content (text), then `toString()` just returns the text without the start and end tags. On the other hand, `toXMLString()` always returns the XML tags regardless of the element's children. For example:

```
var oXml = <name>Nicholas C. Zakas</name>;
alert(oXml.toString());        //outputs "Nicholas C. Zakas"
alert(oXml.toXMLString());     //outputs "<name>Nicholas C. Zakas</name>";
```

In the previous code, the first alert displays just `"Nicholas C. Zakas"` because the `toString()` method is called. The second alert displays the full XML code, `"<name>Nicholas C. Zakas</name>"`. If, however, the element has complex content, both methods return the same value:

```
var oXml = <name><first>Nicholas</first><last>Zakas</last></name>;
alert(oXml.toString());        //outputs
"<name><first>Nicholas</first><last>Zakas</last></name>"
alert(oXml.toXMLString());     //outputs
"<name><first>Nicholas</first><last>Zakas</last></name>;";
```

In this code, `toString()` and `toXMLString()` return `"<name><first>Nicholas</first><last>Zakas</last></name>"`.

Both methods use a variety of settings on the XML constructor to determine how to output the XML code:

- `XML.prettyPrinting` — When set to `true`, the methods normalize whitespace between elements.
- `XML.prettyIndent` — Specifies the line indent in the methods. By default this is set to `2`.

All the constructor flags are stored in an object that can be referenced by using the `XML.settings()` method. This object can then be used to restore the settings later by using the `XML.setSettings()` method, as shown in this example:

```
var oXmlSettings = XML.settings();      //save these settings
XML.prettyIndent = 4;
XML.ignoreWhitespace = true;
//do something here
XML.setSettings(oXmlSettings);     //return to the original settings
```

Here, the settings are initially saved to `oXmlSettings` before being changed. The settings are then reset using the `setSettings()` method. It is also possible to retrieve the default settings of the parser by using the `XML.defaultSettings()` method:

```
XML.setSettings(XML.defaultSettings());
```

As for XML object instances, you have a large number of methods available to manipulate XML data. Some of these methods are inspired by the DOM; others are not, but all are useful.

The first group of methods deals with namespaces and `Namespace` objects. Most of these are pretty straightforward: `addNamespace()` adds a given namespace to the element and `removeNamespace()` removes a given namespace from the element.

```
var oWroxNS = new Namespace("wrox", "http://www.wrox.com/");
var oXml = <message>Hello World!</message>;
oXml.addNamespace(oWroxNS);
//do something else
oXml.removeNamespace(oWroxNS);
```

It's also possible to retrieve arrays of namespaces by using the `inScopeNamespaces()` and `namespaceDeclarations()` methods. Each of these return an array of `Namespace` objects, with `inScopeNamespaces()` returning only those namespaces from the current element down and `namespaceDeclarations()` returning all namespaces represented from the root element down.

To deal with individual namespaces, you can use `namespace()` to retrieve a namespace and `setNamespace()`, as you might assume, to set a namespace for the current element.

```
var oXml = <wrox:root xmlns:wrox="http://www.wrox.com/">
    <wrox:message>Hello World!</wrox:message>
</wrox:root>;
var oWroxNS = oXml.namespace();
var oNewNS = new Namespace("ncz", "http://www.nczonline.net/");
oXml.setNamespace(oNewNS);
```

Attributes are very easy to access in E4X by using the `attribute()` and `attributes()` method. The `attribute()` method returns the value of the attribute. The `attributes()` method returns an `XMLList` (which is covered in the next section) containing all attributes for the given element.

```
var oXml = <value type="string">Hello World!</value>
var sType = oXml.attribute("type");  //set to "string"
var oAtts = oXml.attributes();
```

Children of an XML element can be accessed using either the `child()` method, which returns a single `XML` object indicated by either the child's index or name, or the `children()` method, which returns an `XMLList` of all children. Additionally the `childIndex()` method can be used to determine the location of an element among its siblings. For example:

```
var oXml = <employees>
    <employee position="Software Engineer">
        <name>Nicholas C. Zakas</name>
    </employee>
    <employee position="Salesperson">
        <name>Jim Smith</name>
    </employee>
</employees>;

var oFirstEmployee = oXml.child(0);
var oFirstEmployeeToo = oXml.child("employee");
var oAllEmployees = oXml.children();
var iFirstEmployeeIndex = oFirstEmployee.childIndex(); //0
```

This code shows two ways of obtaining the first employee in the XML code. First, the `child()` method is used with the position `0`, the location of the first element. Then, the `child()` method is used with the tag name of the element. Each of these calls returns a reference to the same employee element. To get all employees, the `children()` method is called. Finally, the first employee's `childIndex()` method is called, which returns `0`.

The methods discussed previously return all types of child nodes for the given element. However, if you want to return only child nodes of a specific type or nodes that relate to the element in different ways, several methods are available:

- `comments()` — Returns only comment child nodes
- `elements()` — Returns only element child nodes
- `processingInstructions()` — Returns only processing instruction child nodes
- `descendants()` — Returns all nodes that descend from the given element
- `parent()` — Returns the parent node of the element

A variety of methods are available to alter child nodes:

- `appendChild(`*`child`*`)` — Adds a new child to the end of the children
- `prependChild(`*`child`*`)` — Adds a new child to the beginning of the children
- `insertChildBefore(`*`child, refchild`*`)` — Inserts a child before a given reference node
- `insertChildAfter(`*`child, refchild`*`)` — Inserts a child after a given reference node
- `replace(`*`childname, newchild`*`)` — Replaces the child with the given name (or position) with a new child
- `setChildren(`*`list`*`)` — Replaces all children with children contained in a given `XMLList`

These methods are incredibly useful and easy to use:

```
var oXml = <employees>
    <employee position="Software Engineer">
        <name>Nicholas C. Zakas</name>
    </employee>
    <employee position="Salesperson">
        <name>Jim Smith</name>
```

```
    </employee>
</employees>;

oXml.appendChild(<employee position="Vice President">
                     <name>Benjamin Anderson</name>
                 </employee>);

oXml.prependChild(<employee position="User Interface Designer">
                     <name>Michael Johnson</name>
                  </employee>);

oXml.insertChildBefore(oXml.child(2), <employee position="Human Resources Manager">
                                          <name>Margaret Jones</name>
                                      </employee>);

oXml.setChildren(<employee position="President">
                     <name>Richard McMichael</name>
                 </employee> +
                 <employee position="Vice President">
                      <name>Rebecca Smith</name>
                 </employee>);
```

This code illustrates some of the methods discussed previously. Note that you can use XML literals in place of `XML` objects in all methods. First, the code adds a Vice President named Benjamin Anderson to the bottom of the list of employees. Second, a User Interface Designer named Michael Johnson is added to the top of the list of employees. Third, A Human Resources Manager named Margaret Jones is added just before the employee in position 2, which at this point is Jim Smith (because Michael Johnson and Nicholas C. Zakas now come before him). Finally, all the children are replaced with President Richard McMichael and Vice President Rebecca Smith (maybe there was a major layoff). Note, in that line, the plus symbol between the two employee literals. This indicates that the values are contained in an `XMLList` object. The resulting XML looks like this:

```
<employees>
    <employee position="President">
        <name>Richard McMichael</name>
    </employee>
    <employee position="Vice President">
        <name>Rebecca Smith</name>
    </employee>
</employees>
```

There has been a lot of talk in this section about the important concepts of simple and complex content. They are so important, in fact, that the XML object has methods to help out: `hasComplexContent()` and `hasSimpleContent()`. Each of these methods returns a Boolean value indicating whether the element contains the type of content indicated. By rule, only one of these methods can return `true` for any given element.

```
var oSimpleXml = <message>Hello World!</message>;
var oComplexXML =
<message><greeting>Hello</greeting><target>World!</target></message>
var bSimple = oSimpleXml.hasSimpleContent();    //returns true
var bComplex = oComplexXML.hasComplexContent(); //returns true
```

If you want to create a complete (deep) copy of some XML, you can use the `copy()` method. This method returns an exact copy of the node and all its descendants (no ancestors are copied).

```
var oXml = <message>Hello World!</message>
var oNewXml = oXml.copy();
alert(oNewXml.toXMLString());     //outputs <message>Hello World!</message>
```

The XML object has a method called `length()` which always returns `1`. This may seem a silly, but it was done to blur the distinction between `XML` objects and `XMLList` objects when writing code. Another method, `contains()`, is equally useless in the context of XML objects, but it is included to make the code compatible with `XMLList` objects as well. The `contains()` method returns `true` only when you pass in the XML object calling the method, like this:

```
oXml.contains(oXml);
```

Again, these two methods have actual uses in `XMLList`, but aren't terribly useful in `XML`.

The `nodeKind()` method determines what type of node an XML object represents, returning either "text", "element", "comment", "processing-instruction", or "attribute". Consider the following XML object:

```
var oXml = <employees>
    <? Don't forget the donuts! ?>
    <employee position="President">
        <name>Richard McMichael</name>
    </employee>
    <!-- just added -->
    <employee position="Vice President">
        <name>Rebecca Smith</name>
    </employee>
</employees>
```

Given this XML, the following table shows what `nodeKind()` returns depending on which node is in scope.

Statement	**Returns**
`oXml.nodeKind()`	"element"
`oXml.child(0)`	"processing-instruction"
`oXml.employee.@position.nodeKind()`	"attribute"
`oXml.employee.nodeKind()`	"element"
`oXml.child(2)`	"comment"
`oXml.employee.name.child(0)`	"text"

The `normalize()` method works the same way as in the DOM: It normalizes (combines) whitespace and text between elements to create single text nodes instead of multiple ones. Not very exciting, but necessary for dealing with XML code.

Four methods are used to deal with the names of XML nodes:

- `name()` — Returns the qualified name of the node, which is a `QName` object
- `localName()` — Returns the local name of the node, which is equivalent to `name().localName`
- `setName(qname)` — Sets the qualified name of the node
- `setLocalName(localname)` — Sets the local name of the node

Example:

```
var oXml = <message>Hello World!</message>
oXml.setLocalName("msg");          //changes the code to <msg>Hello World!</msg>
oXml.setName(new QName("mess"));   //chnages the code to <mess>Hello World!</mess>
```

Here, the XML code is changed twice, changing `<message/>` to `<msg/>` and then `<msg/>` to `<mess/>`.

The last method is `text()`, which returns the text (simple content) of an element:

```
var oXml = <name>Nicholas C. Zakas</name>;
var sName = oXml.text();    //returns "Nicholas C. Zakas";
```

The XMLList Class

The `XMLList` class, briefly introduced in the previous section, represents an array of `XML` objects. Just as with the XML object, you have a number of ways to create an `XMLList` object.

First, you can use the constructor and pass in an XML string containing a number of elements that aren't enclosed by a root element. For example:

```
var oXmlList = new XMLList("<name>Nicholas C. Zakas</name><name>Michael
Smith</name>");
```

In this example, a string of two `<name/>` elements is passed into the `XMLList`, which creates two separate `XML` objects and stores them. Alternately, you can use the plus sign with existing `XML` objects to create an `XMLList`:

```
var oXml1 = <name>Nicholas C. Zakas</name>;
var oXml2 = <name>Michael Smith</name>;
var oXmlList = oXml1 + oXml2;
```

These three lines perform the exact same function as the single line shown previously, creating two `XML` objects and storing them in a new `XMLList` object. But you also have one more way to create an `XMLList`:

```
var oXmlList = <><name>Nicholas C. Zakas</name><name>Michael Smith</name></>;
```

This form is the XML literal for an `XMLList` object. The important syntax is the empty opening and closing tags, indicating this isn't a typical `XML` object (empty tags are illegal in XML).

As mentioned in the previous section, the `XML` and `XMLList` objects are purposely similar to blur the distinction between the two. As such, `XMLList` objects have all the same methods as `XML` objects, although they behave a bit differently.

In the `XMLList` object, methods generally call the method of the same name on each `XML` object in the list and return the results in another `XMLList` object. For example, if you call `attribute("id")` on an `XMLList` object, it calls the `attribute("id")` on each `XML` object. If the `XML` object returns an attribute, that attribute is added to the result `XMLList` object. Once all `XML` objects have contributed, the result `XMLList` object is returned. Here's a list of all the methods that act this way:

- `attribute()` — Returns an `XMLList` of the given attribute from all `XML` objects
- `attributes()` — Returns an `XMLList` of all attributes from all `XML` objects
- `child()` — Returns an `XMLList` of all child nodes with the given name from all `XML` objects
- `children()` — Returns an `XMLList` of all child nodes from all `XML` objects
- `comments()` — Returns an `XMLList` of all child comment nodes from all `XML` objects
- `descendants()` — Returns an `XMLList` of all descendant nodes from all `XML` objects
- `elements()` — Returns an `XMLList` of all child elements nodes from all `XML` objects
- `normalize()` — Normalizes each `XML` object
- `processingInstructions()` — Returns an `XMLList` of all child processing instruction nodes from all `XML` objects
- `text()` — Returns an `XMLList` of all child text nodes from all `XML` objects

The two methods that didn't make sense for the `XML` object, `length()` and `contains()`, make much more sense when used in the context of an `XMLList`. The `length()` method returns the number of objects in the `XMLList`; the `contains()` method determines if a given XML object is contained within the `XMLList`, for example:

```
var oXml1 = <name>Nicholas C. Zakas</name>;
var oXml2 = <name>Michael Smith</name>;
var oXmlList = oXml1 + oXml2;
alert(oXmlList.contains(oXml1));  //outputs "true"
```

In this example, `oXmlList` is created by combining `oXml1` and `oXml2`, so when the `contains()` method is called with `oXml1`, the result is `true`.

Four other methods behave somewhat differently from the `XML` object:

- `copy()` — Returns an exact duplicate of the `XMLList` object
- `hasComplexContent()` — Returns `true` when the `XMLList` contains one element with complex content or when the `XMLList` contains more than one `XML` object
- `hasSimpleContent()` — Returns `true` when the `XMLList` is empty and when the `XMLList` contains one `XML` object with simple content
- `parent()` — Returns an `XML` object if all objects in the `XMLList` have the same parent; otherwise returns `undefined`

Together, the `XML` and `XMLList` classes provide a very powerful interface to manipulate XML data.

Implementations

The only implementation of E4X is in BEA Weblogic Workshop (not surprising, because BEA initiated the definition of E4X). In Weblogic Workshop, E4X is called JavaScript for XML (JSX) or Native XML Scripting, and it is used on the server to manipulate XML. JSX files are compiled into Java classes during execution in Weblogic Workshop and can then be used in any other Java classes, including Web services.

For more information about JavaScript for XML in Weblogic Workshop, see `http://dev2dev.bea.com/products/wlworkshop/articles/JSchneider_XML.jsp`.

According to Mozilla's roadmap, E4X is anticipated to be included in Mozilla 2.0 (indeed, the code for Rhino, Mozilla's JavaScript interpreter, already contains code relating to implementing E4X), making it the first freely available E4X implementation.

Summary

This chapter looked at the future direction of JavaScript as it relates to certain standards. ECMAScript Edition 4 is on the horizon (and has been for years), but it is not yet released. This chapter gave an overview of the Netscape Proposal for ECMAScript 4 and discussed what parts, if any, are currently implemented.

It also discussed the new standard called ECMAScript for XML, which adds native XML support to the ECMAScript language. Although this standard isn't available in client-side scripting for Web browsers, it is supported in BEA Weblogic Workshop, and the Workshop will continue to push its use in the next few years.

The bottom line here is that JavaScript is continuing to evolve, and no one can be sure where it will end up. However, the future is looking bright as JavaScript is being adopted by more and more platforms and applications. For instance, the soon-to-be-released MacOS X Tiger features a new programming platform called Dashboard that uses JavaScript to make lightweight applications that can run on the MacOS desktop. With this sort of support, along with Microsoft's JScript.NET, don't be surprised to see JavaScript moving more and more out of the world of the Web and onto your desktop.

Index

SYMBOLS

A

C

E

F

G

H

J

K

L

M

N

P

S

T

V

W